ROBERT
MENZIES

ROBERT MENZIES

A Life

Volume 1
1894–1943

A. W. MARTIN
assisted by Patsy Hardy

MELBOURNE UNIVERSITY PRESS
1993

First published 1993
Designed by Lauren Statham, Alice Graphics
Typeset by Syarikat Seng Teik Sdn. Bhd., Malaysia.
Printed in Australia by McPherson's Printing Group
for
Melbourne University Press, Carlton, Victoria 3053
U.S.A. and Canada: International Specialized Book Services, Inc.,
5602 N.E. Hassalo Street, Portland, Oregon 97213–3640
United Kingdom and Europe: University College London Press,
Gower Street, London WC1E 6BT

This book is copyright. Apart from any fair dealing for the
purposes of private study, research, criticism or review, as
permitted under the Copyright Act, no part may be reproduced by
any process without written permission. Enquiries should be made
to the publisher.

© Allan William Martin 1993

National Library of Australia Cataloguing-in-Publication entry

Martin, A. W. (Allan William), 1926– .
Robert Menzies: a life. Volume 1, 1894–1943.

Bibliography.
Includes index.
ISBN 0 522 84442 1.

1. Menzies, Sir Robert, 1894–1978. 2. Prime ministers—Australia—
Biography. 3. Australia—Politics and government—1922–1945. I.
Hardy, Patsy. II. Title.

994.042092

Contents

	Preface	xi
1	From Jeparit to the University of Melbourne	1
2	The Young Lawyer	32
3	'A Certain Amount of Public Work'	53
4	The Coming of the UAP	68
5	State Politician and Minister	94
6	Federal Attorney-General, 1934	120
7	The Discovery of England, 1935	143
8	Qualifying for 'Omniscience', 1936–1937	177
9	The Narrow Squeak	203
10	England and Europe, 1938	219
11	Days of Unsettlement, 1938–1939	240
12	Prime Minister of Australia, 1939	266
13	Political Uncertainties, 1939–1940	287
14	Encountering Churchill's England, 1941	316
15	Ireland, Churchill and Disillusion	337
16	And Bleed Awhile	356
17	In the Wilderness	388
18	Phoenix?	408
	Reflections	425
	Sources	432
	Index	435

Illustrations

	page
Roy Street, Jeparit, in the 1890s *National Library of Australia*	5
The Menzies children, about 1900 *National Library of Australia*	6
Jeparit and the Wimmera in Victoria	8
The Students' Representative Council of the University of Melbourne, 1916 Melbourne University Magazine, *October 1916*	21
Selborne Chambers *F. M. Bradshaw*, Selborne Chambers Memories, *Plate III*	34
Handbill for the 1928 East Yarra Province election *by courtesy of Mr G. Menzies*	62
The young barrister Table Talk, *25 April 1929*	71
'Illira' *Menzies family*	73
The Young Nationalists go to the people, 1931 Young Nationalist, *1 January 1931*	76
Nationalist victory in Tasmania Australian Statesman, *1 June 1931 National Library of Australia*	91
Christmas cheer Argus, *24 December 1931*	93
The Argyle Ministry, 1933 *Menzies family*	103
Egon Kisch *Egon Kisch*, Australian Landfall (*London, 1937*)	131

ILLUSTRATIONS

The handsome Minister, 1935 Sun-News Pictorial, *Melbourne, 20 February 1935*	142
Reception at the Capitol Theatre, Perth *National Library of Australia*	146
The Australian ministerial party in London, March 1935 *Menzies family*	149
Empire Parliamentary Association luncheon, 1935 The Times, *5 July 1935 National Library of Australia*	161
A family holiday at 'Illira' Table Talk, *6 February 1936 Menzies family*	191
'Recruits Wanted' Bulletin, *19 February 1936*	193
The Australian Academy of Art Argus, *6 May 1937*	197
The Lyons Cabinet, 1937 *National Library of Australia*	215
With Peter Heydon in London, 1938 *Menzies family*	225
Ministers at the trade talks in London, 1938 *National Library of Australia*	227
The unveiling of the Villers-Bretonneux Memorial Age, *2 August 1938*	231
The Christmas Ham Argus, *6 December 1938*	253
The troubled Lyons Cabinet, March 1939 Daily Telegraph and Morning Post, *London, 15 March 1939*	259
The new Prime Minister, 28 April 1939 *Austin-Murcott*	273
Mr and Mrs Menzies senior arrive in Canberra, May 1939 *Menzies family*	277
The first Menzies Cabinet, 1939 *National Library of Australia*	279
The Lodge in 1939 *Menzies family*	281
Convivial relaxation with Mrs Stewart Jamieson Independent Monthly, *August 1989*	283
Convivial relaxation with journalists in Launceston *National Library of Australia*	283

ILLUSTRATIONS

Announcing the outbreak of war, 1939 *National Library of Australia*	285
A Lionel Lindsay bookplate *National Library of Australia*	286
Stan Cross on Menzies' reluctance to send troops Smith's Weekly, *4 November 1939*	289
Stan Cross on Menzies' task as wartime Prime Minister Smith's Weekly, *11 November 1939*	290
With Lord Gowrie on an Australian cruiser, 1940 *Australian War Memorial (AWM 521)*	292
Campaigning in the 1940 election *National Library of Australia*	304
The 'outstanding candidates' Bulletin, *25 September 1940*	307
The Advisory War Council, Canberra, 19 November 1941 *National Library of Australia*	309
H. V. Evatt's anxiety for office Bulletin, *11 December 1940*	311
A dinner in Cairo *Australian War Memorial (AWM 5857)*	319
North Africa in February 1941 *National Library of Australia*	321
A press conference in London, 1941 *National Library of Australia*	322
Addressing factory workers at Coventry, 1941 *National Library of Australia*	331
Menzies with Churchill outside No. 10 Downing Street, March 1941 *Australian War Memorial (AWM 6414)*	333
With de Valera, 1941 *National Library of Australia*	340
Conferring of degrees at Bristol, April 1941 *Australian War Memorial (AWM 7465)*	346
Taking movies of Mackenzie King, 1941 *Menzies family*	357
Emerging from the office of the Australian High Commissioner, Ottawa, 1941 *National Library of Australia*	358

Menzies and Casey in New York, May 1941 *Australian War Memorial (AWM 7424)*	360
Notes for the Sydney Town Hall speech *Menzies family*	363
The triumphant reception at home, 26 May 1941 Daily Telegraph, *27 May 1941*	366
Frith on the resignation of the Prime Ministership Bulletin, *6 August 1941 National Library of Australia*	373
Frith comments again Bulletin, *27 August 1941 National Library of Australia*	384
Norman Lindsay comments on Menzies' dilemma Bulletin, *13 August 1941*	392

Preface

In this volume I offer an account of R. G. Menzies as man and politician, up to 1943, at least as I have come to see him. Menzies' later years, as Australia's longest-serving Prime Minister, have received much attention from historians and journalists but his earlier career, and the formative influences he experienced before entering politics, are not well known. 'Objectivity' is now an unfashionable aspiration but in looking at the younger Menzies I have nevertheless tried to distance myself from the prejudices and preoccupations of a later period, to examine the making of the man as a process shaped in its own terms and accessible in large degree to the careful observer. What one judges Menzies to have become—whether for good or ill—in his later years, of itself tells little of the *process* of becoming. On the contrary, it may too easily lead to selection of evidence, unconscious as well as conscious, to shore up the image of a persona already established in the investigator's mind.

Writing a book such as this involves another difficulty which I have laboured against but which has probably defeated me. An extraordinarily high proportion of Australians in the 1990s were either not in the country or not yet born when Menzies was an active politician. They thus have no personal picture of him or any clear understanding (unless they are among the few who have made a special study of it) of the political history of Australia in his times. One cannot therefore assume much if one wishes to communicate with more than a small, well-informed audience, the more especially as Menzies has long been caricatured for their own purposes by politicians as well as television, radio and print journalists, often in one-liners more notable for their cleverness or scurrility than their accuracy. I have tried, accordingly, to make my story stand on its own feet, to explain simply, when it seemed necessary, what the issues—political and otherwise—were, what the sequence of governments was, who the politicians were. To colleagues who know this terrain well and will suffer boredom as well as possibly disagreeing with my emphases I can only say apologetically that I am writing for a wider audience, though I hope that they will find some new tit-bits in what I say.

Finally, though this is a biography, the history behind it is unashamedly political, and that requires little apology since, after all, its subject is a dedicated politician and we are trying to understand what, at least in his public life, motivates him. The materials for probing Menzies' personal life are sparse, but I have used what is available, supplementing it with interviews, and am hopeful that what has emerged is something closer to a real live man than the ogre conventionally pictured on one side of Australian politics and the saint conventionally pictured on the other. None of the areas of Australian history which today preoccupy many scholars—Aboriginal, environmental or women's—is formally dealt with in this book (though there are many implications for the last-named) as much as anything because, as Dr Coombs once remarked of a slightly later period, they just 'weren't then on the agenda'.

I am indebted to a number of people who kindly permitted interviews to discuss Menzies, or made available to me relevant papers in their possession. I list these in detail in my note on 'Sources', at the back of the book. A multitude of others have over the years of my research offered help in a variety of ways. In enumerating those I remember, I ask others I do not mention to forgive me for this human weakness and consider themselves thanked too: Hartog Berkeley, Geoffrey Bolton, Paul Bourke, Judith Brett, Stuart Cockburn, the late Manning Clark, Cecily Close, Mark Cranfield, Sir Walter Crocker, Peter Crockett, Chris Cunneen, Christopher Daniell, Graeme Davison, David Day, John Eddy, Peter Edwards, Tom Fitzgerald, the late Ron Gilbert, Helga Griffin, Peter Gronn, Judith Harley, Cameron Hazlehurst, Bill Hudson, Robert Hyslop, John Iremonger, John Jost, Di Langmore, David Lee, John Legge, Les Louis, Jamie Mackie, Jan McDonald, Graham Menzies, Oliver MacDonagh, James Merralls, Tom Millar, John Mulvaney, John Nethercote, Larry Noye, John O'Brien, Mark Richmond, John Ritchie, Martha Rutledge, Peter Ryan, Alan Shaw, Gavin Souter, Jim Stewart, Frank Strahan, Hugh Stretton, Maurice Timbs. Characteristically, my old friend Geoff Serle always remembered me when he came across a snippet of information about Menzies, and Noel Webb has been a constant and stimulating correspondent. Sir Paul Hasluck has shown interest in this work from its beginnings and has given valuable judgements on a number of matters. For long I seemed a permanent fixture in the manuscript room of the National Library of Australia and wish to record the constant and cheerful helpfulness of the librarians who preside over that remarkable place. Other libraries and repositories where I have experienced similar courtesy include the Mitchell, in Sydney, the Menzies, at the Australian National University, the La Trobe, in Melbourne, the Flinders University Library and the Mortlock, in Adelaide, the Noel Butlin Archives Centre (formerly the ANU Archives of Business and Labour) and the Australian Archives, in Canberra, the Archives of the University of Melbourne, the Cambridge University Library, the Archives of Churchill College, Cambridge, the Bodleian Library, Oxford, the B.B.C. Written Archives, Reading, and the Public Record Office, London. In addition, Dr Benedikz, of the Library of Birmingham University, kindly answered my queries about the Avon Papers and provided photocopies of several important letters therefrom.

There are special debts. First Janet Penny, then Patsy Hardy, worked with me, more as enthusiastic colleagues than as research assistants. Patsy Hardy edited the various versions of the manuscript on disk and was responsible for the final formatting. My colleagues Ken Inglis and Barry Smith read the whole manuscript in draft, as did Heather and Peter Henderson. All four commented on minor errors and stylistic lapses, for which I am grateful. Of course I accept final responsibility for what has eventually gone into print. I wish also to emphasize that although I was asked by the Menzies family to undertake this study it is not an 'official biography' if by that is meant a work in any sense scrutinized or censored. Family papers have been made freely available to me with the understanding that what I do with them is my responsibility alone. Likewise on other, public material my independence is absolute.

I must finally record my appreciation of the skill of Drs Hurwitz and McGill and of Dr Nikolic and the sisters of his Intensive Care Unit of Woden Valley hospital, Canberra, without whose ministrations at a time of crisis this book would never have been finished. The latter is true at that and at all times of the contribution of my wife, to whose companionship, encouragement and erudition I owe more than can ever be expressed.

A. W. Martin
Canberra, 1992

1

From Jeparit to the University of Melbourne

ROBERT GORDON MENZIES was born at Jeparit, a tiny township in the Wimmera district of Victoria, on 20 December 1894.[1] He was the fourth of five children of James and Kate Menzies. His parents were among the first-born of that generation of gold-rush migrants which the historian of the colony of Victoria, Geoffrey Serle, has shown to have been in their youth, literacy and skills the most remarkable wave of newcomers to Australia in the history of European settlement. A Scots strain in the family, and the rural setting of his entry into the world, were accidents of fate of which Menzies was in his later manhood often to boast. Of the two, the Scots parentage was the most deeply internalized: the rural setting came to be a useful symbol for a particular Australian self-identification, but a physical reality to be quietly escaped from.

Robert's paternal grandfather, also named Robert, had reached Melbourne from Scotland in 1854. A seaman of twenty-two on the vessel *Thomas Feildon*, this Menzies jumped ship and joined the exodus from Melbourne to Ballarat in search of gold and a fortune. Born and bred in the Glasgow region, he had little incentive to return to Scotland. His parents, James and Catherine Menzies, had both died, leaving him no property. Father James, in his time a bleacher, chargekeeper and gardener, owned a little land in a rocky valley between the parishes of Port Glasgow and Greenock. But he died in 1832, leaving some of the property to the children of his first wife, Agnes, and the rest to Catherine, who was his second spouse. On her death this property passed to Hugh, her eldest son

---

[1] The two main sources for the origins and earliest history of the Menzies family in Australia are Hugh Menzies, 'An Australian Menzies Family', *Menzies Clan Society Magazine* (Aberfeldy 1987), 6–13 (my copy by courtesy of Mr G. Menzies, and Mrs P. Henderson), and Frank G. Menzies, 'Reminiscences of the Menzies Family', a 35-page roneoed document prepared for private circulation in the family (my copy from the late Mrs I. Green). Except where otherwise stated, these works provide authority for the early part of this chapter.

and Robert's brother. A seaman also, Hugh sold the land, spent a short time in Quebec and then followed Robert to the Victorian diggings. According to a niece, he was later drowned in a wreck off the New South Wales coast when on his way to Queensland for a health trip.[2] On his voyage to Australia, Robert had made a number of ship-board friendships. Some survived. The most notable of them was that of a Fife cobbler, Thomas Brand, who was emigrating with his wife and family. In 1855, the year after their arrival in Melbourne, Brand's eldest daughter, Elizabeth, married Robert Menzies, in Collingwood.

Robert took his bride to a tent home beside Ballarat's Yarrowee Creek, where he had already established himself as a digger. There is no indication that his work brought more than a competence, though he remained a miner until 1861 mostly, it seems, as an employee of one of the numerous mining companies soon formed to tackle the expensive task of following Ballarat's deep leads.[3] In his first Australian years, the rough community to which Robert had come matured with astonishing speed. Gold was the motor of change, though more of the newcomers who quickly swelled the population came to service rather than engage in mining. Permanent buildings rapidly replaced canvas offices and dwellings; hotels, stores, churches and schools were built; courts, government offices, a hospital and even a share market were institutions which told of a population with diversified specialist skills. Metalworking was one industry firmly established at this time: the initial incentive was the demand for mining equipment, but Ballarat's workshops were soon producing a variety of implements. The town's first foundry appeared late in 1856; by 1861 there were ten, eight specializing in mining equipment, the other two in agricultural implements. These and the other trades established in the town enjoyed until the coming of the railway in 1862 the natural protection of distance from Melbourne manufacturers and importers. The same natural protection also assisted farmers, so that in the surrounding districts a notable expansion of local agriculture of all kinds accompanied the town's remarkable growth.

Paradoxically, the town's expansion was not matched by good fortune in the mines; indeed, from a peak in 1856 gold production steadily declined until in 1861 it was a quarter of what it had been four years earlier. The difficulty of tracing deep leads, often through a basalt covering and in the face of endless pumping to

[2]Margaret Adair to R. G. Menzies, 17 July 1952, Menzies Family Papers (in the care of Mrs P. Henderson, who generously gives me permission to quote from them.)
[3]My discussion of Ballarat is based on Weston Bate, *Lucky City: The First Generation at Ballarat, 1851–1901* (Melbourne 1978), especially 84–5, 118–28.

clear shafts of underground water, for a time frustrated many companies and led in the early 1860s to sometimes drastic lay-offs of workers. Robert Menzies was one who lost his job. After trying several other occupations he set up a business in partnership with one Josiah Pawsey, selling imported mining machinery. It flourished briefly, helped no doubt by the coming in 1862 of a rail link between Ballarat and Geelong. But as local engineering was well entrenched and a movement for protection was strong in the colony's politics, the future of an importing business of this kind was far from secure. It was ailing in the later 1870s and Robert left it, to put his talents where the strength was, by engaging as a travelling salesman for Ballarat's Phoenix foundry. As such he became widely respected. Then in 1879, at forty-six, he died suddenly from pneumonia, having caught a chill when helping to rescue a wagon from a fire.[4] Several of the town's leading companies closed as a mark of respect and many of their employees joined the cortège to the cemetery. His employers erected an obelisk over his grave in what is now the Old Ballarat cemetery.[5]

At the time of Robert's death he and his family lived in a modest cottage in Dana Street, Ballarat. There were nine surviving children. Left with few material resources, the widowed Elizabeth Menzies faced a dour time rearing this brood. Her three older sons, Hugh, John and James (later to be the father of Robert Gordon) had initially to become the family breadwinners. Their hard work and their mother's frugality and strength of character made the family's survival possible at a time when self-help was all that could be relied on. In the end Elizabeth survived thirty-two years of widowhood, becoming for her numerous grandchildren a strong and somewhat formidable matriarch.

At the time of his father's death James Menzies was apprenticed to a Ballarat coachpainter. The manufacture of high-class horse-drawn vehicles was by this time one of the many specialties of the town's tradesmen and the intricate painting of these conveyances a highly skilled craft. When he had served his articles the young journeyman persuaded his employer to pay him at piece rates rather than by wage, so that by working longer hours he could boost his income. Subsequently he briefly established his own coachpainting business, and was a neighbour and friend of the inventor Hugh Victor McKay who in the 1880s perfected a stripper-harvester combine, a revolutionary machine which could strip the heads of a wheat crop, then winnow and bag the grain

[4] R. G. Menzies, *Afternoon Light*, 5.
[5] Ballarat *Courier*, 28 January 1879.

for carting direct from the paddock. Menzies painted the first of these machines and gave it a name subsequently famous throughout rural Australia: 'Sunshine Harvester'. Then, in the late 1880s, Menzies joined the Phoenix foundry, becoming head painter. Secure in his new position, he married, on Christmas Day 1889. His bride was Kate Sampson.

Like her husband, Kate came from a large family. Her mother, Mary, died when Kate was twelve, leaving seven children. Her father, John Sampson, remarried. His new wife, Mrs Besemeres, was the matron of Creswick hospital, a widow with four children of her own. She and Sampson had two more offspring, so that in the end the combined family in their care numbered thirteen. An immigrant of 1854 from Cornwall, Sampson, like Robert Menzies, had joined the gold rush, in his case settling at Bald Hills, Creswick. He worked for some years as a miner and became president of a miners' union of which W. G. Spence was secretary and which was the predecessor of the Australian Workers' Union. At Creswick Sampson led a strike for an increase in the miners' weekly wage from forty to forty-two shillings, and suffered for his pains a mine owners' boycott so effective that he was never able to work in a mine again. Helped by his oldest sons, Sydney and Edward, he made his living as a wood carter supplying timber for the mines from the Bullarook forest. John Sampson's formal education was limited, but he took an avid interest in politics and was—as his grandson Robert was to put it—'a keen and discriminating reader'.[6]

James Menzies' marriage exacerbated his extravagant work habits. Kate later told her children that 'Father frequently collapsed on arriving home from work. He was always intense in anything he undertook, with an inner urge to carry out thoroughly any duty assumed by him—particularly where it concerned others'. One's impression is of a compulsive, neurotic personality who in the ugly jargon of our own day would be described as a 'workaholic'. Four years of married life convinced Kate that a change of lifestyle was vital if she were to avoid becoming a widow bringing up a family of young children. The marriage had by now produced three: James Leslie (1890), Frank Gladstone (1892), and Isobel Alice, or 'Belle', as she came to be known (1893). Hope for a way of improving James's condition came when he was advised to find a drier, warmer climate than Ballarat, and Kate's brother, Sydney Sampson, suggested a move to the tiny Wimmera township of Jeparit. Sampson had bought a general store there and in 1893, from the rear of this store, began the production of a newspaper,

---

[6]Menzies, *Afternoon Light*, 5.

The vista down Roy Street, Jeparit, in the 1890s: the Menzies store is past the Mechanics' Institute, on the left.

the *Jeparit Leader*. A few days after the *Leader* was first published, Sampson offered the store to Menzies. The aim was to effect the latter's needed change of scene, and to allow Sampson himself to concentrate on the new paper. Menzies agreed. Living quarters were built behind the store (on the corner of Roy and Charles streets) and late in 1893 the family moved in. There a fourth child, Robert Gordon, was born on 20 December 1894. Sampson ran the *Leader* until 1897, when he sold out and moved to the larger town of Warracknabeal, to take over the local paper, the *Warracknabeal Herald*.[7]

Jeparit owed its existence to settlers who in the 1880s selected land in the extreme north of the Wimmera, braving low rainfall, summer heat, poor soils and the daunting task of clearing a stubborn cover of scrub, mainly mallee.[8] The Wimmera area,

---

[7] A. J. Williams, 'Jeparit's Early History', part 47. A series of articles from *Jeparit Leader (JL)* 1955–56, newspaper cuttings held by the Royal Historical Society of Victoria.
[8] The account of the Wimmera and Jeparit which follows is based on Land Conservation Council, Victoria, *Report on the Wimmera Area* (Melbourne 1985); and H. J. Gloury, *"Our Jeparit": the History of a Small Country Town* (Back to Jeparit, October 1980).

The Menzies children, as caught in a carefully posed period photograph, about 1900: from the left, Frank, Belle, Bob and Syd.

containing almost 17 000 square kilometres of land adjoining the South Australian border, had for its first European exploiters squatters who followed the tracks of the explorers, Thomas Mitchell and Edward Eyre. Eyre, seeking an overland route between Melbourne and Adelaide, in 1836 followed the Wimmera

River northwards, to find it flowing into what he reported to be 'a large freshwater lake about forty miles in circumference'. He called it Lake Hindmarsh, after the Governor of South Australia. After the Victorian land legislation of 1869 selectors spread into the lower Wimmera above Horsham, but it was another decade before the less hospitable north was seriously settled. Many of the farmers there were Lutherans of German origin who came overland from South Australia: hardy and experienced agriculturalists leaving often exhausted land to settle afresh. Together with other newcomers from the south and east of Victoria these were the people who created the needs which small settlements like Jeparit grew up to meet.

The parish of Jeparit (thought to be an Aboriginal term for 'home of small birds') appeared in survey plans in 1876, but a township was not so named until 1889. By 1891 the settlement had become a tiny reality, with a population of fifty-five. The Menzies arrived as the Depression of the 1890s was having its most devastating effects in Melbourne and other large centres, but Jeparit was too remote and too new to suffer the real ravages caused by the collapse of the colony's land boom. In fact, Jeparit was at that time going through a Lilliputian expansion of its own. By 1893 the town had two newspapers, boasted a variety of small businesses and was about to be linked by a branch railway line, through Dimboola, to Ballarat and Melbourne. There was a subsequent period of considerable suffering when a run of poor seasons in the late 1890s culminated in the terrible drought of 1902. Then things looked up again, with better seasons and improvements in farming techniques. The census of 1911 registered the population of Jeparit at over 800. The Menzies, who left the township at this stage, had thus lived through its vital first decade and a half of growth. They made a major contribution to its development, in a variety of ways.

The store survived rather than prospered. Kate looked after the millinery and drapery departments and supervised a dressmaking service. James managed the groceries, the boot and saddlery sections and the various insurance and stock and station agencies he held for external firms.[9] Sometimes he took his small boys out on hawking expeditions, most notably to sell to the railway construction navvies who after 1894 were working on the mallee extension beyond Jeparit.[10] His children remembered James as being, by ordinary commercial lights, too kind to be a good businessman. He gave extensive credit to the poor farmers who were his main

---

[9] How the store was managed is revealed in advertisements in *JL*, sampled for 1902, 1909, 1910.
[10] Frank Menzies, 'Memoir', 10–11.

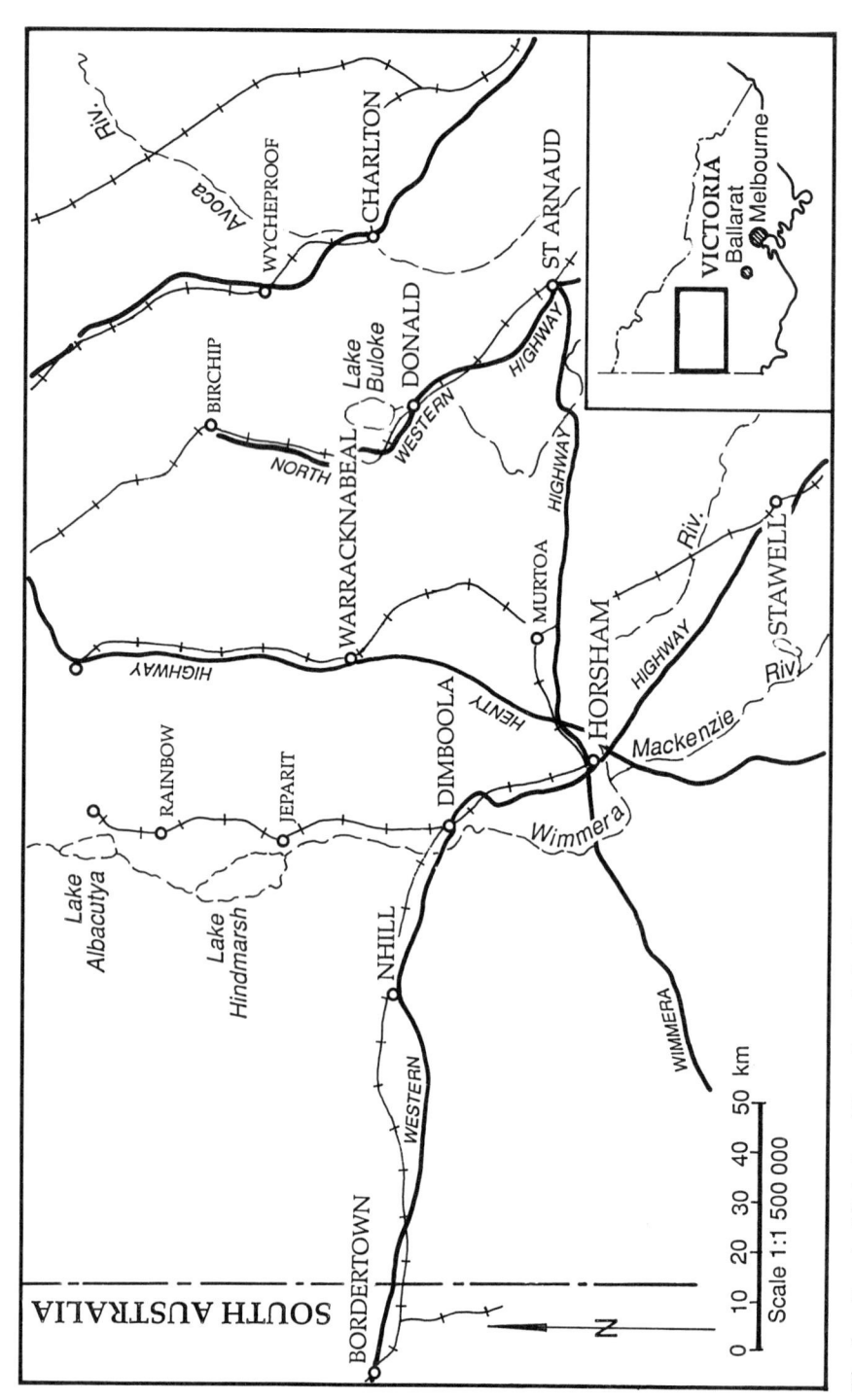

The location in Victoria of Jeparit and the Wimmera

customers while struggling himself to meet the demands of his Melbourne suppliers. But Kate's hope that Jeparit would bring her husband better health was vindicated, perhaps for the unexpected reason that his business at once put James intimately in touch with the people of the little township and drew much of his attention outwards, to community problems and welfare. A vigorous man in his early thirties, he blossomed in an environment which brought about the discovery in himself of leadership and speaking skills which had only been latent in his Ballarat days. Frank Menzies' description of his father at this time seems apt: 'intemperately generous, he was consumed with a passionate determination to help other people'.

One old Jeparit identity, Vere Patterson, proprietor of the *Jeparit Leader* between 1907 and 1918, in later years remembered James Menzies as the most notable of the town's early citizens: he was 'the daddy of them all. He occupied every presidential chair Jeparit had to offer, political, civic, social and sporting. His tales of the earlier Jeparit days always made entrancing stories'.[11] Menzies was a member of the Dimboola Shire Council, in whose jurisdiction Jeparit fell, from 1898 until he left the town, serving twice as shire president. He was a founder of the Jeparit branch of the Australian Natives' Association and was prominent in establishing organizations ranging from the Progress Association and the Caledonian Society to the rowing club. He was always in demand as a speaker at the Mutual Improvement Society and was the inevitable chairman for any important meeting to do with local affairs. One of the more notable instances of his authority occurred during the 1902 drought, when the government promised licences to graze starving stock on the dried bed of Lake Hindmarsh. A meeting of farmers held in the Mechanics' Hall to decide how and to whom the licences would be issued elected Menzies chairman of a management committee which subsequently set fees and procedures for issuing licences and adjudicated in disputes between licensees.[12]

The church was a special focus for James's energy. In Ballarat he was always a firm Presbyterian, in his last years there being a prominent 'elder' at Scots Church, Soldiers' Hill. But on arriving in Jeparit he threw his lot in with the Methodists, who were the strongest non-Catholic group, with their own church building, which had been erected in 1891. As he always liked to say afterwards, James was 'a Presbyterian by conviction and a Methodist

[11] Gloury, *"Our Jeparit"*, 24.
[12] Farmer's meetings re Lake Hindmarsh: *JL*, especially 31 October and 14 November 1902.

by adoption'.[13] While the Presbyterian conviction bred in him a somewhat narrow Calvinism, the Methodist adoption allowed him to give reign to a highly emotional temperament. One manifestation of this was the development of a fiery lay-preaching style; another was an unashamed tendency to display emotion on certain public occasions. In 1902, for example, he set off for Melbourne, intending to establish a business there and leave Jeparit (a plan which, fortunately for the little town, eventually misfired). His friends mourned his impending loss: 'By the removal of Mr Menzies', lamented the *Jeparit Leader*,

> Jeparit loses a citizen that it can ill afford . . . Connected with all movements of religious, social and public interest, Mr Menzies was regarded at all times as an authority and more than one will miss his right-minded and governing influence which unconsciously placed him in a position to command the respect of all with whom he had dealings.

At a parting Sunday ceremony he was presented with a handsome bible by the young men's class he had been teaching at the Methodist church. 'In accepting the gift', the *Leader*'s reporter wrote, 'Mr. Menzies was so overcome with emotion, that for a time he was unable to reply'. Eventually he expressed his thanks and 'offered a few words of friendly advice to the young men, that they may adopt the proper lines to pursue and live good and honourable lives'.[14] As his son Bob was later to describe him—in the perspective of another half century—James was

> a strongly built man of little more than medium height. His hair was prematurely grey, and became a splendid silver. He had a fairly full moustache, in which he took some pride. The nervous tension which he had tended to make him both dogmatic and intolerant; in a very modified sense, a 'Barrett of Wimpole Street'. His temper was quick. We, his sons, got to know that 'whom the Lord loveth, he chasteneth'. We were not a little frightened of him . . .[15]

This was an important aspect of James's emotionalism. When almost ninety his daughter Belle still remembered the aftermath of one childish sin, when she and her brothers were caught feeding the animals of a visiting circus. Her father severely beat the boys, then turned to her: 'You're a girl and I won't hit you, but I hope you've been sufficiently punished by hearing what happened to your brothers'.[16] Frank's recollection of his father as a disciplinarian was as vivid as, if a little more benign, than Bob's:

---
[13]Frank Menzies, 'Memoir', 15.
[14]*JL*, 11 April 1902.
[15]Menzies, *Afternoon Light*, 9.
[16]Mrs Green recollected this incident in an interview on 27 February 1984.

Father was strict, to put it mildly, and certainly believed the scriptural injunction 'Spare the rod and spoil the child'. He had a fine fleshy hand and that part of my anatomy which 'seems to have been specially designed by nature for chastisement' was peculiarly receptive. Many a thrashing I received and I was never aware that punishment was not deserved but I'm afraid that Father's enthusiasm (he was intense in everything he did) often made the punishment exceed the crime. I held no resentment and retained the greatest affection for him throughout life.[17]

In the recollections of Frank and Bob their mother Kate appears as a foil to James, both at home and in public. Writing of the children's 'fear' of their father, Bob remembered years later how they 'found ... regular refuge in the embracing arms of our mother, who afforded us the comfort of her own understanding, balance and exquisite humour'. And, in larger affairs,

Where [Father] was positively intolerant, she ... in the end would secure a victory for sweet reasonableness. [He] was a great one for getting things done. In this he was completely unselfish, for all his greatest crusades were for others. But in the battle he could inflict wounds. My mother healed them.[18]

Chastisement aside, the children had the normal enjoyments and camaraderies of a small country town. They had no inkling of their parents' dour struggle for economic survival. They played football and a rustic form of hockey, with paper sticks and empty jam tins for balls; they yabbied, fished and swam in Lake Hindmarsh and the Wimmera River.[19] They began their education at the first Jeparit school—Victoria number 2988—in a small timber room that had in 1894 been shifted bodily to the township from a hamlet, Woolshed, near Dimboola. John ('Daddy') Livingston, the Head Teacher in their time, was not a forgettable man. A liberal wielder of strap and cane (even kind Frank Menzies remembered him as having been 'a bit sadistic'), his other memorable trait was an uncanny skill in catching flies from the swarms which came into the schoolroom from its ungauzed windows. 'Woe befall one that got between his face and forefinger. It would inevitably add to the semicircle of dead comrades in front of the Head Teacher's desk.' Livingston made the speech, so moving to James Menzies, for the young men who presented him with the bible in 1902. In due course he became one of the grand old men of the town: 'He could be depended upon to attend any public meeting convened for the

[17] 'Memoir', 16.
[18] Menzies, *Afternoon Light*, 12.
[19] Frank Menzies, 'Memoir', 15–16.

welfare of Jeparit. He had an orderly mind, and was a reporter's delight in the way he summed up disorderly meetings'.[20] To posterity he sounds like a minor James Menzies. Certainly Bob Menzies always remembered him with awe and a sort of nervous affection.

Neither Kate nor James Menzies had had much formal schooling, though both were keen readers who extended the range of their knowledge and above all (a prime virtue in son Bob's eyes) spoke educated English. This, Bob thought, showed that 'schooling is wonderfully advantageous, but is not all'. The Menzies were nevertheless anxious that their children should have the best education that could be afforded, once they had exhausted the resources Jeparit had to offer. The four eldest—Les, Frank, Belle and Bob (a fifth sibling, Syd, was born a decade after Bob)—were sent in turn to Ballarat, where they attended State School no. 34, in Humffray Street. This school's 'scholarship', or upper sixth, class had a State-wide reputation for excellence. The sixth class stood at the apex of the system. High schools had yet to be established in Victoria: pupils with limited means could hope to get to private schools and secondary tuition only by aspiring to one of the forty scholarships offered each year for competition among State school pupils aged fourteen and a half or under. Les and Frank went to Ballarat first, leaving Jeparit in 1904, to board with their father's mother, the redoubtable widow Elizabeth, who still lived in the old family home in Dana Street. Belle and Bob followed a year or so later.

Les was not academically inclined though the work he did at the school allowed him later to undertake commercial training. In the scholarship exams Frank missed out on a full scholarship by nine marks but was awarded a half scholarship to Grenville College, in Ballarat. Then came the greatest family achievement. In 1907, at the end of his second year at Humffray Street, Bob topped the State in the scholarship examination. He was 13 and his achievement Jeparit's sensation of the year. Frank was beside himself with joy:

> The train to Jeparit in those far off days was a three-week event and we all waited with impatient expectation the publication of the scholarship results. I was then sixteen and was always the first to scan the pages of the Age. At last the great day arrived. Bob was on top of the list with 672 marks, 36 ahead of the second place! At the time we boys were on our vacation and were busy painting the side of the house. I dropped my brush, mounted the family bicycle and believe it or not,

---

[20] Gloury, *"Our Jeparit"*, 24.

in century heat rode across the country 26 miles which took me six hours with frequent rests under the mallee scrub bordering on the rough track to break the news to Uncle Jack Sampson on his farm at Yellanjip, six miles out of Warracknabeal. Could enthusiasm and admiration have done more?[21]

The two teachers of Menzies' class were John McDonald and Thomas Jones, who both appear in an old photograph of the 1908 scholarship group published half a century later in the Ballarat *Courier*. The occasion of the photograph's resurrection stirred Menzies to reminisce, to an old classmate, about McDonald's insistence on making the children sing ('Hearts of Oak' was the favourite song) and about Jones's achievement in 'teaching us to work out the most complicated arithmetical problems on the smallest possible piece of paper'.[22] Menzies never forgot his debt to Jones. In 1936, for instance, he described him as 'quite the best teacher of arithmetic I have ever known. Not the least of his achievements was his success in changing me from an extremely dull, to quite a creditable arithmetical scholar'. Indeed, Menzies received a personal letter from the examiners after the 1908 results came out, congratulating him and specially mentioning the excellent 'short cuts' displayed in his arithmetic paper.[23]

Interviewed once in old age, Menzies still vividly recalled Ballarat's impact on him when as a schoolboy he came to this metropolis from the small, dusty township that had always been home. He spoke of simple but unforgettable things experienced for the first time in his life: the smell of asphalt; the shouts of newsboys on the long platform of the railway station; the traffic in the streets and the electric lights. Ever since that first encounter, he said, Ballarat 'has meant something special to me'.[24] In hindsight's glow, perhaps he remembered the Ballarat experienced then as the gateway to a new world; or was it, in adulthood, that the memory of noise and bustle symbolized a clutch of the preferred values—development and prosperity, winnable through self-help and hard work—for which he knew the Ballarat story stood? In memory's patterning there was, however, something else

---

[21] Frank Menzies, 'Memoir', 14. *Melbourne Punch*, 6 February 1908, published a photograph of the 13-year-old boy, announced his achievement and hailed the 'promise of a successful scholastic career'.

[22] A photograph of the class and a letter to Menzies' old class-mate, Dorothy Richards, are in the Menzies Papers, MS. 4936, series 17, box 426 (MS. 4936/17/426), National Library of Australia (NLA). The original of the photograph was presented to the Ballarat Historical Society by Margaret Adair, R. G. Menzies' aunt.

[23] Menzies to Norman Jones, 17 August 1936, Australian Archives (AA), CP450/7/1, bundle 5, folder 243.

[24] NLA, Oral History Unit, Interview with Menzies, 25 February 1969, 1169/293.

that remained clear and sharp about his Ballarat experience. That was its overwhelmingly Scots flavour, concentrated in Grandmother Menzies. She was a short, round old lady, usually dressed in black bombazine and wearing a widow's lace cap. Though not well educated, she had, in Bob Menzies' words, 'the root of the matter in her'. The only books permanently permissible in the house were the Bible, the Presbyterian hymn book, *Ingoldsby Legends* and *Pilgrim's Progress*. But Grandmother did allow bona fide schoolbooks and stood firmly over her charges: her regular order at 6.30, after an early evening meal, was 'now Robert, get to your book' (she apparently always referred to 'your book' in the singular, as if it were some kind of universal compendium).[25]

Somewhat narrow-minded, devout and lacking in humour, she was also frugal. The children got from their parents threepence a week pocket money. For Bob and Belle, one penny of this was earmarked for the tram fare to make regular visits to their maternal grandfather, John Sampson, who lived in East Ballarat. On one occasion Grandmother Menzies discovered that the children sometimes walked to the Sampsons. She immediately accused them of doing so to save one penny for self-indulgent purposes, like buying their favourite lubricant for hours of study—peanuts—and promptly docked it from their allowance.[26]

His regular visits to Grandfather Sampson, who had what Bob Menzies once called 'the divine facility of not talking down to children' became the most important informal element in the education Ballarat gave him. Though a boy, Menzies came to Ballarat already alert to the interest and many of the nuances of politics. Besides his awareness of his father's public work, there were the many discussions he had had, unusual for such a young boy, often on constitutional matters with his uncle, Sydney Sampson, who edited the Warracknabeal newspaper and represented the Wimmera in the Commonwealth parliament between 1906 and 1919. Grandfather Sampson, now in his seventies and 'an upright man with a good forehead ... and full white beard', gave instruction in the union cause for which he had in his time suffered. When Bob came over from West Ballarat to see him, it was a habit of Sampson's to give the lad a recent editorial from the Sydney *Worker* to read, then to ask his opinion of it and to

---

[25]This picture of Grandmother Menzies is from an unpublished, part-completed, biography of R. G. Menzies by A. Dawes, now in the Menzies Family Papers. Menzies approved of and may have instigated this work, providing interviews and reviewing the draft as it was written (oral information from the late Ian Fitchett, who was also implicated). I therefore take Dawes' assertions and quotations as genuine, if often superficial, representations of Menzies' opinions and account of events.

[26]Interview with Mrs Green, 27 February 1984.

argue over the issues it raised. Years later, in his recollection of this experience, Menzies was sure that he had expressed views more conservative than those of his grandfather but could not forget how tolerant the old man was as he listened to his 'ark of the covenant' being dealt with unkindly. But there was no question in Bob's mind that what he had learnt from the old Labor man was one of the most important elements in his earliest political education.[27]

On his scholarship Menzies followed brother Frank to Grenville College, probably because his parents felt he was still too young to leave Ballarat for one of the great public schools in Melbourne. For a time it seemed likely that what Humffray Street had given him Grenville might very well take away. This respectable but declining school (it expired, in fact, in 1910) had in Menzies' time only thirty boys and two teachers: the headmaster, Arthur ('Boss') Buley, and an assistant. An excellent, if weary, classicist, Buley was an indifferent teacher of other subjects. Menzies' promise as a mathematician rapidly faded: Buley, he was always to aver, was to blame. And in his second year at the school Menzies performed poorly in the public examination for the 'leaving' certificate because, he believed, Buley had an exaggerated opinion of his abilities, and overloaded him with subjects—six of them, as well as Junior Public Latin and Greek, neither of which the boy had touched before. Nor could Menzies carry away from Grenville any reputation for sporting prowess: he played football and cricket, but reluctantly and without great success. Legend has it, however, that he was noted for a gift which he was to go on to develop with remarkable effect: that of mimicry. His special subject was William Henry Judkins, the most prominent Methodist reformer of the day, whose targets were prizefighting, gambling, racing, drinking, dancing and barmaids and who reserved a special hate for Catholics in general and John Wren, the Melbourne entrepreneur of gambling, in particular. Judkins' florid style of fiery, righteous oratory invited lampooning, and Menzies proved himself to be the uncannily accurate lad for that. Once his talent had been discovered, he was repeatedly put up to 'do' Judkins for the boys. That gave him a Grenville nickname, 'Judkins'—'Juddy' for short.[28]

It was inevitable, given his articulateness and prominence in local affairs, that James Menzies should be pressed to stand for parliament. As early as 1902 the opponents of the then premier, Irvine,

[27] Menzies, *Afternoon Light*, 6.
[28] The picture of Grenville College is from Dawes, 46–8.

whose electorate of Lowan took in that part of the Wimmera which embraced Jeparit, tried to get Menzies to stand for the seat. He declined, refusing 'to be a party to any action that might tend to complicate political matters at present', an ambiguous excuse which probably reflected the fact that for him it was financially impossible to contemplate spending long periods in Melbourne. He agreed, however, to stand for the seat in 1911, after Jeparit admirers had engineered his preselection for the 'People's Party', a kind of country party which emerged in the run-up to the election. As the preselection ballot approached, a Jeparit committee quietly built up the local membership of the party. 'Hardly a man refused to join', we are told, and the final vote for Menzies, over his Nhill rival, one McLennan, speaks eloquently of his ascendancy as, virtually, Mr Jeparit.[29] In the election campaign that followed he was a prominent and popular speaker at meetings, socials and picnics organized throughout the Wimmera by branches of the various anti-Labor bodies of the day.[30] He won the seat comfortably against a single Labor opponent, and entered parliament as a supporter of the Ministry headed by John Murray. A Presbyterian of Scots parentage and noted for his maverick radicalism, Murray promised progressive policies of rural development, in which he linked closer settlement, railway extension, assisted immigration and the establishment of State secondary education.[31]

What made it practical for James to take on this new phase of public service was that the eldest children's completion of their schooling disrupted the family's settled Jeparit life and heralded a move to Melbourne. By 1909 Les and Frank were in Melbourne in public service jobs, boarding there with a widowed aunt, Mary Moulton. Bob was about to take up his scholarship in one of Melbourne's public schools. Sometime in 1909 the parents decided that the family's changing circumstances required new arrangements: Kate would move to Melbourne and establish there a family home, while James would for the time being somehow keep his business interests going in Jeparit. The good citizens of Jeparit sent Kate away with every mark of admiring affection. In December 1909 they arranged a nostalgic farewell ceremony in the Mechanics' Institute. 'No more popular and philanthropic lady than Mrs Menzies has ever resided in this district', declared the *Jeparit Leader*. A concert was given in her honour, she was presented with a handsome tea and coffee service, and 'Daddy' Livingston delivered a long eulogy. Kate replied, the *Leader*

---

[29] Williams, 'Jeparit's Early History', part 31.
[30] *Nhill Free Press*, 14 December 1911.
[31] *Australian Dictionary of Biography (ADB)*, 10: 644–5.

reported, 'in a noble speech, logical and fluent'. There was a more conventional response at another ceremony, this time to allow the adherents of the Jeparit Methodist Church to present Mrs Menzies with a handsome hot water kettle. James, as the head of the family, spoke on his wife's behalf. 'Mrs Menzies' going away', he said, 'was solely in the interests of her family, the sons being now residents of the city, and they felt it was demanded of them that the family should not be robbed of those character building elements that only home life could instil into their young lives'.[32]

The Menzies briefly set up their new ménage in Coventry Road, South Melbourne, then moved to Grey Street, East Melbourne, where they lived at the time of James's election to parliament. This was home to James during parliamentary sessions, but at least until 1912 he kept up his Jeparit business, and lived there much of the time. Contemporary directories list Jeparit as his 'private address' and the Melbourne house as his 'town address'; and for several years after Kate's departure he still served on the local Shire Council and remained generally active in Jeparit affairs. The family moved house again in about 1912, this time to Fairholme Grove in Camberwell; after a few years there they settled briefly in a newly built house called 'Lowan', close to the river in Rockley Road, South Yarra. It was from this address that Frank enlisted in 1916 and Bob travelled each day to the University. By then James had disposed of the Jeparit business and joined the family permanently in Melbourne. Then, apparently in 1918, the family moved into what became their permanent home, a two-storey house in Wellington Street, Kew.[33]

It is not clear why the Menzies made so many moves before finally settling down. Perhaps, as strangers to Melbourne, they took time to find practical and congenial surroundings. What partly sold the Kew house to them was its size: once the Jeparit business had gone an uncertain economic future turned Kate's mind to the possibility of taking in lodgers.[34] But in any case, after their experience of more congested suburbs, Kew must have seemed especially attractive to them as country folk. As its historian, F. G. A. Barnard, proudly wrote in 1910, 'Kew has, ever since its first settlement, borne the distinction of being Melbourne's prettiest and healthiest suburb'. Its elevation, extensive parklands and fine views over the Yarra and the city contrasted favourably with the circumstances of its lower-lying and more densely

---

[32] *JL*, 23 December 1909.
[33] The account of the Menzies' movements after their arrival in Melbourne is the result of resourceful detective work on the directories of the day by Ms Patsy Hardy.
[34] Information from Mr G. Menzies.

populated neighbours, Hawthorn and Camberwell. There the completion of the Camberwell railway in 1882 had brought a transformation: as Barnard puts it, the populations of Kew and Hawthorn were to that point much the same; after the railway came, however, Hawthorn 'simply walked away from Kew and doubled its population in no time, but as it could not double its size, the inevitable consequence is that for people to the acre Kew possesses only about two and a half to Hawthorn's ten'. As might be expected, there were some notable mansions in Kew, which was a socially desirable address. That was perhaps important to James as a new member of parliament.[35]

At the beginning of 1910, just before the family move, James sent Bob to Melbourne with instructions to present himself to the headmaster of Scotch College to seek enrolment in that school. But close friends from Grenville days, the sons of a Methodist clergyman, naturally chose to go to Wesley College, and Bob wanted to be with them. So he went for interview to Wesley's formidable headmaster, L. A. Adamson, and was accepted. Father James was not pleased and the disobedient boy found himself on his mettle: 'You may suppose that having had this bad year at Grenville and having been given the rounds of the kitchen by my somewhat peppery parent about it, I knew that when I went to Wesley I had to put my nose down, otherwise all hope of the University was out'.[36] A contemporary at Wesley, Percy Joske, later described the fifteen-year-old lad who arrived at the school for his first term at the beginning of 1910: 'he was a gangling type of boy, growing rapidly, with intense energy and tremendous self-assurance'. Joske says that on closer acquaintance Menzies seemed never to stop talking. 'His tongue was derisive. He did not hesitate to throw his weight about, and his common term of scorn for those with whom he disagreed ... was "you're a dag" '. So he soon received the nickname 'Dag Menzies', which stuck to him throughout his schooldays.[37]

By the time Bob arrived at Wesley, Adamson, who had become headmaster in 1902, had put his impress firmly on the school. An Englishman and a product of Rugby and Oxford, Adamson extolled 'strenuousness and sentiment', and the first period of his rule, the years from 1902 to 1913, were for the school 'the golden age of sport'. If ever in the past a boy went to school solely for study that time had gone by, Adamson said.

[35] F. G. A. Barnard, *Jubilee History of Kew. Its Origin and Progress 1803–1910* (Kew 1910), 10, 57.
[36] Dawes, 51.
[37] Percy Joske, *Sir Robert Menzies, 1894–1978*, 7.

> The Rhodes Scholarship has changed things in an extraordinary way. Now, if a boy has brains and has the slightest chance of winning the scholarship, he pays attention to his sports as well as to his study, and he is twice the boy for doing so. If a student does not feed his brain with healthy blood he will run the risk of petering out.

Though as a man Menzies was to enjoy following football and cricket, observing each as an art rather than a mere game, he was at Wesley not very interested in and certainly incompetent at sport. Probably because of this, Adamson never made him a prefect.[38] Preparing himself for examinations was Menzies' overriding consideration.

In his first two years at Wesley he did not particularly shine, but his third year of work was more successful: at the end of it Menzies won one of the twenty-five exhibitions, each worth £40, awarded by the State for university study, as well as the highest honours in English and History. Menzies attributed this happy outcome to two teachers in particular: Harold Stewart and Frank Shann. Stewart was a strict disciplinarian with a formidable directness, a man who by precept taught clear and honest thinking. Shann was the principal English teacher whom Menzies credited with remedying the stilted style he brought from his Ballarat schools. He was also an important influence in encouraging Menzies to memorize thousands of lines of poetry, chiefly Shakespeare, which beside their imperceptible effect on his vocabulary must have been important in cultivating that sense of timing and balance evident later in his work as barrister and public speaker.[39]

Menzies at last began in 1913 the university studies he had so ardently hoped for, enrolling in first year Law. At the end of 1916 he duly graduated, with first-class honours. Academically this undergraduate career was a triumph, very much something to atone for Grenville and please his peppery parent. In 1914 Menzies won the Dwight Prize in British History and Constitutional History; in 1915 he was awarded the John Madden Exhibition in Jurisprudence and the Jesse Leggatt scholarship in Roman law, the law of contract and the law of property; in his final year he won the coveted Bowen prize for an English essay. The last-mentioned,

---

[38] Impressions of Wesley are from Geoffrey Blainey, James Morrissey and S. E. K. Hulme, *Wesley College: the First Hundred Years* (Melbourne 1967): 'the golden age of sport', 108; Adamson on the Rhodes Scholarship, 111; Menzies' habits and achievements at Wesley, 76; also Joske, *Sir Robert Menzies*, 8, and Cameron Hazlehurst, *Menzies Observed*, 20.
[39] Menzies and his teachers at Wesley: Dawes, 53, 55. Mr Ken Menzies asserted at interview, 11 November 1985, that his father could all his life recite many lines of Shakespeare.

on *The Rule of Law During the War*, was printed as a thirty-six-page brochure in 1917—Menzies' first publication—with the signal honour of an introduction by William Harrison Moore, the Professor of Law and Menzies' hero. University records show that he had earned the Master of Laws degree by early 1918.[40] His sister Belle was in later years fond of explaining these feats by describing the undergraduate Menzies at his table in the family home behind a monumental pile of books, eschewing social life and sport to plough night after night through one tome after another, with a bowl of peanuts always at his elbow. The picture is apt enough in one sense: no set of achievements like his would have been possible without a hard slog, and father James and— more ruthlessly—Grandmother Menzies had taught him the necessary self-discipline for that. But the story has another dimension, one that tells of intellectual energy exceeding the demands of academic work and, perhaps more important, of a burgeoning drive towards public prominence and leadership in an environment where, for the first time in his experience, both were there for the taking.

The tip of the iceberg here was a recommendation of the Students' Representative Council (SRC) to the University Council, late in 1915, that Menzies should be the 1916 editor of the *Melbourne University Magazine (MUM)*. The Council approved and then, early in 1916, the undergraduates elected Menzies to the presidency of the SRC itself. By now a senior in a student body of 1200, he had from his freshman days taken a keen interest in student affairs. He was a founder of the Historical Society, which in the absence of a debating society became one of the few forums in which student views could be aired. An active member of the Law Students' Society, he established an early reputation as a notable debater.[41] He also contributed to *MUM*, initially as a writer of verse which, though often painfully sentimental to the modern eye, handled metre well and used the 'poetic' clichés of the day as effectively as most. By the time of his elevation to editor he had established a reputation as an unusually bright and articulate member of the undergraduate community.

It should also be said that, within that community, his thinking was 'sound'. There was as yet no Labor club and radical students were few. One of these, Guido Baracchi, has described the student

---

[40] The principal documents recording Menzies' undergraduate career are in Melbourne University Archives (MUA): Professional Board Minutes, IX, 451; Student Administration, enrolment no. 130119; application for lectureship in Law of Contract, 26 April 1920, 1920/239.
[41] *Melbourne University Magazine (MUM)*, October 1915.

The Students' Representative Council of the University of Melbourne, as photographed in 1916: *(standing)* I. B. Fabrikant (Engineering), L. E. B. Stretton (Laws), P. Kelynack (Veterinary Science), A. H. Edgar (Medicine); *(seated)* K. A. McCarthy *(Medicine,* Hon. Treasurer), Miss Norah Crawford (Arts, Vice-President), R. G. Menzies (President), Miss E. M. Kelly (Science), L. W. Craig (Medicine, Hon. Secretary).

body of the day as 'bourgeois in its social background',[42] a definition which, while implying that wealth and privilege were represented, also allowed that many students came from respectable though not particularly prosperous families, who were either making economic sacrifices to send their children to university or, like the Menzies, were fortunate to have offspring bright enough to compete successfully for the relatively few free scholarship places which were available. In some of his first contributions to *MUM* Menzies caught well the earnest spirit and decorous behaviour conventionally expected of such students. The teaching staff of the University and affiliated colleges set an example in at least one important matter. In April 1915, just after the Gallipoli landing, a well-attended staff meeting passed, *nem con*, a series of resolutions pledging their services to the country's war effort. The

[42]Baracchi, 'What's new, Professor Derham?', ibid., 1970.

first and most important of these was the vow to abstain from the use of alcohol, except under medical advice, for the duration of the war.[43] But not all the students followed this worthy precept, as an article of Menzies'—'An Evergreen Topic'—disapprovingly related. One student audience, stimulated by the demon drink, had heckled a group of lady students—'The Girls Who Stayed at Home'—who put on a cabaret show in the ' "sweet cause" of charity'. For Menzies this disturbance was 'boorish and ill-mannered', the work of 'the gilded heroes of "the order of the tankard" '. These were the students, he wrote, who cultivated 'the friendship of the billiard room' and, forgetting the purpose of university life, 'freely squander their parents' money, and acquire a manly contempt for him who is so far lost to self-respect and the claims of society as to study laboriously for examinations'.[44] What was missing at the University was the discipline students had known at school, and without that many were lost.[45]

This moralistic tone was to be the hallmark of *MUM* during Menzies' editorship. The magazine, he wrote in his first editorial, existed to record 'our fleeting fancies, both grave and gay ... that we may learn to express ourselves with clearness and dignity, or failing that, with piquancy and wit'. A second part of the editorial, on 'Education and Truth', while a little short on clarity and wit, certainly had dignity. It defined education as an 'eternal struggle towards completed truth', a 'refining and purifying process', forming the 'foundation on which every one of us, be he or she an earnest student, must go on building through life'.[46] Most of Menzies' editorials and signed articles were in this serious vein, canvassing a variety of subjects ranging from the question of war aims to the tercentenary of Shakespeare's birth.[47] There were also several extraordinarily flowery appreciations of the natural world: 'A Mountain Fancy', telling at length of an eerie night-time hike at Mt Macedon; and 'Night Skies', bush reflections on a clear evening when 'my mind, freed of its shackles, wanders up and up from star to star, until it is lost in the infinite glories of worlds beyond worlds'.[48] Each piece has for its central point the recording of a mystical moment when, experiencing a profound sense of the supernatural, 'My spirit bows down and worships in silence and alone'. Since at the time he was also president of the Students' Christian Union Menzies was no doubt

[43] *MUM.*, June 1915.
[44] Ibid., October 1915.
[45] Ibid., May 1916.
[46] Ibid.
[47] Ibid., May, October 1916.
[48] Ibid., August, October 1916.

expected to promote such themes, though beneath the mannered prose one senses some strain, as if in the experiences he talks about he is almost pathetically grateful for the imagined 'signs' of faith confirmed.

Not that, outwardly, there was doubt about himself or anything he stood for. One contemporary, Brian Lewis, describes Menzies at this time as 'massive and dignified ... At the University he was a big fish in a pool depleted of males by the war', a remark given special point by the fact that at the height of his influence as a student, Menzies was briefly engaged to Lewis's sister, Phyllis. According to Lewis, it was a strange match which no one quite understood, given Menzies' lordliness and Phyllis's flippancy and impertinence. 'There was no obvious affection between them and none seemed to develop', says Lewis. 'Both were prominent at the University and there was the air of an arranged dynastic marriage'. Such criticisms notwithstanding, Lewis recalls that he and his brother Neil, then schoolboys, 'liked Bob a lot. He showed no stiff dignity with us and was easy and natural; he did not condescend but dealt with us in an adult sort of way'. Here was a side of Menzies not often commented on at this time and one for which the Lewis family was soon to have special, and sad, reason to be grateful. Brian and Neil had four brothers at the war and in 1918 one of them, Owen, whom Menzies had known at Wesley, was killed. Neil was at school when the news came through and 'was eating his ... lunch beside the Front Turf when Bob Menzies found him and gently told him. Bob has done many things in his life, important things, kind things and cruel things, but none kinder than this'.[49]

The 1916 SRC had eleven members. Four of these were medical students; there was a representative each from Engineering, Science, Veterinary Science, Arts and Dentistry; and Menzies and Len Stretton, probably his best undergraduate friend, came from Law. The only woman on the Council, Norah Crawford, represented Arts and was Menzies' vice-president.[50] Her name and his were sometimes linked in campus gossip, with what degree of truth it is not possible to tell: she was in due course to marry Stretton. The routine work of the Council as recorded in its minutes included the arrangement of debates with Sydney University, the organization of socials and theatre nights, and the supervision of the sports union. A surviving programme for the 'Varsity Theatre night' of 6 October 1916 shows how even the war

---

[49] Brian Lewis, *Our War* (Melbourne 1980), 261–2, 264, 300.
[50] There is a photograph of the SRC of 1916, with a caption identifying individuals and their constituencies, in *MUM*, October 1916.

could not dampen the normal puerile humour of the undergraduate review. Called—for no reason that is obvious—'The Geisha', the show consisted of the performance of a series of songs (words supplied with the programme) written to fit various well-known tunes and full of in-house references to people and incidents. The one serious note came at the end of a humorous piece describing Prime Minister Hughes going to England to 'expound his martial views' and returning to say:

> 'They want more men back there, and I propose to send 'em,
> A stiff-backed crowd oppose me, but egad, sir, I will bend 'em,
> The people shall decide conscription by a Referendum!'
> Said little—Billy Hughes.
>
> Good boy, Billy Hughes,
> We like a man who's game to back his martial views,
> We like your fighting spirit, and we want the world to know
> That the boys who wear the blue and black have never been too slow,
> And whether all the votes are for the 'yes' or for the 'no',
> Three cheers for—Billy Hughes!

A programme note explained that this piece had been 'written, after consultation, to express the views of the S.R.C., by R. G. Menzies, Club House, University'.[51]

Later that month the conscription issue came up in the University in a much less light-hearted way. Outside, the campaign for the first referendum was being savagely fought, and the SRC decided to convene two meetings and invite distinguished speakers to put the 'yes' case at the first and the 'no' case at the second. Two barristers and graduates of the University, J. G. Latham and G. Maxwell, accordingly gave a large audience at the Melba Hall the arguments for a 'yes' vote. They were well received, listened to attentively and loudly cheered, so that an *Argus* reporter concluded that 'with the exception of very few, the students were enthusiastically in favour of conscription'.[52] The second meeting, convened a few days later to allow the opposite case to be put, quickly confirmed this judgement. The invited speaker was Maurice Blackburn, Labor MLA and Melbourne's best-known pacifist and opponent of conscription. When the hall was opened students crowded boisterously in and a male student commandeered a piano at the back of the hall to accompany loud singing of the national anthem, 'Tipperary' and 'Till the boys come

---

[51] SRC Minute Book, MUA. Geisha Programme: Varsity Theatre Night, 6 October 1916, MUA. I wish to thank Dr Cecily Close for drawing my attention to this programme.
[52] *Argus*, 20 October 1916.

home'. The singing continued after Menzies, as chairman, and Blackburn climbed on to the stage. In a lull Menzies came forward to appeal to the audience:

> On Thursday last we had two distinguished graduates—(cheers)—to put before us the case for conscription (cheers). No one could be more strongly in favour of conscription than I—(a storm of cheers)—but, as logical men, we must recognise that if Mr. Blackburn's arguments are bad, they will prejudice his case, and if they are good ones, as sensible men we should hear him (Cheers, countercheers). I appeal to the sporting instincts of the undergraduate body for fair play by both sides. (Cheers, and the National Anthem).

The appeal had little effect: the national anthem was again sung and when a section of the audience (mainly women) remained seated there were shouts of 'stand up', and 'traitors'. Blackburn did his best: 'you do not honour the King by singing the National Anthem as an obstruction to free speech', he managed to shout in one lull. 'I say you do not represent the sense of University opinion, nor the good sense of the University.' Miss Lush, an undergraduate, climbed on to the platform and tried to speak but was counted out and aggressively asked by a student who followed her why she had not stood up when the national anthem was sung. 'When you sang it legitimately to open the meeting I stood', she replied, 'but not when it was used for obstruction'. ('Uproar, and a loud voice, "We're counteracting disloyalty". Cheers'). At length Blackburn gave up: 'Now, ladies and gentlemen and others present'— (laughter and a voice, "Maurice, you wrong me")—'I am deeply grateful for the kind hearing', and with that he walked out of the hall. In the dying minutes of the meeting a Mr Sinclair, M. A. Oxon, spoke in support of Blackburn and a medical student, Mr Dinwoodie, replied. The national anthem was sung, cheers were given for conscription, and the *Argus* reporter counted only twenty hands held up when a vote of thanks was moved for Blackburn.[53]

The best-known case of an individual student being made to suffer for radical anti-war views is that of Guido Baracchi, who when eighty-three wrote for *MUM* in 1970 a witty account of his exploits as a law student in 1917, his *'annus mirabilis'*. An enthusiastic guild socialist, Baracchi had debated his views in the Historical Society where, he says, even radicals would chide him for mentioning the class struggle, or 'tut tut' him for wanting to abolish the wage system. Few took Marx seriously. 'Bob Menzies, very slim and handsome, would reassure us for the twentieth time that he

[53] Ibid., 24 October 1916.

believed in the "via media", uttered with unction even then'. In 1917, after Menzies' stint as *MUM*'s editor was over, Baracchi served on the journal's editorial board. For the first issue of that year he wrote an article entitled 'National Guilds: Capital and the State', which offended most of the university community and was angrily taken up by the Professorial Board. 'The war', it began, 'whatever the jingoes and junkers tell us, is not primarily our affair. Essentially it is an European war, fought by the Allies against Germany to maintain the balance of European power. This is the true explanation of our recruiting figures, the exact index of the nation's war interest'. The Professorial Board interviewed Baracchi and its more extreme members pressed for his expulsion. Moderate counsel, however, prevailed after Harrison Moore, in helpful mood, asked Baracchi the leading question (which he answered in the affirmative): 'You wish to stress the word "primarily" '? But the reprieve was brief: in less than a week Baracchi was summoned before the Board again. This time his offence was to have responded to published letters of complaint about his views with a sardonic reply inviting his critics to prove their commitment to the war by either enlisting or taking up useful war work like knitting socks. Expulsion now seemed certain, until Baracchi narrowly saved himself by scribbling a declaration of loyalty to the British Empire. But students inflamed by Baracchi's behaviour were not so easily mollified: a crowd pushed him up to the boot-tops into the university lake and at an impromptu meeting resolved that he must publish in the next issue of *MUM* an apology for having expressed views which were calculated to reflect discredit on the University. When Baracchi agreed, the incident was declared closed.

Baracchi thought that Menzies took no part in this affair: he did not see Menzies at either the lake dunking or the subsequent meeting and he was later 'positively informed' that Menzies was not among the crowd.

> I accepted this [opinion] the more unreservedly because someone else assured me Menzies had said he wouldn't have a bar of my views, but thought I should be allowed to express them. Many years later, I had this confirmed to me by a man who had been his friend and fellow student ... I concluded: if in nothing else, on that occasion Menzies was like Voltaire. 'For', as he has written with truth in his memoirs, 'even I had my good moments'. This was one of them.[54]

As a member of the *MUM* board of management Baracchi would have seen a reply Menzies wrote in his best florid style to the offending article. In it he pressed Baracchi to 'come up from his

[54] What's new, Professor Derham?', *MUM*, 1970.

digging in the miry clay, and stand upon some little eminence, whence we may see a goodly landscape, and breathe the fresh air of God's heaven'. There he would see a free Australia, with a priceless British heritage, 'fighting beneath the banners of truth, and justice, and honour, and all that counts for much in the world's future'. Menzies' piece, though it reached galley proof stage, was never published. The management board, in view of the furore caused by Baracchi's first article, decided not to print a second from him, and in fairness to exclude Menzies as well.[55]

The Baracchi incident and the pro- and anti-conscription meetings were boisterous expressions of a jingoism which, as the war progressed, bred in the University, as outside its doors, a dark spirit of persecution against 'shirkers' and those fancifully thought of as potential 'traitors'. In one notorious case a vendetta in the University Council led by the warden of Trinity College, Alexander Leeper, issued in the virtual dismissal of two German-born members of the university staff, despite their marriages to Australians and their clear Australian sympathies.[56] The Council member who moved the final motion to prevent the offenders' appointments being renewed at the end of 1915 was L. A. Adamson, headmaster of Menzies' Wesley College. Another Wesley man who forthrightly pressed similar views was Menzies' idol, Harold Stewart. Brian Lewis relates how his brother Ron, then president of Queen's College Students' Society, hosted a dinner at which Stewart was the guest of honour. Ron Lewis, just twenty, had reluctantly agreed to an appeal from his mother (who already had four sons at the war) to finish his university year before joining up. In his thank-you speech for the Society's hospitality Stewart attacked Lewis for not having enlisted. Such lapses of taste emphasize the savagery of the 'patriotic' persecution of youth. The Medical Students' Society refused to admit candidates for membership who could not satisfactorily explain why they had not enlisted, and the Presbyterian college, Ormond, would not allow men over twenty to stay in residence unless they had been rejected as medically unfit—a stand which the Church's General Assembly approved when it was challenged. As Lewis observes, it was in this atmosphere 'far easier to make the sacrifice of enlistment . . . than to accept the insults for non-enlistment'.[57]

Even crueller was the scarification occasionally meted out by men who were actually serving and could therefore with a certain smugness assume the right to speak. Menzies' *MUM* and his SRC

---
[55] David Walker, *Dream and Disillusion: a search for Australian cultural identity* (Canberra 1976), 111.
[56] G. Blainey, *A Centenary History of the University of Melbourne* (Melbourne 1957), 138.
[57] *Our War*, 310.

were the butts of one particularly vicious assault of this kind at the end of 1916. In the last issue he edited, Menzies closed his editorship with a modest farewell, 'De Nobis'. 'To please everybody', he wrote, 'is manifestly impossible'.[58] This issue of the magazine had scarcely gone to press when a letter arrived from one A. D. Ellis, 'somewhere in France'. 'A couple of your latest issues reached me in the trenches', he wrote, 'and when I read them I was sorry to have received them. How little the war seems to have affected you all!' College, club and society activities still went on, and eligible men, it seemed,

> were still nobly grappling with the difficult problem of whether they should finish their courses or fight for their country. They were not certain which way their duty lay !!! As an old student of the University ... I am grieved beyond measure at the editorial utterance of such preposterous rot. It can originate only from sublime ignorance, sublime conceit, or sublime selfishness.

As an old Melbourne man he found it humiliating to hear from Oxford and Cambridge men how as a matter of course their colleges emptied as all students volunteered within a few months of the outbreak of war. He thought candidature for office in clubs and societies, and especially in the SRC and management of MUM, should be made conditional on recent rejection for military service. In that way the taint of selfishness might disappear and there would be 'at least an early collapse of this strange exotic M.U.M., with its vapid reveries and its unmistakable, if intangible, air of pulseless patriotism'.

Menzies insisted that this letter be published in full in the first issue of 1917, despite the new editor's belief that Ellis's 'very arbitrary judgement might have been withheld', given his inability to examine personally 'the real conditions prevailing at the University at the present time'. In a letter to the editor Menzies wrote:

> ... Of much 'editorial rot' I plead guilty, but I do not think I am either sublimely ignorant, sublimely conceited, or sublimely selfish when I say that the path of duty does not always lead to the recruiting depot— duty has to many in this respect been a hard taskmaster.

> ... On the question of the M.U.M. and the S.R.C, in both of which I occupied a leading position, I will say nothing, deeming it better to leave your readers to their own reflections than to enter into any controversy with one who is, I freely admit, fighting for me.[59]

[58] *MUM*, October 1916.
[59] Ibid., May 1917.

The reference to duty as a hard taskmaster suggests how close to the bone Ellis had cut. That Menzies did not enlist puzzled some contemporaries and in later years was a subject for snide and uninformed comment, some of it by historians. The extent of the pain Menzies himself suffered on this issue cannot be known, but that he suffered is undoubted. Throughout his life he took the view, which few sensitive people would today contest, that the reason for an individual's decision in such a matter was absolutely personal, a question on which an outsider could have neither the knowledge nor the right to make a judgement. To take that attitude in the overcharged atmosphere of the University in 1916 and 1917 required courage, especially as for some it might seem discrepant with his intense patriotism and approval of Australia's involvement in the war, his enthusiastic support for conscription and the obvious enjoyment of the taste of military life he got by being a member of the Melbourne University Rifles. A small but obvious connection between the last two matters is that if conscription had come into force, Menzies would have been one of the first to be drafted—a fact which he must have known and which would have overridden (possibly to his relief?) whatever other loyalties or scruples were keeping him out of the AIF. But certainly his reputation in the eyes of those who persecuted 'shirkers' was not helped by his obvious pleasure in membership of the University Rifles in which, between 1915 and 1919, he served the necessary stint of compulsory military training then required of his age group to provide a militia for the domestic defence of Australia. By late 1915 he had attained the rank of lieutenant, was writing in *MUM* of members' pride and sadness at the loss of old comrades at Gallipoli and—perhaps inadvertently—jocularly revealing that, although the unit was now a three-company battalion, its standard of training still had a long way to go:

> Musketry is to be gone into more thoroughly this year, and a four days' 'musketry camp' will be held shortly. This will mean that instead of a few hurried shots with a borrowed rifle in a failing light, and with only the very haziest notion of which target to fire at, the science of shooting will now be carried out in a dignified manner. The recruit will be taught the elements ...[60]

The allegation that Menzies resigned his commission and so in effect rejected the idea of service in the war is incorrect: he held his commission until his mandatory period of service was over.[61]

---
[60] Ibid., August 1915.
[61] Joske, *Sir Robert Menzies*, 11; Dawes, 68; Menzies' reply to Page's attack in 1939, see below p. 275.

Brian Lewis, who knew Menzies well and was one of those puzzled by his failure to enlist, wrote years later: 'I believe that Bob had a deep reason for not going but could not reveal it without hurting others. I believe that he deliberately damaged his career knowing that he was making a sacrifice in doing so'.[62] Evidence for the last assertion is lacking, but the first is certainly correct. Menzies' two elder brothers, Frank and Les, joined the AIF with their parents' approval, but a family conference decided Bob must stay. As Frank was later to explain it, to have two out of the three boys at the front seemed 'a pretty good contribution'. One grown man was badly needed at home, to stand by parents who were ageing, not well off (James's parliamentary salary of £6 a week was their only regular income), and who had just been through the trauma—in their eyes, indeed, perhaps the disgrace—of losing Belle. She eloped, soon after Frank's enlistment, with a soldier of whom the other members of the family deeply disapproved. This happening, Frank said, had broken his father's heart. Family solidarity was Scots and notable: as Frank put it, 'if you scratched one you scratched the lot'.[63] Family conferences were to remain important in Menzies' scheme of things for a long time: that their conclusions were influential, and sometimes even binding, must be partly attributed to the firm disciplinary tradition in which the children had been brought up. Of incalculable importance too, one suspects, was the quiet but steely dominance of mother Kate. On the enlistment issue she never wavered.

In academic achievement and leadership in student affairs, Menzies' undergraduate years have to be considered triumphal, and this even despite the fact that in his time the absence of many men at the war so reduced potential competition. His intellectual gifts were outstanding and he had a remarkable fluency of expression which was the fruit of a variety of experiences ranging from watching at close quarters the actions and sayings of his father and uncle in public affairs to the 'liberating' effect of his English studies at Wesley. That his speeches and writings were couched in the conventional idiom of the day and that they expressed received rather than original views has sometimes made him look to modern—and anachronistic—eyes to be dull and conventional, especially by comparison with the occasional non-conformist, like Baracchi. But his strength derived from his very skill in articulating majority opinion, and he did this so well because he agreed with that opinion himself. In a special way, he was the sounding board

---
[62] *Our War*, 263.
[63] Interview of Frank Menzies by Lady McNicoll, NLA Oral History Unit, 1169/350.

of the wartime university community. What we cannot easily gauge at this distance is the kind of person, or how popular, he was. Elegant in deportment and handsome in appearance, he seems to have made some good friends, and incidents like his sensitive treatment of Neil Lewis at the time of Owen's death suggest a capacity for kindness. On the other hand he could display a pomposity which opponents enjoyed pricking and, if contemporaries like Joske are to be believed, his sharp tongue made him something of a 'controversial figure':

> ... his habit of denigrating people caused him to be greatly disliked ... His friends vainly sought to support him by expiating on his outstanding capacity. It was not unusual for other people, who may not have possessed his ability but who had to measure up to him, to discover that he had made derogatory remarks about them. This may have led to the statement afterwards often repeated, that he did not suffer fools gladly. The trouble was that his opponents frequently were *not* fools and that he tended to say things that were not only cutting and unkind but that were unjustified.[64]

[64] *Sir Robert Menzies*, 19–20.

2

The Young Lawyer

UNDER THE headline 'Threshold of a Career: Happy Hour in Banco Court' the Melbourne *Argus* carried in 1922 a rather whimsical account of how a batch of a dozen barristers and solicitors—with 'smiling, happy, hopeful faces'—had recently been admitted to practise. 'Each was followed by a father, a mother or some young person whose friendship (on her oft repeated assurance) was "purely platonic".' On the courtroom's second bench, at which on ordinary days instructing solicitors and waiting barristers would have sat, was a row of twelve bibles on which the new barristers were to 'swear true allegiance, and that they would "so demean themselves" '. English tradition, the reporter said, was never more rigidly observed than here. The barrister moving admission of a candidate rose and performed his office in set language, in exactly the same manner as the Lord Chancellor of England 'intones his address'.[1] Four years earlier, in May 1918, having served the required twelve months articles of clerkship with a solicitor, Menzies had been through just this ceremony. Unfortunately there is no record of how he felt about it or of which family members—or other close friends—watched.

Victoria's legal profession was what was known as a 'fused' one: following an Amalgamation Act in 1891, legal practitioners were admitted as both barristers and solicitors of the Supreme Court. Occasionally—mostly in country areas—one person might actually practise both callings, becoming what was known in the parlance of the profession an 'amalgum'; but this was rare. More usually, an entrant to the profession chose between the work of an advocate and that of an office lawyer. The latter normally could plead only in magistrates' courts; the former generally signed the Bar Roll of barristers, undertaking 'to practise exclusively as a barrister',

[1] *Argus*, 2 June 1922.

mostly in the higher courts. To sign the Roll was also to agree 'to comply with the rules made [by the barristers] in general meeting and with rulings of the Committee elected by such barristers'. This committee, the 'Bar Association', was the real definer and enforcer of barristers' standards of professional conduct. In signing the Roll Menzies was being admitted to a small and tight-knit professional élite.

No more than seventy or eighty strong, the Victorian Bar, as its historian, Sir Arthur Dean, has put it, 'began its post-war existence somewhat heavy at the bottom and light at the top'. Between 1919 and 1921 most of its leaders were elevated to the Bench and in 1919 there were only three King's Counsel in practice. The 'heavy bottom' grew quickly after the war, swollen initially by returned servicemen who had qualified before the war or completed their training soon after. In the decade to 1920 the number of barristers on the Roll more than doubled, competition for available work became keen and there was an acute shortage of accommodation. Selborne Chambers, the established home of the Victorian Bar, was full to overflowing by 1923.[2] Menzies, however, had managed to get rooms there before then. He would in fact remain a tenant in this hallowed building almost until his death.

Built in 1881, Selborne Chambers was named for the then Lord High Chancellor of England, Baron Selborne. Close by the law courts and with a frontage on Chancery Lane, it had developed by the post-war years what its historian, F. Maxwell Bradshaw, calls 'that combination of dignified severity with a slight suggestion of the down at heel, that is so often found in association with the law'. On the ground floor a wide central corridor ran the building's whole length and opened upward to an encircling gallery on to which the upstairs rooms opened. Above was a high-pitched, sawtooth ceiling. That central corridor, with its openness to the upper floor, created a sense of unity which made the place 'a cross between professional chambers and a club'. Little knots of barristers formed and dissolved there, some leaning over the balcony, to joke or discuss issues ranging from the latest appointment to the judiciary to cricket and football. Within this club-like atmosphere Bradshaw notes one routine happening which may be of particular importance in the Menzies story: the 'very audible remarks coming from one member of the Bar to another in this passageway', in which individuals' legal competence, religious beliefs and political views were 'challenged in broad Australian'. Passers-by might be

[2] Details of the Melbourne Bar for this period are from Arthur Dean, *A Multitude of Counsellors*, and Julian Disney, John Basten, Paul Redmond, Stan Ross, *Lawyers* (Sydney 1977).

Selborne Chambers, with its internal balcony over which barristers lean to chat and, in lighter moments, exchange badinage.

staggered, but 'this was merely part of the traditional comradeship of the Bar'.[3] Sir John Norris, a near-contemporary of Menzies in the 1920s, has made the same point. In those days, according to him,

[3] F. Maxwell Bradshaw, *Selborne Chambers Memories* (Melbourne 1962), 84–5.

the Bar was so small that everyone knew everybody else. There were no inhibitions about what they said about or to each other: they were good friends who neither took umbrage nor suffered real hurt. Time may have somewhat romanticized this memory of uninhibited friendship, but the atmosphere so recalled seems not in general terms to be gainsaid. Sir John is also of the opinion that an element in Menzies' later reputation for acerbity and seeming arrogance was his having often unthinkingly carried over into a political world with wildly differing assumptions about behaviour the ease, indeed intellectual fun, of personal criticism and argumentation appropriate to a close-knit lawyers' community.[4] Menzies' son, Ken, agrees, vividly recalling boisterous arguments and cutting epithets exchanged over the meal table by Menzies and his friend Len Stretton, especially during holidays shared at Mt Macedon. Others, friends and family members, who joined in had to be prepared to 'have their heads chopped off'; a stranger overhearing it all could only sense murderous overtones, instead of the good-natured game it really was. The observation helps to explain, if it does not excuse, the insensitivity Menzies sometimes showed to the atmosphere of a non-legal milieu. In due course, for example, it needed his wife to warn him against the habit of carrying into politics the legal convention of referring to people by their surnames.[5] On the other hand we need to note how misleading it would be to accept as the whole truth this explanation of one of Menzies' most prominent foibles. That something deeper was also involved is clear from judgements like that of his contemporary, Percy Joske, who knew him well:

> Menzies' strength at the Bar and subsequently in politics lay in his personality. He had an incredible degree of charm and good looks. His personality was forceful and determined, and like many another Scot he would ride roughshod over his opponents. He employed his cutting tongue without hesitation. As he always spoke with great authority and was readily quoted, his talk could and did cause harm to the unfortunate at whom it was aimed . . . [He had] a fierce determination to succeed, which made him cause offence to others, often thereby doing himself harm.[6]

As a newly called barrister Menzies had the good fortune in 1918 to read with the leading Victorian junior, Owen Dixon. Menzies was the first pupil Dixon took on, even though by this

---

[4]Interview with Sir John Norris, 20 May 1988. Sir Sydney Frost, who was also present, confirmed the point.
[5]Interview with Mr Ken Menzies, 24 November 1988.
[6]*Sir Robert Menzies*, 26.

time he had built up 'an enormous practice' (Menzies' description) and would in 1922 take silk—which by strict convention brought to an end the possibility of his accepting further neophytes.[7] Apart from the special privilege of working with somebody so eminent Menzies was fortunate in being able to undertake such an apprenticeship at all: it was expensive, and some of the leading lawyers of the day—Cussen and Dixon himself were examples—had not been able at the appropriate point in their careers to afford it. The cost was fifty guineas for six months. How Menzies met it we do not know, but perhaps an admiring family helped him to spin out the proceeds from early briefs. To be a pupil meant that one was privy to all papers and meetings to do with cases that the master was engaged in, could be asked by him to undertake devilling in the preparation of cases, and sat in court to observe and learn from him in action.[8] Menzies himself has put the purpose of it all well. The pupil

> is, of course, free to accept briefs of his own and, if he is lucky, as I was, gets a few. But his great advantage is that he sees a busy junior at work, and at close quarters. The law comes alive for him. He begins to know how little he knows and what a world of difference there is between academic learning and the same learning when applied to the tangled facts of life... I soon lost any self-conceit which may have been induced by my success as a student. When Dixon would invite my views on some matter that had come on to his table, and I nervously offered them, he would nod gravely and then go on to develop an argument that, invariably, though in a kindly way, showed me that I had no more than touched the surface of the matter, that it had aspects of which I had not dreamed. I did not take long to learn that I had almost everything to learn.[9]

In these circumstances 'an occasional simple brief of my own for some case in a court of Petty Sessions was useful ... in restoring some of my confidence'. The first of these briefs he remembered well, but perhaps embroidered a little in the telling. It took him to the small country town of Mansfield, where he appeared in the Mining Warden's Court before a Police Magistrate, one Knight. His fee was six guineas, from which he had to pay his train fare and accommodation. Still, to him it was 'a great case':

---

[7]For a brief but telling appreciation of Owen Dixon, see Sir Ninian Stephen, *Sir Owen Dixon: A Celebration* (Melbourne 1986).
[8]Interview with Sir John Norris, 20 May 1988.
[9]Menzies, *Measure of the Years*, 229–30.

Right through the night I kept thinking about it. Every time I conjured up a new point I would sit up in bed, light the candle on the bedside table and make a note of the point... The next morning, walking across to the Court, I saw my opponent. He was a dark-jowled, lugubrious fellow, the local solicitor. Though I got to know him well eventually and he proved a very fine chap, I remember saying to myself: 'Well, all right, if I can't beat this chap, that's too bad'. We went in. We argued the case. The magistrate, with a bit of a twinkle in his eye, said to me at one stage: 'But, Mr. Menzies, you put that particular point pretty confidently. Suppose I disagree with you?' 'Well', I said , 'Your Worship'—he reminded me of this years afterwards—'if you do that, it will be unfortunate, because it will involve me in an appeal and I will certainly carry it on appeal and have that put right'.

This cheeky remark notwithstanding, the magistrate decided the case in Menzies' favour, though through a final throw of irony it was in the end lost on appeal to the Court of Mines, despite the fact that Dixon was brought in to lead Menzies on the appeal case.[10]

Menzies made his first appearance in the High Court less than a year later in a case, Troy v. Wrigglesworth, which he liked to remember whimsically as having come his way by accident. The senior counsel originally engaged for the case suddenly fell ill and the instructing solicitors, who were only paying a small fee, looked hurriedly for a junior who knew something about constitutional law. So Menzies got the brief, and his father came to sit at the back of the court and listen to the arguments.[11] For a junior to appear alone for the first time before the High Court of up to seven judges could be a fearsome experience. Used to single judges or juries in his own State he could find it difficult to follow a planned argument in the face of a panel of judges, each of whom had at every point the right of interjection and cross-examination.[12] The case concerned a Commonwealth employee, an army driver who had been caught speeding in St Kilda Road, Melbourne. The fact that he was taking a patient to the base hospital did not save him: he was convicted and fined by a summary court consisting of two Justices of the Peace. Menzies' brief was to conduct the appeal of this man, Edmond Troy, before the full High Court Bench. The technical

---

[10] Menzies' words are recorded by Dawes, 83–4. Menzies' Fee Book for the period (in the possession of Mr Hartog Berkeley, who kindly made it available to me), records that the fee he received for this case was six guineas. Also, in July 1954, a representative of *John Bull Who's Who* asked Menzies for details of his first case. He replied: 'Mining Case before Warden's Court, at Mansfield, Victoria. Fee £6.6.-. Expenses (travelling, etc) £5.-.- Profit £1.6.- !! (Won)', NLA, MS. 4936/17/427/17.
[11] Dawes, 85–6.
[12] Dean, *A Multitude of Counsellors*, 195.

argument he advanced was that by Victorian law and precedent a Commonwealth employee committing such an offence could not be tried by anything less than a Police Magistrate's Court. Three of the five judges ruled in his favour, and ordered a retrial in the proper Victorian court. In presenting the verdict of the majority, Judge Edmund Barton complimented both sides on the able way in which the argument had been conducted, and Judge Gavan Duffy, who dissented from the final decision and who had given Menzies 'a pretty torrid time', told Menzies that he had been 'very much impressed by the ability with which you have presented your argument'. This case netted Menzies 10 guineas, and he always enjoyed recounting the family sequel:

> Well, you know, the Old Man went out, and afterwards went back to my mother and said: 'You know, my dear, I have been underestimating Robert'. That was very good. It almost revolutionised his outlook on his third son's talents.[13]

The effect of this case in bringing Menzies favourably to the notice of the High Court judiciary was seconded by his performance at a celebrated Bar dinner in Melbourne a few months later. In October 1919 illness forced Sir Samuel Griffith, Australia's pre-eminent constitutional lawyer and Chief Justice of the High Court since its establishment in 1903, to resign. Sir Adrian Knox, a leading Sydney barrister, was appointed in Griffiths' place. In courtesy the Melbourne Bar gave him a dinner. As the most recently called barrister present, Menzies was 'Mr Junior', who by tradition would normally have the task of proposing the distinguished guest's toast. But the senior barrister managing the programme, H. E. Starke, did not have a high opinion of Menzies and arranged that the chairman of the proceedings, Sir Edward Mitchell, should propose the toast. Though a senior and distinguished lawyer, Mitchell was noted for his dreariness as a public speaker. His toast for Knox went according to form and an exasperated Starke, having second thoughts, scribbled on a placecard the curt note: 'Menzies, propose Barton's health!' It was a sudden but congenial summons: Barton, a father of federation, former Prime Minister and the most venerable of Australian judges—with 'fine brow and a lambent eye'—was a man in whose honour one such as Menzies could warm. Perhaps, as he has written, he did it 'probably the better for having had no warning'.

---

[13]Troy v. Wrigglesworth, *Commonwealth Law Reports (CLR)*, 1918–19, 26: 307; Fee Book, 4 June 1919, 46; Dawes, 85–6.

I remember quoting Swinburne's verse to Walter Savage Landor:

> I came as one whose thoughts half linger,
>   Half run before;
> The youngest to the oldest singer
>   That England bore.

The speech had a *succes fou*; made me known to the judges; and restored me, permanently, I believe, to Starke's good graces ... [14]

By the end of 1919 briefs for cases in the Victorian County and Supreme courts were combining with opinion work to keep Menzies busy and lay the basis for a sound income. The reported cases show that he was soon developing a general practice, handling such matters as divorce, contracts and disputes over land, debts and wills. From the beginning, as he put it himself, he 'had no taste for criminal work, and did but little of it'.[15] In one way this is mildly surprising, for Menzies quickly developed the skill most necessary for success in such work: cross-examination. Joske attributes much of Menzies' success to the aplomb he showed in court from the beginning, his readiness when under pressure to withdraw or reconstruct an argument:

> It had become second nature to him to be always acting. If he got the wrong answer in cross-examination, he never let either the witness or the jury realise that it was, for him, the wrong answer. Even the best cross-examiners—and Menzies certainly deserves to be ranked among the best—on occasion get the wrong answer, and it is important to be able to take it without flinching. Menzies was too astute a cross-examiner to get the wrong answers often, but where this did occur, he took it as if it were the answer he was seeking in order to lead on to something else, making recovery that delighted the temporarily horrified solicitor instructing him.[16]

Menzies followed Troy v. Wrigglesworth with further appearances in the High Court in 1920, one of them of singular importance. In February he was Owen Dixon's junior in a case which involved the interpretation of an old man's intentions in a home-made, ungrammatical will.[17] But in other instances that year he appeared singlehanded, most notably in cases involving constitutional law, an area which he was to make peculiarly his own. The most momentous of these cases, Amalgamated Society of Engineers v.

---

[14]Dawes, 79; 'Mitchell' in *ADB*, 10: 527; Menzies, *Afternoon Light*, 322–3.
[15]Menzies, *Measure of the Years*, 255.
[16]*Sir Robert Menzies*, 267. Dean, *A Multitude of Counsellors*, also comments warmly on his skill, 220.
[17]McRobert v. McRobert, *Argus Law Reports*, 1920: 37.

Adelaide Steamship Co. Ltd (the so-called 'Engineers' case) marks a turning-point in both Commonwealth–State relations and in Menzies' own professional career. It brought him what Sir Arthur Dean has called 'sudden fame' which put him, while still a junior, remarkably near to the head of the Victorian Bar.[18]

The case concerned the respective powers of the Commonwealth and State arbitration tribunals. Jealous of the rights of their separate colonies—soon to be States—the founding fathers had in the Federal Constitution given the Commonwealth only specific powers, reserving all unnamed, 'residual' powers, to the States. Arbitration was one of the latter, except that in industrial disputes which spilled over more than one State boundary, the Commonwealth Arbitration Authorities had—by grant of a specific power—the right to act. It was in the interest of a union to get if it could an award from the Commonwealth Arbitration Court because such an award was superior in its widespread, interstate coverage of the workers in an industry. However, up to 1919 a string of High Court cases had supported a doctrine known as 'Implied Immunity of Instrumentalities', which read the Constitution to mean that neither the States nor the Commonwealth could legislate or otherwise act to interfere with each other's instrumentalities or organs of government. Following this doctrine, the High Court had consistently held that the Commonwealth arbitration system could not legally intrude in disputes between State employees and their government employers. The Engineers case raised this issue afresh, because what the Union wanted was the right to seek a federal award covering employees in two Western Australian government enterprises: a sawmill and a machine shop. Briefed to represent the union, Menzies arrived for the main proceedings to find himself faced with 'a thickly populated, and from my lonely point of view, hostile Bar table'. All the States except Queensland had briefed counsel to support Western Australia's fight against the Engineers. A serious issue of State rights was clearly felt to be at stake.

The argument, which occupied six days, was complex and—for the layman at least—arcane. But essentially, in a series of brilliant moves, Menzies challenged the doctrine of Immunity of Instrumentalities, and focused attention instead on the actual words of the Constitution. A specific grant of power to the Commonwealth, he argued, had to be fully defined before the residual powers were appealed to; and an express grant could only be reduced by express limitations. In the relevant Section of the Constitution, the only limitation he could find was the word 'industrial', and it was logical

---

[18]Dean, *A Multitude of Counsellors*, 195.

that 'what is industrial if done by a private employer is industrial if done by a State'. The judges, with one dissentient, agreed, and in upholding Menzies' case made a landmark constitutional decision. Its wider significance has been lucidly summed up by Geoffrey Sawer:

> The practical effect of this decision was to expand greatly the potential scope of Commonwealth power, because the Constitution operates by way of gift of power to the Commonwealth, not to the States, and the decision requires that powers so granted be given the fullest amplitude of meaning possible before one can begin to speak of the powers left to the States.[19]

Menzies won two other significant, if less revolutionary, High Court judgments for unions in 1920. The first was for the Federated Engine Drivers' and Firemen's Association, which had made a log of claims in Victoria, New South Wales, South Australia, Western Australia and Tasmania. An interstate dispute thus existed and the federal Arbitration Court became the appropriate body to handle it. But separate agreements and awards made within the States before the case came on reduced the dispute to one State, Tasmania, and that raised the question of whether the federal court was still competent to act. Contrary to previous rulings the High Court now held that once an interstate dispute exists, it has to be treated as such whatever happens, thus strengthening the position of the federal Arbitration authorities, as the unionists wished.[20] In the second case, for the Merchant Service Guild of Australia, Menzies persuaded the High Court that the Commonwealth Arbitration power encompassed pilotage and other State government activities—thus applying for the first time the precedent established by the Engineers' judgment.[21]

Besides being a constitutional landmark, the Engineers victory was for Menzies a personal landmark too. 'I was the sole counsel for the successful party. I was very young, twenty-five years old, and a success meant a great deal to me. In fact, I got married on the strength of it.'[22] These words, delivered with a flourish to an American university audience many years later, caught well a

---

[19] Geoffrey Sawer, *Australian Federal Politics and Law, 1901–29* (*AFPL* 1), 126–8, 216–17; *Australian Federalism in the Courts*, 121–31; Menzies, *Central Power in the Australian Commonwealth*, 30–42; L. Zines, *The High Court and the Constitution* (Sydney 1988), 335.
[20] Federated Engine Drivers' and Firemen's Association of Australia v. Adelaide Chemical and Fertiliser Co., Ltd, and others, 28 *CLR* (1920–1), 1; Sawer, *AFPL* 1, 220.
[21] Merchant Service Guild of Australia v. Commonwealth Steamship Owners' Association, 28 *CLR* (1920–1), 495; Sawer, *AFPL* 1, 220.
[22] Menzies, *Central Power*, 31.

spirit of remembered elation. Engineers put the seal on what was already a promising practice. Marriage was a luxury in which the young barrister could certainly indulge.[23]

Menzies' bride was Pattie Maie Leckie. They were married in the Kew Presbyterian church. Five years younger than her husband, Pat had been born at Alexandra, in central-eastern Victoria, where her father was at that time a farmer and storekeeper. Her mother died when Pat was only seven, and the girl was educated first at the Presbyterian Ladies' College, East Melbourne, and then at Fintona, in Camberwell, being a boarder at each school. John William (Jack) Leckie, Pat's father, had been educated at Scotch College, where he distinguished himself as an athlete and footballer. For two years he studied medicine at Melbourne University, but left medical studies to settle as a farmer and storekeeper at Alexandra. In 1913 he won a seat in the Victorian Legislative Assembly and in 1917 he moved to the Commonwealth House of Representatives. Defeated in the election of 1919 he remained out of politics for a decade and a half. In the meantime he moved to Melbourne and established the firm of Leckie and Gray, lithographic printers and canister manufacturers. He thus entered the business life of Melbourne, becoming a leading member of the Chamber of Manufacturers, serving in due course on its executive. In 1917 he remarried. With his daughter Pat he had a particularly close relationship, the product no doubt of the years without wife on one side and mother on the other, but strengthened by the fact that as she grew up she shared his political interests and travelled with him on election tours.[24]

As a boarder at PLC and Fintona, Pat routinely sat with her schoolmates in Sunday services at the appropriate Presbyterian churches, Cairns Memorial church in East Melbourne in the first case and Trinity church, Camberwell, in the second. In overlapping periods the Menzies family also attended these churches: she had seen Robert from a distance and the families—both of them prominent in church circles—knew of each other. But the couple seem not to have met formally until after she had left school and he was practising at the Bar. It was at a party at Camberwell and it became a kind of family legend that he walked into the room, strode across to her, and said: 'You're Pattie Leckie; you used to make eyes at me in church'. Pat always asserted its truth but he for his part humorously denied it: he hated to think, he said, that he was such a gauche young man, even in those days. After the

---

[23] The Fee Book shows receipts for each year ending in June as follows: 1919, £9 9s, 1920, £525 10s; 1921, £2149. The last two were respectable sums at this time.
[24] *ADB*, 10: 43–4.

party Robert escorted her to her home in Hawthorn: the friendship subsequently ripened and in a few months the two became engaged to be married.

After the marriage the couple lived briefly in a flat in Gellibrand Street, Kew, and then had houses in Charles Street and Grange Road, before moving to what was to be their home for twenty-five years in Howard Street, Kew. It was clear that they were very happy, though the young Mrs Menzies found her new in-laws a formidable family, close-knit and with narrow puritanical ideals which often made them self-righteously critical of others whom they saw as having less rigid standards. And they—especially the mother—were inordinately proud of and ambitious for Bob: Pat, as a girl not long out of school, felt them often to be cold and disapproving of her, as if she (or indeed anybody else?) was not really good enough for him. Time was to mellow this tension, but never quite to remove it. Children duly came: two sons, Ken in 1922 and Ian in 1923 and a daughter, Heather, in 1928. Home and children—as was normal in young middle-class professional families—was Pat's primary care. Bob, who as an up-and-coming barrister had been living at home in the Wellington Street house ruled by his capable mother, had few domestic skills and no incentive to learn any. In his new family circle his uselessness about the house, particularly his bumbling in the kitchen, became legendary. His children observe that he shrewdly cultivated the legend. His role was to work at his profession; and indeed he did.[25]

In later years Menzies was impatient of exaggerated stories which attributed his success in the courts simply to a brilliant intellectual gift for quickly mastering a brief. He told one author who wrote that Menzies could look over a brief as he walked into court and then deal with the case effectively that he was 'falling into a popular error'.

> No barrister could ever perform such a feat. The secret of whatever success I had as an advocate was that I always went into Court having devoted hours of work to the study of the brief, and having to the best of my ability mastered all its details. This I think is true of all the successful advocates I ever heard of. Flexibility in the course of argument is, of course, desirable but preparation is vital.[26]

The testimony of other lawyers who knew his court performances confirms the claim. Sir Arthur Dean, for example, has noted of Menzies that: 'In the presentation of legal argument to the Courts,

---

[25] The account of Menzies' meeting with Pat Leckie, their marriage and early life is from Dawes, 93–6, and interview with Dame Pattie Menzies, 1 October 1987.

[26] Menzies to Seth (a British author who wrote a book on him for children in the 'Red Lion' Series), 5 July 1960, NLA, MS. 4936/17/426/10.

notably to the High Court, he was outstanding: he knew his law when he came into court; his argument was well-prepared ... No Court could turn him from his course'.[27]

In the 1920s—over his principal years as an advocate—Menzies worked, as Dame Pattie remembers it, 'fantastically hard'. He estimated that at this time his weekly hours of work would average not less than eighty.[28] The Melbourne courts sat from 10.30 a.m. to one o'clock and from 2.15 to 4.15 in the afternoon.[29] Menzies' habit was to work at his desk long into the night and to get up as late as court or conference obligations permitted. In the first years of marriage this work routine and the demands on Pat of home and children meant that they lived what she calls 'a very quiet life'. Almost always, however, Menzies took Sunday off, to rest and spend time with his family. Though they sometimes went to church they took no part in wider church activities and Sunday was a day for reading, and occasional picnics and outings.

For Menzies himself there were other diversions, somehow compatible with the stern demands of his profession. Thus, for example, like most self-respecting Australian males of his day he avidly followed cricket, that spectator sport treated as at once a deadly serious element of social and national life, and an artform for sophisticated study and discussion. When test matches were played in Melbourne he joined, whenever he could get away, the grey hordes of felt-hatted, soberly dressed onlookers who crowded the cricket ground to give it an air of seriousness and dignity strange to the modern eye. He also began in 1925 a congenial association which was to last throughout his life by becoming a member of the Savage Club.

The famous London Savage Club—'a Club of Merry Fellows'—was established in 1857 as a place of meeting and mutual amusement for creative artists of all kinds: writers, painters, actors and musicians. It was and remained jealously exclusive. As late as 1976 it still had its Qualifications Committee to examine minutely the credentials of would-be members, 'to see that no-one, however wealthy or socially upstage, seizes the name Savage under the wire'. A Melbourne copy of the Club, founded in 1894, could never be so exclusive if it wanted to build a viable membership. Besides those of artistic bent others—chiefly professional and businessmen—were from the beginning admitted. The Club's rooms—a three-storey Georgian building in Bank Place, a short but charming cul-de-sac off Collins Street—are located in the heart of

---

[27] Dean, *A Multitude of Counsellors*, 220.
[28] Menzies, *Afternoon Light*, 316.
[29] Interview with the late Sir Reginald Sholl, 24 May 1985.

Melbourne's business and banking area, and hard by are the law courts and barristers' chambers. By Menzies' time lawyers formed a large part of the Club's membership. This was a place to rest, take refreshment and enjoy good fellowship. There were jovial dinners and socials, and clubrooms decorated with spears and clubs and sketches of cannibals around stewpots. The origin of the name 'Savage' was lost in obscurity, but often otherwise sober members found in it clues to the way of levity. For Menzies it must have been a welcome place of release from the hard work of his office. It was to prove important to him in another way too: as a place where informally he came to know a wide variety of influential men in the business and legal worlds.[30]

In the earlier 1920s opinions, retainers, the County Courts and the Victorian Supreme Court appear to have provided the staple fare of Menzies' practice.[31] County Courts had jurisdiction in both equity and common law cases up to £500 and it was natural, as his reputation grew, for Menzies' work there to diminish in favour of better briefs in the higher courts. But later on, when he had left his legal career far behind, he looked back at his experience of the County Court 'with a sort of nostalgic affection'. It was certainly one of the main sources of the legal recollections he loved to retail in an after-dinner speech or when relaxing with cigar and a drink in a congenial group. 'For all I know', he wrote in later life, 'the County Court has become the preserve of businesslike lawyers, pressed for time. But there were characters in my day. Their entertainment value was in some cases superior to their legal attainments'.[32]

Menzies was briefed in two High Court cases in 1921, did not appear in that Court the following year, but in 1923 had four cases there. From then on, clearly well established, he took High Court briefs which annually ranged in number between five and eight, until 1931 and 1932, when there were eleven and twelve respectively. Up to 1929, when Menzies took silk and Owen Dixon was appointed to the High Court bench, the two appeared together in more than a dozen cases. Menzies was Dixon's junior also in many cases in the Victorian Supreme Court. The two made a formidable combination, and the continued close association with his old teacher must have been important to the honing of Menzies' skills as an advocate. Over this period, either singly or with Dixon, Menzies had a number of High Court briefs on arbitration matters,

---

[30]Matthew Norgate and Alan Wykes, *Not So Savage* (London 1967); David Dow, *Melbourne Savages* (Melbourne 1947); K. D. Gott, 'Sir Robert as Savage', *Nation*, 7 March 1964, 5–7.
[31]Evidence from Fee book and surviving list of retainers.
[32]Menzies, *Measure of the Years*, 245.

frequently to appear on behalf of unions.[33] Though this was, in terms of total cases, only a minor part of his work in that jurisdiction, its importance is enhanced when we note that at this time he was also very active as an advocate in the Commonwealth Conciliation and Arbitration Court. Menzies was clearly developing, in the wake of the Engineers' case, an interest and expertise in industrial relations and the law associated with it. He was of course not alone among barristers in this: the 1920s were marked in Australia by bitter social tensions and intermittent industrial conflict which put the arbitration system under great strain and produced much litigation. But in Menzies' case a close concern with the legal problems created by these troubles was to have a special significance: indirectly it became one of the major influences which drew him into active politics. Most of his early work in the Arbitration Court was routine: unremarkable cases involving the meaning and application of awards. But in the mid-1920s, in both Arbitration and High Courts, Menzies became professionally involved in a number of cases which had notable implications for the federal politics of the period. The most important of these resulted from disputes which tied up the waterfront, and which the Commonwealth Ministry of the day interpreted as constituting a sinister threat to its central policies, and indeed to the capitalist system itself.

The Prime Minister, Stanley Melbourne Bruce, had come to office in 1923 at the head of a Nationalist–Country Party coalition. A Cambridge blue, barrister of Middle Temple, Gallipoli hero and Melbourne importer, Bruce represented himself as a simple businessman, opposed to socialism but unenthusiastic about 'party politics'. Government, he thought, was best conducted by the application to public affairs of good business methods. His Treasurer, Country Party leader Earle Page, a disarming but ruthless country surgeon and farmer, agreed. General prosperity during their first years in office encouraged optimistic planning for new national economic growth. Bruce's slogan was 'Men, Money and Markets': it envisaged attracting British finance and British migrants as the driving forces of an expanding economy.

Prosperity, however, also encouraged unionists, especially seamen and wharf labourers, whose work was arduous and circumstances harsh, to step up their traditional struggle for better

[33]The estimate of Menzies' activity in the High Court is based on a complete survey of the cases reported for the period in *CLR*. I wish to thank Ms Janet Penny for collecting the raw data for this. The figures for arbitration cases in the High Court are: 1920, 3 of 4 High Court briefs; 1921, 1 of 5; 1923, 2 of 4; 1924, 2 of 7; 1925, 3 of 8; 1926, 1 of 5; 1928, 1 of 6. Unfortunately there is no way to enumerate accurately Menzies' extensive work in the Arbitration Courts and the Victorian Supreme Court.

working conditions. In the 1920s this struggle took on a special bite from the radical zeal, some of it avowedly Communist, of the maritime unions' leadership. For several years up to 1925 the Seamen's Union carried on a kind of guerrilla warfare over 'job control': who should decide, unions or employers, how, when and under what conditions, ships' crews should be chosen. After a number of holdups and alleged union defiance of court orders, the Commonwealth Arbitration Court, in response to an application from the shipowners, deregistered the Seamen's Union. This move cancelled existing awards and the shipowners refused to sign a collective agreement to maintain the awards. Union leaders called a nation-wide shipping strike. It was to last seven weeks— and goad an exasperated Commonwealth Government into direct industrial action.

Menzies became involved in much of the litigation leading up to the strike. He appeared for the shipowners in a number of cases about job control, including in 1922 an unsuccessful attempt to have the union deregistered.[34] Early in 1925 he and Dixon won a High Court verdict dismissing a union appeal against an Arbitration Court ruling on job control,[35] and in the same year, with Dixon again, he was a principal in the final saga of having the Seamen's Union deregistered. Briefed by the shipowners, Dixon and Menzies first won a High Court ruling which confirmed that the President of the Arbitration Court had the power to deregister the union and then, in that court, effectively argued the case for deregistration.[36]

To represent the owners against the union may well have been personally congenial to Menzies, though that is certainly not simply to be assumed, as the fact of his earlier briefings on behalf of the Engineers and other unions makes clear. His work as a barrister was to represent his client's case to the best of his ability. What was important was that absorption in this litigation gave Menzies technical expertise in a branch of law which in those troubled years addressed what seemed intractable social and political conflicts. This work led him to apply his mind creatively to the scope and structure of arbitration in the special circumstances of his day: to ask how, given its existing form and the

---

[34] 16 *CAR* (1922), 1246. Menzies appeared in this case with John Latham, a distinguished but prim and cold Melbourne barrister, who had served during the war as a naval intelligence officer, and who in 1922 both took silk and won the Kooyong seat in the House of Representatives (*ADB*, 10: 2–6).

[35] Australian Commonwealth Shipping Board v. Federated Seamen's Union, 36 *CLR* (1925), 442.

[36] Application by Commonwealth Steamship Owners' Association and Australian Shipping Board for the Cancellation of the Registration of the Federated Seamen's Union of Australasia, 21, 22 and 29 May 1925; 1, 5 June 1925; 21 *CLR* (1925), 724.

traditional assumptions on which it was based, the arbitration system could be refined and improved, and whether in fact it served a good purpose at all.

Questions of this kind took on a special importance as the results of the Bruce Ministry's intervention focused attention more and more on the possibility of a new approach through root and branch restructuring of the arbitration system. Government efforts in 1925 to defeat the seamen by amending the Immigration and Navigation Acts failed. Bruce's one victory was at the general election of 1925, which he won by appealing to basic forms of prejudice: 'no dirty, greasy foreigner', he said, must be allowed to interfere with Australia's industrial system.[37] Subsequently claiming a mandate for a stern attack on 'subversive' agitation, Bruce appointed Latham as his Attorney-General and endorsed the latter's draconian Crimes Act, which outlawed strikes and lockouts in all transport industries. Bipartisan agreement allowed a Conciliation and Arbitration Act which gave judicial tenure to the leaders of the Arbitration Court and established the Court's power to police its own awards. But that scratched the surface: at the heart of the industrial problem, the Government moved to secure, by referendum, another change which would give the Commonwealth Arbitration Court the power to deal with *all* disputes, whether interstate or not.

Bruce and his ministers had discussed this idea with State governments, business and union leaders for some three years, and the final form of the proposal (which included sweeping new powers over trade unions, employers' associations, corporations, trusts, and combinations in restraint of trade) was agreed on by negotiation between Bruce and the leader of the Labor Opposition, Charlton.[38]

The legislation to authorize the referendum passed peacefully enough through parliament, and assuming that the same would be true when the proposals reached the electorate, Bruce allowed time for only a short campaign. But he miscalculated: as soon as discussion began there was a storm of opposition and the far-reaching implications of the proposals were explored. The hot debate that followed extended from mid-July to August 1926 and in it a number of people who had not before taken any active part in politics were drawn into the fray. One of the more notable of these was the young Robert Menzies.

This, as Menzies himself always observed, was the beginning of his political career. Though at home in the courts, he had done little public speaking, none of it on politics. But in 1926, as he

---

[37] I. M. Cumpston, *Lord Bruce of Melbourne* (Melbourne 1989), 59.
[38] The most insightful discussion of the background negotiations is G. Powell, 'Bruce, Latham and the 1926 Industrial Powers Referendum', *ANU Historical Journal*, 1979–80, 14, 28. See also Sawer, *AFPL* 1, 280 for Bruce–Charlton agreement.

later wrote, 'being a well-known junior at the Victorian Bar, I was induced to oppose [Bruce's] proposals'.[39] How and by whom he was so induced is not recorded. No doubt the referendum was a subject well canvassed in those informal discussions and arguments that always echoed in the corridors of Selborne Chambers. In any case, he was present when a large public meeting on 21 July agreed to establish a Federal Union 'to oppose the unification proposals now before the Country'.[40] The leading spirit was Sir Arthur Robinson, a wealthy 54-year-old barrister and politician. He had briefly served as a minister in two Victorian State governments. He was hard-hitting and skilful in debate. His brother, the industrialist W. S. Robinson, described him as 'a dyed in the wool conservative'. His legal firm, Arthur Robinson and Co., owed a good deal of its prosperity to the business it handled for the Collins House group of companies, in which his brothers William and Lionel were prominent.[41] Robinson became president of the Union, and thirty-five others were elected as a committee to support him. Menzies was one of these. The Union claimed to be non-party, to represent 'all sections and classes of the community':

> It is Federal because it seeks to maintain the true Federal attitude, and it is a union in active co-operation with similar activities in the various states of the Commonwealth. It regrets that the present Government has seen fit to adopt measures which are in serious conflict with the policy with which Liberals and Nationalists have been identified, and which has led them to oppose similar proposals when introduced by Labor Governments.[42]

When the Committee met to fashion a plan of campaign, Menzies was chosen as one of a handful of speakers to be deployed around the State to address meetings for the 'No' case. In an early skirmish he spoke at Geelong;[43] and then at the formal launching of the Union's campaign in the Prahran Town Hall he was one of two speakers to support Sir Arthur Robinson's inaugural oration.[44]

According to a story Menzies told years later, his experienced Uncle Sampson went to hear this, his nephew's first political speech. Asked afterwards for his reaction to it, the old man's

---

[39] Autobiographical article drafted for *Rydge's*, n.d. but *c*. 1950, NLA, MS. 4936/17/426/9.
[40] *Age*, 22 July 1926.
[41] *ADB*, 11: 422–3.
[42] *Age*, 22 July 1926.
[43] Ibid., 5 August 1926.
[44] Ibid. and *Argus*, 17 August 1926.

judgement was withering. Crisp, polished and learned, he said, the speech would have made an excellent address to the High Court, but as a political effort it was abysmal. The politician's task was different from the barrister's: though each had to produce a case, the politician must take care to speak simply, introduce a little humour and, above all, keep repeating, albeit with variations in his choice of words, a few uncomplicated ideas.[45] The criticism was not unfair. Seeking rapport with his audience, Menzies had indeed begun with humour, but it was very heavy-handed. 'Mr Bruce', he said, 'had referred to "self appointed experts who were broadcasting free legal opinions around the country". Sir Arthur Robinson and he seldom gave a free legal opinion, and seldom had an opportunity to broadcast it. (Laughter)'. The referendum, he continued, offered 'legalistic proposals' for constitutional amendments of a kind never before put to the voters:

> very few lawyers could agree on what they meant ... To vote for the changes would be to take a leap in the dark. It was clear that the Commonwealth Government wanted to control all the industrial matters now controlled by the States—and that included such peculiarly local functions as workers' compensation, legislation about shops, factories and even unemployment. It had yet to be shown that in questions of conciliation and arbitration federal were more likely than State institutions to secure industrial peace. Indeed, the record suggested otherwise, for in the area it already controlled, the Federal Parliament had ... created an almost indescribably bad feeling in industry. The old method of strikes had in its favour that everything was above board; there was no hypocrisy. Strikes were admittedly costly and clumsy, but were they any inferior to the present system of litigation, in which employers and employees were made parties to a dispute in Court? Each side in the court was intent on winning, as a lawyer was, and no consideration was given to the third party, the public.

Bruce himself had admitted that instead of settling disputes the arbitration court created them; but there could be no doubt that if given the powers it sought the Government was bound to 'apply the same nostrum more generally'. Bruce's proposals, Menzies declared in another bout of humour which brought a little laughter, 'were analagous to the audacity of the manager of a department in a store who, having made a hopeless failure of the department, said there was only one thing to do—make him managing director of the [whole] store with absolute authority'.[46]

[45] Dawes, 5: 4–5; Menzies to W. M. Hughes, 27 November 1947 (telling the story), NLA, MS. 1538/1/9325.
[46] *Argus*, 17 August 1926.

Robinson contrasted the present 'hurricane campaign' of three weeks with the two months allowed in 1913 by the Fisher Labor Government, in an almost identical referendum. The federal parliament was about to move from Melbourne to Canberra and that, Robinson said, made the reason for a negative vote 'tenfold stronger than on previous occasions'. In an early sample of 'Canberra bashing', he explained that 'the safeguards of an active public opinion and a vigilant press will be absent when the Federal Parliament meets in the bush. It will legislate and administer in an atmosphere of 1000 or 2000 public servants, a few score of traders and 100 politicians. [Laughter and applause]'.[47] Throughout the campaign there were constant complaints at seeming obscurities or downright contradictions in the proposals. Businessmen behind the Federal Union, for example, bitterly opposed the request for power to control corporations, on the ground that Labor might come again to office in the federal parliament and 'try to bring about nationalisation without compensation'.[48] The All Australian Labour Congress, on the other hand, declared its belief that the 'Bill contained in the referendum proposals of the Federal Government has been deliberately drafted by the political representatives of the employing class for the purpose (1) of destroying all effective trade union organisation, and (2) of nullifying all important working-class reforms introduced by the existing State Labor Governments'. The Congress rejected explanations from the federal parliamentary Labor leader, Charlton, of his party's 'yes' position because of negotiations he had himself had with Bruce, and by a vote of 144 to 10 directed all members of the Australian Labor Party (ALP) to vote 'no' in the referendum.[49]

Both the *Argus* and the *Age* gave generous coverage to speakers on both sides. As the campaign progressed Menzies seems to have been deployed as a kind of workaday speaker, to do country tours and be on call when the Federal Union was asked by particular bodies for expositors of the 'no' case. The experience was a useful apprenticeship, which reached its high point when he was one of two speakers commissioned to wind up the country 'no' campaign at the Ballarat Town Hall.[50] But at the final rally in Melbourne on the night before the vote his task was a little less elevated: simply to move the vote of thanks to five more prominent speakers headed by Robinson and Theodore Fink, the respected 71-year-old newspaper proprietor and educationalist.[51]

[47] Ibid.
[48] A. J. Helmsley, *Age*, 7 August 1926.
[49] *Age*, 9 August 1926.
[50] Ibid., 1 September 1926.
[51] Ibid., 3 September 1926.

The electorate finally rejected the Government's proposed constitutional amendments with majorities in all States except Queensland and New South Wales. The warning of the *Argus* editorial on the morning of the vote—it was headed 'The States in Jeopardy'—caught at the overwhelming feeling in Victoria.[52] In most 'no' arguments, States rights had in various forms been a dominant theme. It was ironical that Menzies, whose signal victory in the Engineers case had brought an *extension* of Commonwealth power should in this campaign feature as a vigorous defender of States rights. But his intimate understanding of the arbitration process was undoubtedly what made him so effective a campaigner against remedies he genuinely thought undesirable. Indeed in his speeches in 1926 he was well on the way to a radical position that he elaborated in a series of celebrated articles in 1929: rejecting existing arbitration courts as needlessly confrontationist, and proposing a novel system of industrial tribunals on which employers, employees and the public would be represented and which would eschew compulsion.[53]

---

[52] Ibid., 4 September 1926.
[53] Four articles on 'Industrial Peace', *Argus*, 18–21 June 1929.

3

'A Certain Amount of Public Work'

MENZIES' PROFESSIONAL experience in industrial law, and the strong views he held on arbitration were, as we have seen, a sufficient explanation for his involvement in the referendum campaign of 1926. That he found through this experience that he was good at and enjoyed public speaking no doubt also accounts for his drifting, almost immediately, into Victorian politics, which had not hitherto interested him. But later, when telling his biographer, Dawes, of his decision in 1927 to stand for a seat in the Legislative Council he professed to remember something else. Menzies' reasoning, Dawes wrote, had gone something like this:

> 'Well, here you are; you are practising your profession; you are earning a lot of money'—as money was thought of in those days—'and you've got an enormous amount of work to do. But isn't it rather a narrow sort of existence? Isn't it about time that you cut out of this, and did a certain amount of public work?' The family tradition was beginning to ooze out and in his innocence he told himself: 'All right; I'll give it a go! The Legislative Council won't occupy all my time. I'll be able to take an interest in public affairs, perhaps contribute something to them, and at the same time I'll be able to do most, if not all, of my legal work'.[1]

If the family tradition of public service influenced him it could only draw strength from the Melbourne that was now moulding him. The economy of the place was dynamic, and the expanding social class in which he moved and of which he was a part had a rich associational life the thrust of whose ideology was towards stability, patriotism and responsibility. The referendum having awakened his public talents, the imperative to use them was strong.

[1] Dawes, 5: 14.

The 1920s saw considerable growth in the city of Melbourne and its suburbs, both in numbers of people and in geographical spread. Industrial expansion was the most important motor of change, for industry, already spurred during the war by import shortages, was encouraged anew by post-war tariff protection. Between 1918 and 1926–27 almost 2500 new factories were established in Victoria, and Melbourne's factory workforce increased by a third. A buoyant economy drew into the metropolis investors and immigrants from the State's rural areas, from other States and from overseas. Melbourne absorbed approximately 80 per cent of Victoria's population increase over the decade, to give it by the beginning of the 1930s a million people and the highest metropolitan concentration in Australia. Fast, economical tram and train services (the latter electrified by 1923) brought a new outward push of suburbs, particularly south towards the bay and east towards the hills. By the end of the decade Melbourne's two largest residential suburbs were Caulfield and Camberwell, housing more people than each of Victoria's three major provincial cities, Geelong, Ballarat and Bendigo. Put together, both were soundly middle class in complexion, extensions of that curve of established suburbs—Toorak, Hawthorn and Kew—which bordered the southern side of the Yarra River and overlooked from the ramparts of elevated ground the factories and more congested working-class districts spreading out from the opposite bank to the flatter north and west. It was in that direction that most of the new factory development took place, though hard by the city itself, in East Melbourne, and in salubrious high spots like Heidelberg and Eaglemont, there were pockets of gracious living.[2]

Trade, commerce and every kind of service and professional activity naturally received an enormous boost from industrial expansion. Melbourne was also soundly established as Australia's financial capital, an ascendancy symbolized by the fact that the country's two most powerful entrepreneurial groups, the Broken Hill Proprietary Company (BHP) and the 'Collins House' companies, had their headquarters there. Banking, insurance and the retail trade absorbed a considerable managerial and clerical workforce, whose steady growth was the main impulse behind the suburban spread to the east and south. How self-conscious at least some of these people could feel about their social position was instructively demonstrated when at the beginning of the decade, in 1920, a handful of enthusiasts set out to establish what they actually

---

[2]This account of Melbourne's expansion draws chiefly on the excellent *Victorian Year Book* of 1984, especially 17–18.

called a 'Middle Class Party', to enter State politics to protect the interests of 'unorganized' people in the community who were neither blue-collar workers nor wealthy employers. A degree of status insecurity was reflected in their stress on self-improvement and the need, as one supporter put it, to preserve 'the reward of being on a higher social plane by educating themselves'.[3]

There were other organizations, however, which reflected a middle-class confidence simply assumed as the natural order of things, requiring no self-conscious definition. The powerful Australian Women's National League (AWNL), for example, could trace its origins back to 1904: it was pre-eminent in opposing socialism, demanding loyalty to the Crown, and taking a lead on social questions which crossed class boundaries. A good example of the latter was the early post-war fight against venereal disease which Dr Fetherston, war-time director-general of medical services for the AIF, in 1922 told the South Yarra branch of the AWNL 'was not confined to the vicious of the lower classes, but was working tremendous havoc among the best of the community in all classes'.[4] In the same year the AWNL led in the establishment of a Melbourne branch of an Australian Association for Fighting Venereal Diseases, in which twenty-eight 'public bodies' became affiliated under the presidency of Sir James Barrett, a colourful ophthalmologist and later Vice-Chancellor of Melbourne University.[5] Other women's organizations, like the Gentlewomen's Aid Society and the Australian Women's Association (with—at its twenty-second anniversary in 1922—forty-one branches and a membership of over 3000) had primarily charitable objectives but were also interested in matters like the policing of professional standards and the training of domestic servants.[6] The Women's Citizens' Movement, by contrast, was more overtly political, forming in 1922 a council to work towards the direct representation of women in parliament.[7]

The war's legacy of grief had intensified rather than diminished the conviction of bourgeois Melbourne that Britain and Australia were one. The memory of the conscription crisis was raw; continuing sectarian tensions were still closely related to the issue of loyalty. The St Patrick's Day march, for example, was for a few years a source of conflict, even after Archbishop Mannix pulled off the coup in 1920 of having the procession headed by thirteen Victoria Cross winners in full AIF uniform and mounted on grey

[3] *Argus*, 3–4, 10–12 March 1920.
[4] Ibid., 2 March 1922.
[5] Ibid., 15 March 1922; 'Barrett' in *ADB* 7: 186–9.
[6] *Argus*, 4, 14, 17 March 1922.
[7] Ibid., 15 September 1922.

horses.[8] That was in answer to such Protestant demonstrations as a recent farewell organized by a body called the Loyalty League to a cleric noted for his aggressive patriotism: the Rev. T. E. Ruth of the Collins Street Baptist Church. The hall was filled half an hour before the proceedings began. The audience sang patriotic songs, waved Union Jacks and gave cheers for King and Empire. Ruth called on the Lord Mayor of Melbourne to ban the 'disloyal' St Patrick's Day procession, and declared that 'the Freemasons were loyal to the flag and that was enough to incur the enmity of those who cut the Union Jack out of the Australian flag'.[9]

Rather more balanced were organizations like the British Empire League, formed in mid-1920, which 'took no heed of political party, creed or class, and welcomed to its ranks all who possessed the one qualification of loyalty to the Throne'.[10] The longer established Royal Society of St George boasted a similar inclusiveness. At a typical social it organized in 1922, the League had as its guest of honour the Anglican archbishop of Melbourne, Dr Harrington Lees. The Society's president, Arthur Robinson, introduced Dr Lees as 'a truly representative Englishman' and said that members wanted him 'to feel that throughout the community there was love and affection for England which nothing could shake'. In a graceful response Dr Lees likened his own position to that of a former governor of South Australia who had spoken of himself as being 'a better Englishman for being an Australian and a better Australian for being an Englishman'.[11]

In 1924 the received notion of Australia's proper relationship to Britain was most neatly put by the young historian, W. K. Hancock. After a distinguished undergraduate career at Balliol, Hancock was now returning to Oxford to take up a fellowship at All Souls. The Melbourne University Graduates' Association entertained him at a farewell luncheon, and there he gave a short address on contemporary nationalism. Of Australia and Britain he had concluded that:

> The more one saw of other countries, the more one came to respect the achievements of Britain in the direction of conserving a sane nationality and at the same time forming a community of communities. This had been done by the specially British gifts of liberty and culture, and the successful future of Australian nationalism lay in the cultivation of British principles.[12]

[8] Ibid., 22 March 1920.
[9] Ibid., 9 March 1920.
[10] Ibid., 10 June 1922 (second annual meeting).
[11] Ibid., 9 September 1922.
[12] Ibid., 11 June 1924.

One enthusiastic, but short-lived, champion of Imperial patriotism, the Australian Legion, believed that the most urgent need of the day was to find and train 'young men of character and ability' who would eschew class politics and become effective legislators in the common interest. Some of its members wanted the Legion to become an actual political party, to enter parliament and serve the same purpose as the once-dreamed-of middle-class party, 'with its fighting face on, and meet the swashbuckling, gasconading champions of Labour'. Nothing came of that, but the Legion's main work, that of organizing lectures and speaking classes, pioneered methods of education soon taken up by the most important political club of the decade, the Constitutional.[13]

The Constitutional Club was formed in October 1925, frankly to support Bruce's 'law and order' election campaign. Bruce himself was present at the Club's foundation meeting, where he declared himself 'very impressed with the spirit of service that actuated the young men who were taking an active interest in these clubs'.[14] An executive elected at this meeting formally established the Club the following week, and its members subsequently took an active part in the election campaign, drawing up a fighting platform against Communism and mounting street-corner rallies in the Government's interest. The election was subsequently described as 'remarkable for the interest taken in it by young men who outside the Labour movement had previously been inclined to neglect politics'.[15]

Its formal rules declared that the Club was to consist of members 'pledged to loyalty to the Throne and Empire and the maintenance of constitutional government'.[16] Here, then, was another Melbourne organization emphasizing loyalty, Britishness, the sanctity of British institutions and the sound virtues of true citizenship. It was in fact formed just in time to take a prominent part in an impressive rally of likeminded associations to assert their principles, implicitly against the dark forces of subversion. This was a large public meeting held on 10 March 1926 at Anzac House, at which those appearing together on the platform included delegates from the Royal Colonial Institute, the Royal Society of St George, the Constitutional Club, the Royal Caledonian Society, the Navy League, the Cambrian Society, the Loyal Orange League of Victoria, the Sailors' and Soldiers' Fathers' Association and the

---

[13]Ibid., 10 June, 11 July 1922; 8 May, 25 August, 18 December 1923; 29 March, 15 April, 20 May, 3 June 1924.
[14]Ibid., 27 October 1925.
[15]S. Sayers, *Ned Herring*, 94.
[16]*Rules and Regulations of the Constitutional Club* (Melbourne 1925).

Returned Sailors' and Soldiers' Imperial League. The meeting agreed on the need for continued co-operation, and enthusiastically endorsed a proposal 'To unite by means of representation on a central Council all those existing voluntary organizations whose constitution is founded upon ... loyalty to the Crown and Constitution and the duty of good citizenship'.[17]

By May 1926 the Constitutional Club was well established and boasted a wide range of activities. A model parliament and debating groups met each week; there were classes in public speaking and study groups on public finance and industrial relations. The Club had taken rooms and established a library which, it was planned, would in due course 'contain all the best modern references on economic, political, industrial and other subjects'. Membership had reached 850. The Lord Mayor of Melbourne, Sir William Brunton, when formally opening the Club's rooms on 14 April, declared that its formation 'filled a much-needed place in the life of Melbourne':

> There is a necessity to form in the minds of the younger men of the nation the strong and firm principle of constitutional government as it is known under the British flag ... This Club stands for loyalty, and what greater purpose can any organization have? ... It will, one hopes, build up a band of men willing to serve their country, and able to frame legislation which will mean its progress, uplift and prosperity.[18]

It is not clear whether Menzies was a member of the Constitutional Club though he must have been well informed about its work. Its rooms were near to the courts and to the Savage Club, and prominent among its officials were individuals who would soon be working with Menzies to establish a ginger group of younger men within the Nationalist party. The most important of these was Wilfred Kent Hughes, a Rhodes scholar of 1914 and returned soldier, who at thirty-one was six months younger than Menzies. The two met in discussion groups at the time the Constitution Club was formed and, greatly impressed, Kent Hughes is reputed to have said of Menzies to a friend: 'He's a good type, and we hope to get him into State parliament next election'.[19] A State election took place early in 1927, soon after the 1926 referendum campaign, and although Menzies did not himself stand, he took to the public platform to assist Kent Hughes, who sought

---
[17] *Argus*, 11 March 1926.
[18] Ibid., 15 April 1926. The account of the Club's activities is based on a variety of press reports, particularly ibid., 21 May 1926.
[19] Frederick Howard, *Kent Hughes*, 37.

National Party selection for the seat of Kew, and when he failed to get it, stood defiantly as an independent 'Progressive Nationalist'. Kent Hughes's platform certainly contained items progressive at that time for a man on the conservative side of politics: he advocated, for example, a strong afforestation programme, an advanced education policy with generous new grants to the University and an industrial relations system based on co-operation rather than conflict. His campaign secretary was Arthur H. Clerke, a Tasmanian Rhodes scholar who was at the time Speaker of the Constitutional Club's model parliament and at the declaration of the poll Kent Hughes claimed his election as a victory for 'the younger Nationalists'. In subsequent weeks he attacked the Nationalist establishment and the intrigues it fostered in the business of endorsing candidates. In September 1927 he gave his wife an account of a meeting of the Kew branch of the Nationalist Federation which is unambiguous about Menzies' involvement now in the affairs of the party. At this meeting, said Kent Hughes, there was still 'plenty of electricity in the air' about his rebellious capture of the seat over the endorsed Nationalist candidate. But soon Bob Menzies was 'hoeing into them on their pre-selection methods' and in the upshot the 'Old Guard' had 'rather a thin time' of it. 'They asked me to speak, and I gave them a short resumé of the political situation. As they had attacked me on pre-selection I had to reply, and so I supported Bob, and told them that I would never stand for pre-selection again under existing conditions.'[20]

The party in whose affairs Menzies was now dabbling was the Victorian branch of that new anti-Labor political formation which resulted from the conscription split of 1916. Its propagandists in the 1920s naturally made the most of its origins and its name: typical of dozens of declarations of faith was one made in 1922 by the then federal minister for trade, Arthur Rodgers, when he said that the Nationalist Party was different from every other Australian party in that it had been formed for the particular purpose of saving and preserving the safety of the Empire, and for that purpose it embraced all classes.[21] This patriotic tone at a general level chimed in well with the loyal Britishness and Protestantism of respectable Melbourne and tied the Nationalist Party and that other great political exponent of loyalty, the AWNL, together—so closely indeed that the latter was in effect simply a wing of the party. But the Nationalists were also the inheritors of

[20]Ibid., 49.
[21]*Argus*, 21 June 1922.

the liberal–conservative tradition of the 1909 Fusion and thus the nominal champions of free enterprise and the chief opponents of Labor. That gave them their practical role in the State's day-to-day politics, though not always in an agreed, coherent way. By the mid-1920s the parliamentary party was divided into a number of factions and the party organization had at its centre two uneasily related bodies, the National Union and the National Federation.

The National Union was a small, secretive clique which controlled Nationalist funds and sought to dictate policy to the National Federation. The Federation, a public, open body, ran the party organization and such rudimentary constituency associations as it had. Its officials and party workers were for the most part less socially elevated than the members of the Union, and tension between the two was endemic. In the mid-1920s the Union executive consisted of four members under the chairmanship of Sir William McBeath. Probably behind the scenes the most powerful figure in the Nationalist Party, McBeath was until 1925 managing director of a leading wholesale silk warehouse with headquarters in Melbourne and branches in Sydney, Adelaide, Brisbane and New Zealand.[22]

After the Nationalists suffered reverses in the State election of 1924 McBeath spearheaded a drive to raise special funds in business circles to form new constituency branches and revive old ones to campaign for Bruce in the 1925 federal election, under the slogan 'Insurance against Bolshevism'. (It is no surprise to find McBeath also chairing the foundation meeting in October 1925 of the Constitutional Club.)[23] Under his leadership the National Union appears to have achieved between 1925 and 1928 almost complete control of the National Federation. What was happening did not escape the observation of the press. *Smith's Weekly* published a somewhat lurid but nevertheless accurate exposé in 1926[24] and, during the election campaign of 1927, the *Age* talked of 'the capture of the National machine by the secret and conservative National Union', subsequently producing an 'inside story' about a 'Big Four' running Victorian politics from the Melbourne Club.[25] When the party performed badly in 1927

---

[22] For the nature of the Nationalist Party and, subsequently, for the brief analysis of Victorian politics I rely heavily on the excellent thesis of Margaret Vines, Instability in Governments and Parties in Victoria in the 1920s; on McBeath: *ADB*, 10: 204–5. McBeath's firm was Makower, McBeath & Co. Pty Ltd.

[23] *Argus*, 27 October 1925.

[24] *Smith's Weekly*, 20 February, 6 March 1926.

[25] *Age*, 18 April 1927, quoted by Vines, 126–7. Vines says the four were probably the Executive: McBeath, Colonel Holdsworth, Sir Robert Gibson and P. C. Holmes Hunt.

rebels like Kent Hughes blamed the conservative 'dead hand' of the National Union. In the next year or so, capture and revitalization of the National Federation, and with it of the Nationalist Party, would become his main political aim. His friend, Bob Menzies, would be a staunch ally.

For such men, dissatisfaction with the state of their own party broadened into something very like contempt for the character of the State's politics generally. In the 1920s the instability and unproductiveness of Victoria's governments were notorious. Between 1923 and 1929 there were eight separate ministries. Office came to depend on shifting coalitions, in which a faction-ridden Country Party usually held the balance of power between the Nationalists and the Labor Party. Partly for this reason a gerrymander inherited from the nineteenth century was maintained and extended, so that by 1926 the vote of a country elector was worth more than twice that of a person living in the metropolitan area. Since this electoral system made it impossible for either the Labor Party or the Nationalists to hold power in their own right, the tendency was for political principle to dwindle before expediency. It was not a milieu to lure outstanding men into politics: fastidious contemporary critics depicted Victorian politicians, with few exceptions, as men of limited vision and moderate capacity.[26]

It is not altogether clear why, when he finally decided to enter parliament, Menzies chose the Legislative Council. Perhaps he really thought that sitting in the Upper House would involve minimal interruption to his professional life; or perhaps, having finally made up his mind to try parliamentary life, he did not care to wait for the next general election to contest a seat in the Lower House. (That election, in the natural order of things, need not have taken place until 1930.) Or again—what is more likely—men who had watched or been associated with him in the referendum campaign noted his potential and urged his candidature when the first chance of his getting into parliament occurred.

Legislative Council elections were due in mid-1928, and at the end of 1927 Menzies announced that he would be nominating for one of the seats, the East Yarra Province.[27] A month after this the

---

[26] Of the variety of sources on which these general remarks on Victorian politics are based the most important are Vines; *Victorian Parliamentary Debates (VPD)*; excellent short accounts in *Victorian Year Book* 1976, 1984; Frederick Eggleston, 'Confidential Notes on Victorian Politics', Australian National University (Menzies Library), MS. 2; D. W. Rawson, 'Victoria, 1910–1966: Out of Step, or Merely Shuffling?', *Historical Studies (HS)*, 49 (Oct. 1967), 60–75.

[27] *Argus*, 13 December 1927.

Legislative Council Elections
EAST YARRA PROVINCE

POLLING DAY,
Sat., June 2
8 A.M. TO 8 P.M.

POLLING DAY,
Sat., June 2,
8 A.M. TO 8 P.M.

ROBERT GORDON MENZIES
Born at Jeparit, Victoria.   Age 33 years.

Third son of James Menzies, formerly M.L.A. for Lowan. Nephew of Sydney Sampson, formerly M.H.R. for Wimmera.

Educated at State Schools at Jeparit and Ballarat, proceeding as a scholarship winner (head of the list for Victoria) to Grenville College, Ballarat, and Wesley College, Melbourne, and thence as Senior Exhibitioner to the Melbourne University.

At the University he graduated in Laws, finally obtaining the degree of Master of Laws.

During law course obtained highest honors throughout, including the Dwight Prize in History and Constitutional Law; the John Madden Exhibition; the Jessie Leggatt Scholarship; the Bowen Prize; the Supreme Court Prize, and Final Honors Scholarship with first class honors.

During his final year was President of the Students' Representative Council, and Editor of the University Magazine.

Commencing as a pupil in the chambers of Mr. Owen Dixon, K.C., has practised as a Barrister for 10 years. Extensive practice acquired, now almost exclusively in High Court and Supreme Court.

Has been engaged in many notable cases in recent years, e.g.: the famous Engineers' case in the High Court; the Badak cases; the "Herald" art libel case; the 44-hours case.

Standing counsel to some of the largest industrial and mercantile concerns in Australia.

In 1927 appointed by the Metropolitan Daily Newspapers of Australia and the Journalists' Association to act as arbitrator to settle salaries and conditions, and subsequently so acted.

Is a member of the Victorian Bar Committee, the Standing Committee of the Convocation of the University, and the Council of Legal Education.

In 1920 married the eldest daughter of John W. Leckie, formerly M.H.R. for Indi.

How the young Robert Menzies presents himself to the East Yarra Legislative Council electorate in 1928.

sitting member, J. K. Merritt, who had represented that electorate since 1913, and against whom Menzies had expected to contest the seat, announced his retirement, 'owing to increased business interests and responsibilities'.[28] It looked as if in the consequent by-election Menzies would have an easy, unopposed run. But he had barely begun to publicize his policy when a formidable candidate came out of retirement to contest the seat. This was George Swinburne, the much revered 67-year-old engineer, politician and public benefactor. Swinburne had sat in the Victorian Legislative Assembly from 1902 to 1913. He had subsequently been a foundation member of the State Electricity Commission and had served on both the Council of the University of Melbourne and the Board of Trustees of the Public Library. He was a lifelong advocate of liberal education and the founder of the Technical College which came in due course to be named after him. A gracious Gladstonian-type liberal, he was noted for his innate courtliness.[29] Menzies later recalled how Swinburne, after deciding to contest the seat, took him to lunch and expressed regret that they should be opposing each other. 'Well, Sir', Menzies claimed to have replied, 'the moment you announced yourself as a candidate, I knew I had no hope. Of course you will win. But I am not going to start a political life by running away from the first formidable opponent—and so, Sir, I must go on and take my licking'.[30]

Menzies' handbills[31] listed twenty-five electoral committees, naming a chairman and secretary for each. These committees covered every important suburban centre in a large constituency which stretched eastwards from Kew and Toorak through Box Hill and Camberwell to Oakleigh. It was the heartland of middle-class Melbourne. No doubt to claim suburban 'committees' was largely window-dressing, little more than identifying people who were willing to chair election meetings and perhaps distribute handbills. But Menzies' 'Central Committee', which gave its headquarters as 515 Collins Street, was decidedly formidable and indicated clearly the type of backing he could boast. The chairman, R. J. Boyne, was a city woolbroker and a director of the Australian Mercantile Land and Finance Co. There were three vice-chairmen: Essington Lewis, managing director of BHP; Kingsley Henderson, head of a major Melbourne architectural firm and director of a number of companies, including the stockbroking firm of J. B. Were; and W. H. Swanton, managing director of a shipping firm, member of the Chamber of Commerce, and recently president of the Melbourne City Mission. A young public accountant with a

[28]Ibid., 15 February 1928.
[29]*ADB*, 12: 150–2.
[30]Dawes, 5: 15.
[31]I wish to thank Mr G. Menzies for showing me, from his personal papers, one of these handbills.

distinguished war record, J. A. Gray, was general secretary. He was a stalwart of the Constitutional Club and had won the Hawthorn seat in a 1930 Legislative Assembly by-election. The members of this committee all lived in one or other of the suburbs within the electorate.[32]

One of Menzies' more fetching handbills carries his photograph: a handsome face, still very youthful at thirty-three, but with a suitably grave expression. The bourgeois values of that time and place, as well as his own self-identification, are both reflected in his proud introduction of himself as the 'third son of James Menzies, formerly M.L.A. for Lowan' and 'nephew of Sydney Sampson, formerly M.H.R. for Wimmera'. The handbill goes on to give a short biography, including educational history, prizes won, and his achievement as a barrister, having in ten years built up an 'extensive practice ..., now almost exclusively in High Court and Supreme Court'. He was a member of the Victorian Bar Committee. To cap the lot he could announce that he had 'In 1920 married the eldest daughter of John W. Leckie, formerly M.H.R. for Indi'.

In this election the Nationalist Party did not formally endorse either of the candidates, though both said they were Nationalists.[33] However, the first plank of Menzies' platform urged that 'Every effort should be made to unify the non-Labour parties'. It was also now 'more urgently than ever' necessary for Victoria to have a 'strong and effective Legislative Council': any proposal to abolish it must be resisted and voters must increase its usefulness by taking a greater interest in its proceedings. Other general issues which Menzies took up included federalism ('if the State is to do its best work its complete sovereignty within the limits imposed upon it by the Commonwealth Constitution must be strictly respected') and State finance. Public utilities must be given 'financial independence without meddlesome political interference'; and in general the State's policy should be one 'not of parsimony, but of close economy'. In two other, more idiosyncratic matters, afforestation and university education, the young Menzies was almost ahead of his time. 'The planting of trees as distinguished from the mere protection of existing trees ought to be regarded as one of our great primary industries. From every point of view an extensive policy of afforestation will pay for itself many times over'. And money spent on the University was well spent: 'The

---

[32]Essington Lewis, *ADB*, 10: 87–92; Kingsley Henderson, *ADB*, 9: 257–8; W. H. Swanton, J. Gibbney and A. Smith, *A Biographical Register 1788–1939*, II: 291; R. J. Boyne and J. A. Gray, *Who's Who*, 1935, 80, 207.
[33]*Argus*, 15 May 1928.

true progress of the State requires that University training shall be as readily accessible as possible to all children who display the necessary mental qualifications'.

On the eve of the election, the *Argus* ruminated on the dilemma confronting the electors. Either candidate would make a good member. One was blessed with 'experience and long association with politics'; the other represented 'the younger school of trained men who are showing a commendable desire to take their parts in public life'.[34] The electors, however, seem not to have been in a lather of anxiety over the choice. Voting was not compulsory; only 23 per cent of those enrolled went to the poll. Menzies' prediction proved correct: an overwhelming majority (9127–5451) preferred Swinburne. He, at the declaration of the poll, described Menzies as 'able and clever' and said that he hoped the young contender would in due course be elected to parliament in one House or the other. Menzies for his part congratulated Swinburne, thanked him for a contest 'entirely free from personalities' and described Swinburne as 'a more useful member of the Legislative Council than I would have been'. But he hastened to add that he would not want that remark ever to be used against him in the future![35]

No special significance is to be placed on the fact that so few people voted. Poor turnouts were traditional at Council elections. Complacency was no doubt as important in this as mere lethargy. In 1928 the suffrage was still what it became after a mild revision in 1903. It was restricted to males with £10 freehold property, £15 leasehold, or who belonged to certain professions. With such a franchise it hardly mattered how many, or even who, voted. The Council's conservative reputation, first earned in bitter nineteenth-century clashes with the colony's Lower House, the Assembly, lived on into the mid-twentieth century.[36] Menzies was not upset by this. Defence of the Legislative Council was high on his list of priorities. He fought against any suggestion that its franchise should be liberalized: if it should ever happen that the two Houses were elected by the same constituency the result, he said, would be 'a fiasco'. It was necessary that the Council should be a real House of review, elected in such a way as to have a viewpoint of its own. In Victoria this was the classical conservative attitude.[37]

As it happened, Swinburne was to hold his seat in the Council for only three months: tragically, on 4 September 1928, he collapsed and died in the Chamber. In the by-election that necessarily

[34] Ibid., 29 May 1928.
[35] Ibid., 5, 6 June 1928.
[36] The standard reference on these matters is Geoffrey Serle, 'The Victorian Legislative Council, 1856–1950', *HS*, 22 (May 1954).
[37] *Argus*, 24 May 1928.

followed, Menzies stood again. He was opposed this time by E. C. Rigby, a respected Kew Councillor. The contest was again conducted with gentlemanly courtesy, made easy, no doubt, by the fact that the candidates' policies hardly differed. Menzies stood on the same platform as in his May campaign, though this time he spoke rather more frequently and sternly about political interference in the management of state enterprises like the railways and about the general danger to good management and good government threatened by the factional nature of contemporary politics in Victoria. 'We expect our Parliament to form its judgement on one consideration only', he said in his final election address, 'the good of Victoria—but we witness the remarkable spectacle of a number of small groups bargaining about the price of support'.[38]

The election took place on Saturday 6 October 1928. This time only 19 per cent of those on the roll turned out, and at the declaration of the poll both candidates called for legislation to establish compulsory voting. Menzies won by over 2000 votes, a decisive victory if—given the voters' apathy—a somewhat inglorious one.[39] On 9 October he was sworn in by the president of the Legislative Council, Sir Frank Clarke.

So began a political career triggered at the outset by hostility to Bruce's arbitration proposals and then largely sustained by a genuine sense of public responsibility. The parlous state of Victorian politics, in which governmental instability inhibited the achievement of much needed legislation and gave notorious scope for ministerial connivance with pressure groups, could not be remedied, Menzies believed, unless the intellectual and moral quality of those entering public life underwent a dramatic transformation. This was a view he had put forward long ago, in his *MUM* days, but it took on a new relevance in the light of the stirrings among the young professionals and businessmen of Melbourne which centred on the Constitutional Club. To the extent that he stood for the same reforming zeal as such contemporary critics of the status quo, Menzies was entering politics as a sort of respectable radical, and indeed would quickly be—as his alliance with Kent Hughes already suggested—in the van of those anxious to give new life and relevance to his natural party, the Nationalists. 'Respectable' is, of course, the operative word. The changes he wanted were changes in method and quality, not in ultimate aims. He stood for constitutional democracy and jealous preservation of

[38] Ibid., 5 October 1928.
[39] Ibid., 8 October 1928.

existing institutions. He believed in the rule of law, the sanctity of contracts and the superiority of free enterprise except for certain public utilities, and these must be made independent of political interference. He was suspicious of the Labor Party, which talked of abolishing or emasculating the Legislative Council, which was frankly dedicated to the advancement of the interests of a class rather than of the community generally, and parts at least of which did not share in the simple identification of Australia and Britain. Menzies, by contrast, in education, instinct and professional training proudly assumed such identification as a natural and unalterable strand in the web of his life. In all these respects, he was the quintessential representative of the Melbourne bourgeoisie of the 1920s.

4

The Coming of the UAP

MENZIES' MEMBERSHIP of the Legislative Council turned out to be brief, though he achieved momentary fame by winning ministerial office after only a few weeks in the House. At the time of his election a minority Labor government tenuously held office with the support of the Country Progressives, a group which had broken away from the Country Party. But soon after Menzies took his seat the Labor Premier, E. J. Hogan, dared to bring down in the Legislative Assembly a redistribution bill, to reduce the country bias of the State's electoral gerrymander. The Progressive Party forthwith withdrew its support and forced Hogan to resign. Sir William McPherson, recently elected leader of the Nationalist Party, accepted the commission to form a new ministry. He chose Menzies as one of three Legislative Councillors to become Ministers Without Portfolio. Menzies' friend, Kent Hughes, still in the Assembly as member for Kew, also received ministerial rank, as Secretary to the Cabinet. The rapid elevation of these two young men was as much a reflection of the mediocrity of the more longstanding members of the Party as of their own brilliance, though McPherson was soon to rue the choice. Parliament adjourned before Christmas 1928 and did not reconvene until July 1929. Over this long recess the Government laboured behind the scenes to consolidate its position, which was very precarious. The Nationalists held only 18 of the 65 seats in the Legislative Assembly and needed the support of the two wings of the Country Party to govern. Then, two days before parliament met, a major sensation occurred which did little to help McPherson.

In a blaze of publicity, three of the new ministers—Kent Hughes, Menzies and another Legislative Councillor, Marcus Saltau—resigned from the Government. They did so in protest at a concession Cabinet had decided on to hold Country Progressive Party support. This was to underwrite a bank guarantee of up to

£60 000 against losses by the Amalgamated Co-operative Freezing Works, to enable them to operate in the coming season. These works, for freezing country-killed meat, had received successive government guarantees since 1921–22 and already involved a debt to the State of over half a million pounds. The resigning ministers were disgusted that, at the behest of a pressure group, further money should be spent on such a doubtful enterprise. The freezing works entanglement might intrinsically seem a small matter, said Menzies, but it epitomized something much larger and more serious: 'By a wonderful mixing up of vague ideas of democracy with still vaguer ideas of finance, the State was doling out money recklessly, regardless of whether the money would ever be returned'. He spoke of other manifestations of the evil: the terrible mess which he said government departments had made of financing rural settlement, and constant political influence, in the interests of individual user groups, in the management of railways. It was essential that this political influence be fought, to free the Railway Commissioners from all external pressure and allow them to conduct their business in a businesslike way. Issues of these kinds were made especially important by the present strained position of the State's finances. Victoria's by now established tradition of low taxation (a matter on which the National Union and the Country Party were as one), extravagant government spending and a public debt built up by borrowing in the prosperous years of the mid-1920s, were combining to threaten the State's solvency. Explaining his resignation, Menzies said that though he remained a supporter of the Government's general policy, he was leaving the Ministry on what he saw as a vital matter: the urgent need to stem the drift in public finance.[1]

In the weeks that followed it became evident that the shock of the ministerial resignations would have no effect in galvanizing the McPherson Government into positive action. By now economic circumstances were rapidly deteriorating, as depression took hold. Unemployment was perhaps the most ominous harbinger of things to come. Already during Hogan's premiership it was known in mid 1927 that at least 10 000 people were out of work in Victoria; by the autumn of 1929 the numbers had taken a new surge forward.[2] On this and other serious matters the Government lacked a policy. McPherson, who was ill as well as unimaginative, provided no leadership. Unwilling or unable to do so, the Government had still failed to produce a budget for 1929 when, late in

[1] *Argus*, 2, 19 July 1929; *VPD*, 179: 408–9.
[2] Janet McCalman, *Struggletown* (Melbourne 1985), 152.

October, it was defeated in the Assembly by a combination of Labor and its erstwhile supporter, the Country Progressive Party. Forced to make a financial statement, the Government admitted to a deficit of over a million pounds. It then had no alternative but to secure a dissolution and go to the country. A general election was scheduled for December 1929. It would be at this election that Menzies would seek his first seat in a lower House, the Victorian Legislative Assembly.

The first half of 1929, the parliamentary recess which ended with his dramatic departure from the 'trite and unpicturesque Cabinet of Sir William McPherson', marked Menzies' emergence as a public figure in Melbourne's little social and political world. In April the society journal *Table Talk* carried, in its series on 'prominent personalities', a long article introducing Menzies as 'one of the most interesting young men in the country'. He had just taken silk, and his mounting reputation made him 'one of the most employed at the Victorian bar'. The writer, having spent an hour and a half interviewing Menzies in his chambers, came away impressed. Physically, the new minister was 'six feet one in his socks. He has a manner that is disinclined to diffidence, a figure that is a tribute to the porridge of his ancestors and a voice that can woo or command'. He was personally warm and human. In politics a Nationalist 'paying due devotion to the trinity—the Flag, the Throne and the Constitution', he also displayed 'a critical Liberal strain that may have been derived from his maternal grandpa'. He showed every sign of becoming 'a statesman of the deepest dye'.[3]

Especially after the drama of his resignation, and largely through the vehemence of his pronouncements on public morality and his palpable attractiveness as a public speaker, Menzies became more and more a sought-after performer, particularly on the popular platform. It was, for example, at this time that he began to appear before an audience with which he quickly became a special favourite—the Methodist Central Mission's Pleasant Sunday Afternoon. Here he displayed a by now rapidly developing skill which Uncle Sampson no doubt found pleasing: that of weaving an attractive address around a few simple points, and pitching it at the level appropriate for his audience. He was much at home with the middlebrow folk of the Pleasant Sunday Afternoon, with whom his campaign for a new sense of responsibility in politics went down well. In May he delivered a homely elaboration of it by talking about the kind of parliamentarian Victoria so sadly

[3] *Table Talk*, 25 April 1929.

Table Talk discovers an elegant young barrister in 1929.

needed. That man's first characteristic must be a well-informed brain: 'Many persons had a first-rate intellect but fifteenth-rate industry. The world consistently obtained more from persons possessing a second-rate intelligence, coupled with a first-rate capacity for hard work, than from those who possessed a first-rate brain but had little capacity for hard work'. Even more important, the ideal legislator should be able to contemplate the needs of the State as a whole. He should lead and educate the people. He should not go into parliament as a delegate but as a representative, obliged after debate and study to form his own judgements and be capable of defending them.[4] In a subsequent talk to the same audience he added to this firmly Burkean view of public affairs corollaries about citizenship and the law: how the community's acceptance and implementation of law must be an essential accompaniment to sound government.[5] Increasingly in demand as speaker on less formal occasions, Menzies took every opportunity, his words always tailored to the audience, to press his reformist ideas. As an example we may note his remarks at a luncheon of the Old Trinity Grammarians' Association. There he observed how 'the political occupation is regarded as one which a really intelligent and decent person does not bother about'. The trouble was that in too many ways abuse had become the main content of politics. At school one learnt the sporting viewpoint that the other fellow's school was as good as one's own. That spirit was needed in politics: 'I favour the introduction of a few ideals into politics. The point of view that is needed is the one which gives a place to generosity and fair play, and an endeavour to understand and judge cases on their own merits'.[6]

In private life also the parliamentary break was important: it saw the opening of a new chapter in the Menzies family's way of living. This was the decision to buy a holiday cottage at Mt Macedon, a lovely wooded retreat fifty-eight kilometres from the city, much prized for its healthy air, fine views and exclusiveness. The move reflected both the sound financial position Menzies' practice had achieved and a wish to enrich a family life which must sometimes have seemed narrowed by the father's strict work habits. As additional incentive, his son Ken was a delicate boy, for whom brisk walking in mountain air was recommended: an activity in which Menzies himself, whose favourite exercise was walking, could happily share.[7]

[4] *Argus*, 6 May 1929.
[5] Ibid., 14 October 1929.
[6] Ibid., 10 October 1929.
[7] Interview with Mr Ken Menzies, 11 November 1985.

The stimulus for this move came chiefly from a man who by this time had become a good personal friend, Staniforth Ricketson, a stockbroker and a fellow Savage. Managing partner of the firm of J. B. Were and Son, Ricketson was a major—and sometimes thought sinister—power in Melbourne's tight financial world. He was also noted for his charity and his capacity for great kindness. In the 1920s Ricketson purchased 'Illira', a modest house at Macedon, and when in 1929 another property, 'Hascombe', came on to the market, he tried to persuade Menzies to buy it. But Hascombe was beyond Menzies' means or needs: it was set in 26 acres of wooded grounds and had eleven bedrooms, a ballroom and two tennis courts. Menzies persuaded Ricketson to buy it himself and then took on 'Illira'.[8] The family thus joined a select coterie of weekenders and holiday-makers which included leading citizens like the Herbert Brookeses and the Nicholases of 'Aspro' fame. The neighbours formed a congenial social group. On walks or over drinks the men exchanged reminiscences, talked over common literary interests, discussed political and social issues. But most memorable for all family members were the happy times they and their guests spent

'Illira' offers the peace and relaxation of Mount Macedon.

[8] Ibid.; Robert Murray and Kate White, 'Staniforth Ricketson' in R. T. Appleyard and C. B. Shedvin (eds), *Australian Financiers Biographical Essays* (South Melbourne 1988), 309–30.

as a kind of *ad hoc* community over holiday periods, like Christmas and New Year, when most left Melbourne to rest and take the air at their Macedon retreats. Almost all had children, and one daughter of Ricketson's—now an elderly lady—still remembers with sparkling eyes the happy times when they came together, at tennis parties or on occasions when all the fathers and the children of both sexes played *ad hoc* cricket matches. Most vivid of all is the memory of Menzies, his endless fertility in devising activities for the children—from paper chases in verse to exciting bushwalks— his great sense of fun and his natural ease with children.[9]

The Victorian general election of December 1929 took place in the shadow of a momentous change in Australia's national politics and at a moment when it became clear beyond doubt that the world was passing into the grip of the Great Depression. At a federal election in October 1929 Labor, led by James Scullin, swept Bruce's Nationalist–Country Party coalition out of office. By an ironic throw of fate, Scullin formed his Government (the first Commonwealth Labor Government since 1916) just as the crash of the New York stock exchange signalled the Depression. Bruce had been destroyed in the climate of mounting economic unease, by the effects of bitter industrial conflicts which he had once hoped to cure through those 1926 powers which Menzies had played so important a part, in Victoria at least, in denying to him.

Labor's Commonwealth victory on the eve of the Victorian State poll could only alarm Nationalists like Menzies, who felt that their own party, with its uninspired leadership and lack of policy, was at its nadir in 1929. Labor's sweeping victory in the federal election, Menzies said, was bound to be repeated in Victoria 'unless the non-Labour parties seriously considered the pressing economic problems confronting the State'.[10] Kent Hughes was equally alarmed. As he told an audience of students at the University, the only hope for the future was a rejuvenated form of Nationalist ideology, around which liberals, independents and moderate Country Party members could sink their differences and present a united front to Labor. For this purpose he was anxious to see the bright young Bob Menzies leave the relative backwater of the Legislative Council and help give new life to Labor's opponents in the Lower House. A chance for the transfer providentially arose when, before the election, a friend who held the semi-rural seat of Nunawading, Edward Greenwood, decided for health reasons not to stand again. Greenwood and Kent Hughes called on Menzies

[9] Interview with Mrs Elizabeth Alder, 4 May 1989.
[10] *Argus*, 18 October 1929.

at his Kew home and urged him to nominate.[11] Soon after, at a meeting of 'friends and supporters' at Box Hill, Greenwood recommended Menzies, one of 'a new force of young men who have given added strength and vision to the party', as his replacement. The meeting unanimously agreed.[12]

Menzies opened his campaign on the evening of 13 November, at the Rialto Theatre, Box Hill. 'What we want in politics today', he told an attentive audience, 'is plain speech about plain subjects for plain people'. All candidates had an urgent duty to grapple with the question of public finance. The loan indebtedness of the State had so increased as to raise the interest bill from £3 250 000 to £7 500 000 in the previous ten years, and the auditor-general's explanation was a text on which any man might hang a sermon. So Menzies warmed to his favourite theme: the evils of a 'predatory' party system, in which groups in parliament all too often imagined that they were there 'for the sole purpose of getting what they could for their constituents'. The most rapacious of all was the Country Progressive Party, which he condemned as 'the country division of the Labour Party': besides being greedy, it advocated co-operative marketing schemes which were really socialist in conception. He himself was unequivocally a Nationalist, but it was not the duty of a Nationalist 'to be a sheep, and follow blindly'. The party needed wide-ranging reform to stop its present downward slide.[13]

That same day he had begun practical steps towards giving the Party new vitality. He was one of three Nationalists who decided to call a private meeting of selected lawyers and businessmen to launch 'a movement to attract younger men into politics as representatives of the Nationalist Party'. The other two were Kent Hughes and T. S. Nettlefold, a considerable figure in the Melbourne business world. Aged 50, Nettlefold was general manager of the Hume Pipe Co., manufacturers of concrete pipes and slabs. He was a leading light in the Constitutional Club, and a member of both the Chamber of Manufacturers and the Stock Exchange.[14] The proposed meeting duly took place next day, in Menzies' rooms in Selborne Chambers. There the new movement, at once dubbed 'Young Nationalists', was born.[15]

After the meeting Menzies explained to the press that the intention of the organizers was certainly not to add to the 'already unnecessary multiplicity of parties': the Young Nationalists would

[11] Howard, *Kent Hughes*, 55.
[12] *Argus*, 9 November 1929.
[13] Ibid., 14 November 1929.
[14] *ADB*, 11: 3–4.
[15] *Argus*, 5 May 1933. Address by Menzies to Young Nationalists recalling origin of the movement.

The Young Nationalists pioneer new ways to go to the people, not scorning to copy, frankly, the methods of their Labor opponents: as Menzies once put it, to put orthodoxy in the manner adopted by unorthodoxy.

work within the Nationalist Party. They in fact believed that 'a vigorous Nationalism is the political hope of Victoria, and we are determined to show that Nationalism has at call the vigorous services of many young men'. As a first task they planned to organize a team of speakers to be on call for concerted attacks in key electorates. Premier McPherson gave the movement his blessing, declaring it 'highly desirable that those who are to be our political leaders should begin their training as early as possible'. 'Youth in Politics', trumpeted the *Argus* hopefully. Menzies and Kent Hughes thought they could organize for this election the services of at least fifty young men, a not over-optimistic aim, given the number of trainees who would by then have graduated from the Constitutional Club's public-speaking classes. How successful they were is uncertain; but press reports of the campaign, and its results, do not suggest that the Young Nationalists had much impact yet. But the organization had been born: and a great spurt forward was to come *after* the election, the results of which proved a sad blow to Menzies' fondest hopes.[16]

Menzies took the Nunawading seat with ease, offering at the declaration of the poll no apologies for his outspoken criticism of the habit of 'spoon-feeding country districts' and his advocacy of an equitable redistribution of seats.[17] As usual, no party won a mandate to govern and when parliament met it was an open secret that Labor expected to cobble together enough votes from uncommitted members, including the notorious Country Progressives, to win office. Menzies seconded the Address-in-Reply motion with a graceful reference to his own father, James Menzies, who seventeen years before had stood in the same Chamber and spoken on the same motion. He provoked much hilarity from the Labor benches when, on a favourite topic, he remarked that the railways were a great national undertaking upon which the prosperity of the State depended:

> Mr. Hogan: Upon which the solvency of the State depends.
>
> Mr Menzies: Yes, I would go so far as to agree to that.
>
> Mr. Bond: (Lab., Glenelg): Good, come over here, brother. (loud laughter).
>
> Mr. Holland (Lab., Flemington) No, there is no need to do that. Stay there and we will join you tomorrow (renewed laughter).[18]

[16] Young Nationalist meetings and statements: *Argus*, 14–16 November 1929.
[17] *Age*, 11 December 1929.
[18] *Argus*, 12 December 1929.

The prediction proved all too correct: Hogan moved a hostile amendment to the Address-in-Reply motion, and the Ministry, defeated 36–28, resigned. Hogan formed a Labor administration. Of course Menzies did not obey his temporary 'friends', and faithfully joined the Nationalists on the Opposition benches.

Though Hogan was generally respected personally, the coming of a Labor government in Victoria, following so closely on Labor's triumph in the federal election, and coinciding with a rapid worsening of the Depression, was deeply disturbing to some sections of the community and gave a new spur to the Young Nationalist movement. Its leaders quickly set about active recruiting. In March 1930 a general meeting of Young Nationalists adopted a constitution and set themselves up, within the existing Nationalist organization, as 'an inner body of members', a ginger group, organized as a kind of élite. Under a committee of nine the membership would be limited to 440, organized for active work in units of 100, with a leader for each group of ten. Two of the 100s were to be metropolitan and two country: the plan was that 'by this means a force of trained speakers and workers will be available in every electorate that the Nationalist Party chooses to contest'.[19] The larger party organization welcomed these moves and gave the Young Nationalists three representatives on its Central Executive. Nettlefold was elected chairman of the new Young Nationalist body and Menzies and Kent Hughes became vice-presidents. The leaders of the metropolitan 100s were two Constitutional Club men, J. A. Spicer and A. H. Clerke.[20] Menzies was one of the three representatives elected to the Central Executive of the Victorian National Federation. He thus got, as a Young Nationalist, what was soon to prove an important foothold in the central party organization. Writing to the *Argus* a few months after this general meeting, Nettlefold urged young men to join the new movement, claiming that there was now 'an extraordinary wave of enthusiasm almost unknown in political circles'. As evidence he cited the excellent turnout for all Young Nationalist meetings—'almost every member who has been invited has been in attendance'—and his observation that 'more and more thoughtful men must be coming to realise that leaning on the State will never get us through our difficulties. The cure for most of our troubles must be the effort, initiative and independence of individual citizens'. And as youth was 'the natural period of individual effort', it followed that the Nationalist Party should hope and work for support from the young.[21]

[19] Ibid., 3 March 1930.
[20] Ibid., 9 June 1930.
[21] Ibid., 3 March 1930.

As Nettlefold wrote that, in the winter of 1930, Sir Otto Niemeyer, an emissary from the Bank of England, was arriving in Perth, to begin an examination of Australia's public finances. Depressed export prices and liabilities contracted in the expansive 1920s had by now brought the difficulty of meeting debt charges in London to crisis-point: Niemeyer had come virtually to decide how Australia's credit-worthiness could be restored. He delivered his verdict, that Australia could no longer live beyond its means, to a specially convened Premiers' Conference in August. The so-called 'Melbourne Agreement' followed: all premiers undertook to balance their respective budgets in 1930–31, a promise understood to involve cuts in wage rates and government expenditure, including outlays on social services. But as unemployment deepened, it quickly became clear that to achieve the goals agreed to in Melbourne was impossible and a bitter debate developed over what was to be done. Though in practice there were many nuances to it, this debate was, essentially, between those who advocated severe Niemeyer-type deflation and others who pressed for an expansion of credit, chiefly to finance public works programmes to generate jobs for the unemployed. Over the last months of 1930 the debate wracked and split Labor Parties at Commonwealth and State levels, producing extremist rhetoric which in turn added to the alarm of those people, Labor and non-Labor alike, who feared social disorder.

Menzies was one of these. In the Victorian manifestation of the debate he was firmly on the side of orthodoxy: of balanced budgets and strict adherence to the letter of the law. He was cold to the dismay of Labor men who saw the cuts associated with budget-balancing as an assault on traditional verities. Given his Burkean view of parliamentary representation, Menzies was impatient with the relationship of Labor members to their trades union and organizational base. His special animus was directed at J. T. Lang, the turbulent premier of New South Wales, and E. G. Theodore, Scullin's Treasurer before July 1930 and after January 1931. Lang won a State election in October 1930 on a programme which rejected the Melbourne Agreement and included promises running wildly contrary to that document's deflationary spirit. He was to move on and advocate a moratorium on the payment of interest to British holders of Australian bonds and a reduction of interest on internal loans. Theodore, who in the faction politics of Labor in New South Wales was an enemy of Lang's, regarded such 'repudiation' as anathema. But he did favour credit expansion. A man of considerable political experience, Theodore had read Keynes, entertained liberal views about monetary management and was intellectually the most gifted man in the Scullin Cabinet. He was obliged to resign the Treasury after a Royal Commission accused him of corruption in mining deals when he had been Premier of Queensland. But his influence behind the scenes remained strong.[22]

Menzies harped constantly on the danger of Langism coming into Victoria. He lauded Hogan for steadfastly defending the Melbourne Agreement, but castigated him when, just before the New South Wales election, he sent a message of good luck to Lang—the man, in Menzies' words, 'whose name in politics is a byword for dishonest repudiation ... the most reckless financier in Australia today'. He warned the Nationalist faithful that Lang's doctrines 'may be forced on the Victorian Labour Party at any time. Whatever Mr. Hogan's honesty might be, he is controlled by an outside authority which dictates to him its policy'.[23] This was a pointed reference to recent events at a special Victorian ALP Conference when the majority expressed such bitter criticism for Hogan's acceptance of the Melbourne Agreement that he challenged it to order him and his ministers to resign. In fact the issues at stake in this confrontation were complex, and to call Hogan's critics Langites was facile as analysis, however effective as propaganda.[24] More hard-nosed were the sometimes arresting statements Menzies made of his own position. Once, when in the House he was attacking Lang and heaping faint praise on Hogan, an interjector interrupted him: 'Humanity is greater than finance, and Labor stands for humanity'. Menzies replied sternly:

> Unfortunately, humanity is not greater than finance ... Unless we cure our troubles at the centre we shall not be able to make more than a weak, unsuccessful attempt to meet the problem of unemployment, and to dispense that just treatment which we want to give to every man and woman of every class and condition. It is because we know that no good turn can be done to the underdog in a community which is insolvent that we have realised and publicly stated that our first aim is public solvency.[25]

He told a Pleasant Sunday Afternoon that 'Young Australia' must show a 'willingness to work' and to accept 'sacrifice on all sides',[26] and reminded Nationalist and AWNL rallies that both employers and employees must recognize that costs of production

---

[22] *ADB*, 12: 197–202.
[23] *Argus*, 30 September 1930.
[24] The complexity of the Labor situation has been unravelled with skill and scholarly authority by L. J. Louis, in his *Trade Unions and the Depression*, a work which has been of inestimable value in the preparation of this chapter.
[25] *VPD*, 188: 3019.
[26] *Argus*, 3 March 1930.

had to be lowered.[27] In Parliament he fought against a Farmers' Relief bill, enunciating the principle of which he rapidly became Victoria's most eloquent spokesman: sanctity of contracts. The proposed legislation, to effect a moratorium for farmers in distress, was unacceptable, he declared, 'because it permits the State to cut across the ordinary liabilities which debtors accept in relation to their creditors'. Were parliament to countenance such legislation, future outside investment in Victoria was not to be hoped for.[28] Invited to speak to the Conservative Club at the University he delivered a stout anti-socialist address replete with the standard homily on balancing budgets and disregarding 'parrot-cries' about standards of living:

> Today the most popular thing that a politician can do is to stand on a platform, thump the table, and say, 'Whatever happens we are going to protect the Australian standard of living'. We are all entitled to the standard of living that we can afford. I have nothing but contempt for the man who insists on a standard of living at the expense of those from whom he borrows money.[29]

In the later months of 1930 and into 1931 Menzies' speeches, like those of other orthodox conservatives, began displaying a new emphasis: on the threat of inflation and on denouncing expansionary monetary policies increasingly pressed by left-wing members of the federal Labor Caucus. This subject lent itself to witty simplifications to which public audiences—most of them already converted—readily warmed. So, for example, he told a Nationalist rally in Warrnambool that whereas when private citizens found their incomes reduced they cut down expenses, Labor governments said: 'we have a better way. Put a little more water in the whisky'.[30] Young Nationalists chuckled when he told another rally at Camberwell that Frank Anstey and J. A. Beasley, two radical members of Federal Caucus who had until recently 'lived in decent obscurity' but were now demanding deficit budgeting, 'had derived the whole of their political education from the soap box in the days before the Young Nationalists had lent lustre to that article'. The real object of people like Anstey and Beasley was the destruction of capitalism, and they knew that the best way to do that was to 'monkey' with the currency.[31] Speaking at Caulfield in November he declared that the 'imperative need in public life' at

[27] Ibid., 7 July 1930.
[28] VPD, 182: 759.
[29] Argus, 28 June 1930.
[30] Ibid., 20 January 1931.
[31] Ibid., 4 February 1931.

the present time was for a few businessmen of the first calibre. The 'financial geniuses now coming to the surface' in the Labor Party had the idea that they could 'pull the country out of the bog by printing banknotes'. Without a doubt inflation 'is going to be the next great political issue in the country'.[32]

The travail of the federal Labor government towards the end of 1930 made this prediction all too apt. Scullin was in England for an Imperial conference, having left James Fenton as acting Prime Minister and Joseph Lyons as acting Treasurer (in place of Theodore). Both accepted as mandatory the principles of the Melbourne Agreement. They and those of like mind in Cabinet and Caucus were in any case locked into these commitments by political and financial powerlessness. With a majority in the Senate the non-Labor parties could block any radical monetary legislation. And the Commonwealth Bank, the key institution for shaping national credit policy, was sternly controlled by the chairman of its independent board, Sir Robert Gibson. Gibson, who had been largely responsible for Niemeyer's visit, believed that it was the bank's responsibility to manage the currency, and insisted that budgets must be balanced before substantial credits could be made available to government.

Gibson's steeliness brought him no friends among Labor Caucus militants, who wanted the Melbourne Agreement rejected and a credit expansion substituted for wage cuts. Lang's success in the New South Wales election was a great boost to their morale and the debate between them and the orthodox cabinet leadership became more and more fiery, as new revenue became increasingly necessary. Matters came to a head at the end of October when Caucus was considering a Cabinet scheme for cautious ministerial and civil service salary cuts and increased public works expenditure. A newly elected member, G. A. Gibbons, primed by Theodore, moved as an amendment to the official proposals that the Commonwealth Bank be required to provide credit to finance a £20 million public works programme, to assist primary and secondary industry and to meet maturing internal loans for which provision had not yet been made. Amid pandemonium that lasted for some days a majority of Caucus passed the Gibbons amendment, and then approved a new resolution that the conversion of a £28 million loan falling due in December 1930 be deferred for one year. Caucus had thus approved a large move towards deficit financing, and an additional measure which both Lyons and Theodore correctly stigmatized as repudiation. From London Scullin condemned the resolutions as 'dishonest and disastrous',

[32] Ibid., 7 November 1930.

and Lyons announced that he would defy Caucus and go ahead with the loan conversion. Eventually, on 12 November, Caucus voted to adjourn the dispute until Scullin's return; but the party's unity was shattered, wounds which would not easily heal had been opened up and the alienation of Lyons had begun.[33]

Lyons's decision to defy Caucus was in fact to herald a turning point in his career. The campaign to convert a loan of £28 million—a seemingly quixotic enterprise at a time of such deep depression—brought him into the limelight and disclosed political talents which to many seemed extraordinarily well attuned to the needs of the time. Lyons was a man of great principle, buoyed up by the simple faith that government debt was like personal debt and all commitments had to be fully honoured. In Tasmanian politics, where he had shone before his election to the Commonwealth parliament in 1929, he had become well versed in the arts of tactful persuasion. He had a kind of populist appeal in which he used patent honesty and ordinariness of mien with quiet calculation.[34] But most important of all, through his much publicized struggle with Caucus, Lyons had won the favour of financiers, businessmen and prominent conservative politicians. The loan conversion campaign brought a number of such people into direct and open co-operation with him, and this was to be of crucial importance in the future shaping of Commonwealth politics. In particular, a small Melbourne committee known in due course as 'the Group of Six' became close advisers and did much to organize the campaign. Menzies was one of them.

The Group's leader was Menzies' good friend, Staniforth Ricketson, the stockbroker. The other members were C. A. Norris, general manager of the National Life Association;[35] Sir John Higgins, formerly chairman of the British Australian Wool Realisation Association Pty Ltd (BAWRA);[36] Kingsley Henderson,[37] a leading Melbourne architect; Ambrose Pratt,[38] novelist and journalist. Menzies was the only practising politician; all the others were in some way or other directly involved in business or financial affairs. The obvious interest of such men in preserving economic stability has conventionally—and correctly been taken as an explanation for their having acted together in December

---

[33] For these and other general points on the Depression I rely on C. B. Schedvin, *Australia and the Great Depression: a study of economic development and policy in the 1920s and 1930s* and J. R. Robertson, 'Scullin as Prime Minister: seven critical decisions', *Labor History* 17 (1970): 27–36.
[34] *ADB*, 10: 184–9.
[35] Murray and White, 'Staniforth Ricketson', 318.
[36] *ADB*, 9: 289–90.
[37] Ibid., 9: 257–8.
[38] Ibid., 11: 274–5.

1930 and later. We should not, however, be misled into concluding that because that interest was usually expressed in moral terms, the morality was shallow. As events were soon to demonstrate, especially in Melbourne, repugnance at 'repudiation' was wide and deep: for an overwhelming number of people it was a national disgrace to be fought against at all costs. There is no evidence to deny to any member of the Group genuine commitment to this outlook or, as Pratt once put it, a 'desire to influence public opinion for the public good'. In lighter vein, a diversion for conspiracy theorists might be to wonder where the 'plot' was first hatched. Could it have been in the bar beneath the spears and cooking pots of the Savage Club? After all, at least four of the group—Ricketson, Menzies, Henderson and Pratt—are known to have been members.

The conversion campaign which Lyons and his advisers mounted was a 'patriotic' and highly emotional one. Rallies, advertisements in the press, on radio and in the newly arrived 'talkies' were accompanied by a variety of schemes which the organizers devised to enable even people without savings to become investors. Thus some employers bought bonds for their employees, contributing a part of the cost and deducting the rest in instalments from their wages. Banks and insurance companies offered advances to investors on sometimes radical terms. The day before the loan closed, Friday 12 December 1930, was declared 'All for Australia Day': many businessmen announced that they would put into the loan all their takings for the day. Lyons urged all Australians to do their Christmas shopping on that day.

Though the campaign was intense throughout Australia, it was particularly enthusiastic in Melbourne.[39] The Young Nationalists took the lead in waging with gusto what they insisted was a 'non-political' campaign for the loan. It began on 28 November with the first of a series of open-air meetings. Outside the Commonwealth Bank in Collins Street two lorries, decorated with appropriate posters, were used as platforms: from the first, Young Nationalist speakers harangued passers by while, on the second, Commonwealth Bank staff offered bonds for sale.[40] Similar demonstrations were arranged by the organization's country 'hundreds', pamphlets were prepared and distributed, and the Young Nationalists' campaign won special thanks from the federal ministry and Commonwealth Bank officials.[41] Young Nationalist speakers also appeared on the platform beside prominent

[39] *Age*, 17 December 1930.
[40] *Argus*, 28 November 1930.
[41] Ibid.

drawcards like Sir John Monash in a series of crowded midday rallies in the Melbourne Town Hall.[42] There too Lyons and his organizers staged the climactic rally of their campaign. At this meeting, crowded to the doors, the two key speakers were Lyons and W. A. Watt, a leading Nationalist who had served in both the Victorian and Commonwealth parliaments. This juxtaposition symbolized the need to put aside party differences for a patriotic end. Amid great cheering Lyons declared that 'when such an assembly could show its enthusiasm on such a drab subject as a loan, one need not despair about the future of Australia'. In a fine peroration Watt commended the 'clean strong men' in the Labor party who were standing up and doing 'the right and honourable thing and refusing to take the easy course of succumbing to Party prejudice'. Four days later Lyons announced to parliament that the loan had been subscribed and the Government was therefore closing it. But when all the returns came in, it was found in fact to have been oversubscribed by £2 million. It was a great, almost astonishing victory, and congratulations poured in from people of many different political hues. 'Please accept the congratulations of a Nationalist who admires a good honest Australian of any party', ran a typical example. 'With such men as you in power the honour of Australia is in safe keeping ... Wishing you every success in your splendid struggle with the wreckers'.[43] Most important of all, it is evident that Lyons's performance and his public appeal deeply impressed Menzies and Ricketson, who during the campaign had worked in the background as organizers and facilitators. Lyons had obvious leadership potential if it should become possible for a new political combination to be devised to resist radical Labor excesses. Ricketson appears already, while the loan campaign was still in progress, to have privately canvassed the need for a new political party to 'restore the confidence of the people of Great Britain in the financial honesty and political integrity of the people of Australia'. He cabled Lord Glendyne, a partner in the British stockbroking firm of Nivison & Co, which handled Australian government borrowings on the London market, to investigate the possibility of securing help from the London financial world to fund a new party, but to no avail. 'We have no politics', Glendyne replied, 'our sole duty being to advise and act for existing government, such advice and action transmitted through recognised government channels'.[44]

[42]Ibid., 3, 4, December 1930.
[43]N. Robinson to Lyons, NLA, MS. 4851/1/2.
[44]*National Times*, 27 May 1978, which quotes from cables but does not give their provenance. Murray and White, 'Staniforth Ricketson', 318, accept the evidence.

Events were, however, quickly to show that no external help was needed to give birth to the kind of party Ricketson hoped for. In the first weeks of 1931 two political developments in fact presaged its coming: renewed dissension in the Scullin Ministry and a simmering on of the 'patriotic' excitement stirred up by the loan conversion campaign. The first resulted in Lyons's detachment from the Ministry and, ultimately, from the Labor Party; the second provided the atmosphere for a groundswell of agitation and organization as alarm grew, especially in Middle Australia, at fears, however exaggerated, of national bankruptcy and social dislocation.

On his return from England in January 1931 Scullin, with Caucus endorsement, reinstated Theodore as Treasurer, though the latter stood by the main thrust of the Gibbons resolution and had not yet been cleared of the Queensland corruption charges. A horrified Lyons resigned from the Cabinet and in Melbourne on 4 February met the Group in Ricketson's office, where Menzies as spokesman asked him to leave the Labor Party and promised the Group's support if he were prepared to become leader of whatever political forces could be marshalled against the Scullin Government.[45] After much agonizing and a final unsuccessful attempt in Caucus to defeat Theodore's financial proposals, Lyons crossed the floor, with four other Labor members, to join a Nationalist vote of censure on the Government for having reinstated Theodore. Lyons, in great distress, thus automatically expelled himself: 'To deliberately break the associations of a lifetime', he told the House, 'is a step which no man, unless he is utterly bankrupt of sensibility, can take without sharp pain and mental suffering'.[46]

Lyons's defection coincided with an extraordinary phenomenon akin to, and in subtle ways fed by, the spirit of the December loan conversion campaign. This was the burgeoning in South Australia, New South Wales and Victoria of citizens' leagues which expressed malaise and dissatisfaction with existing party politics. Australia was 'on the brink of a precipice', declared the chairman at a monster meeting of one of these leagues held early in March. 'What were the peoples' representatives doing? Not one thing except talk, and even the talk was not of the country. It was of party, nothing but party'. At another meeting, at Drummoyne in New South Wales, hundreds of people unable to get into the hall listened to the star speaker's voice amplified into the street outside. He was Professor Tasman Lovell, Sydney University's first

[45] P. R. Hart, 'Lyons: Labor Minister—Leader of the U.A.P.', *Labour History* 17 (October 1970): 44.
[46] *Commonwealth Parliamentary Debates (CPD)*, 128: 236.

professor of psychology. What he said, in its strange transcendentalism, catches well at the ill-focused emotion that swept many into the movement. The League, he said,

> was one, not of mushroom growth, but rather of spontaneous combustion. The League and its idealism were so urgently needed just now that people were seeking membership with an ardour for which it was difficult to find a parallel. It was not supported by banking and industrial interests, nor was it begun by persons desiring to form a new party by which to elevate themselves... It was a strenuous opponent of selfishness, snobbery, extremism, and materialism, and it hoped to purify public life by its struggle against these four curses standing in the way of morality, merit, sweet reasonableness, and culture.[47]

The first of these bodies to be formed was the Citizens' League of South Australia, which had 30 000 members by the end of 1930. In New South Wales an All For Australia League, conceived originally by a group of Rotarians, was launched early in February 1931. The League was not in its origins quite as innocent of 'banking and business interests' as the starry-eyed Lovell thought: its initial executive has been shown to read largely as a roll-call of top managerial and commercial men.[48] But one reporter's description of the audience at the inaugural meeting is closer to the Lovell picture. That audience, he said, swept him 'back on a wave of memory to the camps and enlistment depots of 1914 and 1915. Clerks, bank managers, labourers, small shopkeepers, accountants, barristers, a mixed audience but all inspired by a wave of patriotic ardour'.[49] The growth of this League was astounding. Three weeks after its foundation it had 30 000 members; the number had leapt to 130 000 by the end of June. The Victorian parallel, another Citizens' League, was launched on 19 February at a monster meeting at the Melbourne Town Hall. The South Australian League had taken the initiative which originally led to its formation by sending its 'honorary organizer', E. D. A. Bagot, to Melbourne in January to stir interest there in the movement. Bagot first approached the Constitutional Club and 'found the members most receptive', then addressed a meeting of the 'Citizens' Committee' (principally Ricketson's Group) which had worked the previous month on the conversion loan campaign. The Citizens' Committee, chaired by the Collins House businessman and chair-

---
[47] *Sydney Morning Herald (SMH)*, 25 March 1931.
[48] Trevor Matthews, 'The All For Australia League', *Labour History*, 17 (October 1969): 138–9.
[49] Quoted by Stuart Macintyre, *The Oxford History of Australia, 1901–1942*, 268.

man of the National Union, R. W. Knox,[50] and with Constitutional Club representatives co-operating, subsequently founded the Melbourne Citizens' League.[51] By the time the Victorian League held its first State convention in May 1931, it had 80 000 members in 320 branches. Before then, early in March, it amalgamated with the New South Wales All For Australia League, and took that name.[52]

The generalized fears that spurred the Leagues' growth were exacerbated by continuing political crisis over the unsuccessful Melbourne Agreement. A meeting of premiers in February rejected an appeal from Theodore for recovery through modest monetary expansion, and in March and April the Senate foiled his attempt at legislation to secure the same end. Then in mid-March the nightmare happened: Lang defaulted for the first time, on interest due to the Commonwealth from New South Wales. Three days later Lyons offered his support to Latham, now federal parliamentary leader of the Opposition, and spoke of meetings he was planning in the eastern States.[53] He would harness for political purposes the great wave of feeling which the Leagues represented.

The campaign began in Adelaide on 9 April under the auspices of the Citizens' League, whose officers, led by the redoubtable Bagot, arranged his meetings and organized a convention of delegates from kindred associations in all States.[54] As his train drew into Adelaide station Lyons shouted from his carriage door to the waiting crowd: 'We shall strike a match tonight which will start a blaze throughout Australia'. That night, in the Exhibition Building, he addressed an audience of 3000 who, the Adelaide *Advertiser and Register* reported,

> Thundered their approval. The meeting was an amazing demonstration of the feeling of confidence Mr. Lyons has inspired in people that he is the leader Australia is seeking . . . The imagination and complete concurrence of the densely packed rows of people were captured, not by any display of fiery rhetoric, but by the man's transparent honesty

[50] *ADB*, 9: 630.
[51] Minutes of meetings of Executive Committee of South Australian Citizens' League, 21 January 1931, NLA, MS. 1186/1/2; E. D. A. Bagot to H. E. A. McCarthy, and Bagot to R. W. Knox, 17 January 1931, NLA MS. 1186/2. Bagot thought Knox would not be a suitable person to continue to take a prominent part in the League because of his political position, there being an 'absolute necessity for bringing in from the outset all classes of the community and making it a real Citizens' movement'.
[52] Matthews, 'The All For Australia League', 139–40.
[53] Hart, 'Lyons: Labor Minister—Leader of the U.A.P.', 46.
[54] Delegates were from AFA League, NSW; AFA League, Vic. (Kingsley Henderson); Producers' Advisory Council, Tas.; Sane Democracy League, NSW; Citizens' Federation, WA; Proportional Representation Group, SA; Citizens' League, SA. Citizens' League Executive minutes, 8 April 1931, NLA, MS. 1186/1/2.

and commonsense. Here was someone who thought and felt as they did, who had a home like them to lose or save, talking to them in a conversational way, but putting the country's plight to them with devastating clearness, and with equal clarity, step by step, showing them how he proposed to apply the remedy for which he was enlisting their aid and sympathy. It was no miraculous cure, no sudden waving of a wand that he offered them; it was merely the ancient rules for keeping the wolf from the door ... Old heads nodded in agreement, young eyes glistened with eagerness, misted with the emotion of strong sympathy ... [55]

Next day Lyons addressed other meetings, then caught the Melbourne express. Meantime the convention of delegates from the various leagues had agreed on 'unity of purpose and action in supporting the Hon. J. A. Lyons as the leader for creating a non-party Government' and sent telegrams to Latham and Page calling on them to co-operate under his leadership.[56] Events were moving quickly. In Melbourne on 13 April Lyons and his wife received a rapturous reception in the Town Hall at a rally graced by a platform full of notables including, as leaders of the Young Nationalists, Menzies and Kent Hughes.[57]

In a secret meeting with Lyons, the Group and the National Union made clear their wish that he replace Latham as leader of the Commonwealth Opposition.[58] Four days later, on 17 April, under severe pressure and after complex discussions, Latham resigned the leadership of the federal Opposition in Lyons's favour. Menzies, as fellow barrister, leading member of the Group and key Victorian Nationalist (he had been elected president of the Young Nationalist organization in February), was at the heart of these negotiations. Kent Hughes, Menzies' close friend, was one of many who hastened to congratulate Latham on his self-abnegation. 'You have known for some time past what my feelings were', he wrote. 'The public won't have the Natls as their rallying point, therefore we have got to find some other course ... I trust the sacrifice will not be in vain and that the service will not be unrewarded in the future.'[59] Perhaps he knew something already about a 'reward'. Latham was to become Chief Justice of the High Court in 1934 and it was later commonly understood in Melbourne legal circles that the appointment had been promised as a quid

---

[55] 9 April 1931.
[56] SA Citizens' League Executive minutes, 13 April 1931, NLA, MS. 1186/1/2; Hart, 'Lyons: Labor Minister—Leader of the U.A.P.', 49.
[57] Hobart *Mercury*, 14 April 1931.
[58] Hart, 'Lyons: Labor Minister—Leader of the U.A.P.', 49.
[59] Kent Hughes to Latham, 19 April 1931, NLA, MS. 1009/49/240.

pro quo for resigning the leadership and preserving the appearance of unity by staying on as Lyons's deputy until party reorganization could be completed.[60]

That quickly happened. Two days after Latham's resignation, a meeting in Melbourne mapped out plans for a 'United Australia Movement', through which the Nationalists, the AWNL, and the various citizens' leagues could 'act in harmony' and develop through State committees an organization 'to secure the return of United Australia candidates' at the next general election. The meeting which thus laid the basis for a new political party was small and exclusive. It consisted of thirteen men, including Lyons, four members of the Group (Menzies, Ricketson, Henderson and Higgins), two leaders of the South Australian Citizens' League, two representatives of the Victorian National Union and two representatives of the New South Wales All For Australia League. The meeting declared the Movement to be 'not anti-labour, but ... opposed to all such proposals as inflation, repudiation and communism'.[61] The Victorian section of the new party was formally established several weeks later when, under Lyons's chairmanship, a small group met privately at Scott's hotel and resolved that a United Australia Movement should be formed, with a Central Council composed of representatives of the bodies taking part in this inaugural meeting. The organizations represented were the National Federation, the All For Australia League, and the Young Nationalists Organization. This conference declared itself the first meeting of the Council, of which Kingsley Henderson, now secretary of the All For Australia League, was elected chairman, and Staniforth Ricketson temporary secretary.[62]

Menzies was not present on this occasion. The Young Nationalists were represented by Kent Hughes, Nettlefold and Manifold. Menzies had just sailed for Burnie: Tasmania was in the throes of a State election and he went to campaign on behalf of the sitting Nationalist Ministry, under Premier J. C. McPhee. Menzies was particularly welcome as president of the Young Nationalists and was wanted to address meetings against the propaganda of

[60] Hart, 'Lyons: Labor Minister—Leader of the U.A.P.', 50; Diary of Owen Dixon, 16 April 1952: 'I had lunch at the Aust. Club and talked to Starke who spoke about Latham's appointment as a job with Lyons in exchange for his making way for the latter as P.M.'.
[61] Minutes of conference in Melbourne on 19 April 1931, NLA MS. 1186/1/2.
[62] *Argus, Mercury*, 6 May 1931. The 'convention' began on 5 May but went on for more than one day. Hart says, without giving documentation, that on 7 May 'the parliamentary Nationalist Party transformed itself into the UAP with Lyons and Latham as its leaders. All Lyons' ex-Labor followers except Gabb joined the new party, along with the remnants of W. M. Hughes' Australian Party', 'Lyons: Labor Minister—Leader of the U.A.P.', 51.

Theodore, who had spoken in Hobart and Launceston the week before in support of the Tasmanian Labor Opposition. In the days just before this trip Theodore had come to rival Lang in Menzies' gallery of dangerous men. He told one AWNL meeting that 'Mr. Lang is just a crude swashbuckler, but Mr. Theodore is the "big noise" in the Federal ministry, and we must do all in our power to repel his insidious promises'.[63] At the end of April a large meeting

Menzies returns as a hero, in Young Nationalist eyes, from his 'demolition' of Theodore in the Tasmanian election campaign of 1931.

[63] *Argus*, 24 April 1931.

in the Melbourne Town Hall organized by the Young Nationalists heard Menzies, Kent Hughes and J. A. Spicer revile Lang and denounce Theodore. When Menzies declared that the immediate result of the 'inflation' threatened by Theodore's policies would be that government bonds would fall and interest rates would rise an interjector shouted: 'It will do a lot of damage to the other side'. 'Yes', replied Menzies, 'some people want to do a lot of damage to "the other side". Some people, and a few of them are in politics, are so anti-British that they cannot contain themselves. I thank God that the Australian people are not!'[64] He seized on the same theme the following weekend in a Pleasant Sunday Afternoon talk, 'At the Crossroads', delivered just as he was preparing to leave for Tasmania. But this time he used unfortunate words which, while they did not disturb his respectable audience, were seized on by enemies anxious to depict him as a ruthless conservative. Some of them have been quoted, usually out of context, ever since:

> If Australia were going to get through her troubles by abating or abandoning traditional British standards of honesty, of justice, of fair play, of resolute endeavour, it would be far better for Australia that every citizen within her boundaries should die of starvation during the next six months. To look for the easiest way out was about as traitorous a thing as any Australian could engage in at the present time. (Loud applause).[65]

On 7 May the federal Nationalist Party transformed itself into the United Australia Party (UAP) and formally elected Lyons leader of the Opposition. That evening, at his first Hobart meeting, Menzies made a great hit by dramatically announcing Lyons's new position as 'a piece of information which had just come to hand and which he believed was fraught with very great significance'. He prophesied that before many months a Tasmanian would be Prime Minister of Australia.[66] And 'if a federal ministry were put in power under the leadership of Mr. Lyons (prolonged cheers), it would so far restore the confidence of English investors that they could hope for prompt financial accommodation'. Menzies' elation was understandable. Though formidable impediments had yet to be overcome before Lyons reached the desired goal, the new political party that Menzies and his friends had worked to create was now in being. He spent three days vigorously speaking in Tasmania, always to enthusiastic audiences,[67] and presumably had a part in the outcome

[64] Ibid., 1 May 1931.
[65] Ibid., 4 May 1931.
[66] Hobart *Mercury*, 8 May 1931.
[67] Ibid., 6, 7, 8 May 1931; *Argus*, 7 May 1931.

Christmas cheer in a dour time: 'Soon after his return from Tasmania yesterday the leader of the United Australia Party (Mr J. A. Lyons), in the Fox Movietone studio at West Melbourne, recorded a message through the cinema apparatus' (Melbourne *Argus*, 24 December 1931).

of the election, which returned McPhee and the Nationalists with an enlarged majority.[68] He came home just as the thirteenth Victorian parliament reconvened, for its third session. For a time Victorian politics would again occupy most of his attention.

[68] *Argus*, 11 May 1931. Nationalists won 18 out of the 30 seats, Labor representation fell from 14 to 11.

5

State Politician and Minister

THE VEHEMENT anti-Theodore rhetoric of Menzies' Tasmanian campaign might be good anti-Labor propaganda, but the truth was that by the end of April 1931 the Treasurer, defeated by the Senate and the Commonwealth Bank, was powerless, his policies in tatters. The Loan Council therefore appointed a committee to find a new scheme for achieving budget equilibrium by June 1934. This committee in turn appointed a sub-committee of 'experts'—four economists and five State under-treasurers—who, after conferring with banks and other financial institutions, submitted a plan which Scullin summoned a Premiers' Conference to consider. The Conference met over the period 25 May to 10 June and hammered out what became known as the Premiers' Plan. Though the medicine it prescribed was bitter, this Plan was the first that seemed likely to succeed. It was made possible through a compromise by which the banks agreed that reduction in government expenditure and interest rates could take place simultaneously: earlier schemes had foundered on the insistence that budgets should be balanced before loan interest could be reduced. It also introduced the idea of 'equality of sacrifice'. Interest rates were to be lowered by converting the existing internal debt: under a refloated loan bondholders would receive reduced incomes, just as wage and salary earners would from cuts in government expenditure. As finally agreed to, the Plan had three main elements: reduction by 20 per cent of adjustable government expenditure; increases in Commonwealth income and sales taxes; reduction of public and private interest rates. A conversion loan would reduce the interest rate on Government bonds by 22.5 per cent; banks would voluntarily reduce their interest rates and rate reductions on private mortgages were to be effected by State legislation. The conference also resolved that the plan was an indivisible whole—the various parts depended intimately on each other.[1]

For Labor governments and the Labour movement generally the acceptance of cuts which meant a reduced standard of living was a heavy blow and an immediate source of tension between unions and radical politicians on the one hand and Scullin's supporters, in State and federal parliaments, on the other. Outside Labor ranks, the cry of 'repudiation' was strong, especially when the premiers agreed that a special tax should be levied on bondholders unwilling voluntarily to convert. Melbourne financiers exerted pressure through Lyons and Latham against this compulsion and the premiers, aware that the Plan needed Opposition approval to get through the Senate, invited the leaders of the federal parliamentary Opposition to the conference, where they won their point and had the conversion made voluntary. Further, though the premiers had at the Conference pledged themselves to the Plan, each State parliament had to enact legislation to put it into effect. This was a complex task, which proved the major political preoccupation of the next session of the various legislatures. In Victoria this was the session to which Menzies returned after his Tasmanian trip and Lyons's defection.

Hogan had barely formed his Labor ministry in December 1930 when the leadership of the Opposition changed: McPherson resigned through ill health, and was replaced by his former Chief Secretary, Sir Stanley Argyle. A 63-year-old Collins Street specialist medico of some standing, Argyle had entered the Legislative Assembly in 1920, winning the Toorak seat as an independent Nationalist against the endorsed candidate. His criticism of secretive, National Union sponsored, party selection procedures made him something of a forerunner to Kent Hughes and Menzies and as a 'metropolitan liberal' he favoured and won important public health and hospital reforms. But by the time he took over the Nationalist leadership the urge to press imaginative policy seems to have deserted him. On the Depression, he criticized those who wasted time arguing about responsibility: all sections of the Australian community, he said, were equally blameworthy for the economic sufferings of the time, having lived since the war 'in a fool's paradise'. What mattered now was that Government should follow sensible policies, which in his eyes meant reducing wages,

[1] The section which follows, on the formation of and agreement about the Premiers' Plan, is drawn from Schedvin, *Australia and the Great Depression*, especially 244–55, and Peter Cook, 'Labor and the Premiers' Plan', *Labour History*, 17 (1970): 97–110.

increasing taxation and economizing wherever possible.[2] With so simple a philosophy it was easy for him to accept the main thrust of the Premiers' Plan, leaving it to his more brilliant subordinate, Menzies, to mount the main attack on aspects of the Plan which the Opposition found it difficult to accept.

Two major measures were in question: the first, a Financial Emergency Bill, designed to effect reductions in expenditure; the second, a Debt Conversion Agreement Bill, to authorize conversion of government loans to reduce interest charges. Hogan insisted that the legislation was 'indivisible': to reject any part of it would in effect be to reject the Premiers' Plan itself. The Financial Emergency Bill was in five parts. Parts I to III and V provided for cuts in salaries, pensions and permanent appropriations, Part IV provided the means by which a private borrower in difficulty could apply to the courts for a reduction in the interest he was paying. In the second reading debate Part IV was the main target for the Opposition. Menzies led the attack with spirit, for the proposal here raised an issue fundamental to his social and political outlook: the sanctity of contracts.

'It is one of the principles of the political philosophy of members on this side of the House', he said, 'that it is no part of the legislative function of government to impair the sanctity of contracts between citizen and citizen'. Contract was the very cement of modern society. Menzies cited Sir Henry Maine's dictum that the history of our legal institutions has been the history of a movement from status to contract. He appealed to Bentham, and read from Alexander Hamilton and the *Federalist*, with its eloquent assertion, in no. 44, that 'Laws impairing the obligation of contracts are contrary to the first principles of the Social Contract and to every principle of sound legislation'. No emergency should be allowed to impair these principles and, taking a phrase from the *Federalist*, Menzies explained in these words why he must vote against the Bill: 'it is because I for one believe so profoundly in the overshadowing importance of giving some regular course to the business of society; it is because I believe that without that regular course and without the security that it engenders, there can be no hope for our salvation'. It was a fine speech, which earned ironic congratulations from the Labor benches: 'the privileged sections have a worthy representative in the hon. member', declared Jackson of Prahran.[3] John Cain, Labor Minister for Railways, offered a backhanded compliment when he argued that the compromise nature of the Premiers' Plan was the reason it should be supported;

---

[2] *ADB*, 10: 92–4.
[3] *VPD* 185: 1250–2.

it had been framed at a Premiers' Conference at which men of all shades of opinion were represented, from red Laborite to Tory, the latter 'so ably represented in this House by the hon. member for Nunawading. In fact, we have had no more died-in-the-wool Tory in any of our parliaments during the last half century'.[4]

Given the pledge each premier had implicitly made at their crucial Conference, however, there was little the House could do but pass the measure. The same was true of the Debt Conversion Agreement Bill. An agreement to convert the entire internal public debt of Australia had already been negotiated, put in order by the solicitors-general of the Commonwealth and States, and signed by the State Premiers and the Commonwealth Prime Minister.[5] The bill before the House was simply to register the formal agreement of the Victorian parliament. Argyle reluctantly accepted it, as did Menzies and the other opponents of interest rate reduction. All, however, took the opportunity to explain why, though inevitable, their action went against the grain. In a long and troubled speech, Menzies reiterated his opposition to the breaking of contracts, though he was at pains to make it clear that he accepted the correctness of everyone being made to contribute fairly. But he believed that this should be done through taxation, not the alteration of contracts.[6]

The loan was floated successfully in August. If anything, the conversion campaign was more highly organized than that of the previous December. It was directed by a National Appeal Executive whose leaders were Gibson, Scullin and Lyons, and a committee of leading journalists, headed by the ruthless owner of the Melbourne *Herald*, Keith Murdoch, co-ordinated the press campaign. In a remarkable response, all but £16m, or 3 per cent, was converted. Great—indeed unexpected—as this result was, it was widely felt that, because inequity would result if a small section of the community did not share in the general sacrifice, the bondholders of the £16m should be somehow made to pay. Theodore's answer was to force conversion on them, and a conference of premiers which met in September finally agreed that, distasteful as it was, this course was the best available. Thus the premiers committed themselves, a Debt Conversion Bill (no. 2) was framed, and each agreed to put it through his parliament.[7]

As Deputy Premier (Hogan, his health deteriorating under the strain of events, was in hospital), Thomas Tunnecliffe introduced the new Conversion Bill into the Assembly at the beginning of

[4]Ibid., 1307.
[5]Schedvin, *Australia and the Great Depression*, 262.
[6]*VPD*, 185: 1576.
[7]Schedvin, *Australia and the Great Depression*, 262–5.

December 1931. By then it had been passed by the parliaments of the Commonwealth, New South Wales and South Australia, and there was no chance that any action by Victoria could stop it. In the Assembly the Opposition furiously attacked the Bill—Menzies called it 'the grossest form of dishonesty'—but to no avail.[8] In the Legislative Council it passed quickly through all stages in one day. One member, bluff Dr Harris, summed up the prevailing attitude there by applying the moral of 'Aesop's fable about the fox who lost his tail': those who had not converted had not responded to the

> call of love of country ... I regard the talk of repudiation, as applied to the compulsion of these people to come in with the rest of Australia, as mere nonsense. I support the Bill ... I object to having my tail lopped off whilst the other fellow is allowed to run about with his on.[9]

Throughout the various debates during 1931 on measures to deal with Depression conditions, Menzies maintained his steely views on the sanctity of contracts. Thus, for example, in May 1931 he 'condemned, root and branch', an Unemployed Occupiers and Farmers Relief Bill by which the Government legislated for a moratorium for tenants, mortgagors and farmers on payments due if they could show they were unemployed. What was being set up, he said, was not a true moratorium, but simply an arrangement by which landlords and mortgagees were in effect subsidizing the debtors.[10] Again, in September, he fought against a Landlord and Tenant (Rent Reduction) Bill, which sought to reduce rents for long leases contracted when money values were very different from those of 1931. 'To talk of restoring confidence by methods of this sort', he told the Assembly, 'appears to me to be the greatest paradox'.[11] There was, for Menzies, no compromise on this issue.

The second half of 1931 saw continued growth in the strength of the Young Nationalist movement, and consequently in the influence of Menzies in wider party affairs. Indeed, in something that looked very much like a Young Nationalist takeover of the party apparatus, he won in September the presidency of the National Federation itself. People who, like Kent Hughes, had always resented obscurantist control by the National Union must

[8] *Argus*, 17, 22 October 1931.
[9] *VPD*, 187: 5595.
[10] Ibid., 185: 214.
[11] Ibid., 186: 2363, 2847.

have rejoiced. Menzies himself certainly spoke ebulliently at the first meeting he chaired as President: the Federation's fifteenth annual conference, held in September and attended by 200 delegates from all over the State. He had accepted the presidency, he said, in the belief that 'as he was a Young Nationalist the innovation might, for that reason, have a useful effect on the Federation':

> The party to which you and I belong has of recent years suffered almost a regular series of reverses, at least in Victoria. If we cast about for an explanation I believe that we will find the answer to be this—that we have to too great an extent been looking for political expedients ... I believe that a large majority of the public today is perfectly ready to give its adherence to a party which will display political principle and political courage... We have suffered far too much from people who have no political convictions beyond a more or less genteel adherence to our side of politics. That kind of adherence is worthless. We must have people who believe things, and who are prepared to go out and struggle to make their beliefs universal.[12]

In other words, for the whole party to appropriate Young Nationalist ideology was the key to future success.

Early the following month (November 1931) the Young Nationalists followed this general conference with a weekend convocation of their own, to prepare a fighting platform for the next elections. More than 100 delegates attended, Menzies presided and after two days of discussion the meeting issued a very detailed statement of agreed policy. Its 'principal objective' was forthright and orthodox: 'We stand for Imperial unity under the Crown, individual freedom, and the encouragement of a sturdy independence among the people'. On matters of detail State and federal issues were intermingled under general headings: this was a statement of position to serve in whichever election came first. So, for example, under 'Government Finance', it declared the balancing of budgets to be essential to full recovery, repudiated 'any Government interference with private contracts', and insisted 'that all income-earning persons should contribute equally to the cost of Government'. Overall, the platform was a crisp elaboration of the Depression policies of Menzies and the other makers of the UAP.[13] The *Argus* hailed it with an editorial, 'Youth in the Forefront', which praised the Young Nationalists both for providing an overdue and principled statement of party objectives and for their developing crusade in the electorates:

[12] *Argus*, 24 September 1931.
[13] Ibid., 9 November 1931.

Young Nationalist speakers have carried the war into the enemy's camp by organising street meetings in industrial suburbs. Their success has been such as to indicate that there are no Labour strongholds too impregnable to be challenged at election time. The virility of the Young Nationalists' campaigning has infused a new strength into the Nationalist movement.[14]

The exuberant mood of the Young Nationalist at this time reflected as much as anything else a sniff of coming political victories. The Premiers' Plan might be in process of being approved and implemented, but both the Victorian and the Commonwealth Labor Governments were reeling before its impact on their supporters. As Menzies pointed out, Hogan, vilified by the unions and the more radical section of his parliamentary party, could not have passed much of the legislation endorsing the Plan without the support of the Opposition, and in fact was kept in office by the vote of a handful of Independents.[15] In the Commonwealth parliament Scullin's Government, desperately weakened by the defection of Lyons and his followers, was dependent on the good grace of a group of five members who in effect constituted a separate Labor party of men who followed Lang's policy and were in fact at his beck and call. And Lang was not only at loggerheads with the Scullin Government over economic plans, but also, in the Byzantine world of New South Wales Labor politics, harboured a savage enmity towards Theodore.

The Scullin Government was the first to go when, only a few weeks after the Young Nationalists' conference, the Lang group crossed the floor of the Representatives on a vote of confidence concerning allegations that Theodore had misused unemployment relief funds.[16] A short, bitter election campaign followed. All over Australia economic suffering and the conflict between traditional loyalties and pragmatic panaceas inflamed social antagonisms. There was, in truth, much in the assertion of a writer in the *Round Table* that the campaign was one of terrors more than of promises: 'Each side claimed support because of the danger of putting the other into office'.[17] The election resulted in a staggering defeat for the Government. In the House of Representatives the ALP lost thirty seats, nine of them Victorian. The effect on the Party's leadership was calamitous: eight members who had served in the Scullin ministry were defeated. Included in these was Theodore, who left

[14] Ibid., 10 November 1931.
[15] Ibid., 31 October 1931.
[16] For an excellent analysis of Lang's part in these events see Bede Nairn, *The 'Big Fella': Jack Lang and the Australian Labor Party 1891–1949* (Melbourne 1986), 247–9.
[17] Quoted by L. J. Louis, *Trade Unions and the Depression*, 136–7.

politics for good. Lang Labor survived with five seats, the UAP won thirty-nine seats and the Country Party sixteen. Lyons became Prime Minister, forming an all-UAP Cabinet.[18]

Labor's federal catastrophe was soon matched by collapse in Victoria. The strains of 1931 so told on Hogan that by the later months of the year he suffered periods of nervous illness which put him intermittently into hospital. At the end of January 1932 the annual State Conference of the Party resolved that members of parliament who further supported the Premiers' Plan would be expelled. Parliament met, after an adjournment, in April. On a vote of confidence on the Plan Labor split and the Government fell. Parliament was dissolved on 14 April 1932.[19]

In the federal election that followed Scullin's fall, Menzies played a key role in organizing the Nationalist, now officially called 'UAP',[20] campaign in Victoria, though his own appearances on the platform were not frequent. But in the State election brought on by the Hogan Government's collapse he travelled and spoke more frequently than any of his colleagues, fulfilling the role of leader of his party's organization with energy and flair. His articulateness and skill in dealing with interjectors made him the idol of his supporters and the *bête noire* of his enemies, particularly the less well-educated, who thought him snobbish and over-bearing—a reaction typified by the interjector who interrupted a homily on the meaning of 'confidence' with a contemptuous 'Go on, University man'.[21] It was, throughout, a bitter campaign. There was much talk, on both sides, of the menace of Communism, talk which in Melbourne had a special edge in view of Communist organization there of an Unemployed Workers' Movement whose demonstrations and physical resistance to evictions of tenants brought periodic bouts of disorder and vigorous—sometimes brutal—police action. The weeks of the election, moreover, co-incided with dramatic events in New South Wales: the climax of the Commonwealth Government's conflict with Lang over his repudiation of interest payments; the preparations of the New Guard to take over should law and order break down; and, finally, the dismissal of Lang by the Governor of the State, Sir Philip Game—on 13 May, the day before the Victorian poll. Throughout

---

[18] Sawer, *AFPL* 2, 42.
[19] The meticulous and moving account by Louis of Labor's Victorian travail is the source for this bare summary, and of other remarks in this chapter on the Victorian situation.
[20] By the time of the federal election, Nationalist parties had merged with other anti-Labor forces under the umbrella of the United Australia Organisation. For practical purposes this occurred at different times in different States. In Victoria the Nationalist Party was formally renamed UAP in September 1931.
[21] Albert Park, *Argus*, 29 April 1932.

the campaign the UAP, and Menzies in particular, used the Lang bogey to considerable effect. As Menzies sloganized to the Warrnambool electors on 9 May, they faced 'only one choice: honesty or Langism'; there was no middle course. Throughout his campaign he denounced, as the mechanism through which Langism threatened Victoria, control of the parliamentary Labor party by its external organization. By contrast he claimed to know, as himself both a member of the UAP and president of the United Australia Organization in Victoria, that there was no discussion between the organization and the parliamentary party about what the latter 'is to do or what its policy is to be. The United Australia Organization is an organizing body pure and simple. This story that there are some mysterious interests which issue instructions to the party was always a foolish one and always a false one'.[22] For a man who, ever since his entry into politics, had resisted National Union control that 'always' had to be tongue in cheek.

On the eve of the poll Menzies put his party's simple case in a black-bordered, signed statement in the *Argus*:

> The United Australia Organization, confident of Australia's recovery and progress under good government, asks for a definite verdict in favour of prudent and honest public finance.
>
> No party which has not the assurance of definite support in Parliament and in the constituencies can hope to exhibit that degree of promptness and resolution which is necessary for dealing with our present chaotic financial position.
>
> The major task of the next three years is to give commerce a chance of recovery, a chance upon which effective re-employment depends, by reducing and ultimately destroying the dead weight of Government deficits.[23]

The final poll registered a devastating defeat for the ALP. Its thirty Assembly seats were reduced to sixteen.[24] The press hailed 'Victory for the Plan', Tunnecliffe resigned and, as president of the United Australia Organization, Menzies issued a statement on the 'great triumph' represented by the election result, which 'showed that the people of Victoria had no mind for weird financial tricks'.[25]

Commissioned to form a new government, Argyle chose five UAP men, three Young Nationalists, three members of the Country Party and one of Hogan's ex-ministers. Menzies received the

[22] Ibid., 11 May 1932.
[23] Ibid., 13 May 1932.
[24] Louis, *Trade Unions and the Depression*, 210.
[25] *Argus*, 16 May 1932.

The Argyle Ministry is presented to the Victorian public, 1933: *(standing, left to right)* Menzies, Linton (Secretary to Cabinet), Manifold, Chandler, Kent Hughes; *(seated)* Cohen, Goudie, Jones, Allan, Pennington, Dunstan, Macfarlan, Argyle.

Attorney-Generalship and the Railways portfolio. The *Age* reported that 'the Young Nationalist section of the U.A.P. is frankly disappointed that only one of its members, Mr. Menzies, has been given full Cabinet rank'. The other two, Kent Hughes and Manifold, were honorary ministers.[26]

Menzies assumed control of his new bailiwicks on 19 May, with something of a flourish. In the morning the retiring Labor minister, Cain, took a somewhat emotional farewell of the Commissioners and heads of departments at the railway headquarters and introduced Menzies as his successor. In reply Menzies paid a tribute to the work Cain had done and said that the task of saving public finance from ruin could only be achieved by 'hard work and co-operation'. Compared with other departments, Menzies added, 'the Railways Department had nothing to fear'. Having delivered this gnomic statement he went to the more familiar setting of the High Court, where he was appearing in a case and where, after

[26] *Age*, 19 May 1932.

the luncheon adjournment, he said: 'If the Court pleases, before argument resumes, I have the honour to announce that I have been appointed His Majesty's Attorney-General for the State of Victoria'. Justice Rich, the senior judge presiding, offered the Court's congratulations, and later in the afternoon the outgoing Attorney-General, William Slater, took Menzies to the Crown Law Department and introduced him to the chief officers there.[27] As if to seal all this new eminence, Menzies was elected deputy leader when the parliamentary UAP had its first meeting a few weeks later. The *Argus* attributed this largely to the influx of Young Nationalists at the election, for whereas in the last parliament there were only six of these men, now there were sixteen.[28]

After the new Government had been formed, the Young Nationalists had a great, self-congratulatory fling, in a smoke social they held at Rumpelmayer's Cafe on the evening of 6 June. Kent Hughes, their president since Menzies' elevation to the headship of the Party organization, said they had heaps of reasons to justify the occasion: the election victories to which they had contributed so much in Victoria and New South Wales; the need to congratulate Argyle on his accession to the premiership; the need to congratulate Menzies on being elected deputy leader of the UAP. Special guests included Argyle, E. S. Cunningham, late editor and now leading trustee on the board of the *Argus*,[29] E. H. Willis, the influential behind-the-scenes secretary of the National Union,[30] and G. S. Maclean, secretary of the United Australia Organization. During the evening a telegram of congratulations was received from the UAP Premier of New South Wales, Bertram Stevens, who had just had a sweeping electoral victory over Lang. Young Nationalists who had taken part in the New South Wales campaign talked of their experiences, and amid derisive laughter a bust of Lang, crowned with a dunce's cap, was 'unveiled' on the platform. The two formal speakers of the evening were Argyle and Menzies. Argyle's theme was joy and hope at the effects of the new interest of the young and the respectable in politics:

> When I first entered parliament 12 years ago, it was made clear to me that I had lost caste by becoming associated with politics. That, unfortunately, was the opinion which a great many people held of those who then entered public life. The revival of interest in politics, coupled as it has been with the entry into Parliament of so many men who

[27] *Argus*, 20 May 1932.
[28] Ibid., 16 June 1932.
[29] *ADB*, 8: 177.
[30] Ibid., 12: 51.

have proved themselves and demonstrated their capacity for leadership in private life, must surely remove this reproach. I would like to warn you, however, not to let your enthusiasm wane.

Menzies gave an assurance that the vigour of the organization would be maintained:

We recognise a good deal of truth in the cynical saying that a Ministry begins to die as soon as it is born. In everything we do to carry out the policy on which we were elected, we tread on a few corns or offend a few interests, and so we begin shedding votes. This organization intends to expand to counteract that tendency, and to maintain the confidence and enthusiasm of the people.[31]

The new Government started well enough: its initial plans for economies, novel charges and taxes and other measures to meet obligations under the Premiers' Plan received general commendation: the *Age*, for example, described them as 'unexceptionable', a 'triumph over political affiliations and the prejudicial outlook of party politicians'.[32] But the day-to-day bite of economic suffering in the electorates and the inexorable pressure of sectional interests were soon eating away at concensus. At the annual meeting of the AWNL, soon after the election, Menzies warned against this, urging a crusade to improve party organization and to guard against those 'little cold whispers that did more to destroy a ministry than all the blasts of opposition . . . There was no surer way to undo the good work of an election than to allow it to be nibbled away by the rats afterwards'.[33] Though he was never to put it as crudely as that, the 'rats' for Menzies were the more radical members of the Country Party. Indeed, the most important legacy of the two years he was now beginning as a State minister was to be his hardening distrust of the Country Party as a selfish sectional interest.

It was perhaps inevitable that as Minister for Railways, Menzies should displease the largest single group of his customers, the farmers. Victorian freight rates, admitted on all sides to be high would, if reduced, theoretically give important benefits to the man on the land. But the railway 'problem' was one of the Depression's worst: with a capital value of £75 000 000 the railways represented half the State's public debt and, like other ministers before him, Menzies was desperately anxious to see the railways pay. In the

[31] *Argus*, 17 June 1932.
[32] *Age*, 24 August 1932.
[33] *Argus*, 20 September 1932.

three years up to March 1933 8000 railway employees had been made redundant and Menzies claimed that the ratio of working expenditure to revenue was the lowest in the history of the State, comparing favourably with any system in the world.[34] He could see no more fat to cut and firmly told a long string of delegations that rates could not be reduced without increasing taxes which would unfairly penalize other sections of the community. A further complication was the development of road competition against the railway system, especially virile as the operation of motor lorries and service cars in country areas was one of the few initiatives that small investors and unemployed people who at least had a driver's licence could try to exploit in such desperate times. Country people often benefited from such competition: they were not all enchanted when Menzies took determined steps to eliminate it by legislating to set up a Transport Regulation Board which would license, and thereby control, commercial vehicles in non-urban areas.[35]

More explosive still was that issue on which Menzies' outspoken views were by now legendary: the sanctity of contracts. He fought several schemes advanced in and out of parliament to help ailing primary producers reconstruct by easing interest rates through legislation.[36] Tension on this and related matters led Menzies and other Young Nationalists to make speaking tours in country areas to criticize a number of Country Party demands. Country Party officials threatened to contest all UAP-held constituencies at the next election, and the *Age* speculated about a possible ministerial reconstruction in which 'the Country Party, in its quest for the Attorney General's scalp, would try to force Mr Menzies out of the Cabinet'.[37] Then in June 1933 the Central Council of the Country Party issued a directive to the three Country Party

---

[34] Ibid., 2 March 1933.

[35] Menzies introduced the second reading debate on his Transport Regulation Bill on 29 August 1933 (*VPD*, 191: 1083 ff). As Hazlehurst (*Menzies Observed*, 89) has correctly remarked about this speech: 'Of all the parliamentary speeches Menzies made, at federal as well as State level, none displayed greater mastery of detail or fluency of argument'. The measure stirred much excitement and brought a variety of unexpected vested interests out of the woodwork. For a particularly lively example of meetings on the issue see Menzies before a Lilydale audience, *Argus*, 1 September 1933. The measure was in the end badly mauled in the Legislative Council, after long negotiations between the two Houses, in which Menzies earned unstinting Labor praise for his patience, clarity and fairness (see esp. Tunnecliffe, *VPD*, 193: 4175).

[36] The most important of these was a plan advanced by a Melbourne-based body, the Primary Producers' Restoration League, which wanted tribunals established throughout the country to help primary producers on the edge of bankruptcy to 'reconstruct' their affairs (*Argus*, 8 November 1932).

[37] *Age*, 15 May 1933.

members of the Argyle Ministry to resign unless the Government accepted a series of demands which included reduction in railway and interest rates, and a guaranteed home consumption price for primary products.[38]

The immediate crisis was weathered when there was a change in the Country Party leadership, but for Menzies and the Young Nationalists tension remained. In September 1933, for example, as newly re-elected president, Menzies launched at the United Australia Organisations' second annual meeting a hard-hitting appeal to the UAP to be true to its principles, if necessary even at the cost of temporary political defeat.

> The Country Party purported to be an ally of the United Australia party. What was its policy? It was concerned merely with procuring any temporary advantage for one section of the community. A Labour member of the Legislative Council had said to him with some bitterness, 'The Country party would vote for Communism tomorrow if it meant 3d. more a bushell in the price of wheat' (Laughter). The United Australia Party believed in private enterprise, and in the much-abused capitalist system. It was time that the party ceased to apologise for its opinions ... The party's danger was that it seemed to be bargaining away its belief for a mess of political pottage.

As he went on to explain it, that mess of pottage was composed of those sectional, and in his view largely socialistic, demands set out in the Country Party's June ultimatum and called for ever since.[39]

Despite ministerial responsibilities, parliamentary duties and the continued demands of his legal practice, Menzies' public performances as a speaker increased in volume and variety in 1933-34, partly because of what was obviously now his sheer pleasure in the easy rapport he could establish with most audiences, and partly because he felt a genuine sense of mission as the advocate of traditional democratic values, as he saw them, in the face of incipient threats, at home and abroad. On the lighter side he is to be observed in the many everyday settings that the ordinary round of constituency responsibilities created: introducing Lyons to open a bazaar at the Mitcham Scout Hall and speaking jocularly about the failure of cigarette manufacturers to put prime ministers, as well as cricketers and footballers, on their cigarette cards;[40] opening a fete at Box Hill Grammar School and telling the boys that they were more important than even 'a good and able headmaster'

[38] Ibid., 22 June 1933.
[39] *Argus*, 27 September 1933.
[40] Ibid., 17 July 1933.

in establishing a school tradition;[41] giving an address at the Gordon Institute of Technology on the need in Australia for a greater interest in art and literature.[42] But the major themes of his more serious talks remained political, for the most part extensions of that call for quality and integrity in public life which the Young Nationalist movement itself symbolized. He never tired of insisting on what he called in one broadcast the 'supreme duty' of a member of parliament to 'disagree violently with his electors if he thinks them wrong'. The question was of far-reaching importance: 'a strong Parliament was the only protection against dictatorships and Communism', and parliament could only preserve itself through independence and strength.[43]

Menzies' anxiety to widen, however simply, the perspective in which Australian affairs were considered was an essential part of the reform programme which he and the more intellectually-minded leaders of the Young Nationalist Organisation were still pressing. In May 1933, for example, Young Nationalists from the University—Professor K. H. Bailey, G. L. Wood and P. D. Phillips—established for members a course of lectures in international affairs, and at a meeting to launch these Menzies eloquently exhorted as many as possible to seize the opportunity of learning how to speak 'from the comfort of a background of sound knowledge'.

> In his five years of experience [in politics], he had often been ashamed of the lack of knowledge on the part of the men who stood beside him on the platform. There might have been a time when a man could get through in politics with a little general knowledge so long as he had mastered the arts of osculation for the benefit of babies, and of being a good fellow for the grown ups. Today, however, questions tended less and less to be political in the local sense and more and more economical and international.[44]

Serious Melbourne newspapers meantime carried foreign news which he could exploit, in a simple way, with popular audiences. Thus, in December 1933, he asked a large UAP rally in the Camberwell Town Hall: 'Can anyone here prove that we are Hitler-proof or Mussolini-proof, or that the Parliamentary system in Australia

---

[41] Ibid., 14 October 1933.
[42] NLA, MS. 4936/1/1/1.
[43] Talk on 3LO, reported in *Argus*, 3 November 1933.
[44] *Argus*, 5 May 1933. Note also Wood's remarks: 'There was possibly no more self-contained, self-satisfied country than Australia, and he was glad to see the young representatives of the more stable section of the community at last waking up to the value of the study circle which earnest and thoughtful people in the opposite camp had long realised'.

has an immortality denied in other parts of the world?[45] Early in 1934 he could preach to a Pleasant Sunday Afternoon on a text taken from the slogan of a shop in the city: 'Our shirts are wide in the body and long in the tail'. The world, said Menzies, had developed a peculiar interest in shirts, 'not in the width of them or in the tails, but in their colour and association ... In many ways we have come to associate all forms of aggressive nationalism with the adoption of the shirt as a symbol'. Implicit was a serious threat to the Menzies ideal: a rational, contract-based polity.

> It was hardly necessary to demonstrate how private semi-military organisations like most of the 'shirt' organisations could breed danger. They were not of the State. They developed the idea of primitive justice and wild justice. Inevitably, too, the formation of one such organisation in a community of high-spirited people led to the formation of counter-organisations. An Englishman, born into liberty won through centuries of struggle, would not tolerate a system whereby he enjoyed liberty only as a concession by the Government of the day, a 'temporary grant'.[46]

In what became a celebrated broadcast some months later he addressed the rhetorical question 'Is democracy doomed?', and outlined a number of 'diseases' with which it was alleged that democracy was beset. But none of them was incurable. The safeguard against the most threatening was in the hands of the electors themselves: 'Some people—and I am one of them—think that the greatest danger to democracy lies in the readiness of the popular elector ... to be bribed by promises of political and pecuniary advantage'. But 'as economic and political problems become more and more interwoven, men of all sorts and conditions will more and more realise that an interest in politics is vital to their own well-being'.[47]

Other bearings on the questions which preoccupied Menzies in these popular talks received a heated airing when eighty Young Nationalists held a weekend conference at Healesville in November 1933. This developed quickly into a meeting of highly engaged young men not so worried that the existing form of government might succumb in the face of external attack as that it should be choked by its own accumulated defects. The central issue for debate was the question: 'What is our attitude toward the present system of government?' Speakers uniformly expressed dissatisfaction with the tone of contemporary politics and the way parliament

[45] Ibid., 12 December 1933.
[46] Ibid., 5 March 1934.
[47] Ibid., 22 May 1934.

operated, dwelling on the time-wasting nature of current parliamentary procedures and the supposedly poor quality of parliamentarians. Thus, for example, a pioneer Young Nationalist now a member of the Legislative Assembly, Vinton Smith, catalogued ways in which parties on both sides of the House constantly brought forward 'potboilers to keep the show going' and observed that 'for men accustomed to the direction of business . . . such time-wasting devices were extremely irritating'. Some suggested wild remedies, like P. D. Phillips's plan to remodel State parliaments by abolishing parties and reconstituting the parliaments as purely administrative machines to carry out policies decided federally. Others—a small but vigorous group—thought the same ends might be achieved by adopting some form of Fascism. The Young Nationalists' paper, *The Australian Statesman*, had already fostered discussion of this issue, its most notable piece being an unsigned editorial of 1 May: 'FASCISM! The Spirit of the Age'. When historians come to sum up the events of the present era, it argued, 'they will undoubtedly call it the Fascist Age or the Age of Youth'. It was not possible to understand Fascism until it was divested of all the trappings with which it had been adorned:

> Fascism has really nothing to do with black or brown shirts, Swastika badges, the castor oil of Mussolini, the muddled mind of a Mosley, or the heroic hail of a Hitler. Fascism has still less to do with the comic capers of Colonel Campbell. If the New Guard wishes to adopt Fascism as its creed it must first of all learn something of politics and political leadership, and secondly it must be able to differentiate between mummery and material things . . .

But when it came to saying clearly what Fascism *was* about, the author seemed to be somewhat muddled, talking in the end in the jargon of the day about how it was 'necessary to replace traditional syndicalist anarchy by a complete organisation of all interests', with the State 'forcing syndicates into the ordered social organism'. Largely muddled too were the Young Nationalists at Healesville who declared themselves to be 'Fascist in sympathy'. Kent Hughes had, it seemed, become one of these. He explained, a trifle obscurely:

> He did not wish it to be thought, however, that he was advocating a melodramatic dictatorship in Australia. He did not believe that Australians were fond of saluting. The existing parliamentary system, nevertheless, needed moulding in such a way that urgent problems, such as production and marketing, could be dealt with more promptly than they were at present.

Menzies could not stand idly by and listen to anybody advocate, in however muddled and naive a way, dictatorship for Australia. Fascism, he firmly said in reply, was inconsistent with parliamentary government:

> Before we can determine whether we are Fascists or not, we must determine whether we believe in Parliaments. Under a very great dictator like Mussolini you may produce a degree of efficiency and control which Parliament is unable to produce, but that is the product of the genius of a man and not of a system. We may not produce 100 per cent of efficiency under our Parliamentary system, but we do produce a very high percentage of liberty, and as a British people we are not inclined to change freedom for some form of dictatorial control.

Of course the system stood in need of renovation, and again Menzies outlined those ideas for improvement which he had made his own: attract 'first class men' into parliament; see that they were not 'occupied with petty details which could be dealt with by a capable administrative officer'; and eschew 'the wretched notion that when a man entered Parliament he took on a full-time job, and should be perpetually at the beck and call of the electors'—a return to amateur government would be an important step to re-establishing parliament as an efficient machine.

Though spirited, the discussion proved inconclusive, and at the end of the conference Menzies moved and carried an instruction to the Executive (of which he remained the dominant member) to prepare for a new conference, in March 1934, a series of policy proposals on parliamentary procedure and on the question: 'what should be the relationship of the State to industry?'[48] Meantime, in February 1934, the Young Nationalists had their annual meeting, which coincided with a Premiers' Conference being held in Melbourne, so that Lyons and Latham were able to attend as guests. The annual report recorded sound progress: the organization now had 852 members, new and larger premises in Collins Street, and in 1933 had held five general meetings as well as the Healesville conference. Lyons described the Young Nationalists as 'the spearhead of the Party they represented' in Victoria and Latham complimented the Young Nationalists on the way they were 'standing for the ideals of democracy, which were being threatened in nearly every country'. The newly-elected president, Vinton Smith, declared that: 'The great attraction of this organization is its tolerance of individual opinion and conviction. It is to

---

[48]Ibid., 27 November 1933, for report of the conference, from which all quotations are drawn.

be hoped that the entry of its members into Parliament means the end of representation of the people by political errand-boys and seat-warmers!'[49]

At the time of this meeting Argyle was seriously ill and Menzies was at the beginning of what would turn out to be a three-month stint as Acting Premier of Victoria. He was therefore the State's representative at the Premiers' Conference for which Lyons and Latham were in Melbourne. There he made a great impression. His most important contribution was a two-hour speech on 19 February about the serious threat to federalism implicit in the steady development of Commonwealth financial power. On the evening of that day the Young Nationalists held their annual meeting and there Lyons enthusiastically described Menzies' speech to the Premiers' Conference as 'an address which is worthy to rank among the greatest efforts of the statesmen who have built up this great Commonwealth'. Less extravagantly, and more accurately, the press hailed it as a 'striking analysis'.[50]

Argyle's illness kept him on the political sidelines until the first week of June 1934. He was back just in time for the reconvening of parliament, which met on 20 June after a recess of six months. The Government announced that the new session would last only three months. In October Victoria was to be visited by the Duke of Gloucester, making a royal tour as part of the State's centenary celebrations, and it was felt proper that parliament should be in recess for that. As elections would then be shortly due the Ministry thought it pointless to reconvene until the new House could be constituted: it fixed March 1935 for the election and decreed extension of the recess until then. As the *Age* acidly observed, that meant that in 1934–35 the State legislature would have sat for three months out of a year and a half—'scarcely enough to vary the monotony of a private member's placid existence'.[51]

By contrast, for Menzies the long recess up to June 1934 was an immensely busy time. Argyle, on his return, paid 'a graceful tribute' to his 'excellent work' as Acting Premier,[52] and the compliment was well earned. Menzies' performance at the Premiers' Conference in February was the most dramatic of his public appearances in Argyle's stead, but there were many other workaday situations in which he acted as an effective spokesman for the Ministry. More important, he had to meet the heavy administrative demands of the Premier's Department in addition to

[49] Ibid., 20 February 1934.
[50] Ibid.
[51] *Age*, 19 June 1934.
[52] Ibid., 13 June 1934.

his own, and was responsible also for the general oversight of the Treasury. As the financial year came to an end there were particular worries when unexpected losses on the railways and soldier and closer settlement promised a deficit that would markedly exceed the £800 000 allowed to Victoria for 1933–34 under the Premiers' Plan. Menzies issued every department with orders that 'the most rigid economy' must be practised. 'Whatever might be the position about certain signs of recovery', he told a delegation of unionists who waited on him in April to protest against the Railways Commissioners having recently dismissed eighty employees, 'the State has reached a crucial testing-point'.[53]

The most troublesome problem to confront Menzies over those months was a prolonged strike at the Wonthaggi State coal mine, so serious at one stage as to threaten the continued existence of the mine and, through that, of the town itself. The underlying issue was the miners' resistance to wage cuts decreed under the Premiers' Plan: the strike began in March 1934 when two men were dismissed by the mine management for 'disobedience to orders' and seven wheelers were suspended for having refused to work on the ground that they were being paid less than award wages. The stoppage lasted five months, keeping over 1100 miners out of work for a total wage loss of £110 000. Menzies finally managed to persuade Cabinet to agree to concessions which led to a compromise agreement. The wheelers were reinstated and new machinery set up for consultation between management and unions: face was saved on both sides. While the acting president of the Miners' Federation could congratulate the miners on their 'splendid fight', Menzies happily observed how good it was that 'wise counsels have at last prevailed'.[54]

Meantime Menzies continued his work in the courts. At one extreme he would take on without remuneration cases like that of a girl from the Melbourne City Mission's Maternity Home to win maintenance for her child—a fight which he took successfully to the Supreme Court, at the cost (as the Mission's superintendent put it in a letter of appreciation) of 'much time and trouble on your part'.[55] On the other hand there were the lucrative cases like that celebrated by Colin Fraser, of Collins House, who in June 1934 wrote to thank Menzies for the way 'you handled our case'. 'The difference between yourself and Bradman', he added, 'is that you

---

[53] *Argus*, 6 April 1934. The principal reason for the railway loss was that the wheat harvest was not being cleared to the seaboard as it normally was, presumably as growers waited in the hope that prices would rise.
[54] Ibid., 11, 12, 13, 20, 25 July 1934; *Age*, 20 July 1934.
[55] Bruce to Menzies, 12 May 1934, NLA, MS. 4936/1/1/1.

are never "off your bat" so that we always take your heavy scoring for granted'.[56] More run-of-the-mill cases still earned heartfelt gratitude, as suggested by a letter the Registrar of the Dental Board of Victoria, E. Joske, wrote in April 1934 to Menzies to record appreciation of 'your great and never to be forgotten services'.[57]

Notwithstanding all the energy and commitment to Victoria which Menzies displayed before and during his acting premiership, the feeling was distinctly abroad by mid-1933 that he was destined for something greater. Among private admirers there was a sense of quality which G. H. Knox, the distinguished soldier and UAP member for Upper Yarra, expressed well when writing at the end of 1933 to give Menzies his Christmas greetings. He spoke warmly of 'your fine work in our House ... your straightforwardness and your even temper in very trying circumstances' and asked what was ahead: could it be the Chief Justiceship?[58] S. M. Bruce, in Australia during the early part of 1934, had talks with Menzies and, when embarking to return to England, at the beginning of May, wrote to say 'how greatly my journeyings to & fro have convinced me that there is a great part for you with your personality & ability to play in Australia'.[59] The following month a journalist, G. E. Terry, who, though he disagreed politically with Menzies, had received in reply to an expression of that disagreement an 'exceedingly kind letter' from him, wrote that 'of the many who are watching your own upward starry course, few, if any, do so with more joyful hope than does ... Yours'.[60] By the time Terry wrote this, occasional newspaper speculation that Menzies' 'upward starry course' was destined to take him out of State into Commonwealth politics was almost a year old.

In July 1933 the *Argus* had observed that changes brewing in the federal Cabinet made it seem likely that an attempt would soon be made to entice Menzies to Canberra. There had indeed been 'a desire that Mr. Menzies should enter Federal politics for nearly four years': specifically, a strong attempt had once been made to persuade him to stand for the federal seat of Ballarat. Though at the time Menzies had been adamant that he would not leave State parliament, 'recently he has been less communicative regarding his future'.[61] The particular point of this observation was that, although no official announcement had yet been made, those

[56] Fraser to Menzies, 10 June 1934, ibid
[57] Joske to Menzies, 18 April 1934, ibid.
[58] G. H. Knox to Menzies, 28 December 1933, ibid.
[59] S. M. Bruce to Menzies, 1 May 1934, NLA, MS. 4936/1/5/38.
[60] G. E. Terry to Menzies, 22 June 1934, NLA, MS. 4936/1/31/252.
[61] *Argus*, 13 July 1933.

in the know expected that Lyons would soon be losing three of his most experienced ministers and would thus be in urgent need of new blood in his Cabinet. Bruce, as honorary minister, had since September 1932 been the Government's 'resident minister' in London but, as Lyons himself put it, this arrangement could not be continued indefinitely since 'it would involve a departure from the collective responsibility of Ministers'.[62] Bruce was consequently tipped to become the first Australian High Commissioner, and indeed did so in October 1933. The Assistant Treasurer, Sir Walter Massy-Greene, a captain of industry, was for business reasons expected to leave the Cabinet and in fact resigned in the same month as Bruce.[63] And it was by this time an open secret that the Attorney-General, Latham, would almost certainly give up federal politics in order to take the Chief Justiceship of the High Court when Sir Frank Gavan Duffy took his impending retirement. If this came to pass it would be a neat solution for Lyons if Menzies stood for Latham's blue-ribbon UAP seat of Kooyong, to become, on election to the House of Representatives, the Commonwealth Attorney-General. What remains obscure is whether this had been contemplated long before, when in 1931 Latham gave way to Lyons as leader of the federal Opposition.

In May 1934 the Lyons Government decided to dissolve the existing Commonwealth parliament in the following August and to schedule the election of its successor for September. When reporting the decision to dissolve, the *Argus* added that it was 'nearly certain' that Menzies would contest a federal seat in the September election: 'Mr Menzies has consented to make the change as soon as circumstances permit'.[64] 'Circumstances' became propitious in less than two months, when on 5 July Latham announced a decision, 'for purely private reasons', not to seek reelection to the federal parliament in the coming contest. Lyons expressed regret, paid Latham an eloquent tribute, and persuaded him to stay on as Attorney-General until the election.[65] So Kooyong and the attorney-generalship, as political reporters had expected, both became available. Menzies, however, did not jump at once, despite immediate approaches from all non-Labor political organizations in the constituency. Before consenting to stand, he intimated to the press that he would need to be satisfied about major questions of federal policy then under discussion between the UAP and the Country Party for an electoral pact. He had also

[62] Ibid.
[63] Sawer, *AFPL* 2, 44.
[64] *Argus*, 18 May 1934.
[65] Ibid., 6 July 1934.

to consider the implications for his family and for his legal practice of spending long periods in, or even moving to, Canberra.[66] Hesitation, and behind the scenes discussion, went on for almost three weeks before, on the evening of 23 July, Menzies formally accepted an invitation to stand for Kooyong. The final decision had clearly been made some days before. The invitation itself was issued by a convention representing the Kooyong branches (twenty-four in all) of the United Australia Organisation, the AWNL and the Young Nationalists, meeting in the Glenferrie Masonic Hall. It was embodied in a motion that was formally presented to Menzies after he and his wife had been summoned from their home by telephone to the meeting. In accepting, Menzies observed that 'Canberra is not attractive, either personally or professionally, for obvious reasons, but I feel that the Commonwealth Parliament must still attract the services of men who are interested in public affairs if the Federal system is to continue effectively'.[67]

The sincerity of this almost rueful remark is not to be doubted: it accorded with every protestation Menzies had made in the previous five years about the responsibility of men of probity and talent to make their services available to the public. It would have been false modesty of the most ludicrous kind to pretend to doubts about the qualities and experience he would bring to federal politics. It would also have been politically unwise as well as simply indelicate to intimate too manifestly the other—and quite legitimate—urge that was taking him to Canberra: ambition. In any circumstances, given the experience of his remarkable rise in State politics, Menzies could expect to make his mark speedily in the federal sphere. But there was one special circumstance about his decision which suggests that ambition must have tipped the balance. It is most baldly put in words which Lyons would use a little later when reminding a UAP party functionary that 'we induced Menzies to come in in the expectation that he would succeed me'.[68]

The Victorian parliament was only four weeks into its 1934 session when Menzies, having opted for Canberra, resigned his portfolios and then the Nunawading seat. He had handed the Premiership back to Argyle at the beginning of the session, and in these final weeks played an inconspicuous role in the Ministry's affairs. His last two preoccupations were the settlement of the Wonthaggi dispute and the handling of a disturbing outbreak

[66] Ibid.
[67] Ibid., 24 July 1934.
[68] Lyons to his wife, n.d., NLA, MS. 4552, box 28. I am indebted to Dr Di Langmore for drawing my attention to this letter.

of disease among cattle on a Board of Works sewerage farm. The 'war' with the Country Party, so positively threatened in the summer of 1933–34, failed to explode, thanks primarily to Argyle's instinct for compromise and Menzies' understanding of the futility of fighting further on a stage he was about to abandon. Argyle reconstructed the Cabinet as soon as Menzies announced he would be leaving, giving the railways portfolio to the other leading Young Nationalist, Kent Hughes. The *Argus* opined that 'it would be idle to suggest that the present State Ministry is as strong as it was before reconstruction. The times require moral as well as intellectual fibre in members of the Cabinet, and Mr. Menzies possesses both'.[69] 'Ariel', in the paper's 'Above the Speaker' column, thought there were nevertheless brief compensations, 'because for two days an intelligent-looking man was added to the number already on the back Ministerial bench. In those few days of calm Mr Menzies gave a passable imitation of a man watching the world go by ... there being still other fields to conquer, he has not yet wept'.[70]

Meantime, the conventional compliments were exchanged. Menzies, Argyle told the Kooyong nomination meeting,

> has been a tower of strength in the Cabinet, not only because of his legal knowledge but also because of his general administrative ability. I appreciate the fact that in going from Victorian politics to the Federal sphere he is doing so at considerable personal sacrifice, and on the grounds of public duty, and offering his services where they are most required.[71]

As instances of Menzies' 'outstanding ability' Argyle cited his handling of the Wonthaggi dispute and of the recent beef disease problem at the Board of Works farm. Was it a pointed omission to highlight such relatively minor matters and say nothing about the contributions which Menzies would have considered his greatest in Victorian politics: his pioneer work in the creation of the Young Nationalists movement and the sharpening up of conservative ideology; his steady insistence, in the face of bitter—especially country—opposition that Victoria honour her obligations under the Premiers' Plan; his efforts, as Minister for Railways, to find ways of rationalizing Victoria's transport muddle? It is difficult to resist the conclusion that Argyle was not entirely sorry to see Menzies go. The latter's outspoken criticisms of

---
[69] *Argus*, 26 July 1934.
[70] Ibid., 28 July 1934.
[71] Ibid., 24 July 1934.

contemporary political groups, when considered along with the key position he had won for himself in the party organization, must have been uncomfortable for Argyle, as parliamentary leader, to live with. It was in fact easy to sense in Menzies a prickly ambition not attuned to the cosy understandings of traditional Victorian politics. He had also become the greatest obstacle to the achievement of a workable alliance with the Country Party, and that was the basic requirement to keep an Argyle Government in office.

When Menzies resigned his seat he left a letter for the Speaker to read to the House. Despite the sharp passages at arms he had had with some Country Party and Labor members, there was a ring of sincerity in much of what he wrote:

> Though I am proposing to contest a seat in the Federal Parliament and to enter a new political arena, I will always value what I have learned to appreciate in the Victorian Parliament—namely that vigorous political differences and conflict are not inconsistent with mutual respect and warm personal friendships.[72]

The decision to move to federal politics brought the messages of congratulation to be conventionally expected but two of them had a peculiar extravagance and carried resonances important to our picture of the man as he left for Canberra. The first was from father James, written on the day after Robert accepted the Kooyong nomination:

> We cannot allow so eventful a chapter in your already eventful career to be opened without putting on record the parental pride which has a place in both our hearts for our own Rob.
> Mother and I trust that in the good providence of our Heavenly Father you may be preserved to the continued accomplishment of still wider service (than the scope of the State of Victoria afforded) in this your response to the call of the Commonwealth. We know that 'sound views' the product of diligent and trained investigation will always make a stronger appeal to you than the glamour of a cheap popularity.[73]

The second was written by Menzies' friend Professor Kenneth Bailey, of the University Law School, to congratulate him when in September he had actually been elected for Kooyong. In a rather more sophisticated fashion, Bailey pondered on Menzies' course so far, and came to the conclusion that 'it really has been a trium-

---

[72]*VPD*, 194: 182.
[73]James Menzies to R. G. Menzies, 25 July 1934, NLA, MS. 4936/17/427/17.

phant political career. I should think that one would probably have to go back to Palmerston or Peel or Pitt for parallels'. As to Menzies' impending membership of the federal parliament,

> It is a considerable comfort to folks like me to know that your courage and persuasiveness and robust liberalism will be there. My ideas on social adjustment you will probably think unsound. But I think at heart you probably agree with me in fearing the Fascist and the Militarist a good deal more than the Communist.[74]

It was, at least for the 1930s, a prescient remark.

---

[74] Bailey to Menzies, 28 September 1934, NLA, MS. 4936/1/1/1.

6

Federal Attorney-General 1934

IN THE federal election of August–September 1934 Menzies played a key role for the UAP, both as campaigner and organizer. His itinerary was as strenuous as that of Lyons himself: in three weeks he toured five States and addressed more than fifty meetings.[1] Since he was president of the Victorian UAP, he was also much involved in the organizational side of the campaign in his home State.

The speaking tour was an important 'blooding' experience, an initiation into the feel, in unfamiliar places, of federal politics. Menzies had already spoken in Sydney and had campaigned against Labor in a Tasmanian State election. But to go to Ipswich in Queensland (and on a special aeroplane), or to talk to country folk in New England, were new experiences. He enjoyed, and performed well in, such novel settings: his striking presence and oratorical skills were superior to the ordinary expectations of those who heard him. In Adelaide, if the Melbourne *Argus* is to be believed, his visit 'ended election apathy': his was the first 'overflowing meeting of the campaign in South Australia', and his audience came alive as he castigated Labor and stirred interjectors.[2] By contrast he had a strangely silent reception at the New South Wales mining centre of Wollongong—no questions and no interjections—which led him to declare, rather naively, that his reply to those who predicted a swing to Labor must be 'the words of the American, "Oh yeah?"'[3]

At the outset of the campaign Menzies predicted that nationalization of banking would be the main election issue but, as Scullin's policy speech soon made clear, Labor stopped short of that. Instead, it promised a full inquiry into the banking and

[1] *Argus*, 11, 17 August 1934.
[2] Ibid., 24, 25 August 1934.
[3] Ibid., 5 September 1934.

monetary systems and undertook to establish a new means of regulation through a central bank with a single governor who would execute general policy decided by parliament. This was interventionism unacceptable to the UAP. As Menzies put it: 'in my simple philosophy I believe that two things have worked to the good of Australia in recent years ... the non-political control of the Commonwealth Bank and the non-political control of the Australian currency'.[4] To inveigh against 'political tinkering with the banking system' quickly became the central theme of almost all his speeches—a theme which lent itself to many colourful variations. Thus, while the UAP prescribed for the banking system 'sound doses of confidence', Labor offered 'pink financial medicine purveyed from a large, showy bottle'; the electors had to guard against the danger of 'putting the banks of the Commonwealth into the hands of people not fit to run a banana stall'.[5]

For the rest, Menzies followed Lyons in promising increased federal aid to the unemployed and to primary producers, though such relief was not to be 'indiscriminate'. What that meant for the unemployed he left unexplained; in the farmers' case 'the principle to be applied is simple—that adequate protection should be afforded to efficient farmers on suitable farming lands', though what that meant in practice seemed to be anyone's guess. He also spoke of the need for constitutional reform to redistribute taxing powers and reiterated his faith in an 'intelligent protective policy' to help restore employment.[6] But in most matters the essence of the UAP's position was simply continuance of the Ministry's existing course: at one meeting Menzies denounced what he called 'the parrot-like cry of "Give us your policy"': if asked for his policy for the next three years he would simply say "Honest Government" '.[7] Above all, that meant 'sound' financial policy. A poignant interjection at one of Menzies' Adelaide meetings brought out the basic argument with cold clarity. The recovery of Australian credit since the fall of the Scullin Government, said Menzies,

> has been so profound that we have been able to convert £110,000,000 of our overseas debt.
>
> *A Voice:* But what about giving us some food, clothes, and shelter?
>
> *Menzies:* That is being provided by the increasing confidence which the Federal Ministry is creating ... We offer you increasing employment and prosperity. We offer to release credit by the only way it can

[4] Ibid., 16 May 1934.
[5] Ibid., 22, 24 August 1934.
[6] Hawthorn, ibid., 16 August 1934.
[7] Wollongong, ibid., 5 September 1934.

really be released—by building up confidence. If you want to use the currency as a mere instrument of bribery then by all means vote for Labour.[8]

For people still short of food, clothes and shelter this was scarcely an argument to bring much immediate comfort.

As expected, Menzies took Kooyong effortlessly, and the election as a whole resulted in another victory for the non-Labor parties. But Labor made sufficient gains to deny the UAP the majority which would allow it to govern in its own right. After initial bickering and one false start Lyons and Page negotiated a coalition. The new Ministry was announced on 12 October 1934. As prearranged, Menzies was Attorney-General (a month before his appointment, Latham wrote him a very detailed memorandum explaining the organization and work of the Attorney-General's Department, briefing him, in effect, for the work ahead).[9] He also became Minister for Industry. Lyons remained Prime Minister and Treasurer; Page was Minister for Commerce and unofficial Deputy Prime Minister. The UAP had seven full ministers and the Country Party two. The Country Party's deputy leader, Thomas Paterson, a farmer and founder of the Victorian Country Party, took the Interior Ministry.[10] The UAP ministers included two New South Wales veterans, Archdale Parkhill and W. M. Hughes, whom Menzies was now encountering at close quarters for the first time. At fifty-six, Parkhill had in the previous parliament been the most senior UAP member after Lyons and, while a staunch admirer of Lyons, saw himself as the natural successor to the leadership, though despite his urbanity and experience, he was not particularly popular within his party. A dandy who affected extravagant dress and manners, he was nevertheless a vigorous debater who had been important in the building up of Nationalist morale in the last days of the Scullin Ministry. In the new Cabinet he took over Defence from the much respected Senator George Pearce, whose intermittent experience of that portfolio dated back to 1908 and included the whole of the First World War.[11] Hughes, at seventy-two, was brought in from outer darkness to become Minister for Health and Repatriation, his first ministerial post since in 1923 the Country Party under Page forced him out of the Prime Ministership in favour of Bruce. Hughes had had his revenge by helping to vote the Bruce–Page Government out of office in 1929:

[8] Ibid., 24 August 1934.
[9] NLA, MS 1009/53/96–9.
[10] *ADB*, 11: 158–9.
[11] Ibid., 142–3 (Parkhill); 177–82 (Pearce).

to be Page's fellow minister now was a further irony which must have amused him. Though past his prime Hughes was still a figure to be reckoned with politically, and for fellow ministers never a dull colleague personally. His mercurial temper and satirical and abrasive turn of phrase could at times be curiously softened by acts of kindness and charming behaviour.[12] Menzies appears quickly to have developed towards him an amused tolerance which could shade off at times into a kind of affection. It could only have helped the relationship that Menzies brought from Victorian politics so strong a dislike for Country Party aims and tactics. That dislike would hardly be assuaged by closer association with Page. Amid universal sympathy, Page had withdrawn from active politics for almost all of 1933 after his eldest son, the manager of a family station, had been killed by lightning. But by 1934, just as Menzies came to federal politics, Page was fully engaged again, his tough bargaining with Lyons over the coalition demonstrating that he had lost none of his political shrewdness or his single-minded commitment to the rural interest above all others. Moreover, Page's special devotion to the needs of his own constituents in northern New South Wales and his attempts to promote the idea of a separate State in the New England area symbolized the kind of parochialism for which Menzies always felt contempt. And personally, there was little about Page, who personified the limitations of a country surgeon and businessman, to impress the urbane Melbourne barrister. He was a poor speaker, whose 'torrent of high-pitched words' outran ideas and easily fell into garrulousness. His public as well as private talk was punctuated with the refrain 'You see, You see' and he had a giggle which amused some and irritated others.[13] For an often cutting mimic like Menzies it must have been difficult at times to refrain from entertaining friends by 'doing a Page'.

He knew Victorian ministers better. T. W. ('Tommy') White, who had received Trade and Customs in the previous Lyons Ministry and now stayed on in that capacity, had won the Balaclava seat in 1929 under the aegis of the Young Nationalists: Menzies had been one of those who campaigned for him. The manager of a small family business and an experienced officer in the pre-war militia, White was a war hero, a pilot who had spent time as a prisoner of the Turks and later wrote of his adventures in a book

[12] On Hughes see L. F. Fitzhardinge's two-volume biography (Sydney 1964, 1979) and his excellent summary in *ADB*, 9: 393–400.
[13] *ADB*, 11: 122. Note also that Dame Pattie commented on the giggle etc. at interview, which makes it clear that it was a subject of amusement and perhaps—considering the tone in which she referred to it—distaste among the Menzies.

he called *Guests of the Unspeakable*. His diaries in the 1930s reveal private prejudice against Menzies for his lack of war experience, a prejudice in which there was also evident some jealousy of Menzies' superior gifts.[14] There is no way of telling how far Menzies himself was aware of these feelings at the time of the formation of the Ministry. But more congenial and important to him were the two most impressive UAP junior ministers, Henry Gullett and Richard Gardiner Casey.

At fifty-six Gullett held a 'junior' portfolio only because ill health had forced him in 1933 to resign as Minister for Trade and Customs. He had held this important portfolio twice, most recently with Bruce, representing Australia at the Imperial Economic Conference of 1932 at Ottawa. There, through determination and a fiery temper, Gullett had been chiefly responsible for winning unexpectedly favourable terms for Australia in the trade agreements. He had been war correspondent and historian, and had served on Hughes's staff at the Peace Conference. After returning to journalism he was elected as a Nationalist for the Henty seat in the House of Representatives, and held it for the rest of his life. As an experienced and senior Nationalist from Victoria he became a staunch friend and, later, supporter of Menzies.

Casey, then forty-four, had begun his political career in the previous parliament, having won the Victorian seat of Corio in 1931. Menzies assisted in that campaign and subsequently the two men appear to have seen a good deal of each other and begun what was to be a chequered friendship.[15] Thanks to the self-made wealth of his businessman father, Casey had grown up in affluent South Yarra, receiving his education at Melbourne Grammar and Cambridge University. He served with some distinction, chiefly as a junior staff officer, at Gallipoli and in France. On his return to Australia he seemed destined for a business career but in 1924 applied for and won a newly established position in London: political liaison officer between the British and Australian governments. In this position, held with one short break until 1931, Casey was directly answerable to the Prime Minister, Bruce, who began by being something of a patron but soon became a genuine friend. It was an extraordinary opportunity for a young man to learn about the inner workings of government. He was given a room in 2 Whitehall Gardens, the offices of Sir Maurice Hankey, the powerful Secretary to the British Cabinet and to the Committee of Imperial Defence. Hankey told Bruce that he had been instructed

---

[14] I have consulted White's diaries through the courtesy of his daughter, Mrs Judith Harley.
[15] W. J. Hudson, *Casey*, 91.

by the Prime Minister, Baldwin, 'to show him [Casey] everything which I should show you if you were in England. In fact I show him a good deal more, because he is a whole-timer on this job and I do not mind overburdening him'.[16] Casey's efficiency, charm and polish and, above all, his almost boyish enthusiasm—'his evident capacity', as it has been happily called, 'to be made agog'[17]— quickly made him *persona grata* with most of the British ministers and officials with whom he had dealings: Hankey, in particular, warmed to him as 'an ideal man'. When eventually Casey left the job it was chiefly because his mentor, Bruce, was gone, and under Scullin the work lost its savour. Bruce was the person most responsible for Casey's decision to enter politics: he fondly saw his young protégé as a potential prime minister. Menzies' arrival on the scene, and his immediate elevation to senior Cabinet rank, however, rather complicated that picture. By 1934 Casey might have a firm foothold in that London world of Imperial affairs and power of which Menzies yet knew nothing at first hand. But the political nous which Menzies had so speedily acquired in the years of Casey's absence from Australia would more than make up for that.

One omission from the 1934 Cabinet disappointed Menzies: Charles Hawker. A South Australian pastoralist who by sheer willpower overcame terrible war injuries to force himself to lead an active life, Hawker had entered the House of Representatives in 1929. President then of a new Liberal Federation of South Australia, he made many overtures to the South Australian Country Party for amalgamation and succeeded in 1932 in negotiating the formation of a Liberal Country League. This achievement at once won Menzies' admiration: here was the kind of fusion of anti-Labor forces which seemed so unattainable in his own State but which might have put paid to the Country Party greed and parochialism which had always so disgusted him. He was even more impressed when at its first election the new League, with Hawker as its campaign director, had resounding success in 1934. After the election Hawker wired his congratulations on Menzies' Kooyong win and Menzies wrote:

> I will feel extremely sorry if you are not in the Cabinet. Though I am sure we would from time to time disagree most heartily, I have always felt that you and I could work effectively together in the political world.[18]

---

[16] P. G. Edwards, *Prime Ministers and Diplomats*, 73.
[17] Quoted, ibid., 71, from W. J. Hudson and Jane North (eds), *My Dear P.M.: R. G. Casey's Letters to S. M. Bruce 1924–1929* (Canberra 1980).
[18] Menzies to Hawker, 5 October 1934, NLA, MS. 4847/7/5.

It was the message of one strong and principled politician to another, and in response Hawker assured Menzies that 'I and my friends in South Australia are sincerely anxious that there should be stable political conditions—we are glad to join up or to stand aside according to whichever will best help general harmony'. But it was not to be: the tortuous negotiations at federal level between the UAP and the Country Party displayed what Hawker called 'mutual bickering over non-essentials' which the South Australians were not prepared to countenance.[19] When the coalition was finally arranged, Hawker was left out of the Ministry, almost certainly in penance for a characteristic if seemingly quixotic action he had taken when a minister in the first Lyons Government. At the 1931 election he had promised his constituents to vote for the maximum reduction of parliamentary salaries as a Depression measure. When in its Financial Emergency Bill (to implement the Premiers' Plan) the Government included a reasonable reduction, a member of the Opposition moved an amendment to enlarge it, and Hawker felt honour bound to cross the floor, vote for the amendment, and thus expel himself from the Ministry. Nevertheless, there were some in the party who thought of him as of future leadership material and few, however much they might disagree with his political ideas, who questioned his integrity. His friend the historian Keith Hancock spoke for many when he described Hawker as representing 'the best that an Australian can do or be'.[20]

The Duke of Gloucester was not the only important Englishman drawn to Australia at the time of Melbourne's centenary celebrations. Another who arrived just after the federal election was Casey's old London mentor, Maurice Hankey. Hankey claimed to be merely on holiday with his wife, to observe a particularly interesting set of festivities in a country which he had never before visited. But in fact he was in Australia principally in his capacity as Secretary to the Committee of Imperial Defence, for secret talks on Australia's defences. The festivities provided a cover, but they and Australian work habits were also an impediment to his confidential task. Hankey was impressed with the 'wonderful reception' he received behind the scenes: 'Cabinet Ministers, Chiefs of Staff, and officials, one and all have treated me with exactly the same degree of confidence as their opposite numbers in London ... show towards me', he wrote to Ramsay MacDonald.[21] But his work was slowed by his ministerial hosts' preoccupation with

[19] Hawker to Menzies, 9 October 1934, ibid.
[20] *ADB*, 9: 231–2. On Hawker's resignation, Sawer, *AFPL* 2, 43–4.
[21] Hankey to Ramsay MacDonald, 15 November 1934, Public Record Office, Kew (PRO), PREM 1, 174.

Cabinet formation, by the centenary celebrations and by the relaxed attitude of Australian public servants to their office work ('they knock off work religiously at 5 p.m.', he told Baldwin, and don't go to [the] office on Saturdays! I could have done a lot more but for the incessant functions, parties, public holidays, etc.').[22] He found ministers 'living a harassed life in the attempt to attend both the ceremonies and the meetings of the Cabinet'. In this connection Hankey found Lyons 'a frightfully decent old boy':

> His obvious sincerity and extreme frankness create a most agreeable impression. When I congratulated him on the delightful speech he had made the evening before at the parliamentary dinner to the Duke of Gloucester and expressed admiration at his ability to produce it at a time of great pressure of work, he at once told me that most of it had been written by Mrs Lyons—a wonderful woman, a good mother of twelve, and no mean politician.[23]

Hankey thought Lyons seemed somewhat depressed and 'doubtful of his own future', an impression confirmed by one of the Prime Minister's colleagues (unfortunately we are not told which) who said to Hankey: 'I believe your friend Casey will be P. M. before long'. In the late Cabinet, Hankey learned, 'my old friend J. G. Latham seems to have been the strong hand':

> He ruled Lyons with a rod of iron. Rather a hard man and above all a realist he was a constant check on Lyons' sentimentalism. But Latham, who is poor but extravagant, has retired to the Bar to make some money and no-one has yet quite taken his place. For this role Mr. Menzies, the leading figure at the Bar apart from Latham, is generally cast. He enters Commonwealth politics for the first time as Attorney-General, a post with a far more important status in Australia than in England. Menzies . . . is regarded in inner circles as the coming man . . . He is, according to British standards, rather a rough diamond; very contemptuous of soft and soppy policies, but a good fellow at bottom and quite fearless of responsibility. He has literally changed places with Latham, the former becoming Attorney-General and the latter taking his place at the bar.

Hankey noted that the 'inner ring' of Cabinet consisted of Lyons, Page, Menzies, Gullett and Casey, together with 'the "elder Statesman"' Sir George Pearce, 'tremendously trusted and universally liked'. Unfortunately Pearce seemed to be in bad health,

---

[22]Hankey to Baldwin, 17 November 1934, Churchill Archives Centre, Cambridge, HNKY 4/26.
[23]Hankey to Harding, 28 November 1934, PRO, CAB 63/70, PFF/9573, 121. Lyons as 'frightfully decent old boy', Hankey to Baldwin, ibid.

though a tee-totaller '(probably too much tea, like many Australians)' and that was why he had given up the Defence portfolio, 'which most people consider a disaster'. This inner ring notwithstanding, Cabinet procedure 'is evidently very loose and rambling'.

> There is a nominal agenda paper, but they don't stick to it and wander all over the place... Casey gets exasperated at the waste of time. Menzies, entering the Commonwealth Cabinet for the first time, was appalled and contrasted the procedure unfavourably with that of the Victorian Cabinet. He asked a lot of details as to how we conduct cabinet business, as did other ministers.[24]

Menzies made his first speech in the Commonwealth parliament on 2 November 1934, in the address-in-reply debate. It was at once apparent that some members thought him ineligible for the courtesy of silence normally extended to 'maiden' speakers. Perhaps as a veteran of the Victorian legislature he was thought to have exhausted his right to such immunity. The main argument of his speech was that an inquiry was urgently needed into the basic economic and social problems of the day—the extent and causes of unemployment, how to train more skilled artisans, problems associated with the employment of women in industry—to gather data and (though this was implied rather than stated) even to facilitate bipartisan agreement on at least some remedial policies. The Langite Jack Beasley interjected that the Lyons Ministry had taken a long time to get round to acting on these issues and Frank Brennan, Melbourne solicitor and erstwhile Attorney-General in the Scullin Government, sneered that the Government 'must have been waiting for the advent of the right hon. gentleman [Menzies]'.[25] Menzies ended his speech with an observation which at least earned him some press plaudits:

> May I conclude by saying something which hon. members may choose to regard as a criticism, but which I choose to regard as a perfectly frank admission. I make it as one who, it is true, is a completely untried member of this House, but has some experience of both office and opposition in another parliament. When we are not in office, we all too frequently regard the task of thinking as unnecessary and, indeed, as irrelevant; and when we are in office we are so busy that we have little time for thinking. The result is that thinking about large problems tends to be discounted, and any government which says boldly in its policy speech or a Governor General's speech, 'we propose to think' is at once accused

[24] Hankey to Harding, ibid.
[25] *CPD*, 145: 166.

of having idled for years past . . . Whether we are in opposition or in office, the time has come when we must pool all our mental resources and engage in some concerted thought about these most elementary and fundamental features of the greatest problems which confront us.[26]

Though the Opposition was not greatly moved by this speech, the *Argus* was: calling it 'An Essay in Statesmanship', the paper remarked on how it gave 'dignity and point' to the debate on unemployment.[27] In the House Brennan, by contrast, reiterated the Labor view that money should be made the servant and not the master of the people. If the Lyons Government had recognized this three years ago, he said, 'many men could be at work today, many desolate homes could have been brightened'. It was 'effrontery' for the Government 'to tell the people that in 1935 it proposes to make a comprehensive survey of the root causes of unemployment, which are obvious'. As for Menzies, his advent in federal parliament resulted from being 'not altogether wanted' by 'poor Sir Stanley Argyle', who saw him as the chief obstacle to rapprochement with the Country Party and had muttered the words of a famous English king: 'of the cowards that eat my bread, is there none that will rid me of this turbulent priest?'[28]

The session which thus opened lasted only a few weeks: parliament adjourned for the Christmas break on 14 December. When it reconvened in March 1935 Menzies was not in his place. With Lyons and several other ministers, he was on his way to England. But in that brief pre-Christmas period a group of Opposition members singled Menzies out for especial vituperation. They made two particularly virulent attacks on him, the first on a trumped up matter but the second on an issue that stirred up considerable public controversy.

The minor matter was the fact that, when Victorian Attorney-General, Menzies had appeared before a Commonwealth Royal Commission into the petrol industry on behalf of the Shell Oil Company. The charge was brought forward by W. R. Maloney, the widely respected veteran Labor member for Melbourne,[29] who moved formal assertion of the principle that

> The position of an Attorney-General, whether of State or Commonwealth, being a sacred one, no Attorney-General should under any circumstances accept any . . . reward . . . to represent individuals, combines or corporations against his country or the interests of its people.

[26] Ibid., 167.
[27] *Argus*, 7 November 1934.
[28] *CPD*, 145: 168, 172.
[29] *ADB*, 10: 389–90.

A phalanx of Labor members—Makin, Beasley, Brennan and Blackburn—supported Maloney, but Menzies in a formidable speech demolished their arguments, quoting precedents to show that, while in Royal Commissions appointed by the Commonwealth Government no Commonwealth Attorney-General would consider himself at liberty to appear, State Attorneys-General were professionally quite properly at liberty to do so. In arguing thus he was supported especially stoutly by Hughes, and in a vote on party lines his critics were defeated. Brennan again seized the opportunity for a personal attack on Menzies. 'It is sometimes necessary', he said,

> in this, as in other unions, to stand shoulder to shoulder with one's colleagues to protect their rights and submit the viewpoint of the profession or calling concerned. As I have said on other occasions the Attorney-General and I are not members of the same union. I am a member of the union which habitually does the work: the hon. gentleman is a member of the union which habitually draws the fees [i.e., solicitors *v.* barristers].

Menzies: That has not been the fashion in my time.[30]

The more serious matter was the so-called Kisch case, whose eruption produced, especially among the nation's small 'l' liberal intellectual circles, a scandalized outcry against what many saw as a denial by the Lyons Government of the right of free speech. Menzies was not involved in the early stages of this contretemps, but as Attorney-General he inherited it and became the affirmer and to some extent the scapegoat of Government policy. That does not of course mean that he did not agree with it. What critics saw as persecution of Kisch Menzies saw as necessary action to defend the state against subversion.

Egon Kisch, journalist, author and a leading member of the European anti-war movement founded by Henri Barbusse, was invited as guest and chief speaker to an All-Australian Congress against War and Fascism scheduled for August 1934, to coincide with Victoria's centenary celebrations. The promoters of this conference, the Australian Movement Against War and Fascism, have been described by one historian as 'a tiny and little-known group of communists, radicals and anti-conscriptionists from Great War days'.[31] But contemporary conservatives, particularly in

---
[30] *CPD*, 145: 711.
[31] A. T. Yarwood, in the Foreword to the Macmillan edition of Kisch's *Australian Landfall* (S. Melbourne 1969), viii.

The temporarily crippled Egon Kisch, with his fellow fugitive, Gerald Griffin (far right), talks to some of his admirers: from left, Max Meldrum, Vance Palmer and Katharine Susannah Prichard.

Melbourne, saw the Australian organization as more sinister and widespread than this. The *Argus*, for example, published a long unsigned article in July 1934 under the heading 'Origin of the Anti-War Movement, Communism's Soft Voice', claiming that the movement was well established, with headquarters in Sydney and fifty-two branches in New South Wales alone. The organization, it claimed, had spread to Queensland and South Australia, and in Victoria was using the centenary celebrations to target returned soldiers, sailors, nurses and youth generally. The author asserted that the three prongs of 'the trident of Communistic penetration in Australia today' were the Friends of the Soviet Union, the Minority Movement (whose aim was to engineer the election of Communists to official positions in unions) and the Anti-war Movement. From this claim it was an easy step to a smear by association: to the assertion that the anti-war movement favoured for the achievement of its aims the weapons recently endorsed at a Brisbane congress of the Communist Party. These included a general strike of munitions workers, a hold-up of shipping and a 'gigantic' strike of all miners.[32] In the atmosphere of the time such allegations were calculated to make the blood of many of the good citizens of Melbourne run cold.

The organizers of the Melbourne anti-war Congress checked ahead with the Immigration Department to be sure that Kisch would not be debarred from entry into Australia on account of his German nationality and were assured that entry would be permitted as long as his expenses in Australia were guaranteed locally.[33] But early in October 1934, long before Kisch's arrival in Australia, H. E. Jones, the Director of the Investigation Branch of the Attorney-General's Department, informed the Department of the Interior that the intending visitor was a member of the international Communist anti-war movement and recommended that his baggage be searched at Fremantle for Communist literature. If any were found he should not be permitted to land.[34] By 16 October Jones had secured further information about Kisch: his physical description, and his connections. 'He is an important Communist member of the International Society of Proletarian Authors, a Communist organization founded in Moscow ... also an international speaker for the Communist anti-war and anti-fascist cause ... His Majesty's Government in the United Kingdom has declared him a prohibited immigrant and he is not allowed to land there'. This information, wrote Jones, 'strengthens my recommendation that he should be refused entry into Australia'. At this point, his immediate post-election negotiations with Page having broken down, Lyons had just formed a minority UAP Government. One of the first acts of the new—and temporary—Minister for the Interior, Eric Harrison, was to sign, on Jones's advice, a declaration of Kisch as an undesirable immigrant. It was still almost a month to Kisch's arrival and Harrison's decision received no publicity.[35]

The examination of Kisch's baggage duly took place on 6 November, when he reached Fremantle on the liner *Strathaird*. No incriminating literature turned up, but that did not matter now. Kisch had been declared a prohibited immigrant on other grounds.

[32] *Argus*, 31 July 1934.
[33] Statement by Blackburn, *CPD*, 145: 262.
[34] The original initiative seems to have come from Victoria: Roland S. Browne, Inspector, Attorney-General's Department, Investigation Branch, Melbourne, to The Director, Canberra. Secret. Quotes various rumours about Kisch and paragraph from the *Herald* of 5 October 1934 which says Kisch 'a German novelist, whose writing satirising the Hitler regime caused him to be sent to Nazi concentration camps for political prisoners'. Will be visitor to Centenary celebrations here, 'according to a provate [sic] cablegram received in Melbourne today from Henri Barbusse the French novelist and editor of the French journal "Monde" '. Advises thorough search of his baggage at first Australian port of call. AA, A6119/1, item 24.
[35] Ibid.

Lyons and Page having settled their differences and formed their Coalition Ministry it was the new, Country Party, Minister for the Interior, Thomas Paterson, who formally imposed the ban on Kisch. The precise evidence on which this (originally Harrison's) decision rested was never officially made public and when forced to justify its action the Government asserted—correctly, but without giving its source—that, though once admitted to the United Kingdom for a speaking tour, Kisch had now been declared by the British Government a prohibited immigrant. Kisch was not permitted to land in Fremantle and was ordered to remain on the ship, virtually as the captain's prisoner, until it cleared Australian ports and took him away from the country. The ban was effected under section 3(gh) of the Immigration Act, which defined a prohibited immigrant as

> Any person declared by the Minister to be in his opinion, from information received from the Government of the United Kingdom or from any foreign government, through official or diplomatic channels, undesirable as an inhabitant of, or visitor to, the Commonwealth.[36]

As soon as the Kisch reception committee in Melbourne learned of the ban, and while the *Strathaird* was still on its way from Western Australia, the members met, passed a resolution of protest and arranged a follow-up public meeting.[37] On the same day, in his first statement on the case Menzies, now Attorney-General, said that Kisch 'had not been allowed to enter Great Britain because of his subversive views'. The Commonwealth, he added, 'feels under no obligation to receive persons of this type'. For the same reason the Government was also denying entry to the New Zealand delegate to the Congress, Gerald Griffin.[38] Menzies' old antagonist, Brennan, meantime pounced on his first assertions about Kisch and, given that no official statement had been made about the source of the Government's information, accused Menzies of having 'made up his mind about Herr Kisch on a very unreliable type of hearsay evidence'.[39] But an official transcript of a meeting next day between Menzies and a delegation from the Trades Hall shows such an assertion of Menzies' responsibility to be very wide of the mark:

> I do not know about the Kisch case, it was dealt with before I came in, but information telephoned from Canberra disclosed that Kisch was excluded from England, and they do not exclude people there in a

---

[36] Yarwood, 'Foreword', xii.
[37] *Argus*, 8 November 1934.
[38] Ibid., 10 November 1934.
[39] Ibid., 8 November 1934.

hurry—there is probably a very much stronger tradition in England as regards free speech than there is here...The Griffin case did actually come before me and was considered by Cabinet.

Menzies went on to explain that Griffin had spent a considerable time in Russia where he had held official positions. The Government had photographic copies of documents he had issued in connection therewith, as well as irrefutable evidence that he was a vigorous Communist propagandist. While Russia was rearming, propagandists of Griffin's kind were associating themselves with anti-war movements 'with a view to eliminating armies in other countries'. Australia was 'exposed from a defence point of view': to admit people who advocate disarmament was dangerous.

> Any man prepared to advocate a peaceful change of system of government can always say just what he likes. When we touch upon Griffin we touch upon something affecting ordinary national security. Judging from the way the Griffin case was considered I know that Cabinet was reluctant to come down unfavourably in the matter of exclusion—other things being equal, let him come in.[40]

By the time the *Strathaird* reached Melbourne Kisch's supporters had in train a court action to challenge the right of the ship's captain to detain him in accordance with Government instructions. It failed, and on 13 November, as the ship was pulling out of the wharf to leave Melbourne, Kisch leapt over the rail and landed on the quay, breaking a leg but giving himself an inspired title for a subsequent volume of memoirs: *Australian Landfall*. Despite this heroism, the injured man was somewhat ignominiously carried back to imprisonment on the ship, which resumed its way up the coast towards Sydney.

Next day Brennan moved in the House of Representatives an adjournment to allow discussion of the Kisch case. He opened the debate with a hard-hitting attack on Menzies for having allegedly 'butted in' and ineptly attacked Kisch before getting all the facts of the case. Banning Kisch was indefensible: existing laws 'lack nothing in drastic and even oppressive qualities' to deal with anything Kisch might actually *do* if he were allowed in. In reply Menzies delivered a long legalistic homily to show how under the Immigration Act the Government's power to exclude people advocating subversion was beyond doubt. He declared that 'information in the hands of the Government'

---

[40]Notes of a Deputation which waited upon the Federal Attorney-General ... at Melbourne, on Friday, 9th November, 1934, AA, A432/1, item 34/1736 PT2.

indicated that 'this so-called congress against war and fascism' was simply 'the expression in Australia of the international communistic organisation'. Kisch had been in England in June and July of 1933, but as a result of his activities had in September been banned from further entry into the United Kingdom. Menzies denied that the Government opposed free speech, but 'Communism connotes revolution', Kisch's denials that he was a Communist were not to be taken at face value, and 'the limits of free speech are passed by propaganda which aims at the overthrow by violence of the government of a country'.[41] A most acrimonious debate followed in which every variety of prejudice from extreme left to far-right found expression, often crudely. One speaker, however, briefly raised the tone of the discussion: Maurice Blackburn, a Labor member who had served in the Victorian Legislative Assembly and, like Menzies, had just been elected to the Commonwealth parliament. Thought of even then as the conscience of the Victorian Labor movement, Blackburn was admired by almost everyone who knew him.[42] Menzies, he said, was unfortunate in finding himself defending a decision that someone else had taken: a brief, moreover, that for him must have gone deeply against the grain.

> Those who have known the Attorney-General for any length of time must have viewed with disgust and surprise the attitude which he adopted today. I have known him for a great many years. Although we have differed politically, I have always thought that, if there was anything for which Robert Menzies would lay down his life, it was for the right of freedom of speech, for the right of people to express their opinions.

Though not himself a Communist, Blackburn said, he had concluded through earnest study that Communism was a reasoned position and that Communists 'are perfectly entitled to express their opinions'. He believed, in fact, that the stand Menzies was taking in this case did not reflect his real feelings. Blackburn knew of an instance when, as Minister for Railways in Victoria, Menzies had once taken up the case of a man alleged to have been dismissed because he was a Communist.[43]

By this time letters were pouring in, chiefly to the Attorney-General's Department, objecting to the exclusion of Kisch and Griffin as undemocratic and a denial of the Australian tradition

[41] CPD, 145: 254–9.
[42] ADB, 7: 312.
[43] CPD, 145: 262 ff.

of 'fair play'. Clergymen, academics and creative writers were prominent among the protesters, though the brunt of the attack was made by leading trade unionists.[44] Kisch's defenders meantime mounted a habeas corpus action and in a High Court hearing in Sydney on 15 and 16 November, Justice H. V. Evatt ruled that in making the original exclusion the minister had not satisfied the requirements of the relevant section (3gh) of the Immigration Act. The source of the information on which Kisch had been banned had not been precisely stated and it should moreover have come from a government.[45] This verdict meant that Kisch had to be released and permitted to land, but as soon as he did so he was detained and given a dictation test. It was in Scottish Gaelic and, when he failed, Kisch was charged with being an illegal immigrant. A police magistrate heard the case on 17 November and granted a remand until 23 November; bail of £100 was found by Kisch's friends and he was freed.

Next—to the horror of many good Scots—Kisch's indefatigable mentors took to the High Court, and won, an action asserting that Gaelic was not a European language within the meaning of the Act. The Government, however, persisted. Returning to section 3(gh) of the Immigration Act, the Minister, Paterson, set out to effect a watertight banning while at the same time not revealing anything of the operation of the Investigation Branch. Under Lyons's signature he cabled the Secretary of State for the Dominions to ask for 'advice by telegram in plain language position in regard to the exclusion of Egon Kisch from the United Kingdom'. The reply brought no new detail but was unequivocal:

> Position is that Egon Kisch was refused leave to land in the United Kingdom in September, 1933, on account of his known subversive activities. Permission to enter the United Kingdom would not now be granted to him.[46]

Kisch's litigious supporters were preparing to resist this new challenge when in February 1935 the Government decided to cut its losses and give up. It offered not to proceed with the case against Kisch and to pay his court costs if he undertook to leave Australia at once. Kisch agreed and sailed from Fremantle on 11 March.

---

[44] Correspondence file, AA, CP450/6, bundle 2, for sample of protesting letters. A Kisch–Griffin Defence Organization formed to conduct a campaign against the Government had a committee composed almost exclusively of trade unionists, AA, CP450/6, bundle 2, f. 28.
[45] 52 *CLR* (1934–35), 221–333.
[46] Quoted in *Argus*, 10 January 1935.

Kisch was effectively free in Australia between his release on bail in mid-November 1934 and his departure in March 1935. Meanwhile Griffin, deported after failing a dictation test in Dutch, slipped back into Australia on 14 November under an assumed name and disguised in horn-rimmed glasses. Both Kisch and Griffin missed the Congress, which had begun on the 10th, but Kisch travelled widely in Australia and addressed a number of crowded rallies. Griffin eluded the police long enough to address meetings in several States and then somewhat dramatically gave himself up in the Sydney Domain on 25 November. For the Government and for Menzies in particular the whole affair was altogether embarrassing. The victories won by the Kischites in the High Court could only be galling to the Attorney-General and his officers, who were after all the Government's legal advisers. On the larger question of free speech the Government's image suffered in some quarters and, though it was doubtless enhanced in others, Menzies firmly denied that free speech *per se* was at stake. 'I may be perfectly tolerant of opinions expressed in my own household', he wrote in one of his many defensive letters to academic critics;

> I may be quite unmoved by even violent abuse entertained by people not in my household; but I surely am entitled to say that I will not admit the latter to my family circle.
>
> ... The real activities of movements or individuals are not necessarily in line with their platform pronouncements. The man who confines his activities to bellowing at a street corner will never cause me the loss of a moment's sleep.[47]

But few cases were so clearcut, and Blackburn's words about Menzies' sudden illiberality must have stung. That Menzies escaped the last ignominious phase of the Kisch case must have been cold comfort to him. By the time the final negotiations were taking place, he was in England.

The move into federal politics brought the Menzies no temptation to move house to Canberra. When accepting nomination for Kooyong Menzies, as we have seen, had made plain the distastefulness to him of Canberra, both physically and professionally. It was indeed hardly a tempting time: the population of the 'bush capital' was only 7500, almost 9 per cent of them unemployed. Thanks to the Depression, construction of roads and buildings had

---

[47]Menzies to Professor Allan G. B. Fisher, 16 November 1934, AA, CP450/6/1, bundle 2/31.

effectively ceased. Canberra was in the doldrums.[48] One visitor who thought the climate the best in the world nevertheless described the city as half a dozen scattered nuclei leaving the gaps to posterity; the houses and shops 'are as much alike as Chicago sausages, and there is the sham American socialism which prevents a man from putting up a fence to his own house'.[49] J. P. Moffat, the Consul-General for the United States, observed that Menzies and White 'hate Canberra, stay there the minimum time possible, never bring their wives and families, and count the hours till they can get back to Melbourne'.[50] Apart from the town's intrinsic unattractiveness to him, time spent in Canberra was for Menzies an additional burden on a professional life already disrupted by his political commitments. As he had told interjectors at one Hawthorn meeting during the late election campaign:

> While I have been in politics I have had the very doubtful pleasure of seeing three-quarters of my legal practice go to the winds. I am a barrister by profession and I want to make it perfectly clear that whenever I have any chance to appear in court consistent with my political duties I will do so.[51]

In fact, as he said this, Menzies knew he was soon to realize what the *Argus*, in announcing it, called 'an ambition which is cherished at some time by most lawyers in the British Dominions—the opportunity to argue, or at least to appear, before the Privy Council'.[52] A trip to England sometime in 1935 would be involved and, if any were needed, here was an additional reason for rejecting the idea of spending unnecessary time in Canberra.

The Melbourne solicitors for a firm called Paper Sacks Pty Ltd had won from the Privy Council leave to appeal against a decision of the Australian High Court in a patent action about the manufacture of heavyweight paper bags. Menzies had led a distinguished Bar before the High Court in the original case and lost; but the firm's solicitors were still anxious that he take on the Privy Council appeal. This was litigation, observed the *Argus*, in which 'Australian commercial and industrial interests, particularly in the cement trade, are taking keen interest'. The letters patent for the manufacture of these bags had been granted in 1925 to an American firm, which in turn granted a perpetual licence to a New South Wales company, Bates (Australia) Pty Ltd. Since then, many

---
[48] Jim Gibbney, *Canberra, 1913–1953* (Canberra 1988), 159, 163, 186.
[49] John Bedford in the *North Queensland Register*, quoted by Gibbney, ibid., 176.
[50] Quoted by Gavin Souter, *Acts of Parliament*, 306.
[51] *Argus*, 16 August 1934.
[52] Ibid., 25 July 1934

millions of bags had been made and sold, and Paper Sacks Pty Ltd was now asking for the revocation of letters patent on the ground chiefly that 'the invention ... is not novel, and has previously been used and published'.[53]

The Privy Council hearing was set down for May 1935. For Menzies—and the Government—it was a happy coincidence that in the first half of 1935 strong Australian ministerial representation was needed in London for two important Imperial events: the Silver Jubilee celebrations of George V's reign, and an associated conference of the Empire Parliamentary Association. Lyons was to head the party and the two ministers most concerned with trade and commerce, Gullett and H. V. Thorby, were to accompany him. The addition of Menzies, with his legal expertise and impressive public presence, would be a great bonus, especially since the private business taking him to England would relieve the taxpayer of most of his expenses. The less ceremonial aspect of the party's mission was the real reason for Gullett and Thorby's inclusion: talks with the British authorities about trade under the Ottawa agreement of 1932, and in particular the trade in meat. The chief aim here was to forestall the renewal of British agreements with the Argentine on the import of chilled beef and to prevent restrictions on the entry of the Australian product. As Gullett wrote to Hawker at the end of January 1935, he was eager to begin a 'vigorous offensive' against restrictions and had received 'excellent assistance' from Menzies in drafting the agenda for forthcoming talks. The matter was urgent, so the Australian ministers were leaving early in the hope of forestalling Argentine–United Kingdom negotiations.[54] They were booked to travel on the *Otranto*, scheduled to leave Melbourne on 19 February.

With various officials and secretaries the party would number sixteen, which the *Age*, in statistical mood, sourly asserted was the largest overseas delegation ever to eat up taxpayers' money. The reporter counted 131 trunks and packages being loaded as baggage at Melbourne, estimated their weight at five tons and in a wild flight of fancy declared that 'their aggregate cubic content would be almost sufficient to hold Parliament House itself for shipment to London'.[55] Extravagant farewells to Mrs Lyons reflected both the degree to which she had captured the respect, sometimes affection, of the Melbourne bourgeoisie and the importance,

[53] Ibid.
[54] Gullett to Hawker, 31 January 1935, NLA, MS. 4848/3/6/III–IV; *Sun-News Pictorial*, 22 February 1935.
[55] *Age*, 20 February 1935. Other members of the party included the chairman of the Tariff Board, a special officer of the Customs Department, a meat consultant and Menzies' private secretary (Stirling).

especially in those days of dignified shipboard travel, attached to an official visit to the heart of Empire. At what the press described as a 'brilliant gathering', held in the music-room of her mansion at Toorak, Lady Knox, wife of Sir Robert (the National Union president who had been associated with the Group in Lyons's original elevation), wished Mrs Lyons *bon voyage*. In long, tight-packed columns the *Argus*'s social reporter described the dresses worn by seventy-eight of the guests—Mrs R. G. Menzies' wore 'a charming white silken dress with a flower design and a little garland at the neck'.[56] Mrs Lyons was also formally farewelled at occasions organized by the Victorian Women's Citizens Movement and by representatives of Roman Catholic Women's philanthropic and welfare bodies.[57]

Four days before Menzies' departure the Young Nationalists gave him a farewell luncheon in the banqueting hall at the Victoria Palace. He used the occasion to celebrate the success of the Young Nationalists in bringing new dynamism to a party whose fortunes had in 1929 'reached their lowest ebb for thirty years'. As he spoke, Victoria was in the throes of a State election campaign and it seemed appropriate to stir the spirits of the faithful. 'The real charm of the organization', he declared,

> is that its members have never been great respecters of persons. Some of my friends in the organization have even addressed me in unmeasured terms. (Laughter) . . . I want it to remain thoroughly critical and not to accept the views of anyone conspicuous in public life. I hope that individualism, although it has been suffering in politics, will remain alive in this organization. It was created not to make followers, but to make leaders, and so far it has been successful.[58]

On the day he sailed, 19 February, Menzies wrote two important valedictory letters. The first was to Hughes, briefly discussing several minor Cabinet matters and adding the final flourish:

> May I add that my highest hope for England is to do nothing that may diminish the reputation which you, in an outstanding fashion, created for us in the old world.[59]

We can perhaps sense a note of irony in these last words. But there was no irony in the other, unaffected letter he wrote that day. It was to Staniforth Ricketson:

---

[56] *Argus*, 19 February 1935.
[57] Ibid., 21 February 1935.
[58] Ibid., 16 February 1935.
[59] Menzies to Hughes, 19 February 1935, AA, CP450/6/1, bundle 2, f. 23.

> I cannot leave Melbourne to go abroad without telling you how much I appreciate all your many acts of kindness and friendship during the past few years. I cannot imagine that any man who ever went into public life in Australia has enjoyed more loyal friendship.
>
> My chief regret is that I do not better deserve the self-sacrificing goodwill which you invariably exhibit.
>
> Pat and I will carry with us tangible souvenirs of the generosity of Gwen and yourself and our little group, but I can assure you that the most valuable souvenir will be the constant recollection which we will carry with us of 1000 acts of kindness.[60]

The details are no doubt lost for ever but fragmentary evidence such as this lends weight to the supposition that in the transformation of Menzies the politician in the crucial first half of the 1930s Ricketson was perhaps the primary single influence. One feature of this was his readiness to handle aspects of Menzies' personal finances, in which the latter's lack of practicality would soon become notorious. To help release Menzies from such worries was perhaps at this point, where political activity was seriously interfering with his professional life, the most practical gift Ricketson could confer on his friend.[61] But there is a note of affection in this letter which, given Menzies' normal reticence, is striking and suggests that Ricketson's support had for him a psychological as well as bread-and-butter meaning. We have to remember that those were the years of growing attachment to Macedon, of relaxed and companionable contact there, in an atmosphere where kindness and mutual respect must have specially flourished.

As for Hughes, we have no way of knowing whether he had received Menzies' letter before, on 20 February, he wrote to 'My Dear Attorney-General' to wish him 'bon voyage' and 'an interesting and profitable sojourn in Britain'. That morning the *Sun-News Pictorial*, Melbourne's morning tabloid, had carried on its front page a series of photographs of travellers being farewelled on the *Otranto*. One depicted a particularly handsome Menzies in smiling pose with his two well-dressed schoolboy sons, Ian and Ken. The sight triggered off one of Hughes's more wildly impish effusions:

> I'm sorry I did not have the opportunity of 'seeing you off', but I am consoled in some measure by gazing with admiring eyes on the artistic and lovely portrait of 'A Gentleman & His Two Sons' which adorns

---
[60] Menzies to Staniforth Ricketson, 19 February 1935, ibid.
[61] Dame Pattie Menzies avers that Ricketson's management of Menzies' affairs was of crucial importance in releasing his energies for politics. Menzies' lack of interest in money is stressed by all his family and many outside observers.

The vision of the handsome Minister, farewelled by his two fair sons, which arouses Billy Hughes's mock jealousy.

embellishes and makes priceless the columns of one of our 'junior morning contemporaries'. Hoblein [sic], Reynolds Raphael—to name no more—must gnash what is left of their teeth when from their cold shades they see this beautiful picture, and curse the fates which sent them on and out of the earth far, far too soon.

When I look at it I feel something like these poor wretches only more so: Far more so! For I have had my likeness took! And my picture painted by... gifted men. And when I look at—or even think of—the 'orrid thing they made of me, I weep hot scalding tears & say in futile, petulant but vicious protest, O, God why didn't you give me a face like Bob Menzies?[62]

---

[62] Hughes to Menzies, 20 February 1935, Menzies Family Papers.

7

The Discovery of England 1935

> Flowers, books, coloured streamers, tears, smiles, earnest consultations in corners about 'a certain cure for seasickness', the slow agony of farewells that reach the 'oh well' stage at 4.30 P.M. and peter out miserably at 6 P.M. A good dinner in the quiet waters of the bay, and early to bed.[1]

THUS, ON 19 February 1935, Bob and Pat Menzies, aboard the *Otranto*, went through the farewell rituals of their day. To part from their children for the first time was especially trying, the greatest 'agony of farewells'. Next morning, however, Pat seemed 'more cheerful ... and in a moment of exuberance throws letter of credit out of window with mass of wrapping papers and dead flowers'.[2] Another day, and they were in Adelaide: 'Ring up home and hear the small voices over the wires. For once I don't curse the telephone'.[3] And then, in Fremantle, there were letters from home, 'each so characteristic of the writer that one can only marvel at and be thankful for the early development of personality and character in the three children'.[4]

As these first glimpses intimate, the story of this trip has for the outsider a special flavour. For the first time in his life Menzies kept a diary. He began it on the day the *Otranto* steamed out of the Bay and ended it, 400 handwritten pages later, on 8 September, when he could happily record on another ship, the *Aorangi*: '... right ahead, a few hours away, is the Rip—and Port Phillip—and HOME!'[5] He would later explain that the real credit for this achievement lay with his wife who saw the expedition as a great adventure, thought the children would in time come to value a

[1] Overseas Diary, 1935, NLA, Menzies MS. 4936/13/396, 19 February 1935.
[2] Ibid., 20 February 1935.
[3] Ibid., 21 February 1935.
[4] Ibid., 25 February 1935.
[5] Ibid., 8 September 1935.

careful record of what their parents had seen and done, and stood over him to be sure he made an entry each day.[6] In *Afternoon Light*, the memoir he wrote thirty years later, Menzies observed that he had never been a serious diarist but went on to note that even his limited experience suggested to him that 'a private diary, kept as a reminder of past error, may serve a useful human purpose'. For,

> when a man heavily engaged in affairs sits down, at the end of a long and arduous day, or even next morning, when he has the great advantage of *'l'esprit d'escalier'*, he tends to be either hasty or defensive. He will tend to condemn others and to justify himself.

The context makes it clear that this remark was prompted by his having dug out a second diary, recording a crucial trip he had done in 1941, to jog his memory on events about which he was planning to write in his memoirs. A little unnerved by what he found, Menzies observed that he could not read this diary 'without blushing for my readiness to make snap judgments and to resort to easy epigram':

> I was, of course, many years younger than I am now, and consequently more prone to intolerance and hasty judgments. 'My salad days, When I was green in judgment'. My executors will do me good service if they use the incinerator freely.[7]

Happily, Menzies' executors did not use the incinerator freely, at least on the diaries. So, through them, we find ourselves suddenly in touch with a real live person: the Menzies lurking behind the public mask, a mask created by, among other things, his distaste for the public display of emotion and his deep concern for the sanctity of privacy in personal and family life. Moreover, Menzies seems in his remarks in *Afternoon Light* to be almost at pains not to associate any observations on 'past error' with the 1935 diary. It is almost as if there remained for him something authentic, perhaps magic, about the experiences of that year, and something pristine about the record he had kept of them. Symptomatically, he drew upon that record in 1936 to write a book, fortunately never published, which he evocatively called 'Jubilee Pilgrim'. That title suggested what was profoundly true: that for Menzies the 1935 trip was an emotional experience of great

---

[6] He explained this in the preface to the unpublished book he wrote in the next year, 'Jubilee Pilgrim'. In asserting that he had only kept two diaries Menzies forgot a few other fragmentary efforts, most notably one in 1948.
[7] *Afternoon Light*, 44–5.

importance, a voyage of discovery—the discovery of England. That what he found there was what he had from childhood been conditioned to find did not in the least take away from the excitement and significance of it all.

On the Australian leg of the journey Menzies began by being irritated by reporters at Adelaide who interrupted him while shaving: 'why are reporters so frequently crude, illiterate and lazy? Pride of craftsmanship seems to be dying out fast among these people, who once (see H. L. Mencken) essayed to style themselves a profession'.[8] Crossing the Bight brought a 'rediscovery' from *Macbeth* (which he was then re-reading) that had its lesson for an agony not obviously in Shakespeare's mind as he wrote: seasickness, and the 'formidable "if" ' in

> If it were done when t'is done, then t'were well
> It were done quickly.[9]

The Lyons joined the ship in Perth in time to be given a civic reception in what Menzies describes as a crowded and suffocating picture theatre, with an 'incoherent acting Lord Mayor ... and industrious band of 6 instruments' which played 'for he's a jolly good fellow' when Lyons appeared. Then, as the ship sailed out into the Indian Ocean, Menzies notes how the 'combination of heat and necessities of social chatter (of which he knows nothing) make the Prime Minister hors de combat'. Menzies himself, however, seems to have enjoyed to the full the fun of shipboard life. On 28 February Enid Lyons noted in her diary how 'Mr. Menzies is favourite for the ball tennis tournament',[10] and he himself recorded a few days later a rather hilarious encounter:

> Most abbreviated shorts on record appear on Miss D. Harrowing incident. She reclines on deck-chair, all legs and admiring attendants. She (to me), after some preliminary badinage, 'what do you think of my shorts?' I (offensively leaning over the chair and peering at her), 'Sorry, but I hadn't noticed them!' (Sensation !)[11]

The day after this incident, 2 March, was Pat's birthday, and Menzies threw a cocktail party for about 60 people, 'with merriment continuing through evening. First breaking up of the ice between number of people'. Enid Lyons, by now 'very homesick'

---
[8] Diary, 21 February 1935.
[9] Ibid., 23 February 1935.
[10] Enid Lyons Diary, 1935, NLA, MS. 4852.
[11] Menzies Diary, 1 March 1935.

Ministers, *en route* to the Silver Jubilee of George V in London, are honoured in what Menzies records as a crowded and suffocating picture theatre with an 'incoherent acting Lord Mayor'.

('God bless all my darlings') was cheered by the occasion, especially when one passenger sang 'Phil the Fluter's Ball, unaccompanied, with great success'.[12]

Landfall at Colombo and Aden brought the first foreign scenes and vivid descriptions as Menzies' fresh eye took them in. British imperialism provided unfailing blinkers, as ingrained assumptions were confirmed by first-hand experience. Aden, for example, stirred reflections on

> the persistent Englishness of the English. Here is a golfcourse, there a soccer football ground (in this climate!); here a cricket ground. The town is clean. A few hundreds of Englishmen rule it and clean it and water it. The more I see of such people the more satisfied I am that while doctrinaires and theorists speculate about self-government for

[12] Menzies, and Lyons Diaries, 2 March 1935.

natives (who are chiefly experts in idleness and the demanding of baksheesh), the British calmly go on their way giving to these peoples what they could never give themselves.[13]

In Colombo they lunched at Kandy with the governor, Sir Reginald Stubbs: *'very* English', Menzies records, 'sherry, champagne, port— Governor (who has ruled Jamaica and Hong Kong) says with pride that he has never worn a white dinner jacket. No wonder these English are unbeatable'.[14] Indeed, sartorial symbolism was one piece of Britishness which Menzies effortlessly embraced. Soon we find him acidly noting the performance of his ministerial colleague Thorby, farmer and grazier and one-time Minister for Agriculture in New South Wales, a man whom the *London Daily Express* would shortly describe as 'Tall, dour and rugged: [one who] might easily be mistaken for a plainclothes cop shadowing Lyons'.[15] By the time the ministerial party was in Egypt Menzies records how

> the true Australian touch [is] throughout provided by H.V.T., who attends everything dressed in a white (or near white) panama hat, a baggy grey suit held together with a white belt, and a pair of white tennis shoes. Our dislike of dressing properly on proper occasions is a queer form of inverted snobbery, and the sooner we realise it the sooner will English people cease to regard us as a set of outlandish yahoos.[16]

But Egypt itself overwhelmed Menzies. The valley of the Nile— 'the greenest thing I have seen'—reminds him of a 'vast irrigated lucern field', and 'Cairo is immense. Where did I get the idea that this city of a million people was a broken down village of huts surrounding some place called Shepherd's Hotel?'[17] Then, sailing up the Italian coast, he broods on the classical associations of the place and, landing at Napoli, is greeted by 'a young and spruce representative of Mussolini, complete with eyeglass'. This worthy says Mussolini would be pleased to receive Menzies and Lyons but the appointment he offers is several days hence and so, though 'desolated', they have to press on to meet commitments in London.[18] So they catch the Rome Express and cross a countryside calculated to entrance someone used only to the Australia of the 1930s ('houses with lovely proportions, white with green shutters,

---

[13] Menzies Diary, 12 March 1935.
[14] Ibid., 6 March 1935.
[15] *Daily Express*, 23 March 1935.
[16] Diary, 16 March 1935.
[17] Ibid.
[18] Ibid., 20 March 1935.

perfect doorways and moulded cornices. Many of them shabby, but all showing more than a trace of that widespread artistic judgment which is so rare with us'). There is a brief break at the end: 'we dine and I drink ASTI SPUMANTI—a great day!'[19] Then across France and on to the Channel ferry, which has them in Dover harbour in 55 minutes:

> As we enter, we have the White Cliffs on our right and crowning them the Dover castle. At last we are in England. Our journey to Mecca has ended, and our minds abandoned to those reflections which can so strangely (unless you remember our traditions and upbringing) move the souls of those who go 'home' to a land they have never seen. Dover: it has for centuries been the gateway of romance and high endeavour. I feel a tang in its air that no mere state of wind or weather could possibly create.

And that night, in London, 'at 10.30 p.m. I sneak out and look at Trafalgar Square and one of the Wren churches by starlight. And so to bed'.[20]

So began Menzies' 'discovery' of England. That first act in London—sneaking out to glimpse Trafalgar Square by starlight—caught at what would be its essence: an *experiential* discovery of institutions, a culture and a people which, at the age of 41, he already knew and in the profoundest sense assumed to be his own. Literature, photographs and paintings could etch the beauty of the English countryside in his mind, but that was not a reason for failing to respond to its actuality; and as for most educated Australian visitors of his and the next few generations, who had been implicitly taught that their own country had little—and certainly no independent—history, the palpable immanence of British history, in stones and architecture, was to him overwhelming. What is remarkable, given his age, his forensic sophistication and the practicality of his political experience, is the intensity of the emotion—sometimes perilously close to sentimentality—which this discovery of England was to arouse in Menzies. A little to our surprise we learn that, even at this stage, he was extraordinarily romantic and, as that often means, somewhat naive.

---

[19] Ibid.
[20] 21 March 1935. Not all the party felt the same thrill. Enid Lyons records: 'Reached Calais & boarded Channel boat. Met by Chief of Police. Capt. of boat knows Austr. well. Asked for autographs. Saw Dover castle and cliffs but got no thrill. What's wrong with me? Mr. and Mrs Bruce met us at Dover. Came through Kent. Very like home. Savoy Hotel. Too much luxury. Flowers everywhere'. NLA, MS. 4852.

The Australian ministerial party arrives in London, March 1935. Lyons is greeted by the Secretary for the Dominions, J. H. Thomas. On the far left Bruce watches, while Hankey (in the black overcoat) and Menzies are part of the centre stage.

Dover harbour and Trafalgar Square were the beginnings of his sense of place; what came next was somewhat less serene: a 'nightmare' tour of London conducted by an old friend, Ronald Mackay, once a teacher of philosophy at Sydney University and now a London solicitor. 'Mackay drives in the light of nature and by means of a series of approximations', Menzies recorded. 'In intervals of panic we see Houses of Parliament and Temple and "the City" '.[21] But tranquillity next day brought clearer impressions: 'a few worth recording', he wrote,—and so began the first of a long series of often extensive set-piece descriptions of places and scenes that were to be the hallmark of this diary. It was of Parliament, 'the most impressive building so far':

> a beautiful design, lovely stone, and of course a wonderful stimulus to the mind and imagination. How so much of it came to be built by a generation responsible for the Albert Memorial I cannot understand.

[21] Diary, 23 March 1935.

> Enter the great hall of William Rufus, and find on the floor a brass plate marking where Warren Hastings stood his trial nearly 150 years ago. Stand beside it recapturing the great description by Macaulay and listening for echo of ringing tones of Burke's great denunciation. For the moment almost imagine I am Hastings (mens aequa in ardius) until I remember that 'his person was small and emaciated' and realise I am not cast for the part.

'English history becomes a new thing', he ruminated, and shortly afterwards, when he and Lyons were welcomed by Ramsay MacDonald and Elliott Thomas at Downing Street in the Cabinet Room, Menzies noted Robert Walpole looking down from the mantlepiece and reminded himself that 'In this room have sat and presided Walpole, Chatham, Pitt, Disraeli, Gladstone, Asquith, Lloyd George. If walls could only speak!'[22] The apogee of this communion with the past came a few weeks later, when on the way back to London from a weekend at Chequers he and Pat visited Milton's cottage at Chalfont St Giles and then stood, starry-eyed, in the driveway of Hampden House (it and the nearby church, he notes, 'are practically as they were in Hampden's day: they would stir the soul of an Australian Trade Union Secretary!'). But 'what a day!':

> I have literally been in the presence of the great charter among the barons assembled at Runnymede: I have seen the very handwriting of the man whose sword and character made England a free country [Cromwell]: I have stood where stood many times the great John Hampden, and have sat awhile in the invisible presence of the greatest poet of liberty. How could any Englishman tear down the temple built by these great hands? The survival of a free Parliament in this land is not to be marvelled at. One realises that a Parliament for England is something growing from the very roots of English soil.[23]

But the Australian ministers were in Britain to work as well as to dream, and Menzies records how, on his first morning in London, Bruce took him to a conference with legal advisers to the Foreign Office, to discuss an agreement the United Kingdom had made to import a large quota of Argentinian meat. Menzies found his opposite numbers at this meeting 'as impressive as Chinese ambassadors, elusive, and unwilling to argue legally about any point of difficulty. They annoyed me as lawyers always do when they behave politically and not legally'.[24] But the issue in fact was

---
[22] Ibid., 25 March 1935.
[23] Ibid., 14 April 1935.
[24] Ibid., 22 March 1935.

in an important sense political—the one vital bread-and-butter matter on which the Australians were there, virtually as antagonists, to negotiate. In 1932, thanks chiefly to the tough, at times brutal, tactics of the negotiators, Bruce, McDougall and Gullett, Australia had emerged from the Ottawa conference on empire trade with large gains for which few concessions had had to be made. Except in one case—that of meat—the Ottawa agreements gave Australia free entry to the British market with many of her goods enjoying a preferential tariff over those of foreigners. At a time when the Depression had brought disastrous falls of prices and contraction of markets for primary goods, these were precious gains for Australian producers. In the case of meat, the British negotiators had dug their toes in against a demand for tariffs against foreigners and the Australians had made their one concession: agreement that the British might fix quotas on imports from all sources, Dominion and foreign alike. It was important to the British that they have freedom of manoeuvre, since in deciding on quotas they faced a difficult balancing act. Beside Dominion interests they had to consider those of local producers and also to bear in mind traditional and extensive British capital investments in Argentina. Argentina's continued viability at this time of acute economic difficulty depended on finding markets for her major export: meat. For the Australians, on the other hand, to limit or even eliminate British freedom of movement through a new, fixed agreement was highly desirable. That was what the forthcoming negotiations were, essentially, about. The prospect of success was not helped by the fact that, as has recently been graphically shown, senior British civil servants and politicians were still bitter at the Australians' adeptness at 'screwing concessions out of us' at Ottawa.[25]

In fact, over the whole four months between their arrival in late March and their departure at the end of July, the Australian delegation would endure almost continuous negotiations on the meat question. As they dragged on, Menzies recorded an increasing sense of frustration and ennui. Noting, day after day, 'more meat conferences', he writes in exasperation 'we are circumnavigating the entire globe of irrelevancy', and on 12 April crankily registers encountering R. A. Butler, 'who thinks the meat problem, of which he knows nothing, on which I have worked every day since we arrived, "very simple" '. The principles at stake might have been straightforward enough but, as extant records of prices

---

[25]This account of the meat issue depends primarily on the work of Dr John O'Brien, of University College, Cork, and most particularly his article in *Historical Studies*, 22 (October 1987): *passim*, but especially 574–7.

and quotas prepared for the endless discussions show well enough, the details were complicated and, for anyone not personally connected with the rural interest, boring. The long wrangle, Menzies records, 'almost persuades me to become a vegetarian, until I remember that the joint hopes of the farmers of Great Britain and Australia depend upon increased consumption. Whereapon I groan, set to, and reach for the indigestion tablets'.[26] In the end, the long effort was not worth it; the ministers went home largely empty handed.

There was much other work too: conferences with British and Dominion ministers and civil servants on airmail services, broadcasting and shipping problems; and then came the Empire Parliamentary Association Conference, which entailed long sessions, preparation of papers and speeches, much travelling and endless banquets. We catch Menzies close to the end of his tether on 18 July when, as one of the Association's touring party, having endured days of travelling, civic receptions and inspections of industrial establishments, he found himself in Birmingham, being carted over Dunlop's biggest works, observing in the B. S. A. factory the manufacture of everything from small arms to motorbikes, and in the evening attending a banquet as a guest of the mayor and corporation. There he had to respond to the toast to the guests: 'despite some allusions to the great Joseph Chamberlain manage to do most indifferently. The municipal meal is beginning to pall on me'.

As a visiting Dominion minister engaged in important official discussions Menzies would in any circumstances have come into contact with a wide spectrum of British officials and politicians. It is, however, certain that he received more notice because of the word that went ahead of him from the influential Hankey. As we have seen, Hankey had on his recent Australian trip been much impressed by Menzies. On his way back from Australia at the end of 1934 he wrote to tell Baldwin that Menzies was coming to London on a Privy Council case: 'We ought to make much of him. He is a strong man and very pro-British, and most anxious to meet our leading men'.[27] Hankey sent the same message to Sir Edward Harding, head of the Dominions Office: Menzies was 'intensely pro-British and, as his wife (who accompanies him) told me, very keen to meet our leading men. It is essential that he should be shown every attention'.[28] On 12 January 1935, a week after his

[26]Diary, 23 April 1935.
[27]Hankey to Baldwin, 23 August 1934, HNKY 4/26, Churchill Archives Centre, Cambridge: copy from Baldwin papers, Bodleian Library, Oxford.
[28]Hankey to Harding, 28 November 1934, PRO, CAB 63/70, PFF/9573.

return to England, Hankey was invited to Sandringham for the weekend, to report to the King on his trip to the Dominions. The Duke and Duchess of York were also there, and Hankey had long conversations with these members of the royal family about Dominion affairs, on which he found them very knowledgeable. His diary does not record who the individuals Hankey spoke of were, but it would be surprising if Menzies' name was not mentioned.[29] Once Menzies arrived, Hankey saw him frequently on official occasions and the two lunched privately with Baldwin on 11 April, only weeks before the latter took over the prime ministership from the decrepit Ramsay MacDonald. Menzies found Baldwin 'just what I expected':

> I tell him of Father's regard for his speeches and of my own interest. His position here is most important. Critics say he is lazy and deficient in ideas, but the best informed people I have met... credit him with real and constructive ability. A good face and head, and, after some early reservations, spoke to me in a very interesting fashion.

Next month the Menzies spent several days in Surrey at Hankey's home, whose 'perfect rural setting' included a 'view like that from our house at Macedon in spring'. They played tennis, drove round the countryside, and after lunch on the second day Hankey and Menzies walked over to visit the former's neighbour, Winston Churchill. 'Much good conversation en route', Menzies records:

> What a wise and well-informed little man Hankey is. When one recalls his presence and influence at almost every war and peacetime conference of the last 20 years one does not wonder that more than one observer considers that some day he may be regarded as the greatest Englishman of his day. But it is part of his technique to be self-effacing.

They found Churchill wallowing in a pool he had himself constructed, wandered through his walled garden, and at tea listened to their host working himself up on the parlous state of national defences.

> My impression is of a remarkable man who lives too well and lacks that philosophical mental self-discipline which prevents a man from going to excesses either of mind or body. But an arresting person—and I had no delusions of grandeur in his presence![30]

[29] Diary of weekend at Sandringham, Churchill Archives Centre, Cambridge, HNKY 1/8.
[30] Diary, 25, 26 May 1935.

The other person of especial importance in bringing Menzies into contact with 'the leading men' was the Australian High Commissioner, Bruce. They dined or lunched together often, and after a dinner hosted by Bruce early in the visit, a dinner at which he met a galaxy of notables, Menzies observed: 'Bruce's contacts are amazing, ... we clearly pay him too little'.[31] Menzies had privately not been hitherto particularly well disposed towards Bruce but the experience of working with him soon changed that. As he wrote following one of the first of the interminable conferences on meat,

> On our side there is a disposition to ramble, but Bruce grows on one more and more as clear-headed, strong and persona grata with the men who count in England. All my old prejudices are melting away.[32]

However initiated, Menzies' contacts and discussions gave him a lively sense of being momentarily at the centre of things. He met all the current British ministers and some of the top civil servants, and got their views first-hand on a variety of public issues. The civil servants in particular impressed him. After talking with Sir Edward Harding of the Dominions Office and Sir Horace Wilson of the Board of Trade, he labelled the latter 'prince of public servants' and bemoaned that Australian ' "democratic" stupidity' which 'makes it so difficult to make special provision for attracting the best brains (and many of the best men of their years at Oxford and Cambridge) into the Civil Service'.[33] He lunched with Sir Robert Vansittart, Permanent Head of the Foreign Office, and listened to a long anti-Hitler diatribe: that Germany was the only threat to peace in Europe, that Hitler was a megalomaniac, that war was certain within four or five years unless England made it clear that Germany's ambitions would be stopped.

A month earlier, at a House of Commons luncheon, he had sat next to Chamberlain, who 'explains' both Germany and Japan 'by saying they have an inferiority complex' and observed that 'the best guarantee of peace in Europe would be the concession of some power and self respect to Germany'.[34] At the beginning of May he listened to the Commons debate on the 'Stresa front'. It was a tense time: in January the Saar had returned to Germany by plebiscite; in March Hitler had repudiated the clauses in the Versailles Treaty on German rearmament, announced compulsory military training and told the British Foreign Secretary, Sir John Simon, that Germany now had an air force on a par with England's. In April

[31] Ibid., 28 March 1935.
[32] Ibid., 1 April 1935.
[33] Ibid., 20 May 1935.
[34] Ibid., 1 April 1935.

Simon and the Prime Minister, Ramsay MacDonald, met French and Italian representatives in the Borromeo Castle on Isola Bella off Stresa and issued a statement agreeing to oppose 'by all practicable means any unilateral repudiation of treaties which may endanger the peace of Europe'.[35] After hearing the Commons debate Menzies noted that the temper of the House clearly favoured 'a real measure of rearmament by Britain' and that 'Hitler's lies and untimely truculence have gravely shaken [the] average Englishman's desire to be generous to a former foe'. But he was sour about Churchill's performance in the debate: 'the idol has feet of clay'. Not only did he *read* his speech but 'his theme is a constant repetition of "I told you so", and first class men usually don't indulge in this luxury. If a first-rater has once said an important thing, he doesn't need to remind people that he's said it'.[36]

However grave, foreign affairs appear not to have been the topic of conversation at Menzies' first meeting with Anthony Eden. It was on 5 July, when the Menzies lunched at the House of Commons with the Speaker, Eden and his wife. Eden, since June Minister for League of Nations affairs, was just coming into prominence. Menzies thought both the Edens 'very young, and he surprisingly nervous'. Sober matters were clearly not on the agenda that day: 'chatter purely social', Menzies records, 'my stock of small talk really astonishes me'. He was having, it was clear, plenty of practice. Once discovered, he was endlessly in demand for luncheons and dinners, and he and Pat were guests at some notable weekend house-parties. Though he was being treated to a kind of duchessing, he managed, more often than not, to keep his head. He was quizzically amused by English country families and the ease with which they mixed the sacred and the secular (nicely symbolized for him by the Swinton gentleman who had a beautiful spire built on the local church to celebrate having won the Derby) and their notion of the real man: 'he must be intelligent without making too much of a point of it; he must attend to the rites of the church but leave the public discussion of religion to the nonconformists; ... he is rather of the opinion that it is better to ride badly to hounds than to face up to a stiff problem of the intellect'.[37]

Even royalty did not quite faze him. Certainly, early in May, in minister's uniform, with sword and cocked hat, he enjoyed the pomp and colour of the formal Jubilee service at St Paul's,[38] and

---
[35] A. F. Havighurst, *Twentieth Century Britain* (New York 1966), 245.
[36] Diary, 2 May 1935.
[37] Ibid., 7 June 1935.
[38] Ibid., 6 May 1935.

at a Buckingham Palace dinner a few days later he rejoiced in being the man chosen to take the 'bright and talkative' Mrs Winston Churchill in on his arm, subsequently to talk across her to Lloyd George and afterwards to have a ten-minute chat with the King.[39] But there's an almost larrikin Australian touch to his account of a Buckingham Palace ball he and Pat went to in June,

> I in sober black knee breeches and an enveloping mantle of self-consciousness. It is a gay sight—uniforms and white tiaras, with the Royal Family industriously dancing in a small cleared space at the throne end of the ballroom, and a vast concourse of the elect packed tightly into the rest of the room admiring the orchestra and the gold plate. However, the champagne is good and the great very friendly, and we enjoy ourselves.[40]

Again, though captivated by the Duchess of York ('delightfully pretty, charming and natural'),[41] he was under no illusions about the princes. The Duke of Kent, he decided, was 'a good trier but with a certain amount of the schoolboy's diffidence and shakiness on the facts. These Royal sons are all triers, but they have a late flowering'. The main point to record about the Duke of York was that he seemed to be controlling his stammer.[42] The Prince of Wales, however, had better moments. Menzies talked to him at tea at St James's Palace:

> For once, he is in a state of physical and nervous repose, and the result is a natural and interesting talk about Fairbridge farm schools, land settlement, Theodore, Billy Hughes, *et hoc genus omne*. The prince clearly leads the family in grey matter.[43]

But to observe these weak vessels of royalty in no way diminished for Menzies the power and social significance of the institution they embodied. At the cup tie final at Wembley in April he watched spellbound as in the presence of the Prince of Wales '93,000 bareheaded and *motionless* people' sang 'Abide with Me' and 'God save the King'. 'An irreligious communism', he opined, 'has no chance with these people'.[44] Again, at the trooping of the colour, on the King's birthday, '[George V] and all four sons

---

[39] Ibid., 9 May 1935.
[40] Ibid., 13 June 1935. There is a serious misquotation in C. M. H. Clark's account of this incident where 'self-consciousness' is rendered as 'consciousness', thus fundamentally altering the sense of the passage, *History of Australia* (Melbourne 1987), VI: 487.
[41] Diary, 9 May 1935.
[42] Ibid., 11 July 1935.
[43] Ibid., 9 July 1935.
[44] Ibid., 27 April 1935.

are on horseback, and the public feeling is again most intense. These are poor days in England for the reds'.[45] Earlier, at the jubilee celebrations, he describes 'streets lined with thousands of soldiers and millions [sic] of people, with a blue sky, a golden air and the bursting green of the parks [making] a radiant setting'. 'There is here', he reflects, 'a real bond between the monarch and his people, that defies all the academic arguments of the so-called revolutionaries' and he quotes a conversation with 'a barber of the old school' who 'illuminates the whole problem by waving a razor over me and saying "Did you notice the weather on Monday, sir? You can't tell me that God didn't have a hand in that. It was more than a coincidence. My Mates and I are all for the old man (meaning the King and not God) because he's one of us" '.[46]

This 'barber of the old school' is one of the only two members of the English lower orders to appear in the whole of the diary. The other is a Sunday orator in Hyde Park to whom, we might say, Menzies responded as one pro to another: 'a little Cockney', as he describes him,

> surmounted by a red flag, preaching the Russian gospel and quoting Stalin as if he was fresh from the most intimate disclosures of that statesman's mind; a poor speaker, all emphasis and callisthenics, but with a complete knowledge of the golden rule that crowds love to be insulted.[47]

Both barber and orator are oddities: Menzies, it is clear, had no meaningful contact with working- or lower middle-class English people. Nor does he record having remarked ugly slums or industrialized districts on any 'voyage of discovery' (his phrase for a sightseeing trip), though he travelled from one end of the country to the other by train and must have passed through many depressed areas. Insulated socially, his vision was selective: England's impact was spiritual and romantic, its keynotes beauty and serenity, to be imbibed through rural scenes, hallowed historical places and architecture.

[45] Ibid., 3 June 1935.
[46] Ibid., 6, 9 May 1935. Enid Lyons's appreciation of this day makes an interesting contrast. 'Probably the most wonderful day of my life—at least part of it, the procession. The sunshine was hot and bright. Went to St James' palace yards at 9 o'clock. Talked other PM's wives ... The crowds along route wonderful. Cheers & cheers & hand waving to which I immediately responded. Daddie raised his hat. Australians all along the route calling "lovee" or "Good Old Joe" or "Aussie". Perfectly thrilling. Scene in St Paul's beautiful. Wonderful uniforms etc. Royalties arrive much later than we. Queen looked marvellous. Palest pink lace over silver white and silver lame coat white fox collar; pink and silver toque'. Lyons Diary, 6 May 1935.
[47] Menzies Diary, 5 May 1935.

At Oxford he found All Souls 'one proof, among many, that England is the most civilised country in the world': a country 'impatient with those hustling and superficial people who think the getting of money is the chief end of man'. Oxford, indeed, brought profound 'peace ... and a spirit upon me which it is worth while travelling thousands of miles to experience'.[48] In London, Westminster Hall, with its stone walls 'stained with age and fire' and its great Eastern window 'a splash of colour in the pale gloom', seemed to him 'the most real place in all England'.[49] In the countryside, meantime, he was 'learning to understand, as I never understood before, the secret springs of English poetry ... This green and tranquil country sends forth from its very soil the love of good humour and contentment'.[50] The Cotswolds, predictably, entranced him, 'with marvellous vistas of field and tree and a cold clear sweeping wind that sends joy tingling through you'. And he noted, as if it was an original observation (had he really never heard it before?) how the stone houses of the villages seemed to grow out of the very soil. In modern times architecture had ceased to be an art: 'Why do architects and builders now war with nature instead of entering (as the Gloucester builders did) into a pact of mutual assistance?'[51]

As the definitional woolliness of some of these observations suggests, Menzies' 'discovery' of England can be understood largely as an emotional discovery of the England already in his mind. But in the practical world of day-to-day action England had an equally important personal significance for him. 'Discovery' is too strong a word here: 'confirmation' would be more accurate— confirmation of certain of his powers, and therefore, in important ways, of self. The principal roles here are Menzies as lawyer on the one hand, and as speaker and politician on the other. In neither case could he of course have doubts about his achievements at home, but it might be a question of how he would match up as a smaller fish in the bigger pond of England. His outward radiation of confidence and charm, publicized progressively by the English press, which throughout received him well, masked a degree of private diffidence, almost, at times, of insecurity, which bred in turn a frank hunger for praise. The artlessness with which these needs are recorded is in fact one of the more fetching characteristics of the diary: beyond simply recording fact and emotion it is at times a real dialogue with himself.

[48] Ibid., 18, 19 May 1935.
[49] Ibid., 11 July 1935.
[50] Ibid., 11 May 1935.
[51] Ibid., 20 May 1935.

The Paper Sacks case began in the Privy Council at the end of May, in proceedings which impressed Menzies as 'informal, courteous and efficient'. He was quickly at home: courts were his milieu, their procedures and the work of preparing a brief second nature to him. The case lasted a month, ending on 25 June when, Menzies records, 'my own form ... fortunately, good. Trevor Watson [the barrister who appeared with Menzies] most flattering. "That is the best reply in a patent case I have ever heard" '. At dinner at the Inner Temple next night two leading barristers were 'very pleasant about my reply in the Paper Bags case, B. saying that it let the breath of common sense into the case for the first time'. Then, a few weeks later, new evidence of his acceptance by the English Bar: 'Letter from Gray's Inn making me Honorary Master of the Bench—an honour usually reserved for Prime Ministers !!!' Hughes, he noted, was the only other Australian minister to have been made a Bencher.[52] His cup was almost full. The crowning drop came on 26 July, in the middle of 'a fierce rush of work to get things cleaned up before departure' for Australia next day. 'Privy Council gives judgment in my favour. Hooray. Specially pleased because chief point argued by me is the chief ground of their decision.'

In this legal sphere Menzies had not been worried by diffidence, but it was still good to collect and cherish the crumbs of praise. It was the same with public speaking, though here a greater degree of self-doubt was curiously mixed with a note of arrogance as the British, with some exceptions, proved after all not to be exemplars of the great art. In the first few weeks he spoke not at all, partly because he was not asked, but partly also to avoid overshadowing his chief. At the first official luncheon Lyons, who spoke for the Australians, 'makes most admirable speech! He is doing famously and I may well be content to be in the background while he does as he is now doing'.[53] But Lyons was not at the Empire Society's banquet a week later and Menzies, who was, noted: 'on the whole speeches bad, and I longed to make one'.[54] Visiting the Commons he heard Chamberlain's budget speech ('excellent and delivered from scanty notes') but was again displeased with Churchill. On the night of the Jubilee ceremonies the British Government dined Dominion visitors at Claridges but, writes Menzies,

Ramsay MacDonald's speech misses a great opportunity—all 'wuds, wuds wuds', and Bennett's [the Canadian Prime Minister] reply remarkable only for an American accent and pointlessness. I become

[52]Ibid., 9 July 1935.
[53]Ibid., 26 March 1935.
[54]Ibid., 3 April 1935.

more and more gloomy—where are the after-dinner speakers? Perhaps the quality of such speeches is in inverse ratio to the quality of the wines, which here are always excellent.[55]

But by the time he wrote that his own performances had begun: a luncheon address at the Constitutional Club ('performance fair');[56] a speech at the Devonshire Club ('for the first time I satisfy myself');[57] an address ('well received') to a luncheon at the London Australian Society.[58] Then, at a dinner at the Canada club to honour that Dominion's new governor-elect, John Buchan (Lord Tweedsmuir), Menzies replied for the guests, as he remembered, late in the evening 'to an audience grown very restive and, in the case of some, slightly alcoholic, and to my pleasant surprise I get away with it—the greatest ovation I've ever had!' His theme was that the sole remaining bond of Empire was their common kingship. It must have been quite an evening: 'I had a sort of levée afterwards; and was elected an honorary Canadian a couple of dozen times'.[59] In noting the occasion the *Sunday Times* described Menzies in flattering terms:

> He has the reputation of a brilliant lawyer, and he is without doubt a remarkable speaker. He has an impressive appearance—the strong face which we expect from Dominion statesmen, made most attractive by a twinkling humour ... As an after-dinner speaker he is a model of urbanity, and his speech at the dinner to Lord Tweedsmuir last Monday could hardly have been bettered. Mr. Menzies is Australian-born, but he speaks precisely in the manner of a cultivated Englishman.[60]

Less than a week after this tribute, the conference of the Empire Parliamentary Association began. On 4 July the Speaker of the Commons presided at a luncheon held in Westminster Hall to welcome delegates from overseas legislatures of the Empire. There, before a gathering of 500, Stanley Baldwin, who had just taken over the Prime Ministership and was thus chairman of the United Kingdom branch of the Association, delivered the key oration of welcome. Menzies, his reputation in London as a speaker now soundly established, was asked to reply on behalf of the visitors. It was quite appropriate that he should be the one

[55] Ibid., 6 May 1935.
[56] Ibid., 16 April 1935.
[57] Ibid., 17 April 1935.
[58] Ibid., 21 May 1935.
[59] Ibid., 26 May; *Argus*, 29 May 1935.
[60] 2 June 1935.

The Empire Parliamentary Association luncheon in Westminster Hall, 4 July 1935, where Menzies, responding to Baldwin, makes his first triumphant speech in England.

Australian to speak: Lyons, having fulfilled the ceremonial functions directly connected with the Jubilee (and having, as Menzies noted on several occasions, fulfilled them well) had left on 17 June to travel home via Europe and America. What followed was for Menzies the high point of the whole trip, the climax, we might almost say, of London's discovery of him and of his own confirmation of himself. The story is best told in his own words:

> A redletter day. I speak with Baldwin in Westminster Hall; possibly the first Dominion Minister ever to speak in this historic spot. We lunch first, and I am terrified to be sitting with the Speaker, Baldwin, the Duke of Athlone, Ramsay MacDonald, Neville Chamberlain, Bruce and John Simon. A great occasion, and I have for once written out my speech so that I shall not collapse in the presence of the shades of Edmund Burke and Fox and Sheridan. Baldwin speaks magnificently; he has vigour, eloquence, a rich historical imagination and an immense prestige. My heart sinks. He, contrary to the common practice here, does not read his speech, so I put mine on the table and commit myself to the mercy of providence. I think of Mother and Father listening in 12,000 miles away and trust not to dishonour them and get to my feet, and *mirabile dictu*, get away with it.

> A magnificent audience gives me an ovation at the finish, and I am deluged with congratulations. Tonight, at the Imperial Institute, I am quite excited to find my speech, so to speak, the talk of the room. Even the Duchess of York (sweet creature) has heard of it.[61]

He did not exaggerate. Next day there were more congratulations, and *The Times* hailed the speech with a verbatim report and a leading article.

Baldwin had called the spot where they met 'sacred ground': the hall of Rufus, nursery of the English common law and parliament. 'The English parliament', he declared, 'had no one man for its maker, neither Simon de Montfort nor even King Edward. No man made it, for it grew'. Menzies' theme was the same: their parliamentary system would endure because 'its roots were deeply set in the history and character of the British people'. No one in his audience, except perhaps Pat, could know how much this speech drew on the words of the emotional diary he had been writing, almost as if the phrase-making there had been rehearsals for public performances. He spoke of his feelings as he stood before Hampden House and of how for him the rafters of Westminster Hall still rang with the voices of the past. Freedom in Britain had been 'no concession granted either by a mob or by a dictator'; 800 years of national history made British institutions like the grey stone villages he had lately seen in the Cotswold Hills:

> He understood the Prime Minister, that great lover of the English countryside, better when he had seen them. Far beyond the activities of the ribbon-builder and the sub-divisional expert, they stood as the lovely embodiment of a pact of mutual assistance between the old stonemason and the landscape on which he built. They seemed to him to illustrate most perfectly that harmony which was the essence of the best things which England had given to the world.[62]

Its flourishes and the predictability of its sentiments notwithstanding, this speech bears the ring of sincerity. And it neatly complements Baldwin's, though Menzies' artless account of the circumstances of its delivery makes it clear that there had been no prior conferring to make it so. The truth was that Menzies was now well attuned to Baldwin and to his conservative ideology. The two men had met and talked freely, and Menzies' previous readings of Baldwin's sayings had also gained life from the

---
[61] Diary, 4 July 1935.
[62] 5 July 1935.

experience of actually hearing a number of speeches displaying that 'vigour' and 'eloquence' which so swept him away at the Parliamentary Association luncheon. Baldwin's neo-populism, his careful avoidance of the language of class and his stress on nation, tradition and consensus as the cement of the status quo, made his identification of constitutionalism with conservatism irresistible for Menzies. Indeed, Baldwin's insistence on the legitimacy of English institutions deriving from their historical evolution, and their consequent soundness in the face of 'contrived' systems like Bolshevism and Fascism, was identical with the argument which Menzies had long been propounding at home. The extra dimension he learned from Baldwin—and his own starry-eyed reaction to the English countryside happily bolstered this—was the urge to transpose the sanctity of history to the natural world. It is easy now to think of many of the speeches Baldwin made embodying these sentiments as, in the words of one recent commentator, merely 'evocative flights of homespun philosophy'.[63] But with their constant images of harmony and continuity as the core of Englishness these invocations of nature's rhythms, with family and state almost mystically attuned to them, constituted at the time a powerful conservative ideology.

It is not surprising that Menzies was impressed. For him 'home' was indeed Britain: a fact not at variance with his Australian background but given new immediacy by the experiences of 1935. English images of the kind Baldwin evoked caught his imagination: what mattered was that tradition, truth and stability lay in the inheritance which, as Britishers, antipodeans like himself shared with those who in the homeland knew at first hand, in their day-to-day world, how past and present merged. What the Baldwin message meant to Menzies by the time he left for home is suggested in a letter he wrote from Quebec to thank the Prime Minister 'for your very great courtesy to me on my ... visit to England'. He asked Baldwin 'to forgive my impertinence if I say two things in addition'.

> One is that my chief political impression, after four months in the middle of English politics, is that your own personal power and prestige are much greater than you may be disposed to think yourself. If I may say so, your capacity to excite enthusiasm among the English people for something *above* their average level of thinking strikes me as without equal in our own time. Popular leaders can so easily, as

---

[63]Roy Jenkins, *Baldwin* (London 1987), 138. 'There was', says Jenkins, 'a lot of "this dear, dear land of ours", of "the level evening sun over an English meadow", of "the rooks tumbling noisily home into the elms"'.

every politician knows, rouse selfish and unworthy emotion, that I hope you will not regard it as an impertinence for a young and obscure political visitor to record his delighted impression of your own rare and invaluable power.

I can assure you that one of your minor good deeds will be the fact that you have inspired me to a greater faith in the people and a greater desire to serve them honestly and well'.[64]

There is no reason to doubt the sincerity of this letter, which clearly registers an important phase in the development of Menzies' thinking about the opportunities and the duties of a politician who takes his role seriously.

On their last full day in London the Menzies lunched Australian friends who had been good to them and took their leave of Maurice Hankey. Next morning at seven o'clock they rang Mother, Father and Belle Menzies: 'Hope Mother could hear—I arranged the call because I thought it would be a thrill for her and Father to hear our voices from the other side of the world'. Later, at Waterloo station, they were seen off by Sir Edward Harding, of the Dominions Office, the Bruces, the Mackays and Keith Officer,[65] 'and are quite sad to leave so many good friends'. From Southampton they sailed on the *Empress of Britain* for Canada, crossing the Channel to pick up passengers at Cherbourg: 'and thus it is that the chatter of French voices and the broad shovel hat of a French curé are our last impressions of the old world'.[66]

To return home via Canada and the United States as they were scheduled to do seemed, to one as homesick as Menzies had become, 'an irritating delay'; but still, 'there is something of a thrill in going into what is to me a new land, with language, ideas and even physical appearance very different'. There was a nice touch at their landfall at Quebec; 'as we left the wharf and passed through an almost entirely French crowd, one girl said (of Pat) "comme elle est belle!" ', a remark which Menzies recorded with spontaneous pleasure.[67] One consistent theme, indeed, of the whole trip, is Menzies' pride and joy in his wife's beauty and conquests. In a visit to Court on 25 June, Pat 'looks lovely and would

---

[64]Menzies to Baldwin, *c.* 1 August 1935, Baldwin Papers, Bodleian Library, Oxford.
[65]Officer had had experience in the colonial service of Nigeria before joining the tiny External Affairs Branch of the Prime Minister's Department in 1927. In 1933 he was appointed Australian Liaison Officer with the British Cabinet (the position Casey had vacated in 1931). For an excellent description of Officer and his work see Peter Heydon, 'Keith Officer (1889–1969), Pioneer and Symbol', *Quadrant*, July–August 1970, 30–41.
[66]Diary, 25–27 May 1935.
[67]Ibid., 1 August 1935.

put any bride of 21 into the shade'. And on the day they left England he ruminates on the many friends they had made: 'Pat in particular may claim to have had a real triumph. Her quiet but cheerful friendliness and naturalness have obviously appealed very much to the English taste'.

Though in London at that celebrated evening for Lord Tweedsmuir he had enjoyed being made an 'honorary Canadian', the colder reality (as he saw it) of Canada at once sparked Menzies' dislike. 'The Canadians, I regret to say', he wrote on his first day in Ottawa, 'seem to me to be excessively Americanised', a fact particularly irritating since 'the Yankee genius expresses itself more freely in "quick fire" conversation than in thought'. He was, however, well treated, being dined and lunched as a kind of semi-official visitor, and though not greatly impressed with most of those he met found one Graham Towers, at thirty-seven Governor of the Bank of Canada, 'slim and elegant ... quietly intelligent and English rather than American'.[68] In Montreal they tasted at the cabaret Chez Maurice 'the night life of a great pseudo-American city'. The crowd was badly dressed, 'something like the crowd of yesteryear at Warracknabeal or Horsham'. White trousers and golf coats were the most popular dress, and there was a 'bedlam of noise, partly produced by a wooden-faced orchestra dressed in some synthetic Tyrolese costume and partly by the "wal, I'm tellin yuh!" of the life and soul of the party at the next table'. But such irony soured into frankly puritan distaste before the evening was out:

> Then comes the cabaret show. The legs have waved, the eyes rolled, and the funny men arrive! My hat! For obscenity I have never heard their equal. When they had exhausted the resources of their anatomies and physiological knowledge (to the accompaniment of shrieks of mirth from those present!) we crept out, ashamed. No civilised English-speaking country would tolerate these foul perverts for five minutes. Yet in America they pass for humorists![69]

On to New York. Distaste again welled up on the 'tube railways, with their freights of Jews and Wops and the mixed races of the world' but, as subsequent pages of graphic description testify, New York nevertheless 'thrilled' him despite himself.[70] Next day, *en route* for Washington, in a quaint throwback to his days as a railway minister, Menzies was invited to travel in the electric locomotive ('streamlined and massive and therefore called "Mae

[68] Ibid., 2 August 1935.
[69] Ibid., 3 August 1935.
[70] Ibid., 5 August 1935.

West" '), that drew the train the 230 miles from New York. He liked the physical ambience of Washington, especially ' "water in the landscape" (what a blunder the selectors of Canberra made!)' In Washington, too, the Menzies had their first taste of the South, and liked it. At a 'young-old tavern' they ate fried chicken, Southern-style, and cherry pie 'and feel that in some ways it was a pity the South didn't win the Civil War'. What melted them most was 'the soft Southern accent with its accompaniment of friendly good manners ("I just guess you folks must be from out of town; yessuh! Yes ma'am!")'[71]

Washington of course also meant government and politics and here, predictably, Menzies was acidly critical. Interviews with Secretary of Commerce Roper and Secretary of State Cordell Hull went well, and he met and was duly impressed by Roosevelt. But otherwise there was little to be admired. He thought the Capitol 'a fine building' but its corridors

> are cluttered with statues of mediocrities and its debates beneath contempt. Messengers and visitors wander about in shirtsleeves, collarless and noisy: one misses the reverent quiet of the visitors to the Houses of Parliament at Westminster.

In Chicago Menzies liked the university, principally because its buildings were 'intelligently modelled on Oxford' thus producing 'a pleasant campus, and a sort of suggestion that civilisation is coming'.[72] Perhaps that was generous, for the verdict which Menzies, proud and intolerant Britisher, finally passed on the United States of 1935 was bleak indeed:

> One thing which impresses the mind is that we err if we regard the Americans as our blood cousins. The majority of them are not Anglo-Saxons; their appearance is different; their language is by no means identical; their ideas are cruder; their standards are lower; they engage in a nauseating mixture of sentiment ('Mother's Day') and dollar chasing not palatable to the English mind; they have no consciousness of responsibility for the well being or security of the world; no sense of Imperial destiny except in terms of collaring the world's trade and washing their hands of world responsibility. The best Americans are pathetically conscious of this; they admire Great Britain and secretly envy her; the first thing one of them will tell you (if he can) is that his uncle or grandfather or mother in law came from the British Isles. More and more the minority American—the American who derives from before the alien invasions of the twentieth century—turns impatiently from the racketeering, corruption, violence, intolerance and

[71] Ibid., 6, 7 August 1935.
[72] Ibid., 9 August 1935.

selfishness of contemporary America to look with envious eyes at the quietness, the tolerance, the sense of values, the ordered justice, the security of England.[73]

Perhaps, after all, Menzies *did* have reason, if in later years he looked back at the 1935 diary, to blush at his 'readiness to make snap judgments'. That they were so attuned to the England he had newly discovered perhaps excused him. It is also apparent that he was getting very homesick. On 3 August, as he was leaving Montreal, he admitted to himself that 'the fact overshadowing all, [is] that I dislike the American accent and blaloney [*sic*], and "want to go home".'

The trip home across the Pacific was in the main uneventful. Menzies, especially with more time to write, continued to revel in description of places and people: Honolulu, Fiji (lovely scenery, but 'I am pleased when the boat sails. It must be conceded that natives and foreign parts per se have no great attraction for me. I am a degenerate modern; with a taste for cleanliness and good plumbing').[74] In the first leg down the American coast the ship had carried a large party of elderly delegates to a British Medical Association Conference—general practitioners from the provinces, Menzies concluded waspishly, since they 'have that ineffable look of omniscience which characterises the second-grade medical man the world over; their wives occupy such an unassailable social position in Muddleton-On-Slush that they have forgotten the arts of dress'.[75] He himself assiduously exercised. In England—to the surprise and admiration of some journalists—he had frequented a gym and played squash and tennis; on board ship quoits and energetic walking round the deck were the best he could do. He carefully recorded the distance walked each day; it varied between eight and ten miles, but even so he had to admit to himself that 'the adipose residue of many official dinners will take a lot of moving!'[76] They surfed at Honolulu, where they tried out the large surfboards of the day, and Pat, 'guided by her "gentleman" [instructor] stood up valiantly on hers with complete success'.[77]

They reached Sydney at last on 6 September, and that night Hughes and a group of lawyers gave Menzies dinner at the Hotel Australia, where he records making 'a rambling speech'. Two days later the diary comes to an abrupt end outside the Rip. For the reunions that follow we have to depend on imagination.

[73]Ibid., 15 August 1935.
[74]Ibid., 29 August 1935.
[75]Ibid., 13 August 1935.
[76]Ibid., 17 August 1935.
[77]Ibid., 20 August 1935.

Lyons and his wife had arrived home some weeks before the Menzies. They were given an enthusiastic civic reception in Melbourne on 16 August. Mrs Lyons redeemed a promise by telling a packed Melbourne Town Hall her remembrance of England 'Through Australian Eyes'.[78] It was a homely tale somewhat different in its emphasis from the declaration of that other returning expert on Britain and Europe, R. G. Menzies. On arrival in Melbourne he told reporters that he was returning from England with a new faith in democracy, the one hope of the world. He was also profoundly convinced of the need for personal contact between Australian statesmen and the statesmen of other parts of the world.[79] It was essential that Australians remedy their 'narrow outlook' on foreign affairs. In England, thanks to the currently threatening aspect of Europe, interest in foreign affairs was intense. In Australia apathy could no longer be afforded: at least in the Commonwealth parliament we should try to develop discussions as serious and as well-informed as those in the British Commons. But Menzies did claim to bring home one positive message: on migration and economic development. In migration the emphasis of the past had been on recruiting people for farming, but he found in England now a 'growing recognition that the development of Australian secondary industries must be sympathetically regarded as part of a process of establishing an all-round and secure nationhood'. That view, he said, had been particularly evident in Empire Parliamentary Association discussions, where opinion was decidedly against putting 'more people into the business of producing primary products for export'.[80]

Federal parliament had adjourned on 11 April, while the Australian ministers were away. It reconvened on 22 September. The Labor Opposition at once moved censure, protesting against the Government's failure to call parliament together for five months, its powerlessness to solve the problem of unemployment, and its ineptitude in the trade talks with Britain. The acting leader of the Labor Party, Francis Forde, launched the attack. He denounced the meat negotiations as a complete 'washout' and observed that as much could have been accomplished through the High Commissioner 'without a single minister leaving our shores'. Considering the ennui he had endured over the weeks of agonized bargaining, it is understandable that Menzies should react angrily to this attack. He was not, he said, apologetic about the negotiations: Australia had won increases in import quotas of chilled beef

[78] *Argus*, 17 August 1935.
[79] Ibid., 7 September 1935.
[80] Ibid., 10 September 1935.

and frozen lamb and mutton. But in reality these were very modest, and Menzies' case was not strong. It was therefore gratifying when the respected Hawker came to his rescue and spoke warmly of 'the patient and capable negotiation of the Australian ministers' and argued that the concessions on mutton and lamb would in practice give the Australian exporters unrestricted entry to the British market for likely production in the current season.[81]

The censure motion was easily defeated in a vote on party lines: it annoyed ministers but hardly stirred widespread passion. That was not true, however, of the other matter which engaged attention as soon as the session opened: the international crisis brought to a head by the ripening of Italy's designs on Abyssinia. 'I should like to see the Australian point of view thoroughly thrashed out in a special debate in the federal parliament', Menzies had said on his arrival home.[82] He got his wish when on 22 September, the day after the session began, Lyons presented to the House of Representatives a long ministerial statement on the dispute.[83] While in London Menzies had talked much with Bruce and others about Mussolini's ambitions and the troubles of the League of Nations. He came away convinced, as he had told his diary on 10 June, that 'the peace of the world hangs on a rotten thread'. Britain was 'the one country which consistently acts as if the Covenant [of the League of Nations] were a real and operative thing' but, as he knew, it remained uncertain what that would mean in a real crisis. The French, under the leadership of Pierre Laval, were fearful of pushing Italy into Germany's arms and were inclined to think of Abyssinia as the necessary price for Italian friendship. There were British politicians and officials—particularly fierce Nazi-haters like Vansittart—who took the same view. The Admiralty was known to be uneasy at the thought of possible hostilities in the Mediterranean. Such fears and doubts were an important part of his input into the Government's statement of position.

After a brief but lucid summary of the history of Italy's 'dispute' with Abyssinia Lyons announced that a critical phase had just been reached. The Conciliation Committee of the League Council had drafted settlement proposals which involved a considerable loss of Abyssinian territory to Italy. The Abyssinians were prepared to accept this, but Mussolini rejected it. Would he resort to war to enforce his demands? If he did, since Abyssinia was a member of

[81] *CPD*, 147: 118ff.
[82] *Argus*, 10 September 1935.
[83] *CPD*, 147: 30ff.

the League, Italy would be deemed automatically to have committed an act of war against all League members, who in that case must sever trade and financial relations with her and contribute armed forces if further action were needed. The recently appointed British Foreign Secretary, Sir Samuel Hoare, had made to the League Assembly what Lyons called 'a momentous statement on British policy'. Lyons summarized its gist, though he did not quote the ringing words Hoare had used: 'The League stands, and my country stands with it, for the collective maintenance of the Covenant in its entirety, and particularly for the steadfast and collective resistance to all acts of unprovoked aggression'.[84] Australia's representative, Bruce, had spoken more gingerly: as Lyons reported it, he 'urged that, while the Conciliation Committee of the League Council had the problem under review, speakers should avoid dealing with the dispute in any manner which might add to the difficulties of a solution'. This was the present view of the Commonwealth Government.

When Lyons moved that his statement be printed each of the two Labor leaders in opposition, Forde for the ALP and Beasley for Lang Labor, launched vigorous attacks. Lyons, they said, had not contradicted statements in the press that the Government had committed Australia 'up to the hilt' in support of the policy announced by Hoare. So it had 'blundered into a decision that might involve Australia in war'. Beasley, in a long pacifist speech, declared the attitudes of France and Britain to be no more than imperialistic rivalry with Italy, and moved amendments to express parliament's 'profound horror at the prospect of a second world war developing out of the conflict of Imperial trading interests' and to order the Government not to support sanctions. In the debate that followed, Menzies attacked the notion that Australia could declare its neutrality of all wars outside its boundaries, since it was not an independent entity in world affairs, but part of the British Empire 'or, if honorable members prefer the modern jargon, part of the British Commonwealth of Nations'. For him the real cement of this Commonwealth was fealty to a common king: Great Britain's position would necessarily be Australia's.[85] After a vitriolic debate, Beasley's amendments were rejected.

Mussolini invaded Abyssinia on 3 October. This brutal attack on so helpless an African state brought a public reaction in Britain and France that has been compared to the revulsion caused in 1914

---

[84]Havighurst, *Twentieth Century Britain*, 246. 'At this time, his aside went almost unnoticed "if risks for peace are to be run, they must be run by all" '.
[85]*CPD*, 147: 578–82.

by Germany's invasion of Belgium.[86] Support for firm action by the League was overwhelming. On 8 October the League's Council declared that Italy had resorted to war in violation of her obligations as a member of the League, and at a subsequent meeting of the League Assembly fifty-four member countries endorsed the declaration and approved the imposition of sanctions. In the Australian parliament, at the end of the month, Menzies moved the second reading of a Sanctions Bill, to impose Australian sanctions against Italy and affirm the Government's determination to stand behind the League and the Covenant.

A debate followed that was a fiery re-run of the argument over Lyons's earlier statement. In his introductory speech Menzies presented a largely legalistic assertion of Australia's obligations as a member both of the League and of the British Commonwealth. John Curtin, now Opposition leader, argued in a powerful speech that sanctions could never be effective, given the international character of oil and armament companies, and quoted an impressive array of politicians—among them Latham, Baldwin and Cripps—to the effect that it was useless to imagine that economic sanctions might not also entail military sanctions. Menzies announced that the Bill was urgent and set 7 November, a week from its introduction, as the deadline for its passage. It was then guillotined through, in the face of vociferous Opposition complaints.[87] So sanctions were imposed: it remained to be seen how far the dire predictions of their opponents were correct.

A few days before the sanctions debate began, the *Argus* noted that Menzies might soon have another overseas task: he was under strong pressure, especially from sections of the Country Party, to represent the Commonwealth if the Privy Council agreed to hear an appeal by one Frederick Alexander James, a South Australian dried-fruits grower and merchant, against a recent High Court decision for the Commonwealth against him. 'It is understood', the report added, 'that he [Menzies] is not anxious to make another journey so soon', but in fact as Attorney-General he had little choice.[88] On 6 December, the day parliament rose for the summer recess, Menzies told the House of Representatives that word had arrived that the Privy Council had granted James leave to appeal and would allow several State governments to intervene in the case. In a little over a month he would be embarking for England again.

[86] Rhodes James, *Anthony Eden*, 152.
[87] *CPD*, 147: 1284–7.
[88] *Argus*, 25 October 1935 and 55 *CLR* (1936).

James was challenging the validity of an important piece of Commonwealth legislation, the Dried Fruits Act, 1928–32. What was at stake was the competence of the Commonwealth Government to regulate marketing of dried fruit (and, by implication, other rural products, especially wheat and dairy produce, for which schemes were already in operation) by establishing for individual producers or traders quotas above which it was illegal to sell such fruit in Australia. The object was to manipulate the market in the growers' favour by controlling local supplies and thus keeping the Australian price up. Production over and above the quota had to be exported, to what was a depressed world market. By the late 1920s soldier and other closer settlement had resulted in overproduction, at a time when overseas prices were collapsing. An Australian Dried Fruits Association, comprising most growers and dealers, tried to effect voluntary regulation, failed, and then persuaded the Commonwealth and four State governments to set up Boards to supervise domestic and overseas sales. It was the legislation surrounding the work of these Boards that became the subject for James's litigation.

James was an aggressive entrepreneur who had developed his dried-fruit processing business in the 1920s. His painstaking quality controls were such that fruit marketed under his brand name was generally in high demand, and many smaller growers gladly sold their fruit to him. He did not join the Dried Fruits Association and repudiated regulation. The story goes that James learnt typing and shorthand for business purposes and practised by repeatedly copying out the Commonwealth of Australia Constitution Act. The familiarity thus gained with the Constitution led him to suspect that the marketing legislation which frustrated his freedom of action on Australian markets might be in conflict with Section 92 of the Constitution, which stipulates that interstate trade must be 'absolutely free'. James obtained a licence for his packing shed and registered as a dealer, but obeyed quota regulation only when it suited him. When in 1926 he contracted to sell 240 tons of fruit above his quota to dealers in New South Wales and Victoria the South Australian Board prosecuted him. James resisted, and the legal action which followed was the opening shot in what was to become a bizarre but for a time all-too-successful vendetta against marketing regulation by governments and statutory authorities. It was the first of what turned out to be for James a series of twenty-eight law-suits.[89]

[89] *ADB*, 9: 464–5.

The details were complex but essentially James first won a series of cases which by the application of Section 92 ended in denying the South Australian Government and its instrumentalities the right to regulate his marketing of dried-fruits. But if Section 92 so prevented State action, did it equally fetter the Commonwealth? This issue was tested when in 1932 the Commonwealth Dried Fruits Board confiscated fruit, above his quota, which James tried to sell in New South Wales. James took the Board to the High Court and lost: the Court ruled, in other words, that the Commonwealth did have powers superior to Section 92. James sought and won the right to contest the Court's decision before the Privy Council, and it was this appeal which Menzies was required to fight in 1936. The case was of great importance: if James won, the whole of the existing scheme of controlled marketing of primary produce in Australia would be in jeopardy. Thus the New South Wales, Queensland and Victorian Governments—impelled by their concern to preserve their marketing schemes—sought leave to intervene in support of the Commonwealth. Tasmania and Western Australia were granted leave to support James. Their position was first and foremost a states-right one, contending against any confirmation or extension of Commonwealth power. On 29 December the Victorian Premier, Albert Dunstan, announcing that his Government would be permitted to be represented before the Privy Council, added that arrangements had been made for Menzies to appear for Victoria as well as the Commonwealth.

There was a second, and far less significant, case in which Menzies was briefed as Attorney-General to appear while in England. This was Arthur Payne v. the Federal Commissioner of Taxation, and concerned the taxation of income, earned by Payne and kept in London in sterling. When the Australian Taxation Commissioner insisted that the tax be calculated on the Australian exchange equivalent, Payne took the case to the High Court. He lost his case and lodged an appeal to the Privy Council.[90]

Just before the House of Representatives went into recess, in December 1935, the UAP parliamentary party held an election to fill the deputy leadership, which had been vacant since Latham left it more than a year earlier. What impelled the decision to fill the post at this juncture was not publicly stated but it is clear that at this time Lyons was weary, and anxious for a deputy to be ready to take over from him when the time became opportune.[91]

---

[90] 55 *CLR* (1936), 158–65.
[91] Lyons made this explicit in a letter to Menzies on 26 April 1936. See below, p. 189.

It is also likely that Menzies, whose ambition and meteoric rise already gave him strong influence in Party counsels and made him an obvious candidate, did not want to risk seeing the deputy leadership settled while he was away in England. Rivalry was strong behind the scenes. The ageing Archdale Parkhill, with solid New South Wales backing, was a formidable contender.[92] Casey had some support though he was also at that time trying to persuade Bruce to come home and re-enter politics, as a potential leader under whom he could happily serve.[93] Bruce finally refused in November: the ballot took place a month later and Casey, though he had just become Treasurer, was no match for Menzies. The same was true of White, the Minister for Customs whose jealousy and contempt for Menzies were always thinly veiled. Cabinet decided that only ministers should be candidates, a proviso that ruled out Hughes and Hawker, two possible rivals of Menzies. Menzies won with Parkhill as runner up.[94] So he could leave for England feeling his position in Government and Party to be secure.

Menzies' election to the deputy leadership gave another dimension to Hankey's private observation that Menzies had 'literally' changed places with Latham. He was now in a position to carry out the role in Cabinet which Hankey saw as Latham's: to 'rule Lyons with a rod of iron'. He was also, in various public forums, making clear his ambition to see the provincial-like slackness of Australian ministerial practice tightened up. So, for example, in an address to the Constitutional Association in Sydney, he advocated the creation of an inner cabinet, to devote itself to matters of detail, leaving large matters of policy to be dealt with by ministers attending larger cabinet meetings[95]—a notion that brings to mind Hankey's observation of Menzies' impatience with the loose procedures of the Lyons Cabinet. Again, at a farewell luncheon given by his faithful Young Nationalists as he left for England, Menzies attacked, in statesmanlike fashion, the view that visits abroad of ministers were useless and expensive. Some industries send two or three men overseas every year, he observed, but 'when one of the ministers responsible for the time being for the Government of Australia is sent abroad his journey is referred to contemptuously as a jaunt'. But in fact

---

[92] See especially Melbourne *Herald*, 21 September 1935, which depicts Parkhill and Menzies as the two most significant contenders, citing Parkhill's solid New South Wales backing but observing that Menzies was believed to 'command practically the whole of the interstate support'.
[93] Hudson, *Casey*, 94–6.
[94] *Argus*, 5 December 1935.
[95] Ibid., 1 October 1935.

there is little doubt that the Government of Australia would be better if every Cabinet Minister experienced personal contact with statesmen of other countries. The constant criticism of such visits is merely a sign of inferiority complex and of a belief that we have nothing to learn from the rest of the world. What we need in Australia very urgently is a sense of proportion.[96]

Clearly, as he saw it, his own trip in the first part of 1935 had taught him much.

Still, as he left Australia again Menzies, if in reflective mood, might in the light of recent events in Europe have wondered a little whether 'statesmen of other countries' always had wisdom of judgement to teach. Ever since his return from England he had assured audiences that the events of 1935 had proved the soundness of British statesmanship, on which, he said, Australia's security ultimately depended. 'While men of the calibre of Mr. Stanley Baldwin, Sir Samuel Hoare, and Mr. Anthony Eden controlled British foreign policy there was no cause for alarm'.[97] In the Italian crisis Britain, under the guidance of these men had, he claimed, stood four-square for upholding of the Covenant. But his enthusiasm was soon to appear, at least in part, misplaced. Under pressure from those who wanted to keep Mussolini out of Hitler's arms, Hoare's enthusiasm for sanctions wilted, and early in December, *en route* to a skating holiday in Switzerland, he stopped in Paris to confer with Laval. There the two 'statesmen' worked out a set of proposals for 'a friendly settlement of the Italo-Ethiopian dispute'. Leaked next morning to the Paris press, this extraordinary document was greeted with stunned incredulity in Britain. It proposed handing over half of Abyssinia's territory to Italy, in return for a narrow corridor through Eritrea as an outlet to the sea. The flood of protest that followed is perhaps best typified by the *Spectator*'s comment: 'The Foreign Secretary has jettisoned in a day both his own personal reputation and his country's'. Hoare, at first unabashed, was summoned home and permitted, on 18 December, to resign. Baldwin renounced the Hoare–Laval agreement next day in the Commons but the humiliation could not so easily be removed. With only a little hyperbole, Robert Rhodes James has written of the outcome:

> Throwing Hoare to the howling mob could only be a temporary palliative to British opinion. A dictator had won a great victory. His air force and troops butchered their way into Abyssinia, in one of the

[96] Ibid., 14 February 1936.
[97] Ibid., 9 October 1935.

most ghastly one-sided campaigns in modern history, where the ranks of the dead, maimed and blinded were literally uncountable. It marked the lowest point of British prestige abroad since the worst days of the South African War.[98]

From this failure of British policy Menzies could draw at least one consolation. Hoare's demise made way for the man for whom he had developed a growing admiration. Just before Christmas 1935, at the age of thirty-eight, Anthony Eden was appointed Foreign Secretary. He was the last minister to receive his Seals from the dying George V. One wonders whether he ever told Menzies what the King, who was 'very down on plan of Paris', told him he had said to 'Sam' [Hoare] when accepting his resignation: 'Poor fellow—no more Coals to Newcastle, no more whores [Hoares] to Paris!'[99]

[98] Rhodes James, *Eden*, 155–6.
[99] Ibid., 157.

8

Qualifying for 'Omniscience' 1936–1937

MENZIES SAILED, this time without his wife, in February 1936. As he explained to an English friend, the two boys had just gone to Geelong College as boarders, 'leaving only a small daughter at home. Under the circumstances, Pat thought that she could not very well get away again so soon'.[1] Hughes, having again failed to say goodbye in person, penned one of his notes for Menzies. 'This looks like "The great Cryptogram" ', he scribbled across the top. 'But with intensive concentration—and copious drafts of beer—iced—you'll understand enough of it to get a fleeting glimpse of my meaning.' Tinges of irony and affection laced the typical madcap humour: it was a missive Menzies no doubt added to the fund of Hughes stories which he used as conversation pieces with men of affairs—from the King down—in England. Hughes did not want Menzies 'to go without [my] wishing you every good thing':

> And this I now do: when you departed in 1935 I gave you my blessing, and to that fact, O Sceptic, is to be attributed not only your safe return but the triumph you were by general consent of a grateful populace, duly accorded.
>
> You have been so diligent in your studies of the law that I fear you have neglected that most fascinating of all branches of knowledge I refer of course to Antigonus of Syracuse—one of the wisest and certainly the sanest of the ancients... and so I refrain from more than passing reference to the curious stories which Heliogabolis tells us in his magnum opus "The Caul of the Wyld". But one thing cannot have escaped you: the marvellous prophylactic properties of the Caul of a seven months child, when hung around the neck attached to an amber necklace.
>
> You simply can't drown with one of these contraptions. That fact is well established, as you *must* know.

---

[1] Menzies to O. W. Darch, 18 February 1936, AA CP450/7/1, bundle 5, f. 24.

> Well, my blessing is like a Caul, only much more so. Its sovereign properties have a far wider range: and like a Comprehensive Householder's Policy cover all risks, fire, earthquake, war, sudden death and Privy Council Appeals.
> And this I give you!! Go forth Sir Galahad.[2]

Leisurely at first, the trip to England allowed Menzies and his little entourage (Alfred Stirling, as secretary, and Vinton Smith) to visit Cairo and, from Naples, to have a look at the excavated ruins of Pompeii. But at that point Bruce intimated that the party should get to London promptly. So they disembarked at Villefranche, drove to Nice and caught the Blue Train to Paris, then travelled to Bologne and crossed to Folkestone. That night Menzies dined informally with Bruce, bringing him up to date with the political gossip from Australia, and learning from him about recent sittings of the Council of the League of Nations, of which Bruce was currently the president.[3]

A strenuous round of social engagements began at once. Menzies reported these to the folk at home in long, diary-type letters, repeatedly telling Pat how disappointed everyone he met was that this time she had been left behind. There were luncheon parties like that hosted by 'our old friend Lord Swinton (Under Secretary for Air)' where another of the guests was Douglas Fairbanks and 'his latest wife, formerly Lady Ashley':

> I rebuked Fairbanks for arriving in such a humdrum fashion in a motor-car, telling him that the least I expected was that he would have appeared over the parapet of the house and to come down hand over hand passed [sic] the windows. He is an unusual looking fellow, with a yellowish brown complexion and black straight oily-looking hair. However, he is a man with a good deal of experience and turned out to be good company. His wife struck me as having a fashionable figure, a face which was at the same time plain and decorated, and a pretty good capacity for having her own way.[4]

Lunching soon after at 11 Downing Street, Menzies found Mrs Chamberlain 'as pleasant and as vague as ever'. She said that 'she had listened in to a speech of mine last year; that she thought it very good; that she couldn't remember what it was about, but that in some way it always seemed to remind her of trees' (so much

---
[2]Hughes to Menzies, 10 February 1936, Menzies Family Papers.
[3]Menzies to Pat, 27 March 1936, Menzies Family Papers. Stirling, a law graduate, come soon to hold posts in External Affairs and became an indefatigable correspondent of Menzies. Vinton Smith, stockbroker and leading Young Nationalist, was on a private business trip to Germany.
[4]Ibid.

for the conceit about cottages growing out of the Cotswold soil!).[5] Later, he and Vinton Smith had a weekend in Paris. They shopped, and saw a cabaret show at the Bal Tabarin in Montmartre. To describe it on paper was beyond his power, Menzies told Pat, but he was sending an illustrated programme, 'and when you have seen it you will realise that you must never allow me to go to Paris unattended again'. At the end of the second day he and Smith, worn out,

> sat like two old boulevardiers in front of one of the footpath cafes in the Champs-Elysees and drank our coffee and watched the world walk past. We saw enough to indicate that French women and girls have a tendency to be extremely goodlooking, with very neat feet and ankles (unlike those you see in Bond Street) and with a real flair for wearing their clothes well.[6]

Of his many sightseeing expeditions the one which excited Menzies most came later in his stay—a trip on the Flying Scotsman to Edinburgh in June and several days in Peebleshire. He lovingly catalogued the historical scenes crossed by the Edinburgh train-line after Berwick-on-Tweed: the battlefields of Dunbar, Preston Pans and Carberry Hill, then the Pentlands and Arthur's Seat. When driving through the village of Peebles he was reminded of a famous story: 'An old resident of Peebles was, by some stroke of luck, enabled to visit Paris, and when he came back was asked what he thought of that great city. His reply as—"Paris a' things considered was a wonderful place—but still Peebles for pleesure"'. He visited Melrose, Dryburgh and Jedburgh Abbeys, at the last of them intrigued by 'the spirited conversation of the little Scots woman who acts as caretaker and guide and who spoke of the attacks made on the Abbey 500 years ago with an indignant glint in her eye, just as if she was describing something that had happened to her own family the day before'. And so the description ran on over four close-typed pages—till it ended with an apology for such a 'tedious and long-winded letter', for which the only excuse was that 'there is something about this Scotland that comes bubbling up in my blood'.[7]

As in most of such family letters from abroad—especially about scenes he had so recently shared with his wife—Menzies dwelt on impressions of people, places and experiences belonging, so to speak, to 'off duty' hours. Of the less colourful, more arcane and

[5] Ibid., 3 April 1936.
[6] Ibid., 28 April 1936.
[7] Ibid., 5 June 1936.

serious matters of the strenuous working part of his life he wrote little, with the exception of an issue all-consuming to men of affairs in England and, Menzies thought, too little noticed in Australia: the terrible danger of war in Europe and the dilemmas with which that confronted Britain. On 7 March 1936, only a few weeks before Menzies reached London, Hitler had made his first coup by re-occupying the Rhineland, repudiating both the Locarno treaties and those clauses of Versailles which stipulated that the area must be kept free of military garrisons. Neither Britain nor France, though both were committed to do so, took any action to resist. Such supineness underlined the failure of nerve reflected in the non-enforcement of sanctions imposed at the end of 1935 against Italy. In an early letter home Menzies explained how the full implications of collective security had never been properly worked out: Britain was irresolute because the Government, and Eden in particular, had been put in an embarrassing position by their own people. 'The overwhelming majority of the electors of Great Britain are favourable to Germany, see no possible objection to the Germans marching into their own territory, and scoff at the idea of helping the French to turn them out.'[8]

After Mussolini's troops, on 2 May, entered the Abyssinian capital, Addis Ababa, Menzies told Eden that in his view sanctions should be lifted, 'admitting quite freely that the experiment had not been a success, and getting to work at once on such an alteration of the Covenant of the League of Nations as will bring it more into line with the realities of public opinion'. By that he meant turning the League into an investigating body, whose function would be to pass judgement on international disputes, but not to enforce penalties: 'the events of the last few months have shown quite clearly that public opinion stops far short of supporting the idea of any threat of collective war to enforce the Covenant . . .'[9] It did not occur to him to think how perilously close this position was to that recently elaborated in the Australian parliament by his political opponents.

Eden had come by late May 1936 substantially to agree. Till then (the time of his conversations with Menzies) he and Chamberlain had in the British Cabinet held out against majority opinion which had come to favour cutting off sanctions. But on 10 June Chamberlain, as Chancellor of the Exchequer, announced that sanctions would end.[10] This was, effectively, the beginning of appeasement, an approach to international affairs strengthened at

[8] Ibid., 17 April 1936.
[9] Ibid., 28 May 1936.
[10] Rhodes James, *Anthony Eden*, 166–7.

the end of the year when Italy and Germany announced the formation of the Rome–Berlin Axis, Germany and Japan concluded an anti-Comintern pact, and Britain did nothing except begin rearming. Menzies probably contributed his mite to the final decision to lift sanctions. A letter which Hawker received from a friend in England at this time offers tenuous evidence: 'Sanctions have been lifted and in this your Mr Menzies played, I imagine, some considerable part ... He made an extremely good, ante [sic]-sanction speech to the Empire Parliamentary Association'.[11] And after he had returned home, Menzies wrote to Eden to rejoice about views they held in common:

> There was an ancient legend about a mouse having helped a lion to get out of an awkward position. The recollection of this story emboldens me to say that you have no stronger or more willing supporter than myself, and that I hope that if on any future occasion you feel that a supporting public opinion in this Dominion would be of value to you, you will not hesitate to communicate with me. I also hope that you will, under no circumstances, permit the Beaverbrooks and other newspaper Bumbles to get you out of the superb habit of occasionally laughing at your troubles.[12]

Soon after his arrival in London Menzies had moved into a small flat on the ground floor of no. 7 Park Place, a few doors off St James's Street. It was most conveniently placed, within easy distance of Green Park, Buckingham Palace and Whitehall and even, at least for an enthusiastic walker like Menzies, the Strand and Australia House. A blind street, Park Place was reasonably quiet, the flat had a good sitting room, bedroom and bathroom, 'and although I found Brown's Hotel very good in an old-fashioned way, I am not sorry to be able to get all my things unpacked and feel that I have a castle of my own to which I can withdraw and do a little work'.[13] He was in fact quickly involved in somewhat more than 'a little' work. There were his two Privy Council cases to prepare for and he had always to be properly informed for his many official discussions with British ministers and civil servants: 'My days', he was soon writing, 'have been fully occupied at Australia House and in various conferences which have a strong family resemblance to the ones I took part in last year'.[14] Earle Page also arrived in London, sent by the Australian Ministry at a point of crisis in trade relations, again on the never-ending

---

[11] Bill Austruther-Gray to Hawker, 15 July 1936, NLA, MS. 4848/3/6/iii–iv.
[12] Menzies to Eden, 18 August 1936, AA CP450/7/1, bundle 5, f. 242.
[13] Menzies to Pat, 27 March 1936, Menzies Family Papers.
[14] Ibid., 9 April 1936.

question of meat exports to Britain, and he gladly roped Menzies into the negotiations. The two also talked with the British authorities on a range of other matters, of which the most important were the development of the Empire airmail service and plans for establishing aircraft manufacture in Australia. At the end of May Menzies, having determined to leave for home on the *Strathaird* on 28 June wrote home complaining how 'the rate at which you can get negotiations finished in London is extremely slow'.

> We have yet to conclude our discussions on air mail, aircraft manufacture, marketing problems generally, and three or four minor matters. Practically all of them are at present in a very rudimentary state of progress, and as the Whitsun holidays will make it practically impossible to get anything done next week, . . . you will see that I am coming to the conclusion that when I leave I will probably have to abandon Earle Page to conduct the negotiations alone. Of course, the longer one is available in London, the more people come in who discuss new matters, and I am already so heartily sick of being an exile from my own family that my sailing date, from that point of view, cannot come too soon.[15]

As before, the trade talks were the most difficult of Menzies' encounters with the British. In the Cabinet in Canberra the feeling was strong that the Ministry's very survival might depend on winning significant concessions for some interests believed to be essential for UAP and Country Party support in the electorates. For Australian wheat and wool, whose external markets were relatively wide, preference in Britain was less crucial than for meat, dairy and other farm products which were almost totally dependent on the British market. Meat was especially important. New horizons were developing as technological advances increasingly facilitated the long-distance carriage of chilled beef, far superior to and more lucrative than established exports of frozen meat. There was also the complicated question of placating pressure groups like the Chambers of Manufactures by finding ways of encouraging Australian 'import replacement' in secondary industry without breaching those sections of the Ottawa agreements which promised British manufactures 'reasonable' competitiveness.[16] Indirectly related were some aspects of trade with the United States. Motor cars were the most important case. Since American vehicles suited Australian conditions far better than

---
[15]Ibid., 28 May 1936.
[16]Kosmas Tsokhas, *Markets, Money and Empire: The Political Economy of the Australian Wool Industry* (Melbourne 1990), 95.

others, they had won the lion's share of the local market. That both embarrassed English exporters and was the major element in a serious imbalance of payments between Australia and the United States, exacerbated, as that was, by the fact that America had a prohibitive duty on wool imports. It had become an issue whether government could curb American imports to divert the trade more to the British while at the same time encouraging local manufacture of chassis and bodyworks, preferably through American and British investment and participation in Australian industry.

Page arrived in London just as Britain was about to sign a new trade treaty with Argentina, Australia's great rival in the meat trade. He and Menzies insisted that no treaty should be finalized without Australian approval, and tense talks began. Inevitably these also involved the Lyons Government's recent 'trade diversion' moves against Japan, which it depicted as an attempt to aid Lancashire's textile manufacturers. Japanese imports had progressively made serious inroads on Britain's traditional Australian market for rayon and cotton goods: to stem the tide, the Government now placed heavy restrictions on the trade in these items. Australia bought this curb on Japanese trade at high cost: Japan retaliated by boycotting Australian wool and a period of great unease began between the Lyons Government and powerful grazier and broker lobbies. Menzies wondered, somewhat artlessly, whether the British would agree to 'an international rayon conference to be appointed in Australia to enable Lancashire and Japan to sit down with one another and to divide up the available market between them'.[17] But old stagers like Gullett and Bruce had little time for such finesse: the real issue for them was how best to use trade diversion as a weapon in the negotiations with Britain. At the height of the controversy with Japan Gullett impressed on Page how closely—and critically—the two questions were related:

> ... we have got the greatest Press we have ever had on anything—but of course we could be entirely lost on the whole matter if we did not get restriction on foreign beef. Every Australian Newspaper has rallied to the Government, and this Japanese question has submerged everything else; if we get a set-back now, probably the Government will go.[18]

On 12 June Malcolm MacDonald, Secretary of State for the Dominions, informed Page and Menzies that the British Cabinet had just decided on a new proposal: that a moderate duty should

---
[17]D. C. S. Sissons, 'Manchester v Japan: the Imperial Background of the Australian Trade Diversion Dispute with Japan, 1936', *Australian Outlook*, 30 (1976), 496-7.
[18]Quoted in Tsokhas, *Markets, Money and Empire*, 109.

be imposed on foreign beef and that Dominion beef should be let in free, provided that for two years imports from both the Argentine and the Dominions be fixed at their present levels. Lyons reacted with a violent cable which denounced the proposal as 'totally unacceptable'. 'I am not exaggerating', he said, 'when I say that if your Government's proposals made to Page and Menzies were published in Australia national sentiment would be deeply shocked and the whole trade diversion policy and my Government would be placed in a hazardous position'.[19] In the upshot the British set a quota and a heavier duty on foreign meat, reiterated that Dominion meat should be duty free and substantially increased the Australian quota for the next three years.[20]

Menzies had no choice other than to back Page and his other Cabinet colleagues in pressing their sometimes harsh tactics. That, however, did not mean that he either liked these tactics or approved of the conflict with Japan. As he wrote to his father when that conflict was at its height:

> Our political negotiations have not been altogether happy. Page has discovered what we learned last year, which is that the problem of the British Government in dealing with our meat exports and reconciling our interests with the interests of the British grower and of British foreign trade is not easy ... On the whole, my feeling is that the sooner one gets back to Canberra the better for I am not at all satisfied that we are not too rapid over things on which we ought to be slow and far too slow over things on which we ought to be prompt and clear.[21]

A formal agreement with Japan on acceptable quotas for textile imports into Australia and wool exports from Australia to Japan was finally reached in January 1937. The negotiations were delicate and labyrinthine, involving private as well as ministerial intermediaries. As Attorney-General, Menzies played some part in the discussions, chiefly as one of a Cabinet committee of four set up in October 1936 to maintain liaison on the Japanese dispute with a Special Wool Advisory Committee, consisting of three top leaders of graziers' and woolbrokers' organizations. By keeping these men informed of what was going on, and allowing their opinion to be registered, the Government managed to persuade the interest which was in fact suffering most from its policy not to criticize it publicly. Throughout, Menzies was of course loyal to the Government line but he almost certainly had misgivings about Gullett's diplomacy and the whole trade diversion policy.

[19] Ibid., 108.
[20] Page, *Truant Surgeon*, 244.
[21] Menzies to Father, 24 June 1936, Menzies Family Papers.

The diary of J. P. Moffatt, the United States consul-general, suggests that this was understood on the Canberra grapevine by February 1937:

> 11 & 12 February 1937 ... Squire also picked up from Townsend, who was with Page and Menzies in London last year, the story of the trade diversion measures from that angle. He said that Menzies had disliked it from the beginning ...[22]

A. R. Townsend was an officer of the Department of Trade and Customs, who as part of the negotiating team must have been privy to Menzies' opinions.

'Work' in London also included something Menzies had never set out to do before: the writing of a book. He was assiduous, if nervous about it. On 3 April, for example, early in his stay, he recorded having 'remained in my flat for the whole of the weekend, doing some writing on the proposed book, which is making slow but steady headway though, I dare say, when I have finished it I will decide not to publish it but to keep it as a sort of skeleton in the family cupboard'.[23] Later, when saying how much he hoped that his weekly letters home would serve the family as an adequate record of his doings, Menzies added: 'I am afraid that I have not been writing a diary this time; any spare time I have has been devoted to licking last year's diary into shape'.[24] That was it: the spell of 1935 was still upon him and the urge to share it irresistible. 'Licking' the diary 'into shape' did not mean editing it for publication itself—that, he wrote, 'would be too personal'—but rather writing a book 'based upon it'. Since the diary is an attractive, spontaneous document, the decision not to publish it was perhaps an unhappy one. But, equally, Menzies' instinct to refrain from giving the public the manuscript he did ultimately produce was fortunate. It might just have gained an appreciative audience in its own time, though its almost jejune tone might not have gone down well even then; but it would certainly not have stood the test of time and would have been a gift to the great tribe of his later mockers.

Menzies chose for the book the title 'Jubilee Pilgrim', and explained in a subtitle that it was 'some account of the voyage of an Australian to England and Scotland and of his sojournings there

---

[22] Quoted by D. C. S. Sissons, 'Private Diplomacy in the 1936 Trade Dispute with Japan', *Australian Journal of Politics and History*, 27:2 (1981), 151. This paragraph draws on Sissons' article generally, also Tsokhas, *Markets, Money and Empire*, 111–18.
[23] Menzies to Pat, 3 April 1936, Menzies Family Papers.
[24] Ibid., 23 April 1936.

in the great year 1935 when King George V came to his jubilee'. In it he expressed a wish to improve Australians' and Englishmen's knowledge of each other 'which is the beginning of all wisdom and understanding'; but for the most part explanation is subordinate to, or simply implicit in, description, especially of travels and of 'the educated Englishman of London'. The manuscript moves between different levels of seriousness and jocularity, with bursts of astounding naivete, and it was indeed wise to leave it as a skeleton in the family cupboard.[25]

The 'great case',[26] James v. the Commonwealth, began in the Privy Council on 4 May. It was to continue for nine subsequent sittings, the last on 19 July. The minor case—Payne v. Commissioner of Taxation—followed immediately, over the two days 21 and 22 May. In the major case two South Australian barristers, Wilfred Barton and Kevin Ward, appeared for James, and Sir Stafford Cripps for the Tasmanian and Western Australian governments. (Menzies regarded Cripps as his most formidable opponent. He had met Cripps socially several weeks before the case began, and found him 'a very pleasant man', though he could not forbear making one mordant remark for the family: 'Cripps is, as you know, regarded as one of the more extreme Socialist leaders ... but like so many eminent Socialists here, he sees his dreams of a future Socialist state through the rosy spectacles of an income of £15,000 a year'.)[27] On the other side, the New South Wales Attorney-General, Henry Manning, appeared for his Government and that of Queensland. Menzies, as Commonwealth Attorney-General appeared for the Federal Government and was also briefed to appear for Victoria. The one appearance in practice served both purposes and, while Menzies as Attorney-General received no remuneration from the Commonwealth, Victoria was to pay him a fee.

Barton opened the case and Menzies was momentarily cheered: his opponent, he thought, 'never succeeded in getting on top of his material, and when he finished ... left the Privy Council in a state of considerable confusion as to what the precise issues were'.[28] Cripps followed, explaining that Tasmania and Western Australia were concerned with the broader interpretation of Section 92 rather than with the particular legislation which was being challenged. In a lucid and hard-hitting address he declared

---

[25]Menzies Family Papers include a typescript copy of the MS.
[26]Menzies to Pat, 8 May 1936, Menzies Family Papers.
[27]Ibid., 23 April 1936. A brilliant barrister, Cripps had been elected Labour member for East Bristol in 1931. An ardent socialist, has was the hero of Labour Party militants on the left wing.
[28]Ibid., 8 May 1936.

that while in the wording of Section 92 there was no qualification to the assertion that trade between the States should be 'absolutely free', in Section 51, which gave the Commonwealth power over trade and commerce, there was. This power was given 'subject to the Constitution'. Cripps argued that, since Section 92 was part of the Constitution, it overrode Section 51 and so denied the Commonwealth the power to put any impediment whatever upon trade between the States.[29]

Menzies was impressed: 'Sir Stafford Cripps has an admirable delivery and style, and when he sat down my prospects were not as good as they had been a day or two earlier, at least three of their lordships showing a strong disposition to be against me'. But after replying to Cripps, he felt better: 'I am glad to be able to say that I have never been in better form in Court, ... had a really excellent hearing and, when I finished my argument, ... even the other side were prepared to agree that we have at least as good a chance of winning as they have'.[30] Menzies' principal argument was that in its origins Section 92 was about border duties and the need for intercolonial free trade: as the words in the Constitution had it, 'on the imposition of uniform duties of customs, trade, commerce and intercourse among the States, whether by means of internal carriage or ocean navigation, shall be absolutely free'. But what the Privy Council was being asked to determine was something quite different: whether the Commonwealth had the power to legislate to establish schemes of marketing for the whole country. Previous verdicts, won by James, had confirmed the powerlessness of the States in this matter. If the Commonwealth was similarly judged 'the result would be that the totality of power in Australia will prove to be less than the totality of power in other civilized countries'.[31] The Privy Council gave its decision on the Payne case on 24 June: in Menzies' favour, as he had expected. But it did not deliver the verdict on James's case until 12 July and by then Menzies was at sea on his way home. In mid-June he had flown to Holland via Paris, conferring at the Hague with the Dutch Prime Minister, Dr Colijn, and the President of the Permanent Court, Sir Cecil Hurst.[32] A week later he boarded the *Strathaird* at Marseilles, having flown to Paris first to make a speech at the International Chamber of Commerce. We do not know when he first heard the Privy Council's verdict or what his reactions were. But he must have been disappointed.

[29] 55 *CLR* (1936), 17–19.
[30] Menzies to Pat, 14 May 1936, Menzies Family Papers.
[31] 55 *CLR* (1936), 20–36.
[32] Menzies to Father, 24 June 1936, Menzies Family Papers.

In a 25-page judgment their Lordships concluded that Section 92 *did* apply to the Commonwealth. So the Dried Fruits Act was invalid, and so too was a range of other existing legislation on the marketing of primary products. It was a verdict delivered a little sadly, given that it prevented the Commonwealth from controlling prices and markets 'even though ... satisfied that such a policy is in the best interests of the Australian people'. But the Privy Council saw its task as being to interpret the Constitution, not to rewrite it. And in that process 'the true test must, as always, be the actual language used'. The intentions of the Constitution's framers might certainly be ascertainable, but 'new and unanticipated conditions of fact arise'. In 1898–1900 the Constitution makers were certainly thinking of border tariffs and were anxious to eliminate them. However,

> they presumably did not anticipate those commercial and industrial difficulties which have in recent years led to marketing schemes and price control, or traffic regulations such as those for the co-ordination of road and rail services, to say nothing of new inventions, such as aviation or wireless. The problems, however, of the Constitution can only be solved as they emerge by giving effect to the language used.[33]

So decisive a rejection of his chief argument made this a signal defeat for Menzies. He could, however, draw some comfort from the fact that in their final remarks their Lordships expressed their 'appreciation of the help given to them by the counsel who have argued in this appeal, in particular the Attorney-General for the Commonwealth, the merit of whose admirable argument is in no way diminished because it has not succeeded'. But there was one notably unpleasant political side issue to the case. At home, a month before it came on, Blackburn moved an adjournment in the House of Representatives to discuss the propriety of Menzies representing Victoria as well as the Commonwealth before the Privy Council. Victoria was to pay a fee of 200 guineas, said Blackburn, but for Menzies to accept this would involve a breach at least of the spirit of the Constitution. For the Constitution prohibited, on pain of forfeiting his seat, any member of the House of Representatives from taking a fee for services rendered to the Commonwealth. Since Menzies would be presenting the one case for both Commonwealth and Victoria, it would be improper for him to receive any fee. If he did, he would be being paid merely to say 'the State of Victoria concurs with the Commonwealth's argument'. Curtin supported Blackburn but Hughes, Holt and

---

[33] 55 *CLR* (1936), 44.

Lyons asserted Menzies' right of private practice and indignantly denied that there was anything improper in his accepting the Victorian brief.[34]

Behind the scenes, however, the ministers felt some unease at Blackburn's attack. At Easter, just after the incident in the House, Lyons took a break in Tasmania, and on his return to Canberra was approached on the 'delicate question' of Menzies' fee by Senator Tom Brennan, the acting Attorney-General. Lyons and Brennan then consulted Casey, and Lyons, as was his normal wont, talked the matter over with his wife. All agreed that as Prime Minister Lyons should write privately to Menzies and urge him 'to accept a nominal fee only from Victoria'. Lyons duly wrote the letter, in his own hand, on 26 April 1936. He put the proposal gingerly for Menzies' consideration, representing it purely as a matter of strategy. 'I agreed with your action in the first place and did my best to justify it in the House, and I still agree with it.' But there was a danger that 'your name may be bandied about on the hustings in an atmosphere of untruth, misrepresentation, exaggeration, etc, some of which at least may find acceptance in the minds of the electors'. This would be bad for the party and could be worse for Menzies himself:

> The day must come when, in the ordinary course of events, the leadership of the Party will devolve on you. You have in a comparatively short time established a position in our public life without parallel in the recent annals of Australia. It would be a national calamity if an opportunity should be given to our opponents to dim the lustre of your reputation by distortion of a position which on purely moral and legal grounds is unassailable. No monetary advantage could compensate you, *or Australia*, for that.

Then came what seemed the unequivocal promise that Menzies must surely have assumed since having originally been lured into the federal arena and then elected to the deputy leadership of the party: 'for some time I have felt that the time had come for you to step into my shoes both because you should be given the opportunity to use your talents for Australia's benefit and because I feel that I have done a pretty good job ... and am entitled to a rest'. Though foiled so far by officials in the party organization, who 'always seem to think that I bring in something to the voting strength', Lyons promised now to press for the changeover as soon as Menzies returned.[35]

---

[34]*CPD*, 149: 685ff. Harold Holt, a 22-year-old Melbourne lawyer, Young Nationalist and protégé of Menzies, had recently entered parliament, having won the Fawkner seat at a by-election.
[35]Lyons to Menzies, 26 April 1936, Menzies Family Papers.

Menzies' response to this letter seems not to have survived, but neither of the possibilities it canvassed was realized. Lyons continued in office and Menzies, it seems, took the fee. When he came home his enemies in parliament pursued him again on this question but now Menzies could reply in person and the leader of the attack was the strident Frank Brennan rather than the civilized Maurice Blackburn. After Cripps, Brennan was easy meat and Menzies demolished him with relish. Quoting previous cases on Section 92 Brennan accused Menzies of going to England to 'whip a dead horse', denounced him for arguing in the court a view opposite to one he had presented in the *Australian Law Journal* in 1928 and asked whether Menzies spoke before the Privy Council 'as a private advocate drawing a fee from the State of Victoria or as a Public Trustee for the Commonwealth'. Menzies replied that the arguments he presented followed the instructions of the Governments of Victoria and of the Commonwealth. There had been no complaint from either of his clients, and on this matter and on the charges of inconsistency with his previous cases and writings, Menzies read Brennan an eloquent—and contemptuous—lesson on the duties of an advocate:

> When a man goes into Court as an advocate his own views do not matter. He has no right to have his own views in his mind. He is there to represent his client... When an Attorney-General goes into Court to argue on behalf of the Crown, he has exactly the same duty as any other advocate. He owes to his client all the zeal, all the industry, all the honesty, all the skill that he possesses. If he allows his own personal views and prejudices to cloud the submission that he will make, then he fails in his duty as an advocate. If it were not so—if an advocate presenting a case were at liberty to say 'I will not have that because I hold views to the contrary'—he would be acting as a judge rather than as an advocate.[36]

Menzies arrived back in Australia on 28 July and at once plunged into a punishing round of writing, public speaking, departmental work and—after the House reconvened on 10 September—parliamentary duties. Summing it all up, he wrote in October to Keith Officer in London:

> ... I have been almost painfully loquacious on political platforms, to say nothing of having to do a tremendous amount of parliamentary work. People out here seem to think that an official trip to England

[36] *CPD*, 151: 702ff., 770.

A *Table Talk* photographer captures in 1936 a happy family group: the Menzies on holiday at 'Illira'.

qualifies one for omniscience. Although I am afraid I have done nothing to foster such a reputation I am still being asked to speak on every subject under the sun.[37]

---

[37]Menzies to Officer, 12 October 1936, AA CP450/7/1, bundle 4, f. 178.

The disavowal was disingenuous: Menzies in fact courted and revelled in such 'omniscience'. Before leaving London he wrote five articles to go ahead of him to the *Argus*; articles drawing on his 'exceptional opportunities of hearing at first hand the views of many British statesmen, publicists and men of affairs'.[38] These had for their subjects the future leaders of Great Britain, the League, Germany, France, and British public opinion.[39] 'In them', he told Officer, 'I make various observations about people which you may regard as tactless. I did this because I felt that there was a great educational value in a lively first-hand account of people and things that are important to Australia'.[40]

In the many talks he gave during the month after his return, Menzies naturally varied his emphasis according to the audience: folk at the Pleasant Sunday Afternoon heard mostly about his sentiments on visiting the Roman Wall in Northumberland;[41] the Chamber of Manufactures was told how his experiences in England convinced him that received views of Australia's position in world trade needed drastic revision.[42] But there were key themes which always broke through. The most important was also the simplest: that the world was on the brink of war and that was primarily to be attributed to the decline of democracy. Britain was rearming, but 'nobody in Europe believes that Great Britain threatens war against anybody'. The preservation of peace depended on others doing 'what I believe Great Britain is doing—preserving balance, sanity and judgement'. That could happen only in democracies, where private citizens could say what they thought and press their views on the governments that ruled them. That was all the more reason for the British self-governing Dominions to rally to the peace-preserving causes of the motherland: they also had a responsibility to see that their democratic institutions were safe and in good working order. In Australia that meant that there must be less apathy and more individual participation in public affairs: 'The price of democracy is the energy with which we as democrats are prepared to work the machinery that has been given to us'.[43]

His not always happy experience of trying to negotiate trade agreements in Britain lay behind another of Menzies' preoccupations at this time: advocacy of a vigorous resumption of British

[38] *Argus*, 1 August 1936.
[39] Ibid., 1–6 August 1936.
[40] Menzies to Officer, 18 August 1936, AA CP450/7/1, bundle 5, f. 242.
[41] *Argus*, 7 September 1936.
[42] Ibid., 14 August 1936.
[43] Ibid., 10 August 1936.

RECRUITS WANTED.
(A Victorian Laborite suggests that the poster would be more effective.)

In the 1930s travel takes time, is costly and raises eyebrows when, as in the long-drawn-out trade talks of these years, the necessity for a ministerial presence at negotiations abroad is difficult to demonstrate. So, in the popular press, trips become junkets.

migration to Australia. He told the Chamber of Manufactures that Australia should aim immediately to create a population of twenty millions by the middle of the century. Two successive years of involvement in talks about the export of Australian products had convinced him that the United Kingdom 'does not present an unlimited market for us'. And 'the moment you begin negotiating for markets in other parts of the world you are met by negotiations on the well-known gastronomic axiom, 'a cutlet for a cutlet'. Thus we are more and more driven to consider our own market—and that means population. He was sceptical of land settlement schemes run by governments as a means of promoting immigration; busy factories were needed 'and a growing population supplied and maintained by its own efforts'.[44]

One aspect of Menzies' admiration of British governmental practice which now spiced his public utterances about democracy was the respect he had developed for the upper echelons of the British civil service. Two official London visits, in which he had come into regular contact with these superior beings, convinced him that accepted practice in the Australian civil service needed drastic revision. Very few senior positions were open for proper competition or appointment from outside the service. Having negotiated with and been entertained by men like Vansittart he forgot others whose obscurantism had irritated him on his earlier trip and told his Melbourne audiences how in England he had been impressed by

> the high calibre of the public service. The Government there was willing to pay large salaries to large men. Yet when it had been decided recently to reserve a proportion of places in the Commonwealth civil service to university graduates there had been an outcry by so-called democrats against the creation of a privileged class. If the placing of the best educated and most intelligent members of the community in the service of the country was the creation of a privileged class, he was all in favour of it (Applause).[45]

Among the many statements of opinion Menzies made at this time by far the most controversial were on art. Scarcely a month after his return he opened an exhibition by the portraitist, William Rowell, and in doing so bought aggressively into the smouldering controversy in the Melbourne art world between a traditionalist establishment and artists who were seeking inspiration from 'modernist' work abroad.[46] During his recent travels, said Menzies, he had been to the Louvre, to Dutch galleries and to exhibitions in London where he had seen the work of surrealists. 'I can say that I have seen some of the greatest pictures in the world and also those that must undoubtedly be amongst the worst'. Rowell's work, he thought, was of high quality 'when contrasted to the

[44] Ibid., 14 August 1936.
[45] Ibid., 25 August 1936.
[46] Of the numerous and excellent accounts of this controversy see, e.g., Bernard Smith, *Australian Painting, 1788–1960* (Melbourne 1962), 205–25; June Helmer, *George Bell: the Art of Influence* (Richmond 1985), 81–92; Humphrey McQueen, *The Black Swan of Trespass* (Sydney 1939), 26–42; Geoffrey Serle, *From Deserts the Prophets Come* (Melbourne 1973), 159–66. 'Modernist' influences went as far back as Van Gogh and included Picasso, Matisse and Braque.

singularly ill-drawn pictures of "modern" art, described by their authors as having a symbolic value unintelligible to the unilluminated mind. My own Philistine philosophy is that there can be no great art without great beauty'.[47] He had privately expressed what this philosophy meant to him when, on his first visit to London, he had gone to the opening of the Royal Academy. 'Great disappointment', he told his diary, 'and not unlike Victorian Artists. Query: Do they really reject anybody's work? Fifty per cent of the stuff on the walls looked like the efforts of untrained inebriates'.[48]

This melancholy experience did not, however, still a conviction Menzies had developed that Australia needed an Academy of Art (preferably 'Royal'). In February 1936, before leaving again for London, he had had talks with artist friends about the establishment of such an Academy, the object being to create the means for artists throughout Australia 'to speak with one voice on important matters associated with art'.[49] Conferring subsequently in England with officials of the Royal Academy and of the Dominions Office, he came home as keen as ever to see an Australian Academy founded, and confident that he now knew all the formalities through which this might be done.[50]

What gave a particular purport to Menzies' aggressive remarks at the Rowell opening was the freshening up, during his absence, of the art controversy in Melbourne, in which two incidents were especially important. The first was the publication in May of an article, by the respected Melbourne artist and teacher, George Bell, which denounced Academies as bodies that 'use every means in their power to defend art and themselves from any discovery made by an original thinker'.[51] The second was an address by Justice H. V. Evatt when opening in June an exhibition of paintings by Adrian Lawlor. Lawlor was an experimentalist whose previous exhibition, in 1930, had been greeted by George Bell as 'the first one-man show, by a local artist, of pictures painted in the mode of thought current in the art world for the last forty odd years'.[52] In opening the 1936 exhibition, Evatt said that 'Australia lagged far behind the standard of art in England, America and Europe'.

---

[47]*Argus*, 25 August 1936.
[48]Menzies' Diary, 3 May 1935, NLA, MS. 4936/13.
[49]*SMH*, 7 February 1936.
[50]*Argus*, 27 June 1936.
[51]Bell, in Bernard Smith's words (*Australian Painting*, 215), 'had worked out his own aesthetic position, not without difficulty, during a lifetime'. He wrote the quoted words in an article published in the *Sun* of 16 May 1936 (Helmer, *George Bell*, 84).
[52]Helmer, *George Bell*, 67.

He attributed this 'chiefly to the fact that our national galleries are controlled by men who suffer from an intense abhorrence of anything that has been done since 1880'.[53]

In October 1936 the President of the Sydney-based Society of Artists, Sydney Ure Smith, announced the imminent formation of a Royal Australian Academy of Art, which would have its headquarters in Canberra, and hold annual exhibitions in Sydney and Melbourne.[54] Provisional committees formed in Sydney and Melbourne were soon working on a constitution but by early 1937 a variety of dissensions had become evident. The conservative–modernist controversy lay behind some but by no means all of them. A tangle of personal, institutional and interstate jealousies was also involved. The Sydney committee resented what it saw as Melbourne's arrogance; there were quarrels about methods of election to the Academy and the failure of the prime movers to consult all art societies; in Melbourne Bell led an outcry against the alleged secrecy and selectivity of the organizing committee there.[55] At first Menzies treated these squabbles as a storm in a teacup. He was not, he said, concerned about the organizational details of bringing the Academy into being: what mattered was that it should be formed, so that it could carry out tasks like representing Australian artists overseas, or arranging exchange exhibitions with its counterparts in Britain and Canada.[56] He was in fact to have his way in mid-1937, when at a meeting he presided over in Canberra, the Academy was launched. There were fifty foundation members from the leading art societies and a Council of ten, representing between them all the States. But conservatives predominated on the Council, and the birth of the organization was preceded by such controversy that its hopes of flourishing and of representing the art world in general were not bright.

The most publicized squabble followed a speech Menzies made when launching, early in 1936, another art show, the Victorian Artists' Society's annual exhibition to which, by invitation, a handful of 'modernist' painters from the Melbourne Contemporary Art Group contributed. He repeated provocatively the sentiments he had expressed some months before at the Rowell opening. Exhibitions of Academies in other countries, Menzies observed, had raised the standards of public taste by directing attention to good work. It was evident from this exhibition that the Victorian Society

[53]*Argus*, 3 June 1936. Evatt was a consistent champion of modern art. His wife, Mary-Alice, was an artist, one of George Bell's students.
[54]*SMH*, 27 October 1936.
[55]Ibid., 10, 15 February 1937 (note especially letter of Sydney Long); *Argus*, 6 March 1937; Helmer, *George Bell*, 85.
[56]*SMH*, 11 February 1937.

Menzies addresses a meeting of Victorian artists who have accepted invitations to become foundation members of the controversial Australian Academy of Art, 1937: (*from left*) Max Meldrum, James Quinn, Paul Montford, the Attorney-General, W. B. McInnes and Arnold Shore.

was encouraging people in every type of painting. But 'certain principles must apply to this business of art as to any other business which affects the artistic sense of the community. Great art speaks a language which every intelligent person can understand. The people who call themselves modernists today talk a different language'.[57] Many in the audience were shocked at these remarks and a vigorous press controversy followed. It began with a letter to the *Argus* from Norman MacGeorge, a landscape painter of the older generation who was nevertheless interested in modern art. Menzies' speech, he said, indicated that 'the "Royal Australian Academy", of which he admits the paternity, is obviously intended as a disciplinary measure to those whose conception of art is not his'.[58] Menzies' reply produced a great storm:

> Mr. Macgeorge [sic] has been misinformed about the object of the proposed Australian Academy. It is true, however, as Mr. Macgeorge claims, that I find nothing but absurdity in much so-called 'modern art', with its evasion of real problems and its cross-eyed drawing. It

[57] *Argus*, 28 April 1937, quoted by Smith, *Australian Painting*, 216.
[58] *Argus*, 1 May 1937.

is equally true that I think that in art beauty is the condition of immortality—a conclusion strengthened by an examination of the works of the great European masters—and that the language of beauty ought to be capable of being understood by reasonably cultivated people who are not themselves artists. I realise that an Academy should find room in its membership for all schools of artistic thought provided they are based on competent craftsmanship.[59]

'What does a layman know of craftsmanship or draughtsmanship?', asked George Bell, in a first unmannerly assault.

Anything new revolts the man of pedestrian mind. He finds it difficult to appreciate fully any form of expression to which he is not accustomed. Just as it would be ludicrous for an artist to argue a knotty point of law, so is it ludicrous for Mr Menzies to say what is good art and good drawing.[60]

While, on the other side, conservative artists, like Harold Herbert, sprang at once to Menzies' defence ('modern art ... is embraced by poor artists who need some outlet for their incompetence. I agree with everything that Mr Menzies has said'),[61] Menzies rose to Bell's bait with a reply that has been generally lampooned by historians of Australian culture—most of them whiggish in their working assumptions—as 'classically mistaken'.[62] 'Mr Bell', he wrote, 'is correct when he says that I am not a painter. He might be right when he says that I have a pedestrian mind. But in spite of these disabilities, the fact remains that I am a typical person of moderate education, and I hope of reasonably good taste, with a lifelong interest in the fine arts'. That such a person, as consumer, had the right to make judgements about which artists pleased him individually, and could in the process develop an understanding of artistic techniques, was the unexceptionable burden of Menzies' argument. Provoked by Bell's contemptuous words, however, he went on to make the extreme assertion that lay exhibition-goers and purchasers of his kind would be the class of people who would 'over the next 100 years, determine the permanent place which will be occupied in the world of art by those painting today'.[63] Bell's reply was to agree sardonically: 'Exactly—and if he could be here in a hundred years' time he would be wiser, and his opinion of these [modern] works would then no doubt more

---

[59] Ibid., 3 May 1937.
[60] Ibid., 4 May 1937.
[61] Ibid.
[62] Serle, *From Deserts*, 163.
[63] *Argus*, 5 May 1937.

nearly approach criticism'. But for taste and understanding to evolve properly, the danger of an Academy imposing restrictions had to be firmly resisted.[64]

Menzies' part in this argument, and his work to establish his Academy, have generally received a bad press. They are taken as evidence, variously, of his bourgeois taste, his conservatism, his arrogance, his worship of Imperial models and, in the words of Ure Smith, his being 'too influenced by pomp and ceremony, by the outward appearance, by "names" and "labels" as such'.[65] Each of these generalized charges may to an extent be sustained. That they express, and with the advantage of hindsight, an élitist view of art appreciation has, however, also to be clearly registered. Menzies had no specialized training in this field, as he admitted, but his sincerity in feeling that traditional art was superior to much contemporary art is not to be doubted. Nor is his ultimate right to say so, as well as the fact that a strong body of recognized art critics agreed with him. That that 'much' so often came to be interpreted as 'all' was due both to his opponents' readiness to misinterpret him and his own tendency to exaggerate in the heat of argument. Both as lawyer and politician Menzies was also prone to over-simplistic categorization, so that at times he missed subtle and often cantankerous gradations and groupings in the artistic world. These, quite as much as the broad 'modernist' *v.* 'conservative' dichotomy were a source of difficulty in getting the Academy off the ground and winning for it wholehearted support. There is no reason seriously to doubt the genuineness of Menzies' hope that an Academy would give Australian artists a voice abroad: his error was to think that artists could be easily organized and to assume that the issue of organization would not be muddied by doctrinal controversy. The timing of his main agitation about the Academy is also important: those feelings of 'omniscience' which he commented on to Officer generated zest and self-confidence in all he did in the first months after his return from England. For him there could be no doubting that the Academy was needed and its foundation correct and certain. He was not put off by the fact that colleagues like Henry Gullett had contrary views, as did influential opinion-makers like Keith Murdoch. And, if anything, his certainty about the need to combat some forms of modernism drew strength from their outspoken support by Justice H. V. Evatt.

---

[64]Quoted in Adrian Lawlor, *Arquebus* (Melbourne 1937), 39. This collection of documents and commentary on the controversy is generally regarded as a *tour de force*, though Humphrey McQueen (*Black Swan of Trespass*, 27–30) argues persuasively that, 'dazzling as Lawlor was as a polemicist, he had almost nothing to say'.

[65]Ure Smith to Norman Carter, 8 February 1938, quoted by McQueen, ibid., 27.

Evatt's complaint about conservatives controlling Australian galleries seemed well exemplified in Victoria when in September 1936 J. S. MacDonald was appointed Director of Victoria's National Gallery, Melbourne. Trained as a painter at Melbourne's Gallery Art School and in London, Paris and New York, MacDonald had been art critic on the Melbourne *Herald* and Director of the Sydney Gallery. He was a friend of Menzies and an arch-conservative of whom Menzies once wrote that 'his severe standards of judgement, his detestation of humbug and his rejection of the shoddy, were at once the delight of his friends and the tooth-grinding of his opponents'.[66] He arrived in Melbourne in good time to support Menzies on the Academy issue. The Victorian Cabinet, in exercising its prerogative to appoint the Director, overrode a recommendation of the Gallery Trustees that the post be offered to W. Hardy Wilson. This action caused a brief sensation and was never fully explained. It has been suggested that lobbying by Menzies was a factor in it, but that is doubtful in the extreme. Menzies himself wrote to MacDonald, 'when I saw that the Trustees had recommended somebody else I must confess that I saw no hope left. It was quite useless for me to approach the Victorian Government, which is not to be numbered among my warmest supporters'.[67] This was indeed true: Albert Dunstan, the radical leader of the Country Party, had in 1935 begun a long rule as Premier of Victoria, his Ministry initially supported by Labor. It was a combination that could happen only in Victoria, and one with whom co-operation by Menzies was unimaginable. Menzies had certainly tried to solicit votes in the Trustees' choice for the post, but in the final decision that was irrelevant.[68]

Menzies' reputation for conservatism in matters artistic derived from outbursts he personally made and then resolutely stood by. But on the other controversial cultural issue of those years, book censorship, his name was associated with a collective policy which in Cabinet he might influence but which in its final form he had to stand by, whether or not it fully reflected his private views. What went on in Cabinet we cannot know, but it does seem that Menzies was not a wholehearted abetter of the extreme censorship for which the Lyons Government came to stand.

[66]Foreword, J. S. MacDonald, *Australian Painting Desiderata* (Melbourne 1958), viii.
[67]Richard Haese, *Rebels and Precursors: the revolutionary years of Australian art* (Ringwood 1988), 53, makes the allegation of Menzies' lobbying. Menzies to MacDonald, 8 October 1936, NLA, MS. 430/4.
[68]Murdoch, who was one of the Trustees, had tried to get the post for his art critic on the *Herald*, Basil Burdett, but the Trustees had become deadlocked between him and MacDonald, and Hardy Wilson was chosen as a compromise candidate.

Regulations which dated back to Hughes's wartime prime ministership gave the Government extensive powers to ban the import of books on grounds of seditious intent or indecency. The Labor Government under Scullin had modified these powers but most were restored when Lyons came to power in 1932. By December 1933 sixty-six political works alone were banned: thirteen months later the number had swollen to 156, most of them Communist works, many of which freely circulated in Britain.[69] Late in 1934 a public reaction took place in Melbourne, when a group of intellectuals established a Book Censorship Abolition League. In conjunction with this League an evening newspaper, the *Star*, sponsored a great public debate on the issue in the Town Hall,[70] and the League opened a campaign of lobbying and petitioning. The League's President, W. Macmahon Ball, was a lecturer at the University of Melbourne who had in 1932 established for law and honours history students what became a celebrated course in Modern Political Institutions. His difficulty in getting past the censor books he needed for this course was the initial spur to his work in the formation of the League. Macmahon Ball had met Menzies at the University in the late 1920s. Both lived in Kew and both were enthusiastic walkers. They often took together the long walk along Victoria Parade into town, to their respective places of work. Macmahon Ball later recalled that foreign affairs and political theory were favourite subjects of discussion on these walks.[71]

Censorship was administered by the Commonwealth Customs Department, and its Minister, 'Tommy' White, was an avid and one-eyed anti-Communist censor, who treated Macmahon Ball's League with disdain. But when doubtful cases arose, the standard procedure was for Customs to refer to Attorney-General's, Menzies' Department, for advice. By 1934, after the Seventh Congress of the Comintern, the stress in Communist propaganda changed from advocating revolution to agitating for a common Democratic front against War and Fascism, thus ostensibly preaching peace and co-operation and taking a position which could hardly be called, in the technical legal sense, 'seditious'. Attorney General's began recommending the release of most Communist books and, when this happened, White ordered his officers to ban books without reference to Menzies' Department. Between

---

[69]Peter Coleman, *Obscenity, Blasphemy and Sedition* (Brisbane n.d.1963?), 110–11. Except where otherwise stated, Coleman is my authority for the account which follows of how the censorship system worked.

[70]Melbourne *Star*, Report of 'Public Debate Held in the Melbourne Town Hall 26 February 1935: "That Political Censorship Be Abolished" '.

[71]Personal interview with the late W. Macmahon Ball, 13 November 1985.

1933 and 1935 Customs banned about one hundred political books in this way. But late in 1937 Cabinet decided, presumably after disagreement between the Ministers concerned, that the Attorney-General's Department was superior to Trade in this matter and the books banned without reference to them were released.

Tensions between Trade and Attorney-General's departments were no doubt exacerbated by personal tensions between the two Ministers. On the censorship issue Menzies certainly lacked White's fanaticism. Herbert Burton, of the Council for Civil Liberties, described him in 1937 as a 'liberal influence in Cabinet'[72] and Macmahon Ball always remembered Menzies' reply to one request from him for an interview to discuss a number of books that had been banned. It was terse: 'Neither of us has time to waste. The banned books to which you refer will be unbanned in the morning'. And, as Macmahon Ball remembered it, they were.[73]

---

[72]Deputation on the banning of the *Napredak*, 9 November 1937, AA CRS A432/57/36/216.
[73]W. Macmahon Ball, interview, 13 November 1985.

9

The Narrow Squeak

AFTER MENZIES' return from England, in July 1936, there was a short parliamentary session, from September to the beginning of December. A recess till March was planned, but Lyons had briefly to recall parliament before Christmas to deal with the constitutional crisis which arose in Britain over King Edward VIII's wish to marry Wallis Simpson. It was out of the question for Mrs Simpson, a twice-divorced woman, to become queen. The British Cabinet dismissed the alternative of a morganatic marriage and the Dominion prime ministers all took the same view, Lyons being the most adamant of them.[1] When, as the alternative to giving up his attachment to Mrs Simpson, the King chose on 10 December to abdicate, special legislation was required in the United Kingdom to vary the succession to the throne, and the assent of Australia was required.[2] After some lively discussion, this was carried in parliament without division.

The most important political result of the abdication for Australia was indirect: in May 1937 the coronation of George VI took Lyons and two of his senior ministers to England where they stayed on for an Imperial Conference, the first to be held since 1930. Their absence, following the recent six-month trip of Menzies and Page, weakened the Government at a time of mounting difficulties and was an important factor in making 1937 a notoriously thin year for parliamentary sittings. Menzies hoped to be in the Prime Minister's party again, but Cabinet decided that he should not go this time. 'There is a general feeling', he wrote to an English friend in February 1937, 'that an unbroken year in

---
[1] Roy Jenkins, *Baldwin* (London 1987), 52.
[2] This was simply a matter of convention, in that Australia had not at this stage adopted the Statute of Westminster whose preamble required Dominion assent to such legislation. In a learned speech, Menzies as Attorney-General explained the position to the House.

Australia will be politically good for me, as we have a general election before December'.[3] In that election the omens for Government success were not good. With the removal of Lang as a threat, and an improvement in the economic outlook, the sense of crisis on which Lyons and the UAP had ridden to power was receding. The Government had won two elections, but could it take the third? Such a thing had not happened since the beginning of Commonwealth politics in 1901; and in 1937 the Lyons Ministry scarcely looked the right combination to break the record. It had developed no dynamic or coherent policy. The trade diversion conflict with Japan had offended some sections of the electorate. Its policy on book censorship, while pleasing to bourgeois conformists, had stirred formidable antagonism in intellectual circles. Under the bumbling Paterson, the Minister for the Interior, a damaging *cause célèbre* had eventuated through the prohibition of another 'immigrant', Mrs Mabel Freer, from entering the country. As Murdoch put it to a close friend in May, 'there has been a great and disastrous drift in political leadership'.[4] And on the other side, there were signs that a viable Labor Opposition was firming up. Scullin had retired and John Curtin, elected to replace him, headed in 1936 a newly united party, after Federal Caucus in February of that year readmitted the Lang Laborites.

The issue in the Freer case was not, as in the Kisch case, any supposed threat to Australia's security but one of moral censure. Cabinet solidarity held the other ministers behind Paterson, but Menzies, for one, disagreed profoundly with Paterson's actions and, while publicly keeping himself sternly in check, did all he could behind the scenes to right the wrong he was convinced had been done, and to persuade his colleagues of the damage the case was doing to their ailing political fortunes.

Mrs Freer arrived at Fremantle on the R.M.S. *Maloja*, from India, on 20 October 1936. Travelling on the same vessel was an Australian army officer, Lieutenant Dewar, who—as Paterson put it in an explanation to the House—had 'become entangled' with Mrs Freer, though he had a wife and child in Australia. Though Paterson did not say so, Dewar and Mrs Freer planned ultimately to marry. Mrs Freer was given a dictation test in Italian, on failing which she was declared a prohibited immigrant. When the *Majola* reached Sydney, Mrs Freer was allowed to land and trans-ship to a vessel bound for New Zealand. After repeated questions in

---

[3]Menzies to W. Trevor Watson, 25 February 1937, AA, CP450/7/1, bundle 6, f. 279.
[4]Murdoch to Clive Baillieu, 25 May 1937, NLA, MS. 2823/29.

parliament Paterson baldly declared on 11 November that 'information received from India was of such a nature as to indicate that Mrs. Freer was a person of undesirable character'. He refused to divulge the source of his information or to enlarge on what it consisted of.[5] Next day Jock Garden, the newly elected Lang Labor member for Cook, moved the adjournment to censure 'an arrogant Minister setting himself up as a censor of morals' and a long debate ensued, in which two UAP backbenchers, Holt and McCall, were bitter critics of the Minister.[6] On the same day, one G. P. Finlay, a solicitor engaged by Mrs Freer in Auckland, wrote to Menzies as Attorney-General to request an 'impartial consideration by some form of judicial tribunal' of the decision to exclude his client from Australia. Since no proper explanation had been given, he said, public speculation on the case had run wild:

> It was freely rumoured that Mrs Freer was an International Spy, that she was engaged in the White Slave Traffic, that she was a dope fiend. Indeed, the public imagined, and no doubt still imagines, that she is anything and everything that in its view would be alone sufficient justification for the peremptory [sic] harshness of the treatment she received ... To say, in such circumstances, that her character is ruined, is to phrase the position in moderate terms.[7]

But Cabinet turned down the request for an inquiry and upheld the exclusion.[8] The press had a field day at the Government's expense: Warwick Fairfax of the *Sydney Morning Herald* told Menzies that he could remember no previous issue on which the Australian press had shown such unanimity.[9] Throughout the controversy in parliament Menzies refused to be drawn, except when at question time on 17 November Garden asked him what legal remedies Mrs Freer had to test the action of the Minister in excluding her from Australia. Menzies replied that he was sure the House would excuse him 'from undertaking the task of giving legal advice to a private citizen who contemplates proceedings against the Crown'.[10] In Auckland Finlay meantime engaged a

---
[5]*CPD*, 152: 1659.
[6]Ibid., 1769–74.
[7]Finlay to Menzies, 12 November 1936, AA 432/1 36/360.
[8]Menzies to Finlay, 2 December 1936, ibid. The decision was made on Menzies' advice. He arranged for Lyons to see Finlay's letter and wrote 'I still think only two possible courses—first reversal former decision. Second sit tight and let controversy die away. I still prefer latter course of action. I cannot see how the Government could agree to a special investigation by special tribunal to meet purely individual case'. AA CP290/1/1, bundle 1, f. 16.
[9]Fairfax to Menzies, 5 April 1937, AA 43/119.
[10]*CPD*, 152: 1873.

barrister, Matthew Barnett, who, after writing officially to Menzies on the 'grave injustice' that had been done to Mrs Freer, sent a personal letter to inform him that

> Mrs. Freer is at present living quietly in Wellington a rather lonely and isolated existence, waiting until such time as I may be able to advise her on the prospects of the appeal which I promised to make on her behalf. She desires no compensation and will definitely undertake to make no claim for compensation, and to take no part in instigating legal proceedings, in the event of the prohibition against her entry into Australia being lifted.[11]

Menzies was spared further harassment in the House by the fact that parliament did not meet in the six months from the beginning of 1937 until July. In March he wrote confidentially to Barnett suggesting that if he came over to Australia, 'quite privately, yourself, and discussed this matter with me in three or four weeks' time', there was a distinct possibility of 'some useful position being achieved'. But he emphasized the need for privacy, since 'it is politically embarrassing for any of my colleagues to recede from an already adopted position because of newspaper clamour. Silence ... seems to me to be the only condition upon which any satisfactory outcome from this unhappy matter can be hoped for'.[12]

Whether Barnett came to Australia or not is unclear, but within a month Menzies brought the Freer case up again in Cabinet, seeking to have the ban lifted, without success.[13] He persisted, however, and on 2 June Cabinet did indeed decide that Mrs Freer could be admitted. The Melbourne *Herald*, in announcing the decision, reported a trans-Tasman telephone conversation with Mrs Freer, in which she said she had been in constant correspondence with Lieutenant Dewar, had an unchanged relationship with him, and would now come to Australia as soon as she could.[14] A little over a month later, on 12 July, she arrived in Sydney.

Why Cabinet made the decision it did is not recorded. But pressure from press and public, Menzies' lack of sympathy with the ban, his unsought contact with Mrs Freer's representatives and a general anxiety to hose down the political damage of the whole affair were of obvious importance. So too was the failure of Paterson's despairing attempts, after the event, to find precise evidence to damage Mrs Freer's reputation. These included urgent telegrams, all sent *after* the declaration of her status as a prohibited

---

[11] Barnett to Menzies, 18 February 1937, AA A432/1 36/360.
[12] Menzies to Barnett, 12 March 1937, 'Private and confidential', AA 43/119.
[13] Menzies to Barnett, 13 April 1937, ibid.
[14] *Herald*, 2 June 1937.

immigrant, seeking confidential reports on Mrs Freer's background and reputation from the Dominions Office, Scotland Yard and, through the Home Department there, of police in India. Precise information came to light about who Mrs Freer was, but nothing to her discredit emerged.[15] Nor do the files reveal anything conclusive about why the ban was imposed in the first place. It seems unlikely that Dewar's Australian wife had lodged a complaint. Dewar claimed that he and she were 'living apart and intend to do so for all time'. A report from the Indian police revealed, however, that Dewar, as a member of the Australian staff corps returning to Australia, had applied for two tourist tickets for himself and his wife, in lieu of the first-class government ticket to which he was personally entitled. The authorities disallowed this since their records showed that, in fact, Dewar's wife was already in Australia. Was this the incident which alerted wowserish authorities to the moral issue into which Paterson blundered?

The extent of the damage which the Freer case caused the Government can scarcely be exaggerated. Menzies took great trouble to counter it by writing personally to the many electors who privately intimated their disillusion.[16] More ominous, in April Warwick Fairfax warned Menzies that it was 'quite impossible for you to conduct any discussions with Mrs. Freer's representatives without the knowledge of the Press' and declared that in his view the Government ought to 'gain the maximum of credit by coming out into the open and making an immediate announcement that if Mrs. Freer returns to Australia she will be admitted'.

> If she decides to take legal action against the Commonwealth let her take it, and if she succeeds let the Government take its medicine like a man. I think it tolerably certain that it will have to take worse medicine at the Gwydir by-election and undergo a major operation later in the year.

Gwydir in New South Wales had been recently vacated when the sitting member, C. L. A. Abbott of the Country Party, was appointed as Administrator of the Northern Territory. The second ominous reference concerned the federal election due later that year. Fairfax added that he and his closest colleagues were 'getting severely alarmed at the Government's position and prospects ... It is going to prove difficult for the "Herald" to be of help to a Government in so far as it will not help itself, and I say this with every sympathy for your own position'.[17]

[15] AA CP290/1/1, bundle 1/96.
[16] See e.g. Menzies to G. A. R. Wilson, AA CP450/7/1, bundle 7, f. 295.
[17] Fairfax to Menzies, 1 April 1937, AA 43/119.

The Gwydir by-election came up early in May 1937, almost a month before Cabinet made its decision to admit Mrs Freer. The *Sydney Morning Herald* did not in fact follow Fairfax's implied threat to damage the Government but Labor nevertheless won the seat. This was for Labor the first electoral test after the amalgamation of its politically warring factions. A Lang candidate, W. J. Scully, stood for the seat. 'I am afraid we are in for a very tough struggle', Menzies wrote to Hawker. 'From what I hear the Lang man seems to be more than adequate. However, Lang is still a bogey in New South Wales and we shall see that his depredations are not forgotten by the electors'.[18] This was whistling in the dark. Curtin and Lang appeared on the same platform at Gunnedah on 13 April and though Lang briefly acted in character (Lyons, he said, was on his way to London with the most expensive delegation ever to leave Australia with the express mission of handing over Australian foreign policy 'absolutely to Downing Street')[19] the new alliance held. The appearance together of the two Labor leaders was in some sort an answer to Menzies' disbelief, expressed somewhat sneeringly two weeks earlier at the annual general meeting of the UAP, in 'any visible sign of the "united front" which Mr. Curtin and Mr. Lang had been talking about so profusely'.[20] The Labor victory was in fact mainly due to an extraordinary case of vote-splitting: the Country party, factionally divided, fielded three candidates. Even so, most of the press was inclined to read the defeat as a sharp rebuke to the Government. In view of the Gwydir result, wrote the *Age*, 'Federal Ministers could wisely engage in some severe self-analysis'. They were too aloof, too indifferent to public opinion and too dependent on the barren slogan 'Keep out Labor!': 'it is unreasonable to go on recalling the blemishes in the past record of opponents and expect intelligent people to respond to that appeal alone'.[21] Part at least of Fairfax's prediction about medicine seemed to have come true.

There had been an even more ambiguous reproof to the Government a month earlier when, by referendum, it tried to rescue the marketing system wrecked by the Privy Council's decision in the James case. Its main proposal was for a constitutional amendment to free Commonwealth marketing laws from the restrictions of the guarantee in Section 92 of interstate freedom of trade. The request was rejected by large majorities in every State. In fairness to the Government it has to be said that, once the campaign began, the

[18] Menzies to Hawker, 3 April 1937, AA CP450/7/1, bundle 8, f. 297.
[19] Adelaide *Advertiser*, 14 March 1937.
[20] Ibid., 2 March 1937.
[21] *Age*, 14 May 1937.

cross-currents of opinion were bewildering. Labor men who might have been expected to approve extensions of Commonwealth power resented the restriction to marketing alone, and there was some support for this view from the Government benches too. On the other hand, many State UAP and Country branches opposed the proposal from their almost instinctive reaction against any extension of federal power.[22] As Menzies put it when writing to a friend in England, 'marketing has the States by the ears, and, strangely enough, a large measure of the opposition is coming from the very section which the amendment is designed to help, id est the farmers'.[23] Again, describing the situation in South Australia, Hawker told his friend Duncan-Jones how the referendum campaign 'took all the early part of the year. We had visits from Menzies (2), Tom Paterson, Hardy and Lyons. All the time it was like hoeing in treacle'.[24] Despite the confusion, a writer in *Round Table* saw the result as an indication of the political malaise of the time:

> In the defeat of the referendum anti-Commonwealth sentiment was equalled by anti-Government feeling. The elector who is not bound to the Labour party by class-consciousness has scant opportunity of telling the Federal Government how much he dislikes some of its actions. While Mr. Lyons is respected everywhere, and deservedly retains a great measure of personal confidence, some of his Ministers are unpopular. The trade diversion policy, the book censorship, the exclusion of Mrs. Freer, and the unimpressive record of Ministers during the last two years reinforced the opposition, encountered by any referendum proposal, from people who desire to reject it because they distrust or dislike the Government that sponsors it.[25]

When parliament finally met in July 1937 Curtin, as Leader of the Opposition, deplored the long recess and wanted to know why Lyons's implicit promise that the session would begin in March had not been kept. Page, the Acting Prime Minister in Lyons's absence, offered a wishy-washy answer 'explaining' the delay in terms of the unexpected length of the referendum campaign and the lateness that year of Easter. In a hard-hitting speech on the

---

[22]Sawer, *AFPL* 2, 83, has an excellent brief analysis of the main cross-currents.
[23]Menzies to J. G. G. Kevin, 8 February 1937, AA CP450/7/1, bundle 6, f. 279.
[24]Hawker to Duncan–Jones, 20 April 1937, NLA, MS. 4847/7/4. Hawker spoke of a meeting in the Adelaide Town Hall when Menzies' 'claws' were well and truly out. He had asked Menzies to come over and help because 'people are committing themselves by driblets to oppose the referendum ... You can do a lot to check the rot. The Young Liberals have committed themselves to NO'. AA CP450/6/1, bundle 3, f. 35.
[25]*Round Table (RT)*, 27 (June 1937): 655–6.

Address in Reply, Curtin castigated the Government for its failure to allow parliament to debate a range of vital matters and he and his more outspoken followers taunted the Government on the loss of the referendum and of Gwydir, as omens of things to come.[26] Menzies warned Labor members not to 'shout too much about having won the Gwydir by-election, otherwise they will, in the opinion of the average person, resemble nothing so much as a man who, being entirely unaccustomed to the strong drink of success, has become inebriated by one small glass'.[27] And as the session quickly came to an end Hawker was reporting that

> things have run our way in the main. Labour is pretty divided. They arrived at Canberra very cocky after Gwydir but their tales [sic] lost some curl under fire in the House. The Lang crowd did not follow Curtin too well and the most was made of the leadership from behind. Menzies was less flippant and more ruthless and in that guise was more appreciated.[28]

The most important test, however, would be the election that still lay ahead. Lyons meantime arrived home, reaching Perth on 20 July. He confidently predicted victory for his Government and said that Cabinet meetings beginning in Sydney on the 27th would decide policy for the elections. He gave away only two significant political points. One was that during his four-month absence he had been in constant touch with his ministers on the subject of National Insurance and agreed with them that this matter must be proceeded with 'as rapidly as possible'. The other was that he had 'no intention of withdrawing from federal politics'.[29] A great UAP rally of 2500 people greeted Lyons and his wife with a standing ovation at the Melbourne Town Hall on 30 July and heard him assert his Government's endorsement of the message of the Commonwealth Prime Ministers' conference that, given 'the inherent dangers of the world situation', it was crucial to have 'an Empire strong and undivided, not as an instrument for war, but as an instrument for peace'. In this, as in all other matters, 'the United Australia party stands for all classes today, as it did when it was formed'.[30]

Until the election campaign formally began, Lyons made no other important public appearance, other than in parliament. Parliament reconvened on 24 August, to begin a session that lasted

---

[26]*CPD*, 153: especially 94–5.
[27]Ibid.
[28]Hawker to Duncan–Hughes, 11 July 1937, NLA, MS. 4847/7/4.
[29]*Argus*, 21 July 1937.
[30]Ibid., 31 July 1937.

only three weeks until it dissolved for the election, now fixed for 23 October. The most important business of this brief session was to hear Lyons's report to parliament on the Imperial Conference he had just attended. Defence had, predictably, been the Conference's most important preoccupation.[31] Given the threatening European situation, Britain was rearming and the Conference's concern was for the safety of the Empire as a whole. Its main conclusion was scarcely epoch-making: the best contribution each Dominion could make to general Imperial security was to exert itself to provide for the defence of its own region. And the underlying assumption was what it had been at earlier Imperial Conferences on defence—most notably those of 1923 and 1926—that naval power was for the whole Empire the crucial element of common defence. This was the 'blue water' strategy which Hankey had reasserted in his report on Australian defences in 1934 and which had clear policy implications. Expenditure on the navy must take priority over the other armed forces so that Australia could play its proper part in the task of keeping British sea-lanes open. But no one imagined that the tiny Australian navy (it consisted, by 1937, of four cruisers, four destroyers, one seaplane carrier and a few smaller vessels) could in reality meet by itself the naval threat with which large-scale war in the Pacific would confront the Commonwealth. So an essential element in the strategy was for Australia to be able to depend for protection on the larger British naval forces which could theoretically be based at Singapore. 'Theoretically', because in 1937 fortifications at Singapore had still to be completed and strong naval and air forces deployed there. In emphasizing his agreement with the stategy endorsed at the London conference, Lyons told the House:

> It is an unavoidable geographical fact that the first line of defence of the Commonwealth is naval, and if we expect a British fleet to be based on Singapore, as a safeguard to Australia, we must be prepared to co-operate and provide for the squadron necessary in our own waters. With such security provided, the enemy is kept at arm's length, our shores are made inviolate, and our overseas trade moves freely to its markets throughout the world.[32]

Curtin responded with a powerful speech which made it clear that defence would be a central issue in the coming election campaign. Already in debates of 1936–37 on the estimates for the

---

[31] The brief treatment which follows of Lyons's report on defence discussions and their background draws on *CPD*, 154: 21–37, *RT*, 28 (December 1937), 125–34, and J. M. McCarthy, *Australia and Imperial Defence 1918–39: a Study in Air and Sea Power* (St Lucia 1976).

[32] Quoted, *RT*, 28 (December 1937), 126.

Department of Defence he had challenged the Government's expenditure on the navy (in the three years to 1937 it was 45 per cent of the defence budget) and declared that 'the dependence of Australia upon the competence, let alone the readiness, of British statesmen to send forces to our aid is too dangerous a hazard' on which to found a defence policy. 'The Labor party's policy', he subsequently wrote, 'is against participation in foreign wars and for the reservation of all Australia's strength for the defence of the land in which we live'. This was the thrust of the argument with which he now confronted Lyons. Self-reliance, not dependence, was his party's watchword. That meant that costly naval units, which in a war could so easily be diverted for Imperial purposes other than the strict defence of Australia, should not be favoured at the expense of a sound supply and munitions system, a well trained and mobile army and, above all, a greatly expanded air force. And both army and air force should not be thought of as having any primary purpose other than the defence of the Australian continent: 'we on this side of the House insist that in the final analysis this nation shall not be committed to warlike activities outside Australia without the absolute and established consent of the Australian people'.[33]

In a gracious note to his son Kenneth, who with brother Ian was then a boarder at Geelong College, Menzies wrote on 2 September:

> I find myself becoming very tired of political affairs, and the prospect of having to go out electioneering all over Australia in the next month or two is a very depressing one. However, two of the best rays of sunlight in a politically gloomy world are at Geelong College.[34]

It was more than a mere gesture of affection. In a sometimes whimsical way, and despite his aggressive statements in public, Menzies was apprehensive about the coming election. He had, for example, written in late June to Keith Officer, who was now the Australian representative at the British Embassy in Washington, to tell him that Casey would be passing through on his way back from the Imperial Conference (in Casey's absence, Menzies had been Acting Treasurer):

---

[33] Ibid., 130. McCarthy, *Australia and Imperial Defence*, reveals that the Government was still sitting on Hankey's recommendation that the army should be reorganized for a dual purpose: to defeat any attack which fell short of full-scale invasion, and to be capable of expansion into an expeditionary force which could then be dovetailed into Imperial units. This would of course have been anathema to Labor. McCarthy is also most illuminating on traditional behind-the-scenes service jockeying for expenditure, principally between the army and the navy, both of whom tended to see the air force as ancillary to their operations.

[34] Menzies to Kenneth, 2 September 1937, AA CP450/7/1, bundle 6, f. 280.

I think I will be thoroughly relieved when Dick gets back from England. To be a Treasurer immediately before an election is to be the most unpopular man in Cabinet. When I am not being menaced I am being wooed with soft words and bombarded with persuasive letters, most of which come from W. M. Hughes. Dick, as you probably know, is returning via America. I envy him the trip, but judging by appearances here, it may be the last one he takes, officially, for some time.[35]

Curtin began the five-week electoral campaign by delivering Labor's policy speech at Fremantle on 20 September. Lyons would not launch the UAP campaign until the 28th, but it was arranged that Menzies would immediately give a nationwide broadcast replying to Curtin's speech.[36] Curtin catalogued the Lyons Government's broken promises and declared that the return to 'prosperity' which it claimed to have achieved in reality affected only the privileged few: '... the maldistribution of the fruits of prosperity has never been greater in the history of the country'. Labor would introduce unemployment insurance, establish a system of pensions for widows with dependent children and 'take every legislative step' to establish a 40-hour week. In line with what he claimed to be the main thrust of the report of the recent Royal Commission on monetary and banking systems, Curtin promised that Labor would legislate to restore to the Commonwealth bank control of the nation's credit, and to the people control of the Commonwealth bank. On his other major preoccupation, defence, Curtin reiterated the position he had by now explained on many occasions. Industries must be built up 'until every possible requirement to self defence could be supplied within the Commonwealth'. Far less stress must be placed on naval arrangements and far more on the air force as the key element in local defence.[37]

In a somewhat lacklustre reply Menzies denounced Curtin's promised social services and public works as inflationary, denied the claim that Labor's banking policy was endorsed by the Royal Commission's report, and asserted that the 40-hour week was a matter for arbitration courts, not parliament. With heavy-handed humour he made fun of Curtin's demand that the Australian people must give their consent before the nation should be committed to warlike activities outside Australia:

[35] Menzies to Keith Officer, 21 June 1937, AA CP450/7/1, bundle 8, f. 296.
[36] More than fifty B Class stations were to be linked to the broadcast. Such dissemination of propaganda seems still to have been novel. Note *RT*, 27 (December 1936), 208, re trade diversion: 'In informing the people later of developments in the trade dispute with Japan, the Prime Minister has twice used an instrument of propaganda unprecedented in Australia—a broadcast over all networks in Australia. These tactics have produced a considerable impression'.
[37] *Argus*, 21 September 1937.

Suppose someone attacked Singapore ... Would Labour require that before Australia did anything about it there should be a referendum? Should Australia be put in the ridiculous position of sending delegates to the attackers to say, 'Look here, gentlemen, you have come too soon. You must wait at least six weeks. We must issue writs, prepare a pamphlet, and obtain a decision of our people'?[38]

The Government's relatively simple policy was agreed to at a series of Cabinet meetings. Lyons promised the electorate what the *Argus* described as 'safe, sound government'. His Government, he said, had balanced the budget in each of its six years in office, had reduced taxation and had restored practically all the cuts that were imposed in the worst period of the Depression. Financial responsibility of this order could be looked to in the future. Defence would be safeguarded within the British naval system, but with a proper balance between navy on the one hand and air force and army on the other. Banking reform would be promoted along the lines recommended by the Royal Commission and a 'balanced' tariff policy would be pursued. Most important of all, when confirmed in office, the Government would present parliament with a practicable scheme of National Insurance through which, for modest weekly contributions, 'there would be available for the great majority of the employed population guaranteed benefits during sickness, medical treatment at all times, pensions for widows and orphans, and superannuation'.[39]

Ministers worked hard in the campaigning which followed. Lyons covered 6000 miles and addressed forty-three meetings in twenty-six days.[40] Menzies had almost as strenuous a programme. There were piquant moments, like Menzies' visit to Jeparit, where he addressed 'one of the largest political meetings ever held in the district', found his initials which he had carved in a school desk, observed the growth of a tree he had planted as a boy, and was given a civic reception.[41] On another evening Lyons and Curtin addressed audiences, one after the other, in the Town Hall at Creswick. Journalists relished the 'gracious gesture' Lyons made when ending his, a rowdy meeting, by asking that Curtin be given a fair hearing, for 'in view of his position of leader of the Opposition it must be a proud thing for Mr. Curtin to return to Creswick, which was his former home, on a public mission'. The *Argus* noted 'what is probably a new record in municipal hospitality. Both

---
[38] Ibid., 22 September 1937.
[39] Ibid., 29 September 1937.
[40] Ibid., 24 September 1937.
[41] Ibid., 19 October 1937.

The Ministers of the Lyons Cabinet of 1937: (*from left*) Brennan, Thorby, Page, Parkhill, Pearce, Lyons, Menzies, Hughes, Paterson, McLachlan, Casey, Gullett.

Mr. Lyons and Mr. Curtin were accorded civic receptions. In view of the delicacy of the situation, the receptions were held one after the other, ... both ... after 9 p.m.'[42] Menzies' denunciation of Labor's demand for the 40-hour week earned from the trade union leader Albert Monk the sobriquet 'political weathercock with the vision of a cyclops'. Menzies' majority was in fact markedly reduced in Kooyong which, thanks to his speaking tour, he neglected and where he was opposed by an independent, L. H. Hollins, a Douglas Creditor who argued that 'the only remedy for the exploitation of the world was Christ's standard of absolute love'.[43] At Sunshine Menzies stood on the same platform with Casey and declared him 'the hardest working public man in Australia today: his capacity for industry amounts to genius'.[44] And on defence, which by the mid-point of the campaign had been accepted on all sides as the leading issue, Menzies was unequivocal. As he told the Kooyong branch of the AWNL, 'The protection of Australia lay in British naval power, and that was why the Lyons Government, in co-operation with the British Government, was preparing to make the navy the first line of defence'.[45]

A question which ominously came up more than once in the election campaign was that of Lyons's leadership of the UAP. We have seen Lyons on his return from England denying rumours that he might leave federal politics: he became even more adamant as election day drew closer. Lyons flew to Tasmania on 21 October to complete his Australian campaign in his own electorate, and there he declared:

[42]Ibid., 20 October 1937.
[43]*Age*, 5 October 1937.
[44]Ibid., 15 October 1937.
[45]*Argus*, 16 October 1937.

... To me, Tasmania is a haven—a place of rest and happiness, and I would like to spend all my time here. However, the job I am doing now is, I believe, my duty, and I shall continue to do it as long as I am wanted.

The statement has been made repeatedly that I am to relinquish the leadership of the Government. It has just been revived in this State as part of the lie that the Government intends to introduce conscription. The statement is as true today as it was six years ago, when it was said that I would make way for Sir John Latham, or as it was three years ago, when it was said that Mr. Menzies would take my place as leader. We are going to win this election—win it easily—and I am going to continue as leader for a long time yet. (Applause)[46]

In effect, the party managers had triumphed again: Lyons, whatever his faults in Cabinet, was an election winner. It is doubtful whether any other UAP leader could have saved at the hustings in 1937 so divided and faltering a party. As it was, the coalition won the election with ease. The overall position in the House of Representatives was little changed. The UAP lost four of the seats it had held in the previous parliament, but two of these went to the Country Party and one to an independent who inclined towards the Government. There was a swing to Labor in the Senate elections, but not enough to give that party control of the House.

A brief footnote should be added about the Freer affair. If Menzies hoped that the decision in June to admit Mrs Freer meant the end of the matter, he was soon disappointed. In August Mrs Freer, now in Australia, wrote to Menzies to raise the question of compensation. She had thought, she said, of writing to the Prime Minister, but 'you have been so fair, and have shown such sympathy and understanding in my case that I decided to write to you first, knowing you would do your best to assist me in my fight for justice'. No one knew, she said, what 'anguish and mortification' she had suffered, having her name 'bandied about from mouth to mouth', so that 'now wherever I go crowds of people stare at me as if I were a strange animal. This kind of publicity is shattering my nerves'. She could have made a considerable sum by publishing her story without reservation

> with all the correspondence and all the paper that I have, but I have always refused these offers. I am writing a biography for one of the weekly magazines but it does not include any reference to any of the correspondence from any people connected with the Government.

---

[46] Ibid., 22 October 1937.

... I appeal to you as an upright and fairminded man to put my case before the Government to clear my name of the vile and untrue things which have been said about me and to grant me fair and proper compensation for the very heavy loss I have been put to.[47]

Menzies' response to this rather alarming letter was to 'suggest that it would be wise to consider the matter very carefully before taking any definite steps' and to remind her of the undertaking Barnett had given the previous January when appealing for Cabinet reconsideration of the exclusion: that Mrs Freer promised, if granted entry, to make no claim for compensation. 'I know you would not wish to violate an undertaking of this nature', Menzies wrote, and he sought, in confidence, to arrange a meeting in Sydney on 4 September. Mrs Freer was, however, in Brisbane, and asked that a meeting be arranged in Canberra, promising to 'refrain from taking further steps until I have seen you, as I wouldn't for the world let you down'.[48] Menzies sent regrets and said the interview could perhaps be arranged when she returned to Sydney. When this did not happen Mrs Freer wired on 1 October threatening action unless an early meeting was arranged but Menzies replied that he would not be in Sydney until after the elections. Mrs Freer finally wired on 15 November: 'Have waited in vain given stories Smith's Weekly'.[49] Menzies replied that Cabinet had not met except formally since the election and that he regretted her decision. At that Mrs Freer wired that she had cancelled the contract with the paper and was 'awaiting further news from you'.[50] Either as a result of this virtual blackmail, or because he was still genuinely concerned that Mrs Freer be justly dealt with, Menzies prepared a long Cabinet submission detailing the steps in the case, concluding that there could be no doubt that Mrs Freer 'suffered severely as a result not only of certain statements made in relation to her exclusion but also as a result of the non-disclosure in detail of the reasons for her exclusion'. He recommended that an allowance be made to her, on condition that she understood that 'any payment is made as an act of grace and without any admission of liability on the part of the Commonwealth'. The matter was discussed on 6 December; Menzies' copy of the submission bears at the end, in his own hand, a record of what happened: 'Cabinet decides no action. Robert

---

[47] Mabel Freer to Menzies, 14 August 1937, AA 43/1139.
[48] Ibid., 27 August 1937.
[49] Ibid., 15 November 1937.
[50] Ibid., 16 November 1937.

Menzies, Dec. 1937'.[51] He had promised to wire Mrs Freer after the Cabinet meeting. Whether he did so or not is unknown. But she appears to have been satisfied that a genuine attempt to secure compensation had been made, for she made no further blackmail threats and appears not to have moved again to publish her story. It is understood that eventually she married not Dewar but a Sydney fish merchant named Cusack.[52]

---

[51] 6 December 1937, AA 432/1 36/360.
[52] Souter, *Acts of Parliament*, 305.

10

England and Europe 1938

THE RE-ELECTED Government, confident in its renewed strength, showed signs of complacency ominous in the light of its parliamentary record before the election. It did not convene parliament until December 1937, and that sitting lasted only six days. Then, at the end of January 1938, it announced that a new session would not begin until the last week of April or the beginning of May. Given that over the whole of 1937 up to the election in October parliament had sat for only twenty-four days, this renewed delay was something of a scandal. People had hoped that the election would 'inaugurate a new era', observed the *Age*, 'but already that hope is shattered'. The Ministers had forgotten that they were the servants of democracy: 'Rarely in Australia's parliamentary history has there been heaped up such a mass of questions ripe for legislative attention ... yet the Parliament in which they should be fully discussed is kept closed'.[1] Among a number of public figures who made the same complaint was the former Governor-General, Sir Isaac Isaacs.[2] Reg Pollard, the member for Ballarat (the only seat in the House of Representatives which Labor had wrested from the UAP in the election), claimed that parliament was being kept inactive because three ministers were about to go abroad and the team was so weak that the 'Government would be unable to face the House and carry on public business'.[3] Events would prove that an exaggeration, but it was true, especially given Lyons's growing ill health, that the absence in 1938 for four months of three key ministers, Menzies, Page and White, seriously weakened the Ministry.

[1] *Age*, 28 January 1938.
[2] Souter, *Acts of Parliament*, 309–11.
[3] *Age*, 29 January 1938.

Cabinet decided that the three should travel to London to complete those protracted trade negotiations with Britain that had begun with the Ottawa Agreement of 1932, due to expire in August 1937. Though there was no immediate need to renegotiate it Canada had done so and New Zealand, South Africa and Rhodesia had intimated to the Dominions Office that they wished to follow suit.[4] For Australia, the incentive which these moves by the other Dominions naturally provided was heightened by the pressure of the local manufacturing lobby, represented primarily by the Associated Chambers of Manufactures and the Australian Industries Protection League. After the modest concessions on meat won in 1936, the British market was almost completely open to Australia's primary products. But as a quid pro quo the United Kingdom insisted that its manufacturers have on the Australian market 'full opportunity of reasonable competition with Australian products on the basis of the relative costs of economical and efficient production'.[5] In the real world this was ambiguous. The Agreement, tacitly allowing that both the market and Australia's manufacturing capacity would change over time, left it to the Australian Tariff Board to make periodical recommendations to Government on the level of duties required to guard local interests, to assure fair competition to the British and to keep foreigners out. Australian manufacturing interests wanted more precise arrangements, which would stipulate clearly a level of protection designed to give them an expanding share of the local market. At the beginning of 1938 manufacturers' representatives put their case in private talks to the three ministers. Menzies accepted the manufacturers' position and from the beginning became the most forceful of the delegates. He it was who wrote the submission upon which Cabinet based its instructions to the delegates: the central one being that the articles of the Agreement which contained the existing arrangements to ensure British access to the Australian market (articles 8–15, but especially 10) should be deleted.[6] Page later claimed that he (as Minister for Commerce) had been 'given the task of leading the delegation',[7] but those in

---

[4] Under the terms of the Agreement, the treaty remained in force after August 1937, subject to 'six months notice of denunciation and subject to the further provision that the Agreement may be varied by consent after consultation between the two governments'. There was thus no compelling reason why revision should take place in 1938. For this quotation I am indebted to Dr J. O'Brien, whose unpublished paper 'The 1938 re-negotiation of the Ottawa Agreement' forms the basis of much of the treatment of the 1938 negotiations which follows. I wish to acknowledge the generosity with which Dr O'Brien has made his work in progress available to me.
[5] Quoted by O'Brien, ibid., 3–4, 5.
[6] O'Brien, 8.
[7] *Truant Surgeon*, 250.

the know recognized, as the journalist Roy Curthoys put it, that Menzies was 'the real, though not the titular, head of the delegation'.[8] This was to be one source of ill-feeling between Menzies and Page.

The Australians feared that the negotiations would be complicated by the fact that Britain was currently engaged in talks with the United States, designed to produce a new commercial agreement for Anglo-American trade. Such an agreement, it was thought, was likely to have repercussions on the existing system of imperial preference. Australian trade officials, bound for the London discussions, were sent ahead via Washington to observe the progress of the British negotiations there, and to conduct preliminary discussions with the Americans in case a separate agreement with Australia should prove desirable. Menzies meanwhile wrote for the *Age* an article on the Anglo-American 'Attempt to Make a Treaty'. It was short on specifics but noted the anxiety with which producers and exporters in Australia watched from the sidelines, and assured readers that 'the Government proposes to do nothing that will not, in the long run, forward the interests of Australia—your country and mine'. If some immediate sacrifice were to prove necessary, it would be justified 'by a far greater measure of prosperity than we can ever hope to have if Great Britain and America stand apart'.[9] The *Age* sardonically remarked a few days later that it was inconceivable that the Government had not decided on clearer instructions for the Australian delegation than these vague words reflected, but 'on this, as on so many other vital subjects of national interest, the public is left to grope in the dark'.[10] The Government in fact had made no statement about any briefing of its emissaries by the time the first of them, Menzies and White, sailed from Melbourne, in the *Strathmore*, on 22 March. The impression cultivated was that the real work was to be done on the voyage to England. As the *Argus* put it: 'The party will be a self-contained unit, with a

---

[8]Curthoys to Deakin, 8 April 1938, NLA, MS. 2994/2. Curthoys, a senior journalist, was editor of the *Argus* between 1929 and 1935. His letters and identifiable published writings reveal remarkable accuracy and insight in reporting. He was Australian correspondent to *The Times* and Deakin was his main London contact on that paper. 'Though, for pretty obvious political reasons not much publicity has been given to the fact in Australia', Curthoys added on this occasion, 'Ministers ... will make a big effort to facilitate the opening of European markets'. He sent an article about this, 'written after conversations with Mr Menzies'. Note also that on 1 March 1938 Herbert Brookes wrote to Menzies sending articles from the American press 'dealing with the contemplated Trade Agreement' and offering any advice 'which might be useful to you as leader of the Australian delegation', NLA, MS. 1924/1/14133.
[9]*Age*, 1 February 1938.
[10]Ibid., 7 February 1938.

reference library of 150 volumes and several trunks of important documents. The ministers and their secretariat will prepare themselves for the London conversations on the voyage'.[11]

It was indeed an impressive 'party'. Menzies and White were accompanied by their wives, and Lady Page,[12] whose husband was to travel overland and join the ship at Fremantle, also embarked at Melbourne. Officials included the Assistant Controller-General of Customs; a representative of the Trade Treaties Section of the Customs department; and a publicity officer. Menzies and White had personal secretaries. Also travelling to England on the vessel, and clearly available for consultation, were the President and Secretary of the Associated Chambers of Manufactures and the Chairman of the Australian Meat Board.

It had not been all work for the Menzies prior to their departure. In January the family, in common with others fortunate enough to have holiday homes there, had relaxed at Macedon.[13] There were also luncheons and dinners to attend and address, the most important being the farewell in Melbourne to the Australian Test Cricket team then leaving to contest the Ashes in England. It was a great occasion, with representatives present from all the State cricketing associations. Justice H. V. Evatt, vice-president of the New South Wales Cricket Association, presented the captain of the Australian team, Don Bradman, with an Australian flag. Speaking to the toast, 'The Australian Team', Menzies recalled amid laughter having done the same at farewell luncheons in 1930 and 1934. On both occasions Australia had won the Ashes, so that Harry Brereton, of the Victorian Cricket Association, had said to him: 'You had better come along and make another speech today'. He added that, by some extraordinary coincidence, the Prime Minister had decided that he (Menzies) should visit England to confer with British ministers about 'something or other' this year. He had sent word ahead in the hope that those arranging the meetings would have a full list of cricketing fixtures at hand when doing so and in the meantime offered himself, 'in spite of physical improbabilities' as the team's mascot. Then, in more serious vein, and with his eye no doubt on the distinguished representative from New South Wales, he noted that cricket was a 'unifying factor in Australian society': 'We are all disposed to look kindly at each other in regard to cricket (hear, hear). Many might be very indifferent at it. None were indifferent to it (hear, hear)'.[14] Cricket

[11] *Argus*, 22 March 1938.
[12] Page was made a K.C.M.G in 1938.
[13] *Age*, 12 January 1938.
[14] Ibid., 8 March 1938.

was indeed to be a highlight of Menzies' trip to England in 1938. But as such it was only one aspect of a remarkable set of experiences which made the first half of the year one of the most important in his whole career.

For Menzies the trip did not begin well. Learning that at Bombay, where they were to call, there had been an outbreak of smallpox, Page insisted that the whole party be vaccinated. Menzies reacted badly and in the tropics developed a high temperature and an ugly arm. The experience, he wrote, 'almost settled Pat whose chief task for some time was sponging me down to prevent me from actually bursting into flames', and he got little comfort from the ship's doctors who 'would come and lean on the foot of my bed, scrutinise my arm, and say, with almost diabolical pleasure, that "it was the finest reaction that they had ever seen" '. But things improved once they were through Suez. In Egypt Menzies, Page and White talked with King Farouk and the Prime Minister, Mahomed Mahmoud (the latter 'with all the ease that we expected when we found that he was a former student at Balliol'); at Malta they met the Governor; and at Marseilles they landed and had a day's drive along the south coast of France to Monaco and Monte Carlo. At Monte Carlo they visited the Casino, found it 'rather dingy and second rate looking', though the black-coated croupiers, with their 'quick darting eyes' came up to expectations. Trying his hand at the roulette tables Menzies won 250 francs but then 'went on putting my counters on to the table' and lost the lot—so he was able to assure his strait-laced parents at home 'that I took no tainted money out of Monte Carlo with me'. At the end of April they landed at Plymouth. A train trip through 'glorious Devon', decked as it was with the signs of early spring, brought them to Paddington station and a welcoming committee of the Bruces and Australian and British officials. 'Such is the effect of this place', Menzies wrote in reporting the trip '[that], although we have been here for only a fortnight, I feel as if I have been here for years'.[15] He was once again in his second home.

The official whirl which Menzies relished for a time alienated even faithful Pat: as her husband conceded, 'My official lunches and dinners tend to leave her deserted rather too much, and she frequently feels rather lonely and homesick'.[16] In an uncharacteristic letter she complained to her children that she wished she had not come:

[15]Menzies to Mother and Father, 12 May 1938, Menzies Family Papers.
[16]Ibid.

Daddy knows so many people here and they all want him to dine with them. We have been here a fortnight now and I have had 2 dinners alone with him and 3 with other people present and no lunches. So you see it isn't much fun.

But Menzies' secretary, Peter Heydon, a young man who was tasting London for the first time, was very attentive and thoughtful, taking her sometimes to dine at 'one of the famous restaurants' and sometimes to the theatre:

He found that I was going to have lunch alone today so he came home and had it with me and then went on to the cricket. Dad went there this morning and is no doubt steeped in cricket by now without any other thought in his head, which is quite right as he has a lot of worries ...[17]

Here was another rub: cricket left her cold. For Menzies, of course, it was an obsession. To be in England in the summer when a Test series was on was for him veritable heaven and one of his first engagements was a dinner given at Lord's to the Australian XI. His mind went back to 1935, for Baldwin was in the chair and Menzies was asked to speak too, 'so that I now have completed an admirable double, speaking, with Baldwin, on high matters of state in Westminster Hall, and speaking, with him, on cricket, in the almost equally sacred precincts of Lord's'.[18] He contrived to see something of most of the matches which the Australians played, and to report his impressions of them to brother Frank and father James. Thus, on the day when Pat imagined him 'steeped in cricket' (14 May) he watched Bradman at Lord's—'as big a bogey as ever over here'—making 'his usual double century', helped by a lifeless wicket on which the batsmen 'have been having a harvest'. A week later he was at the Oval, to see the Australians playing Surrey[19] and in June 'I deserted Pat, who detests cricket, and drove off to Nottingham for the Test Match'.[20]

As it turned out, Pat's disillusion was only temporary. Though, as Menzies himself put it, 'too many of my engagements [were] of a purely masculine kind',[21] there were also as the weeks passed mixed parties and dinners, visits to old friends made in 1935 and 1936, even some contact with royalty. Shared occasions buoyed up Pat's spirits and her husband had helpful bouts of thoughtfulness,

---
[17] 'Mother' to Ken, Ian and Heather, n.d. [14 May 1938], Menzies Family Papers.
[18] Menzies to Frank, 30 May 1938, Menzies Family Papers.
[19] Ibid.
[20] Menzies to Mother, 21 June 1938, Menzies Family Papers.
[21] Ibid.

In 1938 Mr and Mrs Menzies are snapped by a street photographer as they walk in London with Peter Heydon (then Menzies' secretary).

as when he arranged before his visit to Nottingham, and 'at a time when my own engagements were such that she would not normally see much of me', for her to have a fortnight's trip to Norway and Sweden with Dorothy Stirling, sister of his former secretary, Alfred Stirling, now Australian External Affairs Officer in London.[22] By then she had written positively to the children about having 'settled down here at last' and about Menzies' work:

> Daddy . . . is very popular here and everyone wants him to go and dine with them. He is meeting some very interesting people and the contacts he makes are doing Australia a great deal of good. He has definately [sic] made his mark in London, more so I think than any other politicians we have ever sent here. You must feel very proud of him.[23]

[22] Ibid.
[23] 'Mother' to Ken, Ian and Heather, 28 May 1938, Menzies Family Papers.

As Menzies himself realized clearly enough, his hosts, in the attention they paid to him, were not always disinterested entertainers. He made the point jocularly to Frank, just as the trade negotiations were about to begin. 'The so-called festive round has continued, that is to say I lunch officially, and dine officially, practically every day, the whole process inducing a state of ultimate exhaustion in which one will no doubt be almost ready to agree to anything. This is known as the British negotiating technique.'[24] As the talks got under way, this whimsical misgiving deepened into suspicion, then downright hostility. British officials did not take kindly to the Australian insistence on renegotiation while trade talks with the United States, the outcome of which would have obvious implications for the Ottawa Agreement, were still going on. Then, soon after the Australians arrived in London there was an unfavourable change of British ministerial personnel when Malcolm MacDonald, the Secretary of State for the Dominions, was transferred to the Colonial Office. MacDonald, a flexible negotiator, was a good friend who, in Menzies words, had 'got to know and sympathise with our point of view'. He was replaced by Lord Stanley who, while 'a charming and delightful fellow, is rather deaf and quite inexperienced . . . the result being that he [is] apt to reflect too much the Board of Trade view'. The head of the Board of Trade was another Stanley, Oliver, who, while Menzies found him 'personally most agreeable', took a narrow and rather unimaginative view of Empire problems.[25]

Since the negotiations on the British side were conducted by ministers and officials of the Dominions Office and the Board of Trade, this did not augur well for the Australians. In fact, by the end of June the talks were deadlocked.[26] Menzies meantime became progressively more disillusioned with the seeming intransigence of British officials, a disillusion which quickly became generalized into denunciation of the tendency he thought he detected in the business world to put material gain ahead of imperial sentiment and the realization of the full potential of the Empire in moral as well as economic terms.

---

[24] Menzies to Frank, 30 May 1938, ibid.
[25] Menzies to [Geoffrey] Syme, 21 July 1938, Menzies Family Papers. MacDonald, the son of Ramsay MacDonald, was at this time Chamberlain's right-hand man. His success in negotiating an understanding with de Valera over the so-called Treaty Ports led to the transfer to the Colonial Office so that he could try his hand at settling troubles in Palestine and Jamaica. Reporting this to Frank, Menzies added at the end of May that 'The change-over [to Stanley] will, I am afraid, render even slower the progress of our negotiations which have, so far, exhibited a great disposition not to get really started at all'.
[26] O'Brien's unpublished article has the details.

Australian Ministers involved in the trying trade talks of 1938 in London look a somewhat dispirited group: (*from left*) Menzies, Page, Bruce, White.

Menzies expressed his new disenchantment most forcibly in his letters home, though he also seized the opportunities which arose in London at dinners or formal occasions when he was asked to speak to needle the locals about their lack of proper Empire-mindedness. Thus, for example, on 17 June, he addressed the Imperial Defence College on the question 'Is the British Empire breaking up?' and 'as the meeting was private, I was able to be more provocative than usual'.[27] In his witty way, he was always on the qui vive for an opportunity to puncture the pomposity of English businessmen, as at a dinner given on one occasion to the Australian ministers by a group of London shipping magnates. There he had 'quite good fun' with Sir Edmund Vestey, of the wealthy firm which dominated the Northern Australian cattle industry, who 'in a rather moaning fashion, kept telling us all of the large sums of money that the Vesteys had lost in a purely

---

[27] Menzies to Mother, 21 June 1938, Menzies Family Papers. Writing on 26 July he told the family that on 23 June he had addressed a number of members of the House of Commons at the Empire Parliamentary Association rooms on Australia's problems in the Pacific. 'I took the opportunity of criticising the inertia of the British Board of Trade on shipping problems. It is practically impossible for a visiting Minister to engage in any such criticism publicly, but I have taken every opportunity of making criticisms where the absence of publicity rendered that course possible.'

disinterested way during their business career'. Menzies delighted others at the table by satirically complimenting Sir Edmund 'upon having for so long been one of the controlling spirits in a philanthropic institution' and, in reporting the incident to his brother, Frank, exploded:

> There is here, as elsewhere, a good deal of sentimental humbug to be found on the lips of big businessmen, the truth being that the City of London owes its position to having a somewhat shrewder eye for a bargain than any other place in the world. The more I see of it, the more I am convinced that, while Imperial sentiment is regarded as an admirable digestive after dinner, it does not count for very much when you get down to the actual brass tacks of an international business deal.[28]

Writing home in a general family letter at the end of July, Menzies summed up the disenchantment with which, this time, he was about to leave England:

> Speaking broadly, I have been in a much more critical mood throughout this journey than on either of my previous visits. Perhaps some of my illusions are beginning to wear a little thin, but I am increasingly convinced that in London whenever a contest occurs between British sentiment and a good business deal, the good business deal wins... Again, if you leave out a few men in the Cabinet and the Departments, the average view undoubtedly is that a country like Australia can be taken for granted and that nothing like the same attention need be paid to our views as would be paid to the views of Turkey or Yugoslavia. In order to get our business concluded at all we had to point out pretty sharply that Ministers apparently thought nothing of keeping us dangling around London subject entirely to the exigencies of their own normal Departmental programmes, although if the representatives of a foreign country had come along for trade negotiations they would undoubtedly have been given continuous attention and their affairs concluded within a relatively few days.[29]

Put at its simplest, what the Dominion envoys were seeking in a new agreement was twofold: enlargement of the United Kingdom market for Australian primary products and British recognition of Australia's right to develop her manufacturing industries, even if that involved a degree of competition with British

---
[28] Menzies to Frank, 30 May 1938, Menzies Family Papers.
[29] Menzies to family, 26 July 1938, ibid.

imports.[30] Given that, with the exception of wine, sugar, spirits and tobacco, upon which duties were imposed for revenue purposes, all Australian goods were admitted to the United Kingdom free of duty, the first aim could only be achieved if the United Kingdom were prepared to discriminate in Australia's favour against foreign producers and/or her own. To the British negotiators that suggestion could only be anathema, given political concern for home farm interests, the importance of primary goods in current trade negotiations with the United States, and the fact that in each year during the 1930s Australia had had a substantial surplus in its balance of trade with the United Kingdom—even during the trade diversion phase of 1936.[31] In 1936–37 the United Kingdom in fact provided the market for almost 50 per cent of Australian exports: and there was some irony in the unadvertised fact that the 1938 delegation had as one of its briefs quiet investigation of trade prospects in Europe.[32] As to the question of industrial development, the United Kingdom negotiators, and particularly officials of the Board of Trade, were affronted by Australian suggestions that certain British manufactures should be discriminated against in the Dominion market to allow replacement by locally produced goods. That such should *not* be the case was the quid pro quo on which free access of most Australian goods to the British market had been postulated under the Ottawa Agreement.

When the most serious breakdown in the negotiations occurred, at the end of June, the Menzies took off for Paris and spent six happy days there:

> In effect, we had, I think, the most perfect holiday we have ever enjoyed; went to all the shops, rubbed our noses on all the windows, risked our lives in scores of Paris taxi cabs, ate perfect dinners at

---

[30] As Menzies saw it, 'The best minds here (such as Malcolm MacDonald, who gets better every year) fully understand that if the British Empire is to include two or three first class powers, instead of one, it is urgently important to concentrate upon the development of a country like Australia, and that that development must, in the nature of things, be more rapid than any development of existing industries in the United Kingdom. But the Board of Trade will have none of this. It regards each Dominion merely as a customer for British goods, and it trembles with horror at the possibility of its customer going into business on his own account', Menzies to Uncle Syd, 12 July 1938, Menzies Family Papers.

[31] O'Brien, 8–9.

[32] Roy Curthoys wrote an article for *The Times* early in April 1938, 'after conversations with Mr. Menzies', to 'throw this aspect into high relief'. Though, he told Deakin, 'for pretty obvious political reasons not much publicity has been given to the fact in Australia, Ministers, particularly Mr. Menzies . . . will make a big effort to facilitate the opening of European markets, because it is beginning to dawn on Australia that there are very serious limitations to the consumptive capacity of the United Kingdom'. Curthoys to Deakin, 8 April 1938, NLA, MS. 2994/2.

pluperfect prices and, in the most orthodox fashion, visited the Bal Tabarin and the Folies Bergeres... we avoided museums like the plague, and drank in purely the modern Parisian spirit. A potent spirit it was, and we will probably both remain somewhat intoxicated by it for a long time to come.[33]

The trade talks came alive again when Bruce, accepting the impossibility of negotiating a new agreement with Britain, suggested that the old (Ottawa) compact simply be renewed, with a covering public statement that talks had taken place 'on the broader basis of the future development of Australia and her position in the British Empire'. On 14 July Menzies and other ministers agreed to this proposal, and a week later the two sides signed a memorandum of ten broad principles which would 'be regarded as the charter of United Kingdom–Australian trade relations'. This document was in one sense little more than a series of pious statements to camouflage a reality in which nothing had changed. But Menzies took it seriously, and strenuously argued that though after months of negotiations the tariffs desired by the manufacturers were still unachieved, the Australian mission had won from British Ministers 'an unequivocal admission (for the first time in an official way) of Australia's right and duty to develop her manufactures'. The relevant 'broad principles' were reminiscent of those developmental aspirations which Menzies had voiced on his return to Australia from England in 1936. British and Australian Ministers agreed:

(a) that in the interests of both countries and of the British Empire as a whole it is desirable for Australia to endeavour to bring about as soon as possible a substantial increase in her population;
(b) that it is impossible to achieve this objective solely or principally by an expansion of Australian primary industries;
(c) that there is therefore a necessity to combine with such expansion the sound and progressive development of Australian secondary industries.[34]

In a brief but emotional interlude at the end of July 1938 Menzies went with the official party to France for the unveiling by the King of the memorial just completed at Villers-Bretonneux to Australians killed in the First World War.[35] This impressive edifice, crowning rows of uniform headstones marking the graves is, as Menzies put it, 'beautifully placed on the top of a slope looking

---

[33]Menzies to family, 26 July 1938, Menzies Family Papers.
[34]Quoted in Page, *Truant Surgeon*, 394–5.
[35]Menzies to Belle, 6 August 1938, Menzies Family Papers.

The Australian Ministers, Page, White and Menzies, represent their
Government at a moving occasion in 1938: the unveiling of the
Villers-Bretonneux Memorial to Australians killed in France in World War I.

out over miles of wheat fields'. Back in March 1938 the Australian Cabinet had authorised the High Commissioner to spend a minimum sum of £4000 on the ceremony, much of it for the guard of honour to be provided by ex-AIF men visiting or living in England.[36] Some hundreds of such veterans attended. The main expense of the occasion was, however, borne by French authorities, who astonished Menzies with the precautions they took to protect the King and Queen. 'All the way out from the village of Villers-Bretonneux to the site of the Memorial the road was completely lined with troops, with a further line of troops out from the road in the fields and, half a mile further out, small groups of cavalry scouts. Any attempt on the lives of the visitors would have required an invading army'.[37] The official visitors subsequently lunched with the mayor and councillors of Villers-Bretonneux.

The unveiling ceremony impressed all who were there. Menzies thought the speeches of the King and the French President excellent: the King's 'full of feeling and dignity' and the President's 'a

[36] Cabinet Minutes, 11 March 1938, AA A2694 XMI, vol. 18, pt 2.
[37] Menzies to Belle, 6 August 1938, Menzies Family Papers.

characteristic piece of French declamation'. The diary of Menzies' colleague, Tommy White, has a long and very moving description of the day's events. White was especially affected by the contingent of some hundreds of ex-AIF men in plain clothes and the action of Lt Col Jacob, the RSL representative at the unveiling, who brought with him an urn containing the ashes of wreaths left at the Melbourne Shrine of Remembrance and the Sydney Cenotaph on Anzac Day, and scattered them on graves at the monument. White, thus aroused, could not forbear making the ungenerous remark common to ex-servicemen of the day who thought of events like the Villers Bretonneux ceremony as their sacred property:

> It was interesting to see who were representing Australia and very definitely some of the party, both ministerial, official and private who were there and looked on it as something in the nature of a spectacular function, if they had any shame should not have been there, having shirked their responsibilities during the sacrifice which was now being commemorated.[38]

Other entries in the diary make it all too clear that the member of the party whom White had most in mind here was R. G. Menzies.

Among the reasons for Menzies' frustation in the initial stages of the trade talks was the difficulty of getting attention to such mundane matters when official London was preoccupied with the current European crisis, the German threat of war over Czechoslovakia. Shortly before the Australian party reached London, Hitler's invasion of Austria had brought the coup of Anschluss; when they arrived, the alleged grievances of Sudeten Germans in Czechoslovakia were being orchestrated into an excuse for Nazi invasion. In England Chamberlain had succeeded Baldwin as British Prime Minister in May 1937 and, while vigorously advancing a programme of rearmament, was also by now committed to appeasement of the European dictators. Tension over aspects of this policy between Chamberlain and his Foreign Secretary (and Menzies' hero), Anthony Eden, culminated in February 1938 with Eden's resignation from the Cabinet. Dining later with Menzies, Eden was to speak 'with great generosity' about Chamberlain but complained that the latter's 'anxiety to come to terms with the dictator countries rather led him into ignoring his Foreign Secretary'.[39] On 25 May 1938 the visiting Australian ministers met

---

[38] T. W. White, Diary, 22 July 1938.
[39] Menzies to family, 21 June 1938, Menzies Family Papers. The dinner with Eden had been on 2 June.

with Dominion High Commissioners and Lord Halifax, Eden's successor as Foreign Secretary, to discuss the Czech crisis. Eduard Benes, a founder and since 1935 President of Czechoslovakia, resisting dismemberment of his country, had set his face against German demands for Sudeten territory and ordered partial mobilization. The general feeling of the meeting of Dominion representatives was that Halifax should make it clear to the Czechoslovak Government that it ought to make concessions to Germany. Earle Page put the parochial Australian position nakedly:

> It was not until Germany had been satisfied that there would be any prospect of easing down on the armament race, or any change from the policy of autarchy which the German Government were at present following, or consequently any general revival of world trade... Germany had formerly been one of Australia's most important markets for her wool and other raw materials, and there could be no revival of this market until more normal trading arrangements with Germany were possible. What Australia desired, therefore, was a politically satisfied Germany which would be ready to take her share in the peaceful development of the world. Would the German Government be satisfied if they got the Sudeten Germans, and if they would be satisfied, would it not be wise to give the Sudeten Germans to them?

More sophisticated, but equally attuned to the majority view, Menzies expressed puzzlement at Benes's policy: 'Was it not bluff, and if so, was it not almost a suicidal bluff?'[40] As he put it to Frank, 'Benes, the Czechoslovakian President, is regarded in well-informed circles here as being what we would call a fairly greasy fellow, and what the polite British diplomat would call "rather tiresome" '.[41] The charge against Benes was that he had not honoured his original undertaking to make Czechoslovakia, a creation of the Versailles treaties, a federation on the Swiss model. Instead, wrote Menzies, he had 'clearly done everything to exalt the power of the Czechs and diminish the rights of the Germans'. It was therefore only just that he should now make concessions to the Sudeten Germans' would-be protectors, the Nazis. British policy, Menzies thought, was moving in the right direction and Chamberlain, 'a man of clear-headedness and determination', would bring to it 'such a degree of horse sense that real trouble may be avoided'.[42] Germans and Englishmen could naturally be brought to understand each other; the evil to be resisted was fanaticism.

---
[40] For *Note* of this meeting from which these quotations are drawn see *DAFP* 1: 157–63.
[41] Menzies to Frank, 30 May 1938, Menzies Family Papers.
[42] Menzies to Mother and Father, 12 May 1938, Menzies Family Papers.

To people in London the Germans every now and then seem to be uncivilised butchers, while the Germans in their turn are constantly misled by their belief that anything said by an irresponsible newspaper or by an irresponsible back-bencher in the House of Commons is to be taken as a serious pronouncement of British Government policy.[43]

Soon after he wrote these words, Menzies and his wife set out ('with true Scotch caution', in different aeroplanes)[44] to see Germany for themselves. It was a semi-official visit: Heydon and Stirling went with them; Stirling sent an official account to Lt Col W. R. Hodgson, Secretary of the Department of External Affairs in Australia and *The Times* commented that the expedition, which lasted four days, 'was a minor landmark in the progress of the Dominions towards an individual European policy'.[45] The German Foreign Office put a senior officer at Menzies' disposal; Sir Nevile Henderson, the British Ambassador in Berlin, gave a dinner at the Embassy in honour of him; Dr Schacht, President of the Reichsbank, gave the Menzies a lunch; and Brinkmann, head of the Reichwirtschafts Ministerium entertained them at a dinner. The principal object of the visit was to observe the political situation but Menzies also made arrangements to see German factories, workers' housing, the new State highways and recently erected Olympic stadia and open air theatre. Menzies had long conversations with ambassador Henderson, whom he thought 'an extremely clear-headed and sensible fellow with a frank and even breezy method of putting the British view to the Germans'.[46] Henderson, who has also been described elsewhere as 'a persistent, able and lamentable advocate of an Anglo-German settlement on any terms',[47] no doubt did much to confirm the attitudes Menzies had absorbed from Government circles in London. After his return Menzies wrote to Halifax that 'if this queer spirit which now occupies Germany is to be exorcised' more and more pressure should be put on Prague, and more and more pressure on the English press 'not to talk dangerous nonsense about "firm stands" and "successful threats" at Berlin'.[48]

None the less, and contrary to one prevalent myth,[49] Menzies did not come away as an uncritical admirer of Nazi Germany. He found Berlin 'drab', with few signs of humour. The overwhelming

[43] Menzies to Hubert Jacoby, 13 July 1938, Menzies Family Papers.
[44] Menzies to family, 26 July 1938, Menzies Family Papers.
[45] Quoted in Stirling's report to Hodgson, *DAFP* 1: 398. Except where otherwise stated, the account of Menzies' visit is taken from this report.
[46] Menzies to Lyons, 6 August 1938, *DAFP* 1: 400.
[47] Rhodes James, *Anthony Eden*, 173.
[48] Menzies to Halifax, 6 August 1938, Menzies Family Papers.
[49] For a particularly egregious example, see Humphrey McQueen, *Gallipoli to Petrov*, (Sydney 1984), 168–9.

majority of younger Germans were certainly in favour of the régime: 'In a gloomy sort of fashion they are content; they are well looked after, wages are high, social services are good, factories are well-planned and humanely conducted'. Public money was being spent like water, but

> Hitler is not spoken of with any warm or spontaneous affection but with the respect which one attaches to a legal fiction ... Hitler is not an administrator, as Mussolini is. He is a dreamer, a man of ideas, many of them good ones. He propounds the idea, Goering gets it carried out, and Goebbels tells the German people how marvellous it is.

What he found difficult to understand was 'the easy acceptance by the German people of execution without trial, the complete suppression of criticism and a controlled press'. He told Schacht 'the real danger of the régime was that the suppression of criticism would ultimately destroy Germany'. Germany's great contributions to the modern world had been in philosophy and the sciences, and both required freedom. Schacht, ever the polite host, agreed: he was certain, though, that the rigour of authority, necessary now, would be relaxed over the coming years. Menzies, however, decided that, gloom notwithstanding, it would be a 'blunder' to think there was no spiritual content in Nazism: 'the Nazi philosophy has produced a real and disinterested enthusiasm which regards the abandonment of individual liberty with something of the same kind of ecstasy as that with which the medieval monk donned his penitential hair shirt.[50]

The Times reported the Menzies' departure for home on 9 August. They were to board the *Cormorin* at Marseilles.[51] In a parting statement Menzies reiterated his call for more effective consultation between London and the Dominions—a call which had been a constant, and much approved, theme in a number of his speeches during the visit[52]—and spoke again of his conclusions about Germany. 'The principles of the totalitarian state', he said,

---

[50] Menzies to F. B. Gamble, 2 August 1938, Menzies Family Papers.
[51] Page went home via America. Note Menzies' catty remarks to Casey: 'Page, with great self-abnegation, is returning through America and the comparatively cool waters of the Pacific, but we are coming back on the "Cormorin" through the Red Sea at its hottest and will therefore arrive even more exhausted and disillusioned than we are at the present moment. I have already written to the Prime Minister, telling him that we must never again send three ministers to conduct a single negotiation. Thereby hands a most curious tale which I will expound to you at our next merry meeting'. Menzies to Casey, 6 August 1938, Menzies Family Papers.
[52] See, e.g., *Times* reports of Grosvenor House Empire Day dinner (25 May), and annual dinner of Royal Institute of International Affairs (22 June). An editorial of 28 June enthusiastically endorsed Menzies' campaign on consultation.

as the Germans freely admitted to me in Berlin, are not suited to the British genius, but I do hope that we British people will not too easily accept the idea that because personal liberties have been curtailed in Germany the result is necessarily a base materialism. There is a good deal of a really spiritual quality in the willingness of young Germans to devote themselves to the service and well-being of the State. If our democracy is to survive and flourish, and the liberty which is its lifeblood is to remain pure and strong, we will have to realise that a willingness to serve the community either in a political or social or industrial way, should come to be regarded as a normal state of mind and not as a mild eccentricity.

The Times, besides reporting these words, carried an editorial endorsing them: 'Mr. Menzies' remarks regarding Germany show him to be a keen and understanding observer. They are excellent as models of the views that we may hope will command the widest assent throughout the Empire'.[53] But by the time Menzies arrived home, it was difficult to maintain even conditional admiration for Germany. The final phases of the Czechoslovak crisis were upon the world.

Menzies arrived in Melbourne on 11 September and next day he, Page and White were welcomed to a meeting of Cabinet, where they 'outlined at some length the method and detail of their negotiations' in London.[54] But for the moment that was less important than the international situation, on which senior ministers were soon to be in almost continuous session. On 12 September Hitler closed a mass Nazi Rally at Nuremberg with a frenzied speech demanding 'justice' from the Czech Government for the Sudeten Germans. War threatened, Chamberlain made his first offer to meet Hitler, and the downward path to Munich began. The meeting at Berchtesgaden followed and Chamberlain agreed to negotiate with France and Czechoslovakia possible secession of Sudeten regions on the basis of the right of self-determination. On the other side of the globe, in the Camberwell Town Hall, less world-shaking events were taking place. R. G. Menzies addressed a capacity house, making his first public speech since his return from London. 'I want to warn you', he said, on the question of the hour, 'against any easy falling into habits, to which we are susceptible, of dividing the sheep from the goats, and of saying that dictators are bound to be wrong and democracies to be right. Australians in the past week have passed through many moments of anxiety, but that anxiety has been dramatically lessened by the

[53] 9 August 1938.
[54] Cabinet Minutes, AA CRS A2694, XMI, vol. 18, pt 5.

intervention of the British Prime Minister'. When an interjector asked him why Chamberlain didn't simply tell Hitler that he would stand by France and Russia (who technically had treaty obligations to Czechoslovakia) in the event of a German attack, Menzies replied:

> If I am going to choose between the gambler's throw for peace in the world by three nations delivering a threat in effect to three others, and the wise, simple understanding intervention by one Government which desires to obtain peace by negotiation, that latter course is the one I stand for (Prolonged applause).[55]

At the end of August Lyons had firmly told the British authorities that the 'Czechoslovakian problem is not a question on which war for the British Empire can justifiably be contemplated'.[56] The return to Australia of a Menzies convinced that peace depended on Benes accepting the 'reason' of Germany's claims subsequently strengthened the Prime Minister's hand as Cabinet, in almost continuous session and radio-telephone contact with Bruce in London, lived through the dark days between Berchtesgaden and Munich. On 26 September, just after British and French pressure forced Czech agreement to surrender the Sudeten lands and just before Chamberlain at Munich accepted Hitler's escalated demands, Menzies and Casey prepared for Cabinet the text of a message to convey to Chamberlain Australia's support for the course he was taking. It was approved, but in a troubled entry in his diary one member of Cabinet, White, remembered the words with which the Czechs had surrendered: under 'irresistible pressure . . . we resolved to sacrifice ourselves for world peace as Christ was sacrificed for humanity. We do not blame those who left us in the lurch. History will pronounce its judgement'. 'I feel thoroughly miserable about it', wrote White.

> It seems all opposed to the traditions of our race . . . I think we should hang our heads that we did not stand up to the bully of Europe . . . It may yet mean peace but at what price? One can expect this attitude from M but Casey is inexplicable . . . I realise of course the frightful dilemma of Chamberlain . . . For though one may go oneself it is another thing to deal in the lives of millions of others. Yet while Hitler lives it seems that small countries will be swallowed up and democracy hangs in the balance.[57]

---

[55] *Argus*, 17 September 1938.
[56] Liesching to Stanley, 31 August 1938, *DAFP* 1: 410–11.
[57] White, Diary, 26 September 1938.

It is doubtful whether many Australians would at that moment have agreed with these reflections. When news came through of Eden's and Churchill's denunciations of the 'surrender of the democracies to Nazi threats', the *Age* caught the prevailing Australian mood: 'In every democratic country these feelings are to some extent shared. Shorn of their rhetorical exuberance they are to be heard on Melbourne streets. But none of these critics faces the dread and awful alternative'.[58]

Menzies made the same point when at the annual dinner of the Victorian Chamber of Manufactures he remarked on 'hearing all sorts of thoroughly well-intentioned people talking of what they are pleased to call a preventive war'. But 'to talk at any stage except at the last moment of a preventive war is the very ecstasy of despair'.[59] He went on believing that, while at the same time appreciating an aspect of appeasement which its fire-eating opponents undervalued and which we now know was a prime motive for Chamberlain: its necessity to buy time to allow British rearmament.[60] And like Chamberlain he insisted that 'Germany would have to learn that the British love of fair play was not a sign of weakness'.

Menzies in fact insisted after Munich that the danger of war still had to be faced and that, for Australia, that was a national problem which demanded a national solution. For this reason, the pre-eminence of the federal arm of government had to be asserted. He personally had experience of government both at State and at Commonwealth level, and knew only too well the difficulty of getting things done. As soon as one tried to overcome this difficulty, 'the voice of the small Australian was heard'.[61] Attacking State parochialism on another occasion, he remembered the strength he had felt abroad as a minister representing Australia rather than a particular State and invoked the lesson, closer to home, of the anguish they had all recently been through: 'During the recent crisis people had been thinking not as residents of Melbourne or Victoria, but as Australians. Everyone's thoughts

---

[58] 23 September 1938.
[59] *Argus*, 4 October 1938.
[60] John Charmley, *Chamberlain and the Lost Peace* (London 1989), 193.
[61] *Age*, 17 October 1938. Though on a few points I am at variance with it, the seminal and most thorough treatment of the general subject is E. M. Andrews, 'The Australian Government and Appeasement', *AJPH*, XIII(1967): 34–46. Chamberlain's public warning to Germany in his celebrated Birmingham speech of 17 March 1939 was not unlike a number of Menzies' statements: '. . . no greater mistake could be made than to suppose that, because it believes war to have been a senseless and cruel thing, this nation has so lost its fibre that it will not take part to the utmost of its power in resisting such a challenge if it were ever made' (Charmley, *Chamberlain and the Lost Peace*, 167).

had turned to Canberra, and he hoped that when the crisis was passed they would not go back to vigorous clanking of the parish pump'.[62]

In making such statements Menzies had in mind a vital test which the 'national spirit' would soon undergo. This was a Premiers' Conference, postponed during the Munich crisis, to be held on 22 October, the explicit purpose of which was to lay the basis for a strong and co-ordinated plan of rearmament and defence. But in this it was to fail abysmally. And in the process it fulfilled the worst predictions Menzies made about the baleful influence of 'the small Australian' mentality. It was also the trigger for a most unhappy period of instability for the Lyons Government. And for Menzies personally it was the outward beginning of a seeming rush of ambition, the inwardness of which was and will probably always remain ambiguous.

---

[62] *Age*, 11 October 1938.

11

Days of Unsettlement 1938–1939

AS THE press remarked, the importance which the Commonwealth Government attached to the Premiers' Conference of October 1938 was attested to by the strength of its representation there. No less than seven federal ministers, including Lyons, Page, Menzies and Casey, attended.[1] Page was the *de facto* leader of the group. Just after the Munich crisis Lyons, 'feeling the strain of intense work through the absence of senior ministers overseas on the trade delegation', took medical advice and had a holiday at his home in Devonport, Tasmania.[2] He came back to Canberra for the Premiers' Conference but, still unwell, performed there indifferently. The Conference agreed to a proposal for the federal Government to borrow an extra £4 million for defence (bringing total Commonwealth expenditure for 1938 to £20 million, by far the largest peace-time expenditure on defence so far in the history of Australia) and accepted in principle the idea that the Commonwealth and the States should co-operate in carrying out defence works programmes. But it rejected out of hand the centrepiece of the Commonwealth's proposals: that an Advisory Council, composed of representatives of State and federal governments and industry, should be appointed to prepare a plan for the orderly development of industry and the encouragement of migration.

The State premiers blamed the Commonwealth for not presenting them with crisp proposals and asking them instead to sign a blank cheque; Commonwealth ministers upbraided the States for parochialism and unwillingness to accept machinery which would make central co-ordination of the defence effort possible. The States were particularly opposed to the idea of a central body dictating the order of priority of State works. Bertram Stevens, the

[1] *Age*, 21 October 1938.
[2] *SMH*, 3 October 1938.

capable New South Wales Premier who had ousted Lang, knew his Keynes, and was toying with the idea of entering federal politics, seized the chance to criticize wider aspects of federal policy. Deeply concerned with problems associated with unemployment and housing, he objected to the diversion of State funds to defence unless this was accompanied by the provision of extra finance, through an expedient which he had been advocating for some years: the expansion of central bank credit. To the Lyons Government this idea was of course anathema, and Casey, as federal Treasurer, at once reacted fiercely. Stevens, he said, was taking advantage of a national crisis to force his views of monetary policy on the Commonwealth Government.[3]

A few days after this unhappy interstate meeting, Menzies made a speech, at the Sydney Constitutional Club, which dwelt on its implications. The speech at once became, and has remained, notorious. Menzies' theme was familiar: the need for what he called 'a national spirit in Australia'. Speaking of the recent international crisis he said that Britain and Australia had mutual obligations towards each other and that war 'might be something that would come to Australia and not merely something that was happening 12 000 miles away'. Australians were a good-natured and easygoing people, who did not want to be troubled with uncomfortable facts. But when they were told the facts, they had 'an unrivalled spirit and capacity to face those facts, and act accordingly'. Therefore

> The first lesson for the Governments of Australia is that in these times of emergency we must not hesitate to take the people fully into our confidence and give them leadership along well-defined lines. These great questions can only be solved by the united efforts of the people.

Menzies' use of the plural, 'Governments', made it clear that he was referring to State governments as well as the Commonwealth and reiterating his appeal against that parochialism which to him was well exemplified in the breakdown of the recent Premiers' Conference. 'The parish pump', he said, 'was an admirable institution when it was kept in its place, but . . . in great vital issues there was no room for the purely State outlook'. A national spirit required that the Commonwealth Government must, in appropriate matters, have national powers: 'Are we a collection of States, a Confederacy, or a real Commonwealth?' It was an appropriate question for a constitutional lawyer to ask at a Constitutional Club.

[3] *Age*, 21, 24 October 1938; *SMH*, 22 October 1938.

In this context Menzies made what at this distance appears as an almost passing remark about democratic and totalitarian leadership: 'Democracies could not maintain their place in the world unless they were provided with leadership as inspiring as that of the dictator countries'.[4] Whether so intended or not, this remark in the circumstances of the hour inevitably lent to the speech the possibility of more than one interpretation, as was at once suggested by the headlines under which the newspapers next day reported what Menzies had said. While, for example, the Melbourne *Age* presented its report of the speech under the heading: 'National Spirit Needed. Mr. Menzies Condemns Parochialism', the *Sydney Morning Herald* chose a different emphasis: 'Need For Inspiring Leadership. Mr. Menzies' Appeal'. This last emphasis gave the speech a significance which Menzies himself was explicitly to reject on at least three occasions: that it was a veiled and 'disloyal' attack on Lyons.[5] That this interpretation of what Menzies said has become virtually the received wisdom has primarily to be attributed to Lyons's wife, whose loss in 1939 of the husband she both adored and dominated bred a festering hostility to the men who, she became more and more convinced, had let him down. Of these by far the most culpable in her mind was Menzies. Dame Enid's most explicit public attack on Menzies is contained in the reminiscences published in 1972, *Among the Carrion Crows*. As a matter of courtesy she sent the relevant chapter to Menzies before publication. She explained that, though she had never intended to say anything about these matters, 'the amateur historians who write books and lecture to University students have forced my hand'. She was resentful of 'the denigration of Joe's reputation which 'always seems to leave him an ageing ailing incompetent hanging futilely to office'. Menzies, at the time in hospital after a stroke, was 'far removed from my office and my personal records', but two of the incidents she mentioned were 'still pretty vivid in my mind'. One of them was the Constitutional Association speech:

---

[4]This, like other quotations already given from the speech, is the version of the *Sydney Morning Herald*, 25 October 1938. The *Age*'s version of the crucial sentence was: 'Leadership as inspiring as that in dictator countries, and with the wholehearted support of the people, was essential if democracies were to maintain their place in the world'.

[5]This interpretation is accepted by the federal parliament's most distinguished historian, Gavin Souter (*Acts of Parliament*, 313–14). For perhaps its most extreme version see Kate White, *A Political Love Story* (Ringwood 1987), 198–9. The charge was denied by Menzies himself in parliament on at least two occasions in 1938–39 and many years later, when Enid Lyons showed him the relevant text of *Among the Carrion Crows*.

It was not a speech about my Leader at all. It was addressed to all people in responsible posts in Australia, including myself. Its theme, as I recall it, was that the Nazis had inspired the belief in their own people in bad things, and that in Australia those who had responsibilities, Federal or State or Municipal, must set out to inspire our own people with high ideals. To do this, it was necessary to take them into our confidence and explain, almost day by day, the reasons for our actions. I would undertake to say that nobody present at that meeting thought I was engaging in such a nauseating occupation as attacking my own leader. On your own showing, Joe did not so interpret my speech, but you did. I am sorry that this matter should now be resurrected to put me in a false light.[6]

In the passage in question Dame Enid wrote of the Lyons's breakfast on the morning after the Constitutional Association speech. As was their custom, they had three newspapers to read: the *Canberra Times*, the *Sydney Morning Herald*, and the *Sydney Daily Telegraph*.

Suddenly I was electrified.
'Joe', I exclaimed, 'have you seen what Bob Menzies said in Sydney yesterday?'
'Yes. Why?' he answered mildly.
'Why?' I almost shouted. 'Why? can't you see it's a direct public hit at you?'
'Not at all', he replied. 'Bob wouldn't be guilty of such a thing. It's just the way it's reported'.
'Don't be a fool, Joe', I adjured him. All my fighting blood was up. I could not accept any theory of mis-report or misinterpretation. The attack on Joe's leadership had for weeks, yes, even months, filled columns of the daily press. He would be a naive person indeed who would expect such a speech at that time to be taken at its face value, and Bob was not noted for naivete. I was brimming over with righteous wrath.[7]

Dame Enid does not record which of the newspapers gave her the impressions which made her so angry. Perhaps the reportage of any one of them would have, given the underlying antagonism towards Menzies which she reveals in the passages leading up to her account of that celebrated breakfast. In commenting on the speech, however, all three spoke of the need for some reconstruction of the Cabinet to obtain 'more drive in the prosecution of the Government's policy'; none questioned Lyons's position as Prime Minister. Indeed the *Telegraph* (which Dame Enid must surely not have read) was uncompromising on that:

[6]Quoted in *Among the Carrion Crows*, 177–8.
[7]Ibid., 62.

> It seems pretty obvious that Mr. Lyons is needed more than anybody. He has had a gruelling time.
>
> It is easy to understand the strain which he underwent a few weeks ago, when the country was within an hour of war.
>
> But, as he himself has put it, he is a long way from being a political corpse.
>
> Whatever changes in Federal Cabinet are likely in the future—and in the interest of efficiency some are necessary—Mr. Lyons is not likely to be affected.[8]

This in fact represented majority newspaper comment, notwithstanding Dame Enid's assertion that an 'attack on Joe's leadership' had for weeks 'filled columns in the daily press'. In fact the press was sympathetic with Lyons's illness; the attack was not on him, but on weak ministers, like Thorby, whom it was thought had to go. If Lyons had a fault, it was in his slowness to reconstruct his Cabinet. The newspaper which most eagerly seized on Menzies' speech as an occasion to reflect on the leadership question was Murdoch's Melbourne *Herald*. As Dame Enid correctly suspected, Murdoch believed that Lyons had outlived his usefulness and must go.[9] But even the *Herald* at this stage concentrated on the need for Cabinet reorganization. Menzies, it said, had used a sentence which 'admirably emphasized the urgency of defence preparations: "I believe, such is the complexity of life, that the next war has already begun" '. Menzies was right in stressing the need for the Commonwealth to have national powers but 'the first move is to make the Commonwealth Government efficient for leadership, to place the portfolios in the most capable, resolute hands'.[10]

Meantime the parliamentary Opposition further muddied the issue by seizing the chance to attack Lyons: on the afternoon of the day after Menzies' speech, Curtin moved censure on the ground that the Government had forfeited the confidence of the House 'because of its lamentable lack of leadership in regard to urgent national problems'.[11] Later that day the parliamentary UAP was to meet and it was a fair guess that those who disliked Menzies would raise what White called in his diary 'the specula-

---

[8] 25 October 1938.
[9] Philip Hart, 'The Piper and the Tune', in Hazlehurst (ed.), *Australian Conservatism*, 115. Murdoch had written in July 1937, before the election, to Clive Baillieu in England: 'The people ... are beginning to dislike the Lyons Government most heartily. Certainly there has been a great and disastrous drift in political leadership'. For the more uncompromising position Murdoch had reached by January 1939, see below, pp. 257–8, NLA MS. 2823, folder 27.
[10] 25 October 1938.
[11] Ibid.

tion as to whether he was criticising the Prime Minister'. That happened, but before it did there was one sensational delay. When parliament met in the early afternoon Lyons got the Speaker's first call and announced to a shocked House that a DC2 airliner, the *Kyeema*, flying in to Melbourne from Adelaide, had overshot Essendon aerodrome and crashed into Mount Dandenong. Details were still unavailable, but there had been extensive loss of life. For the Opposition Curtin expressed sympathy to the bereaved, gave notice of his motion of censure, and the House adjourned in respect for the victims of the crash.[12]

Later, in the party room, John Price, one of those who had followed Lyons out of the Labor Party, moved a resolution of confidence in the Prime Minister. There was no opposition. White, for one, took this to be 'rather discomforting for Menzies', but speculation of that kind came to a halt when grievous tidings from outside took all minds temporarily away from current political tensions. As White recorded it:

> Just at the tense moment when the air was rather electric after the set-back to Menzies, Bell, the Speaker, came in and informed me that Charles Hawker, member for Wakefield, had been in the crash and was killed. The news shocked everybody. Ministers drew off to Cabinet and all sat around listlessly as the news sounded too tragic to be true ... Hawker was one of the brighter minds in our Parliament ... spirited leader of the 'squatter group in the House—McBride, Fairbairn and others following him always slavishly.[13]

Hawker, however quirky, was thought by most to be of excellent ministerial quality, and by some to be a potential prime minister.[14]

Curtin's no-confidence motion was easily voted down on party lines. But the demand, in the press, in the UAP and among some ministers for a reconstruction of Cabinet soon reached something of a crescendo.[15] Cabinet had long and heated meetings, breaking tradition by sitting even on 1 November, Melbourne Cup Day. 'The clamours for Cabinet reconstruction and the criticisms over Defence', wrote White, 'made the meeting essential'. Despite its rejection by all ministers at the 1937 election, conscription had by

---

[12] *Age*, 29 October 1938. All eighteen people on board the *Kyeema* were killed. It was the worst disaster in the history of Australian aviation up to that time.

[13] Diary, 26 October 1938. Philip McBride, South Australian grazier and director of Elder Smith and Co., was elected to the Senate in 1937. James Fairbairn, Cambridge-educated grazier, had served with distinction in the Royal Flying Corps during the war and held the Flinders seat in the Representatives from 1931.

[14] *ADB*, 9: 232.

[15] See, e.g. *Age*, 28, 29 October, 1, 2, 5 November; *Courier-Mail*, 28, 29 October, 12 November 1938.

the end of 1938 become a lively issue in Cabinet. White thought compulsion essential if Australia was to raise an effective army and the continuing international crisis brought Menzies to the same view. At one point White, after an altercation with Hughes (who, ironically, was against conscription), stormed out of the Cabinet room, telling Lyons he would not stay in a ministry which would not support universal service. In the consternation which followed, Casey and Page finally persuaded him to return. But the press was soon full of rumours that Menzies was on the verge of resigning on the same issue. White recorded caustically:

> The lobbies are very active with the newspaper men and their speculations on the new Cabinet. The Argus, very much followed by the Herald, is featuring Menzies as being the greatest brain sighing for leadership and a paragon of all that is wonderful as a patriot and statesman. Casey is usually bracketed with him...
>
> An amazing sidelight to the Cabinet manoeuvring is that Menzies had given out to the press that he would probably resign if scope were not given to his great ability or if compulsory training were not introduced. My temporary resignation apparently upset his plans, though I am sure nothing would drag him from the Treasury benches while he thinks he has a hope of leadership.[16]

The conscription issue was for the time being settled by compromise: Cabinet set up a committee under Hughes to test the voluntary principle by conducting a recruiting drive to increase the militia from 35 000 to 70 000. Lyons accepted that the Cabinet must be reconstructed but before this happened his leadership was formally reconfirmed at a party meeting on 2 November.[17] If White's account of this meeting is to be believed it was rather a stormy one. 'Menzies' talk on leadership had aroused a section of the party to espouse his cause', White wrote and, 'in rather an electric atmosphere', Gullett declared that Lyons ought to 'make way for somebody else'. After some 'wordy by-play', White himself 'thought it proper to say that at this moment we had no other leader and that anybody who imagined that he was ordained to lead the party was flattering himself'. He added that on conscription he was prepared to accept the compromise which had been worked out in Cabinet. 'This', he wrote, 'settled the attack that apparently Menzies was going to launch'.[18]

---

[16] Diary, 1 November 1938.
[17] *Age*, 8 November, for retrospective account of setting up of recruiting committee; 3 November for confirmation of Lyons's leadership.
[18] Diary, 15 November 1938.

Two days later Menzies offered a personal explanation in the House 'to correct a report appearing in the local press that he had issued an ultimatum to the Prime Minister'.

> The story ... is completely untrue. I have not done so directly or indirectly. I can attribute the report only to a malicious desire to create bad blood between the Prime Minister and myself, who are not only colleagues, but friends. Any question of either constructing or reconstructing a Cabinet is for the Prime Minister to determine, and nobody else.[19]

The words have the ring of truth, and exemplify the care Menzies took throughout the events of those weeks to maintain the public proprieties of government solidarity. That could, however, coexist with other sentiments behind the scenes: his longstanding disquiet at Lyons's administrative inefficiencies, his conviction of the urgency of Cabinet reconstruction, even his own frustrated ambitions.[20] He had entered federal politics on the promise of the succession to Lyons and had received from Lyons in 1936 another assurance that he would soon step into the Prime Ministerial shoes. That had not happened. He must have known this was the party managers' doing. Inevitably, perhaps, Menzies was somewhat obtuse about the unpopularity his superior ways had earned him in some quarters. 'The difficulty', as Frederic Eggleston was soon to remark, 'is in his relations with other people. I am yet to find anyone who has made so many enemies in politics and so few real friends'. Somebody, he added, should drop the hint to Menzies that he be more human. 'Why are clever men so stupid?'[21] As different an observer as Keith Murdoch had come by the beginning of 1939 to the same conclusion. In November 1938 he had thought it possible that Lyons, who had 'lost his usefulness' could be replaced by Menzies. But by the following January he was writing to their mutual friend in England, Clive Baillieu:

> But Bob has a curiously disconcerting way of discouraging adherence, whilst in fact eagerly seeking it. He is a most difficult man to work for. I do not know whether it is utter laziness or pride. Certainly he

---

[19] Quoted in *Age*, 4 November 1938.
[20] He had complained to Hankey as long ago as 1934 about Lyons's sloppy method of conducting Cabinet meetings (and on this see Casey's remarks to Bruce, Souter, 300). Similarly note Page's story of Menzies' petulant refusal to write with Casey and Page the speech Page wanted Lyons to deliver at the October Premiers' Conference (*Truant Surgeon*, 263). Note also Bruce's conversation with Menzies on how to handle Lyons—brought on by Menzies' complaint about Lyons's changes of mind and the difficulty of working with him (Edwards, 267–8).
[21] Warren G. Osmond, *Frederic Eggleston* (Sydney 1985), 202–3.

is confiding when one is alongside of him, but he never invites confidence. The public is beginning to actually dislike him, which is a great pity. Each week now he is becoming less likely as Prime Minister.[22]

Lyons announced his new Cabinet on Monday 7 November. As the press was only too quick to remark, it was not a wildly radical reconstruction. There were three principal elements. First, a new minister, Geoffrey Street, received the defence portfolio. A grazier and decorated officer from the first AIF, he replaced Harold Thorby, a Country Party minister whose allegedly indifferent performance in those days of international crisis had been one of the Government's most trying crosses. (Poor Thorby, whatever his faults, was open to the worst of ex-service prejudices, as is illustrated by one of White's most scabrous diary entries: 'Thorby cannot of course be expected to understand the ramifications of his Department without any experience. Like Menzies and some others in our Cabinet, he did not volunteer during the last war and has no service experience'.)[23] Second, Archie Cameron, of the Country Party, became Postmaster-General and, third, a 'senior Cabinet group' of six—in effect an inner Cabinet—was announced.[24]

A most startling result followed almost immediately from this reorganization. White, the aggressive defender of Lyons's leadership and the minister who had most vehemently demanded firmer action on defence, announced his resignation from the Cabinet. He was offended at having been excluded from the inner Cabinet to make way for the new Defence Minister, Street. In a subsequent press conference, White announced that 'If his resignation prevented the dangerous trend towards further Cabinet domination by a reactionary section within the group, it would not have been in vain'. This gnomic pronouncement was without doubt aimed at Menzies, and perhaps Casey too. The resignation provoked a nasty scene in the House when White and Lyons publicly read out the letters they had exchanged over the resignation. White referred piously to his having refrained from resigning over the compulsory training issue to avoid embarrassing the Government. Lyons, clearly exasperated, bluntly rejected White's talk of a reactionary coterie in the Ministry and reminded him that he had not objected to the inner Cabinet until he was left out of it. On the Opposition side Curtin drily observed that the eagerness

---

[22]Murdoch to Clive Baillieu, 4 January 1939, NLA, Murdoch MS. 2823, folder 27.
[23]Diary, 27 September 1938.
[24]*Age*, 8 November 1938.

with which White had resigned had been equalled only by the alacrity with which Lyons had accepted the resignation, and Eddie Ward declared that democratic government had ceased to exist in Australia 'and Fascist round-table methods had been substituted'.[25]

Despite these sorry beginnings the new Government derived a measure of kudos from an expanded defence programme which Street promptly announced. Under it an extra £20 million would be spent over the next three years. Notable features of the programme were the construction of two destroyers and twelve torpedo boats in Australia, a new air force station at Townsville, a dock in Sydney, and a naval and air base at Port Moresby. A Commonwealth loan of £10 million was to be raised to meet part of the expense.[26] But some of the cost would have to come out of consolidated revenue, and this had not been budgeted for. The Treasurer, Casey, drew attention to the implications of this in a paper he presented to Cabinet on 5 December. It showed that, even with a surplus of £1 million to be carried over from the 1937–38 accounts, expenditure would exceed revenue in 1939–40 by £5 300 000, a serious deficit by the standards of the day. The paper showed that, while the principal cause of the difficulty was an unplanned £3 million for defence, an important part of the shortfall was £1 million required to implement a scheme of National Insurance already legislated for.[27] This information played into the hands of members in the coalition who disliked National Insurance and almost brought the reconstructed Government to an untimely end, barely a month after it had been formed.

Casey, who had been Treasurer since October 1935, had by June 1938 piloted through parliament legislation to establish a scheme of National Insurance. Promised by the Government at the election of 1937, this scheme was the end-product of some years of inquiry, including reports by two senior British advisers and much work by local officials, particularly in the Treasury. It was to provide disablement, sickness and medical benefits, as well as old-age and widows' pensions for workers and their dependants, based on contributions by government, employers and employees. There is no doubt that behind the proposals lay a genuine liberal reformism which was one reaction to the social distress of the 1930s. But as well as that, Casey, like other conservative politicians and many

[25] Ibid., 9 November 1938.
[26] *Age*, 7 December 1938.
[27] AA A2694 XMI, vol. 19, pt. 1. On the general points that follow I depend chiefly on my interpretation of the principal historian of National Insurance, Rob Watts, *The Foundations of the National Welfare State: the Australian experience* (Sydney 1987), 7–24, with apologies to Dr Watts for points on which I disagree or have misinterpreted him.

officials, thought that the State would be unable to continue indefinitely providing an ageing population with non-contributory pensions: though it might take some time to build up adequate superannuation funds, the new scheme would in the end relieve the taxpayer of what promised to become an intolerable burden. Menzies was as enthusiastic as Casey on both the social and financial benefits promised by National Insurance. He had been one of a small Cabinet sub-committee which had drafted the policy speech in which the Government in 1937 undertook to introduce a National Insurance Bill if re-elected. He was away in England in June 1938 when the Bill finally got through but rejoiced with Casey, writing to congratulate him on 'your valiant battle with the forces of darkness over the National Insurance Bill, the passing of which must be regarded as a tremendous triumph for you'.[28]

Once the Act had been passed, the Government began in good faith to set up the complex machinery required for its implementation, the centrepiece of which was the appointment of a National Insurance Commission and of a corps of officers to administer the Commission's decisions. The first subscriptions, to set the scheme in motion, were due to be paid at the beginning of 1939. Though, as we have seen, Casey found it necessary to warn Cabinet on 5 December of the coming imbalance in Commonwealth finances, it was decided at the same meeting to go ahead with the work already begun. However, Country Party ministers also forced acceptance of a proviso that rural workers should be temporarily excluded from the operation of the Act,[29] a move which brought to the fore again the antagonism which country employer groups had from the beginning shown against contributory insurance. Two days later a UAP party meeting unanimously rejected this move and resolved that the scheme must be 'nationwide'.[30] UAP ministers took the issue back to Cabinet. Page led a Country Party demand that the whole scheme be indefinitely postponed, which Menzies and Casey bitterly resisted, and the resignation of both from the Ministry was expected if Page had his way. When breaking point had almost been reached late on 8 December, Menzies proposed as a compromise that while they should proceed with the scheme, they should postpone the operative part of it— especially the collection of contributions—from January until September, to allow time for the Government to consider proposals currently being made to remove a number of anomalies. Page

[28] Menzies to Casey, 6 August 1938, Menzies Family Papers.
[29] AA A2694 XMI, vol. 19, pt. 1.
[30] *Argus*, 8 December 1938.

reluctantly agreed, after consulting his backbenchers, who nevertheless remained convinced that if the Act were imposed 'the country would be bled so white that it would never meet its obligations', of which by far the most important in the present disturbed time was to provide for 'adequate defence'.[31]

Thus the Government avoided the disaster of losing two senior ministers and—in the words of two Sydney newspapers— 'stumbled into the recess' still intact.[32] But its morale and reputation were low, and as parliament adjourned for the three-month summer recess it suffered yet another blow: in the by-election for the seat of Wakefield, made vacant by the tragic death of Hawker, the Labor candidate, Sydney McHugh, won.

Meantime, to add to the worries of the Government in general and of Menzies in particular, industrial trouble which had been rumbling in the background reached an impasse just as the Christmas season came. Waterside workers at Port Kembla refused to load the steamer *Dalfram* with pig-iron bound for Japan. The purpose of the ban, they said, was political, not industrial: as the union secretary, Tom Roach, put it, the pig-iron should not go because 'success to the Japanese Fascist militarists in China will according to their own statements inspire them to further attacks on peaceful people which will include Australia'.[33] On 28 November 1938 federal Cabinet decided that the ban must end: if it did not, the Government would enforce the Transport Workers' Act, a much-hated measure passed by the Bruce–Page Government in 1929 and known among unionists as the 'dog-collar act'. It required individuals to obtain a licence to work on the wharves and, by making such licences available to all comers, facilitated the recruiting of strikebreakers. Explaining this decision, Menzies as Attorney-General emphasized that 'the question is not whether the waterside workers are right or wrong in their view on what the international policy of Australia should be'. It was, rather, whether policy should be determined by 'the duly constituted Government of the country or by some industrial section'. On 1 December the Government gave the union a deadline of 6 December to resume

---

[31] T. J. Collins, cited *Age*, 9 December 1938.
[32] *SMH*, 10 December; *Daily Telegraph (DT)*, 14 December 1938.
[33] Quoted Len Richardson, 'Dole Queue Patriots', in Iremonger, Merritt and Osborne, *Strikes* (Sydney 1973). This excellent article traces the background to this dispute, adding as important dimensions the social isolation and depression sufferings of the workers in this area. For a wild, partisan and inaccurate account of the dispute see Rupert Lockwood, *War on the Waterfront: Menzies, Japan and the Pig-iron Dispute* (Sydney 1987).

work. Last-minute negotiations failed, a conference of seventeen unions at Wollongong endorsed the Port Kembla watersiders' stand, the ban on the *Dalfram* continued and on 8 December the Government invoked the licensing system.[34]

However formally correct the Government's position on the central issue, its prestige was severely damaged as the dispute developed. Lyons and his ministers offered no explanation for one strange anomaly in their policy: that while having banned the export of iron ore to Japan on the ground that known deposits would barely meet Australia's own expected needs, they were now prepared to allow the export of the more valuable form of ore smelted into pig-iron. As the *Sydney Morning Herald* put it, 'others besides waterside workers are bewildered by the apparent contradiction in policy'.[35] Bishop Moyes of Armidale expressed the view of many Church and other community leaders when he said that 'the sympathies of the greater part of the community are with the men on the waterfront ... who can see that the iron ore is for the massacre of people against whom the Japanese say they have no war'.[36] Menzies extended the deadline but, after meeting union leaders in a vain attempt to negotiate an agreement, invoked the licensing system.[37] It was soon clear, however, that that would prove ineffectual: no applicants for licences came forward. Then, on 17 December, the Australian Iron and Steel Co, BHP's subsidiary at Port Kembla, announced that its works there would have to be closed as, thanks to the waterfront dispute, its products could not be got away. This move involved 5000 jobs[38] and gave apparent credence to the view that the Government and BHP were in collusion to promote, irrespective of the moral issues involved, a lucrative trade with Japan. Menzies meantime had private talks with the ACTU and the federal executive of the watersiders, but to no avail.[39] Just before Christmas he issued a strong statement warning that the continued refusal of Port Kembla watersiders to load the pig-iron had serious implications for Australia's international relations:

> Is it seriously thought to be either prudent or desirable that of the fifty-odd nations in the League of Nations, Australia should be the only one to adopt such a course? And if this course is to be pursued in relation to pig-iron, which may provide material for munitions

[34] *SMH*, 29 November 1938. Conference of the seventeen unions, *SMH*, 5 December.
[35] Ibid., 30 November 1938.
[36] Ibid., 6 December 1938.
[37] *SMH*, 6, 7, 9 December 1938.
[38] *Age*, 22 December 1938; see also Richardson, 157.
[39] *Argus*, 14 December 1938.

The Christmas Ham: for workers at Port Kembla the Christmas of 1938 is a bleak time. Thanks to watersiders' refusal to load a cargo of pig-iron for Japan, steelworks have been closed and unemployment looms. As Attorney-General, Menzies has to handle the dispute for the Commonwealth Government, which contests the right of a union to make national foreign policy. As the issues become muddied, Menzies wins the well-known soubriquet of 'Pig-Iron Bob'.

must it not also be applied to wheat and wool, seeing that food and clothing are as essential an element in military operations as guns and ammunition?[40]

No one remarked on the ironic closeness of this argument to that which Labor had advanced against the use of sanctions to protest against Italy's policy in Abyssinia.[41] Curtin's silence on the matter suggests that Menzies was not too far off the mark when he observed that 'if a Labor Government were in office today it would be compelled to adopt exactly the same attitude'.[42]

Christmas was hot and the summer dry. At Macedon, gardens had suffered and lawns were withered and burnt, but the place remained an oasis of peace, 'away from the hurrying life of the brighter holiday places with their gaiety and bright lights'. The Menzies, as was their custom, spent a quiet family Christmas there, at 'Illira', and were joined later in the month by Frank's wife and children. It was the kind of break which Menzies loved and, at this busy and somewhat tense time, needed.[43]

After the holiday he made his first public appearance at the inaugural dinner of the Melbourne branch of the P.E.N. literary club at Scott's Hotel. The guest of honour was H. G. Wells, then on a speaking tour of Australia and who, the week before, had been publicly censured by Lyons for referring to Hitler as a 'certifiable lunatic' and Mussolini as a 'fantastic, vain renegade from the socialist movement'. In introducing Wells, Leonard Mann, the president of the club, said he had seldom read 'a more stupid utterance by the Prime Minister'. In the course of his talk, Wells remarked that Lyons had a right to his opinion. Menzies took the occasion of responding to the toast to the guests to mount a warm and witty defence of Lyons. During the previous speeches, he said, he had

> written on the table cloth before me the dignified and pregnant sentence, 'Freedom of speech, even for a Prime Minister'. (Laughter and applause). But of course Mr. Wells, with that omniscience which has become such an unpleasant feature of his writing, anticipated me, so perhaps I need do no more than outline it. (Laughter). I am increasingly conscious that whenever a politician disappoints the expectations

---

[40] Ibid., 22 December 1938.
[41] See above, pp. 169–70. Roach had said of the Port Kembla dispute: 'We are putting into operation article 16 of the League of Nations, which declares sanctions on belligerent nations. The Australian Government is a party to the League of Nations' (*SMH*, 19 November 1938).
[42] *Age*, 22 December 1938.
[43] Ibid., 30 December 1938.

of the people and makes a decisive statement at once he is accused of being Fascist. As a democrat, I resent that bitterly. I have had the great honour of being identified with Mr. Lyons as a member of his Government for some years, and I declare that he is the last man who could be accused of endeavouring to suppress any freedom of opinion. Mr. Lyons was not challenging the right of Mr. Wells to his views but he did want to take the opportunity of making it clear that those views were not the views of the Government.[44]

Less than a week after this, on 11 January, Menzies went through a particularly rowdy form of namecalling when, with considerable pluck, he accepted an invitation from the federal Labor member for the area, Lazzarini, to visit Wollongong and confer on the spot with union officials about the Port Kembla dispute. His coming was well prepared for. Four thousand South Coast miners went on strike for the day, and men, women and children lined the road from Bulli Pass to Wollongong, waving placards and booing and hissing as Menzies' car went past. At Corrimal a huge banner stretched across the road announced that 'The People of the South Coast Fully Support the Wharfies in the Pig-iron Struggle'. Some miners' lodges had sent their members by special buses into Wollongong, to take part in the main demonstration there. Street speakers worked on the crowd, which when Menzies arrived greeted him with aggressive banner-waving and shouting. Protected by police, Menzies went into the Town Hall for discussions from which the press was barred. Neither side, as delegates later reported, would 'budge an inch': while Menzies declared that it would be extremely provocative and dangerous for Australia, alone among the nations, to impose sanctions on Japan, the secretary of the Port Kembla watersiders, Roach, depicted his union as 'fighting the fight of Australia'.[45]

It was estimated by mid-January that 7000 were out of work in the Wollongong–Port Kembla area and at an urgent conference in Sydney on the 16th Menzies offered to lift the dog-collar act and arrange talks between the unions and the Government about

[44] Ibid., 9 January 1939. Lyons, holidaying in Tasmania, explained that his criticism of Wells was prompted simply by his conviction that in the present delicate state of world affairs 'actions or statements which brought the possibility of war nearer should be subject to careful scrutiny'. Wells seems not to have been impressed by Menzies' performance. On part of the trip home he travelled with Frank McIlraith, the London representative of *Smith's Weekly*. McIlraith later reported to H. V. Evatt: 'Wells did not form a very high opinion of Australians he met. He thought Menzies and Bruce had second-rate minds. Resented Menzies trying to talk down to him and declared that both Menzies and Bruce might have been born in Hoxton, a slum area in London (McIlraith to Evatt, 16 February 1939, Evatt Papers, Flinders University, Correspondence, 1939a).
[45] *DT*, 12 January 1939.

future exports of pig-iron if workers agreed to load the *Dalfram*. Despite recommendations from both local and federal leaders that they accept these terms, the Port Kembla men at stormy meetings at first rejected them; further Government threats followed, a 'combined unions committee' urged proper talks with the Government on banning future exports and on 21 January the unionists returned to work on the conditions Menzies had adumbrated. At the same time they issued an 'appeal to the Australian people to continue the struggle against aggression' and had the satisfaction of forcing Lyons at length into a proper statement of why the Government was banning the export of iron ore.[46]

That Menzies had in this dispute so valiantly defended, at some personal cost, what was in many respects a shaky position, does not seem to have earned him on his side of politics much of the prestige he might have hoped for. From early January 1939 even the reconstructed Lyons Government appeared to many supporters to be, as Sir Sydney Snow, wealthy businessman and head of the UAP organization in New South Wales, told Lyons, 'done for', unless a drastic remedy could be found. In Melbourne Murdoch, as we have seen, thought the same. Both were convinced that 'new blood' was needed, but neither thought of Menzies as a possible saviour. 'I can find no animus against you personally', Snow wrote to Lyons. 'On the other hand all the leading Ministers are subject to hostile criticism in one form or another—whether justified or not need not be discussed here'. To restore public confidence there was only one thing to be done: a 'triumvirate' must be formed by taking Stevens, now Premier of New South Wales, into the Cabinet and luring Bruce back from England. If Lyons could add these two to the Cabinet he would have worthy henchmen and which portfolios they accepted would not matter: 'I have no wish to disparage any of your present team but the public gaze would chiefly focus on the "big three" '.[47]

Whether Menzies saw this letter we do not know, though it seems improbable. Given how insulting its implications were to him personally, a considerate colleague like Lyons would not be likely to

---

[46]The intricate story of intra-union intrigue in this dispute has yet to be properly studied. It is clear that the old story—on which the 'pig-iron Bob' fable is based—of an uncomplicated Government *v.* watersiders clash, is unacceptably simplistic. That the Port Kembla men's first vote against the Menzies proposals, against the recommendations of federal and local officials, was made on the urging of the *State* president of the union, Findlay, makes it clear that internal union conflicts were involved. See, for the various matters discussed here and in the text, the press of these weeks, especially *Argus* and *SMH* of 14, 17, 19, 21, 23 and 25 January 1939.

[47]Snow to Lyons, 4 January 1939, NLA, MS. 4851/2/12. Snow foresaw that since Bruce was not well off 'in his case financial considerations may be important—if so I think that side could be arranged'.

flaunt it before him. But, equally, we do not know whether Menzies discovered that, soon after this, and despite all the previous understandings about the succession, Lyons briefly tried to persuade Bruce to return to Australia and take over the Prime Ministership. In the unpleasant debates still to come about Menzies' 'betrayal' of Lyons, this betrayal of Menzies by Lyons received no mention.

Bruce arrived in Melbourne on 26 January on a mission to urge Australia, in common with the other Commonwealth countries, to take part in urgent preparations for possible war. He was met officially in Melbourne by Lyons, Street and Menzies and subsequently addressed a meeting, in the Town Hall, on the current international situation. Later, at Lyons's request, he received a deputation from the National Union headed by E. H. Willis, the party functionary who had long impressed on Lyons the unsuitability of Menzies as future leader. The deputation asked Bruce to come back to Australian politics; he, however, declined on the ground that he would be accused of wanting 'to get rid of Joe Lyons'. But soon Lyons himself intervened: according to Bruce, at 'a somewhat pathetic interview', Lyons said to him: 'Look here, you've got to come back. I am absolutely beat. I can't carry on . . .' Bruce agreed to take over, on condition that Lyons recommended this to the Governor-General and was prepared to serve as a minister in a Bruce Cabinet. Lyons accepted these terms, but next day came back to Bruce, accompanied by Casey, to say that he had changed his mind. As Bruce later observed:

> Whether Joe's wife, Dame Enid, had intervened, or whether Richard had persuaded Joe that the course I suggested was too extreme I do not know, but Joe had changed his mind. Joe's attitude was that while my proposal might be a practical one in wartime, the people would not accept it in peace-time. He couldn't accept my terms.[48]

The balance of probabilities is that Dame Enid Lyons had intervened to keep her husband in office. Her later writings make it clear that she was of course perturbed about his weariness and had a certain wish to see him released from the cares of office. But it is evident, too, that pride in him and the certainty that her own influence would come to an end made her ambivalent at the thought of his demise. Keith Murdoch, by now convinced that war was inevitable, found Lyons's failure to act on rearmament with real resolve extremely vexing, and blamed Enid:

[48] Cecil Edwards, *Bruce of Melbourne: Man of Two Worlds* (London 1965), 263. This paragraph, generally, is based on Edwards, 261–3. Note that I. M. Cumpston, *Lord Bruce of Melbourne* (Melbourne 1989), 168–9, also provides evidence of the attempt to get Bruce back as leader.

... his wife is an ardent pacifist, even a belligerent pacifist. When he speaks she speaks; when he gives a Christian message she gives one. When he appears at the microphone she wants to appear also—and she does. Her message always is that if we love our neighbours enough there will be no war. It is very pitiful, and our country is in some trouble about it.

'We all remain on very cordial terms with Lyons', he concluded, 'but there is a great deal of disgust being bred'.[49]

In the first week of February Cabinet met in Hobart where, according to Dame Enid, 'a happier mood prevailed than had been known for a long time. Members enjoyed the climate and the scenery, and Menzies was at his charming best'.[50] After the terrible heat of Melbourne, Hobart's more equable temperatures must indeed have been a relief. The sense of Cabinet tranquillity was the more notable in view of the revival, out of doors, of the universal training issue. In Melbourne a newly formed 'Citizens' Defence Movement' on 1 February organized a rally in the Town Hall to demand that the Government reintroduce compulsory training for Australia's defence. The audience, reported the *Age*, 'predominantly comprised young men, and marked enthusiasm was displayed'. Menzies' friend Vinton Smith was the leader who moved the key motion. He argued that the target of the present recruiting campaign, 70 000, was ludicrously inadequate: Australia needed as a minimum an army of 150 000 and a similar reserve.[51] In reply Lyons maintained that the present recruiting campaign was proceeding well, that the Government had undertaken at the last election to depend on the voluntary system and that he found it 'inconceivable' that in a democracy like Australia young men should not be allowed the opportunity to show that they are prepared voluntarily to respond to the defence needs of their country.[52] That the agitation out of doors brought no sign of support in Cabinet for compulsory training suggested that on this major divisive issue, at least, a concensus had been achieved.

It was, however, soon to become evident that consensus was far away in the case of that other profoundly troublesome matter, National Insurance. By the second week of February it had become an open secret that a new attack on the National Insurance scheme was under way. Cabinet decided to call a meeting in Canberra of all supporters of the Government on 1 March to thrash out the issue. It was freely rumoured that a Cabinet majority would be

---

[49] Keith Murdoch to Clive Baillieu, 4 January 1939, NLA, MS. 2823/27.
[50] *Among the Carrion Crows*, 63.
[51] *Age*, 2 February 1939.
[52] Ibid., 3 February 1939.

On the eve of Menzies' resignation as Attorney-General and deputy leader, the troubled Lyons Cabinet meets in March 1939.

putting forward a proposal to shelve the scheme and what Menzies would do if this were accepted became a major matter of press speculation. Sydney's *Daily Telegraph* put most clearly what was the near-unanimous opinion. Under the headline 'Mr. Menzies and the Stand-Over Party' it opined:

> If the Attorney-General (Mr. Menzies) resigns because of the Government's abandonment of National Insurance, the public will be solidly behind him.
> We have seen so many Ministers clinging to their portfolios at any cost that the example of a man putting principle before position will be widely acclaimed.[53]

It did not, however, come at once to that point. After the two coalition parties met separately and jointly, Lyons announced that National Insurance would not be abandoned but that the

[53] 1 March 1939.

Government would be drafting proposals for modification of the recently passed Act. He did not say so, but it was clear that his chief concern was a long and rambling resolution which the Country Party meeting had passed. This asserted the Party's approval of 'the principles of National Insurance', but made no mention of old-age, widows, orphans or invalid pensions and urged that:

> consideration be given to the preparation of a family medical service scheme, with sick pay and provision for dependent children, to replace the present Act, and that, with this end in view, the State governments, friendly societies and B.M.A. be invited to co-operate with the Commonwealth Government and assist in the formulation of such a measure, and that, pending the enactment of these proposals, the present National and Health Insurance Act be rendered inoperative.[54]

This resolution was taken to a joint party meeting but after discussion on it no vote was taken. Rank-and-file feeling had been expressed with unexpected vehemence in the UAP against any emasculation of the existing Act.[55]

Cabinet began at once a series of what became stormy meetings to decide what should be done. Out of doors the enemies of National Insurance stepped up their propaganda and its supporters—especially officials of friendly societies—expressed alarm at the new threat to a scheme they had assumed to be settled. As W. H. Best, secretary of the Consultative Committee of Friendly Societies of Australia, observed: 'Thousands of pounds were spent by the approved societies in preparing for the scheme's adoption, and it was an obligation of the Government to have it brought in as soon as possible'.[56] Curtin meantime wryly remarked that, while the Prime Minister had declared that National Insurance would go ahead, 'what he did not say, but what was the truth, was that it was held up until it was found what the Country Party would accept'.[57] That, it seemed, is what happened when on 14 March, two weeks after the Country Party's resolutions had been presented to the joint party meeting, Cabinet decided to repeal the pensions provisions of the existing Act, to concentrate on a scheme of family medical benefits, and to arrange discussions between the interested parties (the National Insurance Commission, the British Medical Association, friendly societies and medical benefit

---

[54] *Age*, 2 March 1939, also, generally, same date: *Argus, SMH*, Adelaide *Advertiser*.
[55] Ibid.
[56] Ibid., 3 March 1939.
[57] Ibid.

associations) to work out the details of a completely new scheme. The majority of ministers, whatever other explanations they might subsequently offer, had in fact bowed to the Country Party's ultimatum.[58]

When Cabinet reached this decision, Menzies walked out of the meeting, went to his room, called for a typist and at once drafted a letter to Lyons tendering his resignation.[59] In an atmosphere of high drama, the resignation became public immediately after Lyons announced to the press that, due chiefly to the unexpected financial burden of new defence expenditure, the Government had resolved to shelve all the National Insurance scheme except for health benefits, and in this case a new and less expensive system would be negotiated. Menzies issued a statement recalling how he had been at odds with the Cabinet majority more than once since his recent return to Australia but had refrained from resigning because of the need, in the face of severe difficulties, to maintain solidarity. The decision on National Insurance was, however, 'the last but weighty straw'. That decision 'virtually either cripples or destroys National Insurance for years to come'. Cabinet was proposing to repeal measures, already on the statute-book, which provided for old age, widows' and orphans' pensions, and to substitute for the rest of the Act a new medical scheme whose details still had to be worked out.

> I frankly do not think we can expect to be taken seriously if we start off again with conferences and drafting committees at a time when we have already so notoriously failed to go on with the Act which represents two years of labour, a vast amount of organisation and considerable expenditure of public and private funds.

On the compromise which in the previous December had effectively postponed the operation of the Act until September 1939, Menzies noted how he had replied to criticism in his electorate with a circular letter reaffirming his own commitment to the Act:

> I am not unaware of the manner in which certain interests, which would seek to defeat me or take my place in the representation of Kooyong, are using National Insurance against me. Let me say quite categorically that I stand by National Insurance, and that a defeat in defending it would, in my opinion, be an honourable one.

---
[58] Ibid., 15 March 1939.
[59] Ibid. The draft resignation, typed and with corrections and alterations in Menzies' hand, is in Menzies Family Papers. The terms of the resignation and Menzies' public statement about it appeared in the press throughout Australia on 15 March.

As no financial or political considerations had changed since he wrote that, Menzies could not deny what he had said then: 'I am making no cheap criticism of the decision of the Prime Minister', he concluded, 'or of any other of my colleagues. In particular, I make no attack upon my friend and colleague, the Treasurer, who has worked manfully on this matter, but each of us must determine his line of action according to his own lights and obligations'.

Acclaim for Menzies was widespread. As the *Age* put it: 'Having regard to the many circumstances with which the public have for some time past been familiar, his action does him honour'. Fairbairn and Holt issued statements expressing, in Fairbairn's words, how 'refreshing' it was 'to find Mr. Menzies giving a lead to those who put personal integrity before political advancement'. John Lawson, Menzies' Parliamentary Secretary, wired the news that he would also resign from the Cabinet: 'Accept my congratulations on your notable contribution to the cause of good government stop I am following your lead today and will support you to the last ditch'.[60] Predictably enough, the Melbourne *Herald* was ecstatic:

> Admiration for Mr. Menzies will run high today. His work and his talents raised him to one of the highest posts in a successful political career. As deputy leader of his party he stood in direct line of succession to the Prime Ministership. On grounds of principle and conviction he has deliberately and voluntarily stepped out of the line to easy success. Thereby, he has given new and welcome proof of his fitness for leadership in national affairs.[61]

By contrast, Casey's initial silence was thought peculiar.[62] Subsequently he explained that he was concerned at 'the huge Commonwealth financial commitments' which he now believed the scheme would involve.[63]

Dame Enid's claim that, in the prevailing climate of international tension, Menzies' resignation was, to many, 'an outrage', seems an exaggeration.[64] The most critical newspaper, the *Argus*, questioned Menzies' judgement and adaptability as a Cabinet minister at a time when defence should have priority over social reform, but admitted his 'impeccable' adherence to principle. Mild as it was, this rebuke was judged by the journalist, Roy Curthoys, to be

---

[60] Fairbairn and Holt, quoted in *Age*, 15, 17 March 1939; Lawson to Menzies, 15 March, Menzies Family Papers.
[61] 15 March 1939.
[62] The *Herald*, while praising Menzies, archly remarked on the peculiarity of his leaving the Cabinet unaccompanied. On 17 March the *Age* editorialized unfavourably on 'The Silence of Mr. Casey'.
[63] *Age*, 18 March 1939.
[64] *Among the Carrion Crows*, 65.

'inexpressibly contemptible', and another friend, Sir Alan Newton, wrote to tell Menzies how glad he was that he had sold shares he once had in the *Argus*.[65] Another correspondent, one B. Kelley, wrote that Menzies' resignation would cause 'some uneasy searchings of conscience'. 'Numbers of my friends', he said, '(some of them not 100% with you on all occasions) have become ardently pro-Menzies'. And as Arthur Griffith, the old anti-Lang Labor warhorse from New South Wales, wrote, it was 'encouraging to know that amongst the milk-and-water crowd in the present parliament there is one real *man* at least'; though he was certain that 'A govt [sic] led by you or Hughes would put the Foot-Rot-Cattle-Tick minority where it belongs and would win the confidence of the people of Australia'.[66] Lyons's reaction to Menzies' resignation has been described by his wife as one of anger, followed by relief. Dame Enid's account, written many years after the event, is somewhat incoherent and self-contradictory, but probably comes closest to the truth when she writes:

> Joe's desire—and his power—to cast off bitterness lay in his strong religious faith, but his feelings of relief when Menzies left the Cabinet sprang from his belief in the man himself, in his basic integrity. In Joe's eyes, incomprehensible to many, Bob Menzies had redeemed himself by his resignation.[67]

Though in such matters convention demands polite forms, there was something especially warm in some of the words Lyons used when accepting the resignation:

> You have always expressed your views to your colleagues fairly and fearlessly, and at all times we have been aware that your opinions have been based on high and unprejudiced considerations... I shall look back on our association with feelings of great happiness, particularly as, despite this political breach, our mutual regard, I am most happy to say, remains unimpaired.[68]

Menzies himself expressed appreciation for 'the friendly references to him by the Prime Minister', and insisted to reporters that 'there had been no bitterness over his resignation'. That night he motored to Goulburn and caught the Melbourne Express. In Melbourne next

---

[65] *Argus*, 15 March 1939; Curthoys to Menzies, 17 March 1939; Newton to Menzies, 15 March 1939. Menzies preserved 32 congratulatory letters and 13 telegrams, Menzies Family Papers.
[66] Kelly to Menzies, 16 March 1939 and Arthur Griffith to Menzies 22 March 1939, Menzies Family Papers.
[67] *Among the Carrion Crows*, 65.
[68] Lyons to Menzies, 14 March 1939, Menzies Family Papers.

day he appeared in his Chambers for a professional conference and in the evening he spoke on 'Australia and the United States' at the annual meeting of the English-Speaking Union. His chairman, Justice Lowe, remarked when introducing him that Menzies' latest action had been consistent with his reputation for acting in accord with his principles. Menzies himself made no reference to his resignation other than a jocular observation that he had been 'determined to get to Melbourne to address the meeting at any cost'. The main burden of his talk was an attack on American films. Since they tended to portray Americans 'as those who all lived in a kind of thieves' kitchen, or in a gilded palace with an entrance hall 100 yards long, and with bathing girls on every terrace, it is no wonder that the real America is never known'.[69] Writing a few days later to Hughes, he remarked: 'I feel almost like a schoolboy whose holidays have unexpectedly arrived'.[70]

Over the next few weeks the stocks of the Government seemed briefly to improve. On 28 March Lyons made a broadcast in which, the *Age* asserted, he 'set himself to render the dual service of applying a sedative to the nation's nerves and a tonic to the nation's spirit'. Though the international situation was still alarming, Lyons said, defence preparations were going well, industrialization was proceeding apace, and a better economic outlook generally was to be looked for.[71] Next day he announced an agreement between the British and Australian Governments for the supply by Australia to Britain of 300 Bristol Beaufort planes. It was the first step in the establishment in Australia of a considerable aircraft manufacturing industry and was expected to net £7 000 000 and create at least 4000 jobs.[72] Then, on the 30th, Lyons and Street presented a Premiers' Conference with a new plan to establish a National War Council to advise on the implementation of the defence programme. An important function of the Council would be to facilitate co-operation between the Commonwealth and the States for civil defence in the event of an emergency.[73] When the Premiers agreed to the scheme the Government won something very close to that instrument of co-operation whose loss some five months before had been the occasion for Menzies' controversial Constitutional Association speech. It was a quiet victory, but one suddenly made poignant by the occurrence of the seemingly unimaginable. On 7 April Lyons died.

[69] *Argus*, 16 March 1939.
[70] Menzies to Hughes, 23 March 1939, Menzies Family Papers.
[71] *Age*, 29 March 1939.
[72] Ibid.
[73] Ibid., 1 April 1939.

He had caught a chill when travelling from Canberra to Sydney to open the Easter Show. Admitted to St Vincent's Hospital on 5 April, Lyons suffered a series of heart seizures; Dame Enid came by aeroplane from Tasmania and was at his side when he died. Earle Page who, as Deputy Prime Minister, announced the death, observed: 'The premature ending of this wise and useful life is really due to the intense strain and anxiety which accompanied his efforts to help Australia and the British Empire in their present extremity. If ever a man could truly be said to have given his life for his country, that man is our Prime Minister, whom we mourn'.[74]

---

[74]Ibid., 8 April 1939.

12

Prime Minister of Australia 1939

FOR SOME days Lyons's body lay in state in St Mary's cathedral, where an unending procession of people came to pay their last respects. From Melbourne Archbishop Mannix made a statement which, for once, caught at the sentiments of all Australians: 'The unexpected, almost tragic, death of the Prime Minister brings grief to Australia and far beyond its borders. The misunderstandings and criticisms of public life are hushed in the nation's sorrow'. It was a time, naturally, for eulogies, but few seemed merely conventional. It is hard to doubt the genuine affection in what Menzies, for example, had to say:

> ... while I admire beyond the power of words to express his public services, my clearest and most poignant memories will always be of Joseph Lyons, the man with whom I worked during some of the greatest and most distinguished years of his life. And my memories will not be of a Prime Minister, the Privy Councillor, the friend of kings and rulers, but of a simple unaffected human being who had practised the moving art of humanity, and who never lost the appearance of an almost small boy's bewilderment at the great things that had come to him.
>
> It was my honour to know him intimately in 1931 when the greatest crisis of his political life was upon him. Thereafter, our friendship was, I am glad to remember, unbroken. Even when I felt compelled to leave his Government, only a few weeks ago, his attitude was generous and understanding. We parted with expressions of mutual affection and good will. It would have been impossible to quarrel with him in a personal sense.[1]

On Lyons's death, Page, as Deputy Prime Minister, summoned for consultation the ministers immediately available in Sydney. Hughes, as Attorney-General, gave the opinion that on the Prime

[1] *Age*, 8 April 1939.

Minister's death all ministerial commissions lapsed. Due to Menzies' resignation, the UAP did not now have a deputy leader, so the Governor-General should be advised to commission Page, as Deputy Prime Minister, to form a government. This was done, and the new Cabinet was simply a reinstatement of the old. Announcing this, Page said that he had accepted the Governor-General's Commission on two conditions: that he would resign as Prime Minister as soon as the UAP had chosen a leader; and that if Menzies was elected leader he would not join the new Cabinet. Explaining this last condition later, Page would write: 'I could not recommend my Party to place itself in pawn with a Prime Minister who, I felt, would not achieve that stability in government necessary for an effective approach to the pressing problems of approaching war'. Lyons's death, combined with Menzies' unsuitability as a successor made it seem to him, Page claimed, an ideal time to form a National, all-party government.[2] The Page Caretaker Government took office on 7 April 1939, the day of Lyons's death.

Speculation about Lyons's successor as UAP leader, and therefore the likely Prime Minister, began almost at once. The *Age* immediately came out forthrightly for Menzies. It was imperative, it declared, 'that no sectional rivalries, no personal preferences, should be allowed to act as obstacles to securing for the nation the finest service in leadership'. And Menzies was indisputably the man:

> His natural endowments and intellectual attainments have been enriched by administrative experience. Overseas he has an established reputation as a statesman and public speaker, and no other Minister has within recent years done more to make clear to the British people Australia's special problems, Australia's place within the Commonwealth of Nations.[3]

On the morning of 13 April Menzies called on his old legal mentor, Owen Dixon, who recorded their conversation tersely in his diary: 'Expects to be P.M.: to be elected leader of the Party'.[4] Menzies, clearly, was full of confidence. The *Melbourne Herald*, if

---

[2] Page, *Truant Surgeon (TS)*, 269–70. This is Page's own account of the sequence of events, written in 1963. Although he claims to have made his position *vis-à-vis* Menzies clear at the outset there was some ambiguity in the press, which to the last moment seems to have thought a coalition between Menzies and Page possible (see e.g. *SMH*, 19 April 1939). And on Page's own account of it, the Country Party did not pass a resolution that it would refuse to co-operate with Menzies until the meeting of 18 April (*TS*, 274).
[3] *Age*, 8 April 1939.
[4] Owen Dixon, Diary, 1939.

a trifle less enthusiastic than the *Age*, nevertheless came out in his favour.[5] That evening Menzies spoke, like a true leader, to the Melbourne Junior Chamber of Commerce on the need for the business community to recognize its national and social obligations and to co-operate with the Government for the welfare and defence of Australia.[6] Perhaps that helped to convince the *Herald*, which was soon much more enthusiastic:

> Mr. Menzies is a man of great attainments. In his low gears he may be given to idle a bit, but leadership would, in the view of those who know him best, stimulate him in performance of the kind Australia today so sorely needs. Certain it is that with him in command, Cabinet would function like the very best of business boards: that Parliament would move with dignity and expedition.[7]

Was this, perhaps, the authentic voice of Murdoch?

Menzies' sanguine hopes were premature. The Government parties were due to meet on Tuesday 18 April and the UAP election would take place then; in the ten days between Lyons's death and the meeting a complex series of machinations occurred behind the scenes. Fragments of them are all that can be glimpsed now, but it is clear that the most important revolved around Menzies and a number of rivals, of whom the most serious were Bruce and Hughes.

On 15 April the *Age* reported, under the heading 'Summit of Audacity', that a move was being made to persuade Bruce, who was on his way back to England after his visit to Australia, to return and take the leadership. This move was alleged to have begun in Melbourne, the work of the 'secret junta' behind the UAP—the National Union. Although no official announcement was made, it was 'reliably reported' that the National Union, at a secret meeting in Melbourne on the 14th, decided to 'recall' Bruce. This action, said the paper, was an impertinent attempt by an outside body to take control of the situation: 'Australia needs competent leadership ... it cannot wait months while the National Union tries to pull political strings'. It obviously did not know that Page had already made an approach to Bruce. On 12 April he cabled to ask Bruce to come back to the leadership and offered his own seat of Cowper to facilitate the move. Bruce replied that

---

[5] *Herald*, 12 April 1939. Editorial, 'Mr Bruce or Mr Menzies for U.A.P. leadership' said Bruce would be probably more acceptable, but the difficulty of recalling him was great, and if the Party did not decide to do this 'the alternative is the immediate election of Mr Menzies to the leadership'.
[6] *Age*, 14 April 1939.
[7] *Herald*, 14 April 1939.

he was not prepared to return as a member of any political party, but would certainly consider leading a national government if that were feasible. Casey, who in a somewhat bizarre correspondence had tried in 1935 to persuade Bruce to return to Australian politics,[8] and who as we have seen had been party to Lyons's attempt just before he died to get Bruce to take over, now fully supported Page's move. He agreed to join Page in a radio-telephone conversation with Bruce on 18 April, the day of the crucial UAP Party meeting.[9] The *Argus* also supported Bruce, spreading the rumour that if Bruce accepted, Menzies would become High Commissioner in London, thus releasing the Kooyong seat for Bruce.[10]

Press speculation that a web of intrigue lay behind the push for Bruce was correct. It was explained in a frank letter which Roy Curthoys sent to his friend J. R. Darling, headmaster of Geelong Grammar, who was then on a visit to England. Curthoys was writing to tell Darling about 'the aftermath of Lyons' passing', which he described as 'disgusting'. His principal source of information was Kingsley Henderson, Chairman of Directors of the *Argus* and, as we have seen, once a political associate of Menzies', though now partly estranged from him. 'Your Melbourne Club friends in the National Union', Curthoys told Darling,

> and their opposite numbers in the Union Club in Sydney, aided and abetted by Page, who not unnaturally hates Menzies for the devastating stories Menzies so openly and so tactlessly spreads about Page's leadership of the trade delegation in London; and by Casey, who, in the opinion of most people, comes out of the whole business very badly, made a dead set on Menzies. He was held to have disgraced himself by his resignation on the National Insurance issue, which, as he himself has said, was one of the more respectable actions of his life ... I think the National Union also felt that Menzies wd not be sufficiently amenable to its orders. Hence the first move was to try to get Bruce back. Casey had sounded the Party and having found that he could not command more than a handful of votes, he backed the move. Page, determined to have anyone but Menzies, offered Bruce his seat.[11]

---

[8] W. J. Hudson, *Casey*, 93–6; I. M. Cumpston, *Lord Bruce of Melbourne*, 110–11. Casey was as critical as Menzies of the sloppy Cabinet procedures of the Lyons Government. Hudson also suggests that Casey either wanted Bruce's patronage or would have been glad to replace him in London.
[9] Page, *T.S.*, 271.
[10] *Argus*, 18 April 1939.
[11] R. L. Curthoys to James Darling, 24 April 1939. Letter in private papers of Sir James Darling whom I thank for kind permission to quote this letter. I have also to thank Drs Peter Gronn and Geoffrey Serle for drawing my attention to its existence.

Lest it be concluded from these remarks that Menzies did not also have formidable *support* from the upper echelons of Melbourne society it should be noted that he received a number of letters like that of the surgeon Sir Alan Newton who assured him on 15 April that 'There is no doubt about the general hope that you will become Prime Minister. Everybody of note in the Melbourne Club to whom I have spoken—and I have talked to many—has been in your favour'.[12] (After the contest was over, Newton wrote jocularly about Page's attacks: 'I am still at your disposal if you wish me to excise some ductless glands from the Leader of the Country Party.)[13] And among correspondents who wished him well were Sir Frank Clarke, President of the Legislative Council, sometime President of the Melbourne Club and a holiday neighbour at Macedon.[14] 'I expect and hope that you will be elected leader of the Party', he wrote, and pressed Menzies to take the External Affairs portfolio if forming a government: 'You are the only Australian who is personally known to the men who matter in England (who speaks their language), and all past history shows that these men as a class will do for their own kind much more than they will do for one they regard as an outsider'.[15]

Curthoys was somewhat contemptuous of Menzies' third rival, Hughes. He told Darling that 'A last minute effort was made to rally votes for Billy Hughes, who, apart from his impishness, is physically so senile that he had almost to be carried into Lyons' funeral'. In fact Hughes was in the race from the beginning and received substantial backing from the State UAP organization in New South Wales. Some believed he would make a good prime minister anyway, especially with war looming, but the strongest pro-Hughes influence was wielded by those who wished to see the State Premier, Bertram Stevens, in federal politics eventually. Sir Sydney Snow, head of the State executive, appears to have seen a victory for Hughes as a stepping-stone to a later success for Stevens. As one of Hughes's friends wrote: 'I understand on most reliable authority that Snow favours you as PM until matters have been arranged for Stevens to take that office, meaning that you would be used as a stopgap'.[16] Meantime locals were lobbying federal members from New South Wales to support Hughes. An undated typescript entitled 'Points to be Stressed', now preserved in the Hughes Papers, sets out the case for Hughes's supporters,

---

[12]Sir Alan Newton to Menzies, 15 April 1939, NLA, MS. 4936/1/23/190.
[13]Newton to Menzies, 27 June 1939, ibid.
[14]*ADB*, 8, 17–18.
[15]Sir Frank Clark to Menzies, 16 April 1939, NLA, MS. 4936/1/8/65.
[16]Mulligan[?] to Hughes, 9 April 1939, NLA, MS 1538/36/f. 1.

and probably the line Hughes himself took at the Party election. It stresses the impending danger of war and the 'imperative need of wise, courageous far-seeing leadership'. To recall Bruce, it says, would be a grave mistake: his outlook is British, not Australian; he would be regarded as the representative of vested interests; his record would be dug up and shouted from the housetops. The idea of recalling him is an affront to the Party: a confession of its bankruptcy in statecraft. Menzies is a fine man, a logical and finished speaker, but a lawyer, wholly ignorant of the lives of the people. He is unacceptable to the returned men, without whose support the UAP cannot hope to win; his policy on National Insurance is not acceptable to the Country Party, and the Country Party will not support any government he leads.[17]

When Page and Casey spoke with Bruce on 18 April, the morning of the crucial party meeting, he insisted, as before, that he would only accept an invitation to return on a non-party basis.[18] Curthoys was not far off the mark when he wrote:

Bruce had said ere he sailed away that anyone who wanted to repeat the experience of being a Prime Minister was a fool and a glutton. He sold the Party a pup by saying he wd return if he cd refrain from belonging to any party, could choose his own team and cd have the support of Labour—terms he well knew were as impracticable as they were unacceptable.[19]

Casey reported Bruce's terms to the UAP meeting and added a suggestion from Page that it postpone the election to allow them to be given proper consideration. This the meeting refused to do, so Casey decided to stand himself. In the end there were four candidates: Menzies, Hughes, Casey and White.

It was a tense day in political circles in Canberra. Not only were Page and Casey known to be on the telephone to Bruce up to the last minute; it was clear by then that Page would not join in a coalition government if Menzies were elected. The UAP meeting was delayed for three hours when Menzies had a severe fall. Before leaving for the meeting he took a walk with Mrs Menzies round the gardens near the public offices. Turning to wave as he left her, Menzies tripped on a protruding curb and fell heavily. Dazed, he was taken to hospital where X-rays showed no broken limbs but an arm and leg painfully bruised and grazed. He appeared in the party meeting with his arm in a sling.[20]

[17] 'Points to be Stressed', typed on 'Attorney General' notepaper. NLA, MS. 1538/36/7.
[18] There is a 'transcript' of the radio-telephone conversation in TS, 271–3.
[19] Curthoys to Darling, 24 April 1939.
[20] *Argus*, 19 April 1939.

Each candidate addressed the party meeting for half an hour before the vote was taken. According to the *Age* all agreed that other things must now be subordinated to the demands of defence. Menzies was asked particularly what his policy on National Insurance would be. He was reported as saying that he favoured the establishment of a select committee composed of representatives from all the parliamentary parties, the medical profession, the friendly societies, trades unions and the National Insurance Commission. Its task would be to 'arrive at a satisfactory scheme providing the widest basis of co-operation'. He was not prepared to recast his views to obtain party leadership.[21] There is no way of telling whether Page's ultimatum helped Menzies when the votes were cast. Some observers thought it did: the *Age* alleged that members of the UAP were 'deeply resentful' of the attempt to dictate to them, and the *Canberra Times*, which in fact had warmly supported Hughes, declared that such 'blackmail must be expunged from the political life of the Commonwealth'.[22] On the other hand, the *Argus* opined that it 'would have been deceptive—not to say deceitful' if Page had failed to tell the UAP what course the Country Party would follow if Menzies was elected.[23] In the upshot Menzies won, defeating Hughes, his closest challenger, by four votes. He at once had a meeting with Page, but the latter remained adamant in his refusal to join the Cabinet, although he did not threaten to withdraw support from a new ministry.[24]

'Throughout Australia there will be intense satisfaction that the member best fitted for leadership of the U.A.P. has been elected', was the predictable enough verdict of the *Age*. Newspapers which had supported other candidates wished Menzies well and the *Sydney Morning Herald*, which had been an earnest advocate of recalling Bruce, printed from the pen of 'A Political Observer' a frank but friendly appreciation of the coming Prime Minister. Maybe, it said,

> we are on the dawn of a new era in Australia—an era when forthrightness will count more than politics and adherence to principles more than the ability to bend to every breeze of expediency. Mr Menzies has always, when he has been convinced of the soundness of his convictions, displayed an unwillingness to bow to popular clamour.

---

[21] Ibid.
[22] *Canberra Times*, 19 April 1939.
[23] 19 April 1939.
[24] *Age*, 19 April 1939.

The new Prime Minister, April 1939

Menzies had qualities 'that lift him high above the other members of the Federal Parliament': his keen intellect, his power to 'expound an argument with crystal clarity', his repartee with 'the speed of lightning and the force of a sledgehammer'. He had been accused of arrogance and superiority. Certainly, 'like many men of considerable intellect, he cannot suffer fools gladly, but it is a mistake to assume that he is always arrogant, self-confident, cocksure. He is often shy and nervous, and the apparent air of self-assurance is a cloak that frequently hides extreme nervousness'.[25]

[25] SMH, 19 April 1939.

Parliament met on 19 April, and then, after Party leaders and a number of individual members paid tributes to Lyons, adjourned as a mark of respect. On the afternoon of the next day Page paid the conventional visit to the Governor-General, Lord Gowrie, to tender his resignation as outgoing Prime Minister and to say to whom the commission should pass. But that morning, in the House of Representatives, he took the unprecedented step of announcing beforehand what his advice to Gowrie would be. At the beginning of his short period of office, Page reminded the House, he had committed himself to retire in due course in favour of whoever the UAP elected in Lyons's stead. He would do so now, but since the new leader was Menzies, he and the Country Party were not prepared to serve any longer in a coalition government with the UAP. In explaining why, Page launched an attack on Menzies which the *Sydney Morning Herald* next day described as 'a violation of the decencies of debate without parallel in the annals of the Federal Parliament'.

With war threatening, said Page, this was a time when the country demanded above all a Prime Minister capable of leading 'a united national effort', but Menzies' public record certainly did not suggest he had the right qualifications for that. Three incidents—one twenty-four days ago, one twenty-four weeks ago and one twenty-four years ago—'give me no basis of confidence that he possesses the maximum courage or loyalty or judgement'. Twenty-four days ago, he resigned as Attorney-General, at a time when it was crucial that the Cabinet be held together as it prepared for war. Twenty-four weeks ago he made in Sydney 'a speech on leadership which was taken by a large section of the people of Australia as an attack on his own leader. I do not say it was, but—'. At this point uproar developed as Sir Frederick Stewart, the member for Parramatta, interjected angrily that six members of his Party had had an assurance from Lyons that he did not regard the speech as such. But this was as nothing to the excitement when Page came to his third charge: that twenty-four years ago, when Australia was in the middle of the Gallipoli campaign, Menzies, after being in the military forces for some years, resigned his commission and did not go overseas. Uproar and cries of 'shame' from both UAP and Labor benches greeted this declaration, but Page pressed on:

> I am not questioning the reasons why anyone did not go to the war. All I say is that if the right honourable gentleman cannot satisfactorily and publicly explain to a very great body of people in Australia, who did participate in the war, his failure to do so, he will not be able to get that maximum effort out of the people in the event of war.

When Page finished, Menzies rose to a chorus of 'hear! hear!' and was listened to in silence as he delivered a dignified reply. He had no apologies to make for his resignation on the National Insurance question: 'on the contrary, I regard it as one of the more respectable actions of my public life'. Nor would he retract one word from his speech in Sydney on leadership: it was, he said, 'a homily that I was addressing to myself and to every other person in Australia occupying a post involving leadership of the people of Australia'. Conversations which he had had 'with my late leader and friend were completely inconsistent with any suggestion that he regarded my speech as an attack on him'.

> After all, is this not getting down pretty low? If we are to be held responsible not only for what we say—I am always prepared to accept responsibility for my utterances—but also for the gloss which some person who may or may not have heard a speech puts upon it, that will be the end of all pleasure in public life. I invite every honourable gentleman in this chamber to ask himself: 'how should I like that standard of judgement to be applied to me?'

But there was real, if dignified, bitterness in his response to the third charge. It was one which was not a novelty and indeed represented 'a stream of mud through which I have waded at every election campaign in which I have participated'. Certain people, of whom Page appeared to be one, 'regard it as their ordained mission in life to pry into the private lives of other people; to put them up against a wall and say, "Why did you not do so and so?"' Page had in the process managed to discover some facts and failed to find others. Menzies had not resigned his commission: he had served out his term like any other young man of his age.

> Then I had to answer the supremely important question—'Is it my duty to go to the war or is it my duty not to go?' The answer to that question is not one that can be made on a public platform. This question relates to a man's intimate and personal family affairs and, in consequence, I, facing these problems, problems of intense difficulty, found myself, for reasons which were and are compelling, unable to join my two brothers in the infantry with the A.I.F. . . . but I am foolish enough to believe that the only judgement as to a man's capacity, a man's courage, and a man's fortitude that has any relevancy to his public conduct is the judgement of the people who have known him and have worked with him.
> Members of the U.A.P. know my many faults and such poor qualities as they think I possess. They believe, and I am conscious of the honour they have done me in expressing the belief, that I can lead them, and

I am vain enough to believe that I have the capacity to discharge that trust. And, in doing so, I shall exhibit none of those miserable attributes suggested by the Prime Minister in the most remarkable attack that I have heard in the whole of my public career.[26]

In the excitement that followed, two Queensland Country Party members, Fadden and Corser, dissociated themselves from Page's remarks and announced that they would henceforth sit as Independent Country Party members. The UAP members of the Ministry at once issued an official statement rejecting the Prime Minister's attack. Menzies' wife, who was in the gallery when Page spoke, stood up and pointedly left during the attack, and never acknowledged Page again. The family closed ranks. Menzies' parents flew to Canberra on 3 May, the day Menzies first met Parliament, and were photographed with their son on the steps of Parliament House. At seventy-three, Mrs James Menzies had never flown in an aeroplane before. In an exclusive interview for the *Daily Telegraph* she told of her 'anger when I read that in the Federal House it had been held out against Bob that he had not gone to the war'. The decision to stay had in effect been forced on him by the family: 'we told him again and again that two sons from a family was as much and more than a country expected ... we needed someone at home to look after us'. It was a difficult decision, 'and I think that is why he was perhaps the bravest of all my boys'.[27] Meantime a spate of spontaneous messages came from parliamentary colleagues who were appalled by the attack. That of Senator Allan MacDonald, a Scottish-born accountant who had served in the AIF at Gallipoli, can be taken as typical:

Dear Bob,

I wish to dissociate myself from the entirely unseemly and unwarranted attack made on you by the Prime Minister in the House this morning. I hope never to hear such brutal remarks again in any Parliament. I would like however to offer you my hearty congratulations on your masterly and restrained reply.[28]

---

[26] This account of the speeches is drawn principally from *SMH*, 21 April 1939, which I have checked with the *Age* and *Argus* of the same day. These three suggest that *CPD* for 20 April (*CPD* 159: 14–18) is slightly sanitized but not to the extent implied, e.g., by Dame Enid Lyons, who claims (*Carrion Crows*, 62) that Earle Page's speech was 'so violent' that 'by permission of the House it was withdrawn from Hansard and replaced by a more restrained version'. Only *SMH* has the critical last line of Menzies' speech: 'I shall show none of those miserable paltry traits shown by the Prime Minister in the most remarkable attack that I have heard in the whole of my public career'. I take the majority version which has the milder attack on Page.
[27] *DT*, 4 May 1939.
[28] Allan MacDonald to Menzies, 20 April 1939, NLA, MS. 4936/1/4/176.

In May 1939 Menzies' parents arrive at Canberra airport to be present at the opening of the first Parliament in which their son is Prime Minister. It has been for the mother, Kate Menzies, a great adventure—at the age of seventy-four it is her first flight in an aeroplane!

Curthoys' report of the incident to Darling was both indignant and revealing about Page's animosity:

> I've always felt, after having listened to the proceedings of Australian Parlts for close on 30 yrs, that for brutal personalities they took the palm, but that speech by Page left all else in the shade. In some ways Menzies deserved it, for I have heard him talk among comparative

strangers in terms so contemptuous of Page that I have gasped; and of course, these strictures have got back to Page, and he has brooded over them so long that when his resentment did find expression, it, too, was something that took one's breath away. The future depends on how Menzies can keep his head. To me it is inconceivable that he will not soon become megalomaniac. He has triumphed in the face of great odds.

When Menzies returned to Melbourne, on the day after Page's attack, he received something of a hero's welcome. At Spencer Street railway station he was piped on to the platform by the Pipe-Major of the Victorian Police Pipe Band and welcomed by the Lord Mayor, the Town Clerk, members of the United Australia Organisation, representatives of the Bar, and other friends. There were bouquets of flowers for Mrs Menzies and vigorous handshakes for her husband, very uncomfortable because he had been silly enough to remove his injured arm from its sling before the train arrived.[29] Perhaps Curthoys's cynical last word on this was only partly true: 'It was amusing to see all the gentry who had done their damnedest [sic] to keep him out assembled to greet him at Spencer St the other day. My word, their welcome was effusive! I suppose they will be forgiven over a jolly good dinner at Menzies [Hotel]'.[30] That weekend, Menzies said, he would be 'in hiding', considering the personnel for his new Cabinet.

Page himself was unrepentant, and secured a good deal of support from a number of extra-parliamentary Country Party organizations. The day after his attack, he was in radio-telephone contact with Bruce again. He told Bruce that before the election he had informed the UAP ministers in his Cabinet he would not serve with Menzies. 'There was only one place I could give my reasons publicly where they could be answered ... I have a personal regard for Menzies. I felt it had to be done and the only straight and courageous thing to do was to put it beyond any dispute'. This position had its grain of decency and Page could draw some strength from Bruce's reply: 'I think your statement admirable and understand perfectly what the position is'.[31] But how 'perfect' Bruce's understanding really was is open to question. Writing to Menzies some months later he observed, rather cynically:

---

[29] *Herald*, 21 April 1939.
[30] Curthoys to Darling, 24 April 1939.
[31] *TS*, 277–8. Note, however, that as Cecil Edwards points out, *TS* contains only a 'glancing reference' to Page's actual speech. According to Edwards, 269, 'Page himself was later so ashamed of what he had said in Parliament that, according to Lady Page, he asked a few weeks before his death in 1961 that it be omitted from his autobiography' (published 1963; Dame Pattie says Lady Page never came back to Canberra again after the incident).

There is no doubt that Page was your fairy godfather, if you had the slightest desire to be Prime Minister. Apparently he had considerable objection to your being one and promptly took the only possible course which would make the job a sitting certainty for you. The working of Page's mind is still a complete mystery to me notwithstanding my very considerable experience of its vagaries.[32]

Why Page acted as he did is not so mysterious, however, when one remembers Menzies' abiding and only half-hidden distrust of the Country Party, a distrust honed razor-sharp by the obstructive role which Page and his followers took in the final battles over National Insurance. But above all there was resentment at that old Menzies superiority which Page, ambitious, though a plodder at best, must have found galling, especially when experienced over the long months they had had to spend together in England and if expressed afterwards in barbed gossip which lampooned the giggly Page dullness.

Menzies announced the composition of his Cabinet on 24 April 1939. There were of course no Country Party ministers: it was a Ministry depending on the support of a minority of the House

The first Menzies Cabinet, 1939: (*at the back, from left*) Fairbairn, Harrison, McLeay, Spender, McBride, Foll, Collett, Lawson, Stewart, Perkins, Holt; (*at the front*) Street, Casey, Menzies, Hughes, Gullet.

[32]Bruce to Menzies, 4 October 1939, Menzies Family Papers.

and the 'discriminating support' of the Country Party. It contained all the previous UAP ministers, though with the exception of Street's (Defence) the portfolios were reshuffled. Casey left the Treasury to head a new Department of Supply and Development. He had as Assistant Minister James Fairbairn, Cambridge-educated grazier, who also became Minister for Civil Aviation. The object was to separate supply problems from Street's portfolio so that the latter's 'great talents will be allowed full play on the all-important problems of defence co-ordination'.[33] Another new initiative was the setting up of a Department of Social Services. Sir Frederick Stewart, a well-known philanthropist, took it and his mandate, said Menzies, was 'to deal with pensions and allied matters and also with National Insurance'. With sixteen ministers the Cabinet was the largest in the history of the federal parliament and, in average age, the youngest: as its most experienced member, the 60-year-old Henry Gullett, remarked to Latham: 'A fair team. All depends on Bob. He has it in him if it can be extracted and applied'.[34] In an emotional broadcast on the night the ministers were sworn in, Menzies appealed for co-operation, and pledged the new Government to two objects: external security and internal justice. 'My Government', he said, 'means business'.

> I come to you as one who has been accused of grave defects—aloofness and superiority. My alleged aloofness is one of those fantastic ideas that obtain currency. I am a singularly plain Australian. I was born in a little town called Jeparit on the fringes of the Mallee country of Victoria and was educated at a country State school, a Ballarat State school and then, by scholarships, at a secondary school, a Public school and the Melbourne University . . . I was not born to the purple. I have made my own way, such as it was, and is. I don't hold the achievement of the Prime Ministership an occasion for foolish vanity: I find in it the acceptance of a responsibility so great that it might well deter much better men than I can ever hope to be.

In his first, honeymoon period Menzies was the guest of the Lord Mayor of Melbourne at a civic luncheon in the Town Hall on 8 May, and of the Lord Mayor of Sydney at a reception on the

---

[33] Page claims (*TS*, 281) that the establishment of the Department of Supply and Development had been prepared by the Lyons Government and in fact was 'the one positive outcome of my submission to the conference of Federal and State Ministers on 21st October 1938'. But at the time of the execution of the idea the real guiding force behind the scenes was Frederick Shedden, the able public servant who was already dominating defence arrangements (J. P. Buckley, 'Sir Frederick Shedden, Defence Strategist, Administrator and Public Servant', *Defence Force Journal*, 50, January–February 1985, 29).

[34] *SMH*, 25, 26 April 1939. Gullett to Latham, 3 May 1939, NLA, MS 1009/1/5312.

15th. At both he was greeted with cheers, and in the Sydney Town Hall the audience rose and sang 'For He's a Jolly Good Fellow' when he came forward to speak.[35] Predictably, the journalists swooped on Mrs Menzies. 'A Special Reporter' for the Melbourne *Herald*, after describing her as 'slim and attractive', quoted her as saying that she was 'simply no good at making speeches' and could 'never hope to be as good as Dame Enid, whom I consider to be one of Australia's most wonderful women'. Meantime the public learned that Mrs Menzies was a gardener, loved reading and was an enthusiastic motorist, who did all the family driving. 'The Lyons tradition of homeliness in our leaders is safe with the Menzies family—that is Mr and Mrs Menzies, their sons Kenneth (17) and Ian (16), their daughter Heather (10)'.[36] On 23 May Menzies took up residence at the Lodge; Mrs Menzies was to follow a week

When in 1939 the Menzies move into their official residence, The Lodge, the house is still in a near-rural setting. Canberra seems in very truth to be what its detractors love to call it: Australia's 'bush capital'.

---

[35] *Age*, 9 May 1939, *SMH*, 16 May 1939.
[36] 22 April 1939. Menzies' ghastly deficiencies as a driver remain legendary in the family. Everyone was grateful for Dame Pattie's skills and all were parties to allowing Menzies' driving licence to lapse when he forgot to renew it.

later.[37] By early June the *Age* was able to observe that a 'notable absentee' from the weekend arrivals at Spencer Street station was 'the familiar form of Australia's new Prime Minister', who in the past had customarily devoted his weekends to his family in Melbourne.[38] But now the family had 'taken up their abode in the official residence of the Prime Minister at Canberra'.

The new Government met parliament in a short session from 3 May until 17 June and briefly showed welcome signs of fresh energy, especially on defence. Casey's Department of Supply and Development was established and, amid much rumbling from Labor, the administrative apparatus was set up to survey and mobilize industry and manpower in time of national emergency.[39] Enemies waiting to pounce on Menzies over National Insurance were not disappointed when, instead of producing any bold new initiative, the Ministry asked for further negotiation between doctors, friendly societies and the National Insurance Commission, with a parliamentary select committee to organize talks 'to see whether a practicable scheme, in which all parties will cheerfully and patriotically co-operate, can be evolved'. Page viciously attacked Menzies again, calling the proposal 'one of the most contemptible volte faces [sic] in Australian political history'. The Government, he said, was now proposing to adopt the very course against which Menzies had resigned in protest only three months before. Though technically correct this was hardly a proof, as Page and others went on to assert it was, that Menzies had been insincere in his original protest. In fact, political circumstances now were very different. Thanks to Page's subversion of the coalition, Menzies led a minority Government. Given Labor's opposition to contributary social services, the Country Party's rejection of anything beyond a health scheme, and the constant difficulties created by an unco-operative medical profession, it is difficult to see what hope there was for anything more than further consultations. Then parliament rejected the request for a select committee, and the skeletal organization set up under the old Act was preserved but set aside for the moment. As defence expenditure mounted and then, finally, wartime preoccupations swamped all else, National Insurance was doomed.[40]

Parliament adjourned during July and August 1939, and Menzies, accompanied by four of his ministers, visited all States to introduce themselves and explain the defence preparations they

---

[37] *SMH*, 25 May 1939.
[38] *Age*, 5 June 1939.
[39] Sawer, *AFPL* 2, 110–11; *Age*, 13, 21, 26 July 1939.
[40] *Age*, 10, 15, 16 June 1939; Sawer, *AFPL* 2, 109.

In a fashionable Sydney restaurant with Mrs Stewart Jamieson, whose husband (no doubt the occupier of the empty place at the table) later became an important Australian diplomat

In Launceston, wrestling with the problems of crustaceans and beer, with old friends from the local paper, the Launceston *Examiner*

were making.[41] Menzies also spoke often about the threatening international situation, his favourite theme being that Britain's course was the right one: 'We must keep open the door of the international conference room until the last moment ... At the same time ... we must devote our energies, wealth, time and enthusiasm to preparing for the time when the door may be closed against us'.[42] On 23 August, after the Nazis and the Soviets made the surprise announcement of their pact, and Chamberlain signalled the end of appeasement by guaranteeing to stand by Poland if her independence were threatened, Menzies declared that if Britain was 'forced into war it will not go alone'.[43] Events moved quickly. In a broadcast on the evening of 31 August Menzies outlined precautionary steps which the federal Government had just taken 'to prepare Australia for an emergency'. Munition factories had been placed on a war-time basis, fixed coastal and anti-aircraft defences were manned, naval ships in commission were ready for sea, dumps of petrol, bombs and munitions were available to the air force.[44] Supply, Casey assured the nation in a broadcast the next night, was fully in order. As Casey spoke, Menzies was on his way to Melbourne by car from Colac, where he had planned to address a public meeting. That address was never delivered. For, as the meeting convened, news came that Germany was attacking Poland.

In Melbourne, at the federal offices, Casey, Gullett, Fairbairn and Holt were waiting for their chief. All Cabinet ministers in Sydney meantime left for Melbourne by a specially chartered aircraft, to begin almost continuous Cabinet meetings.[45] On 3 September the British ambassador handed the German Government a final note calling upon them to withdraw all troops from Poland: when no reply came by the stipulated deadline Chamberlain, in a deeply emotional speech broadcast from the Cabinet room of No. 10 Downing Street, announced that Britain was at war with Germany. On the same evening, Menzies broadcast to Australians that it was his 'melancholy duty to inform you officially that, in consequence of a persistence by Germany in her invasion of Poland, Great Britain has declared war upon her, and that, as a result, Australia is also at war'. And in a clear and succinct speech, he explained how the crisis had developed in the last few months thanks to the 'coldblooded breach' of the series of 'solemn obligations' to which Hitler had committed himself.[46]

[41] *Age*, 19, 27 June, 6, 13 July 1939.
[42] Ibid., 14 August 1939.
[43] *DAFP* 2: 182.
[44] *Age*, 1 September 1939.
[45] Ibid., 2 September 1939.
[46] *DAFP* 2: 221–6.

The sombre moment of announcing Australia's commitment to war, 1939

Later that week Parliament met and Menzies laid on the table of the Representatives a White Paper setting out the text of the documents exchanged between Britain and Germany in the ten days leading up to the declaration of war. He asked for general support as the Government faced the awesome responsibilities now cast upon it. His speech was listened to in silence broken only by murmurs of 'hear, hear' from all sides of the House. Page and Curtin, as Party leaders, pledged their support for all that needed to be done for the defence of the country. Curtin perhaps caught best the sombre mood of the moment; 'we can', he said, 'be a saddened but determined people in this crisis ... We hate and abhor war', but Hitler had 'thrust aside discussion and negotiations and there was no alternative but for this dreadful affliction to come to mankind'. The sentiment was unanimous. Not a speaker queried the correctness of the course the Government had

The artist Lionel Lindsay was an admiring friend of Menzies, and designed for him a number of bookplates. This one is a commemoration of the dour moment when Menzies had to announce the coming of World War II.

taken: the latter-day idea that Australia was fighting 'other peoples' wars' did not occur to anyone. Nor did anyone contest Menzies' assertion that he felt he could appeal for support 'because we are all Australians and British citizens'. From the Opposition benches, even E. J. Ward, while not being 'prepared to give the Government an open invitation to do what it likes', did not hesitate to say that 'we want to see the country defended [and] we want to see the war brought to an early and successful conclusion'.[47]

---

[47] *CPD*, 161: 28–36, 76; *Age*, 7 September 1939.

13

Political Uncertainties 1939–1940

THE GOVERNMENT at once asked for and got what Menzies called 'wide powers of regulation and control in relation to the defence of the Commonwealth and its territories, the safety of the community and efficient prosecution of the war'. The powers were embodied in a National Security Bill, modelled on the War Precautions Act of 1914. Menzies assured the House that the powers asked for would not authorize the imposition of compulsory military service or industrial conscription, and Curtin declared that the Opposition accepted the necessity for such a measure.[1] Behind the scenes, Page told Menzies that the Country Party thought that 'differences of the past should belong to the past' and would in this time of national emergency join a composite government.[2]

Menzies refused to contemplate such an alliance if it meant Page coming back into the Cabinet. 'After four and a half years of what I had imagined was friendly co-operation in the Lyons Government', he wrote,

> you chose—without any warning—to launch a series of public allegations against me. They were not charges which became irrelevant in the event of war; they were deliberately made in view of the possibility of war ... I am not prepared to purchase ... security by inviting into a Cabinet which is composed of men who have confidence in and loyalty to me, one who has repeatedly and bitterly (and I assume sincerely) charged me with want of courage, loyalty and judgement.

In a self-righteous reply Page announced his willingness 'In this war, as in the last ... to serve in any position—in the field, in hospital, in Parliament or Government—in which my experience

---
[1] *Age*, 8 September 1939.
[2] The Page–Menzies correspondence on this matter (letters of 6, 8 and 12 September) are in NLA, MS. 1006/3/28.

and special knowledge can be of public service'. To 'remove the personal aspect', he placed himself in the hands of his party which, after a convoluted internal struggle, elected a new leader, Archie Cameron. Of Cameron, a South Australian soldier settler and dairy farmer, the *Age* remarked that 'his political credo is simplicity itself:—there are only two sides to any question—his own and the wrong one'.[3] When Bruce heard the news he wrote sympathetically to Menzies and recalled a conversation with Cameron, 'when he disposed of Lyons, you, Earle Page and Casey as possible Prime Ministers and then, as an afterthought, cleaned me up in case I had any misguided leanings in that direction'.[4] Menzies insisted on choosing any Country Party ministers to be admitted to Cabinet, Cameron refused, and hopes for a coalition vanished.

Menzies forthwith formed an all-UAP War Cabinet, which in effect became an executive committee to handle the immediate conduct of the war. It took as its secretary the head of the Defence Department, F. G. Shedden, who became the chief architect of much of the country's wartime organization.[5] Menzies arranged for the War Cabinet to consult service chiefs and to report regularly to the full Cabinet. Early press reports told of the long hours it sat. By mid-October Menzies was reporting to Bruce, in London, that the Government had been doing well under difficult circumstances, though there were newspaper critics and Page and Cameron 'are conducting specially poisonous public campaigns'. Criticism was difficult to cope with because 'naturally a great deal of work is not publicly known or appreciated'.[6] Within a few weeks of the outbreak of war, public meetings were being planned to demand the immediate recruitment of an Australian expeditionary force and one friend warned Menzies that 'a whispering campaign is starting with the theme "is the present Prime Minister the right man as a War Prime Minister?"'[7] Even Owen Dixon, visiting Canberra and briefly talking with Menzies on 14 September, 'pressed him with the situation in Melbourne owing to press criticism of inaction'. In fact, as Menzies then told Dixon, he was about to announce, in a broadcast the next evening, that the War Cabinet had decided to raise a volunteer military force of 20 000

---

[3] *Age*, 15 September 1939.
[4] Bruce to Menzies, 4 October 1939, Menzies Family Papers.
[5] P. Hasluck, *The Government and the People 1939–41* (Hasluck, *Government and People* 1), 421–2, is the standard reference for these and similar developments.
[6] Menzies to Bruce, 18 October 1939, *DAFP* 2, 356.
[7] Austin Laughlin to Menzies, 14 September 1939, NLA, MS. 4936/1/30/248. Laughlin himself was disgusted with the whole movement and adjured Menzies: 'Don't, for God's sake, let public noise and clamour affect your judgement'. He had written to a number of newspapers to say 'that it was Australia's good fortune today that you had not been killed in the last war'.

Professor Menzies' crystal refuses to shed any light on the subject.   By STAN CROSS

The cartoonist Stan Cross lampoons Menzies' reluctance in 1939 to rush into sending AIF troops abroad, as the Australian Government had done in World War I.

for service in Australia or abroad. At the same time he made it clear that, in two drafts of 40 000 each, the whole of the militia—available for service only within Australia—was also to be called up for intensive training.[8]

Though the Government was thus well abreast of critics demanding preparations for traditional action to help Britain, it was also attuned to the changed circumstances of 1939. 'If only a kindly Providence would remove from the active political scene here a few minds which are heavily indoctrinated by the "old soldiers" ... point of view', Menzies wrote to Bruce, 'my task would be easier'.[9] In a timely homily to such critics, he declared:

> This is not 1914, when there was no real problem of Australia's security from attack, and when land forces in Europe were the determining factor. People do not adequately realise that in the last war Russia and

[8]Dixon Diary, 14 September 1939; *Age*, 16 September 1939.
[9]Menzies to Bruce, 22 February 1940, Menzies Family Papers.

Italy and Japan were our allies. In this war ... Australia's own security must be attended to. Hence the training of 80,000 militia is of urgent importance, whereas in 1914 militia training was not only minor, but nominal. We cannot send divisions of trained infantry and artillery out of Australia until our own position is clarified.[10]

Before this, in response to an inquiry from Eden about what troops Britain could look for from Australia, Menzies had firmly said that 'upon the Japanese relationship and prospects, I am sure you will agree, must depend absolutely the part other than defensive which Australia will be able to take in the war'.[11] The chronic British failure to develop Singapore as an adequate Pacific bastion had combined with constant complaints by the Japanese consul-general in Sydney, Torao Wakamatsu, about alleged anti-Japanese feeling

Stan Cross tells of Menzies' new responsibilities and expresses confidence in him.

---

[10] *Age*, 26 September 1939.
[11] Whiskard (UK High Commissioner to Australia) to Eden, 11 September 1939, *DAFP* 2, 259.

in the Australian press and community to give bite to the natural apprehensions inseparable from aggressive Japanese policies in China. On accession to the prime ministership Menzies had declared that Australia must play a more active part in Pacific affairs and foreshadowed the establishment of diplomatic relations with Japan and the United States. He suspected that the information which British intelligence provided was inadequate for a country for whom Asia was the Near North, not the Far East.[12] Altogether, despite the anxiety he had accepted in the Lyons era to placate Japan, Menzies displayed at the outbreak of the European war a determination that Australia's security must come before everything else.[13]

That determination was, unhappily, undermined by developments largely beyond his control. A few weeks after the outbreak of war Eden, as Dominion Secretary, invited each Commonwealth country to send a minister to London to discuss war-time cooperation, and Menzies asked Casey to go.[14] When Casey flew out in mid-October, the first drafts of the volunteer force destined to become the 6th Division of the Second AIF were just going into camp. Canada had promised a division for despatch to Europe in December, and New Zealand was recruiting a force for overseas service too. The British were anxious that the Canadian force be followed quickly by the Australian and New Zealand contingents believing, as Eden wrote, that 'the psychological effect on our French friends and on Germany of the knowledge that these troops will be in the field in France, probably in time for a spring campaign, will be most salutary'.[15] In response to Australia's concern about the Pacific the Foreign Secretary ordered an intelligence appreciation, which judged a southward Japanese thrust most unlikely and the Admiralty made its usual assertions about its readiness to send a fleet to Singapore in the event of an emergency. Casey was satisfied and urged that the troops be sent. But Menzies and the Cabinet at home queried whether the need for more soldiers in France was 'sufficiently urgent to justify us incurring risk with our own defensive position', raised the difficulty of transporting the contingent at a time when exports of wheat and wool were suffering severely because of shipping shortages, and expressed the fear that recruiting of more urgently needed aircrew trainees would suffer if men eager for action thought the army the

[12] Whiskard to Dominion Office, 20 September 1939, *DAFP* 2, 277.
[13] See, in relation to this and other points under discussion here, P. G. Edwards, *Prime Ministers and Diplomats*, esp. 116 ff.
[14] *DAFP* 2, 281–2 for invitation; 337 for choice of Casey.
[15] Eden to Chamberlain, ibid., 369.

As war-time Prime Minister Menzies, with the Governor-General, Lord Gowrie, proudly inspects an Australian cruiser early in 1940.

best avenue to get overseas. Menzies cabled the New Zealand Prime Minister, Michael Savage, with these objections and urged that the two governments keep in close touch and act together.[16] But before this message reached Savage the New Zealand Cabinet, on the advice of Peter Fraser, its minister visiting London, had decided to send its contingent and had so notified the British. Thus forestalled, a furious Menzies had no alternative but to agree that Australian troops go overseas too, especially when he learned that the British had miraculously found shipping and had already sent it to convey the Australian troops. Menzies' chagrin is best expressed in the cable he sent to tell Casey that, in the light of the need for co-ordination with New Zealand, the initial AIF drafts would be sent in January 1940 to relieve British garrison troops in the Middle East. But 'Am bound to tell you', Menzies added,

---

[16] Menzies to Savage, and Menzies to Casey, 21 November 1939, ibid., 422–4.

that we do so under protest as we feel that in this matter we have been in effect forced into a course of action which we would not otherwise have adopted. For example, we resent being told that shipping is already on its way for the purpose of collecting our troops on January 2nd when we were not consulted before the departure of the vessels.

It is the general feeling of Cabinet that there has been in this matter a quite perceptible disposition to treat Australia as a Colony and to make insufficient allowance for the fact that it is for the Government to determine whether and when Australian forces shall go out of Australia.[17]

As he told the UK High Commissioner in Canberra, one of the reasons why Menzies was opposed to sending troops abroad at that time was the folly of stirring Labor opposition which certainly existed now and which might disappear later 'if and when activity on the Western Front flares up, and there was visible need for men'.[18] Sure enough, when Menzies announced the decision in parliament Labor opposition erupted. Curtin formally moved to oppose the despatch of the troops and Menzies had to defend a decision he had in fact disagreed with, and to contest some of the arguments which, behind the scenes, he had himself once advanced. It was perhaps most galling of all to be accused, then and later, of being subservient to British policy.[19]

While Casey was in England another crucial matter was settled, and one in which he was deeply involved—the opening of an Australian legation in Washington—but this time Menzies acted masterfully and successfully. Washington and Tokyo were the two centres on which devolved whatever policies Menzies developed towards the Pacific. The preliminaries for establishing embassies in both places had been completed before the outbreak of the war: a Tokyo appointment was delayed, chiefly by British opposition, until mid-1940, but by September 1939 the Government was under great pressure, both from Britain and the United States, to choose the first ambassador to Washington. Menzies favoured Bruce, but the latter wished to keep his post as High Commissioner in London and Menzies offered the Washington job to Casey. He did so after expressing 'reservations about Casey' to Bruce and

[17] Menzies to Casey, 1 December 1939, ibid., 441. Casey replied soothingly that arrangements made by the Ministry of Shipping were only tentative and awaited confirmation by the Australian Government. Note that Menzies' attitude to this and other imperial matters was first discussed by P. G. Edwards, in the light of the documents now available, in 'Menzies and the Imperial connection, 1939–41', in Cameron Hazlehurst (ed.), *Australian Conservatism*.
[18] Whiskard to Dominions Office, 24 November 1939, *DAFP* 2, 432.
[19] *CPD*, 162: 1698ff.

twisting Casey's arm for a quick reply by telling him that the Government was in trouble in parliament over soldiers' pay rates and wheat prices and might have to negotiate a coalition with the Country Party, in which case his vacant portfolio would be useful. Casey said he would prefer to stay in Australian politics but left Menzies to decide: 'If you feel it is desirable that I should go to Washington, I am prepared to fall in with your wishes'. Menzies did so feel, and Casey went to Washington. Whether, as one prevalent myth has it, Menzies used the occasion to get rid of a potential rival is most doubtful. Casey had been thoroughly defeated in the leadership tussle at Lyons's death and had subsequently shown no sign of wishing to challenge Menzies. Their long correspondence over the Washington posting suggests that both Bruce and Menzies saw Casey, by experience and temperament, as the best available man. It was thus extraordinary, not to say dishonest, of Bruce to write to Keith Officer, the Australian Counsellor attached to the UK Embassy in Washington:

> I am frankly somewhat amazed at this decision as the number of Cabinet Ministers of first class calibre in Australia is somewhat limited and our Richard is certainly the outstanding member of the Government apart from the PM. With so few useful colleagues to rely upon, nothing on earth would have induced me to part with Richard if I had been in the PM's place. That, however, is his business and not mine.[20]

As it turned out, Casey's demise was something of a disaster for the Government, though in a different sense from that foretold by Bruce. At the by-election for his seat of Corio, in Victoria, the Labor candidate, J. J. Dedman, won, defeating the UAP's Vinton Smith, longtime Young Nationalist friend of Menzies. As the first by-election since the outbreak of war this was an important test for the Government and was seen on all sides as a straw in the wind for the general election which must take place before the end of 1940. As Gullett told Latham, Corio was 'a lovely political kettle of fish ... Whatever the Government's frailties it has had no chance with a press so hostile'.[21] For a moment Menzies' spirits reached a low ebb. Shedden records that on the Monday after Corio's loss the Country Party demanded Menzies' retirement as Prime Minister. Menzies told Shedden that 'he would never be

---

[20]Bruce to Officer, 12 December 1939, NLA, MS. 2629, box 1, photocopy file. For sensitive discussions which reject the myth, Hudson, *Casey*, 114–16, and P. G. Edwards, *Prime Ministers and Diplomats*, 121–2. With the exception of Bruce's letter to Officer, I base my account on Hudson and Edwards, with consultation of relevant documents in *DAFP* 2.
[21]Gullett to Latham, 5 March 1940, NLA, MS 1009/1/5411.

able to thank me sufficiently for the help I had been to him' and explained that 'he mentioned the matter now lest he should forget it later in case of any change in the Govt.'[22] There was indeed a change, but Menzies' fears of displacement were not realized: instead, he managed to negotiate a coalition with Cameron, who now conceded the Prime Minister's right to veto the choice of Country Party ministers. In a new Cabinet of twelve, five ministers were Country Party men (Page was not one of them) and Cameron became Deputy Prime Minister. This Government was sworn in on 14 March 1940.

Soon after the coalition Ministry took office a dark new phase of the war began. Until mid-1940 the criticism of the Menzies Government's allegedly inadequate war effort had been noisy rather than widespread. These were the months of the 'phoney war', when after the Nazi blitzkrieg on Poland, and the Russo-German subjugation of Finland, there was a lull as the European winter drew in. At the other end of the world, in Australia, it was hard to keep alive that feeling of crisis which the outbreak of war had brought. Menzies himself was partly to blame for the apathy of these months. Wishing to counter panic at the beginning of the war, he had asked the nation 'to carry on through the months ahead with calmness, resoluteness, confidence and hard work'. As a slogan, he hit upon 'Business as Usual', an unfortunate phrase quoted against him ever afterwards.[23] It had to be fought against vigorously when, in the spring of 1940, there was a dramatic change in the war. The Germans invaded Denmark and Norway; after humiliating British losses at Narvik, Chamberlain resigned and Churchill formed his National Government. That was on 10 May, the same day that Italy declared war and Hitler began the 'Six Weeks' War', which opened with the assault on Belgium and Holland and ended with the fall of France. From 4 June, when the last evacuees got away from Dunkirk, there were no British troops on the Continent. The unimaginable had happened. The Battle of Britain was about to begin.

In response to these disasters the reconstructed Menzies Ministry led a drive to arouse the nation for an 'all in' war effort. Menzies secured from parliament, with Curtin's agreement, emergency legislation to facilitate full mobilization. It gave the Government unlimited power to tax, to take property, to direct employers and employees where necessary and to call up manpower for the defence of Australia. 'There will be one limit and

---

[22] Note by Shedden, n.d., AA, A59541/1, box 67.
[23] See Charles Lloyd Jones to Menzies, 6 September 1939, NLA, MS. 4936/1/17/144.

one limit only', Menzies declared. 'There will be no conscription for oversea service.'[24] Of a number of key appointments made to mobilize resources, the most important was that of the masterful Essington Lewis, head of BHP, as Director General of Munition Supply, with virtually dictatorial powers. In what Menzies called 'war programme acceleration' he also announced that a third division of the AIF would be recruited (Cabinet had authorized a second in February), and that 2000 additional men would be taken into the navy.[25] And to stir patriotic feeling as the necessary backing for such initiatives, Menzies was indefatigable in making broadcast talks and speaking from the public platform. The most dramatic of his appearances were those made in his home city, whose Lord Mayor, A. W. Coles, organized in May and June 1940 a series of wildly popular patriotic rallies in the Town Hall. Menzies was usually there. At one, to farewell Sir Thomas Blamey, then leaving to command Australian troops in the Middle East, Coles denounced strikers, farmers who wanted guaranteed wheat prices and businessmen who complained about war-induced trading difficulties: 'we salve our minds with phrases such as "the situation is grave, but not yet disastrous". I imagine that a rabbit feels like that when the first barrel misses him—but can he consider his position very much improved?'[26] Coles advocated virtual nationalization of resources and the elimination of party rivalries by the creation of a truly national government. Though silent on the first, Menzies warmly supported the second of these aims. On 5 June, as the Dunkirk evacuation came to its close, Coles organized a great 'win the war' rally, where Menzies pledged the Government to devote 'all it had' for the cause, publicly thanked Curtin for 'the human friendship and comfort' he had often given in those dark days and reiterated willingness to take Labor ministers into a national Government. The culmination of this meeting was a solemn stage spectacle when, against a background of banners and armed with rifles and fixed bayonets, twenty uniformed members of the original AIF passed a torch to twenty uniformed members of 'the new AIF'.[27]

An element in the patriotic enthusiasm of those days was what Menzies called a 'move against enemies in our midst': the outlawing of the Communist Party and other 'subversive' organizations.[28]

[24] *Argus*, 17 June 1940.
[25] Ibid., 23 May 1940.
[26] Ibid., 18 May 1940.
[27] Ibid., 6 June 1940.
[28] Ibid., 17 June 1940. The other bodies declared illegal were the Australian League for Peace and Democracy, the Minority Movement and Italian organizations in Melbourne, Adelaide, Brisbane, Cairns, Innisfail and Edie Creek, New Guinea.

This was largely a result of coalition with the Country Party. Menzies' preceding, all-UAP, Government had in December 1939 and January 1940 called for Intelligence and State and Commonwealth police investigations into Communist Party activities and accepted their advice that outlawing was not necessary.[29] Page on the other hand consistently demanded a ban, reviling the Menzies Government for what he sneeringly called its 'Hands off the Communists' policy.[30]

The phrase came from a notorious New South Wales ALP State Conference at Easter 1940, which, under left-wing influence, passed a 'Hands off Russia' resolution, opposing the use of force against any country with which Australia was not at war.[31] A consequent declaration by Curtin played into Page's hands: official Labor was 'with Britain and against Germany, because Germany went to war and set the world aflame. If any nation lines up with Germany we are against that nation. In a sentence, we regard Germany's allies as the enemies of Great Britain, and therefore of Australia'.[32] For Menzies the Easter resolution reflected 'an un-British attitude which the Australian people will not stomach'. This view was strengthened by the 'subversive' activities of Communist union leaders, vividly exemplified for him in a strike on the New South Wales coalfields which began early in March 1940 and lasted over nine weeks, seriously affecting transport and the industries which were part of the war effort. The miners' primary grievance, that a recent Arbitration Court decision denying surface workers the same hours as underground miners was not in accord with previous decisions, was a genuine industrial one. But it was also understood that Communist miners' leaders, who conducted the struggle, were at the very least uninterested in advancing the war effort.[33]

A decision by Menzies to intervene in this dispute produced an incident which ranked equally with, if not above, his Melbourne Town Hall appearances. In a plucky act, comparable to his visit to Wollongong during the pig-iron troubles, Menzies arranged to address northern miners in the King's Theatre at Kurri Kurri. As

---

[29] Secret Cabinet Memorandum, 1 December 1939, NLA, MS. 4936/2/36/3; Communist Party—Conference, 22 January 1940, AA, A2671/1/11940; Cabinet Minutes, 8 April 1940, AA, A2697 XR1, vol 4A.
[30] *Age*, 3 April 1940.
[31] Lloyd Ross, *John Curtin: A Biography* (Melbourne 1977), 187–8.
[32] *Age*, 27 March 1940.
[33] On the background to the strike, see R. Gollan, *The Coalminers of New South Wales* (Melbourne 1963), 215; the miners' immediate grievance was clearly set out in a newspaper advertisement: 'Why the Coal Strike?', *Age*, 16 March 1940; Sawer, *AFPL* 2, 119.

Rowley James, the tough member for the Hunter and himself an ex-miner, said from the Labor benches on the day of Menzies' trip, the Prime Minister's mission showed 'a considerable degree of courage. He is going amongst a community which is hostile to him; but even though they be hostile, they are democrats and will give him a hearing'.[34] When Menzies arrived at Kurri Kurri he found an almost empty theatre: the miners' leaders had organized a boycott, providing buses for adjournment to a mass countermeeting at the Newcastle sports ground. Menzies forthwith drove the thirty miles to the Newcastle meeting where, from a boxing ring set up in the centre of the ground, the northern miners' leader, 'Bondy' Hoare, was addressing a crowd of strikers and their sympathizers, drawn from the districts surrounding Newcastle and estimated to number more than 4000. Shouldering his way on to the ground through jeers and boos, Menzies sat at the foot of the ring, heard out the speeches of the miners' leaders, then asked to be allowed to speak himself. Hoare asked the crowd for a decision, and a great roar of 'no!' went up. But Menzies, sitting unmoved, heard out more speakers, the crowd wavered, and a new vote gave permission. Reporters at the scene thought he was listened to with good humour, despite bursts of noisy interjection. The latter, of course, were to his taste. Asked ironically, for example, where his bodyguard was, Menzies replied, quick as a flash: 'The only bodyguard I have here is composed of two or three thousand Australian citizens, who, I believe, will listen to me. I am the grandson of a working miner, who was thrown out of a job because he formed a union'. Eloquent words followed, asking the men to return to work and apply to the Court for a variation of the award—the advice in fact which Curtin, though he did not go personally to the coalfields, was giving them. But after Menzies had spoken, the audience carried a motion repudiating 'the attempt by ... the Prime Minister to break the loyalty of the miners to their leaders' and expressing their determination to carry on the strike.[35]

A little over three weeks later, as strike funds dwindled, a series of conferences brought the strike to an end, with the union representatives agreeing to an undertaking to abide by court awards for the duration of the war. Menzies took the occasion to revive a proposal, so far rejected by the union movement, that it form an advisory panel to assist the Government on industrial matters and

[34] CPD, 163: 149.
[35] Age, 20 April 1940. There is also an account of this incident, and of the strike generally, in Hasluck, Government and People 1, 207.

Curtin agreed to press the unions to reconsider the matter.[36] Meanwhile one man at least, while remaining a political opponent, never forgot Menzies' trip to Kurri Kurri. In 1945 Rowley James, in a private conversation, called Menzies 'the whitest man in Australia today', and in explanation declared that Menzies had 'done a thing that Curtin dare not do and that is go to the coalfields ... I will not hear a word against Bob Menzies, who is a genuine Australian, and probably the best that this country has raised for a long time'.[37]

The fervour of mid-1940 was patchy, and the run-up to the elections late that year saw wide fluctuations in public enthusiasm for the war and many allegations in press campaigns against Government bungling and inefficiency. Meanwhile UAP–Country Party tensions and surviving hostility to Menzies' leadership, exacerbated no doubt by his often tactless impatience with mediocrity, continued. Menzies is to be found more than once referring resentfully to the wasteful irritation of the extra-parliamentary as well as party-political attacks he had to endure. As he told one group of Sydney businessmen:

> at this easily the most difficult pass in our history, I as Prime Minister have to devote at least one-third of my time (and I work fifteen hours a day, seven days a week) to warding off blows aimed at me, not from the front, but from those who are supposed to be my supporters— 'snipers', people who shoot from behind, people who think a fine round mouth-filling destructive criticism is a contribution to make to the war.[38]

In this atmosphere Menzies experienced an especially cruel blow in a disaster that occurred in August, just as he was about to announce the date of the election. On the 13th an RAAF bomber, coming in to land at Canberra airport, crashed on a low nearby hill, burst into flames, and all ten on board were incinerated. The victims included the Chief of the General Staff, Sir Brudenell White, and three federal Ministers: Street, Fairbairn and Gullett. The Ministers were coming to Canberra for a Cabinet meeting. For

---

[36] Hasluck, ibid., 207–8. The panel was formed, after much controversy, by the Government itself, though with Curtin's approval, in July (Hasluck, 234–5. Later references, 290).

[37] Staniforth Ricketson to Frank Menzies, 19 January 1945, sending a letter reporting remarks James had made to an officer in J. B. Were's Sydney branch. Not surprisingly, the regard seems to have been mutual: 'I seem to recall over the years having heard Bob speak in quite a nice way about Rowley James', wrote Ricketson. NLA, MS. 4936/1/33/269.

[38] Quoted, Hasluck, *Government and People* 1, 237.

Menzies their deaths were searing: 'This was a dreadful calamity, for my three colleagues were my close and loyal friends; each of them had a place not only in my Cabinet, but in my heart. I shall never forget that terrible hour; I felt that, for me, the end of the world had come'.[39] His grief was close to the surface in the obligatory parliamentary tributes he paid next day. Of Street: 'he was my friend, faithful and just to me ... In a period of immense personal strain and trial, his steady loyalty meant more to me than I can hope to say'. Gullett could give 'hard knocks' but, the fight being over, the memory lingered of 'the grey-haired, studious-looking man with the quick smile, the tender human charm, the capacity for giving a friendship so understanding and so moving that I can hardly bear to speak of it'. If slightly less affectionate, the picture that Fairbairn conjured up was no less positive: 'He displayed an unusual combination of cheerful fellowship with, perhaps, a hint of Scottish dourness'.[40] It was not appropriate to say that, when Mrs Menzies walked out of the Visitors' Gallery in such distress at Page's attack the year before, it was Fairbairn who noticed and left the House to walk with and comfort her in the parliamentary rose gardens.[41]

A sentiment somewhat different from that which Menzies expressed in the House was reflected in a letter which one E. Telford Simpson wrote on the day of the crash to 'commiserate with you on the loss of three of your colleagues'. A Sydney solicitor, Simpson had since 1936 been chairman of the Consultative Committee, the New South Wales counterpart of the Victorian National Union, and the financing body of the local UAP.[42] Simpson hoped Menzies would not think him 'too mundane and callous' if he made a suggestion about the coming election. It seemed that with three vacant seats, all of them once held by ministers, Menzies had been given 'a rather heaven sent, if I may use that expression' opportunity to launch a new party. It would have one plank, 'Win the War', and would attract into the House 'men of better standing from whom you could select a better ministry'. Simpson wrote that he had been approached by a number of men of this kind who refused to campaign under the UAP banner and who, if nothing were done, would appear

---

[39] *Afternoon Light*, 18.
[40] *Age*, 14 August 1940; *CPD*, 164: 374.
[41] Interview with Dame Pattie, 1 October 1987.
[42] Son of E. P. Simpson (*ADB* 11: 609) and a principal in Minter, Simpson and Co. Alleged by Andrew Moore that at one stage a leading member of the 'Association', *The Secret Army and the Premier* (Kensington 1989), 241.

in the election as independents. He was certain that he could 'switch the funds under my control in support of the new party'.[43] Menzies wired back cautiously that he would 'consider the matter as soon as possible' and Simpson pressed him again with a letter which made it clear that his proposal was partly an emanation of the internal squabbling then wracking the New South Wales branch of the UAP. Dissatisfaction with the present system of preselection, wrote Simpson, was widespread. If a new party open to all sections of the community were not formed, independents were bound to crop up in every constituency, many of them 'backed up by very large financial resources'. These would be the poorest material for effective party action.[44]

Simpson's proposal came to nothing, perhaps because the New South Wales organization was too divided, perhaps because Menzies, grieving at the tragic loss of his closest colleagues and having for months put up with a press campaign demanding 'new blood' in the Ministry, found the attempt to capitalize on the unexpected deaths crude and offensive. As the election campaign approached, the UAP in New South Wales, unable to settle the quarrel about preselection, abandoned it altogether and opted for multiple endorsement.[45] This, plus the cry for 'new men', multiplied candidates and split the vote: later, when reporting on the election to Casey, Menzies sardonically wrote that 'our organization in N.S.W.—made up of the Telford Simpsons and the Horsefields—were just about as willing to support Evatt as they were to support me'.[46]

On 20 August, a week after the air crash at Canberra, Menzies announced the date for a general election, 21 September. Next morning the *Sydney Morning Herald* came out with an editorial, 'the Prime Minister's Opportunity', which deeply offended Menzies. That feeling was no doubt exacerbated by unease at his recent relations with the *Herald* which are not readily to be fathomed at this distance. For some years he and Warwick Fairfax, the proprietor, had been on friendly terms: in his period as Lyons's Attorney-General Menzies had been a frequent visitor at the Fairfax home in Bellevue Hill and a welcome conversationalist during the the Fairfaxes' holidays at Palm Beach; after he became Prime Minister he occasionally lunched at the the *Herald* office, on congenial terms, with Fairfax and his chief lieutenants, the general

---

[43]Simpson to Menzies, 13 August 1940, NLA, MS. 4936/1/28/228.
[44]Simpson to Menzies, 16 August 1940, ibid.
[45]*DT*, 29 August 1940.
[46]Menzies to Casey, 8 December 1940, Menzies Family Papers.

manager, R. A. G. Henderson, and the editor H. A. McClure Smith.[47] The *Herald* had in general looked kindly on Menzies until about May 1940 when it began to be critical of his leadership and his Ministry. The precise reasons for the change are obscure. Pettier issues may have been unrecorded fallings-out over personal matters, or disagreement about Government regulation of newsprint imports. More important, perhaps, was genuine concern at the implications of the darkening atmosphere that had then developed in Europe.[48] But while not withdrawing all support the paper increasingly upbraided Menzies for alleged ministerial weaknesses and bungles, and was joined by the *Daily Telegraph* in demanding that he bring 'big men' into parliament to shore up his Cabinet. In this perspective the editorial of 21 August seemed to Menzies like the culmination of an unjust vendetta against him. He had neither sought new blood, it said, nor had he recognized that growing demands for 'the formation of a new, patriotic, all-embracing party are a significant and natural expression of the country's weariness of party strife. The mass of electors would feel more confidence in Mr. Menzies as a leader, if they were convinced—and they are by no means convinced—that he means to place national needs before party exigencies'. He had missed the chance of inviting 'selected men into the Cabinet in advance of the elections—a step which would have the great merit of showing the country what sort of a Cabinet Mr. Menzies is seeking'.[49]

When Menzies read this, something inside him snapped. He dictated a hurt and bitter three-page draft letter to McClure Smith, then in his neat hand wrote additional, cutting amendments over the typescript. The letter was probably never sent,[50] but it stands as the *cri de coeur* of a tired and maligned man, momentarily near to the end of his tether. The offending editorial, wrote Menzies, was based on the ridiculous idea that the Prime Minister should bring into Cabinet or Parliament 'big men'. It was, as the *Herald* should surely know, constitutionally impossible to introduce into the Cabinet men who had not been elected and were not

---

[47] Gavin Souter, *Company of Heralds* (Melbourne 1981), 184–6. Few documents survive to attest this happy relationship: one is a letter Menzies sent to Mrs Warwick (Betty) Fairfax on the eve of his departure from London in 1938: 'On this occasion I have had very little leisure, although I had an amusing week in Paris and a very interesting, although not very amusing, one in Berlin, so I am quite looking forward to inviting myself out for a drink after my return to Australia, so that I can give you a reasonably veracious account of them' (Menzies to Mrs Warwick Fairfax, 6 August 1938, Menzies Family Papers).
[48] Souter, ibid., 189, thinks the European crisis the most important factor.
[49] *SMH*, 21 August 1940.
[50] Gavin Souter has kindly checked for me in the *SMH* archives and finds no trace of it there.

answerable for their administration on the floor of the House. 'In Sydney, where this theory has some supporters, I have repeatedly but vainly asked various groups who these big men are, whose bigness has so far not persuaded them to go through the pains and discomfort of electoral campaigning in order to serve the people in Parliament'. The coming election would be his own eighth in twelve years:

> every campaign has been personally abhorrent to me. I have waded through the sewer of personal abuse, but I have so far emerged. I have never expected that high office would be handed to me on a plate without pains and without trouble, and, quite frankly, I don't see why anybody else should expect it. I am not entirely out of touch with public opinion in Australia, and I am firmly convinced that the average Australian is on the Government's side. It is indeed ironical to think that the Government's danger of defeat—a defeat which might have tragic results for Australia—does not come from its opponents but from the destructive activities of a relatively small group of men who have failed to realize that if the people are persuaded that this Government is a bad one they will certainly instal [sic] another government which will not be made up of angels of light but of Curtin, Ward, Brennan and Company. That result will not so much be bad for me or my party as ruinous for Australia. I tell you quite honestly that my own defeat would, as such, leave me cheerful. As Prime Minister I have sweated day and night, under recurrent difficulties and disappointments, and sometimes disloyalties. I have gone on in spite of it all, doing my indifferent best, sniped at and loftily admonished [in the original, but deleted, 'by every leading newspaper except the Melbourne "Age" '] until I sometimes curse the day I entered politics. For many months I have done all that any man could do ... to avoid bitterness; to score no cheap party points; to preserve national unity. This policy has frequently disappointed and even irritated my own partisans, but it has left the 'Sydney Morning Herald' persuaded that I prefer 'party exigencies' to 'national needs'.
>
> Do you wonder that men of intelligence prefer to keep out of politics and cultivate their own gardens?[51]

In the election campaign the three main parties agreed that the prime task was to prosecute the war successfully. For the UAP Menzies concentrated almost wholly on this, offering generous representation if Labor would join a national government. For the Country Party Cameron promised full co-operation in the coalition Government and undertook to stand down if a change in his party's leadership would help in the formation of an all-party national government. For Labor, Curtin pledged support for the

[51] Menzies to McClure Smith, 21 August 1940, Menzies Family Papers.

In characteristic pose, Menzies campaigns in the fateful 1940 election.

war effort, including Australian participation in overseas campaigns if home defence were adequately provided for. But much of his policy was also about social justice both as an element in the war effort and an object to strive for in the post-war world.[52]

On the Labor side a noteworthy feature of the election was the resignation of J. B. Chifley and H. V. Evatt from prominent non-political positions to contest important seats. Chifley had been appointed in the previous June as Director of Labor Supply in the Ministry of Munitions and Evatt was stepping down from the High Court, where he had served as a judge for almost a decade.

[52]Sawer, *AFPL* 2, 124–5.

Chifley's decision was made with characteristic quietness and his return to politics at this time of emergency seemed natural enough for one who had been a minister in the Scullin Government. Evatt's action was more dramatic: 'I shall do my utmost to serve my fellow Australians, as so many of them have to face the perils and disasters of war', he declared. Privately, Menzies was, naturally, cynical about that: 'Evatt', he wrote to Casey in Washington,

> whose manoeuvring for a Labour nomination has been notorious for the last couple of years, who applied to me for the post of Minister to America (as you will remember), and who has never ceased to be a politician while on the Bench, resigned to contest Barton. With one common outburst of hysteria the Press, led by the S.M.H., welcomed this great act of self-abnegation as if it restored all the glories of mediaeval martyrdom. They acclaimed Evatt as a high-minded jurist who would bring into politics all of those qualities of detachment and dignity and intellect which it so badly required.[53]

Asked to comment publicly on the candidature, Menzies said that he regarded the precedent Evatt was setting as 'most regrettable. The judiciary should be kept completely detached from politics'. In response Curtin lauded the 'patriotic decision of his Honour, Mr. Justice Evatt, to forfeit a salary of £3,000 and pension rights of £1,500 a year'. For his part Evatt abused the Menzies Government as 'the most irresponsible and inefficient on record', and sought to capitalize on what was clearly in some quarters a New South Wales grievance: that the executive Government, in war as in peace, seemed too 'concentrated and centralized in Melbourne'.[54] Brian Penton, in his regular writings for the *Daily Telegraph*, also made much of the same matter, declaring Melbourne an important issue in the election, and urging voters to return 'big' men, irrespective of party, who would properly

---

[53] Menzies to Casey, 8 December 1940, Menzies Family Papers. On Evatt's ambitions: Spender, *Politics and a Man*, 71, says that about twelve months before the 1940 election, Evatt, whom he had known since their schooldays, invited him to have a cup of tea in his Chambers. 'He was probing ways and means of entering Parliament surveying the lie of the land. He saw the opportunity for greater power in politics than he could exercise on the High Court Bench. He believed, or had convinced himself, that the state of the nation was desperate, and that a national all-party government should be formed. He was wondering whether, if such a government were acceptable to Labor, he would be acceptable to the U.A.P. as its leader, and thus bring about national unity.'

[54] *Age*, 5 September 1940. Evatt wanted to see Canberra 'restored' as the real centre of the country, to counter the 'small and powerful Melbourne coterie who had exercised far too long a dominating influence on Commonwealth legislation and administration'.

represent the strength of New South Wales.⁵⁵ On the eve of the poll the *Daily Telegraph* carried an editorial signed by Frank Packer himself: 'Why We Are Supporting the Best Men'. Such men, it said, were urgently needed 'to assist, in the difficult wartime administration, a Prime Minister who is surrounded by such a weak team that he has to carry four portfolios himself'.⁵⁶ It did not point out that the overloading of portfolios on Menzies was recent and temporary, the result of the air crash.

Menzies' hopes for a decisive result in the election—clear defeat or sound endorsement of the Government's position—were dashed. The UAP–Country Party coalition on the one side and the combined Labor parties on the other won thirty-six seats apiece. There were two independents, A. W. Coles, the doughty businessman Lord Mayor of Melbourne, and Alex Wilson, a Mallee farmer who had held the Wimmera seat since 1937. Both could be expected to support the Government, but there was nothing to prevent either changing his allegiance on snap issues. After providing the Speaker for the House of Representatives, a Menzies Government would have to depend on a shaky majority of one: in practice, one of these Independents. Both Chifley and Evatt won their seats convincingly, becoming formidable additions to the senior ranks of the Labor Party. Of the few new Government supporters, the strongest were J. P. Abbott, a power in graziers' councils, and Eric Spooner, who during a turbulent eight years in the New South Wales parliament had gained considerable experience as a minister. The UAP just held its own in five States: what made the result so close was a marked swing to Labor in New South Wales.⁵⁷

To Menzies it seemed quite clear what had happened. 'The election', he wrote to Casey, 'was a curious affair'.

> It was, as you know, preceded by months in which our clever young friend McClure Smith, of the 'Sydney Morning Herald' and our pugilistic friend, Frank Packer, of the Sydney 'Daily Telegraph' did their very best to discredit the Government and all its works. The S.M.H. people were under the childish delusion that they could wallop

---

[55] 18 September 1940. Norman Cowper, one of those listed by Penton, had backed Bruce in the 1939 leadership tussle and later wrote to Menzies to apologize for not 'barracking' for him and to declare his support. In a postscript to the letter he added: 'Perhaps to satisfy my conscience, I ought to add that a Melbourne man ought never to forget that wisdom, sense and rectitude are to be found in other parts of Australia as well as Melbourne!! and London!!!' (Cowper to Menzies, 24 April 1939, NLA, MS. 4936/1/9/72).
[56] 20 September 1940.
[57] *ADB* 12: 37 and 74–7 for Spooner and Stevens. Hasluck, *Government and People* 1, 256–63, for the most revealing analysis of the election results.

"The result in N.S.W. is to be attributed not to the Government's avowed enemies, but to some of its supposed friends—important sections of the Sydney press."—*Menzies*.
"*This is for your 'outstanding candidates'—they're standing outside in the wet.*"

Menzies sheets home to the *Sydney Morning Herald* (as 'Granny') blame for his Ministry's discomfiture in the 1940 election. Press demands for 'outstanding candidates' produced in New South Wales a plethora of Independents whose competition brought serious losses to the UAP.

the Government and merely produce the pleasing result that their readers would not vote for the Labor Party but would vote for bigger and braver and better men on the Ministerial side of the House. McClure Smith is not without a certain academic intelligence, but etherialised by Balliol. He is, of course, quite a nice fellow, but the utter unreality of his approach to all political problems and his abysmal ignorance of what ordinary Australians think and do have made him a menace.[58]

[58] Menzies to Casey, 8 December 1940, Menzies Family Papers. Though Australian, born in Melbourne and educated at Melbourne Grammar, McClure Smith had indeed gone to Balliol, where he shared rooms with Warwick Fairfax. Before coming home as editor of the *SMH*, he had looked ambitiously at the editorship of *The Times*, a hope, it seems, made futile only by the longevity of Geoffrey Dawson (Souter, ibid., 169).

The *Herald*, which in the end had advised its readers to vote for the Government, admitted that the vote in New South Wales turned the election, and in effect reluctantly admitted that its criticism of Government failings was unfair:

> What told against the Ministry in New South Wales was the very doubt not of its will but of its strength to organize the war effort on 'all-in' lines. It was here, in the most populous, most industrialized and most politically vigorous State, that consciousness of the Government's earlier deficiencies was most acute. Criticism of the Cabinet's lack of imagination, drive and administrative capacity had lost much of its point in recent months, as a solidly-founded war programme developed under the impetus of increasing danger; but some of the distrust formerly engendered remained.[59]

Whatever the reasons for the vote, the stark reality which had now to be faced was that of difficult, perhaps unstable, government, at what was a critical phase in the nation's history. Menzies' immediate instinct was to seek a way out of the impasse through the formation of a national government. But it was not to be. Though the newly elected and ambitious Evatt was prepared to nibble at the idea, Curtin was adamant that Labor, while co-operating fully in the war effort, had other social objectives and could not surrender its freedom of action. A special ALP interstate conference had in mid-1940 ruled against an offer then being made by Menzies for Labor to join a composite government.[60] Curtin would not waver from this position, but he did reiterate an earlier proposal for an alternative: a purely Advisory War Council, on which Government and Opposition would have equal representation, and which the Government could inform and consult on all matters to do with the conduct of the war.[61] Though he accepted this as a second best, Menzies was profoundly unhappy about it. An Opposition which received classified information, gave appropriately informed advice and yet took no responsibility for any decisions that followed was not to his taste. 'A true National Government', he wrote privately, 'or even a true War Cabinet, might be worth a price, but an Advisory Council is worth little or nothing'.[62] But he accepted it and publicly announced that he and his colleagues were determined to try to achieve effective co-operation with the Opposition in the months ahead.[63]

[59] *SMH*, 23 September 1940.
[60] Patrick Weller (ed.), *Caucus Minutes* (Melbourne 1975), 3: 234, 275.
[61] Hasluck, *Government and People* 1, 254, 269–71.
[62] 'Comments on proposals made by the Leader of the Opposition', 22 October 1940, Menzies Family Papers.
[63] *Age*, 23 October 1940.

The Advisory War Council in session in Canberra, 19 November 1941

Menzies was thus left with the unenviable task of reconstructing his Cabinet and continuing the unhappy struggle to keep it afloat. Two ministers had lost their seats in the election, and there were the three vacancies left by the ministers killed in the air tragedy. After the election Fadden, the Queenslander who had revolted against Page's attack on Menzies, defeated Cameron for the Country Party leadership. One of the most popular of men in the parliament—'a hail-fellow-well-met associate of everyone'[64]— Fadden became Treasurer and Deputy Prime Minister. The previous Treasurer, Percy Spender, accepted the Army portfolio. A Sydney lawyer, Spender had first entered parliament in 1937. The *Sydney Morning Herald* saluted his 'really spectacular debut' as Minister for the Army when, with 'Wellsian self-confidence', 'loungesuited, pork-pie hat squarely on head, [he] walked into the beuniformed Victoria Barracks, Melbourne . . . as an aimiable, one-man blitzkrieg'.[65] Spender was matched by John McEwen—'a Byronically different type'—dark-haired and fierce farmer who had served as Minister for the Interior in Lyons's last Government and whom Menzies now chose as Fairbairn's replacement in the

[64]Spender, *Politics and a Man*, 74.
[65]4 November 1940.

Civil Aviation portfolio. Both, said the *Herald* reporter, at once 'set for themselves and their staffs new standards of efficiency which must tauten the fighting fibre of the nation'.[66] Other portfolios were reallocated among surviving ministers, though Menzies took the opportunity to establish a new department of Labour and National Service. As Minister, he seconded the young Harold Holt, who a few months before had enlisted in the AIF. Holt was thirty-two, and had in 1939 served as Assistant Minister to Casey in Supply and Development. He was the new man in the Cabinet who might well be thought of as a replacement for one of the Victorians lost in the air crash. Hughes stayed on as Attorney-General and Minister for the Navy, and a cheeky *Sydney Morning Herald* reporter noted that, while 'there are other competent ministers', the success of Menzies' Prime Ministership 'may depend on his ability to discard the philosophical epigram for the club, when the club, wielded in caveman style, is the weapon needed to deal with permanent inefficiency. The club won't lack targets'.[67] That the club might be needed was suggested by the fact that the new Minister for Commerce was Earle Page. No better indication of his skills as an old political operator is that, somehow or other, Page had made it impossible for Menzies not to include him in this, desperate, Cabinet.

The Government's shakiness and the usefulness, after all, of the Advisory War Council, were both displayed when the Ministry met parliament and Fadden brought down his first full-scale war budget. The Advisory War Council considered it beforehand but discussion there broke down when the Labor members wanted changes the Government was not prepared to concede. In the House Curtin then moved an amendment 'as an instruction to the Government'. In an eloquent speech he did not contest what he called the 'staggering' sum of £186 000 000 sought for 1940–41, but objected to the Government's distribution of the burden and wanted increased payments to pensioners, servicemen and distressed wheatgrowers.[68] Menzies at first treated the issue as one of confidence but the debate suggested that the loyalty of some Government supporters could not be assumed and he agreed to take the budget back to the Advisory War Council. There a compromise was negotiated. Curtin withdrew his amendment when the Government agreed to raise the income tax threshold, in favour

[66] Ibid.
[67] Ibid.
[68] *CPD*, 165: 267–8.

of pensioners, servicemen and drought-affected wheatgrowers, and to appoint a select committee to inquire into the possibility of raising the level of company taxes.

The short-lived crisis revealed the eagerness of a few Labor men, led by Evatt, to overthrow Menzies. 'We mean business', he said of Curtin's budget amendment. 'It was not moved merely so that a useless debate might be held on the subject.'[69] But Curtin had a greater sense of responsibility. 'I am here to make this Parliament workable', he said. 'Government members would like to see this Budget reconsidered. We ought to have an assurance that the wishes of Parliament will be taken into account.'[70] He was obviously not anxious to inherit Menzies' dependence on one Independent. But he also showed, on this and other occasions

"Events are moving towards an all-party Government under Labor leadership."
—Dr. Evatt.

"Hey, that belongs to Labor."
"Who's Labor? You, Curtin or Beasley?"

After the election of 1940 H. V. Evatt's anxiety for office—maybe even the Prime Ministership—is an open secret, and a matter of as much regret for Curtin as annoyance to Menzies.

[69] *Age*, 2 December 1940.
[70] *SMH*, 29 November 1940.

when the Government stumbled, a genuine anxiety to do everything in his power, consistent with his principles, to maintain stability in the face of the war emergency. It is, however, not evident that the nominal Government supporters who at this stage wanted reconsideration of the budget took the same relaxed view as Curtin. The debate on the budget in fact revealed a little group of hard-core UAP dissidents who wanted to get rid of Menzies. Their chief stock-in-trade was an appeal to the now defunct idea of a national government.

The most persistent of them was William McCall, a wool and skin merchant and company director, who had been the member for Martin, in New South Wales, since 1934. 'My support', he had said in September 1940, 'will go to anybody, irrespective of party who ... uses ability as the only criterion in selecting a Government from all quarters of the House'.[71] At the time of the budget crisis McCall alleged that 'there was a big section of the Labor party which would be willing to form a National Government with one of its own members as leader and the support of the more liberal-minded section of the Government and its followers'.[72] On the same day, another incipient rebel, Sir Charles Marr, declared that 'he did not care who was Prime Minister, as long as the Cabinet was as far as possible representative of the full administrative ability obtainable in the House of Representatives'.[73] Member for Parkes, in New South Wales, since 1931, Marr was an electrical engineer who had held office in earlier non-Labor ministries, but not under Menzies. His and McCall's hostility towards Menzies may have arisen from disappointed expectations, New South Wales antagonism to a Victorian Prime Minister, or sheer personal dislike. Whatever the explanation, it was serious and well recognized by Menzies himself. As he told Casey in his report on the 1940 election, both McCall and Marr had scraped in by narrow margins, which pleased him because 'each of them had sought to obtain re-election by the simple and loyal expedient of blackguarding the Government'.[74] Revival at this stage of the issue of a national government can only be interpreted as an attack on Menzies. Curtin had made it clear that he would not condone such a government and had denounced the alternative, another election, as something which 'would weaken the parliamentary system and ultimately strengthen the reactionary elements in the country'.[75]

[71] Ibid., 30 September 1940.
[72] *Age*, 2 December 1940.
[73] *SMH*, 30 November 1940.
[74] Menzies to Casey, 8 December 1940, Menzies Family Papers.
[75] *Age*, 10 December 1940.

There were, however, admirers who sought to shore up Menzies' morale. The most notable of a number of efforts was a complimentary dinner organized for him at the Australia Hotel by 'a General Committee of prominent citizens' and attended by over 300 gentlemen.[76] It was first suggested by F. H. Wright, a prominent insurance broker who knew Menzies well and idolized him. Wright thought that the enthusiasm of those who were asked to assist 'gives the lie to the whisper so often heard in the past that Bob had few personal friends'.[77] Staniforth Ricketson, who agreed, noted how good it was 'to think that we have a man of his calibre at the head of affairs at a period of our history such as this'.[78] Menzies made a stirring speech at the dinner, and later told Ricketson that the function had 'provided much encouragement to me. To know that so many appreciate the work that is being accomplished is a real source of comfort'.[79] He needed such boosts. As he wrote to Casey: 'To be compelled at a time like this to devote about half your waking hours to avoiding political disaster is enough to drive you to despair'. Since a national government could not be formed it looked as if another election would have to be held 'to clear the political atmosphere and enable real Government direction to be re-established'. But there was one consolation: 'thank God, the vast organisation, particularly on the supply and munitions side, that has been set up and is now functioning is month by month producing even more remarkable results. So here's hoping ...'[80]

But despite the political tensions of those days, Menzies could still unbend. At the beginning of December—in the middle of the budget crisis—he happily fulfilled his duties as Vice-President of the Melbourne Scots at their annual St Andrew's Day dinner. After the haggis had been piped in to the traditional slow, rhythmic clapping of hands, the guest of honour, Noel Coward, made a graceful speech and sang 'Mad Dogs and Englishmen'. The President, C. N. MacKenzie, called on 'brother Scots and their guests to make merry', reminding them that the following year, after the tax gatherer had finished with them, they might have to

---

[76] Printed circular invitation of 4 November for the dinner on the 14th so describes the Committee and lists its twenty-three members. A list of those attending the dinner was subsequently printed to show the table plan and reservations. Staniforth Ricketson Scrapbook, MUA.
[77] Wright to Staniforth Ricketson, 13 November 1940, NLA, MS. 8119/2/5. Wright, an ex-army staff officer, wrote in 1942, 'I have served two really great men in my life, one was General Sir John Monash and the other is Robert G. Menzies'. Wright to Sir Robert Knox, 8 September 1942, NLA, MS. 8119/2/15.
[78] Ricketson to Wright, 15 November 1940, NLA, MS. 8119/2/15.
[79] Menzies to Ricketson, 18 November 1940, MUA.
[80] Menzies to Casey, 8 December 1940, Menzies Family Papers.

bring their own sandwiches to the banquet. The Consul-General for the USA proposed the toast 'Australia' and Menzies replied with a witty speech which ended with a stirring affirmation that 'what the Government is saying through its grim budget—saying to rich men living in comfort and to wage earners living from day to day—is this: One in, all in. (Cheers). I have no doubt what their answer will be. (Loud cheers)'.[81] After parliament adjourned on 13 December for its summer recess Menzies travelled to Western Australia to campaign in a by-election caused by the death of the Country Party member for Swan, Henry Gregory. He was at the old settlement of Beverley when on 20 December he turned forty-six. A reference to the birthday in the local press brought a flow of congratulations and a group of supporters came to Menzies' hotel door to present him with a fountain pen. A woman of seventy-eight at one stage pushed through the circle around Menzies to wish him many happy returns and tell him that it was her birthday too. 'The Prime Minister bent over and said something in confidence to her. She smiled and gripped his arm affectionately.' The Premier of Western Australia gave him a walking stick, and Menzies declared it to be the first time he had had a birthday party in years.[82]

When he got back from Western Australia Menzies went with his family to Macedon for the Christmas break.[83] In Victoria it was, the press reported, 'a Bumper Holiday Season'. Tourist officials attributed the increase in holiday travel to something akin to the Melbourne Scots President's exhortation: the spirit of 'make hay while the sun shines'. Others thought, simply, that many people had worked harder and more consistently in the previous twelve months than before, and as a consequence were both in need of a holiday and had more money. Resorts up and down the coast and in the hills were booked out; traffic on the roads was thick. 'People were determined to have their holidays, and [petrol] ration tickets had been carefully hoarded, to be squandered joyously over the holidays'.[84] The Menzies family were fortunate in having 'Illira' as a retreat, but their pleasure in the accustomed break there was not unalloyed. For though it had yet to be publicly announced, they knew that as Prime Minister Menzies was about to make a trip to London, during the parliamentary break, to discuss with the British authorities matters about which his Government was

[81] *Age*, 2 December 1940.
[82] Ibid., 23 December 1940.
[83] *Argus*, 26 December 1940.
[84] *Age*, 28 December 1940.

deeply concerned. Beside the dangers of wartime travel, there was local danger in leaving Australia at this particular time since, as Menzies explained to Bruce, 'political position here precarious and principal lieutenants in Cabinet not very experienced'.[85] Pat was positively opposed to his going,[86] chiefly for this reason but, by Christmas, arrangements had irrevocably been made.

[85] Menzies to Bruce, 3 January 1941, *DAFP* 4, 320.
[86] Interview with Dame Pattie, 18 September 1990.

14

Encountering Churchill's England 1941

THE DECISION that Menzies should make this trip to England arose from concern, in the War Cabinet and on the Advisory War Council, about that running sore, the defence of Singapore. In October 1940 a Far East Defence Conference of British, Australian and New Zealand staff officers, held at Singapore, had prepared a tactical appreciation of defence requirements in the Far East. It underlined what had been evident since the Imperial Conference of 1937: that in military and air strength, quite as much as in naval force, Singapore's defences were gravely deficient.[1] Churchill's penchant for playing down the dangers of this was by now notorious. In 1939, when he was First Lord of the Admiralty, he had in an appreciation of the Far Eastern situation pooh-poohed the idea of Singapore ever succumbing to land-based attack: 'it could only be taken after a siege by an army of at least 50 000 men, who would have to be landed in the marshes and jungles of the Isthmus which connects it with the mainland'. Such a siege must last four to five months at least and could easily be contained 'if at any time Great Britain chose to send a superior fleet to the scene'.[2] The findings of the Singapore Conference of 1940 underlined the hollowness of such a view, and when the Australian War Cabinet received them it cabled London at once to express its grave concern, to offer Australian troops and equipment and to press for more British reinforcements.[3] There was no opposition in Cabinet or the War Advisory Council when Menzies suggested that he should go personally to London to talk over these and other matters with Churchill and his ministers.[4] On 17 December

[1] Paul Hasluck, *Government and People* 1: 295–6.
[2] Paper of 17 November 1939 for meeting of Dominion Ministers on Naval Defence of Australia, PRO, CAB 99/1/141.
[3] Commonwealth Government to Lord Cranborne, 1 December 1940, *DAFP* 4: 212, 285–7.
[4] Hasluck, *Government and People* 1: 313–14.

he informed Bruce that he wished to come to London, visiting Australian troops in the Middle East on the way. Bruce showed this cable to Churchill who asked him to tell Menzies 'how greatly your visit will be welcomed and how much he personally would appreciate your presence here'.[5] In January, just before Menzies left, Bruce warned him that though he might have ready access to all British ministers, Churchill had increasingly taken over control of policy,

> little influenced by other members of War Cabinet who frankly are not prepared to stand up to him. My view is Prime Minister would endeavour treat you in much same way—most cordial welcome—utmost courtesy—invitation to attend meetings of War Cabinet and apparently every possibility for consultation. When however you tried to pin him down to definite discussions of fundamental questions of major war policy I am inclined to think you would find him discursive and elusive necessitating you either (a) taking a line that would mean a considerable show down between you or (b) leaving with a sense of frustration.[6]

Bruce urged Menzies to weigh the political position in Australia against what he could hope to achieve in England. The warning was ominously prophetic.

While Bruce was offering this advice, events in the Middle East added to Menzies' anxiety to visit the troops there. The Australian 6th Division, sent originally to Egypt to train in the time-honoured way for service in France, took instead the leading part in Britain's first North African campaign. France was now out of the war and Italy in it, with half a million troops in Libya and Abyssinia, placing British positions in Egypt and the Sudan under serious threat. Field Marshal Wavell mounted the first drive against the Italians to push them across Libya away from Suez. He had at his disposal the British 7th Armoured Division, the Indian 4th Division and the Australians. The Indians fought the early phase of the campaign by taking Sidi Barrani in December 1940. They were then sent to reinforce units in Sudan, and the British armour and Australian infantry pressed forward in Libya. In a brilliant campaign they advanced 500 miles in a little over a month, taking Italian ports from Bardia to Benghazi, 130 000 prisoners and enormous quantities of equipment and munitions. It was the first notable victory of Allied arms on land since the outbreak of war.

---

[5] Menzies to Bruce, 17 December 1940, and Bruce to Menzies, 18 December 1940, *DAFP* 4: 303, 308. The original of Menzies' cable is drafted in his own handwriting, AA A5954/1, box 613.
[6] Bruce to Menzies, 5 January 1941, *DAFP* 4: 325.

Menzies left Sydney by Qantas Empire flying boat on 24 January 1941. He was accompanied by Shedden, John Storey, of the Aircraft Production Commission, and the secretaries N. C. Tritton and S. Landau. Three of his ministers, Fadden, McBride and Collins, were at the wharf to see him off, together with his wife and father-in-law John Leckie. He was glad to have Leckie there 'because the whole business is distressing to Pat who has vast courage but knows that for once in my life I am off upon a chancy undertaking'.[7] Over the next few days he flew via Darwin and Batavia to Singapore. There he was impressed neither by the state of British arms nor by the quality of the British command. 'Why cannot *one* squadron of fighters be sent out from N. Africa?', he expostulated to his diary. Singapore had just welcomed a new Commander-in-Chief, Air Chief Marshal Sir Robert Brooke-Popham. Brooke-Popham, Menzies decided, looked rather like the late Baden Powell. He had

> borne the white man's burden in many places from Kenya to Canada, and it has left his shoulders a little stooped ... He received us at the landing stage, wearing a pith helmet, a 'bush shirt' of khaki, the tail outside the trousers in the manner of a tunic, and shorts. So complete a type was he that I had much ado not to say 'Dr Livingstone, I presume' ... His attitude throughout our talks was courteous and benevolent, he is a first-class listener, but he left me with a vague feeling that his instincts favour some heroic but futile Rorke's Drift rather than clear-cut planning, realism and science.
>
> Winston Churchill had lunched him in London before he came out to this appointment, and he was boyishly pleased that Winston's farewell exhortations to him had contained more than a hint of the forlorn hope. ('Hold out to the last, my boy, God bless you. If your grandfather had not broken his neck playing polo at Poona he would be proud of you this day!').

Menzies found the other commanders equally unimpressive. General Bond, chief of the army, wore a monocle and spoke 'with that form of mental hiccups which reduces conversation to a series of unrelated ejaculations': if there were action, no doubt he would die gallantly, but so too would many of his men. When Menzies raised broader issues he found that, even on service matters, all the positive talk 'was by myself, with Shedden feeding me with material'. Altogether, 'this Far Eastern problem must be taken seriously and urgently'. On the spot he sent instructions to Australia that three-cornered staff talks (between British, Australian and Dutch officers) should be held at Singapore at once, and the results cabled to him in London.[8]

[7]Diary, 24 January 1941.
[8]Ibid., 29 January 1941; *DAFP* 4: 352–3.

Calls, and talks with officials, followed at Penang, Bangkok, Rangoon, Calcutta. Then, on 2 February, flying west over the desert, the party approached Palestine and Menzies noted how, in this rugged country, 'every patch of soil or hillside or valley [is] cultivated, fallow or green. "He leadeth me beside the still waters" ... Then suddenly the Sea of Galilee and the lone green wonder of the Jordan valley'. At home at 'Illira' Pat was writing a sad letter he would receive some days later:

> We miss you very much and somehow the heart has gone out of these holidays ... At this moment you are approaching Cairo and your first objective, but to us living in this quiet, peaceful place it is very disturbing to know you are reaching Australia's first battleline. If wishes had power and strength ours would turn your flying boat and bring you back to us.[9]

Sir Harold MacMichael, the British High Commissioner for Palestine, with Blamey, met Menzies at Tiberias, took him to see Jerusalem and organized a busy tour around the Australian camps

At Cairo in February 1941 Sir Thomas Blamey gives a dinner in honour of the visiting Prime Minister. At the head of the main table, Menzies sits on Blamey's left, and Sir Miles Lampson, the British Ambassador to Egypt, on his right.

[9] Pat to Menzies, 1 February 1941, Menzies Family Papers.

in the area: 'troops drawn up in many places—salutes—great precision—with only the old and bold cooks calling out "How are you Bob?" ' At one camp after a march past of the 21st Brigade and artillery troops of the 9th Division Menzies addressed the men through amplifiers and reflected afterwards: 'It is a moving thing to speak to thousands of young men, mere boys, in the flower of their youth, many of whom will never see Australia again. War is the abomination of desolation, but its servants are a sight to see'.[10]

For the next ten days, Cairo was Menzies' base. He moved in the local diplomatic circle as the special guest of Sir Miles Lampson, the British Ambassador, clearly creating a good impression. In farewelling him Lady Lampson wrote: 'Noone cd have been a more charming or easy guest—or a wittier! Come back soon'.[11] And 'Chips' Channon, a British MP who was invited to a special dinner party at the Embassy to meet him, found Menzies 'jolly, rubicund, witty, only forty-six with a rapier-like intelligence and gifts as a raconteur'.[12] He gave a successful press interview ('The first Dominion PM they had ever seen') and spoke at dinners in his honour. But his main preoccupation was the pursuit of Australian servicemen: he visited RAN vessels in Alexandria harbour, and flew over the desert to inspect Bardia, Tobruk and Benghazi. Whenever he encountered detachments of soldiers, he spoke to them from an improvised rostrum. 'They all look splendid, but craving for news of home and boyishly pleased when I pointed out the world significance of the campaign they have been winning'. Little incidents bolstered his guileless pride in these men: 'Benghazi goes along. What a tribute to a British conquest. Nobody dispossessed, no loot: good Australians slapping down their money on the bar of an hotel conducted by a "conquered" Italian'.[13] They were clearly on their best behaviour while he was around.

Then, travelling via Khartoum, Lagos and Lisbon the party flew into England on 20 February, low under the clouds and with a tense feeling of 'running the gauntlet' crossing the snow-covered fields of Devon, to land at Poole. Channon, who was on the same flight, noted how 'the excitement of Menzies' Australian entourage was touching to see as they approached England for the first time'.[14] Bruce and a contingent of reporters were there to greet them. Next morning they drove to London, where Menzies was

[10]Diary, 4 February 1941.
[11]Jacqueline Lampson to Menzies, 13 February 1941, Menzies Family Papers.
[12]Robert Rhodes James, *Chips, the Diaries of Sir Henry Channon* (London 1967), 292.
[13]Diary, 11 February 1941.
[14]Rhodes James, *Chips*, 293.

Visiting North Africa in 1941, Menzies talks to all the Australian troops he encounters: here, at Tobruk, he speaks to a small unit he has come upon in the desert.

installed in a suite on the first floor of the Dorchester. 'As the building is modern and there are seven floors above me', he noted, it is considered as good as an air-raid shelter'. That was consoling, for the blitz was still at its height. A busy day followed, with a visit to Australia House and an address at the Ministry of Information to an international audience of 200 journalists about Australia's war effort. Bruce entertained him at lunch at the Savoy to meet a select party of British ministers. Menzies' diary records impressions of these men but only one of the topics discussed: 'Very free talk about Southern Ireland. All present are plainly anti-RC. Bevin convinced that ... now is the time for a commission from the Dominions, chaired by U.S.A., to offer to settle the matter'.[15] Here, on his first day in London, was Menzies' introduction to a subject which, at home, had barely crossed his mind, but which he would quickly discover was an obsession with the British: the peril created by Southern Irish insistence on maintaining neutrality in the war.

The next day, Saturday 22 February, Menzies travelled through the Buckinghamshire countryside to Chequers, where he had been invited for his first weekend with the Churchills. In the celebrated

[15]Diary, 21 February 1941.

After arriving in London in 1941, Menzies at the Ministry for Information briefs a large international press conference about Australia's war effort. Bruce sits on Menzies' right, and Duff Cooper, the British Minister for Information, on his left.

Long Gallery he met Mrs Churchill, and her daughter Mary, 'aged 17, the freshest and best looking girl I have seen for years'. Then the Prime Minister himself swept in, zippered in his Siren Suit ('a dull blue woollen overall ... As worn, I believe, for the sudden alarm and retreat to the basement. As a form of pre-prandial costume it mystified me, for he later appeared at dinner in the white shirt of convention, and forgot all about air raids until 2 am!'). Initial impressions were overwhelming:

> What a tempestuous creature he is; pacing up and down the room, always as if about to dart out of it, and then suddenly returning. Oratorical even in conversation. The master of the mordant phrase and yet, I would think, almost without real humour. Enjoys hatred, and got a good deal of simple pleasure out of saying what he thought of DeValera [sic], who is (inter alia) a murderer & perjurer.

Here again was Ireland, the meat of yesterday's lunchtime discussion. 'There is a growing passion on this subject here', Menzies noted, 'and we may as well get ready for squalls'. Churchill went on to pontificate about the inevitability of America's help, of the likelihood of her involvement in a Japanese war and of Roosevelt's determination to stamp out the Nazi menace from the earth. 'Is he right? I cannot say. If the P.M. were a better listener and less disposed to dispense with all expert or local opinion, I might feel a little easier about it. But there's no doubt about it; he's a holy terror—I went to bed tired!' Next day, 23 February, Menzies walked with the Churchill family in the snow through the winter woods, visited the control room of fighter squadrons and AA guns for the south-east of England, and at dinner that night talked with the heads of bomber and fighter command. Then, 'Momentous discussion later with P.M. about defence of Greece, largely with Australian & New Zealand troops. This kind of decision, which may mean thousands of lives, is not easy. Why does a peaceable man become a Prime Minister?'[16] A definite plan to go to the aid of Greece, then facing German invasion, was to be put next day to the British War Cabinet. At Churchill's request, Menzies would attend this and subsequent meetings of the Cabinet.

The implication of Menzies' note about his 'momentous discussion' with Churchill is that to this point he was not aware that a precise plan to aid Greece existed. This would hardly be surprising, since the decision to recommend such a plan to Cabinet had been made in Cairo only on 19 February, five days after Menzies left the Middle East and four days before he first saw Churchill. It was made at a conference between Anthony Eden, Sir John Dill (Chief of the British General Staff), Wavell and the naval and air force Commanders-in-Chief in the Middle East. Eden and Dill had been sent by the British War Cabinet to investigate and report on the Balkan and Middle Eastern situations.[17] From the Australian point of view the timing and provenance of these events is important. For it has become a common allegation that, as he passed through the Middle East, Menzies was told of the impending campaign, agreed to the use of Australian troops but did not inform either his own Government or the Australian commander in the area (Blamey) of what was afoot. The truth of this allegation is doubtful.[18]

[16] Diary, 23 February 1941.
[17] Field Marshal Earl Wavell, 'The British Expedition to Greece, 1941', *The Army Quarterly*, LIX, 2, January 1950, 179; Rhodes James, *Anthony Eden*, 249.
[18] Of the extensive literature on this subject see especially Norman D. Carlyon, *I Remember Blamey* (South Melbourne 1980), 26–33; and Percy Spender (Minister for the Army at the time), *Politics and a Man*, 128–36. More sophisticated are D. F. Woodward, 'Australian Diplomacy with Regard to the Greek Campaign, February–March 1941', *Australian Journal of Politics and History (AJPH)*, 24, 2(1978) and Jeffrey Grey, *A Military History of Australia* (Cambridge 1990), 156–7, who argue that, on the Greek proposal, the British lied to both Menzies and Blamey.

The Italians had invaded Greece in October 1940, but suffered serious losses and by the end of the year it was obvious that German troops would come through the Balkans to their aid. Would Britain help Greece? At first a little assistance in the air was all that was possible: in the desperate circumstances of late 1940 the first priority was to hold Suez. But then Wavell's North African victories eased pressure there and Wavell became apprehensive lest a German drive on the north-eastern Greek frontier should threaten the port of Salonika, through which the British maintained control of the eastern Mediterranean.[19] Thus by February 1941, when the Greeks appealed for help, both sentimental and strategic considerations were on their side: Churchill in addition became obsessed with the idea that if Britain came to Greece's aid, the Turks and the Yugoslavs, so far neutral, might be persuaded to come into the war on the Allied side.

This was the background when, on 12 February, Eden and Dill left London for Cairo. Bad weather, in which their Sunderland flying boat was almost lost, delayed them at Gibraltar and they did not reach Cairo until the 19th. When Wavell and Eden met, the former remarked, 'You have been a long time coming', and said that he had begun bringing forces together for despatch to Greece.[20] He had indeed: on the day before, he had sent for Blamey whom he informed of 'plans he had made for the organization of a force designated "Lustreforce" ' for operations in Greece. 'I informed him', Blamey wrote later, 'that in my view the matter would require to be referred to Australia, and he stated that he had discussed the possibility of such an operation with the Prime Minister of Australia'.[21] To 'discuss the possibility' of an operation does not imply that a decided plan was spoken of nor, indeed, that Menzies necessarily agreed with such an idea, let alone committed Australian troops to it. Menzies' diary supports the view that any discussions he had with Wavell about future operations were vague indeed. He notes seeing Wavell on a number of occasions, but records only one conversation which had any bearing on future events. It was on 13 February, the eve of his final departure from Cairo: 'Back at 8 pm to an interview with Wavell, who is clearly contemplating the possibility of a Salonika expedition'. Perhaps Wavell was dissembling when he saw Menzies or perhaps he hatched his firm plans for Lustreforce in the next five days, before he saw Blamey and then—as we must conclude—persuaded Eden and Dill to endorse them. Either way,

[19] Wavell, 'British Expedition to Greece', 178.
[20] Rhodes James, *Anthony Eden*, 249.
[21] Blamey to Minister for the Army, 12 March 1941, AA A5954/1, item 528/1.

Menzies' account of his last meeting with Wavell suggests that no clear commitment on his part was made or even asked for.[22] In those circumstances, there was nothing he should have told Blamey about. It was misleading of Wavell to suggest to Blamey that he had Menzies' agreement to Lustreforce, just as it was, later, dishonest to inform the British and Australian Governments that Blamey approved the expedition when fully informed of it.

Menzies' first British War Cabinet met at 5 p.m. on 24 February. In preparation he spent much of the afternoon agonizing with Bruce and Shedden about 'the Greek adventure'. Menzies and Shedden on the whole favoured it; Bruce was more doubtful. At the Cabinet meeting, Menzies made it clear that before Australian troops could be used he would have to consult his Cabinet. He also inquired about the shipping arrangements and equipment to be provided for the force. The Vice-Chief of the Imperial General Staff, Lieutenant General Sir Robert Haining, who was in attendance, assured Menzies that the Australian units were fully equipped, except for artillery and some motor transport which he was sure would be supplied on the spot from British material already in Egypt. Menzies asked what would happen if the enterprise failed: would the price be confined to loss of equipment? Troops, replied Churchill, might have in the end to be evacuated, but 'we ought to be able to evacuate safely all but the wounded'. Menzies stood his ground: 'if the enterprise was only a forlorn hope, it had better not be undertaken? Could he say to his colleagues in Australia that the venture had a substantial chance of success?' 'In the last resort', Churchill snapped back, 'this was a question which the Australian Cabinet must assess for themselves on Mr Menzies' advice'. Cabinet then authorized Churchill to notify Eden that, subject to Menzies getting the agreement of his colleagues in Australia, military assistance would be sent.[23]

Menzies recorded that the whole matter was decided after only three-quarters of an hour's discussion, and would have been despatched in ten minutes but for the queries he himself raised. Churchill's method was brisk: 'You have read your file, gentlemen,

---

[22]Carlyon, *I Remember Blamey*, 27, quotes a signal which Wavell sent to the Chiefs of Staff in London on 12 February saying that a strengthened force could be sent to Greece 'if the Australian Government will give me certain latitude as regards the use of their troops. I have already spoken to Menzies about this, and he was very ready to agree to what I suggest. I shall approach him again before he leaves'. Whatever had been said in earlier conversations, it is evident from Menzies' diary that no clear commitment had come from any 'approach' Wavell made in his last interview with the Australian Prime Minister nor indeed is it manifest that such an approach was made at all.

[23]War Cabinet, 24 February 1941, PRO, CAB 65/21/26.

and report of the Chiefs of Staff Committee. The arguments are clear on each side. I favour the project'. Running round the table, he elicited no more than three or four sentences from anybody. 'I was the only one to put questions, and feel like a new boy who, in the first week of school, commits the solecism of speaking to the captain of the School'.[24] One of the silent observers at this meeting, Sir Alexander Cadogan of the Foreign Office, noted in his diary that night that Menzies had been 'evidently doubtful' about the 'nasty decision' on Greece. Tough Balliol man and career civil servant of long experience and authority, Cadogan had through Eden's machinations replaced Vansittart as Permanent Head in 1936. On the 'nasty decision' he was sympathetic with, if a little more clear-eyed than, Menzies: 'On all moral and sentimental (and consequently American) grounds, one is driven to the grim conclusion. But it must in the end be a failure. However, perhaps better to have failed in a decent project than never to have tried at all. A [Eden] has rather jumped us into this'.[25]

Menzies cabled Fadden canvassing at length the arguments for the action, which would involve three Divisions: two Australian (the 6th and 7th) and one New Zealand. 'Though with some anxiety', his recommendation to his colleagues was that they should concur: if the proposal 'was only a forlorn hope I would not like it and I so informed the War Cabinet. But the view of Dill and Wavell is clearly that it is much more than a forlorn hope'. Fadden responded with the Australian Cabinet's agreement, but pressed Menzies on the matter of equipment, and the thoroughness of planning for evacuation if that should be necessary.[26] Menzies replied that Eden and Dill had given him 'a firm assurance that no Dominion troops will be sent to Greece unless and until they [are] equipped to establishment in all essentials', adding that detailed withdrawal plans were impossible to prepare in advance but no difficulty was anticipated given the abundance of local shipping and the proximity of the Greek islands.[27] He sent that message on Saturday 1 March, before setting out for his second weekend at Chequers. This time Menzies was completely captivated. He drove down with another daughter, Mrs Duncan Sandys: 'like all Churchills, immensely voluble, shrewd, well-informed, and intelligent. This is really the most amazing family. They all admire each other, and a visitor can easily get by if his manners are inconspicuous and his capacity for intelligent listen-

[24]Diary, 24 February 1941.
[25]David Dilks, *The Diaries of Sir Alexander Cadogan*, 18, 358.
[26]*DAFP* 4: 452–5.
[27]Ibid., 465–6.

ing reasonable'. Earlier reservations were wilting: 'Churchill grows on me', despite a feeling that 'his real tyrant is the glittering phrase—so attractive to his mind that awkward facts may have to give way'.[28] Several days later, back in London, Menzies cabled Fadden, reporting his doings and his two weekends with Churchill, whose 'experience since becoming Prime Minister has obviously ripened his judgement and he combines in a unique way most remarkable fighting and driving qualities with an astonishing mastery of the details of both plans and equipment'.[29]

But then, a week later, a new crisis shook Menzies. On 5 March Eden and Dill wired of a 'changed and disturbing situation' in Greece. The Greek commander, General Papagos, had turned 'unaccommodating and defeatist', had failed to fulfil an agreement to consolidate Greek detachments on an agreed defensive line and, drastically reducing the promised number of troops available, wanted to 'dribble' British troops into the line, as they arrived, to take up the slack. After two 'indescribably anxious' days of talks Greek morale had improved but 'the hard fact remains that our forces, including Dominion contingents, will be engaged in an operation more hazardous than it seemed a week ago'.[30] Churchill was at first horrified. 'We must be careful not to urge Greece against her better judgement into a hopeless resistance alone when we have only handfuls of troops which can reach scene in time', he wired Eden. Grave Imperial issues were also raised by the necessity to commit Australian and New Zealand troops and their Governments' agreement in the changed circumstances could not be assumed. This gloomy mood made him, in fact, momentarily clear-eyed: 'Loss of Greece and Balkans by no means a major catastrophe for us provided Turkey remains honest neutral'.[31] But Eden was not in a position to accept this view. 'I need not emphasise to you', he expostulated, 'the effect of our now withdrawing from the agreement actually signed between Chief of the Imperial General Staff and Greek Commander-in-Chief ... This seems to me quite unthinkable. We shall be pilloried by the Greeks and the world in general as going back on our word'.[32]

When these messages came to the War Cabinet Menzies launched a bitter attack. He had had a difficult task, he said, to persuade his colleagues at home that the original decision to aid Greece was correct: now he was being told that there were new and serious

[28]Diary, 2 March 1941.
[29]*DAFP* 4: 469.
[30]Telegram, Eden and CIGS to Prime Minister, 5 March 1940, PRO, CAB 65/22/17–18.
[31]Churchill to Eden, 5 March 1941, PRO, CAB 65/18/13.
[32]War Cabinet, 6 March 1941, PRO, CAB 65/22/23ff.

difficulties. The War Cabinet had simply not been informed of all the facts, and Eden's revelation of a military agreement between Dill and Papagos was, to say the least, embarrassing. Was he, Menzies, to tell his colleagues that the Australians and New Zealanders, who would provide three-fifths of the forces to be used, were committed by an agreement, signed in Athens, which had not even been referred home to Britain, let alone the subject of proper consultation with the Dominions themselves?[33] Churchill at first took the point. He cabled military headquarters in Cairo, observing that since most of the troops who would be involved in the contemplated operation would be New Zealanders and Australians,

> We must be able to tell the Australian and New Zealand Governments that the campaign was undertaken, not because of any commitment entered into by a British Cabinet Minister in Athens, but because the Chief of the Imperial General Staff and the Commander-in-Chief in the Middle East were convinced that there was a reasonable fighting chance. So far, few facts or reasons have been supplied which could be represented as justifying the operation on any grounds but *noblesse oblige*. A precise military appreciation is indispensable.[34]

When this telegram was reported to the War Cabinet, Menzies announced that it 'expressed his own views with precision'; but if he hoped there would be a delay at least until the appreciation arrived, he was mistaken. Suddenly Churchill, his momentary change of heart evidently reversed by Eden's angry message, demanded immediate action. A 'considered military appreciation', he said, 'was on the way here from Cairo [to] supply the detailed arguments; but we know the conclusions already'. The time had come for making a decision. He believed that it was 'our duty to go forward, making the necessary communications to the Dominions whose forces were to take part in the campaign'. The War Cabinet agreed and asked Menzies to seek his Government's assent. At the same time it was informed that, according to a signal from Dill to the War Office, Wavell had explained the situation to Blamey and Freyberg, the New Zealand commander, and both had 'expressed their willingness to undertake operations under new conditions'.[35]

---

[33] Ibid.
[34] War Cabinet, 7 March 1941, PRO, CAB 65/18/19.
[35] Ibid. Blamey later claimed he had expressed no view on this matter. 'On 6th March I was again called in and saw the Chief of the Imperial General Staff (General Sir John Dill) with the Commander-in-Chief. I was informed that following on a visit of the Commander-in-Chief to Greece that there was some doubt as to the plans developing. Although both on this and on the previous visits my views were not asked for and I felt I was receiving instructions, I made enquiries as to what other formations would be available and when' (Blamey to Minister for the Army, Melbourne, 12 March 1941, AA A5954/1/528/1).

In the circumstances there was little more that Menzies could do other than cable Fadden with copies of all the recent telegrams on the Greek question, recommending Australian approval of the expedition on the grounds that Eden, Dill and Wavell thought there was a reasonable prospect of success, that Blamey and Freyberg agreed and that Wavell assured the War Cabinet that the Benghazi front could readily be held despite the drawing off of some forces to Greece. In reply Fadden rehearsed the Australian Cabinet's resentment at Eden and Dill's having entered an agreement affecting Dominion troops without prior consultation, and expressed a fear that should there be a defeat and evacuation it could have a severe effect on Japan's attitude towards Australia. All the same, the message concluded, Cabinet knew that the troops if committed to battle would 'worthily uphold the glorious traditions of the A.I.F'.[36] There, it seemed, the matter rested, at least for the time being. The military appreciation for which Churchill asked Eden and Dill, and whose expected coming he used as final justification for embarking on the expedition, appears never to have been made, let alone sent.[37] And three days *before* Menzies had sent Fadden his recommendation that the Australian Government agree to the expedition the first echelons of the AIF had in fact been ordered to embark for Greece.[38]

Despite these difficulties, Menzies' weekends at Chequers continued. Whatever tensions might develop between them, Churchill (as his private secretary, Colville, put it) considered Menzies one of that category of men with whom, when he was off duty, 'it was agreeable to dine'. Menzies, for his part, genuinely enjoyed the Churchills' hospitality even in the troubled middle weeks of his London stay. The people he met at Chequers were invariably interesting, the conversation was often good and there were many light-hearted moments, like one captured in Colville's diary on 30 March: 'The Duke and Duchess of Kent came to lunch ... Afterwards the Duke inspected the Guard while I struggled with his chauffeur-less car and the Duchess. Mr. Menzies photographed the

---

[36] Fadden to Menzies, 10 March 1941, *DAFP* 4: 486–8.
[37] I have found no document in the British War Cabinet material to show that this appreciation was ever made. Shedden, in an unpublished account of the background to the Greek campaign, quotes Lord Ismay's *Memoirs* to show that Eden, though he carried an 'even graver responsibility than Wavell', had ignored Churchill's request 'at a critical stage to submit a "precise military appreciation" to confirm opinions expressed by him, such as "we believe there is a fair chance of halting a German advance, and preventing Greece from being overrun" ', AA A5954/1 item 766/19.
[38] Gavin Long, *Greece, Crete and Syria* (Sydney 1986 [1953]), 23, notes the embarkation on 5 March 1941. Menzies' cable to Fadden was sent on the 8th.

proceedings assiduously'.[39] The natural ebullience which enabled Menzies to enjoy these and other social occasions made them an important tonic at a time of hard work and threatening gloom. One revealing diary entry tells of his pleasure at entertaining a group of old English test players to dinner, when 'much good talk of cricket'

> helped to take the mind off these dark and hurrying days in London, where the old pleasure of being here has gone, your old friends, all busy, are ships that pass in the night, a new spectacle of ruin meets you at every turn, the air raid warning wails every night, and the only comfort is that the purple crocuses are out in the park opposite.[40]

Sitting in the War Cabinet he listened almost daily to the litany of losses—of civilians killed and wounded in German air raids, of ships sunk and sailors drowned, of aircraft destroyed and pilots shot. In the middle weeks of his stay, Menzies visited a number of provincial cities, where he was appalled by the bomb damage he saw.

Horror at such scenes and admiration for the people who endured them became a central theme in the numerous speeches and talks he gave. 'Impression grows', he had written after one early address 'that best value of this mission is to encourage and lift up the people here. They have had a bad time and want a boost to their spirits'.[41] In mid-March he and Storey visited aircraft and munitions works in Birmingham and Manchester, to inspect them and negotiate with management about the possibility of some processes being carried out in Australia. At the main Avro factory in Manchester he spoke one lunchtime to 9000 workers, about the heavy bombing Germany would soon have to endure, and in Birmingham at the Lucas works he was greeted by a cheering crowd. At Coventry the mayor met him and took him on a tour of ruined city blocks and the remnants of the cathedral. At the Rootes factory he addressed a mass audience in the canteen as 'brave soldiers of Great Britain' and at the Bristol works he spoke through loudspeakers to 20 000 employees.[42] He was in his element as a speaker and full of confidence that the investigations he and Storey were conducting on expanding Australian production of aircraft, munitions and ships were full of promise.

[39] John Colville, *The Fringes of Power* (London 1985), 1, 439.
[40] Diary, 10 March 1941.
[41] Ibid., 26 February 1941.
[42] The quotations in this paragraph are taken as a sample from Diary entries up to 21 March when he spoke at the Bristol works. Menzies kept a careful tally of all speeches he made, great and small, from the time he left Australia. The Bristol one was number 46 (Diary, 21 March 1941).

Menzies addresses factory workers at Coventry in 1941: 'brave soldiers of Great Britain'.

It was thus understandable that he was not greatly daunted by an ominous cable he received from his wife at this time: 'Father and I consider it desirable immediate announcement of probable early return'.[43] A family friend and Sydney wool broker, Jim McGregor, had written on 10 March that Pat, who had just dined with him, was going to Canberra next day, 'and her presence will, I am sure, keep the boys in order'.[44] From then on, Pat spent most of her time in Canberra, greatly frustrated that, in a situation where letters were slow to reach England and security regulations forbade the use of the radio telephone, she could only confidentially communicate with her husband through short, coded cablegrams. Thus she could not adequately convey to him information she in fact soon picked up of intrigues against him.[45] Menzies at first replied that he would certainly make the required announcement, 'but completely impossible leave here before end of month getting home about April 24th'.[46] A week later he cabled again: 'Very important matters under discussion here. Realise that I have no hope of getting away by originally intended date. Will

[43]Pat Menzies to husband, 12 March 1941, Menzies Family Papers.
[44]J. W. McGregor to Menzies, 10 March 1941, Menzies Family Papers.
[45]Interview with Dame Pattie, 18 September 1990.
[46]Menzies to wife, 13 March 1941, Menzies Family Papers.

therefore not leave here until about April 17. Feeling very well, having outstanding receptions everywhere and finding great co-operation from those with whom I am negotiating'.[47]

But in fact, though such co-operation was indeed marked in talks he and Storey had about the production of aircraft and munitions, Menzies faced real frustration on the major issue which had prompted the trip in the first place: the Japanese menace in general and Singapore's defence in particular. Late in February, with Bruce and Shedden, he had a meeting at the Foreign Office with Cadogan and R. A. Butler, the Parliamentary Undersecretary for Foreign Affairs, to discuss the Far Eastern situation; and next day the three conferred on the same question with the British Service Ministers and their Chiefs of Staff. Both meetings were, from the Australians' point of view, dismal failures. At the first of them, Menzies found the British approach to the Far East 'hopelessly disappointing'. Cadogan's attitude was 'one of remoteness and indifference ... I said with some bitterness of spirit: "Well, the only conclusion I can reach is that you have no policy in relation to these matters at all" '.[48] 'Frankly', he confided to his diary that night, 'drift seems policy of F.O. ... Why should we allow an atmosphere of inevitability to drift into our relations with Japan? We need firmness, definition, and friendliness and they are not impossible'.[49] Cadogan, who also recorded the meeting in his diary, took the occasion there to dismiss the Australians with a lordly sneer: 'What irresponsible rubbish these Antipodeans talk!' At the discussions with the service chiefs next day, Menzies pressed for air cover for Singapore, and demanded in vain a clarification of Churchill's vague promise of naval aid if Australia were attacked by Japan. After the meeting he wrote furiously: 'Clear thinking is not predominant here ... What does "cutting our losses in the Mediterranean and going to your assistance" mean? Nobody knows'.[50]

A week or so later, Menzies was momentarily happier about British policy when at the Admiralty he conferred with the First Lord, A. V. Alexander. At this initial encounter, Alexander

---

[47] Menzies to wife, 21 March 1941, Menzies Family Papers. Menzies had a little before this sent Fadden a secret but comprehensive report on the achievements of the visit. It included the following: 'Storey has paid many visits to factories—on the whole delighted with the work being done and has been preparing the ground very skilfully for a proposition which I will make at the appropriate time for the establishment of additional aircraft construction in Australia'. Menzies to Fadden, 4 March 1941, AA A5954/1, box 633.
[48] Quoted in Dilks (ed.), *The Diaries of Sir Alexander Cadogan*, 359n.
[49] Diary, 26 February 1941.
[50] Ibid., 27 February 1941.

Menzies and Churchill in jovial mood outside No. 10 Downing Street, after a War Cabinet meeting in March 1941

'certainly impresses as knowing his department thoroughly'.[51] He agreed with Menzies' emphasis on 'the uselessness of rhetorical phrases such as "cutting our losses in the Mediterranean and proceeding to your assistance" ' and promised to supply a 'realistic statement' of what ships could come east if war with Japan broke out. But when the requested appreciation finally came, weeks later, it revealed even greater deficiencies in the military defence of Singapore than those already known to the Australian Government and was absolutely vague about naval reinforcements: what ships would be sent, it said, could not be forecast with accuracy, for that would depend entirely on the situation of Britain, and the

[51] Ibid., 8 March 1941. Alexander remained one of the few British ministers to impress Menzies. In his report to the Advisory War Council on his return, he described Alexander as 'a very good administrator and the best of the Service Ministers' (*DAFP* 4: 683).

strength and disposal of her enemies, at the time.[52] Menzies' more optimistic hopes of people like Alexander proved in fact to be misplaced. The simple fact which, despite his fulminations, he had quietly to accept personally, was that in her present desperate plight Britain could not make any realistic promises for the future.

These and other negotiations were carried on against the background of a continuing expectation of German invasion, which for Britain was necessarily the key issue of this grim time. Soon after his arrival, Menzies sat through one gloomy War Cabinet meeting which approved plans to thin out the civilian population along the vulnerable coastal strip between Great Yarmouth and Littlehampton. Churchill said that military officers would have to visit people living in this area to make it clear that those who stayed behind would in the event of invasion not be allowed to clog the roads by attempting to leave at the last moment.[53] Menzies was at a meeting held late in March at the War Office to discuss manpower problems, where Sir Robert Haining, Vice Chief of the Imperial General Staff, emphasized that 'the situation was dominated by the threat of invasion, and it would only be possible to spare about two divisions to go overseas until this threat had been reduced'. In other words, significant British relief in the Middle East was not to be looked for. Indeed, the General Staff hoped that the Australians already there would be reinforced at an early date by the AIF 8th Division and an armoured division. More immediately, Haining asked that Australia relieve the pressure on British resources by providing the 'base units' for AIF divisions in the field—such units having hitherto been made up of British troops. Shedden calculated that this would mean finding almost at once an extra 68 000 men and Menzies said that the proposals would have to be examined in the light of the general Australian manpower position, which was affected by other demands.[54]

Despite all its anxieties, the month of March 1941 ended on an upward note thanks to two incidents which in hindsight may look rather trivial but at the time were little gleams of light in the pervading gloom. Both were magnified by Churchill's impetuous, if somewhat crazy, enthusiasm, for which Menzies still cherished a quizzical affection. The first was a *coup d'état* in Belgrade which put a new, anti-German Government in power. The second was the British naval victory off Cape Matapan when three Italian cruisers and two destroyers were sunk in what Churchill called

[52] Hasluck, *Government and People* 1: 349–51.
[53] War Cabinet, 27 February 1941, PRO, CAB 65/17/77.
[54] War Office Meeting, 26 March 1941, PRO, CAB 99/44.

'the tearing up of the paper fleet of Italy'.[55] Both events, occurring within days of each other, were celebrated at a notable Chequers weekend. Menzies was again one of the guests. Churchill's secretary, Colville, recorded how the news of the naval victory stirred his master 'to compose several brilliant telegrams, to Roosevelt, etc., and he has spent much of the weekend pacing—or rather tripping—up and down the Great Hall to the sound of the gramophone (playing martial airs, waltzes and the most vulgar kind of brass-band songs) deep in thought all the while'.[56] The cable to Roosevelt sparked Menzies' admiration: 'What a genius the man has. He has maintained by cable and letter the most easy and informal correspondence with Roosevelt; always treating him as a friend and ally ... "Don't you think we could now do so & so". Result, F.D.R. has passed into the position of an ally without perhaps realising how some of the steps have come about'.[57] Churchill also celebrated the naval victory by sending Matsuoka, the Japanese Foreign Minister, a series of loaded questions about the prospects for Germany and Italy (e.g. 'Will Germany, without the command of the sea or the command of the British daylight air, be able to invade and conquer Great Britain in the spring, summer or autumn of 1941?'), ending with a thinly veiled threat: 'From the answers to these questions may spring the avoidance by Japan of a serious catastrophe, and a marked improvement in the relations between Japan and the two great sea powers of the West'.[58] Again, Menzies was full of admiration: 'Good direct stuff, shocking to the Foreign Office, but pleasing to me'.[59]

There is no record of his reaction to another flight of Churchill's fancy: to seize on the Yugoslav coup to revive the dream of a Balkan front against Germany, and to see in this dream a new justification for the movement into Greece of Australian troops that was at that moment taking place. One of the many messages Churchill sent in this mood of euphoria was a cable to Fadden:

> When a month ago we decided upon LUSTRE it looked a rather bleak military adventure dictated by noblesse oblige. Thursday's events in Belgrade show far-reaching effects of this and other measures we have taken on whole Balkan situation. German plans have been upset and we may cherish renewed hopes of forming a Balkan front with Turkey comprising about 70 allied divisions from the four powers concerned ... everything that has happened since LUSTRE decision taken justifies

[55] Colville, *The Fringes of Power*, I, 439–40.
[56] Ibid., 440.
[57] Diary, 30 March 1941.
[58] Colville, *The Fringes of Power*, 440.
[59] Diary, 31 March 1941.

it ... Result unknowable but prize has increased and risks have somewhat lessened. Am in closest touch with Menzies. Wish I could talk it over with you.[60]

No doubt Menzies went along with this hope: given his own apprehensions about Greece, he was glad to have any straw, however fragile, to clutch at. There was another reason to be pleased to see Churchill in ebullient mood. Menzies was about to embark on a brief diplomatic fling that he knew the British Prime Minister deeply disapproved—to go to Ireland as an outsider to talk to de Valera, in the hope of finding a way out of the difficulties caused by Eire's insistence on its neutrality in the war. Perhaps a Churchill sniffing victory elsewhere might be more amenable than usual to any reasonable arrangements that could be negotiated with the Irish?

[60]Churchill to Fadden, 31 March 1941, PRO, CAB 65/18/54.

15

Ireland, Churchill and Disillusion

MENZIES' INITIAL surprise at the intensity of feeling against Eire for her policy of neutrality in the war soon deepened into alarm as in the secrecy of the War Cabinet he learnt that dreadful shipping losses on the Atlantic lifeline to America were threatening Britain with strangulation.[1] Deprived of any protection from Southern Irish ports and airfields, convoys had to take an extended route around the north, harried to the west of Ireland by long-range German bombers and U-boats which co-ordinated their stalking by radio. It was particularly galling to Churchill that in 1938 the Chamberlain Government, as part of its appeasement policy, had handed over to Eire the so-called 'Treaty Ports'. These five facilities—harbours at Berehaven, Cobh and Lough Swilly, fuel storages at Haulbowline and Rathmullan—had been retained by Britain under the treaty of 1921 which conceded independence to Southern Ireland. Churchill fought desperately for the ports' retention: in the event of war, he told the Commons, Britain might be denied their use and 'we may be hampered in the gravest manner in protecting the British population from privation and even starvation. Who would wish to put his head in such a noose?'[2] When that indeed happened Churchill declared Britain's inability to use Irish facilities 'a most heavy and grievous burden which should never have been placed on our shoulders'. His

---

[1] Between July and October 1940, 245 British vessels were sunk and in November, the worst month of the year, 73 (totalling 304 000 tons) went to the bottom. February 1941—the month in which Menzies reached London—saw the greatest single monthly loss since the beginning of the war—79 ships. Robert Fisk, *In Time of War* (Philadelphia 1983), 247, 260.
[2] Parliamentary Debates, House of Commons, fifth series 335: 1103. R. F. Foster, *Modern Ireland, 1600–1972* (London 1988), 554, notes that Churchill was in a small minority. The ports were handed over with curiously little deliberation on the British side. 'In some ways their upkeep was seen as a liability, and there was a general expectation (not to be fulfilled) that in time of war they might be made available again.'

inflammatory speeches brought intermittent press demands for seizure of the Irish ports, and the chance that Churchill himself would go beyond mere words was great.[3]

Menzies genuinely feared, as he cabled to Fadden, 'drastic measures being considered by Cabinet here' and decided on 'paying quick visit to De Valera'. His hand, he added, 'would be greatly strengthened if Cabinet in Australia could arm me privately with most emphatic expression of opinion that ... Australia cannot and will not remain indifferent to the continuance of a policy which materially helps Germany and may vitally injure us'.[4] The notion that an ingenuous outsider like Menzies might win some influence with de Valera loses some of its outlandishness when we notice a conversation he had, only a few days after sending this message to Fadden, with an American, William Donovan. The two met at a Chequers weekend, just after Donovan had been in Ireland and had talked with de Valera. At the time he was a kind of roving ambassador for Roosevelt and, though Menzies did not know it, had connections with the British secret service and was a privileged go-between in much of Churchill's wooing of Roosevelt.[5] Menzies was impressed by Donovan: 'this is a good man; easy, composed, comfortable looking, with a good blue eye, an orderly mind and quiet speech. I would readily take his opinion on men or affairs'. Donovan told Menzies that he thought de Valera 'worried and troubled of conscience for not having made clear to his own people the real moral issues of the war'. An attempt should be made to establish 'an avenue of personal contact between Dev and Churchill ... The Irish farmer is beginning to discover that neutrality is not profitable, and altogether there are possibilities'.[6]

A few weeks after this, on 24 March, the War Cabinet discussed the effects of restrictions that had been imposed three months earlier, at Churchill's instigation, on trade and shipping to Ireland, and decided to continue, even extend, such anti-Irish measures. Menzies recorded another outburst from Churchill: '700 years of hatred, and six months of pure funk'.[7] At this meeting Menzies announced that he planned to visit Ireland himself. The talks Donovan had had with de Valera had no doubt been valuable, he

---

[3]Martin Gilbert, *Finest Hour: Winston S. Churchill, 1939–41* (London 1983), 43, 433, 574.
[4]Menzies to Fadden, 4 March 1941, *DAFP* 4: 470–1.
[5]For details about this interesting man, who was the founder of the CIA, see Thomas F. Troy, *Donovan and the C.I.A.* (New York 1981), 23–9; Anthony Cave Brown, *The Last Hero. Wild Bill Donovan* (London 1982), 147–55; William Casey, *The Secret War Against Hitler* (London 1989), 14–17.
[6]Diary, 9 March 1941.
[7]Quoted in Diary, 24 March 1941.

said, but they had been confidential and had not been followed by any public statement. He was himself trying to arrange an interview with de Valera, and 'it might be of assistance if this talk was to be followed by some public statement of his [Menzies'] views on the Eire position'.[8] The minutes contain no record of Churchill's reaction to this but Menzies was later to assert that Churchill had said to him privately: 'Never with my approval will you visit that wicked man'.[9]

Menzies planned his trip to include Northern Ireland and flew to Belfast, 'across a wind-tossed and bitter Irish sea', on 3 April. Received by the Prime Minister, J. M. Andrews, he inspected shipyards in the morning and visited the University in the afternoon. In between, a luncheon appearance at the Ulster Reform Club brought great elation. 'They acclaim my speech in extravagant terms', he noted,[10] and so they did: moving the vote of thanks, Andrews said 'they had just listened to a very great speech—one of the greatest ever heard in the Club'. Menzies had begun with jocular remarks hardly tactful for a man due in Dublin the next day: he felt quite at home in the Ulster Club, he said, for the best Northern Irelanders were like the best Australians: improved Scotsmen. But his main theme, clearly directed at Eire, was that of loyalty to the Commonwealth's one King: 'when that ... King makes war and makes it, as on the present occasion, most justly, then I have never felt inclined as a representative of my own country to sit down and engage in vague speculation as to whether or not I should declare war'.[11] That evening he held a relaxed press conference. 'Installing himself in a chair at the head of the table in the Senate Room of Queen's', reported the *Belfast Telegraph*, 'he got a briar pipe going well and then invited questions from all and sundry'. Menzies parried queries about the Treaty Ports, rejected any suggestion that he brought messages from Churchill to de Valera and said his visit to Dublin was being made entirely on his own initiative, to have a general talk with de Valera, convey to him the greetings of the Australian people, see Ireland, and get a first-hand view of her problems.[12]

Next day he travelled down to Dublin by train: 'countryside quite lovely', he noted, 'the white washed cottages making quite a picture in the greenery. In Dublin life goes on and there is no blackout—it seems queer!'[13] Menzies spent the morning, and then

[8] War Cabinet Minutes, 24 March 1941, PRO, CAB 65/18/45.
[9] *Afternoon Light*, 37.
[10] Diary, 3 April 1941.
[11] *Belfast Telegraph*, 3 April 1941.
[12] *Belfast Telegraph, Irish Times*, 4 April 1941.
[13] Diary, Friday 4 April 1941.

Diplomacy in Southern Ireland: 'On the whole I rather like De Valera (though you must tell this to Mother and Father with great discretion), even though I, of course, disagreed with almost everything he said'.

lunch, alone with de Valera, in a 'long conference'. His diary entry is terse, impressionistic and emotional: 'Long, long grey black frieze overcoat, broad brimmed black hat. An educated man. Personal charm. Allusions to history, but not <u>all</u> ancient. He and all his ministers have "done time" as rebels, and family blood has been spilt in the streets. We must remember this—"You have not died on the barricades"!' In the afternoon Sean O'Kelly, the Deputy Prime Minister, and Father Costello, 'a worldly priest', took Menzies to see the Wicklow mountains and the 'lovely ruins and lakes of Glendalough'. Next morning one Beeton, of Irish External Affairs, took him for a drive around Dublin. 'A bigot', Menzies observed, presumably because of Beeton's crisp 'he was not an Irishman', as they looked at the Nelson column and the withering answer he gave to Menzies' triumphant observation at Wellington's equestrian statue: 'Ah, there is Wellington, you can't say he wasn't an Irishman . . . for, dammit, he was born in Dublin'. 'And wasn't it Wellington himself who said that to be born in a stable does not prove you are a horse?' A press conference and an official luncheon followed. Afterwards, 'Dev sees me off at aerodrome. Rough journey in a Rapide to Liverpool and to Heston. Pilot thinks we are pursued in Irish Channel. We grope our way into Heston through fog and balloons.'[14] So ended the short adventure. Before he left Ireland, journalists in Dublin got as little satisfaction out of Menzies as their brethren had in Belfast. Again he refused to be drawn on the Treaty Ports and would not say what he had talked to de Valera about. He was unsympathetic on supply shortages: 'Our shipping problem is much more serious than yours'. Complaints about sugar and tea rationing left him cold: 'Everybody here seemed to live a full life'. And brown bread, it was well known, was far better for one's health than white.[15]

Back in London, Menzies immediately got to work on his report, a long memorandum for the War Cabinet. He submitted it on 9 April and it was briefly discussed in Cabinet on the 10th. *The Times* had meantime printed a summary of his speech to the Ulster Reform Club and a short paragraph noting that he had visited Eire and talked with de Valera.[16] The English press (and particularly *The Times*) were by now giving Menzies great exposure—routinely seizing upon any public statement he made. But, although he had deplored the silence about Donovan's visit to Ireland, Menzies himself now had nothing public to say. The content of his memorandum, and its reception, explains why.

This report is the work of a man untutored in the subtleties of Irish political history but, as lawyer and experienced politician, skilled in the arts of observation and digestion. It also reflects a native sensibility, a strange glimmering of instinctive empathy with a man and a cause utterly alien to his own instincts and loyalties. It is not surprising that it was not a document pleasing to Churchill.[17] It rehearses discussions which Menzies had in Belfast and Dublin and concludes with a series of recommendations drawn from those talks and from other impressions.

Menzies' natural prejudices were at the outset challenged: 'There is a very strong, and indeed bitter, feeling in Ulster about Eire. Though the whole of my own instinctive bias is in favour of Ulster, I was occasionally a little disturbed to find myself wondering whether the Ulster attitude is entirely a reasoned one'. He goes on to make useful comments on the industrial, employment and

---

[14] Diary, Friday 4 and Saturday 5 April 1941. Menzies has a lively account of the tour with Beeton (called 'Mr X' there!) in *Afternoon Light*, 43.
[15] *Saturday Herald*, Dublin, 5 April 1941; *Irish Times*, 7 April 1941.
[16] *The Times*, 4, 5 April 1941.
[17] Copy no. 12 of the memorandum is in NLA, MS. 4936/1/5/36. It is also printed in *DAFP* 4: 549–54. The quotations in what follows are from these sources.

recruiting problems he has observed in Ulster, and the impossibility, in present circumstances, of Ireland being united. It is a rational, if lifeless, account. But when he turns to Eire, 'this "distressful country"', the discussion takes on a new animation. A real live person appears on centre stage: de Valera.

> He interested me very much. He is at first sight a somewhat saturnine figure, particularly when he sallies abroad in a long dark frieze overcoat and a broadbrimmed black hat. Personal contact with him, however, indicates that he is ... I think, sincere, and with a mind in which acute intelligence is found to contain many blind spots occasioned by prejudice, bitter personal experience, and a marked slavery to past history ... He has a large and fanatical following in Dublin. He is the 'chief'. The very clerks in the offices stand promptly to attention as he strides past. His Ministers speak with freedom in his absence, but are restrained and obedient in his presence ... On the whole, with all my prejudices, I liked him and occasionally succeeded in evoking from him a sort of wintry humour, which was not without charm.

Menzies then proceeds to set down de Valera's views, 'not as he precisely formulated them ... but as I inferred them, I think accurately, from hours of discussion'. De Valera sees the British cause in the war as a just one, a view with which 80 per cent of the population of Southern Ireland would agree. But he is equally convinced that the present British Government is hostile and unsympathetic to Ireland, and he is angry about supposed injustices to Catholics in Northern Ireland. He recognizes, however, that Great Britain cannot possibly throw Ulster into Eire. When asked to explain the meaning of a favourite phrase of his, 'the passionate desire in the Irish heart to be neutral in the war', de Valera 'slipped easily and skilfully into a discussion of past history'. But he also came back repeatedly to a quite clear-cut fear: that of German attack, particularly from the air. Strict neutrality is the only feasible Irish defence, since she lacks the munitions and aircraft needed to resist an attacker.

The encounter clearly had its bizarre side. The wily de Valera left Menzies with an impression of almost childlike innocence.

> He stands in front of the map and cannot understand why naval bases in Ireland should be of the slightest importance to Great Britain. I found it necessary to explain to him the importance of air bases as a platform for fighting aircraft. He did not appear to have appreciated the immense significance of even a hundred miles in the zone of operations of fighters. I think he would understand these things much better if he had some of his own...

Other examples were at hand to support the theme of de Valera's innocence, and it is evident that, despite his stern 'improved Scottishness', Menzies was not immune from Irish blarney. That, and his antipodean lawyer-like tendency to assume that rationality could overcome history, led him to a set of final conclusions which he sensed even as he wrote them would not be welcome in London. Still, he did not pull his punches:

> The paragraphs I have written above contain, as I realise, much exasperating information... [de Valera] has in my opinion, some fine qualities. His fixed ideas, like those of his people, cannot be removed by aloofness or by force. They can be removed only by a genuine attempt to get at their foundations by enquiry and, wherever possible, by understanding. To the outsider, like myself, and particularly to one who travelled seventeen thousand miles to confer with his colleagues of the British Government, it is fantastic to be told that De Valera and Andrews have never met, and that I have had more conversations with De Valera than any British Minister has had since the war began. I therefore suggest very strongly that the whole question of the defence of Eire should be looked at, that the Secretary of State for the Dominions should pay an early visit to Belfast and Dublin, and that if he receives the slightest encouragement he should invite De Valera and a couple of his colleagues to come to London for discussions with the Prime Minister and other members of the British Cabinet. I know that such a meeting would be welcomed by some members of the Irish Cabinet who are beginning to realise that neutrality has its defeats no less renowned than war; and I would be by no means pessimistic about the outcome.

As noted above, this paper came before the War Cabinet on 10 April. Menzies' diary tersely records its reception. 'War Cabinet re Ireland. Winston describes my paper as "very readable"—a most damning comment. Beaverbrook, Sinclair & Greenwood rather approve, but Winston & Kingsley Wood exhibit the blank wall of conservatism. There is triangular prejudice on this matter. Winston is <u>not</u> a receptive or reasoning animal.'[18] The minutes of the meeting note that Menzies' opinions 'met with a considerable measure of support', but that Cabinet in the end endorsed the contrary view that it was unlikely that de Valera could be persuaded to come to London, and that if he did no significant results could be expected to follow. 'He already knew that if Eire was prepared to abandon its neutrality (a) we were ready to share our air defences with them; and (b) we would be ready to set up a Defence

[18]Diary, 10 April 1941.

Council for All-Ireland, in the hope that a united Ireland might spring therefrom. There was nothing more which we could tell them.'[19] That, of course, was Churchill's voice, emanating from what Menzies called Britain's one-man Cabinet.

For Menzies himself a public statement was now out of the question. All that was left was the grain of comfort he could draw from a conversation he had at Cliveden at the end of that week with Lord Astor and J. L. Garvin, editor of *The Times*. Garvin 'declared my memorandum ... "the most penetrating account of the Irish position he had ever read" '.[20] Unfortunately for Menzies, few others ever had the chance to read, let alone pass an opinion on, the document. As a War Cabinet paper on a touchy subject, it was classified 'secret', with the conventional legend 'to be kept under lock and key', and had a fifty-year embargo placed on it.[21]

But if in 1941 public expression and defence of his views on the Irish condition were denied to Menzies, he has unwittingly left for posterity a neat, acid summary of them—untutored, perhaps, but the instinctive judgement and last word of a humane outsider. It is in a letter to his wife:

> I had a short and interesting visit to Ireland, about which I cannot write at length, but which I am quite sure you will enjoy hearing about on my return. On the whole I rather like De Valera (though you must tell this to Mother and Father with great discretion), even though I, of course, disagreed with almost everything he said.
>
> Personally, I think the Irish problem is soluble, and I have made an elaborate report on it to Cabinet here. But the greatest difficulty is the prevailing lunacy. They are mad in Dublin, madder still in Belfast, and on this question perhaps maddest of all at Downing Street. Blind prejudice, based on historical events, is the most intractable and almost the most dangerous thing in the world.[22]

The issue of the *Irish Times* which, on 7 April, carried an account of Menzies' last doings in Dublin also informed its readers, in dramatic black headlines: 'Germany Invades Yugoslavia and Greece'. So as Menzies arrived back in London, action on the Greek front was imminent. The hollowness of Churchill's grandiose attempt to justify Lustre as key to a great diplomatic coup was there

---

[19] War Cabinet 38(41), 10 April 1941, PRO, CAB 65/18.
[20] Diary, Sunday 13 April 1941.
[21] In 1986, when I asked for it in the Public Record Office, I found that it was still unavailable there. Australian authorities, not constrained by British rules, had published it in *DAFP* in 1980!
[22] Menzies to Pat, 23 April 1941, Menzies Family Papers.

for all to see. The change of government in Belgrade only meant that, instead of walking peacefully across a pro-German Yugoslavia, Hitler's army would have to attack it. Given Yugoslavia's military weakness, and the fact that Turkey steadfastly maintained its neutrality, the Germans could now be expected in Greece within days. There the 6th AIF and the 2nd New Zealand Divisions were moving into the forward lines. It was planned that they would shortly be joined by the 7th AIF Division, now in Palestine. But this was not to be. A few days before the attack on Yugoslavia, German mechanized units which had been forming in Tripoli since early March mounted under Rommel's leadership a formidable counter-attack in Cyrenaica. Territory that the Italians had lost on the Benghazi front was quickly recovered and elements of the 9th Australian Division, which had been training in the Western Desert, were forced back on Tobruk. The threat to Egypt and Suez was serious, and Wavell decided that the 7th Division could not be spared for Greece.

Menzies learnt of the German armoured thrust in North Africa on the day he got back to London.[23] He was appalled. 'Things have gone wrong in Libya ... and we are in danger of inadequate retreat and grave loss'.[24] At the next War Cabinet even Churchill sheepishly admitted the seriousness of Wavell's miscalculation, for it had been on Wavell's assurance that the Benghazi front was safe that troops had been withdrawn and sent to Greece. 'Our Generals', Menzies told the War Cabinet, 'consistently underestimate Germany's capacity'.[25] In his diary he was much more savage:

> The generals of the War Office are still behind the times. 'We have so many divisions'—as if divisions counted. Armour and speed count, and when we catch up to that idea, we will catch up to the Germans. Only tonight I was horrified to hear Churchill saying, à propos of Tobruk to which we are retreating and where we hope to make a stand, 'If stout hearted men with rifles cannot hold these people until the guns come up, I must revise my ideas of war'. Well, he should revise them quickly![26]

In Cabinet on 11 April Menzies complained again of the way in which the 'capacity of the German armoured divisions had been gravely underestimated', and declared himself 'very uncomfortable about our forces in Tobruk'. Tobruk's perimeter, he said,

---
[23]The news awaited him in a cable from Fadden, passing on a communiqué from Wavell. *DAFP* 4: 546–7.
[24]Diary, 7 April 1941.
[25]War Cabinet, 7 April 1941, PRO, CAB 65/18.
[26]Diary, 8 April 1941.

On 12 April Churchill, as Chancellor of the University of Bristol, confers honorary degrees on Menzies and the United States Ambassador, Winant. The night before, Bristol has suffered a devastating air raid. Menzies remarks in his Diary on the smoking ruins and the indomitable spirit of the university, 'where many a gown was worn over working uniform, and many learned participants had been up fire-fighting all night'.

was too large and scattered to be strongly held by a small force against a German armoured Division. He aggressively quizzed the First Sea Lord about the navy's failure to cut off German supply lines across the Mediterranean to Tripoli and learnt to his dismay that German dive-bombers, based on Sicily and Tripoli and outside the range of the closest British fighters (from Malta), made naval attack on Axis convoys hazardous if not near-impossible. Largely as a result of his insistence, the Admiralty was instructed that 'great risks must be taken' to intercept what Menzies sardonically called the Germans' 'regular ferry service' between Palermo and Tripoli.[27]

[27] War Cabinet, 11 April 1941, PRO, CAB 65/22; Menzies to Fadden, 15 April 1941, *DAFP* 4: 586; Diary, 11 April 1941.

At Chequers on Sunday 13 April, 'we are all depressed by the news of what I call the "botch" in Libya'. It was clear from reports coming in by then that, as well, the Yugoslavs were about to crumble and that inept Greek tactics were allowing the Germans to outflank the main line of defence between the Yugoslav border and central Greece. Next day, in the War Cabinet,

> W. C. speaks at length as the Master Strategist—'Tobruk must be held as a bridge head or rally post, from which to hit the enemy'. 'With what?' says I, and so the discussion goes on. Wavell and the Admiralty have failed us. The Cabinet is deplorable—dumb men most of whom disagree with Winston but none of whom dare to say so. This state of affairs is most dangerous. The Chiefs of Staff are without exception Yes men, and a politician runs their services. Winston is a dictator: he cannot be overruled . . . The people have set him up as something little less than God, and his power is therefore terrific.

For Menzies it was too much: 'Today I decide to remain for a couple of weeks, for grave decisions will have to be taken about M.E., . . . and I am not content to have them solved by "unilateral rhetoric" '.[28]

Thus, a week after his return from Ireland, Menzies suffered extraordinary disillusionment with Churchill, and reached a turning point in their relations. A sufficient explanation for what was happening might have been Menzies' horror at the disasters threatening Australian forces, thanks to British mismanagement which, he now felt, had to be laid at Churchill's door. But Churchill's brutal rejection of Menzies' report on Ireland, into which the author had poured so much of himself, cauterized the wound. When he notified Fadden of his wish to stay on, Menzies made no pretence about the reason: 'Confidentially', he cabled,

> I may tell you that my decision to remain for another week or two arises from the fact that I appear to be the only minister outside the Prime Minister who will question any of his views or insist on points being examined, and as Australia has so much at stake it would be unwise of me to leave here in the middle of a crisis.[29]

With his wife he was more circumspect: thanks to censorship, personal cables lacked the secrecy of official communications. Moreover, surface cordiality had to be kept up. Churchill, perhaps prompted by Menzies himself, cabled Fadden and got official Australian sanction for Menzies to stay for at least another

[28] Diary, 14 April 1941.
[29] Menzies to Fadden, 15 April 1941, AA, A5954/1, box 633.

fortnight.[30] Menzies simply told his wife that decisions affecting Australian troops were impending 'and it would never do for me to clear out just as these matters for decision are about to arise'.[31]

On the day after this exchange of cables Wavell accepted that the position in Greece had deteriorated rapidly and that evacuation was unavoidable: in a communiqué to Dill and the Cabinet he announced that a stand would be made at Thermopylae to cover embarking troops and that all ships still coming to Greece with troops must be turned back.[32] Blamey intimated that, given the almost complete German mastery of the air, Thermopylae could not be expected to hold long. Churchill ordered it to be 'made plain to the Commander-in-Chief that the main thing was to get the men away, and that we should not worry about saving vehicles'.[33] His response to a strong appeal from Menzies for more air cover was less pleasing: air resources had to be divided between protecting the evacuation and sustaining battle in Libya; if these clashed, Libya must have priority. But he did send a telegram to the Middle East Air Commander informing him 'that the Prime Minister of Australia had expressed anxiety on this question' and asking that, 'without prejudice to the immediate safety of Libya', all possible aircraft be spared for Greece 'during the immediately critical days'.[34] This could only be an empty gesture; the lack of air protection remained to the end, as Blamey observed, the greatest source of strain on the troops' morale. The main evacuation took place over several nights from 25 April. Cadogan noted ironically in his diary that this was the 'one thing we're really good at!'[35] At the War Cabinet on 28 April, Menzies, his nerves on edge as final news from Greece was awaited, was again greatly irritated by Churchill: 'Winston says "We will lose only 5000 in Greece". We will in fact lose at least 15 000. W. is a great man, but he is more addicted to wishful thinking every day'.[36]

During those dark days Menzies outwardly kept his head in the face of personal distress at what was happening, of agitated cables from his own War Cabinet and of damaging public criticism at

[30] Churchill to Fadden, 15 April 1941 and Fadden to Menzies, 15 April 1941, AA, A5954/1, box 613.
[31] Menzies to Pat, 15 April 1941, Menzies Family Papers.
[32] 16 April 1941, PRO, CAB 65/22/124.
[33] 21 April 1941, PRO, CAB 65/18/87.
[34] 24 April 1941, PRO, CAB 65/22/135.
[35] Dilks (ed.), *Diaries of Sir Alexander Cadogan*, 24 April 1941.
[36] Diary, 28 April 1941. Menzies' assessment was close to being correct. We now know that 14 000 men (2000 of them Australians) were left behind in Greece: 50 000 were evacuated, but in one respect Churchill was, largely involuntarily, obeyed—the force lost all its vehicles and heavy weapons. Grey, *A Military History of Australia*, 158.

home from some Opposition politicians and the press. He did become tetchy once when his Cabinet bypassed him and communicated directly with Cranborne, the British Secretary for the Dominions: 'you may be assured that I am doing all I can in most difficult and trying circumstances. Canberra is more peaceful than having bombs dropping around you in London'.[37] That last sentence was not mere irony. Menzies had just been through the worst night he experienced in the London blitz. A dozen large bombs fell within 100 yards of his hotel, blew in the windows and filled rooms with acrid fumes. 'Twice the whole building seemed to bounce with the force of the concussion'. Next morning he found buildings blazing in central London streets: 'wherever we walked we crunched over broken glass'.[38] Of this raid Colville recorded that 'bombs came down like hailstones'[39] and Cadogan, walking to the Foreign Office, found the whole area around Piccadilly, St James's Street, Pall Mall and Lower Regent Street 'pretty well devastated'.[40] Menzies could perhaps be forgiven a little impatience with Canberra.

His one achievement in those last days in London was to persuade Dill that the Australian forces should be assembled as soon as possible as one corps under the command of Blamey. Also, Blamey ('instead of some unknown Major General with a hyphen in his name') should be given a definite command such as the Western Desert, so that there would be an effective Australian voice in decisions on the spot.[41] Partly at Churchill's request, he also prepared press and broadcast statements 'to steady the malcontents' whose statements in Australia about the Greek débâcle were 'adversely affecting Australia's reputation'. 'Nobody can even begin to believe how high we stood in London as a result of all we have done', he wrote to his wife, 'and it just drives me to despair to have people told in the cables, in effect, that we grumble in defeat and are cheerful only in victory. There is no grumbling in this place'.[42] 'Evatt's criticisms have been published here and have done harm', he noted in his Diary. 'How can an Australian PM do any good here if his rear is unprotected and unsafe?'[43] In a widely publicized Anzac Day address[44] at the

---

[37]Menzies to Fadden, 18 April 1941, *DAFP* 4: 596.
[38]Diary, 16 April 1941.
[39]Colville, *On the Fringes of Power*, 445.
[40]Dilks (ed.), *Diaries of Sir Alexander Cadogan*, 17 April 1941.
[41]Menzies to Fadden, 19 April 1941, *DAFP* 4: 597; Diary, 19 April 1941.
[42]Menzies to Pat, 23 April 1941, Menzies Family Papers.
[43]Diary, 22–23 April 1941.
[44]Published verbatim in *The Times*, 26 April 1941.

Overseas Club he declared that 'nobody could stand with his head up if we had failed to accept the challenge that the tragedy of Greece presented to us'.

Meanwhile, though the decencies were outwardly preserved, those around him could have little doubt about Menzies' disillusion with Churchill. On the night he decided to stay on for the extra two weeks Menzies gave at the Dorchester to almost fifty men what was originally planned as a farewell dinner. Half the British Cabinet and almost all the Chiefs of Staff were among the guests, though Churchill appears to have been unable to accept his invitation. It was, Menzies recorded, 'a cheery party, at which I made a wicked speech about the Chiefs of Staff: thank God the speech is, by those present, understood to be funny'.[45] Shortly after that he lunched with Churchill, Eden and Attlee at 10 Downing Street: 'Very amusing. I tell Winston he needs Chiefs of Staff who will tell him he is talking nonsense. W. explodes, but it draws him, and he reveals his real opinion of the Chiefs of Staff in terms I could not have equalled! He knows they are Yes-men, and does not love them for it'.[46] Then on Menzies' second-last Cabinet meeting he had another row with Churchill. This time it was over the possible transfer of the bulk of the US Pacific fleet to the Atlantic if America joined the war against the Axis. Behind this suggestion were long and secret internal American service discussions and a decision that in the event of a simultaneous war in the Far East and Europe the proper strategy was to beat Hitler first. Anglo-American staff talks in April, to which Australians were not a party and which reflected concern at German ravages on Atlantic convoys, resulted in proposals for the immediate movement of substantial units of the American fleet from the Pacific.[47] The incident in the British War Cabinet resulted from one of Churchill's ebullient telegrams to Roosevelt. As Menzies recorded it: 'Great argument in War Cabinet. I protest against W. C. deciding what advice to offer USA regarding moving Pacific fleet (or a real section of it) to the Atlantic without reference to Australia, though I was in London!'[48] Cadogan's diary catches the incident rather more graphically:

[45] Diary, 15 April. Though the Diary is somewhat ambiguous as to whether Churchill was there, I conclude from a guest list preserved in the Menzies Family Papers that he was not. Beside his name, in handwriting (presumably that of Tritton, Menzies' secretary) are the words 'No. Lord Beaverbrook's Dinner List', which implies that Beaverbrook was also hosting a dinner that evening. This may also explain why other prominent ministers turned down Menzies' invitation, most notably Beaverbrook himself, Eden, Cranborne, Attlee, Butler and Duff Cooper.
[46] Diary, 21 April 1941.
[47] Hasluck, *Government and People* 1: 353.
[48] Diary, 30 April 1941.

Menzies, quite rightly, made a stink about the telegram sent at 4 a.m., as a result of last night's 'Midnight Follies', heartily endorsing the American suggestion that they should send their Pacific fleet into the Atlantic. Anything more insane! We were able to telegraph Washington to suspend action. But Winston very obstinate that this was the right thing to do ... he suffers from the delusion that any cold water thrown on any hare-brained U.S. suggestion will stop the U.S. coming into the war![49]

Next day, at Menzies' last War Cabinet meeting, the proper courtesies were observed. Churchill declared that Menzies 'had won an outstanding place in the esteem of the British people, and would take back to Australia the admiration and affection of us all'. Menzies thanked Churchill for his remarks and assured Cabinet that 'the experience and knowledge which he had gained during his visit would be of the utmost value to him'.[50] But that afternoon Hankey, after attending a lunch which Menzies addressed and bidding him farewell, walked away down Park Lane with his wife when

We heard someone running, and low [sic] and behold, it was Menzies himself. He burst out at once about Churchill and his dictatorship and his War Cabinet of 'Yes-men'. 'There is only one thing to be done' he said, 'and that is to summon an Imperial War Cabinet and keep one of them behind, like Smuts in the last war, not as a guest but as a full member'. He was very much moved, and left us at the Dorchester.[51]

Until brought into the Cabinet as a full member by Chamberlain, Lord Hankey had been its secretary and secretary also to the Committee of Imperial Defence. Churchill kept him on as a minister, but saw to it that his influence declined. As a loyal Chamberlainite Hankey resented Churchill's leadership and was horrified at his unconventional handling of strategy—'by a series of improvisations', brilliant though some of them might be. Hankey was at this time talking much among people who behind the scenes were alarmed at Britain's desperate wartime position and blamed Churchill for it 'I am puzzled what to do', he told his diary. 'All my friends who were in the Chamberlain Government have been scattered.' One, however, was still in the House of Lords: Sir John Simon. After his exchange with Menzies Hankey went and saw Simon who opined that 'the best plan is to get Menzies to "bell the cat" before he leaves: he has become a great Imperial figure,

[49] Dilks (ed.), *Diaries of Sir Alexander Cadogan*, 1 May 1941.
[50] War Cabinet, 1 May 1942. PRO, CAB 65/18.
[51] Hankey Diary, Churchill Archives Centre (CAC), Cambridge, 1 May 1941. The lunch had been given by the Iron and Steel Federation.

has attended the War Cabinet and the Defence Committee for some weeks, has a big stake in the war, and is entitled to speak his mind'. Hankey phoned Menzies and 'asked him to tackle Churchill when he went to say goodbye'. Menzies said he had already decided to do so, and Hankey 'begged him to urge Churchill to drop his dictatorial methods and to use his military and political advisers properly'.[52] Menzies records the sequel briefly and enigmatically: 'Confusion and hurry. Long talk with Winston regarding the help he needs in Cabinet'.[53] Shedden, who came to say goodbye to Hankey next day, said that Menzies 'got no change out of Churchill': his answer was, in effect, 'you see the people by whom I am surrounded. They have no ideas, so the only thing to be done is to formulate my own ideas'. Hankey exploded: of course they had none; Churchill had got rid of all the people with ideas, because he was 'intolerant of other people's ideas and wants to be Dictator'.[54]

Of those who battened on Menzies' mood of disillusion there was another who, like Hankey, was a man of the past: the 78-year-old Lloyd George. Still a member of the Commons, he had—much to Churchill's relief—fought shy of accepting Cabinet office despite implied offers. Of the many reasons why he could never work in a Churchill Cabinet the most important was that Lloyd George believed Britain could not win the war and was prepared—even preferred—to negotiate peace with Hitler. Though Menzies did not agree with that, he thought of Lloyd George as an elder statesman and knew he was critical of Churchill. A few days before leaving England he travelled down to the old man's country house at Churt, in Surrey, for lunch and a parting chat. The discussion resulted in mutual agreement on a catalogue of Churchill's failings and possible remedies, which Menzies set down for himself afterwards, in an unusually long diary entry. There was the by now standard string of complaints about Churchill's dictatorial ways but the most important point was the 'acute' need for 'a couple of good men to prop up Churchill':

> He is not interested in finance, economics, or agriculture, and ignores the dictates on all three. He loves war and spends hours with the maps and charts, working out fresh combinations. He has aggression without knowledge or at any rate without any love for inconvenient knowledge. His advisers are presumed to have knowledge but haven't enough aggression to convey it to Churchill.

[52] Ibid., 5 May 1941.
[53] Diary, 1–2 May 1941.
[54] Hankey Diary, 2 May 1941.

Menzies and Lloyd George agreed about one at least of the urgently wanted props: the War Cabinet 'must contain a Dominions man, for the Dominions type of mind is essential'.[55] Here, explicitly stated, was the remedy Menzies would a few days later adumbrate in his outburst to Hankey.

Menzies would have been less than human if he did not think of himself as a suitable 'Dominions man' for this job. He had shown a willingness to stand up to Churchill in Cabinet. In the world outside he was effective and admired as a speaker, and valued in the social world in which he mixed. This was his fourth visit to England and, though he had bouts of diffidence and homesickness, it was an environment which he had come to find, on the whole, comfortable. On this trip he had, moreover, received signals that, in some circles at least, any chance of his staying on would be welcomed. He at first treated these a trifle jocularly. Early in March, for example, he addressed at the House of Commons a meeting of the Empire Parliamentary Association on Australia's war effort. 'A remarkable ovation at the finish', he recorded. 'Some of these fellows would not mind my defeat at Canberra if they could get me into the Commons. OMNIS IGNOTUS PRO MAGNIFICO'.[56] But later, after his agony over Greece and his disillusion with Churchill, the jocularity disappeared. Witness, for example, his reference to 'long talk Beaverbrook' the day before leaving England: 'approves of me, and thinks absurd that I should go back to Australia! I am desperately afraid of the future in Great Britain'.[57] Before arriving in London, Menzies had recorded a somewhat lofty disdain for Beaverbrook, the colourful newspaper magnate and minister-crony of Churchill,[58] but when he came to understand Beaverbrook's extraordinary achievements as Minister for Aircraft Production— the provision of the aircraft which won the Battle of Britain[59]— disdain turned into admiration, especially when Beaverbrook proved to be the one minister who was prepared in the War Cabinet to resist Churchill's seeming blindness to the priority of equipment over men. Beaverbrook, on his side, responded well to Menzies, recognizing his courage and his intellectual gifts. Much

[55] Diary, 26 April 1941.
[56] Ibid., 11 March 1941 ('every unknown a magnifico').
[57] Ibid., 1–2 May 1941.
[58] On his way to England, in February, Menzies noted: 'Tales of Beaverbrook's high-handedness come drifting in ... The flashy and the unscrupulous seem to come to the top. The public are very child-like; they like something that rattles. It is the age of publicity, which means that the most illiterate of all trades, that of newspaper writing, becomes dominant'. Ibid., 18 February 1941.
[59] A. J. P. Taylor, *Beaverbrook* (N.Y. 1972), 414 ff.

was implicit in a telegram he sent to Menzies late in May, when the Australian Prime Minister had returned home and was facing a dispiriting domestic political situation:

> If I were an Australian I would welcome you back to your country Stop Being a Canadian ordinarily resident in London I would welcome you back to this country with much more enthusiasm than any other visitor from any other part of the Empire Stop I hope the Australians will decide to send you soon and keep you here for as long as the war lasts.[60]

In response Menzies assured Beaverbrook that 'my association with you was one of the highlights of my journey and I would ask for nothing better than to renew it'.[61]

Given both his success there, and the hostility towards Churchill of a coterie in London, the daring historiographical hypothesis has been advanced that Menzies was tempted, and in fact planned, to overthrow Churchill and step into his shoes as Prime Minister of Britain. It has also been suggested that he was motivated by the wish to escape a parlous political position at home and even to seek a negotiated peace with the Axis powers.[62] Direct evidence to support any of these claims has not yet been found, though the scholar who most forcefully advances them, Dr David Day, has structurally marshalled indirect evidence on the assumption that almost from the time of his arrival Menzies followed a policy designed to win political strength in Britain through his public appearances and his cultivation of anti-Churchill malcontents. That assumption is difficult to accept, given the spontaneous responsiveness to changing circumstances reflected in Menzies' diary, where dominant themes are his strange love–hate relationship with Churchill and his genuine emotion at the changing face of the war. Neither he, nor Hankey, nor Lloyd George, express even at the end of Menzies' time in London any wish to get rid of Churchill. All are practical politicians: what they want, in their own words, is to find a 'prop', perhaps a censor, for him. Nor does Beaverbrook's appreciation of Menzies imply more than a wish to harness his gifts in the fight to save Britain at a desperate time. Certainly, Beaverbrook and Churchill were to some degree at odds during those days but the tension was about whether Beaverbrook's

---

[60]Beaverbrook to Menzies, 24 May 1941, Beaverbrook Papers, BBK D/408, House of Lords Record Office, London.
[61]Ibid., 28 May 1941.
[62]The thesis is most cogently advanced in David Day's *Menzies and Churchill at War* (London and Sydney 1986).

health was up to coping with the important job of co-ordinating munition production and there was certainly no suggestion that Beaverbrook wanted Churchill replaced.[63]

The one document we have which refers directly to the possibility of Menzies taking the British prime ministership is an undated 'Diary' entry in which Shedden ruminated after returning to Australia on 'The Prime Minister's visit abroad'. It recapitulates the difficulties Menzies had overcome, speaks of his 'increasing stature', and observes:

> Mr. Menzies has strongly entrenched himself in public leadership since becoming Prime Minister. His crystal-clear mind and beautiful English explain difficult things that worry the ordinary citizen (in such a simple manner that he feels they are the very things he has been feeling but unable to express himself). While ranking him equal with Churchill and Roosevelt as a public leader, I think he is ahead of them on the practical approach to determining and administering his Policy. Admittedly his responsibilities are not as great, but in the British Empire there is no one on the horizon who approaches him as the successor to Churchill. (Radical as it may sound, why should not a Dominion statesman lead the Empire in war?)[64]

We have no indication that Menzies ever saw this. There is no warrant for describing the passage as a 'frank admission, from within his own camp, of Menzies' ultimate ambition'.[65] To take, without precise evidence to that effect, the flattering words of an acolyte as an expression of the ambitions of the object of veneration raises scary possibilities, to say the least!

On 2 May the King at Buckingham Palace received and farewelled Menzies who, later that day, left London by train for an undisclosed aerodrome. The Bruces and four British ministers, of whom Beaverbrook was one, saw him off. That night he flew out to Lisbon, on the first leg of the trip home via the United States and Canada. It was the end of a ten-week visit of which, in a valedictory editorial, *The Times* observed: 'his presence here, his share in council, and the grace and force of a whole series of eloquent speeches have made a very real contribution to the common cause at a time when the Empire is facing a stern trial ... He has made it unmistakably plain to the world that Australia is with us to the last'.[66]

---

[63]Taylor, *Beaverbrook*, esp. 458–69. Note, 469, 'Of course Beaverbrook still believed that Churchill was the indispensable man. He wrote to Lord Wolmer on 12 May: 'So far as I can see we have only one bold man in the Government, and that is the boss. If we did not have him, God knows where we would be" '.
[64]Prime Minister's visit abroad—1941—an appraisement, AA A5954/1, box 17.
[65]Day, *Menzies and Churchill at War*, 151.
[66]*The Times*, 5 May 1941.

16

And Bleed Awhile

AT LISBON Menzies unexpectedly spent a day waiting for a connection with the American clipper. So he called on Salazar and then took in something rather exotic for him: a bull fight at Estoril ('spectacle of colour, swank and cruelty, worth seeing once'). In New York the Caseys met him at La Guardia airport and gave him dinner at the Ritz-Carlton. Next morning he flew to Ottawa where a detachment of Australian air trainees were drawn up as a guard of honour and the Canadian Prime Minister, Mackenzie King, met him. At a subsequent press conference, 'I sense that King is more criticised in Canada than I am in Australia. But, per contra, he has a loyal following. They stick to their leaders here. He has been P.M. 14 years and Liberal leader 23!'

It was a full ceremonial state visit: Menzies was to stay at Government House as the guest of the Governor-General. Over lunch at the Chateau Laurier, he addressed an enthusiastic audience of 800 Canadian Club members 'on the war and giving all to win it', and that afternoon was taken by Mackenzie King to Parliament House where, in response to an unusual invitation, he addressed the Commons and savoured 'terrific enthusiasm, members applauding by beating on the tables'. Afterwards, with King, Menzies was piped out of the Chamber and spent some hours with the Canadian Cabinet's War Committee, giving them what he described as 'the inside story of Whitehall'. From the steps as he left to go he insisted on taking a movie of King and asked that a screen be provided after dinner that night for him to show films he had taken in England. The Cabinet, the Governor-General, the Chief Justice and other dignitaries were present at the dinner to do Menzies honour. Finally, after a long evening, he collapsed into bed 'dog tired, for I have today made 5 speeches after having 5 hours sleep in about 3 days. What junketings travelling ministers have!' Next morning he breakfasted with his old friend Malcolm

An enthusiastic amateur photographer, Menzies makes for himself a lively movie record of his first encounter in Ottawa in 1941 with Mackenzie King, the Canadian Prime Minister.

MacDonald, now British High Commissioner in Canada, who expressed concern about the Australian political situation. 'His actual words', Menzies recorded, ' "they never know when they have a great P.M., and they never back him". Subject to the fact that I am not great at all, he is right. We are parochial, jealous and ungenerous to those who serve us. The Sydney taint!' Later that morning Mackenzie King and several ministers saw him off in the train to travel to Toronto and thence to New York.[1]

[1] Paragraphs above based on Menzies' Diary, 3–8 May 1941, and Mackenzie King Diary, 7 May 1941, University Library, Cambridge, England.

Menzies is captured in a characteristic mood as he leaves after a visit to the office of the Australian High Commissioner in Canada, 1941.

King, an indefatigable diarist, wrote a long account of the visit, which was clearly, even for him, a great event. Unquestionably, he thought,

> Menzies took this city more or less by storm. He is a fine looking fellow, splendid presence, great vigour, and has a wonderful gift for speaking. He has endless confidence in himself, and does not mind putting himself very much in the limelight... Reveals his Scotch Presbyterian origin in his thoughts and views generally. Has many of

the qualities of a great leader, but, I feel, while his sympathies are broad, he nevertheless is thinking pretty much of Menzies most of the time, and likes very much the environments of high society, palaces, etc, which will cost him, perhaps, dearly in the end.[2]

Menzies' films were what, above all, gave King this last impression. He could not help thinking that when shown in Australia, especially to Labor audiences (bizarre thought, which could only occur to a foreigner!) these photographs would make people feel that 'he has not yet really understood the significance of this war, which is one against place and privilege'. This strange comment reveals more about King than Menzies: to anyone fresh (as Menzies was) from the reality of Britain's desperate struggle for survival and the unity that that had engendered it would have seemed ludicrous indeed to explain the war as being primarily about 'place and privilege'. King's observation about Menzies' pleasure in 'the environment of high society' was more telling, though he missed its element of innocence. The diaries of both men confirm the judgement which Malcolm MacDonald sent home in his official report of the visit. Menzies, he said, admired King's political skill in holding Canada together so well, and had enjoyed King's conversation; King was impressed by Menzies' vigour, forthrightness and charm. 'It does not detract from this picture of friendship if I say that each man is sufficiently shrewd a judge of human character to have detected the weak points in the other.'[3]

King indeed decided that Menzies 'would rather be on the War Cabinet in London than Prime Minister of Australia' and said much to discourage Menzies' obsession with the need for a Dominion minister to counter Churchill's dictatorial excesses.[4] But, whatever he said outwardly, King saw in his heart the point of Menzies' strictures. There was another side to Menzies' photographs:

> Tonight, as I looked at the pictures he showed of the different ministers in the present Cabinet, I confess I felt it was a terrible thing to think that the fate of the Empire is in the hands of the few men we saw portrayed there. I would feel infinitely more confidence in the group that I have around me in Ottawa from the point of view of judgement and wisdom than I do in the men at present in the British administration. There is far too much thought of the role people are playing in history ...

[2] Mackenzie King Diary, 7 May 1941. Subsequent quotations, except where otherwise stated, are from this long entry.
[3] Malcolm MacDonald ('Private & Confidential'), 14 May 1941, PRO, PREM 4/43A/12.
[4] Diary, 8 May 1941.

Menzies arrived in Washington on 9 May, to begin three days of speechmaking, press conferences and talks with American ministers and officials. After a speech Menzies gave to the Press Club the *Washington Post* noted how he 'had observed what was happening to the spirit of Britain. In Miltonic accents he declared that "every time a hammer blow falls, their temper becomes keener, their strength greater." It was, indeed, a tonic to hear this vibrant Australian'.[5] In public utterances Menzies' main themes were that the magnitude and speed of American aid would be what would determine the length of the war and that the fight was America's fight as well as Britain's: 'Not the politics of Europe; but the politics of common humanity!'[6] He had an hour's bedside interview with Roosevelt, who was laid up with stomach trouble, and found that 'he (and Hull) agreed that we all ought to tell Japan where she gets off, but each of them stops short of actually instructing the USA Ambassador to do so'. He obtained assur-

Menzies arrives in New York early in May 1941, on his way home, to be warmly greeted by the recently appointed Richard Casey, the first Australian Ambassador to the United States.

[5] 13 May 1941.
[6] Diary, 9, 15 May; *New York Herald Tribune*, 10 May; *Washington Post*, 11 May 1941.

ances, however, that 'America will not stand by & see Australia attacked', and that the Pacific would not be 'denuded of USA naval forces'. Roosevelt and all the leading ministers, he decided, were 'for war and nothing less'. But the President, 'trained under Woodrow Wilson in the last war, waits for an incident, which would in one blow get the USA into war and get R. out of his foolish election pledges that "I will keep you out of war" '.[7]

After Washington Menzies called and spoke at New York and Chicago, then left Los Angeles for Honolulu, Noumea and, on 22 May, Auckland. On the clipper flights he worked hard, 'writing, in preparation for Australian arrival'. At Auckland he was given a state dinner, slept at Government House and next day received a civic welcome in the Town Hall. That night there was another dinner for him at Government House and when that was over he showed his films ('the later ones', he ruminated, 'are very good indeed'). Afterwards, in the silence of his room, he thought of what lay ahead next day. The press would batter him. There would have to be more speeches. Letters awaiting him at Auckland had already told of things that should be done—all involving hard and unpalatable public appearances—to capitalize on the prestige he had won abroad and resist those who had been publicly attacking and privately plotting against him at home. He had faced the demands of Ottawa and Washington with zest but the more complicated Australian prospect was intolerably different. Something snapped, and he wished that the cup could pass from him. 'A sick feeling of repugnance and apprehension grows in me as I near Australia', he confided to his diary. 'If only I could creep in quietly into the bosom of the family and rest there.'[8] Of course it was not to be.

Unhappily for the historian, Menzies' 1941 diary ends on the eve of his arrival home: we do not therefore have an account of his personal feelings about the events that were soon to overwhelm him. But it is clear that on his arrival at the flying-boat terminal at Rose Bay he was, as one reporter put it, 'tired and grim'[9] or, in the more colourful words of Arthur Fadden, who was at the landing, 'about as happy as a sailor on a horse'.[10] At a brief press conference Menzies said that he had come back 'stimulated to an

---

[7]Diary, 15 May 1941.
[8]Diary, 23 May 1941. The account of Menzies' movements after leaving Washington draws on the diary in the previous days.
[9]*SMH*, 26 May 1941.
[10]Arthur Fadden, *They Called Me Artie; the Memoirs of Sir Arthur Fadden* (Milton, Q. 1969), 58–9.

effort which must surpass any other of my life' and, referring to party divisions in Australia, declared that 'It is a diabolical thing that anybody should have to come back and play politics, however clean and however friendly, at a time like this'. In Britain he had learnt the lesson of unity: there all parties were represented in a real war cabinet; there the bombs fell equally on Buckingham Palace and the slums near the docks. But: 'All the time I was in London the Australian cables would almost continually report alleged political dissensions, rumours of political difficulties, and ill-informed criticisms which added tremendously to the burdens which I was endeavouring to carry'. On Pat's suggestion, wired ahead to Menzies in America,[11] the two spent the weekend together in seclusion, whisked away from Rose Bay to the country house of a friend, at Moss Vale. There, in the quietness he craved, Menzies rested and prepared himself for his appearance at a public welcome which Cabinet planned for the following Monday evening (26th) in the Sydney Town Hall.

Menzies' outburst at the moment of arrival was that of a tired man whose apprehensions were indeed of an Australia which contrasted sharply with the Britain he had left. The formal uncertainty of government remained, with the main parties in the House of Representatives evenly divided, an independent holding the balance of power and a Labor Opposition whose leadership refused to take part in a national government.[12] His attack on continuing party dissension was largely prompted by the fact that at the moment of his arrival a by-election was in progress: for Boothby, in South Australia. It had become vacant because of the death of the sitting member, J. L. Price, who had held the seat since 1928. Originally a Labor man, Price had joined the UAP after Lyons's defection. Menzies' denunciation of the 'divisiveness' which a by-election at this time involved was some index of his agitated frame of mind. A death automatically entailed an election: no other lawful way of replacing the deceased member existed. It was inevitable that, however much they might agree on the necessity for an all-out war effort, the parties which fielded candidates

[11]Cypher Telegram, Menzies to Pat, 18 May 1941, AA A5954/1, box 613.
[12]Menzies had cabled Curtin on 22 April reiterating his appreciation of 'your courtesy and helpfulness' but renewing his offer of portfolios to the Labor Party in a national government (Menzies to Curtin, copy to Fadden, AA, CRS A5954/1, box 633). That the matter was at this stage very much on his mind is indicated by the fact that three days later Hugh Dalton, Minister for Economic Warfare in Churchill's Cabinet, and a Labour man, records having lunched with Shedden, 'who wants to know how British all party coalition came about ... Menzies in some danger'. Dalton did his best to explain the complexities and said frankly that in his opinion Menzies should resign and serve under Curtin (Dalton Diaries, 24: 99 (25 April 1941), Dalton Papers, London School of Economics Library.

```
HOME-COMING SPEECH.                    3.

                                WE HAVE GREAT PRIVILEGES +
                                MUST MAKE GREAT SACRIFICES
THANKS TO FADDEN + COLLEAGUES
                                A.  POLITICAL UNITY.

JOURNEY — TO PALESTINE, EGYPT, LIBYA    NO PARTY NEED GIVE UP IDENTITY
           USA — ROOSEVELT
                                        BUT WE MUST MAKE PARLIAMENT
IMPRESSIONS OF GREAT BRITAIN            AN INSTRUMENT OF WAR AND
                                        NOT OF DISSENTION.
  1.  A GOOD KING AND A GOOD PEOPLE
                                        ACKNOWLEDGE CURTIN'S ATTITUDE
  2.  A GREAT FIGHTING LEADER
                                        BUT WHY SHOULD NOT ABILITIES OF
  3   COMPLETE LOYALTY TO LEADER        LEADING LABOUR MEN BE USED
                                        IN EXECUTIVE CAPACITY !
  4   COMPLETE UNITY
      (3 dissentients on confidence vote)  B.  LOYAL SUPPORT OF GOVERNMENT

      Wonder what sort of govt. if      A FEW REAL FRIENDS, WHO HAVE
      every by-election imperilled      SUSTAINED ME IN THANKLESS TASK
      govt ? Or can we afford these
      things better !                   BUT SO-CALLED FRIEND, WHISPERER,
    LEADER CAN THEREFORE DEVOTE ALL     PAROCHIALIST, SELF-SEEKER — ARE
    HIS TIME TO THE CONDUCT OF WAR      ENEMIES OF STRONG + CONFIDENT
                                        DIRECTION.

                                        A GREAT CRISIS . WE MUST CLOSE UP
                                                           THE RANKS

                        5

            THIS IS THE YEAR OF FATE.
            AUSTRALIAN SOLDIERS, SAILORS, AND
            AIRMEN, UNITED, LOYAL, AFIRE
            WITH A SINGLE PURPOSE, HAVE SET
            US THE EXAMPLE AND HAVE MADE
            A NAME THAT THE WORLD KNOWS
            AND HONOURS. CANNOT WE, AS
            CITIZENS, FOLLOW THEIR EXAMPLE,
            OR MUST WE GO DOWN TO HISTORY
            AS PEOPLE, RICHLY ENDOWED BY GOD
            WITH HEALTH AND WEALTH AND
            GOLDEN OPPORTUNITY, WHO SQUABBLED
            UPON THE STEPS OF THE TEMPLE
            UNTIL THE PILLARS FELL
```

Some of the five brief pages of notes Menzies used for his homecoming speech in the Sydney Town Hall: to write a speech for reading was beneath his contempt. The notes were nevertheless the tips of an iceberg of hard thinking and phrase-making in the Churchill manner.

should in their campaigning lay some stress on the special interests and policies for which they stood. In fact, the candidate who won the seat was as true-blue a non-Labor man as could be imagined: Archibald Grenfell Price, Master of St Mark's College in the University of Adelaide, who in 1931–32 had been chairman of the 'Emergency Committee of South Australia', a conservative body formed to maintain law and order and fight Langism. But when Menzies made landfall, Price's election was still in the future.

The sense of instability, of impending trouble, of course had deeper roots than this. Labor might, under Curtin, provide principled co-operation on war measures, but a faction led by Evatt was eager for power and impatiently pressed for Menzies' removal.[13] More ominous still was disaffection in UAP ranks and the continuing hostility towards Menzies of a section of the Country Party. The latter was an important element in that plotting against him which, while he was away, so worried Mrs Menzies. Spender records having discussed this with Sir Sydney Snow, a leading Sydney official in the UAP organization, after official internal Country Party correspondence accidentally fell into Snow's hands. Menzies must go, it said, if the coalition ministry was to continue in office. On Snow's advice, Spender wrote to Menzies, then on the way home, to tell him 'how his political grave was being dug'.[14] Who was implicated remains obscure, though there seems to be little doubt that Page was a leading conspirator[15]

---

[13] That, at least, was what seemed to be the case as Menzies arrived. He had e.g., already received a long letter from F. H. Wright warning of the 'unholy combination which has sprung up between Dr Evatt and Beasley both of whom profess to be very disturbed indeed that we are not indulging in a much greater war effort'. Wright, Staniforth Ricketson, Frank Menzies 'and one or two others' had conferred with Pat and worked out a programme of public meetings on Menzies' arrival, but this had to be modified when Menzies made it clear to Pat that he needed immediate rest (NLA, MS. 8119/2/15). To add to his confusion, and no doubt apprehension, Menzies received a letter the day after his arrival from Evatt himself, which catalogued alleged inefficiencies in munitions and other wartime production, denied that Menzies' opponents in the Labor Party were 'playing politics', and urged Menzies to negotiate something less than a national government which, while not 'interfering with the rights of opposition or the separation of the two parties', would stabilize the parliamentary situation and allow people like himself to 'serve this country in the most suitable capacity for the period of this war'. Evatt was vague as to the method by which this could all be done, though he seemed to be suggesting that somehow the Advisory War Council should be given executive power. He was also indirectly angling for ministerial status for himself (Evatt to Menzies 24 May 1941, Menzies Family Papers). There is a duplicate of this letter in the Evatt Papers, Flinders University. Hazlehurst, who saw it there, has published this letter in full: *Menzies Observed*, 237–8.

[14] Spender, *Politics and a Man*, 158.

[15] Interview with Sir Allen Brown, 7 November 1991. Note also Shedden, handwritten ruminations (diary?) on fall of Menzies Government: 'Page reported to be the main conspirator', AA, A5954/1, box 16.

and several significant entries in Owen Dixon's diary point to Fadden himself. On the afternoon of 30 August 1941 Dixon called to see the Menzies: 'She was at home & told us of the conspiracy. Sd it was arranged while he was away. Fadden deeply in it. She looked haggard and strained'.[16] The Menzies also thought that Spender was involved, though he and his wife both vehemently denied this in accounts of this period which they subsequently published.[17] Hughes, whose ambivalence towards Menzies was well known, was also widely believed to have been implicated, but he, too, fiercely denied having been involved in any 'intrigue to remove him from the leadership of the Federal UAP'. 'I know nothing', he said, 'of any move in the direction indicated beyond rumours and Press reports'.[18] The discontent of lesser members of the UAP—men like McCall, Hutchinson and Marr—was open and longstanding: that they played a part in the campaign against Menzies is simply to be assumed.

But whatever Menzies' initial weariness and apprehension, his reception was more than promising. On the eve of his arrival, the *Sydney Morning Herald* struck a positive note in an editorial headed 'Native Son's Return. Horoscope for Mr Menzies', which spoke of a 'flood tide' waiting for the returning Prime Minister to take. Fadden had done an excellent job in 'promoting a mutual understanding among Australian political parties', and Menzies' own prestige abroad and commitment to new vigour at this desperate juncture of the war promised inspired leadership.[19] And when, after the initial weekend's rest, Menzies made his first public appearance, in the Sydney Town Hall, he indeed received a tumultuous welcome. He had prepared well, and the adrenalin flowed as he spoke on the subject that most deeply moved him and he made what the *Herald* thought was 'the most stirring speech of his political career'. The Hall was packed, loudspeakers took Menzies' words to the overflow crowd in the Lower Town Hall and the

---

[16]Dixon Diary, 30 August 1941. That there was substance in the suspicion is suggested by the curious allegation Fadden makes in his memoirs that after his arrival Menzies did not 'make any comment of appreciation at the time, in Parliament or out of Parliament, publicly or man to man'. He attributed this to the fact that Menzies had been informed that some of his party were dissatisfied with his leadership and wanted Fadden instead (Fadden, *They Called Me Artie* 60, 62). That Menzies failed to express publicly his appreciation of Fadden's work is manifestly untrue. He did so in the Town Hall speech, in Parliament, and on arrival at Rose Bay. If press reports are to be believed he turned to Fadden, after his initial statement on arrival and said: 'Arthur, I thank you very much for what you have done, and my colleagues, who are also my friends' (*Argus*, 26 May 1941).
[17]Spender, *Politics and a Man*, 156–60; Hazlehurst, *Menzies Observed*, 238–9.
[18]Press release, 24 April 1942, NLA, MS. 1538/36/3.
[19]19, 24 May 1941.

'Native Son's Return': Menzies receives a tumultuous reception in the Sydney Town Hall, 26 May 1941.

street outside. On the platform were Fadden and the other ministers, Evatt to represent federal Labor, and Baddeley, the Deputy Premier of the newly elected Labor Government of New South Wales.[20]

Menzies began by paying a tribute to Fadden's loyalty, to Curtin's courtesy and friendship, and pleaded that parliament be made 'an instrument of war and not an instrument of dissension'. After the unity of purpose and function he had found in Britain, it was sad to come home and realize that

> men sitting on the Opposition benches, men like Mr Curtin, Mr Forde, Dr Evatt, Mr Beasley and Mr Makin, those men who sit on the Advisory War Council, should have no executive function in the direction of the war and should be compelled to stand off and become the critics of an effort to which they might easily be powerful contributors.

But the main thrust of the speech was to tell of the sufferings and courage he had seen in bombed British cities, for 'this war has produced a new order of chivalry and its knights are to be found in the back streets and lanes of Great Britain'. In developing this theme, Menzies was at his best, telling of scenes which for him, and for an audience unacquainted with total war (and not yet made blasé by television), were barely imaginable. In one week, he said, he had visited eight or ten industrial cities, steadfastly producing in their factories all sorts of materials of war, while

> in the centre of them, in every one of them, were great ragged gaps where bombs had fallen; street after street of ruined houses, block after block of cottages, of simple homes, blasted out of existence in a night. In every one of them death had been so widespread and the dead so unidentified that there had been community funerals, with hundreds of victims buried in a common grave. Can you imagine anything so eloquent of utter human anguish than that?

In the Middle East he had met Australian servicemen, his very hearers' sons and husbands, who had made 'English speaking people all over the world ... superbly proud of what Australia

---

[20] Ibid., 27 May 1941, has a detailed account of this appearance. Hazlehurst, *Menzies Observed*, 230–6, has much of the text of Menzies' speech, which the main newspapers were unanimous in branding a speech which 'for passionate eloquence and emotional fervour must surely have been the greatest of his career' (*Argus*, 27 May 1941). Menzies' notes for this speech are still extant. The first item is 'THANKS TO FADDEN & COLLEAGUES' (Menzies Family Papers). Wright thought Menzies on arrival at Rose Bay had 'looked very tired and much older' but 'did not get the impression that his vigour was impaired at all. After listening to him last night I am convinced that my impression was correct and he is at the top of his form'. Wright to Major Douglas Galbraith, 27 May 1941, NLA MS. 8119/2/15.

has done'. He would be the last to subscribe to the cheap remark that Australia had fallen down on the job: on the contrary, miracles of production for war had in many ways been worked over the last two years. Still

> It can scarcely be said by any ordinary citizen of this country that he finds his daily life mode changed from what it was two years ago. We must begin to change our lives; we must make up our minds that war of this magnitude against an enemy of this strength and power can only be won by completely organizing every bit of our energy for his defeat... every bomb I have heard fall, every life I have seen ruined, every experience that I have seen people go through in Great Britain ... has left me more convinced that the time has gone by for the old fights in our country. There is one fight only that matters today and I call on the whole of Australia to GO TO IT!

This speech was wildly cheered by an audience who rose to its feet and spontaneously sang 'for he's a jolly good fellow'. When, at the subsequent Lord Mayor's reception an elated Menzies met Spender he triumphantly asked, 'Well Percy, where is this grave you wrote about?' Spender replied: 'It's been dug all right Bob; it is only waiting for you to be pushed into it'. Remarking on the vividness of Spender's imagination, Menzies strode off.[21] Four days later he received a less happy reception in parliament. In a long and sometimes moving speech he reported the highlights of his trip, paid a tribute to Churchill, and gave a defensive account of the decision to assist Greece. But in an ill-judged peroration he caused an unpleasant party clash by expressing again his 'astonishment' at finding, as he approached Australia, a by-election in progress, such that 'if one party won, the Government would go on, but that if another party won, steps would be taken to remove the Government'. Curtin stilled angry Labor interjections with a dignified reply: 'As the Prime Minister has said, this is the year of fate. I suggest he put aside political catchcries as we put aside political partisanship'.[22] In fact Menzies' reference to the Boothby by-election was sheer propaganda: the campaign was over and the result was known. Grenfell Price had won the seat for the UAP, and the balance of power was unaffected. What Menzies wanted, clearly, was to scarify Labor and raise afresh the issue of a national government.

Next day, in a closed session, Menzies spoke to both Houses of Parliament on aspects of the war which could not yet be made public. In a surprising personal outburst, Page suddenly declared

---
[21]Spender, *Politics and a Man*, 158.
[22]For these speeches, *CPD*, vol. 167, 10 ff.

himself an enthusiastic supporter of the Prime Minister: 'no one could have done more to uphold the interests of all sections of Australia at the heart of the Empire'.[23] Menzies made no comment: he had more important things in view—an adjournment (which he got until 18 June) 'to sort out my ideas and impressions of the journey which I have taken, and to discuss with my colleagues what action is necessary'.[24]

At last, all these trying preliminaries over, Menzies went home to Melbourne. Some thousands were at Spencer Street station to cheer him as he stepped off the train. A kilted piper played him along the platform, and then he and his wife were taken at a walking pace in an open car up Collins Street. They were preceded by four police troopers on grey horses and the police Highland Pipe Band, followed and surrounded by the crowd which had met them at the station. The skirl of the pipes brought thousands of city workers from shops and offices, and Menzies acknowledged many roars, from crowded windows, of 'Good On You, Bob!' From a platform at the Town Hall he made an emotional speech: 'This is the most encouraging thing that has ever happened to me in this city'. The welcome was capped next day at Kew, in the heart of his own electorate, when at an official reception a guard of honour, with fixed bayonets, ushered him into the packed Rialto Theatre, where to the roll of drums the Greek, US and British flags were successively raised and a band played the anthems of the three nations. 'If I live to be 1000 years old, I should never forget what to me is the most immortal passage in the history of the ordinary men of our race', Menzies declared. 'We must nerve ourselves as we have never nerved ourselves before. In a few months to come we shall need every ounce of courage that God has given us.'[25]

On the eve of Parliament's reassembling Menzies made a broadcast to the nation which he called the 'prospectus of an unlimited war effort'. It was the fruit of that consultation within Cabinet and with the Advisory War Cabinet for which he had asked the breathing space of three weeks after his arrival home. The plans he outlined met widespread press approval. They included a drastic revision of the list of reserved occupations, the internment of Communists and the banning of strikes and lockouts in war and allied industries. There was also to be a complete reorganization of Cabinet and the establishment of seven all-party committees to

---

[23] *CPD*, 167: 71–2; *Age*, 31 May 1941: 'Dramatic Event at Canberra. Sir Earle Page Makes Complete Retraction'.
[24] *CPD*, 167: 65.
[25] *Argus*, 2 June 1941.

advise on matters ranging from Manpower and Resources to Taxation and Rural Industry. For Labor, Curtin accepted this approach, though he had reservations about the internment of Communists and the banning of strikes.[26]

Given the enthusiastic reception he received at his homecoming, it might have been expected that such plans would cap the Prime Minister's new reputation. But in politics three weeks is a long time: at a critical moment in a disastrous war it is longer. Just as Menzies arrived in Australia, the German airborne invasion of Crete had begun: within days the newspapers carried long lists of Australian casualties from the Greek and Cretan campaigns. In Parliament, Labor leaders like Chifley were extremely critical of 'errors of judgement' which sent troops to Greece and Crete with poor equipment 'in support of what seems ... to have been a somewhat quixotic notion of honour'.[27] Given wartime restrictions on information, it was impossible for the public to be told how limited a part Menzies had played in the decision to aid Greece, or how desperately he had fought to obtain proper equipment and air cover for the troops once the decision had been made. Inevitably, many Australians associated his name with the ill-starred operation. Chifley was also critical of the Government's ineptitude in manpower control, which had been botched during Menzies' absence and confronted him as a difficult problem to be solved on his return.[28] The Cabinet reconstruction which Menzies now carried out became an inevitable source of further ill-feeling on his own side of the House. Five new departments were created,[29] enlarging Cabinet from twelve to nineteen ministers, and the War Cabinet of six and an Economic and Industry Committee of seven gained sweeping powers. Menzies also took the opportunity to promote to Cabinet three of the elected men who had been among the 'big men' the press had urged on the voters in 1940: J. P. Abbott, powerful among organized graziers; E. S. Spooner, lately Minister for Public Works in New South Wales; and A. M. McDonald, who had served seven years as a prominent member of the Victorian Legislative Assembly. But none of the men who had by now made their dissatisfaction with Menzies open—people like W. V. McCall, Sir Charles Marr of New South Wales and W. J. Hutchinson of Victoria—was promoted, and there were

[26]*CPD*, 167: 107 ff.
[27]Ibid: 113ff.
[28]On this matter see the detailed, and devastating, account Hasluck presents of the interdepartmental committees which attempted to come to grips with the manpower problem before Menzies got home. Hasluck, *Government and People* 1: 387–401.
[29]Aircraft Production, Transport, War Organisation of Industry, Home Defence, External Territories.

others, like A. J. Beck of Tasmania and F. H. Stacey of South Australia, who publicly protested at the Government's failure to choose ministers from representatives of the smaller States. Amid laughter from both sides of the House Arthur Calwell asked Menzies at Question Time on 1 July whether, in appointing Spooner and Abbott to his ministry, he had also considered the claims of Marr, Beck and Hutchinson and whether he had borne in mind the Earl of Clarendon's words to Charles II: 'Do good to your enemies; your friends won't harm you'. The Speaker warned Calwell not to be facetious but nevertheless allowed a second half to the question: 'Now that the preponderance of New South Wales over other States has been further increased in the Cabinet, does the Prime Minister fear a challenge to his leadership from Mr. Hughes or Mr. Spender—that is the old pretender and the young pretender?' Rowley James, the Labor member who had a robust regard for Menzies, flung across the House the interjection 'Throw it in now', to which Menzies replied grimly: 'Anybody who has been Prime Minister for two years in circumstances in which I have been Prime Minister is far beyond fear. I can't describe what emotion it is but it is certainly not fear'.[30]

There were minor consolations. Curtin accepted Menzies' good intentions, endorsed plans for a more concentrated war effort[31] and continued to restrain the group in his party which wanted an all-out attack on the Government. A. W. Coles, the fire-eating Lord Mayor of Melbourne who, after winning the Henty seat as an Independent in 1940, had gone to England at his own expense and come back to attack the Government for its supposed supineness, changed his mind and joined the UAP. As he wrote to Menzies on 25 June, their private discussions had 'revealed to me exactly those things which I desired to find; so that you may now rely upon me to support you through thick and thin'.[32] It no doubt helped that on that same day Menzies was able to announce to the House that the Australian Government was in agreement with Churchill, who had broadcast that Britain would wholeheartedly aid the Soviet Union, which had just been attacked by Hitler.[33] On the other hand, Menzies suffered a serious blow a few days later, when at a Premiers' Conference the States rejected a plan for uniform taxation, which the Government had been advancing for two years and which it considered crucial for war finance.[34]

[30] *Argus*, 2 July 1941.
[31] See, e.g., his speech in the Representatives, 8 June 1941, *CPD*, 167: 107 ff.
[32] A. W. Coles to Menzies, 25 June 1941, Menzies Family Papers.
[33] *SMH*, 26 June 1941.
[34] Ibid., 28 June 1941.

This rebuff may have helped to turn Menzies' thoughts back to the question of his reservations about Churchill's conduct of the war. On 3 July he sounded out by secret cable Smuts and King on the need for a Dominion Prime Minister in the British War Cabinet: Churchill, he said, was a great man, but seriously overworked. But neither of the other Prime Ministers shared his feelings.[35] That Menzies might go back to England to join the British War Cabinet was in fact a common press conjecture,[36] particularly when associated with speculation on the possibility of an early election to sort out the closely divided state of parties in the Representatives.[37] Despite the brave face he presented to the world, July 1941 was for Menzies a month of growing personal travail, the beginning of what was to be possibly the most scarifying time of his whole life. One indication of his state of mind was the letter his mother wrote to him on the 11th, to 'say how much we sympathise with you in your very difficult position' and to remind him that 'the Lord God omnipotent reigneth', however hard it might be to believe this 'at times when one is passing through the valley ... Just keep a stout heart for a stiff brae'.[38] On the very evening on which Mrs Menzies wrote this, Staniforth Ricketson and Frank Menzies hosted a meeting at Mornington between the Prime Minister and a small group of his '24 carat supporters'. 'He feels', Ricketson wrote afterwards,

> that he has lost a tremendous amount of ground in the last month ... I have enjoyed many little gatherings in the PM's company ... but I have seldom been with him in quite the frame of mind that he was in last night. I should say that the nearest to it was when I was with him at Macedon at that Easter time when Joe Lyons died. I don't want you to think from this that the fight has gone out of him—far from it—but I think that he is frankly discouraged that he cannot get himself across to the Australian public better, and also that his actions and motives are so misunderstood even by people whom he has endeavoured so earnestly to inform.[39]

---

[35] Menzies to Smuts and Mackenzie King, 3 July 1941, and their replies, Menzies Family Papers.
[36] E.g., *Argus*, 5 July 1941: tailpiece to 'Early Election threat'.
[37] *SMH*, 7, 14, 18 July 1941; *Argus*, 18 July 1941.
[38] Mother to Menzies, 11 July 1941, Menzies Family Papers.
[39] Ricketson to Wright, 12 July 1941, NLA, MS. 8119/6/23. A bitter letter which Menzies wrote to a friend in London also catches the mood of this time. 'It does not look as if I shall be in England again as Prime Minister. My coldness, selfishness, arrogance, idleness and weakness of mind are increasingly visible to my grateful fellow countrymen.' Menzies to Margaret Gilruth, 20 July 1941, NLA MS. 4936/1/13/109.

END OF THE SECTION.

"I am told that it is the business of a really well-disposed Prime Minister to be extraordinarily pleasant and inoffensive and extraordinarily tactful. Well, I must give up being pleasant and tactful and inoffensive."—*Menzies*.

The cartoonist Frith insightfully suggests that at the heart of Menzies' difficulties is a seeming arrogance which, somewhat sadly, he himself has difficulty recognizing.

Part of Menzies' unhappiness, Ricketson observed, was that some of the press, especially the *Sydney Morning Herald* and the papers controlled by Murdoch, evidenced a 'lack of understanding' which greatly damaged him. That was putting it mildly. Murdoch thought Menzies inadequate as a leader and was not impressed by the Prime Minister's successes in England. The *Sydney Morning Herald*'s antagonism came to a head just at this time in a furious row over newsprint rationing which brought to an abrupt end any surviving friendship between Menzies and Warwick Fairfax. 'It has been clear for nearly two years that politically you would prefer to see me sitting in opposition', Menzies wrote to Fairfax.

On such matters you are unquestionably not only entitled to your own opinion but morally bound to give effect to it. I have never thought that you realised what a Labour administration of Australia during this war would mean but, again, that is merely my opinion. But at the same time I ought to make it clear to you that, with a good amount of inside knowledge as to the real Labour opinions on the conduct of the war, I personally would put up with any sacrifice to keep them out of office.[40]

The disagreement over newsprint rationing involved a particularly faithful supporter of Menzies, E. J. Harrison,[41] who as Minister for Trade and Customs imposed severe restrictions on newsprint imports for established papers while at the same time making available to a Fairfax competitor, Ezra Norton of Truth and Sportsman Ltd, a newsprint licence to allow him to start a new tabloid, the *Daily Mirror*. Fairfax, whose company had prudently built up a stock of newsprint and, from the outbreak of war, had voluntarily reduced its weekly consumption of paper, was aggrieved and virtually demanded that Menzies countermand Harrison's decisions and discipline him. When Menzies refused, an unedifying series of exchanges followed, some of them published in the paper, in which the *Herald*'s profitability became a principal subject of debate.

The newsprint quarrel was not the only cause of the *Herald*'s criticism of Menzies' leadership at this time. Among other factors shaping the paper's attitude were the views of its Canberra correspondent, Ross Gollan, who after the 1940 election had replaced Eric McLoughlin, a journalist who admired Menzies and earned the latter's liking and trust. Gollan was more critical, subtly building up the notion that Fadden had during Menzies' absence proved himself as the coming leader of the Government. 'There is no doubt in the minds of some parliamentarians', he wrote, even before Menzies arrived home,

> that Mr Fadden has done things since he began to act as Prime Minister that might still have been deferred if Mr Menzies were present, and the public has recognized that fact. Country Party member and all, Mr Fadden would, in the common estimation, be the obvious choice for a successor to Mr Menzies, if successor were needed.[42]

---

[40] Quoted by Gavin Souter, *Company of Heralds*, 194. Souter has in his chapter 6 (177–200) a fascinating account of Menzies' relations, 1939–41, with Fairfax and the *Herald*, including a detailed sketch of the controversy over newsprint, a sketch on which I base my remarks here.

[41] Member for Wentworth, 1931–56. On two occasions between 1939 and 1940 he cheerfully gave up portfolios to make room for Country Party representatives to help Menzies form coalition governments.

[42] Quoted, Souter, *Company of Heralds*, 192. I am also indebted to Souter for the points about McLoughlin and Gollan, and their views on Menzies.

And by reporting with zest the manifold rumours in the lobbies about unhappiness with Menzies, Gollan both encouraged dissidents and fostered the atmosphere of instability.

After a Cabinet meeting on 17 July Menzies reaffirmed that the Ministry was not planning a federal election and vigorously denounced Forde and other Labor Party members who had attacked it for not taking over control of BHP which, they alleged, was making undue profits and not pulling its weight in wartime production.[43] That evening internal Government troubles broke into public view when in Melbourne the UAP member for Deakin, Hutchinson, announced that he was calling for a party meeting to consider the question of leadership. What was urgently needed, he said, was 'a more virile policy for prosecuting the war', and Menzies should surrender the prime ministership to Fadden. McCall, who was in Melbourne at the time, announced that he agreed with Hutchinson. It is possible that these outbursts were not independent of a circumstance reported two days before to Menzies by his friend Herbert Brookes. 'Mr Evatt (MHR)', Brookes wrote, 'has been staying in Melbourne lately and has had interviews with several prominent men generally supposed to be on our side politically. I fancy they have not got all from you they felt themselves entitled to'. Brookes quoted 'a leading press proprietor' who had spoken to him of the danger that 'a disgruntled little group' of Menzies' own party might join with Labor to oust him, 'probably in the hope of being included in the new Ministry'. The idea horrified Brookes. 'I take off my hat to you', he wrote, 'for what you have done in Britain and the Americas and here in Australia since your return ... You have grown in spiritual stature and will be permitted (please God) to continue to give a lead to this stumbling democracy'.[44]

Menzies at once announced that he would call a meeting of the UAP to discuss the leadership, a move which Gollan observed 'disappointed no connoisseur of practical politics as a fine art'. The thirteen UAP ministers would provide almost half the Party's voting strength; a challenge was thus bound to fail unless decided at a joint meeting with the Country Party. Fadden declared his loyalty to Menzies and his agreement that the meeting was one for the UAP alone. Their inability to get a joint meeting led the

---

[43] *Argus*, 18 July 1941. Note vigorous reply by H. G. Darling, Chairman of Directors. Price of iron and steel has not been increased since 1938; one and a half million pounds spent on plant essential to the war effort, but which would not have been installed under ordinary market conditions, etc.

[44] Herbert Brookes to Menzies, 15 July 1941, Menzies Family Papers. Rohan Rivett quotes from the same letter in *Australian Citizen: Herbert Brookes, 1867–1963* (Melbourne 1965), 196–7.

chief dissidents to declare themselves. Menzies' old critic, 'Tommy' White, and Sir Charles Marr, member for Parkes, announced their agreement with Hutchinson and called a purely UAP meeting 'sheer humbug'. McCall drew exasperated fire from Menzies by telling the press that the crisis had come to a head because Menzies wanted to engineer a 'law and order' election in an effort to put Labor at a special disadvantage:

> For a member of a Party even to profess to make a statement in public about a private discussion between the leader of his Party and the Executive of the party organisation—a meeting at which he was not present—seems to me to set a new standard of public indecency. I do not believe that such attempted treachery will commend Mr McCall either to his own party or to the Labour Party.

The General Secretary of the UAP, H. W. Horsefield, issued a statement confirming that McCall had not been present at the meeting of the Party's Consultative Committee to which he referred and denying that Menzies had ever made the alleged suggestion. McCall replied that he had been told, not in confidence, what had happened at the meeting by three people who had been there.[45] J. N. Lawson, an ex-minister but still a staunch supporter of Menzies, wrote confidentially on 23 July to tell his leader of telephone conversations he had just had with McCall, who was 'in mortal dread' of an election, fearing he would lose his seat. McCall also told Lawson that Fadden had 'intimated his willingness to accept Government leadership if it is offered to him'. What McCall said led Lawson to conclude that he was privy to Cabinet discussions and that 'his informant is either F or some confidant of F's'. In reply Menzies observed that 'They are ill days for any country when the royal road to publicity, and even fame, is through disloyalty to your Government, your party and your leader'. Still, 'fear may do for our friend from Martin [McCall] what reason could never achieve'.[46]

On the eve of the party meeting the *Sydney Morning Herald* published an editorial viciously attacking Menzies under the heading 'The National Leadership'. It had been preceded a week earlier by

---

[45] This and the previous paragraph are based on *SMH* reports, 18, 21 and 22 July 1941. Also, Menzies on 21 July wired members of NSW UAP Council (Charles Lloyd Jones, A. E. Heath, Sir Robert Gillespie, R. C. Wilson, Telford Simpson) re McCall's press statement 'purporting to reveal private discussion between UAP Consultative Council and myself', asking that prompt steps be taken 'to deal with this gross treachery'. Horsefield's statement was subsequently arranged by Wilson. NLA, MS. 4936/14/417/55.

[46] J. N. Lawson to Menzies, 23 July, and Menzies to Lawson, 24 July 1941, Menzies Family Papers.

another which pointedly mentioned no names but purported to be scandalized at current political bickerings and was a thinly veiled notification that the favour with which the paper had greeted Menzies' homecoming had quite dissolved.[47] Now, it seemed, the high hopes that Menzies would 'unite the country under his leadership and galvanise it into a peak war effort' were not being fulfilled:

> The Prime Minister has brilliant gifts, but the passage of time has tended to show that he has certain defects arising from those very qualities. It is being freely questioned among his supporters whether his judicial tolerance, his keen analytical brain, and his sparkling dialectic, are not better suited to the highest council chambers of the Empire, rather than the post of a man of action which demands rapid decisions, the devolution of responsibility, and hasty improvisations.[48]

That was on Saturday 26 July. The UAP party meeting was held on the following Monday. After the meeting the party Whip, J. A. Guy, issued a statement saying simply that members had 'overwhelmingly expressed confidence in Mr. Menzies'. But the *Sydney Morning Herald* published next day a detailed account of what had allegedly happened, highlighting a clash between Menzies and McCall and intimating that some of the ministers had maintained an ominous silence.[49] Menzies at once asserted that the only acceptable version of the UAP meeting was the official one issued by the party Whip: to him it was

> astonishing to find that the *Sydney Morning Herald* has stooped to ferret out what it must know to be stories retailed by some member or members in gross breach of faith. A more coloured and twisted account of a meeting to that of ... the *Sydney Morning Herald* ... I have never read.[50]

When the paper challenged Menzies to say what errors it had made he declined, with a great show of scorn, 'to rewrite the *Herald*'s report of the meeting for it'.[51] He thus both saved himself the embarrassment of admitting that any of the paper's chronicle of events at the meeting had been accurate (which much of it probably was) and shored up his conviction that he was being viciously persecuted. As he summed up his feelings in a message to Bruce:

[47] *SMH*, 19 July 1941.
[48] Ibid., 26 July 1941. Souter attributes this editorial to McClure Smith. Souter, *Company of Heralds*, 195.
[49] *SMH*, 29 July 1941. See also *Argus* of same date.
[50] *SMH*, 30 July 1941.
[51] Ibid., 31 July 1941.

On my return to Australia Government stocks rose very high. There had apparently been almost complete satisfaction with my work abroad but during the past few weeks newsprint rationing has made recalcitrant newspapers bitter, petty revolts among a few members have been encouraged and whole atmosphere has become murky though fundamentally I have more confidence in underlying sound sense of the people than have some of my colleagues.[52]

Menzies had meantime announced that he would undertake an interstate tour to 'talk about the war': to take to Australians who had not yet heard him the lessons of his recent trip. He was on his way by the end of the first week in August. His closest friends thought the trip could be used to strengthen his position: Ricketson and Wright devised a statement of loyalty to Menzies which they nobbled people in Melbourne to sign and hoped to get other signatures for as Menzies went through South Australia, Western Australia and Queensland.[53] The Prime Minister was in Adelaide on 8 August and gave a stirring talk on the urgent need for unity at a Chamber of Commerce luncheon.[54] Then, two days later, he suddenly cancelled the tour and called a full Cabinet meeting for 11 August. Deteriorating relations with Japan, which had already for some days been the subject of anxious discussion in the Advisory War Council, had reached a new crisis-point. Already Japanese aggression in Indo-China had led to the freezing of Japanese assets in their countries by Britain, the Dominions and the United States; now the Japanese seemed poised to invade Thailand and war appeared to be close. Menzies had also been confidentially informed that Churchill and Roosevelt were meeting somewhere in the Atlantic. He cabled to Churchill his pleasure at that, and urged that in their discussions the two leaders bear in mind the special interests of Australia and New Zealand. When it met, the Australian Cabinet decided that Menzies should go back to London, urgently to represent in the British War Cabinet the dangers and the needs of the antipodean Dominions. That idea was, clearly, more than congenial to Menzies himself. 'I believe',

---

[52] Menzies to Bruce, 13 August 1941, *DAFP* 5: 72.
[53] Ricketson to Wright 6, 8, 9 August 1941, NLA MS. 8119/6/23. On the 8th Wright lunched with Murdoch, whose papers had now openly joined the vendetta against Menzies. Ricketson advised Wright to have in his pocket the list of signatures of those who had declared their loyalty to Menzies, as Murdoch should be interested to see that they included some of his biggest advertisers. He also reported that W. S. Robinson was 'appalled' by Murdoch's papers' attitudes to Menzies and had had a violent argument with Murdoch on the matter.
[54] *SMH*, 9 August 1941.

he cabled to Bruce, 'I am more effective in London than here where at present a hail-fellow-well-met technique is preferred to information or reason'.[55]

But, given the even division of the House of Representatives, Menzies could in practice only go to England as Prime Minister if the Labor Party agreed: otherwise the loss of its slender majority could prove fatal. Curtin, prepared as ever for honourable cooperation with Menzies and shrewdly aware also that as alternative Prime Minister he would almost certainly inherit Menzies' agonizingly uncertain position in the House, was amenable, but that wing of his Party which was anxious for Labor to take office disagreed. On the War Council, and then in Parliament itself, these men, led by Evatt and Forde, insisted that at a time of crisis the Prime Minister's duty was to stay home and provide effective leadership. In Caucus this faction won and Labor refused to agree to a truce. Menzies had to stay if he were to retain the prime ministership. Meantime he asked Bruce to find out whether, if he resigned the prime ministership and went to London as an ordinary Minister, he would be given a seat in the War Cabinet—or even 'If I went as Prime Minister but after a month or two felt my indefinite absence from Australia was creating embarrassment here and then resigned Premiership what prospect there would be of my being asked or allowed to continue to sit in the British War Cabinet'. Bruce replied that he thought it urgent that Menzies come at once to London, as 'the next two or three months will be of transcending importance in which fundamental questions concerning the war and the post war world will be determined':

> In view of the magnitude of these issues it is imperative that our point of view should be fully and adequately represented. This can only be done by the presence here of the Prime Minister of Australia with the prestige and authority attaching to the head of Government of the outstanding Dominion. Out of considerable experience of these people and knowledge of the personalities in the United Kingdom Government I say without hesitation that any Minister of lesser authority than the Prime Minister would be able to accomplish little and even you

---

[55] Menzies to Bruce, 13 August 1941, *DAFP* 5: 72. Except where otherwise stated, the account I give here of the main events of this period draws upon the detailed account of Hasluck, *Government and People* 1, especially 495–502 and 527–36. Note that on 6 August Herbert Brookes had written: 'I have hope that the Japanese move to the South will cause the malcontents and the selfishly ambitious to forget themselves for the time being and get together behind your leadership'. NLA, MS. 4936/1/5/36.

notwithstanding the remarkable impression you created during your recent visit would find yourself frustrated without the status of a Prime Minister.[56]

In the light of Labor's veto on his going to England as Prime Minister, Menzies was thus trapped. He called an urgent Cabinet meeting in Canberra to consider what was to be done. He told his colleagues that the only feasible course was for him to resign and recommend to the Governor-General that he send for Curtin: it would be much better for Labor to be in office under these circumstances than as the result of a forced election 'at which they would probably have a sweeping majority'. This view was received with horror, 'and I have no doubt that it was at this moment that the determination to remove me became crystallised'.

Menzies uses these words in a remarkable personal account of the events of those days which he dictated, sealed and labelled 'most secret', on 1 September 1941, the day after he did in the end resign.[57] 'It cannot be frequently that one has the experience of resigning the Prime Ministership of one's country', it begins, 'and in order that I shall have some record of the circumstances I am now setting them down while they are fresh in my memory'. As background he notes the slenderness of his majority in the House and the hostility of the *Sydney Morning Herald* and the Murdoch Press: 'the former blatantly and crudely, the latter with a little more subtlety, praising me and killing me in the same breath, the technique being that of the skilled slaughterman who calls attention to the beauties of the beast just as he strikes it down'. Hutchinson, McCall and Marr being bitterly hostile, he says, there was, with a budget in the offing, every chance of 'a fatal attack by Labour'.

When in the Cabinet room Menzies announced his readiness to resign in favour of Curtin, Spooner proposed that, instead, a national government should again be offered to Labor and was supported by Page, who 'said that the thing of greatest urgency was for me to be sent to London to put pressure on the British Government to send capital ships to Singapore'. Menzies agreed and drafted a letter to Curtin, offering an equal number of

---

[56]Bruce to Menzies, 13 August 1941, in reply to Menzies to Bruce of the same date, *DAFP* 5: 71–2, 74. The issue was settled by Churchill himself, who cabled to Menzies on 19 August: 'It would not be possible for a Dominion Minister other than a Prime Minister to sit in War Cabinet as this would entail representation by all four Dominions, and would [be ?] too large a permanent addition to our numbers ... From inquiries I have made, there seems no chance that the other Dominions would agree to being represented in the War Cabinet by a Minister from a single Dominion' (Menzies Family Papers). Also PRO CAB 65/19/109.

[57]This document is in the Menzies Family Papers.

ministers to the two sides of the House, and leadership to Curtin or to a compromise leader chosen by any agreed method. At a joint meeting, the Government parties approved the letter. Page and Hughes made public assertions of Menzies' 'statesmanship' in making such a generous offer, and the letter was sent to Curtin, who replied that the Parliamentary Party as a whole, and not he as leader, must decide the matter.[58] The Party meeting would be held on 26 August: Fadden urged that as many ministers as possible should be in Canberra to deal promptly with the result, and Menzies got in touch with all ministers, asking as many as possible to be at hand. The notice was so short that four ministers, McLeay, Abbott, McDonald and Harrison, were unable to be present (Harrison, Menzies' staunchest supporter, could not come because his wife was seriously ill: she in fact died later in the week.) Meantime Menzies himself went for the weekend to Melbourne where, as the *Sydney Morning Herald* put it, he 'took a holiday from politics' to address the Economics Society on the cost of the war. The political situation was inevitably on his mind. He prefaced his address with a description of the bull fight he had seen in Portugal a few months before while waiting for the trans-Atlantic clipper. From the safety of their horses, he said, picadors tormented the bull with thrusts of their lances until it was weak with exhaustion. Then out came the matador for the kill. 'I feel like that bull', he added ruefully.[59]

Menzies met those of his ministers who were available at 2.30 on the afternoon of the 26th, telling them that 'we should clarify our minds as to what we were to do in the event of [Labor's] reply being unfavourable'. Harold Holt said that the prospects of Government success would be greater if there were a new Prime Minister, and suggested Fadden. Senator Foll 'said that my unpopularity in New South Wales and Queensland was such as to be a fatal handicap to the Government should an election come'. Then, just after 3.30, Curtin's reply arrived. Labor would not co-operate in a national government. Menzies asked for 'complete frankness'. The Country Party ministers Page, McEwen, Collins and Anthony said that a new leader was needed. Spender agreed, 'though he had the grace to say that nothing was more unpleasant for him because he owed the whole of his political advancement to me'. Holt, once a dedicated Young Nationalist, declared the same embarrassment. 'I reassured them by saying that I was not taking anything that was being said as a personal attack, but that

[58] *Argus*, 23 August 1941.
[59] *SMH*, 25 August 1941.

all I wanted to get at was the truth of their political views.' Spooner declared for a change of leadership, as did Hughes, 'who had been somewhat quieter than usual, but whose desire to get rid of me was as clearly indicated as usual'. Those who 'stood firm' for Menzies were Leckie, McBride, Collett and Stewart: Menzies guessed that of the absent ministers Abbott would 'favour the Country Party view' and that Harrison, McLeay and McDonald would evince 'complete loyalty'. Fadden 'said little but renewed and reiterated his affirmation of loyalty'. It was, clearly, a deeply divided Cabinet. Menzies called for an adjournment at 5 p.m., until 8.30, to allow each minister to consider his position.

Returning to the Lodge, the Prime Minister went for a long walk with his wife, who was finally persuaded 'that, as my political leadership clearly rested upon nothing better than quicksands, I should resign'. Leckie, who came for dinner, agreed. A call was put through to father James Menzies in Melbourne: 'I left him at the other end of the telephone breathing threatenings and slaughter. He, in fact, at once convened one of our famous family conferences, which reached conclusions similar to my own'. When Cabinet reconvened Menzies announced that he would resign, would certainly not go to London under existing circumstances ('worst possible ambassador for Australia abroad would be a Prime Minister who had just lost the confidence of his own Government and Parliament'), and would insist that the new leader not be nominated by the Cabinet but should be chosen by the joint Ministerial parties and promised unanimous support by them (this last pronouncement, Menzies records, 'caused a sensation').[60]

The crucial party meeting was held on the 28th. Harrison, now up from Sydney, 'passionately urged me to fight the matter in the party room and with the people' but Menzies insisted that he would resign. Other members spoke with regret at what was happening, and the newest UAP recruit, Arthur Coles, 'who up to twenty-four hours before had been among my most acid critics, suddenly became so warm a supporter that he swept out of the room, announcing his resignation from the Party'.[61] A resolution thanking Menzies for his services was carried. 'Many members of the Party were plainly stunned and upset by what was happening, but there was no real attempt to discourage me from the indicated

---

[60] Dixon lunched with Menzies on 1 September 1941 and records in his Diary Menzies' account of events over the last few days. 'Described the treachery. Hughes, Page and Country Party—very bad'.

[61] Dixon noted in his Diary, 29 August, that 'The papers told of the assassination of Menzies, Coles (A. W.) said in the Age that it was the vilest thing he had ever witnessed'.

course.' The Country Party members were sent for and the joint meeting now took place. Hutchinson and Marr nominated Fadden as the new leader; there was no other nomination. At this point Menzies records, simply: 'Issued statement to press, and went home'. His private secretary, Cecil Looker, later remembered that it was somewhat less matter-of-fact than that. He and Menzies, he said, left the party meeting just after midnight. With his arm around Looker's shoulders and tears in his eyes, Menzies blurted out words which Looker recollected as 'I have been done ... I'll lie down and bleed awhile'.[62] The statement for the press was predictably honest and dignified. Labor had rejected his offer of an all-party administration, even without him as Prime Minister:

> It follows that the next task is to get the greatest possible stability and cohesion on the Government side of the House. A frank discussion with my colleagues in the Cabinet has shown that, while they have personal good will toward me, many of them feel that I am unpopular with large sections of the Press and the people; that this unpopularity handicaps the effectiveness of the Government by giving rise to misrepresentation and misunderstanding of its activities; and that there are divisions of opinion in the Government parties themselves which would or might not exist under another leader.
>
> It is not for me to be the judge of these matters, except to this extent, that I do believe that my relinquishing of the leadership will offer real prospects of unity in the ranks of the Government parties. In these circumstances, and having regard to the grave emergencies of war, my own feelings must be set aside.[63]

Next day Menzies returned his commission and wrote gracefully to Curtin: 'Your political opposition has been honourable and your personal friendship a pearl of great price'. 'On my part', Curtin replied, 'I thank you for the consideration and courtesy which never once failed in your dealings with me'.[64] For once the press was muted, generally in admiration, however reluctant: 'Last Generous Gesture', the *Argus*'s editorial heading, typified the mood. For Menzies the outward dignity hid deep hurt, but, as he wrote in response to commiserations from his old secretary and friend, Peter Heydon, 'You can well imagine my feelings ... when they recede further into the distance I suppose I will be able to look upon them more philosophically'.[65] From an extraordinary range of sources came declarations of regret. Even Churchill sent

---

[62]Interview on ABC television, 19 February 1984, with Huw Evans. A similar story is recounted by Souter, *Acts of Parliament*, 340.
[63]*Argus*, 29 August 1941.
[64]Menzies to Curtin and Curtin to Menzies, 29 August 1941, Menzies Family Papers.
[65]Menzies to Heydon, 22 September 1941, NLA, MS. 4936/2/40/35.

"You don't want it, Curtin? Then you shall have it!"

Frith is clear-minded about what has happened to Menzies, August 1941.

a guarded message of condolence,[66] and Blamey sent from the Middle East a warm message of thanks 'for the tremendous support that I had from yourself ... while you were Prime Minister, and for the privilege you gave me in allowing me to approach you directly on policy matters'. Blamey confessed to puzzlement at what had happened but urged philosophical acceptance:

> I am not able to appreciate in its right perspective yet the action of the rats; not so much in leaving the sinking ship as in gnawing right through its timbers and scuttling it. But the wheel of time goes round

---

[66] Churchill to Menzies, 29 August 1941, Menzies Family Papers. *Inter alia* Churchill's message said: 'I went through a similar experience when I was removed from the Admiralty at the moment when I could have given the ANZACs a fair chance of victory at the Dardanelles. It is always a comfort in such circumstances to feel sure one has done one's duty and one's best'.

and in due course will complete its full circle, and though you must be full of disgust at the moment at the reward meted out by their master to those who serve democracy, yet justification will come in the fulness of time.[67]

In an affectionate letter, brother Frank also looked to the future. 'As a family', he wrote, 'we have shared the pride of your high calling ... I believe that if we are spared as a nation your gifts and ideals will be more than ever needed and the period in the political wilderness will strengthen you for further great work'.[68] But it may be that the most affecting message Menzies received came all the way from Alice Springs. 'Dear Bob', it said, 'I do not weep for you. I weep for Australia. This country has sunk to a low level. You did a hell of a good job in the face of overwhelming odds & you crawled to no man. Congratulations'. The writer was one Galloway Stewart, a lawyer whom Menzies had privately coached for the Articled Clerks' examinations in the early 1920s. For this he had refused to accept payment: Stewart was a returned soldier to whom, Menzies said, he owed a debt for having done what he himself could not do.[69]

Menzies' decision not to stay on and fight disappointed supporters like Harrison, who thought that his leader could regain his position if he made an appeal to the people. But Menzies was against an election. He knew Labor stood a good chance of winning, and believed that that would jeopardize Australia's war effort. As he wrote to Curtin when the latter turned down the final proposal for a national government, he was not prepared 'to accentuate the political uncertainties from which this unhappy country is suffering by handing over the Government to the Labour Party'.[70]

---

[67] Blamey to Menzies, 15 October 1941, Menzies Family Papers. Note also letter from Latham in Tokyo: 'I want to congratulate you upon the fine work which you have accomplished under very difficult and trying conditions. Your task has been one of great inherent difficulty—aggravated by petty personal criticism. You have answered your critics by practical achievement—which is the best reply', 30 August 1941, NLA, MS. 4936/1/18/154. Herbert Burton wrote on 8 September, to express his 'admiration both for the dignity and the ability with which you filled the office of Prime Minister for more than two years past. The statement of your intention to resign, as well as your conduct of affairs when in office, must compel the admiration of many, even among those who hold different political opinions', NLA, MS. 4936/2/40/35.

[68] Frank Menzies to Menzies, 19 December 1941, Menzies Family Papers.

[69] Galloway Stewart to Menzies, 6 September 1941, NLA, MS. 4936/2/40/36. For Menzies' reasons for refusing payment I am indebted to Galloway Stewart's cousin, Mr James Merralls, interview on 18 May 1988, and Stewart's son, Rev. J. B. Stewart, of Colac, who kindly provided me with full details of the story.

[70] Menzies to Curtin, 27 August 1941, NLA, MS. 2852/4/23.

His hope was that a change of leadership would strengthen support for a new non-Labor government, at least by making it possible for the few open rebels to toe the line.

But there can be little doubt also that for the moment Menzies' spirit was broken. He had returned from England tired and on an emotional high: his distaste for the Australian political scene after his experiences in Britain reflected genuine shock. Grenfell Price thought that on his return Menzies 'missed the psychological moment' to 'come out with a wider and stronger war policy' to silence his critics.[71] Perhaps this was so: but whatever Menzies said or did would have almost certainly failed to deflect the concerted campaign which the Fairfax and Murdoch press developed against him, or have countered the effects of the 'plotting' that had gone on behind his back while he was in England. In both cases the main allegation levelled against him was that, though his words were fine, he was incapable of taking decisive action to put the country on a proper war footing. Menzies' complaint that he couldn't reveal his achievements for security reasons seems valid enough, and the opinion of the man who worked most closely with him in this area, Shedden, should be noted. 'It was a great experience', he wrote to Menzies in December 1942,

> to be associated with you in the transition to a war footing and the first two years of the war administration. Credit has still to be given to your Government for the planning and preparation that rendered the transition so smooth. Tribute has yet to be paid to the great foundations laid by you at a time when you lacked the advantage of the effect on national psychology and morale of a war in the Pacific.[72]

But in any case, there is a sense in which it is almost beside the point to inquire whether Menzies was or was not a good wartime administrator: the important thing is that the idea that he was not was sedulously cultivated by his enemies in press and party and was widely believed.[73]

On the 'plot' against Menzies during his absence there remains some ambiguity. There is no doubt that he was criticized and envied by many in the Coalition parties and that a wish to unseat him was strong. It seems obvious that sections of the Country Party, which over many years he had despised, were deeply implicated. The same is true of enemies within the UAP, like McCall, who disliked Menzies personally and were also dis-

---

[71] Grenfell Price to President and Secretary of LCL Committee in Boothby, 1 September 1941, Mortlock Library of South Australia, Grenfell Price Papers PRG7/5/3.
[72] Shedden to Menzies, c. 20 December 1942, AA A5954/1, box 67.
[73] Hasluck makes this point effectively, *Government and People* 1, 492.

appointed would-be ministers. It is impossible to judge how far snide chatter among politicians contributed to the 'conspiracy', though that might have been of marginal importance. That Menzies' wife, her ear firmly to the ground during this period, was convinced of a major plot is of considerable significance, and there were indeed slippery customers like Page and Hughes whose enmity was plain. But the loyalty issue was not black and white. Troubled folk, like Spender and Holt, who recognized all Menzies' virtues and personally owed much to him, still wondered whether he commanded enough support and had the right qualities to do the required job. There was, on the other hand, no question that Menzies had firm supporters who believed in his capacity as a leader. It was a major feature of his tragedy that three of the most influential of these—Fairbairn, Gullett and Street—had been killed in the air crash of 1940.

Menzies' brilliance was not denied by his worst enemies. The main charges against him were personal: that with brilliance went arrogance, that he was fatally unable to project himself publicly as a leader, and that, as Curtin once put it to Dixon, 'Menzies never handled his men'.[74] On the same point, there is also Frank's quiet observation, when writing to commiserate with his brother, that he could rejoice in a 'conscience clear of vain regrets, unless it is that you have not sufficiently cultivated the rank and file of your party'.[75] Perhaps that was a major flaw, but it is understandable. Menzies was not gregarious, and would not stoop to (or was not seized of the need to) cultivate popularity. He was absorbed in his task, and could not understand those who, he thought, misunderstood him.

[74] Dixon Diary, 8 November 1941.
[75] Frank Menzies to Menzies, 19 December 1941, Menzies Family Papers.

17

In the Wilderness

THE DIGNITY of Menzies' words at his resignation was matched by courage in his public behaviour in its immediate aftermath. After the swearing-in of the new Fadden Government, he left with his wife for a quiet weekend in Melbourne, arriving at Spencer Street station on the morning of Saturday 30 August. There he was met by his father, his brother Frank and a crowd of about 300 well-wishers, mostly State politicians and supporters from the Kooyong electorate.[1] Later that morning, when friends gathered at the Automobile Club to give him a more formal welcome, Menzies made a short extempore speech in which he asked those present not to allow sympathy for him to distract their minds from the grave issues Australia was facing. At the end there were spontaneous, and to that audience at least, moving words:

> Before I close, let me say again, I'm not going to moan; I mean that—all of it. I've been a lucky man. For no special reasons I've had success beyond the average. I've had health, I've had friends, I've had supremely interesting work. I've poured myself into work but I've been very, very lucky. You see I have been Prime Minister at a great moment in Australian and Empire history. What luck for any man! And I can still make some contribution I hope because I've learned a lot in two years of war. My only desire, my one ambition, is to be allowed to serve in any capacity where I may help to keep this Commonwealth and its people safe.[2]

In the week that followed, Menzies returned to Canberra, where Cabinet discussions on the forthcoming budget, begun before his resignation, were taking place. His replacement by Fadden as

---

[1] *Argus*, 1 September 1941.
[2] 'Extempore speech at the Automobile Club on Saturday morning, August 30th, by Mr. R. G. Menzies on returning to Melbourne after resigning the Prime Ministership'. Roneoed copy generously made available to me by Sir Paul Hasluck, who received it from Professor Douglas Copland in 1948.

Prime Minister had been the only change in the personnel of the Government. Menzies retained his portfolio of Defence Co-Ordination and, indeed, at the swearing-in at Government House, had seemed to one reporter 'the most self-possessed Minister of the new Ministry'. After the ceremony he produced the cinematograph camera which he had taken on the English trip and took shots of his former Cabinet for his personal records.[3] During the budget discussions the Ministry gave Menzies a complimentary dinner at Parliament House; that evening he screened for their entertainment five reels of film he had taken during his trip to England, featuring the London blitz, Churchill, and the Royal family.[4] Shortly thereafter Menzies and his wife went off to an undisclosed destination for a seven-day holiday—the first such break they had taken since he became Prime Minister in 1939. For once their haven was almost certainly not Mount Macedon. A minor family disaster was soon to occur: on the night of Saturday 21 November 1941 'Illira' was destroyed by fire. No one was there at the time; in fact the house had not been occupied for three months. Police who investigated the fire found no indication of how it had broken out and no evidence of malicious damage. But for the family who, as Mrs Menzies told the press, were 'greatly attached' to the place,[5] it was the end of an era. Menzies built no replacement and soon sold the land and remaining outhouses.

During the Menzies' absence the press started various hares about his future, seizing on 'rumours current in Labour circles' that he disagreed with aspects of the budget and might resign from the Ministry, deploring his refusal of a Cabinet request that he go to England as a special envoy to press again the dangers of the Pacific situation, and even speculating that he was looking for a seat in the British House of Commons. Questioned on his return, Menzies' reply was bland: 'I am living a quiet life and I expect to be living one for some time'.[6] A week later, when the debate on the budget came on, the first rumour was decisively squashed: Menzies did not get a chance to speak, but he voted firmly with the Government. The question of England was a little more complicated, though the press failed to discover any details.

Between May and August 1941, while he was still Prime Minister, Menzies' hopes of returning to England had been scotched on a number of occasions by the British Prime Minister himself. Churchill did not relish the idea of having so articulate

---
[3] *SMH*, 30 August 1941. At one point he asked a press photographer to take over the camera so that he could be photographed with some of his ex-ministers.
[4] *Argus*, 5 September 1941.
[5] Ibid., 24 November 1941.
[6] *SMH*, 6, 8, 16 September 1941; *Argus*, 6 September 1941.

and forthright a critic back. 'He would no doubt like invitation to join War Cabinet', Churchill observed in one memorandum, 'but this raises many complications about other Dominions and size of War Cabinet. Although he is unhappy in Australia there is no other man of comparable eminence and knowledge there'.[7] Menzies made repeated calls for a meeting of Commonwealth Prime Ministers but received no support from any of his opposite numbers. Two of them, Fraser of New Zealand and Mackenzie King of Canada, played into Churchill's hands by explicitly rejecting the suggestion that there was a collective Dominion point of view which could be represented by the admission of someone like Menzies to the War Cabinet.[8] It was at this point that the Labor Opposition thwarted Menzies' hopes by denying immunity to his Government if he went to England. After Menzies' resignation Churchill delivered the final blow by stressing to the new Fadden Government that no Dominion Minister other than a Prime Minister would be admitted to his Cabinet.[9]

When Fadden did appoint an emissary to go to London to discuss the Pacific situation, the double irony for Menzies was that the man chosen was Page and that Labor agreed to his going. Fadden argued that since the whole parliament, Government and Opposition, had endorsed Page's mission, his was a special case and Page should be admitted to the British Cabinet.[10] Churchill was greatly annoyed at 'Mr. McFadden's [*sic!*] telegram' but conceded that 'we have got to treat these people, who are politically embarrassed but are sending a splendid army into the field, with the utmost consideration'. So he drafted a message which welcomed Page and, without mentioning the Cabinet, declared that 'we ... will confer with him fully and freely on all matters concerning Australia's interests and the common cause'.[11] On his way to England Page called on Mackenzie King and Churchill was no doubt relieved to hear from the latter that Page had explained that his visit to London was solely with a view to making personal representations on 'Australia's present position vis-à-vis the threatening position in the Far East': he had no thought of urging Dominion representation in the British War Cabinet, and did not himself expect to be invited to attend any Cabinet meetings.[12] Even without this assurance, Churchill must have been pleased that it was Page, and not Menzies, with whom he would have to deal.

[7]Churchill to Lord Privy Seal, 19 August 1941, PRO, CAB 65/19/109.
[8]War Cabinet Minutes, 14 August 1941 and 28 August 1941, PRO, CAB 65/19.
[9]Churchill to Fadden, 29 August 1941, *DAFP* 5: 90.
[10]Fadden to Cranborne, 5 September 1941, ibid., 100.
[11]Memorandum, 6 August 1941, PRO, PREM 4/50/5.
[12]Mackenzie King to Churchill, 25 October 1941, ibid.

Churchill was equally ruthless in blocking another avenue of escape for Menzies: the possibility of his entering British politics. This was first broached by the Governor-General, Lord Gowrie, shortly after Menzies' resignation. In a 'Secret and Personal' cable to Cranborne, the Secretary of State for the Dominions, Gowrie observed that 'it is evident that Menzies' remarkable gifts cannot be fully utilised here', called this a 'deplorable waste of valuable material at these times', and asked whether 'your political organisation' could not find a seat for him in the Commons.[13] Cranborne referred the matter to Churchill who replied that

> from the Imperial point of view it would be unwise of Menzies to leave Australia at the present time. Though he will not be in office, he will occupy an unique position in the politics of the Commonwealth. With his outstanding abilities and experience, he will be able to speak in the Australian Parliament with a voice of combined authority and independence which no one else could command. In this way, he may play a far greater part in moulding the future than would be possible for a newcomer to political life here.[14]

A few months later, when the British High Commissioner in Canberra, Ronald Cross, made the same suggestion, Churchill frustrated it again. By then (February 1942), Fadden had fallen and a Labor Government was in office under Curtin. Menzies, Cross told Cranborne, felt that he had no opportunity of 'pulling his weight in the war effort': the Advisory War Council, on which he sat, advised only on such matters as the Government chose to submit. It would be just as bad if the Opposition came to office: in that case Menzies would have to follow Fadden, 'who to him is (and I can understand it) an exasperatingly stupid man'. Menzies thought he would be more at home in the House of Commons. 'He discusses the matter with me occasionally as a friend ... Ignorance of your views makes it difficult for me to talk with him and I am now in need of guidance as to the line I should take.' Cranborne saw little to worry about. As he minuted to Churchill, nothing had happened to change the view communicated a few months before to Gowrie: 'Australia is none too strong in personnel. I should have thought Menzies' duty and utility was there'. 'I agree', scribbled Churchill.[15]

The Fadden Government lasted barely a month. It was defeated on Fadden's Budget when on 3 October the two Independents who held the balance of power in the House of Representatives voted

[13] Gowrie to Granborne, 10 October 1941, PRO, PREM 4/50/15.
[14] Cranborne to Gowrie, 13 October, ibid.
[15] Cross to Dominions Office, 26 February 1942, with comments by Cranborne (26 February) and Churchill (28 February), ibid.

NOT UNDERSTOOD.
"You couldn't have understood me, sir. I said 'Single or return.'"

The *Bulletin*'s cartoonist, Norman Lindsay, shrewdly catches at the turmoil Menzies feels as 1941 wears on. He is still Prime Minister, but now torn between possible work in London and Canberra.

with Labor in support of the traditional censure motion, moved by Curtin, that the first item be reduced by £1. The Independents had petty (and different) immediate reasons for voting as they did but the fall of the Government is best understood as the culmination of a number of longer-term trends. Among these were the crumbling of the UAP, evident as early as 1938, but which had 'reached its fatal conclusion when Menzies gave up',[16] and the destructive tensions between the UAP and the Country Party. On the other side was the achievement, chiefly as a result of Curtin's principled leadership, of growing Labor unity which made for public respect and the confidence needed to claim the right to govern.

Fadden returned his commission and Curtin accepted the Governor-General's invitation to form a Labor Government. As was its custom, the parliamentary Labor Party elected the ministers and Curtin allotted the portfolios. He also hastened to confirm Page's appointment as special envoy to London. The new Opposition parties, at a joint meeting, elected Fadden as their leader. Menzies had previously resigned the UAP leadership to remove 'any question of personality as between himself and Mr. Fadden and to leave the UAP free to decide, without regard to individuals, whether it should become the official Opposition or combine with the Country Party'. Menzies wanted the UAP to take the former course, thus resuming its traditional role in the coalition as senior partner, whose leader would automatically be leader of the Opposition. But this view did not prevail and Hughes, who favoured joint party action in the fullest sense, was elected UAP leader. Menzies himself did not stand.[17] Thus, as the final humiliation, the erstwhile Prime Minister became a backbencher. It was shortly after this that Gowrie made his abortive approach to Cranborne about the possibility of Menzies entering British politics.

In November 1941 another avenue of escape was briefly and tantalizingly dangled before Menzies' nose. The agent was a British minister, Duff Cooper, sent by Churchill, uneasy at last about Britain's position in the Far East, to examine 'arrangements for the consultation and communication between the various British authorities in that area'. Cooper, who had won renown by resigning from Chamberlain's cabinet in protest against the Munich agreement, had subsequently served Churchill, indifferently, as Minister for Information and was now Chancellor of the Duchy of Lancaster, 'traditionally the odd-job man of the Cabinet'.[18] Cooper was the envied husband of one of the celebrated beauties of London society, Lady Diana, who came with him when he made Singapore the headquarters for his inquiry. After much travel around the area, Cooper concluded that in the 'everchanging

---

[16]Hasluck, *Government and People* 1, 518. Hasluck's is a most sensitive discussion of the significance of the defeat.
[17]*Argus, SMH*, 9 October 1941.
[18]The description is that of Philip Ziegler, *Diana Cooper* (London 1981), 206.

world of the Pacific' the affairs of the British Empire were being conducted by 'machinery that has undergone no important change since the days of Queen Victoria'. He recommended the appointment of a Commissioner-General for the Far East, with permanent headquarters in Singapore, to liaise between the War Cabinet and British civil and military officials in the area, and to prepare the way for the establishment of a regional Council of War.[19] Earle Page, *en route* to London, called on Cooper when passing through Singapore. 'Page seemed to approve the idea', noted Cooper, 'provided Australia was properly represented on it. I said I saw no reason why Australia should not provide the president of such a Council'.[20] Indeed, he was soon thinking that an Australian might be suitable for the initial appointment as Commissioner-General. Lady Diana, who was full of dread lest Cooper himself be chosen ('may[be] Winston thinks Duff comfortably out of the way here— no necessity to find him another job')[21] helped along with a suggestion. She knew Menzies from his English visits,[22] and in Singapore was told by a lady journalist from what Lady Diana called the *Sydney Post* that in Australia he was 'loathed and will never come again. He's bone lazy, tho' head and shoulders bigger than anyone in the Dominion'.[23] That gave her an idea: 'after what the Australians tell me about Menzies then He is indicated', she wrote. 'I mean, if his shares as a P.M. are so low perhaps he needs a job.'[24]

On 5 November the Coopers arrived in Australia for an official visit. Its main purpose was to confer with the Australian Government about Duff's recommendations, which were now on the way to London. At Canberra the visitors stayed at Government

---

[19] War Cabinet. British Administration in the Far East. Report by the Chancellor of the Duchy of Lancaster, 29 October 1941. W.P. (41) 286 (CAC, DUFC 3/8).
[20] Memorandum by Duff Cooper, 4 September 1941, CAC, DUFC 3/7.
[21] Diana Cooper to Conrad Russell, 22 October 1941, CAC, DUFC 9/2. Russell, first cousin to the Duke of Bedford, was a stock-jobber turned farmer, quizzical and quirky, but 'full of the charm that stems from benevolence and joy of life'. He 'relished platonic flirtations with beautiful, high-spirited and usually high-born women'. His friendship with Diana was longstanding and comfortable: 'I love my Conrad with a C', she once wrote to him on his birthday, 'because he is courageous and cuddlesome and courtly and a charmer of charmers' (Zeigler, *Diana Cooper*, 160–2). Her letters to him describing her travels are a delight.
[22] They had first met in 1935. Zeigler tells how, later on, they had been fellow-guests of Chips Channon and she had been 'delighted at his aimiable mockery of their host. "Never knew such a fellow for royalty," he said. "He's like a water-diviner. He'd smell out a prince anywhere". As Channon laughed rather hollowly the butler arrived to announce that the Duke of Kent was on the phone' (Zeigler, *Diana Cooper*, 212).
[23] Diana Cooper to Conrad Russell, 24 October 1941, CAC, DUFC 9/2.
[24] Diana Cooper to Conrad Russell, 26 October 1941, ibid.

House with the Gowries, whom Lady Diana found to be 'unspoilt pets ... no vice regal pomp at all'. She was entranced with the beauty she saw from her window: 'I might be in a tender part of Scotland—no moors, Mary Rose country with blue burn, and blue distant hills and yellow foreground and never a fence or a house'. She was fascinated to go outside to look across at Canberra—'to see an unbuilt town—more fun than Pompei [sic]', with Parliament miles away, a little residential section, and a hill where the Embassies were to be built. In the afternoon of that first day they visited Parliament,

> where my old pal Bob Menzies was delivering an impassioned Opposition speech upon the budget—excellent! but what a beargarden! Only 75 members represent the continent but they are all interjecting at once ... I felt they all hated Bob—even his own side. He came to dinner and gave us an interminable home cinema show of his tour of England, U.S., Canada, etc. Amusing shots of Chequers, Welbeck, all the ministers doing their bit for Bob's hobby. I enjoyed it no end. More particularly as i[t] was so reminiscent of our fathers and their magic lantern—even down to the smell of burning varnish—and upside-downs, and inability to focus.[25]

To complete her pleasure, Cooper sounded Menzies out on the commissioner-generalship, and he intimated that he would be delighted if it were offered to him.[26]

The hope was, however, short-lived—quickly swallowed up by the surge of events as the Pacific situation deteriorated. Back in Singapore by early December, Lady Diana sensed that war was imminent. British warships, including the battleships *Prince of Wales* and *Repulse*, had at last arrived, but little else had changed. Then the blows began. On 8 December the Japanese invaded Thailand, establishing a beachhead at Kota Bahru in Northern Malaya, to begin the two-pronged drive southwards towards Singapore. On the same morning Japanese planes launched their attack on Pearl Harbor and bombed Singapore for the first time. Next day a telegram arrived from Churchill appointing Duff Cooper Resident Cabinet Minister with authority to form and preside over a war cabinet: 'the poor little man is tickled to death', wrote Diana. He was ready to be pleased either with this message 'or one to

---

[25]Diana Cooper to Conrad Russell, 6 November 1941, ibid.
[26]Cooper to Cranborne, 1 December 1941, CAC, DUFC 2/7. 'The position of Menzies is very similar to that which Winston occupied before the war. His worst enemies are the men of his own party. Relations between him and Curtin are quite happy. There seems no prospect whatever of his returning to power in the near future, and therefore he was very much interested when I suggested to him that there might be a job for him in Singapore.'

the affect [sic] that Menzies was on his way'.[27] The truth was that there had not yet been time to consider Cooper's report fully, and the appointment was an emergency measure, not a piece of considered policy.[28] In the upshot Cooper did what he could but was superseded when Churchill and Roosevelt agreed to appoint a military Commander-in-Chief for all Allied administrations in the South West Pacific area and chose Wavell for the task.[29] The Coopers flew out early in January, only a month before the capitulation of Singapore. Had Menzies received the appointment, it would thus have proved short-lived. In the emergency brought by the abrupt outbreak of war with Japan it was natural that Churchill should use Duff Cooper as his stopgap Minister in the area until a comprehensive command could be established. The idea that in more leisurely circumstances Menzies might fill the position was Cooper's own but his and Lady Diana's hopes were extravagant. For given Churchill's successes in blocking Menzies' return to London, he would scarcely have been likely to agree to Menzies' appointment to such an important British post in the Far East.

This point, in fact, was indirectly made clear early in 1942 when the British Cabinet was looking for a Minister of State Resident in the Middle East, a person who would in this region broadly fulfil the function Duff Cooper had envisaged for his Commissioner-General in the Far East. Eden told Bruce that Menzies' name was considered but rejected because 'he probably would not get on with the people in the Middle East, being a somewhat difficult person'. Eden then had a 'brain wave', and suggested Casey. Churchill leapt at the idea.[30] During a visit to Washington at the end of 1941 Churchill had spent a whole evening in the train with Casey and learned that he was 'very anxious for a change'. In asking Curtin to release him Churchill explained that the 'principal Ministers I have consulted and Chiefs of Staff are agreed in wanting Casey for this most important post which requires military experience and knowledge of public affairs both ministerial and diplomatic'. 'I will venture to court your rebuke', he added, 'by asking whether Menzies, with his great distinction and success when passing through America, might not fill the gap caused by Casey leaving Washington'.[31] Was the suggestion tongue in cheek, or merely another example of Churchill's

[27]Diana Cooper to Conrad Russell, 9 December 1941, CAC, DUFC 9/3.
[28]Zeigler, ibid.
[29]See, especially, Churchill to Curtin, 29 December 1941, *DAFP* 5: 387–9.
[30]Note by Bruce of conversation with Eden, 19 March 1942, ibid.: 654–5.
[31]Churchill to Curtin, 13 March 1942, ibid.: 639.

ignorance of Australian politics? He must at least have known, after his conversations with Casey, that the latter's anxiety for a change was chiefly due to his sufferings at the hands of Evatt, now Curtin's Minister for External Affairs, who never hid an arrogant distrust of all appointees of the previous Menzies–Fadden Governments, and hated Casey in particular.[32] The mock-apologetic tone of Churchill's mention of Menzies reflected both his strained relations at that time with Curtin's Government and the fact, no doubt known even to him, that Menzies' name would to Evatt be as a red rag to a bull. Sure enough when Evatt, then on a mission to Washington, learnt of Churchill's proposal, he cabled to Curtin that he had been 'assured in highest quarters that Menzies has no particular influence in this country and that relations I have already established with the President and his special advisers are very close and, I believe, unique for an Australian'. He added, angrily, that 'Churchill's suggesting Menzies was most gratuitous and no doubt caused by a desire to cause political embarrassment'.[33] When Casey left at the end of March Evatt made sure that no immediate appointment of a successor was made so that he could himself act as 'a Minister of the Crown on this spot'.[34]

The speech which Lady Diana had heard her 'Bob' deliver during her visit to Parliament was part of a great duel between Menzies and Curtin during the debate on the first budget of the new Labor Treasurer, J. B. Chifley. Introduced on 29 October, this measure was to replace the budget on which the Fadden Government had been overturned. While Chifley largely accepted his predecessor's predictions of wartime expenditure, he augmented overall costs to allow for increases in pensions and in service rates of pay and shifted the incidence of taxation by raising the rate of income tax on higher income groups.[35] Menzies considered the tax burden unfairly distributed because, he claimed, it would bear heavily on families and on those who lacked the protection of unions. 'Every one of us', he said,

---

[32] Edwards, *Prime Ministers and Diplomats*, 146. The most thorough and insightful discussion of the Evatt–Casey relationship over the Washington post is W. J. Hudson's *Casey*, 127–9.
[33] Evatt to Curtin, 23 March 1942, *DAFP* 5: 675.
[34] Ibid. On 22 March Dixon noted in his diary that he had seen Menzies. 'He seemed downcast at the Casey incident. Thought I should go to US.'
[35] See *CPD*, 169: 130–46, for the Menzies–Curtin exchange. Curtin particularly picked up Menzies' allegation that the budget would cause inflation and finally put it to him 'flatly that his facts were astray, that his memory was at fault and this his imagination was too bizarre'. Hasluck, *Government and People* 1, 520–2, has an excellent discussion of this budget.

whether it be the man who lives in Bellevue Hill on an income of £15 000 a year, or the girl who earns £3 a week as a stenographer, must be prepared to say 'I have a contribution to make'. I am not afraid to go out and say that to the people of Australia.[36]

This was, however, his last major speech for some months: in Parliament he now lapsed into comparative silence. There Curtin won almost immediate stability, when Coles and Wilson voted with the Government at all stages of the budget process and through to the Christmas break steadily supported routine Government business.

Then, in December, the coming of the war with Japan, with the failure of British arms in Malaya and the sinking of the British battleships *Prince of Wales* and *Repulse*, destroyed old verities and ushered in a period of unprecedented national danger. Bipartisan agreement on the urgency of war measures became paramount as national danger mounted with the fall of Singapore, the bombing of Darwin, the Japanese invasion of New Guinea and the possibility that the Australian mainland itself would be invaded. Curtin's stature, and with it his political strength, grew as he provided leadership for new and effective mobilization in these dark days, and Menzies gave him friendship and support so far as prosecution of the war was concerned. Menzies nevertheless retained much of the bitterness that had led him in mid-December to write to his ultra-conservative friend, Lionel Lindsay: 'The press generally has undoubtedly made up its mind that I am to be disciplined, by being converted into a sort of political Trappist. Unhappily, their influence is great because lies are more readable than truth'.[37]

Menzies' parliamentary restraint, and even his periodical urge to quit the Australian scene, did not mean that political ambition was dead. 'As you know', he was later to write to his son, Ken, who was on service in the AIF, 'my own policy has been to wait, and perhaps pay a visit abroad, there being no possibility of success as a leader unless the great bulk of the party wished it'.[38] He made this position clear to Hughes as early as April 1942, following press rumours that he was involved in intrigues to recover the leadership:

> My own position can be clearly stated, as I have stated it to two or three members of the Party who have spoken to me about it: I am not proposing to become a candidate for the leadership of the Party, but if at any time in the future circumstances arose under which for any

[36] *CPD*, 169: 140.
[37] Menzies to Lionel Lindsay, 17 December 1941, La Trobe Library, MS. 9104/1595.
[38] Menzies to Ken, 18 February 1943, Menzies Family Papers.

reason the Party, as a Party, requested me to resume the leadership, I would feel obliged to do so, provided I thought the request represented the real will of the party, but not otherwise.[39]

In reply Hughes noted the 'pregnant but ambiguous qualification' to the denial that Menzies had designs on the leadership, but thanked him for writing in 'this very frank and friendly way'.[40] The leadership, and the whole future of the UAP, were also in Menzies' mind as he developed one of his most important propaganda instruments of these years: the regular radio broadcast.

This idea had crystallized in the last days before his fall. H. W. Horsefield, the UAP Executive Officer in New South Wales, wrote on 20 August 1941 to congratulate Menzies on a speech he had made the night before at a dinner given him by Sydney businessmen,[41] and to commiserate with him over the bad press he was getting in Sydney, for which he suggested a remedy:

> You will remember that President Roosevelt had over 93% of the Press of America against him in his second presidential campaign, but he achieved his greatest majority by talking to the people on the radio. I suggest to you seriously that you should take the gloves off to the Press of Australia and fight them over the National and 'B' class stations, giving the facts and giving the differences between the facts and the facts as presented in the press.

Menzies responded well: 'I was rather interested in your suggestion', he wrote. 'This is something I have been turning over in my own mind.'[42] If anything, the case for thus imitating Roosevelt's 'Fireside Chats' became stronger when he was forced into Opposition. So he began a series of weekly broadcasts on Friday nights through station 2UE in Sydney, relaying to associated stations in Queensland and Victoria. Menzies kept careful tally of the broadcasts, numbering each. In July 1943 he noted that he had been 'giving these talks every week (I will be giving my 76th ... on Friday) since we have been in Opposition, and I have tried to put in simple language the difficulties that face us

---

[39] Menzies to Hughes, 'Personal and Confidential', NLA, MS. 1538/36/3.
[40] Hughes to Menzies, ibid.
[41] *SMH*, 20 August 1941. The burden of Menzies' speech was that a 'New Order' for postwar Australia was being forged through new things learned because of the war: 'new things about human relations, the responsibilities of government, the responsibilities of those who are masters of men and who have capital to invest'. In his final peroration he declared that the yardstick for all Australians must be the question 'Am I measuring up to the men of Tobruk?'
[42] Horsefield to Menzies and Menzies to Horsefield, 20 and 21 August 1941, NLA, MS. 4936/2/40/33.

today and for the future'.[43] In 1943 he published most of the broadcasts he had made in the previous year as a book of essays which took its title from the most celebrated of them: *The Forgotten People and Other Essays*.[44] A short Preface explains that, 'within the acute limits of time and space', the collection represents 'a summarised political philosophy'. The essays are accordingly arranged thematically: 'The Forgotten People' comes first, to strike the keynote of Menzies' thinking; it is immediately followed by six pieces on Roosevelt's Four Freedoms, to amplify the liberal themes of the initial essay; and a set on 'Democracy' (its nature, sickness, achievements and task) brings the collection to a close. In fact, the broadcasts were not made in this sequence. 'The Forgotten People' was given on 22 May and the talks which most directly elaborate its themes came later in the year. In the early months the focus is mostly non-political, with Menzies talking on 'Our American Allies', 'Women in War', and other subjects drawn from his experiences abroad in 1941.

The timing of 'The Forgotten People' is of considerable significance. In the second half of 1942 the war position was still serious, but as the greatest peril waned, the Opposition was less inclined to withhold criticism of the Government and on both sides serious attention began to be paid to the problems and hopes of post-war society. Those discussions were in progress within Labor circles which culminated at the end of the year in the decision to establish a Department of Post War Reconstruction, thought of as a powerhouse of social change and the instrument of future social justice. Menzies, who as Prime Minister had established in 1941 a small Reconstruction Division in the Department of Labour and National Service believed, as he emphasized in one of his broadcasts, in the need to 'provide facilities for competent and practical study of post-war problems by a few sensible and trained people in appropriate places'.[45] But his main fear, which most non-Labor politicians shared, was that before proper study could take place the Government would use its wartime powers to establish socialism by stealth. Curtin specifically rejected this charge, but

---

[43] Menzies to Mrs N. Fulton, 6 July 1943, Menzies Family Papers.
[44] Sydney, 1943. There are thirty-eight essays in the book; since Menzies made a broadcast every week, he chose to leave fourteen texts out. Those printed appear nevertheless to provide a substantial sample of the tone and subject-matter of the broadcasts. These being broadcasts, Menzies had to write down the full texts beforehand. Annotations on original scripts surviving in his papers make it clear that this was necessary to get the timing right and to enable the wartime censor, where necessary, to approve what Menzies proposed to say. The printed version shows the date on which each broadcast was made. Judith Brett has a most insightful article on 'Menzies' Forgotten People' in *Meanjin* 43 (June 1984): 253–65.
[45] Menzies, *The Forgotten People*, 96–7.

his opponents saw straws in the wind that belied the disavowal. They thought, for example, that J. J. Dedman, the Minister of War Organization of Industry, surrounded by doctrinaires, was using his powers to secure permanent government control of industry, and they were alarmed by the unbridled remarks of E. J. Ward, now Minister for Labour and National Service, whose anti-capitalist fulminations remained as extreme as in his most strident Langite days. The difficulty for the UAP was what one of its few intellectuals, Archie Grenfell Price, called in a letter to Menzies the lack of 'a defined and progressive policy'. 'One feels', he wrote, 'that as conservatives our parties are simply attacking the worst mistakes of Labour, without suggesting any progressive altern-atives in their place. Hence we are too frequently damned as "spanners in the War Machinery" '. In a letter to his constituents Price had recently warned of the danger that 'Ward and the extremists' would push the Government into misuse of its wartime powers: to Menzies now he urged that the UAP parliamentary Executive look to the question of policy.[46]

Price was soon rewarded. In less than a month, Menzies made his key broadcast on 'The Forgotten People' and in July he drafted for the Party Executive a comprehensive 'Statement of Common-wealth Opposition Policy for 1942–3'. The statement was generally approved: as one Executive member, Sampson, forthrightly put it: 'I think it good and trust that it will be adopted without stupid manipulation or additions of supposedly vote catching nostrums. If we attempt to outbid Labor we are licked before we start; it can't be done and anyhow, W.M.H. notwithstanding, most of us, I hope, value self respect'.[47] The broadcast led naturally to the statement of policy: it was, in fact, an elegant formulation of the liberal conservatism for which Menzies had always stood and which was now to be at the heart of his bid for political redemption.

'The Forgotten People' is Menzies' attack on what he calls 'our greatest political disease'—that of thinking that the community is divided into the rich and relatively idle on the one hand, and the laborious poor on the other, 'and that every social and political controversy can be resolved into the question: What side are you on?' This kind of class war must always, he contends, be in Australia a false war, for it says nothing of 'the forgotten class—the middle class—those people who are constantly in danger of being ground between the upper and nether millstones of the false class

[46] A. Grenfell Price to Menzies, 13 April 1942, NLA, MS. 4936/14/418/68.
[47] 'Commonwealth Opposition Policy for 1942-3. Drafted by R.G.M., July 1942', NLA, MS. 4936/14/418/68. Surviving replies are filed in this folder.

war; the middle class who, properly regarded, represent the backbone of the country'. In the intervening range between the rich and powerful ('those who control great funds and enterprises') and the mass of the unskilled ('almost invariably well-organized, and with their wages and conditions safeguarded by popular law') are 'the kind of people I myself represent in Parliament':

> salary-earners, shopkeepers, skilled artisans, professional men and women, farmers, and so on. These are, in the political and economic sense, the middle class. They are for the most part unorganized and unself-conscious. They are envied by those whose social benefits are largely obtained by taxing them. They are not rich enough to have individual power. They are taken for granted by each political party in turn ... And yet, as I have said, they are the backbone of the nation.

They are the backbone of the nation because they are people likely to have 'a stake in the country' through the homes—material, human and spiritual—they construct and cherish, often through self-sacrifice, frugality and saving. 'The home is the foundation of sanity and sobriety; it is the indispensable condition of continuity; its health determines the health of society as a whole'. In this and other ways the middle class, more than any other, 'provides the intelligent ambition which is the motive power of human progress'. It finds room in its life for literature, for the arts, for science, for medicine and the law. It 'maintains and fills the higher schools and universities, and so feeds the lamp of learning'. It generates ambition, effort, thinking and readiness to serve, and thus runs counter to the greatest maladies of modern democracy: discouragement of ambition, envy of success, hatred of achieved superiority, sneering at and imputation of false motives to public service. In the post-war world Australia must become a community of people whose motto shall be 'To strive, to seek, to find and not to yield' but that does not mean a return to the old and selfish notions of *laissez-faire:*

> The functions of the State will be much more than merely keeping the ring within which the competitors will fight. Our social and industrial obligations will be increased. There will be more law, not less; more control, not less. But what really happens to us will depend on how many people we have who are of the great and sober and dynamic middle-class—the strivers, the planners, the ambitious ones. We shall destroy them at our peril.

Though the social analysis it represented must be thought approximate and debatable, 'The Forgotten People' was a powerful piece of political propaganda. It is Menzies at his best: presenting simple, arresting ideas in elegant, ardent language. It has the ring of sincerity because so much of it is in fact autobiographical. The middle-class home he idealizes is the home in which he grew up; the child whom his parents see as 'their greatest contribution to the immortality of their race' is himself; the boy who, like a Scottish farmer's son, receives an assured future 'not by the inheritance of money but by the acquisition of that knowledge which will give him power', is Bob Menzies. It is a frankly and fiercely élitist picture:

> That we are all, as human souls, of like value, cannot be denied. That each of us should have his chance is and must be the great objective of political and social policy. But to say that the industrious son of self-sacrificing and saving and forward-looking parents has the same social deserts and even material needs as the dull offspring of stupid and improvident parents is absurd.

By appealing directly to 'the kind of people I myself represent in Parliament', and picturing them as the engines of progress, however 'nameless and unadvertised', Menzies was setting his sights on that ill-defined but potentially vigorous part of the Australian electorate which during the Depression had underpinned the mushroom growth of organizations like the All For Australia League and on which, during its short and chequered life, the UAP had depended. After the disasters of 1941, and in the face of Curtin's success as a wartime leader in the hour of Australia's danger, the conservative parties, if they were to survive in their present form, urgently needed organizational and ideological revivification. 'The Forgotten People' both aimed at this and was Menzies' way of distancing himself from the 'rich and powerful', of whom his most bitter political enemies always depicted him as the champion and representative.[48]

The policy statement which Menzies formulated and which the Party Executive formally endorsed in mid-August 1942 had a preamble extending and particularizing the basic ideas of 'The Forgotten People':

> All our short term activity should be conducted against a background of long term policy so that the people may see not only what we are doing but in what direction we are travelling. Merely to try to outbid Labour is useless and hopeless ...
>
> The dynamic section of Labour, under Ward, is plainly out not for old-fashioned democratic socialism but for a syndicalist system in which industrial and business control will pass into the hands of

[48]The quotations of *The Forgotten People* are from the 1943 edition, 1–10.

Trades Unions and Trades Union officials, thrift will be penalised, and the great middle class of people crushed. We should, to counter this plan—which wartime conditions are powerfully assisting—set out certain principles which will inform our own postwar programmes.

Short-term objectives included full support for effective mobilization, combined with resistance to 'any use of the war emergency for the fowarding of sectional interests or Party/Political ends'; a single Australian army; taxation on a wider field than at present; the outlawing of strikes; resistance to compulsory unionism; research in preparation for post-war reconstruction. Long-term aims included the achievement of secret ballots in unions; simpler arbitration machinery; national insurance on a contributory basis; 'the encouragement by all possible means of thrift, independence and the family home'.[49]

The fears aroused in certain financial and business quarters by the Labor Government's ebullience and the stance of its more extreme members made this for many a timely statement of policy. Admirers like Wright and Ricketson thought Menzies' unpopularity was waning and the time 'fully ripe' for him to make a comeback.[50] Ricketson arranged small group meetings 'for Bob to discuss the present-day political situation and the set-up of the party machine',[51] and Wright wrote to powerful conservatives to press Menzies' leadership claims and underline the need to recruit good men for organizational work behind the scenes. In September, for example, Wright wrote to Sir Robert Gillespie, President of the Bank of New South Wales, about the need for 'first class men' to 'take charge of the organization', and to tell him that the President of the Melbourne Chamber of Commerce had just formed a committee of 'leading financial men' to monitor the developing policies of Labour. 'I write to you', he added, 'because you have had a sympathetic understanding of these problems in the past and you are really the head of the greatest financial organization in Australia'.[52] Gillespie was indeed an old stager in the fight against 'wreckers'. During the Depression he had been Chairman of the Central Committee of the Old Guard, a vigilante group of businessmen and graziers formed to act forcibly to maintain essential services and protect property in the event of Langism getting out of hand.[53] Wright's list of 'leading financial men'

[49] 'Commonwealth Opposition Policy for 1942–3. Drafted by R.G.M., July 1942', NLA, MS. 4936/14/418/68.
[50] Wright to Sir Robert Knox, 8 September 1942, NLA, MS. 8119/2/15.
[51] Ricketson to Wright, 12 September 1942, ibid.
[52] Wright to Gillespie, 21 and 23 September 1942, ibid.
[53] *ADB*, 9: 8.

includes most of the inaugural Council of the Institute of Public Affairs (IPA), an important semi-political organization formed in Melbourne in September 1942, chiefly on the initiative of the Chamber of Manufactures. Menzies himself was present at two of the meetings which led to the founding of this body, which was envisaged as the chief non-Labor fund-raising body in Victoria. It would thus take over the main work of the National Union, to remedy, as one foundation member put it, 'a situation produced by years of intrigue on the one hand, and incompetence on the other'.[54]

Meantime, on one item in the new party platform, the call for a single Australian army, Menzies took a leading part in a major internal controversy which brought Hughes's enmity to a head and threatened a fatal split in the UAP. The occasion was a move by Curtin who, ironically, had fought bitterly against conscription in the First World War, to change restrictions on the use of Australia's conscript militia. Unlike the volunteer AIF, the militia could only be employed for the defence of strictly Australian territory which, however, included New Guinea. Curtin was worried by losses caused by battle casualties and tropical disease, and he was also under strong pressure from the American Commander of forces in the South West Pacific, General MacArthur, who found it politically embarrassing that American conscripts could be made to fight in areas barred to their Australian opposite numbers. At a special ALP Federal Conference in November 1942 Curtin asked that the area in which the militia could be used be extended. He had his way, after the matter had been referred to State Executives, sometimes amid lively controversy. In February 1943, accordingly, Curtin moved in the Representatives a Defence (Citizen Military Forces) Bill, which gingerly revised the range admissible to militia engagement northwards to a line which did not reach Singapore, and eastwards to a line which did not reach New Zealand. It was a weak, almost meaningless, compromise between Labor's traditional policy on conscription and the opposing pressures brought by the crisis of 1942.

[54] For foundation of the IPA see D. A. Kemp, 'The Institute of Public Affairs', Roneo, IPA (originally honours thesis in Schools of History and Political Science, 1963, University of Melbourne); Marian Simms, *A Liberal Nation* (Sydney 1982), 14–18. Those on both Wright's and the IPA lists were: C. A. N. Derham, President of the Chamber of Manufactures; W. E. McPherson and G. H. Grimwade, manufacturers; Cecil McKay, General Manager of McKay Massey Harris Pty Ltd; A. G. Warner, Managing Director of Electronic Industries. Wright's list tails off into 'one or two others', so further overlap is likely (Wright to Sir Robert Gillespie, 20 October 1942; 'Inaugural Meeting of Institute of Public Affairs', 27 November 1942, NLA, MS. 8119/6/23; Kemp, 9). The member who denigrated the old National Union was G. H. Grimwade (Kemp, 8, 12).

The Opposition parties advocated conscription for all areas in which the Japanese had to be fought. But at stormy meetings they agreed that while they would criticize Curtin's Bill they would not move amendments.[55] Behind this decision was a fear that any Labor members still fanatically opposed to conscription might seize such attempted amendment as an excuse for abandoning the measure and thus defeat even the limited advance it represented. Menzies, Spender and Archie Cameron, the fiery ex-leader of the Country Party, were the most vehement opponents of this course, but initially agreed to accept the majority view. When the Bill came before the House, however, all three recanted, amid angry interjections from their own benches. In a sarcastic speech, Menzies called the Bill 'the greatest anti-climax in modern political history': his examination of the map showed that all it did was to add Timor, Amboina and Dutch New Guinea to the places in which conscripts could be used. Australia would only regain some of its lost reputation, he declared, when everyone came to recognize that 'this is a world war, and that no limit can be set in the duty of Australia in relation to it'. He foreshadowed an amendment designed to leave the area of conscript service to the Government's discretion, but a similar amendment from Cameron anticipated it, was defeated, and the Bill went through.[56] In reporting these events to a UAP official in New South Wales Hughes bitterly observed that 'ambitious men and weak-kneed brethren alike find the lure of the limelight irresistible—especially when they can bask in its beams without risk. For as long as there is no danger of the amendment being carried they can safely pose as super-patriots'.[57]

Some observers considered that the rebels had injured themselves by their stand. Mining magnate W. S. Robinson, for example, in reporting the incident to a friend in England, wrote: 'Poor Bob— he and Percy cut sorry figures this week. Both want to retire'.[58] But supporters like Ricketson thought that Menzies had shown himself 'to be the man who can lead Australia', and in private conversations Wright discovered praise even from Keith Murdoch: 'in his opinion Menzies had lost a lot of popularity in political circles in Canberra over his action but had gained in the hearts and minds of hundreds of thousands of people in the street'.[59] After the incident Hughes was forced to call the first Party meeting since his accession to the leadership over a year before. That there

[55]Spender, *Politics and a Man*, 189–98, has a lively account of these bitter meetings.
[56]*CPD*, 173: 304, 317, 604–7.
[57]NLA, MS. 1538/36/41.
[58]W. S. Robinson to Brendan Bracken, 11 February 1943. W. S. Robinson Papers, UMA.
[59]Wright to Sturdee, 17 February 1943, NLA, MS. 8119/2/16.

had been no such meeting was a sore point with Menzies and now the experience proved to be 'singularly disagreeable ... with Billy baring his teeth and snarling threats, and with people like Spooner coming out bitterly in their old colours'. Friends of Menzies wanted to call for a spill of positions, but he persuaded them not to do that lest he be elected leader and have to face 'the bitter hostility of a minority who would ... determine once more to bring me down'. So, said Menzies, an attempt to unseat Hughes was 'defeated by my own friends—and Billy is rejoicing in victory. But nobody was more relieved than I was ... Since then I have been drafting a statement of a very frank kind about the Government and our political problems'.[60]

He completed this statement on 31 March, and persuaded sixteen other UAP members to sign it. They handed it to Hughes at 5.35 p.m. that day. These dissidents, for that is what they were, called themselves 'The National Service Group'. 'We formed the Group', Menzies later told his son, 'for the purpose of gingering up the Opposition[61] (shades of the Young Nationalist movement, a little over a decade before!) Enemies immediately concluded that there was more to it than that: that Menzies was positioning himself to wrest the leadership from Hughes and prepare for an election in which he might take government from Curtin. Archenemies sketched a wilder scenario: as Senator Ashley, the Labor Minister for Information, put it:

> The step taken by Mr Menzies and Senators McLeay and McBride and their colleagues is the only one left to them after their ... deliberate sabotaging of the united war effort in which all political parties have hitherto co-operated. They are the Ishmaels of the political stage. I see they call themselves the National Service Group. In point of fact they are in Australia the National Socialist Group, drawing their fascist inspiration from the very same source as Hitler drew his—the heavy industry combine.[62]

Whatever the interpretation of motive one favoured, one thing was clear: vacillation, for Menzies, was over. He would stay on in politics, aggressively looking for ways to rebuild an ailing Opposition.

---

[60]Menzies to Ken, 30 March 1943, Menzies Family Papers.
[61]Menzies to Ken, 30 June 1943, ibid.
[62]*Canberra Times*, 3 April 1943.

18

Phoenix?

THE NATIONAL SERVICE GROUP'S statement, which they issued to the press on 1 April, recorded 'grave anxiety at the recent drift of events', drawing special attention to 'the refusal of the Government to create one Australian army to render maximum service to the Allied cause' and deploring its 'inadequate appreciation of the War Effort of Great Britain'. Other complaints about the Government concerned its alleged failure to curb price rises, coal strikes and waterside troubles and its extension of social services instead of concentrating on war expenditure. New and vigorous leadership, it declared, was essential for the UAP, 'but in order to avoid dissension we intend to act within the Party as a National Service Group. The differences which exist between us are, we believe, less differences of policy than of action which would achieve that policy'.[1] Menzies' hand was notably evident in a manifesto issued several days later:

> We must abandon the suicidal policy of wiping out the middle class of people. Why should they who have no unions, who draw fixed salaries or modest incomes, who get no cost of living adjustments, whose taxes have doubled and redoubled, who have few capital resources such as the rich have and no drilled and disciplined political party to serve their ends, be required at a time like this to dig into their pockets in order that the waterside workers should be paid amazing wages, or dissipate their own hard-earned savings so that somebody else should get a bigger free pension?[2]

---

[1] Original handwritten memorandum, NLA, MS. 1538/36/3. The members of the Group were as follows: Victoria—Menzies, Senators Spicer and Leckie; NSW—Harrison; Tasmania—Beck; Western Australia—Senator Collett; South Australia—Cameron, Grenfell Price, Duncan-Hughes, Stacey, and Senators McBride, A.J. McLachlan, James McLachlan, McLeay, Uppill and Wilson.
[2] 3 April 1943, NLA, MS. 4936/14/414/41.

In a press statement and broadcast Hughes denounced Menzies and his followers as a 'Group of Wreckers' who could not have helped Labor more effectively had they been its paid agents. A snide attempt was being made to undermine his leadership but it would not succeed and the Group would be 'as helpless in the House of Representatives as a beetle on its back'.[3] In reply, Menzies described Hughes's outpourings as 'full of inaccuracies and reeking with evil suggestion', but said all the same that he would 'refuse to become involved in a competition of personal abuse'. At any time such a competition between two former Prime Ministers would be deplorable; under the present circumstances of the nation it would be unpardonable. 'Such remarks as I feel called upon to make', he said, 'will be about policy and not about people'. He did nevertheless give himself the satisfaction of replying publicly to Fadden, who had slyly remarked on the similarities between the National Service Group's manifesto and the draft Opposition policy. 'If Mr. Fadden's suggestion is that we have just appropriated somebody else's ideas, may I reply by reminding him with great respect that the first draft of the Opposition Policy to which he refers was made by me and submitted to the Opposition Executive over six months ago.'[4]

The press greeted the arrival of the National Service Group cautiously, only the *Sydney Morning Herald* showing downright hostility, and only the Melbourne *Herald* giving a semblance of approval. In a first, signed editorial Keith Murdoch welcomed the Group's desire to sharpen up Opposition ideology and leadership, but criticized it for vagueness about how to improve the war effort.[5]

A week later another editorial, again signed, was kind to Menzies but made it clear that he could not be thought of as the much-needed leader. Menzies' position, wrote Murdoch, was

> a big subject with many complexities, but there is one point on which all should agree. Few men have paid more heavily in family rest and enjoyment, in fortune and in ease of mind than Mr Menzies for the country. Heavy earnings have been abandoned year by year, trains and aeroplanes have been his habitations, and his company has been not what he chose. I point this out because it is one bit of justice to a man in some degree misunderstood, and also because it would be wrong to expect that Mr Menzies should not continue some part of his law work. This part, limited though he makes it, must preclude constant touch with the Canberra lobbies.

[3] NLA, MS. 1538/36/4.
[4] Melbourne *Herald*, 6 April 1943; Press statement, 5 April 1943, NLA, MS. 4936/14/414/41.
[5] Melbourne *Herald*, 7 April 1943.

Menzies, wrote Murdoch, was 'ambitious to take command'.[6] Already in the National Service Group he had seventeen followers: only four more were needed to secure the leadership, and these in due time could no doubt be obtained. But that would split the party even more than the Hughes régime had. The one hope of winning the next election was for the Party to choose a fresh leader and make a fresh start. If both Hughes and Menzies would declare loyalty to him, this new leader would 'bring to the U.A.P. a chance to rise to the full stature of a great creative force. But where is he? ... Names come to the pen: there are several possibilities'. But, wisely or cunningly, Murdoch did not go on to say who they were.[7]

The Group's self-appointed task of 'gingering up' the Opposition was first expressed a few weeks after its formation, when members at a special meeting agreed to urge the Opposition leader to mount a motion of censure against the Government. This, wrote Menzies, 'stiffened up the weaker brethren'[8] and on 21 June Fadden launched a motion of no-confidence. The burden of his attack was that, without a mandate from the people, the Government was developing 'socialist' schemes, which were all the more dangerous because on the left wing of the Labor Party extremists like Ward, now Minister for Labour and National Service, seized every opportunity to talk in class-war terms, at a time when national unity was vital to the war effort and 'industrial lawlessness' had to be curbed. Meantime, through Government mismanagement, rural industries were being starved of manpower, and efforts to check inflation were weak. Most important of all, the Government connived at the notorious story of the 'Brisbane Line', which sacrificed truth to a cynical campaign to depict the Labor Government as having arrived just in time to 'save' Australia.

The tale of the 'Brisbane Line', first 'discovered' by Ward in October 1942, was the high point in a vigorous campaign by a section of the Ministry to depict Australia as being virtually defenceless when Labor came to power, thanks to the lethargy and mismanagement of their predecessors.[9] Ward had himself never been on the Advisory War Council and was not a member of the Labor War Cabinet. But he nevertheless claimed to know that the

[6]Ibid., 13 April 1943.
[7]Ibid.
[8]Menzies to Ken Menzies, 30 June 1943, Menzies Family Papers.
[9]For a balanced account of the 'Brisbane Line' controversy see Hasluck, *Government and People* 1, Appendix 4 ('The "Brisbane Line"—A Study in Wartime Politics'), 711–17. Spender has a more fiery but equally telling account in *Politics and a Man*, 202–17.

Menzies–Fadden Governments had a plan, in the event of Japanese invasion, for abandoning northern Australia as far south as a line drawn through Brisbane: incontestable evidence, he said, of their 'defeatism'. Menzies, Fadden, Hughes, McEwen and McBride, all members of the two previous Governments, made public statements denying the allegations. Curtin, who as Prime Minister had access to any secret documents relevant to the charge, was slow to test his minister's allegations: as has been fairly said, 'his failure on this occasion to repudiate firmly suggestions which he must have known to be untrue fell below his customarily high standards of honesty and courage'.[10] Menzies was particularly incensed by Ward's 'noxious allegations' and the general efforts by Labor to 'besmirch its predecessors' with the allegation that they had left Australia undefended. In the weeks before the censure motion, resistance to this claim was the theme of four powerfully argued and somewhat bitter broadcasts in Menzies' regular series, two refuting 'the Brisbane lie', two asking 'Were we defenceless?', and all accusing Curtin of silent collusion in the false claims of his more irresponsible ministers.[11] On the day after the fourth of these broadcasts Ricketson wrote to convey to Frank Menzies his pleasure that 'at last Bob is taking the gloves off with the Government ... It is late in the day, but perhaps not too late'. What was needed now, he said, was that Menzies develop 'some ruthlessness in his makeup'.[12] Such admirers could hardly have been disappointed at the speech Menzies made in the censure debate a few days later. While accepting the correctness of the alliance with America, he reminded the House that the Battle of Britain and the Battle of the Atlantic, though far away geographically, had been vital to Australia's safety long before Japan or America had come into the war, and spoke of his own Government's contributions, in men and supplies, to this first line of defence. He trounced Labor leaders for having once denigrated him for not taking control of BHP and for putting men like Essington Lewis, 'most of whom are the embodiment of private enterprise and capitalism', in key wartime positions and then, when in office themselves, neither interfering with BHP nor shifting from their posts those whose appointments they had once fulminated against. The truth, Menzies said, was that such men could not be replaced, just as in other aspects of wartime production and management the present Government had succeeded because of the firm foundations he

---

[10] Hasluck, *Government and People* 1, 717.
[11] These were broadcasts on 28 May and 4, 11, 18 June 1943. They are numbered 70 to 73: the full text of each is in the Menzies Family Papers.
[12] Ricketson to Frank Menzies, 19 June 1943, NLA, MS. 8119/6/23.

had left it to build on. He produced statistics to support this argument, and gave short shrift to interjectors like the Minister for Munitions, Makin, 'who seems to think I am going to squirm some day in the witness box of history. I am not. I shall enjoy the evidence more than my friend will'. His final peroration was full of confidence: 'If there is one thing that is clear today it is that there will be no political health in this country until all this miasma of miserable allegations is swept away by the clear draught of a general election. I am for it'.[13]

When the final division came, the Government survived by only one vote.[14] The Opposition returned vehemently to the attack on Ward and a weary Curtin finally announced that after supply had been voted he would seek a dissolution. He also agreed to the appointment of a Royal Commission to investigate the Brisbane Line allegations and stood Ward down from his portfolio until the inquiry was complete. Parliament was dissolved on 7 July and polling day was set for 21 August. A long and bitter campaign ensued.

On the non-Labor side it started badly. Fadden delivered his policy speech at Brisbane on 22 July. One of his promises was for a scheme of post-war credits under which one-third of war-time tax would be returned to taxpayers by instalments after the war. When opening his Kooyong campaign next evening, Menzies said he could not support this proposal: it was something the country could not afford.[15] Fadden angrily declared that

> this stab in the back makes another betrayal in the series for which Mr Menzies has become notorious. The statement came as no surprise to me for I heard last week in Sydney that some such thing might happen because the personal ambition of one man thought it preferable that we should lose this election.

Hughes refused to comment except to say that Fadden's policy was the policy of the Opposition. Menzies said that the tax reimbursement proposal had never been discussed at a party meeting and Senators Spicer and Leckie, both members of the

---

[13]*CPD*, 175: 33–40.
[14]Ibid., 266.
[15]Next morning he sent a memorandum to all members of the National Service Group to explain why he thought Fadden's suggestion could not be carried out and to tell them that he would vote against it if proposed in the next parliament, 24 July 1943, NLA, MS. 4936/14/414/41.

National Service Group, supported him.[16] The *Sydney Morning Herald* dryly observed that the Opposition leaders were offering a prime example of how not to win an election.[17]

Fadden's other planks included immediate pay-as-you-earn taxation, a life assurance scheme for members of the armed forces and the old Opposition demands for an all-party government and a single Australian army. For the rest he depended on what were now established anti-Labor assertions: that the Government's emergency war powers were being used to effect socialism and that the Communists were a sinister force behind Labor. In reply Curtin dismissed the charge of socialism by stealth as a 'dead tiger', giving a formal pledge that his Government had no intention of socializing Australia just because the country was at war. He rested his campaign on the Government's record, particularly its success in placing the country on an effective war footing after the allegedly inadequate work of its predecessors.

Though this was not a formal plank on his platform, Fadden said in one speech that, if elected, the Opposition would again ban the Communist Party. In a dignified reply that Party's Assistant General Secretary, R. Dixon, observed that Communist Party members and those who supported them must now number some thousands of Australian men and women. 'Are they to be denied the rights of free speech and association set out in the Atlantic Charter?'[18] This at least was one matter on which Fadden and Menzies had come to agree. Though the former had for some time talked of banning the Communist Party, the latter was a new convert to that view: at a rowdy meeting in Adelaide he said that 'the recent growth of Communism had been remarkable, and he had changed his mind about it being a small element'.[19] In his regular broadcasts Menzies had already pitted Communism against Christianity, ridiculed Australian Communists who, in lauding Soviet resistance to the Germans, confused Russian patriotism with commitment to an ideology, and warned of the strength of Communists in local trades unions.[20] In this he was naturally at one also with Murdoch who, on the eve of the poll, listed in another

---

[16] Spender, *Politics and a Man*, 219, says that several nights before delivering the speech, Fadden called at his home in Sydney and showed him the draft policy speech and when Spender criticized the tax proposals said the platform could not be altered because it had been approved by the Joint Party Executive. Both Spender and Menzies had, of course, long ago resigned from this body. Spender was certain that Menzies had his eye on the leadership.
[17] *SMH*, 26 July 1943.
[18] Ibid., 9 August 1943.
[19] Ibid., 4 August 1943.
[20] E.g., broadcast of 2 July 1943 (no. 75), 'The Communists', Menzies Family Papers.

signed editorial ('Clear Issues for Australians Tomorrow') twelve unions in which crucial executive positions were held by Communists. He instanced a recent issue of *Labor News*, the organ of the Communist-controlled Munitions Workers' Union, as an example of the propaganda being fed to the membership:

> On the front page of the paper is a despicable cartoon showing Mr Menzies, blackened and bruised, cowering before a worker who has struck him and a soldier who is savagely knocking him about with the butt end of his rifle. The cartoon is given the inciting caption, 'Him or You', and it is the violent Communists' way of depicting the class struggle to be advanced another stage tomorrow at the polls.[21]

Though never clearly urging a vote for him, Murdoch forthrightly demanded that 'persecution of Menzies Should Cease'. 'Mr. Menzies', he wrote in another article,

> is a most distinguished man. As an authoritative voice, an able debater on public questions, and a wise and travelled administrator, he is of great use to the country. One does not need to favour all his policies to agree that he gives expression and strength to the doctrines of life of a large percentage of the people of this country, and on occasions is the best exponent of the thoughts of all.

Again he listed the personal sacrifices Menzies had made in serving as a politician and, conveniently forgetting his own strictures when Menzies was Prime Minister, denounced the 'sickening hypocrisy' of leading ministers who 'lampoon him today as lacking in war-like activity when the truth is that they, themselves, assailed, opposed and derided many of the efforts he made'. Declaring that: 'We Gained Time and Strength', Murdoch went on to put into context, and defend, the export of scrap iron to Japan, the raising and deployment of the AIF, the institution of the Empire Air Training Scheme, and the work of the Menzies Government in creating a munitions industry.[22] Wright, as was to be expected, was delighted. He promptly wrote to congratulate Murdoch on his 'splendid and timely article'.[23]

As usual, Menzies himself worked hard: during five weeks of continuous campaigning he spoke in five States and travelled over 7000 miles. Of the fifty meetings he addressed, he told his son, 'only two were badly obstructed'. With these exceptions, his audiences were 'most friendly in character. There was certainly no

[21] Melbourne *Herald*, 20 August 1943.
[22] Ibid., 5 August 1943.
[23] Wright to Murdoch, 6 August 1943, NLA, MS. 8119/2/16.

superficial sign of any swing in the direction of Labour'.[24] In his best moments, indeed, Menzies felt that, despite the many deficiencies of the Opposition, the Government might be defeated. It was true that there was a plethora of independent candidates and a number of new, *ad hoc* 'parties' and that this chiefly represented disillusion in the electorate with the UAP and Country Parties.[25] It was also true that 'we are, as usual, badly organised, and there is a great shortage of good candidates': a shortage, Menzies thought, 'which cannot effectively be made good until the soldiers are back from this war'.[26] But he thought that the pasting which Curtin had received from the press over the Brisbane Line affair would go against the Government, and he hoped that Labor's attempts to enforce compulsory unionism, and its administration of manpower controls, would be resented in the electorate. Moreover, Frank Packer, the head of Consolidated Press, had invited him to write a special election article for the *Women's Weekly*, 'assuring me that it has six hundred thousand readers and that it is very popular among the troops', and he even had 'unbelievably friendly' talks in Sydney with Fairfax and Henderson ('I don't suppose that it will mean that I will receive ... help from the S.M.H. but if it merely reduces the libellous matter they publish about me by fifty per cent it will be a considerable relief').[27] At the time Menzies' hopes were not altogether ludicrous. There were strange doubts on the other side. For example, when privately asked by R. L. Curthoys what he thought the probable outcome of the election would be Curtin said that 'in

[24] Menzies to Ken Menzies, 2 September 1943, Menzies Family Papers.
[25] For the House of Representatives 338 candidates were standing for the available 75 seats (*SMH*, 31 July 1943). As one correspondent, whose husband was among the organizers of a new party, put it, 'The growth of the Independent movement has really been forced on us by the low standard required of candidates chosen to carry recognised banners', Ella Edwards to Menzies, 11 July 1943, Menzies Family Papers.
[26] Menzies to Ken Menzies, 30 June 1943. Among the many irritations Menzies himself suffered was the failure till the last minute of the Victorian organization to recruit him as a speaker. As he explained to one friend, 'knowing of the carefully fostered belief on my side of politics that my "unpopularity" is rather a drawback, I naturally took no steps to force my services in any direction, despite the fact that there were several key electorates where I was anxious to do anything I could to help' To his annoyance, after he had fixed his itinerary, and indeed, carried much of it out, he was 'beseeched' to visit a number of vital Victorian electorates. Menzies to John Fuller, 13 August 1943, Menzies Family Papers.
[27] Menzies to Ken Menzies, 30 June 1943. Packer was, on the whole, an admirer of Menzies. According to R. S. Whitington, at this time he gave his writers a free hand, 'though he was apt to regard everyone as a Communist'. Whitington reports him as saying: 'I don't care what you say about the other politicans, but I have a terrific respect for Menzies'. Packer, told by his Canberra roundsman, Don Whitington, that Curtin would be sure to win the 1943 election, kept him in Sydney doing little, and organized a victory dinner for Menzies. R. S. Whitington, *Sir Frank* (Sydney 1971), 168–9.

all his experience of politics he had never been so completely in the dark'. When it came, Curthoys said, the election result was 'a staggering surprise and not least to the Government itself'.[28] Curthoys thought when the election began that 'the Govt hadn't a hope', but after ten days of watching the campaign he concluded that the Opposition had presented the Government with many thousands of votes. He listened with the editor of the *Age* (Campbell) to

> Hughes' so-called policy speech . . . and we were appalled. It consisted simply of abuse of Curtin, all grotesquely overdone. The only statesmanship in the whole campaign is coming from Menzies. Why will your friends in the Melbourne Club and Collins House [he was writing to J. R. Darling] not have him as a leader, with all his shortcomings—not that he has more than most of us.

All in all, Curthoys thought, the best thing for the country would be for Curtin to get back and to purge his Cabinet of the Eddie Wards. 'Until we can have a root and branch reform of the U.A.P. . . . it had better remain in the wilderness'.[29]

'Deluge' was the word most often on the lips of the Opposition and its supporters when the election results became clear. Labor won the most spectacular two-Chamber victory seen since the coming of federation. In the Representatives, it secured forty-nine seats (seventeen more than the previous parliament), the UAP won fourteen (nine fewer), the Country Party, with nine seats, was down four, and there were two Independents. Labor gained its first Senate majority since 1914: twenty-two seats as against twelve UAP and two Country Party.[30] Privately, Menzies made the best of a bad job. The new parliament, he told Ken, would be without his enemies Spooner, Marr and McCall, 'a prospect which naturally does not depress me'. Some journalists, particularly in Sydney, 'profess to see in the election results a special vote against the National Service Group and therefore against me. This, however, is mere wishful thinking'. Nevertheless, on his own admission, McBride, Duncan-Hughes, Stacey, K. C. Wilson and Grenfell Price lost their seats in South Australia, where in the previous parliament the Opposition had held eleven out of twelve seats. All were members of the Group, as were Beck, defeated in Tasmania, and Spicer, beaten in Victoria.

[28] Curthoys to Barrington Ward, 13 September 1943, recalling a conversation of 7 August, NLA, MS. 2994/3.
[29] Curthoys to J. R. Darling, 29 July 1943, Headmaster's Correspondence, Geelong Grammar School, cited by kind permission of the headmaster. I am indebted to Dr Peter Gronn for this reference.
[30] I take this succinct formulation of the result from Souter, *Acts of Parliament*, 358.

But when you set against this the defeat of my bitterest critics and the fact that Hughes, Fadden and Page, each of whom can now be credited with at least one poisonous attack upon me in public, are just staggering home in seats which were thought to be overwhelmingly safe, I am not so sure that the election isn't in a personal sense favourable to me.[31]

But not all admirers agreed with this happy judgement. Lionel Lindsay, for example, wrote lugubriously:

Well, My Dear Bob
The Deluge—and worse than I expected ... Ever since your betrayal by Page, the loss of White, Fairbairn and Gullett, the stabs of Hughes and Fadden, the major treason of Wilson and Coles to their pledge, there was no chance of unity. So the chosen of the mob, Ward, Donald Grant, Falstein etc aided by the Communist Union Secretaries will dominate Curtin, and we shall see an outmoded Socialism run this stupid country. They will live to regret you yet, my dear Bob, and as I have little health and energy left, to protect it I intend to read no more politics except when (if) I see your name catch my eye.[32]

Whistling in the dark, Fadden meantime wrote to tell Hughes that he was 'quite confident that nothing can be laid at our door with regard to the disastrous result of the elections'. The fault lay with the National Service Group, which should have listened to the leaders' advice 'and stuck to and by us' on the Militia question. But still, 'As long as we stick together I feel we can rebuild something out of the ruins. We shall have to look to the future instead of holding futile post-mortems, out of which no good can come'.[33]

But there were others with a less naive idea of what had happened, and who saw the very key to the future in proper post-mortems. In August, for example, before the counting of votes had been completed, the Victorian IPA produced a 'Confidential Report on the Federal Election' which dwelt at length on the reasons for Labor's victory and made recommendations for the IPA's future role in non-Labor politics.[34] In the first weeks of

---

[31] Menzies to Ken Menzies, 2 September 1943, Menzies Family Papers.
[32] Lindsay to Menzies, 23 August 1943, La Trobe Library, MS 10375/99. Lindsay was at that stage almost eighty. For points on his friendship with Menzies see Joanna Mendelssohn, *Lionel Lindsay: an Artist and his Family* (London 1988).
[33] Fadden to Hughes, 8 September 1943, NLA, MS. 1538/28/3071.
[34] 'Confidential Report on the Federal Election, 1943', 21 August 1943, IPA Archives, Melbourne, Secretary's Sundry Correspondence, 1942–7. The author of the report is not given. The most likely authors were F. E. Lampe or C. D. Kemp. The Report gave five reasons for Labor's victory: union strength, given the development of industrialization; the one army issue provoked silent resistance; Curtin's personal position; disunity of the Opposition; poor organization of the Opposition in the electorates. It recommended that the IPA should remain the controlling Opposition financial body, but not appear in 'the fighting field'. It should provide research facilities, a library, and encourage young men to enter politics.

September Menzies and F. E. Lampe, President of the Australian Council of Retailers, and a leading member of the IPA, were exchanging detailed analyses of the Labor victory.[35] There is also extant a typewritten 'Preliminary Report and suggestions for the reform and rehabilitation of the United Australia Party', dated 18 September but with no identification of the author, who was clearly not a fan of Menzies.[36] In their assessments both Menzies and Lampe laid great stress on the importance of Curtin's leadership, though Menzies thought that 'the Curtin halo, legend and personality have really been built up by the extraordinarily skilful and devoted service of Mr Curtin's first class press officer, Mr D. K. Rogers'.[37] The moral was clearly that the Leader of the Opposition 'must be provided with an absolutely first class press officer'. Lampe drew attention to the possibility that the Labor Party was regarded as more Australian than the UAP: that the UAP was thought to be more susceptible to English influence. He noted the gullibility of the public in accepting what he called Curtin's half-truths about the work accomplished by the Menzies Ministry for the defence of Australia. Menzies admitted that through advocacy of conscription the National Service Group may have stirred up the silent female vote: 'why should my son have to go thousands of miles from Australia to defend it?' But such points, he wrote, were only guesses: it was in fact essential that 'a small research Organisation be at once set to work to discover, on the ground level, what were the leading causes of the debacle'. Both agreed that new, dynamic leadership was crucial now. The leaders of the U.A.P.-C.P. have fought an election and failed', wrote Lampe. 'They must be replaced. The leader of the U.A.P. should also be the leader of the Opposition'. It was essential, too, that the Party forge for itself a new role:

> in all our thinking and planning we should be ahead, and well ahead, of current politics. There are great brains in the world thinking, reading, writing and planning. We must keep up with that or be thrust

---

[35] Lampe's analysis is dated 1 September 1943, NLA, MS. 4936/14/413/27. Menzies', ibid., 14/414/41, is undated but a note to Lampe written on 14 September makes it clear that he had sent the latter a copy before then.

[36] Ibid., 14/411/16. This may have been composed by the Party organization in NSW, where there was much early perturbation about that State's losses of UAP seats (four out of eight). On 13 September the State UAP Council accepted an Executive recommendation that a Reconstruction Committee be set up to investigate and report on the election and the possibility of setting up proper Australia-wide non-Labor political organization. Sir John Cramer, *Pioneers, Politics and People: A Political Memoir* (North Sydney 1989), 62.

[37] Hasluck, *Government and People* 2, 306n, precisely outlines the role of D. K. Rogers.

ruthlessly aside. Above all we must be a positive, not a negative pole. By our very role of negative pole we have made it possible for Labour to get into power and remain in power.

Lampe thought that for the present this did not necessarily mean that a new party should be formed. But for Menzies 'the wreck produced by the election gives us a great opportunity, if we are ready to seize it', to 'establish a new party under a new name', remedying the lack of viable Opposition party organization and ideology. The new groups and movements which had sprung up in the months before the election were all expressions of dissatisfaction with the UAP. They included some valuable elements: UAP executives must meet the representatives of these new bodies 'freely and frankly with a view to the ... formation of a new body with a clearcut policy'. This new body would need to be Australia-wide, as federally organized as Labor. There must be a properly elected Finance Committee and a regular system of subscriptions, to get away from the widely accepted criticism that the present party was run by big business through such self-appointed bodies as the Victorian National Union. There must be a policy committee, with both parliamentary and non-parliamentary members, 'charged with the duty of constantly revising and restating our political beliefs'. The new organization should have a highly paid executive head and a public relations officer who would be in charge of all propaganda and literature. In addition, the aim should be to place a salaried agent or representative in each key electorate. 'I realise', he added, 'that these proposals involve enormous expenditure, far beyond anything dreamed of in the past, but the simple fact is that unless we are prepared to spend money, hundreds of thousands of pounds of it, between now and the next election, we are quite unlikely to succeed'.

The need for new organization and for new leadership agreed upon by Menzies and Lampe was also the central theme of the third, anonymous, post-mortem, 'Suggestions For Reform', preserved in Menzies' papers. The author remarks on how, in the heyday of its influence, the Party was 'kept fully alive because of the sincerity of Mr Lyons and his political understanding'. Weakened by his loss, the Party suffered another blow when Hawker, Gullett, Fairbairn and Street were killed. At that point, immediate steps should have been taken to groom successors, but the balance of power between the UAP and Labor was so fine that 'old and tried Party hacks were given preference, without due regard to their ability and understanding of the political and social problems of the day'. This dearth of material, allied to internal feuds, contributed materially to the Party's ultimate downfall. No present member

> could be imagined as leading us to victory at the next elections. Propaganda will help but a silk purse cannot be made out of a sow's ear. All that can be hoped for is that if new, young candidates can be recruited for the next election one of them can be groomed for triumphant leadership in a subsequent election. An interim leader is, of course, needed to 'hold the fort'. The ideal man for this job is Casey.

One can only imagine Menzies' feelings as he read this!

He must also have been disappointed by the post-mortem that appeared under Murdoch's signature in the *Herald* a week later. Murdoch said nothing about Menzies, and in a generous tribute gave Curtin credit as the major element in Labor's victory.

> He lifted his own side to a dignified level and tried hard to move it to the middle of the road with promises of moderation that must make the Sydney Trades Hall shiver ... no one will begrudge Mr Curtin his triumph ... He says he stands for Moderation and Victory and the first thing to do is to support him in both lines.

The campaign on the other side 'deteriorated from a bad beginning to a wretched ending, with everyone tired of it, and too many people satisfied that no good Government could be formed out of the present Opposition parties'. A new party was now needed, particularly in the present climate of opinion when a great movement of dissatisfaction with existing social conditions was sweeping through all democratic countries:

> It is expressed not only in the call for more houses, more schooling, more bread, more transport, but in the demand for dynamic and ordered development of the co-operative way of life. This feeling flowed to the Labor party because it declares itself the protector of the weak and the agent of the aspiring, whereas if the forces of Individualism had any life in them they would give spectacular proof that they satisfy the chief ends of man in the way that gives most happiness and strength.[38]

There is, in fact, a general sense in which this was perhaps the most insightful of all the post-mortems.

The new parliament, the seventeenth, was due to begin its first deliberations on 17 September 1943. Before that, the UAP would have to meet to consider its future. It was widely known, as

[38] Melbourne *Herald*, 26 August 1943.

Sydney's *Sunday Telegraph* put it, that many UAP survivors were 'clamorous for an Australia-wide organization, a Federal Secretariat, ably staffed and a new forward-looking policy'. But above all, disaster at the election acutely raised the question of leadership. On that, the *Sunday Telegraph* predicted that 'a new chapter in the political life of stately, silver-templed Robert Gordon Menzies may be written ... A few weeks ago his political enemies were telling one another that Buck Menzies was finished, that he was destined to be a brilliant lone wolf back bencher'. But now he was hot favourite for the leadership of the UAP:

> All Canberra is aware of Menzies' personal and political defects; but Canberra also knows that he is still the most distinguished and gifted personality on the Opposition side; the most brilliant, if not the most astute, figure in the whole parliament ... Many know that Menzies could do the job—he would not be afraid to tread on important toes to bring about inevitable reform.[39]

This prediction proved correct: when the Party met, Menzies was indeed elected to the leadership. There is no record of what lobbying took place, or how he got the numbers, though Spender is probably correct in his assumption that Menzies was unbeatable, given the solid backing of such National Service Group members as had survived the election, the number of Hughes supporters in New South Wales who had lost their seats, and the general disillusion of others.[40] But we do have Menzies' own somewhat acid account of what took place at the meeting. When read between the lines, it catches much of the prevailing atmosphere within the party and of Menzies' own attitude and methods.[41] Hughes's opening gambit at the meeting, Menzies records, was characteristically shrewd: 'Gentlemen, the first question to be decided is whether we shall continue our joint arrangement with the Country Party— if we do, I'll lead, if not, not'. A lively debate ensued. One member put a proposal that negotiations should begin for a complete *merger* with the Country Party.

> This unreal but dazzling prospect of unity appealed at once to some of the elder brethren, the result being that within half an hour there were before the Chair the original motion and at least three amendments,

---

[39] Cutting in Hughes papers, NLA, MS. 1538/28/34. That Hughes kept this cutting suggests how well aware he was of the impending leadership challenge.

[40] *Politics and a Man*, 221. Spender says that, with the losses the UAP had suffered in the election, the National Service Group was relatively stronger in the party than before.

[41] This account is to be found in almost identical letters to Menzies' friend, Lionel Lindsay, 13 October 1943, La Trobe Library, MS. 9104/1601, and to his son Ken, 13 October 1943, Menzies Family Papers.

with most speakers clutching at the idea that the issue of leadership might be evaded or postponed by opening up the indicated agrarian discussions. You'll of course agree with me that the most popular device in politics is postponement. I allowed the confusion to develop, holding my fire to the very last moment. Billy, in the Chair, was incredible. His grasp of procedure has never been very great, and the task of determining in what order and how you put to a meeting of reasonably talkative men a motion, an amendment, an amendment on an amendment, and an amendment on the amendment to the amendment to the motion proved entirely beyond him. For once I was sensible (as your Mother would say) and did nothing to extract him from the tangle, having a vague idea in my mind that his claims to lead an outnumbered party in the hurly burly of Parliamentary debate were rapidly fading.

Hughes finally managed 'to put some sort of upside down question to the meeting', and at that point Menzies rose and reminded members that parliament was meeting next morning and someone 'would have to rise in his place as leader of His Majesty's Opposition'. Months of negotiation would be needed to test and translate into reality the pious aspirations for a merger with the Country Party, and meantime the leadership and deputy leadership of the Opposition would stay with Fadden and Hughes. 'I pointed out that the majority of those in the room must recognise that after our recent drubbing the continuation in office of our election leaders would be hailed with shouts of ridicule and that the public would never take us seriously again'. He then said that he would vote against all the questions before the chair and move: 1. that the UAP should revert to the system under which the majority Opposition party had the leadership of the Opposition; 2. that the Party forthwith choose a leader; and 3. that this leader should be authorized to negotiate a coalition of Opposition forces.

The meeting immediately threw out the existing motion and amendments and voted unanimously for Menzies' motions. Candidates were asked to announce themselves and, 'overcoming our natural modesty', T. W. White, Allan McDonald, Percy Spender and I rose'. On the first ballot Menzies polled thirteen votes out of twenty-six; subsequently the others dropped out and he was elected.

> My first business in the Chair was to conduct an election for the Deputy Leadership. Various members rose as Candidates, and I was just having their names recorded when I noticed that the 79-year-old 'Little Digger', whose qualifications as an up-and-coming understudy to a leader are not obvious, was himself in an erect posture, on my left. I thought he was just adjusting his hearing apparatus, and quite lightheartedly said to him: 'You are not submitting yourself, are you?'

to which—with a diabolical gleam in his rheumy old eyes—he replied: 'oh yes, brother; for the Deputy-Leadership, certainly brother'. The effect of this announcement was cataclysmical. One by one the other aspirants fell away with the result that Billy was unanimously elected, and I have as my deputy in the great work of regenerating a Party and enlivening a political Opposition, an old gentleman, all of whose dynamic force is used retrospectively. But of course the point is that it means that he still has his secretary and his typist and his masseur and his seat on the War Council, and what happens to the political cause with which he is associated does not matter very much.

The press reception of the change was cool, most papers being sceptical of the chance of early, or even possible, UAP recovery, though all recognized Menzies' talents. The most enthusiastic was the *Argus*, whose Canberra correspondent wrote of Menzies having sat on the back-bench for upwards of two years, like the Duke of Plaza Toro, leading his regiment from behind, 'not for the reasons which actuated Gilbert's hero, but because of his great gifts. Now he comes into his own on the Opposition side'.[42] The *Age* was more severe: though he was the right man to tackle it, the task before Menzies was daunting:

> The U.A.P. and the C.P. are more or less wilfully out of contact with many powerful currents in the national life. Their political attitude has become static; much of their political philosophy has become superseded. Rightly or wrongly the majority of Australians are persuaded that the U.A.P. is primarily, if not exclusively, on the side of 'big business'. Whatever reasons exist for this belief, these will have to be completely removed if the U.A.P. is ever to have a political revival.[43]

For this daunting task, even the *Sydney Morning Herald* wished Menzies well, if with supercilious reference to his failures in the past:

> With all his brilliant gifts, Mr. Menzies hitherto has lacked something of the art of managing men, and of the faculty for vigorous execution. A certain intellectual intolerance has not helped him in the past in his relations with colleagues and supporters of lesser mental stature. Political adversity may have corrected these faults. At any rate, Mr. Menzies, who fumbled his second opportunity when he returned from London, now has a third, though of a different kind. He has a Parliamentary party to inspire and reinvigorate as well as to command; and he will not want for good wishes for success in his task.[44]

It remained to be seen whether the wheel had turned full circle.

[42] *Argus*, 25 September 1943.
[43] *Age*, 24 September 1943.
[44] *SMH*, 24 September 1943.

Reflections

By any test Menzies' political career up to 1943 was remarkable, however chequered. Though not yet fifty, he had been a member of the Commonwealth House of Representatives for nine years, a minister for all but two of them and briefly Prime Minister, in the first phase of World War II. Before his election to the federal seat of Kooyong in 1934 he had served a virtual apprenticeship in the Victorian parliament, which he entered in 1928 at the age of thirty-four and in which he had received his first ministerial experience. In the tempest of the Great Depression he was a major player in the complex and chiefly Victorian-led manoeuvres which issued in the coming of the UAP as the new party of 'stability', and in the recruitment from Scullin's Labor Ministry of Joseph Lyons as its leader. Menzies' subsequent transfer to federal politics involved, though that was not for him the only motive, a promise that in due course he would step into Lyons's shoes. This did not happen until after Lyons's death in 1939, and was the source of much ill-feeling, resulting both from Menzies' unpopularity and the insistence of party functionaries on keeping Lyons in office to exploit his electoral appeal. Modern Australian historians also conventionally depict the Lyons Governments of the 1930s as dull and repressive, the agents of the prevailing bourgeois culture, fearful of the unorthodox in art, literature and political thinking. As Attorney-General in those years, Menzies has usually, and in certain cases erroneously, been identified as a blind upholder of these values.

The end of the decade brought Menzies pain, first in the controversy over the succession to Lyons, and second in his Prime Ministership in the first phases of the war. With the best will in the world, it was not easy during the 'Phoney War' to stir a sense of urgency about mobilization in a country far from the scene of real hostilities. But the Menzies Government did its best, dramatically increasing expenditure on defence, calling up troops for local defence and raising, in less than a year, three divisions of a second AIF for voluntary overseas service. The Japanese threat in the Pacific took Menzies to Britain early in 1941 to press for more effective British participation in Far Eastern defence, particularly at Singapore. He fought hard to secure this, but had come to Britain at a time when it was alone, with invasion seemingly imminent, German strangulation of the Atlantic seaways in progress and English cities bearing the full brunt of enemy air attacks. Menzies understood this peril and bled for the English people in their heroic acceptance of sufferings which his own had never yet had to face. The British decision, while he was in London and attending the War Cabinet, to use Australian troops in the ill-starred Greek campaign added to his agony. His ambiguous relations, and final clash, with Churchill on this and other matters concerning the conduct of the war could not be publicly revealed; nor could the extent to which, as a result of his Government's work, the Australian economy had been reorganized to meet the challenge of war. He nevertheless returned to Australia to be initially given something of a hero's welcome, but that soon dissolved in the face of the personal hostility of part of his own and much of the Labor Party, the charge that he and his Ministers were not sufficiently dedicated to meeting the challenge of total war, and the casualty lists that began to come through, almost from the moment of his arrival, of Australian troops lost in Greece and Crete. Late in 1941, with a deep sense of failure and betrayal, Menzies resigned first the Prime Ministership and then the leadership of the UAP.

Relegation to the back bench brought relative parliamentary silence, especially when the opening of the Pacific war seemed for a time to threaten for Australia peril comparable with what Menzies had known so well at first hand for Britain. It was peril which bred a kind of bipartisanship, at least at the apex of each opposing party, as he and Curtin agreed on much and were each strengthened by a sometimes paradoxical personal friendship bred of an almost old-world courtesy and respect. But, especially after Labor came to power late in 1941, this did not prevent Menzies from working to find a coherent ideology to express what he thought might revitalize a crumbling UAP. And when, in concert with world-wide democratic thinking, the Labor Government took steps towards the planning of a new, 'just' society for the post-war world, Menzies and those on his side of politics gave voice to fears. Post-war planning raised for them the question of 'socialism', the more especially since at this time the left wing of Labor, sometimes to Curtin's embarrassment, stepped up loud and simplistic denunciations of the established order. Then, in the election of 1943, the Australian voters overwhelmingly endorsed the Curtin Labor Government. Devastating defeat suffered by the UAP raised crucial questions for that party's future. Would it simply remain a relic of the past, or could it have a positive role in the coming political world? That, indeed, is the major question with which this volume ends: for Menzies, as he took over the leadership again, it was the most challenging question he had yet faced in public life.

As the chapters of this book suggest, to tell the bare bones of the story in this way is merely to scratch the surface of the complex events of the first half of the life of an unusually gifted man. Menzies was a man who might have had a brilliant and lucrative career in the law, but who chose instead progressively to give himself up to the uncertainties of public life. There his success, though not unalloyed, provided rewards which even the highest success in his profession could not have guaranteed. Of these the most important were seasons of administrative power, an admired and—in some quarters—much sought after public presence, and acceptance in social circles, particularly in England, to which he could not normally aspire. There is no doubt, as the conventional wisdom has it, that such prizes enlivened ambition and were among the impulses that drove Menzies on. But the price he often paid for the way of life he had chosen is less well known. To the world he presented a confident, sometimes brash, face. He could be insensitive and domineering. But slights pained him, his outward confidence often hid private nervousness, and in the seclusion of his occasional diaries we catch glimpses of a thirst for approbation by others, almost needed to integrate and confirm his picture of self.

The personal satisfactions of power and recognition were not, however, the only or even the main explanations for Menzies' involvement in politics, especially at the outset of his career. No understanding of the man is possible which does not begin with family, Scots heritage, and the middle-class, Protestant Melbourne in which he spent his university and early professional years. Family and Scots tradition bred an austere sense of public and private responsibility, which Melbourne confirmed and extended. Also deeply involved was his legal training, which for a man of his background and cast of mind confirmed and added to already internalized attitudes.

These influences together bred elevated notions about the responsibility of capable and principled men to take part in political life. That idea was in part created, in part confirmed, by the more general concern which developed in the mid-1920s among young Melbourne men of his class to identify, train and harness recruits for true public service, a concern symbolized by the formation and activities of the Constitutional Club. Menzies' decision to bid for a parliamentary seat was in part a result of his first taste of public agitation in the referendum of 1926, and in part a reflection of his disquiet—which the worthies of the Constitutional Club also articulated—at contemporary Victorian politics. For Menzies, the unsatisfactory nature of public life in the State arose from two related circumstances: the poor quality of those who offered themselves for political service, and the bankruptcy of the contemporary 'party' system. Both would soon induce him to take the leading part in establishing the Young Nationalists movement, designed to revitalize, and in the end to take control of, what he thought of as the only real party in the local legislature, moribund and somewhat corrupt though it was. He saw the other so-called 'parties' of the day as being in reality pressure groups, engaged in political life primarily to secure for their clients the best possible share of the State's largess. The most predatory were the various emanations of the Country Party; the most dangerous was the Labor Party. He believed the latter to be controlled by the outside power of the trades unions and to have socialist aspirations incompatible with true freedom.

By contrast Menzies himself developed from the beginning an almost aristocratic, Burkean view of parliamentary representation. It was the responsibility of a parliamentarian to be his constituents' representative, not their delegate. He should be chosen for his integrity, his ability to think for himself and to make judgements in the light of what he saw as the good of the community as a whole. There were occasions in his earliest years of public speaking when Menzies even voiced as corollaries to this general belief nostalgia that the days of amateur, gentlemanly politics were over and that most politicians saw being a member of parliament as a full-time job and the salaries they got for that their only source of income. In due course experience muted this extreme view of parliamentary representation, but his underlying attitude to Labor and to the Country Party did not change and he carried it firmly into federal politics.

This was one basis of the political conservatism for which Menzies came to stand. The Great Depression highlighted a related but more fundamental source of his position: belief in the contractual foundation on which a stable democratic society had to rest. Everything in his making conspired to support this attitude: his legal training, his family and class background. Contracts symbolized what he saw as the necessary elements of stability: regularity, predictability, reliability. This belief, expressed in his steely advocacy of orthodoxy in the long and distressing debate in the early 1930s over economic policy, certainly made him, as opponents then and since have averred, the defender of the interests of the privileged. There was, however, much more to the debate than that: there is no reason to believe that Menzies did not deeply believe in the view of social arrangements for which he stood, and the mushroom growth of the Leagues of 1931 demonstrated that that view was widely held over a social spectrum well beyond privileged business and financial interests. Menzies no doubt had little direct personal experience of the distress suffered by the unemployed and the working class generally, and was in consequence cold to the human case for unorthodox policies. It remains true that such experience would have been unlikely to move him: he was not well read in economics and, like most of his associates, knew and understood little about the ideas of economists like Keynes. He might intellectually recognize suffering caused by the Depression, but simple economic beliefs combined with a firm view of what made for social stability to convince him that the only hope for amelioration of living conditions lay in balanced budgets to convince future investors of Australia's soundness.

The sanctity of contracts was one fundamental aspect of Menzies' constitutionalism: his respect for British institutions was another. Australia, as he and most constitutional lawyers of his generation saw it, had not only inherited these institutions, but was an integral part of the Imperial polity they constituted and served. And since they had evolved over centuries from English needs and experience and ideals there was about them an *auctoritas* which no theoretically contrived system could match. Menzies' Britishness was thus no garment consciously put on. Education and environment had made it part of his very fibre. He was not a monarchist out of sentiment alone. The monarchy was an integral part of the British structure of government, to be revered accordingly. In relation at least to the period covered in this book the hackneyed allegation that Menzies 'grovelled' to the British and to the monarchy is shallow and anachronistic in the extreme. He had a reasoned understanding of what he and the majority of an almost exclusively Anglo-Celtic community instinctively felt: that they *were* British. On another level altogether, Menzies' 'discovery' of England in 1935 was a confirmation of all he had learned; it was, as he himself said of it, coming home to a home he knew but had never seen. There was certainly some sentimentality and naiveté about that first visit but on later trips he could be very critical of what he experienced. Like any true monarchist he enjoyed meeting and talking to members of the Royal Family and spoke and wrote with pleasure of occasions when this happened. But even in 1935 he wrote with some acidity about the limited intellects of the princes and marvelled at the symbolic significance of the monarchy rather than any admirable human virtues it betrayed other than, perhaps, 'naturalness'. The 1936 and 1938 visits stirred repeated complaints about the obscurantism of top British civil servants and the grasping habits and imperial hypocrisy of British businessmen. And in 1941, though acutely conscious of the desperate danger facing Britain and though glowing with admiration for a people who were so valiantly withstanding the dreadful trial of German bombing, he did not hesitate to criticize and confront Churchill and the British Chiefs of Staff, in and out of Cabinet, when he thought Churchill's ways offensively dictatorial and British decisions inimical to Australia's interests. Such was hardly the behaviour of a 'groveller'.

As to the balance of political forces at home, there can be no mystery about the suspicion, shading into downright hostility, of Labor and Country Party members and supporters towards Menzies. He had never made any secret of his disdain for what they theoretically stood for. On his own side of politics, by common consent, his difficulty, some would say tragedy, was a matter of personal style rather than principle. It was put in December 1941 most simply and candidly by his close friend and admirer, Staniforth Ricketson, in a private letter explaining to W. S. Robinson how Menzies' 'great ability has been discounted ... by certain characteristics':

> his independence of spirit, his inability to 'suffer fools gladly', his alleged 'mental superiority' and his dislike of personal publicity ... I am afraid that there is some basis for this criticism and I feel that if, for example, he could display publicly the likeable personal characteristics of the late Joe Lyons, his acceptance as a popular leader would never have been in doubt. His intimate friends know and appreciate his charm of manner and his many sterling qualities, but unfortunately, the recognition of these qualities has not been general among the people.[1]

Once, when privately interviewed, his brother Frank remarked on Menzies' failure to win and cultivate a group of intimate supporters. Everyone admired Bob and respected him and had to

---

[1] Ricketson to W. S. Robinson, 1 December 1941, NLA, MS. 8119/6/23.

bow to his superior mind and knowledge. But he, Frank, used to say to Menzies that he needed 'to get a body of people around you—twenty or thirty boys who would die for you politically—people you should have in your home, etc. But Bob never had that type of bodyguard around him—just didn't seem to be able to let himself go'.[2] In 1943 Ricketson had made the same point to Frank when he wrote that Menzies would succeed as soon as he realized that he needed 'a loyal band of supporters' whom he should bind to himself 'by deserving their loyalty, rather than always taking it for granted ... and not bothering to make the little acknowledgments which, after all, count for so much in life'.[3] Carelessness about personal relations here shaded into a kind of arrogance, the well-documented Menzies impatience with humdrum stupidity. His cutting tongue and readiness to use his great skill as a mimic were well known. He had in combination with this a seeming aloofness, created in part by his care to avoid public emotionalism and his preference for well-reasoned, logical argument—natural to a lawyer of his kind but also an exemplification of Frank's opinion that 'a lot of Bob's characteristics were reactions against his father'.[4] Withal, Menzies was genuinely puzzled and from time to time privately distressed at his unpopularity and his inability, especially after the outbreak of war, to win the trust of large sections of the public and press. Self-understanding, self-criticism, at least as far as his public persona was concerned, were not his forte.

That had its sad aspect since, on their testimony, those close to him—good friends, children of friends and, especially, family—knew a man who, though sometimes thoughtless, had kindness, loyalty and a great sense of humour.

---

[2] Interview, Lady McNicoll of F. Menzies, NLA, Oral History Unit, 1169/350.
[3] Ricketson to Frank Menzies, NLA, MS. 8119/6/23.
[4] Interview with Lady McNicoll, NLA, Oral History Unit, 1169/350.

Sources

Abbreviations used in Footnotes

ADB	*Australian Dictionary of Biography*
AFPL	*Australian Federal Politics and Law*
AJPH	*Australian Journal of Politics and History*
CAC	Churchill Archives Centre, Cambridge
CPD	*Commonwealth Parliamentary Debates*
DAFP	*Documents on Australian Foreign Policy*
Dawes	A. Dawes, Unnamed, undated, unpublished, part-completed biography of R. G. Menzies
DT	*Daily Telegraph*, Sydney
HS	*Historical Studies*
IPA	Institute of Public Affairs
MUA	Melbourne University Archives
MUM	*Melbourne University Magazine*
NLA	National Library of Australia
PRO	Public Record Office, London
RT	*Round Table*
SMH	*Sydney Morning Herald*
TS	Page, *Truant Surgeon*
VPD	*Victorian Parliamentary Debates*

Interviews

I have been helped in the work for this volume, and in some cases for the next, by interviews with the following: Mrs Elizabeth Alder, the late Professor W. Macmahon Ball, Sir Garfield Barwick, Sir Henry Bland, Sir Allen Brown, Sir John Bunting, Mr Jim Cairns, Lord Carrington, Mr Stuart Cockburn, Sir John Colville, Dr H. C. Coombs, Miss Hazel Craig, Sir Walter Crocker, Sir James Darling, the late Mr Ian Fitchett, Sir Sydney Frost, Sir Martin Gilliat, Lord Glendyne, Mr 'Jo' Gullett, Mrs Judith Harley, Sir William Heseltine, Mr Len Hume, Mr Robert Rhodes James, the late Miss Eileen Lenihan, the late Lord De L'Isle, the Very Reverend Fred McKay, Mr A. H. McLachlan, Mr Ken Menzies, Dame Pattie Menzies, Mr A. L. Moore, Sir John Norris, Mr Hubert Opperman, Mr B. A. Santamaria, Professor Geoffrey Sawer, the late Sir Reginald Scholl, Lady Slim, Lady Soames, Mr Alf Stafford, Sir Arthur Tange, Sir Frederick Wheeler, the late Miss Everil Wilkinson, Sir Roland Wilson.

Primary Sources

I have been systematically through and drawn upon two collections of Menzies papers: the Menzies family papers and the papers of Sir Robert Menzies. The former are in the possession of Mrs Peter Henderson (Heather Menzies), who has kindly given me permission to quote from them. The latter, styled MS 4936, are in the Manuscript Section of the National Library of Australia. Mrs Judith Harley has given me access to the Diary of her father, T. W. White, and Mr James Merralls has allowed me to examine the Diaries and some other papers of Sir Owen Dixon. Both permit me to quote from these materials. I have taken selections from the Hankey and the Duff Cooper Papers, both held in the Churchill Archives Centre, Cambridge. The Master and Fellows of Churchill College kindly permit me to publish from the former, as does Lord Norwich from the latter. At the Australian Archives in Canberra I have examined papers relating to Menzies' period as Commonwealth Attorney-General and the papers of Sir Frederick Shedden.

I have used other, individual items from various collections in the National Library and the Australian Archives, and have found relevant letters in the various repositories which I list in the Preface. All are acknowledged in the footnotes to the text; it would be tedious, not to say pretentious, to list them in detail here. The same is true of Australian newspapers, of which such a subject as the present one requires extensive use.

Publications of R. G. Menzies

To The People of Britain at War. London 1941.
The Forgotten People, and Other Studies in Democracy. Sydney 1943.
Afternoon Light: Some Memories of Men and Events. Melbourne 1967.
Central Power in the Australian Commonwealth. London 1967.
Measure of the Years. North Melbourne 1970.

Selected Secondary Sources

Bunting, Sir John *R. G. Menzies, a Portrait.* Sydney 1988.
Cumpston, I. M. *Lord Bruce of Melbourne.* Melbourne 1989.
Dawes, A. Unnamed, undated, unpublished and part-completed biography of R. G. Menzies. Typescript, in Menzies Family Papers.
Dean, Arthur *A Multitude of Counsellors. A History of the Bar of Victoria.* Melbourne 1968.
Dilks, David (ed.) *The Diaries of Alexander Cadogan O.M. 1938–45.* London 1971.
Edwards, P. G. *Prime Ministers and Diplomats: the Making of Australian Foreign Policy, 1901–1949.* Melbourne 1983.
Fitzhardinge, L. F. *William Morris Hughes: a Political Biography.* 2 volumes, Sydney 1964 and 1979.
Hasluck, Paul *The Government and the People, 1939–41* (*Government and People* 1). Canberra 1952.
—— *The Government and the People, 1942–45* (*Government and People* 2). Canberra 1970.
Hazlehurst, Cameron *Menzies Observed.* Sydney 1979.
—— (ed.) *Australian Conservatism. Essays in Twentieth Century Political History.* Canberra 1979.
Howard, Frederick *Kent Hughes: a Biography of Colonel The Hon. Sir Wilfred Kent Hughes, K.B.E., M.V.O., E.D., M.P.* South Melbourne 1972.

Hudson, W. J. *Casey*. Melbourne 1986.
—— & Stokes, H. J. W. *Documents on Australian Foreign Policy*, vol. IV. Canberra 1980.
Joske, Percy *Sir Robert Menzies, 1894–1978—a New, Informal Memoir*. Sydney 1978.
Lloyd, C. J. The Formation and Development of the United Australia Party, 1929–37. PhD thesis, Australian National University, 1984.
Louis, L. J. *Trade Unions and the Depression: A Study of Victoria, 1930–1932*. Canberra 1968.
Lyons, Dame Enid *Among the Carrion Crows*. Adelaide 1972.
Macintyre, Stuart *The Succeeding Age, 1901–1942*, vol. 4 of *The Oxford History of Australia*. Melbourne 1986.
Page, Sir Earle *Truant Surgeon: the Inside Story of Forty Years of Australian Political Life*. Sydney 1963.
Rydon, Joan *A Biographical Register of the Commonwealth Parliament, 1901–1972*. Canberra 1975.
—— *A Federal Legislature: the Australian Commonwealth Parliament, 1901–1980*. Melbourne 1986.
Sawer, Geoffrey *Australian Federal Politics and Law, 1901–1929 (AFPL 1)*. Melbourne 1956.
—— *Australian Federal Politics and Law, 1929–1949 (AFPL 2)*. Melbourne 1963.
—— *Australian Federalism in the Courts*. Melbourne 1967.
Sayers, Stuart *Ned Herring: A Life of Lieutenant-General the Honourable Sir Edmund Herring*. Melbourne 1980.
Schedvin, C. B. *Australia and the Great Depression: a Study of Economic Development and Policy in the 1920s and 1930s*. Sydney 1970.
Souter, Gavin *Acts of Parliament: a Narrative History of the Senate and House of Representatives*. Carlton 1988.
Spender, Percy *Politics and a Man*. Sydney 1972.
Vines, Margaret Instability in Governments and Parties in Victoria in the 1920s. MA thesis, University of Melbourne, 1975.

Index

Abbott, C. L. A., 207
Abbott, Joseph Palmer, 306, 370, 381, 382
Abyssinian crisis, 169–71, 175–6, 180–1, 254
Adamson, L. A., 18–19
Advisory War Council, 308, 310, 378, 379, 391
Alexander, A. V., 332
All For Australia League, 87, 90
Andrews, J. M., 339
Anstey, Frank, 81
Argyle, Sir Stanley, 95, 97, 102, 103, 112, 116, 117, 118, 129
Ashley, W. P., 407
Astor, Lord, 344
Attlee, Clement, 350
Australian Academy of Art, 195–9
Australian Association for Fighting Venereal Diseases, 1922, 55
Australian Legion, 57
Australian Movement against War and Fascism, 130–1
Australian Women's Association, 1922, 55
Australian Women's National League (AWNL), 55, 59, 90, 105, 116, 215

Baddely, John, 367
Bagot, E. D. A., 87, 88
Bailey, K. H., 108, 118–19
Baillieu, Clive, 247
Baldwin, Stanley, 127, 152, 153, 160–4, 171, 175, 224, 232
Ball, W. Macmahon, 201–2
Ballarat, 1–4, 12–14
Baracchi, Guido, 20–1, 25–7
Barbusse, Henry, 130
Barnett, Matthew, 206, 217
Barrett, Sir James, 55
Barton, Sir Edmund, 38–9
Barton, Wilfred, 186
Bate, Weston, 2n
Beasley, J. A., 81, 128, 130, 170, 367
Beaverbrook, Lord, 181, 353–4

Beck, Arthur James, 371, 416
Belgrade coup, 1941, 334–6
Bell, George, 195, 198
Benes, Eduard, 233, 237
Bentham, Jeremy, 96
Best, W. H., 260
Blackburn, Maurice, 24–5, 130, 135, 188–9
Blamey, Sir Thomas, 296, 319, 323–5, 328, 348, 384–5
Bond, E. E., 77
Bond, General (Singapore), 318
Boothby by-election, 1941, 362, 368
Boyne, R. J., 63
Bradman, Don, 222, 224
Bradshaw, F. Maxwell, 33
Brennan, Frank, 128, 129, 130, 133, 134, 190
Brennan, Thomas, 189
Brereton, Harry, 222
Brisbane Line, 410, 412, 456
British Empire League, 1920, 56
Brooke-Popham, Sir Robert, 318
Brookes, Herbert, 73, 375
Bruce, Stanley Melbourne: introduced, 46; attempt to widen Commonwealth arbitration powers at referendum (1926), 48, 50, 51; predicts great future for Menzies, 114; first Australian High Commissioner in London (1933), 114–15; at Ottawa Conference (1932), 124; as patron of Casey, 124; Menzies' attitude to in London (1935), 154, at Empire Parliamentary Association (1935), 161; and Abyssinian crisis, 170; rejects Casey's urging to re-enter Australian politics (1935), 174; and Menzies, in London (1936), 178; and trade negotiations (1936), 183, (1938), 230; and Czechoslovak crisis, 237; and attempt by Casey and Page to lure him back to Australian politics (1939), 256, 257–8, 268–72; on Page's attack on Menzies (1939), 278–9; and establishment of

Washington legation, 293–4; urges Menzies to come to London (August 1941), 379–80; mentioned, 74, 150–1, 164, 223, 320, 377, 396
Brunton, Sir William, 58
Buchan, John, 160
Burton, Herbert, 202, 385n
Butler, R. A., 151, 332

Cadogan, Sir Alexander, 326, 332, 348, 350–1
Cain, John, 96, 103
Calwell, Arthur, 371
Cameron, Archie, 248, 288, 295, 309, 406
Campbell, H. A. M., 416
Canada, 160, 164–5, 356–9
Canberra, 51, 137–8, 281–2, 394–5
Canberra air disaster (August 1940), 299–300
Casey, Richard Gardiner: introduced, 124; Hankey on (1934), 127–8; and deputy leadership of UAP (1935), 174; and Menzies, in election of 1937, 215; and Premiers' Conference on defence (1938), 241; and National Insurance (1938–39), 249–51, 262; and UAP leadership (1939), 269–72; Minister for Supply and Development (1939), 280; and despatch of first Australian troops abroad (1939–40), 291–2; and Washington legation (1939), 293–4; and Menzies' comments on the 1940 federal election, 305, 306; British Minister of State resident in the Middle East (1942); and post-mortem on 1943 federal election, 420; mentioned, 189, 237, 248, 284, 312, 356
Chamberlain, Neville, 154, 159, 161, 180, 232, 233, 236, 238, 284, 295, 393
Chamberlain, Mrs Neville, 178
Channon, 'Chips', 320, 394n
Charlton, Matthew, 51
Chifley, J. B., 304, 306, 370, 397
Churchill, Winston: Menzies' first impressions of (1935), 153, 155, 159; becomes British Prime Minister (1940), 295; on defence of Singapore (1939), 316; and Brooke-Popham (1941), 318; and Menzies' visits to Chequers (1941), 321–3, 326, 329, 347; and Greek campaign (1941), 323–9, 335, 348; and Ireland (1941), 337–9, 343–4; Menzies' disillusion with, 345–7, 350–3, 372; and Menzies' resignation of Australian Prime Ministership, 383–4; prevents Menzies' return to England (late 1941), 391; suggests Menzies as Australian ambassador to United States (1942), 396–7; mentioned, 378
Citizens' League of South Australia, 87
Clarke, Sir Frank, 66, 270

Clerke, Arthur H., 59, 78
Coles, A. W., 296, 306, 371, 382, 398
Collett, H. B., 382
Collins, T. J., 381
Colville, John, 329, 349
Communist Party, 296–7, 413
compulsory training, 246, 258; *see also* conscription
conscription, 24–30, 245–6, 405–6
Constitutional Club, 57, 60, 66, 75, 77, 88
Cooper, Alfred Duff, 322, 393–6
Cooper, Lady Diana, 393–6
Corser, Edward, 276
Country Party (Victoria), 61, 105–7, 117–18, 129
Coward, Noel, 313
Cranborne, Lord, 349, 391, 393
Crawford, Norah, 21, 23
Cripps, Sir Stafford, 171, 186–8, 190
Cross, Ronald, 391
Cunningham, E. S., 104
Curthoys, R. L., 221, 262, 269–70, 277–8, 415–16
Curtin, John: replaces Scullin as Labor leader, 204; on sanctions against Italy (1935), 171; and Gwydir by-election (1937), 208; on defence (1937), 211–12; in 1937 election, 213; on Lyons's leadership (1938), 244; on Country Party and National Insurance (1939), 260; on outbreak of war (1939), 285; relations with Menzies (1940), 296, (1941), 367, 368, 379, 383, 385; and national government issue, 308, 380–1; becomes Prime Minister (1941), 391–3; on Menzies' handling of his followers, 387; on use of militia (1943), 405; and 1943 election, 415–16, 420; mentioned, 188, 209, 248–9, 297, 415
Cusack, 218

Dalfram, 251–4, 255–6
Darling, J. R., 269, 270
Dawes, A., 14n
Day, David, 354–5
de Valera, Eamon, 322, 338–43
Dean, Sir Arthur, 33, 43
Dedman, J. J., 294, 401
defence (Australia), 210–12, 213–14, 215, 240, 248, 264, 284, 295–6, 313
Dewar, Lieutenant, 204–7, 218
Dill, Sir John, 323, 324, 328, 349
Dixon, Sir Owen, 35–6, 37, 39, 45, 267, 288, 365, 387
Dixon, R., 413
Donovan, William, 338, 341
Duffy, Sir Frank Gavan, 38, 115
Duncan-Hughes, J. G., 209, 408n, 416
Dunstan, Albert, 200

Eden, Anthony: Menzies' first meeting with, 155; becomes Foreign Secretary (1935), 176; and sanctions against Italy (1935–36), 180–1; resigns office (1938), 232; and Greek campaign (1941), 323–4, 327–9; and rejection of Menzies for Middle East appointment (1942), 396; mentioned, 175, 238, 290, 350
Eggleston, Frederic, 247
elections: Victoria (1927), 65; (1929), 74–7; (1932), 101–2; Commonwealth (1929), 74; (1931), 100; (1934), 115, 120–3; (1937), 210, 212–16; (1940), 301–8; (1943), 412–17
Ellis, A. D., 27–8
Empire Parliamentary Association, 152, 160–3, 168, 181
Evatt, H. V.: and Kisch *habeas corpus* case (1934), 136; and art controversies, 195, 199; as vice-president of New South Wales Cricket Association, 222; enters House of Representatives, 304–5; anxiety for office (1940–41), 308, 311, 349, 364, 375, 379; and Menzies' alleged reputation in United States, 397; mentioned, 255n, 301, 367

Fadden, A. W.: and Page's attack on Menzies (1939), 276; becomes Country Party leader (1940), 309; Acting Prime Minister (1941), 318, 329, 335, 338, 347, 349, 367; allegations of intriguing against Menzies (1941), 365; Prime Minister (1941), 381, 388–9, 391–3; Leader of the Opposition (1942–43), 393, 409, 410, 412–13, 417; Menzies' opinion of (1942), 391
Fairbairn, J. V., 245, 262, 280, 284, 299, 300, 387, 419
Fairbanks, Douglas, 178
Fairfax, Warwick, 205, 207, 301, 373–4, 415
Fairfax, Mrs Warwick, 302n
Fascism, 110–11
Federal Union (1926), 49
Fenton, James, 82
Fetherston, R. H. J., 55
Fink, Theodore, 51
Finlay, G. P., 205
Foll, H. S., 381
Forde, F. M., 191, 367, 375, 379
'Forgotten People', 400–3
Fraser, Colin, 113
Fraser, P., 390
Freer, Mrs Mabel, 204–7, 209, 216–18
Freyberg, Major-General B. C., 329

Game, Sir Philip, 101
Garden, Jock, 205
Garvin, J. L., 344
Gentlewomen's Aid Society (1922), 55

George, David Lloyd, 150, 156, 352–3, 354
Gibbons, G. A., 82
Gibson, Sir Robert, 82
Gillespie, Sir Robert, 404
Glendyne, Lord, 85
Gloucester, Duke of, 112, 126
Gollan, Ross, 374, 375
Gowrie, Lord, 391, 393, 395
Gray, J. A., 64
Gray's Inn, 159
Greek expedition ('Lustreforce', 1941), 323–9, 335–6, 344–5, 348, 370
Greenwood, Edward, 74
Gregory, Henry, 314
Grenville College, 15
Griffin, Gerald, 133–4, 135, 137
Griffith, Arthur, 263
Griffith, Sir Samuel, 38
'Group of Six', 83–4, 86, 89–90
Gullett, Henry: junior minister in Lyons Government (1934), 124, 127; and trade negotiations, 124, 139, 151, 183, 184; on Lyons's leadership (1938), 246; in Menzies Cabinet (1939), 280; death, 299–300; mentioned, 199, 284, 294, 387, 419
Guy, J. A., 377
Gwydir by-election (1937), 207–8, 210

Haining, Lieutenant-General Sir Robert, 325, 334
Halifax, Viscount, 233, 234
Hamilton, Alexander, 96
Hancock, W. K., 56, 126
Hankey, Sir Maurice, 124, 126–8, 152–3, 164, 174, 211, 351–2, 354
Harding, Sir Edward, 152, 154, 164
Hardy, C., 209
Harris, Sir John Richards, 98
Harrison, E. J., 132, 374, 381, 382, 385
Harrison Moore, William, 20
Hawker, Charles, 125–6, 139, 169, 174, 181, 208, 209, 210, 245, 251, 419
Henderson, Kingsley, 63, 83, 90, 269
Henderson, Sir Nevile, 234
Henderson, R. A. G., 302, 415
Herbert, Harold, 198
Heydon, Peter, 224, 234, 383
Higgins, Sir John, 80
Hitler, 154–5, 180, 232–5, 236–8, 254, 295, 345
Hoare, 'Bondy', 298
Hoare, Sir Samuel, 170, 175, 176
Hodgson, Lieutenant-Colonel W. R., 234
Hogan, E. J., 68, 69, 77–8, 80, 95, 97, 100, 101
Holland, J. J., 77
Hollins, L. H., 215
Holt, Harold, 188, 205, 262, 284, 343, 381, 387
Horsefield, H. W., 376, 399
Hughes, W. M.: and conscription in World

War I, 24; minister in Lyons Government (1934), 123; facetious farewell to England-bound Menzies (1935), 141–2, (1936), 177–8; and recruitment during World War II, 246, 406; Attorney-General and Minister for Navy in Menzies Government (1940), 310; hostility towards Menzies (1941), 365, 382; UAP leader (1941), 393; and Menzies on Party leadership, 398–9, 407, 421–3; and election of 1943, 416–17; mentioned, 130, 140, 156, 159, 167, 174, 188, 201, 264, 266, 371, 381
Hull, Cordell, 166, 360
Hurst, Sir Cecil, 187
Hutchinson, W. J., 365, 371, 375, 376, 380, 383

'Illira', 72–4, 222, 254, 314, 319, 389
Institute of Public Affairs, 404–5, 417
Ireland, 321, 322, 337–44
Isaacs, Sir Isaac, 219

Jackson, A. R., 96
Jacob, Lieutenant-Colonel, 232
James, F. A., 171–3, 186–8
James, Rowley, 298, 299, 371
Japan, 183–5, 290–1, 332–4, 335, 378, 395–6, 398
Jeparit, 4–13 passim, 16–17
Jeparit Leader, 4–5, 9
Jones, H. E., 132
Jones, Thomas, 13
Joske, E., 114
Joske, Percy, 18, 35, 39
'Jubilee Pilgrim', 144, 185–6
Judkins, William Henry, 15

Kelley, B., 263
Kent, Duke of, 156
Kent Hughes, Wilfrid, 58–9, 61, 66, 68, 75, 76, 89, 90, 103, 104, 110, 117
Kew, 17–18
King, William Mackenzie, 356–9 passim, 372, 390
Kisch, Egon, 130–7
Knox, Sir Adrian, 38
Knox, G. H., 114
Knox, Lady, 140
Knox, R. W., 88
Kyeema disaster, 245

Lampe, F. E., 417–19
Lampson, Jacqueline, Lady 320
Lampson, Sir Miles, 353
Lang, J. T., 79, 88, 91, 100, 101, 102, 104, 208, 240
Latham, J. G., 24, 47n, 48, 88, 89, 90, 111, 115, 127, 171, 280, 294

Laval, Pierre, 169, 175
Lawlor, Adrian, 195
Lawson, J. N., 376
Lazzarini, H. P., 255
Leckie, J. W., 42, 64, 318, 382, 412
Lees, Dr Harrington, 56
Lewis, Brian, 23, 27, 30
Lewis, Essington, 63, 296, 411
Lewis, Neil, 23, 31
Lewis, Owen, 23
Lewis, Phyllis, 23
Lindsay, Lionel, 286, 398, 417
Livingstone, John ('Daddy'), 11, 16
Looker, Cecil, 383
Lovell, Professor Tasman, 86
Lowe, Sir Charles, 264
Loyalty League (1920), 56
Lyons, Enid: Hankey's opinion of, 127; trip to England (1935), 139–40, 145–6, 168; and Menzies' alleged attack on Lyons's leadership (1939), 242–4; and invitation to Bruce to become Prime Minister (1939), 257–8; and Menzies' resignation from Lyons Ministry (1939), 262–3
Lyons, Joseph A.: Acting Treasurer in Scullin Government (1930), 82; first loan conversion campaign (1930), 83–5; leaves Labor Party and becomes Opposition leader (1930–31), 86, 89–90; and second loan coversion (1931), 97; and Menzies' speech to premiers' conference on federalism (1934), 112; and luring of Menzies into federal politics (1934), 116; and coalition with Page (1934), 122; Hankey's opinion of, 127; and George V's Silver Jubilee (1935), 139, 145, 159, 161; and Abyssinian crisis (1935), 169–70; and British trade proposals (1936), 184; and wish for Menzies to succeed UAP leadership (1936), 189; and Imperial Conference of 1937, 211; on Czechoslovak crisis, 237; and Menzies' alleged attack (1938), 243–4; criticizes H. G. Wells (1938), 254–5; offers UAP leadership to Bruce (1939), 257; and Menzies' resignation from Ministry (1939), 263; death, 264–5; mentioned, 168, 173, 189, 372

MacArthur, General Douglas, 405
McBeath, Sir William, 60
McBride, Phillip, 245, 318, 382, 416
McCall, W. V., 312, 365, 370, 375, 376, 380, 386
McClure Smith, H. A., 302–3, 306, 340
MacDonald, Allan M., 276, 370, 381, 382, 422
McDonald, John, 13
MacDonald, J. S., 200
MacDonald, Malcolm, 183, 226, 356–7, 359

INDEX

MacDonald, Ramsay, 126, 150, 153, 155, 159, 161
McDougall, F. L., 151
Macedon, 22, 35, 153, 270, 372; *see also* 'Illira'
McEwen, John, 309, 381
MacGeorge, Norman, 197
McGregor, Jim, 331
McHugh, Sydney, 251
McIlwraith, Frank, 255n
Mackay, Ronald, 149, 164
MacKenzie, C. N., 313
Maclean, G. S., 104
McLeay, G., 381, 382
McLoughlin, Eric, 374
MacMichael, Sir Harold, 319
McPhee, J. C., 90
McPherson, Sir William, 68–70, 77, 95
Maine, Sir Henry, 96
Makin, Norman, 130, 367, 412
Maloney, W. R., 129–30
Manifold, Chester, 90, 103
Mann, Leonard, 254
Manning, Henry, 186
Mannix, Archbishop, 55, 266
Marr, Sir Charles, 312, 365, 371, 376, 380, 383, 416
Massy-Greene, Sir Walter, 115
Maxwell, G., 24
Melbourne Agreement, 79, 80, 82, 88
Melbourne Citizens' League (1931), 88
Melbourne Club, 269, 270, 416
Melbourne University Magazine, 20–3, 27–8
Menzies, Elizabeth (paternal grandmother), 2, 3, 12, 14, 20
Menzies, Frank Gladstone (brother), 4, 10–11, 12, 16, 30, 226, 228, 233, 372, 385, 387, 411, 431
Menzies, Heather (daughter), 43
Menzies, Ian (son), 43, 212
Menzies, Isobel Alice (sister, 'Belle'), 4, 10, 12, 20, 30
Menzies, James (father), 1, 3, 4, 7–11, 15–18, 20, 64, 77, 118, 276, 382
Menzies, James Leslie (brother), 4, 12, 16
Menzies, Kate (mother), 1, 4, 7, 11, 16, 18, 30, 276
Menzies, Kenneth (son), 35, 43, 72, 212, 398, 416
Menzies, Pat (wife), 42, 140, 143, 145, 164–5, 223, 276, 281, 315, 319, 362, 365, 387, 389
Menzies, R. G.: birth, 1; family and boyhood, 1–18; education at Wesley College and University of Melbourne, 18–31; issue of enlistment, 27–30; early legal career, 32–42, 45–8; marriage, 42–3; and 1926 arbitration referendum, 48–52; elected to Victorian Legislative Council (1928), 61–7; Minister in McPherson Ministry (1928), 68; resignation of portfolio (1929), 68–9; elected to Victorian Legislative Assembly (1929), 74–7; and Young Nationalist movement, 75–7, 78, 98–100, 104; orthodox views in Great Depression debates, 79–82, 90–2, 96, 102; and 'Group of Six' in loan conversion, establishment of United Australia Organization and winning of Lyons as political leader (1930–31), 83–93; becomes president of Victorian National Federation (1931), 98–9; Attorney-General and Minister for Railways in Argyle Cabinet (1932), 102–4; hostility to Victorian Country Party, 75, 106, 117–18; as Acting Premier of Victoria (1934), 112–13; elected to Commonwealth House of Representatives (1934), 114–19, 122; Attorney-General in Lyons's second Government, 122; and Kisch case (1934), 130–7; and first English visit (1935), 138–64; and Abyssinian crisis (1935–36), 169–70, 180–1; and James case (1936), 171–3, 186–90; and visit to England (1936), 177–92; and art controversy (1936–37), 194–200; and book censorship, 200–2; and Freer case (1937), 204–7, 216–18; and visit to England and Europe (1938), 223–36; and Nazi Germany, 234–5; and danger of war (1938–39), 238–9; alleged attack on Lyons's leadership (1938), 241–5; and National Insurance issue (1938–39), 249–51, 258–63, 282; and pig iron dispute (1938), 251–4, 255–6; and Lyons's death, 266; and the succession struggle (1939), 267–73; and Page's attack (1939), 274–9; and accession to Prime Ministership (1939), 279–80; and declaration of war against United States legation, 293–4; and loss of Fairbairn, Street and Gullett in air disaster (1940), 299–300; and 1940 election, 303–8; and visit to England (1941), 316–55; and Ireland, 337–44; and Greek campaign ('Lustreforce'), 323–4, 335–6, 348, 370; and resignation of Prime Ministership (1941), 379–87; and 'The Forgotten People' (1942), 400–3; and National Service Group, 405–7; and election of 1943, 412–20; and regaining of UAP leadership, 421–3
cricket, 15, 19, 44, 222–3, 224
legal cases mentioned: his first, at Mansfield, 36–7; Troy v. Wrigglesworth, 37–8; Engineers, 40–1; Federated Engine Drivers' and Firemen's Association v. Adelaide Chemical and Fertilizer Co. Ltd, 41; arbitration litigation (1920s), 45–6; Paper Sacks case, 138–9, 159; James v.

Commonwealth, 171–3, 186–90, 213–16; Payne taxation case, 173, 187
others' opinions of, 18, 31, 35 (Joske); 26 (Baracchi); 70 (*Table Talk*); 96–7 (Cain); 114 (Bruce, G. H. Knox); 118–19 (James Menzies, Bailey); 198 (Bell); 202 National Insurance, 1939); 270 (Sir Frank Clarke); 272–308 (reactions to his winning UAP leadership, 1939); 299 (Rowley James); 320 (Lady Lampson, 'Chips' Channon); 353–4 (Beaverbrook); 358–9 (Mackenzie King); 372 (Ricketson); 383, 387 (Curtin); 384 (Blamey); 385 (Stewart); 386 (Shedden); 394 (alleged *Sydney Post* journalist); 247–8, 409–10, 414 (Murdoch); 421 (*Sunday Telegraph*); 302, 365, 376–7, 423 (*SMH*)
Menzies, Robert (paternal grandfather), 1–3
Menzies, Sydney (brother), 12
Merritt, J. K. , 62
Middle Class Party (1920), 55
Mitchell, Sir Edward, 38
Moffatt, J. P., 185
Monash, Sir John, 85
Moyes, Bishop, 252
Murdoch, Keith, 97, 199, 204, 244, 247–8, 256, 257–8, 268, 406, 409–10, 413–14, 420
Murray, John, 16
Mussolini, 111, 147, 169, 254

National Federation, 60
National Government issue (1941), 303, 308, 312, 380–1
National Insurance, 210, 249–51, 258–62, 282
National Service Group, 406–7, 408–10, 416–17
National Union, 60, 88, 268
Nettlefold, T. S., 75, 78, 90
Newton, Sir Alan, 263, 270
Niemeyer, Sir Otto, 79
Norris, C. A., 83
Norris, Sir John, 34
Norton, Ezra, 374

Officer, Keith, 164, 190, 199, 212, 294
O'Kelly, Sean, 340
Ottawa Agreements, 139, 150–1, 182, 220, 230; *see also* trade talks with Britain

Packer, Frank, 306, 415, 415n
Page, Earle: as Bruce's Treasurer, 46; and coalition with Lyons (1934), 122; Menzies' initial reactions to (1934), 123; and trade talks in London (1938), 220–2, 227; advocates appeasement of Germany, 233; and National Insurance, 250–1, 258–61, 282; announces Lyons's death, 265; intrigue with Bruce and Casey over UAP leadership (April 1939), 268–9, 271; parliamentary attack on Menzies, 274–5, 276–9; resigns Country Party leadership (September 1939), 287–8; and Communist Party, 297; Minister for Commerce (November 1940), 310; and the plots against Menzies (1941), 364, 381, 387, 424; declares self admirer of Menzies (May 1941), 368–9; emissary to London (1941), 390, 394; mentioned, 89, 127, 209, 285, 417
Papagos, General, 327
Paris, 179, 229–30
Parkhill, Archdale, 122, 174
Paterson, Thomas, 122, 133, 136, 204–5, 206, 207
Patterson, Vere, 9
Pawsey, Josiah, 3
Pearce, George, 122, 127
Penton, Brian, 305
Phillips, P. D., 108, 110
pig-iron dispute, 251–4, 255–6
Pollard, Reginald, 219
Pratt, Ambrose, 83, 84
Premiers' Plan, 94, 96, 100, 101, 105
Price, Archibald Grenfell, 364, 386, 401, 416
Price, J. L., 245, 362
Privy Council: Paper Sacks case (1935), 138–9, 159; James case (1936), 171–3, 186–8, 213–16; Payne taxation case (1936), 173, 187

referendums: 1926, Bruce Government, on arbitration powers, 48–52; 1937, Lyons Government, on marketing, 208–9
Rich, Sir George, 104
Ricketson, Staniforth, 73, 83, 85, 90, 140–1, 372–3, 378, 404, 406, 411, 430, 431
Rigby, E. C., 66
Roach, Tom, 251, 255
Robinson, Sir Arthur, 49, 50, 51, 56
Robinson, W. S., 49, 406
Rodgers, Arthur, 59
Rogers, D. K., 418
Rommel, 345
Roosevelt, Franklin D., 166, 335, 378, 399
Rowell, William, 194
Royal Society of St George, 56
Ruth, T. E., 56

Saltau, Marcus, 68
Sampson, Burford, 401
Sampson, Edward, 4
Sampson, John (maternal grandfather), 4, 14
Sampson, Sydney, 4, 5, 14, 49–50, 64, 70
Savage, Michael Joseph, 292
Savage Club, 44, 58, 84
Sawer, Geoffrey, 41
Schacht, Dr Hjalmar H. G., 234, 235

Scullin, James, 74, 82–3, 86, 97, 100, 120, 204
Scully, W. J., 208
Selborne Chambers, 33–5, 49
Serle, Geoffrey, 1
Shann, Frank, 19
Shedden, F. G., 288, 318, 325, 352, 355, 386
Simon, Sir John, 154, 161, 351
Simpson, E. Telford, 333–4
Singapore, 239, 323, 349, 351, 417, 431
Slater, William, 104
Smith, Sydney Ure, 196, 199
Smith, Vinton, 110, 111, 178, 179, 258, 294
Smuts, Jan, 351, 372
Snow, Sir Sydney, 256, 270, 364
Spender, Percy, 309, 364, 368, 371, 381, 387, 406, 422
Spicer, J. A., 78, 92, 412, 416
Spooner, E. S., 306, 370, 380, 382, 407, 416
Stacey, F. H., 406, 416
Stanley, Lord, 226
Stanley, Oliver, 226
Starke, H. E., 38
Stevens, Bertram, 104, 240, 256, 270
Stewart, Sir Frederick, 274, 280, 382
Stewart, Galloway, 385
Stewart, Harold, 19
Stirling, Alfred, 178, 225, 234
Stirling, Dorothy, 225
Storey, John, 318, 332
Street, Geoffrey, 248, 280, 299, 387, 419
Stretton, Len, 23, 35
strikes: Seamen's (1925), 46–7; Wonthaggi miners' (1934), 113; Watersiders', Port Kembla ('pig-iron', 1938), 251–4, 255–6
Swanton, W. H., 63
Swinburne, George, 63, 65
Swinton, Baron, 178

Terry, G. E., 114
Theodore, E. G., 79–80, 82, 86, 88, 90–2, 94, 100, 156
Thomas, Elliott, 150
Thorby, H. V., 139, 147, 244, 248
Townsend, A. R., 185
trade diversion (Japan), 183–5

trade talks (with Britain), 139, 150–2, 168–9, 182–5, 192–4, 220–2, 228–9, 230
Tritton, N. C., 318
Tunnecliffe, Thomas, 97, 102, 106n

Union Club (Sydney), 269

Vansittart, Sir Robert, 154, 169, 194, 326
Vestey, Sir Edmund, 227–8
Villers-Bretonneux, 230–2

Wakamatsu, Torao, 290
Wales, Prince of, 156
Ward, E. J., 286, 401, 410–12
Ward, Kevin, 186
Watt, W. A., 85
Wavell, Field-Marshal, 317, 323–5, 345, 348
Wells, H. G., 254–5
Wesley College, 18–19
White, T. W., 123–4, 174, 220, 221, 222, 230–2, 237, 244–6, 248, 271, 422
Willis, E. H., 104, 257
Wilson, Alex, 306, 398
Wilson, Sir Horace, 154
Wilson, K. C., 416
Wilson, W. Hardy, 200
Wilson, Woodrow, 361
Women's Citizens' Movement (1922), 55
Wood, G. L., 108
Wren, John, 15
Wright, F. H., 313, 378, 404, 406, 414

York, Duchess of, 153, 156, 162
York, Duke of, 153, 156
Young Nationalists: foundation of, 75–7; constitution, 78; in first bond conversion campaign (1932), 84–5; celebration of 1932 election victory, 104; and education of politicians, 108; development of fighting platform, 99–100; Healesville Conference (1933), 109–11; strength of, by 1934, 111; farewell luncheons for Menzies (1935), 140, (1936), 174; mentioned, 98–9, 106, 112, 116, 117, 128, 129, 407